W9-AGQ-001

COLLECTED WORKS OF

IBSEN

COLLECTED WORKS OF IBSEN

Including *Ghosts*, *Hedda Gabler*, *Peer Gynt* and *A Doll's House*

GREYSTONE PRESS
New York

BY GEORGE MC KIBBIN & SON; BROOKLYN, NEW YORK
PRINTED IN THE UNITED STATES OF AMERICA

CONTENTS

CONTENTS

HEDDA GABLER

PERSONS OF THE PLAY

George Tesman.
Hedda Tesman, *his wife.*
Miss Juliana Tesman, *his aunt.*
Mrs Elvsted.
Judge Brack.
Eilert Lövborg.
Berta, *servant at the Tesmans'.*
The action takes place at Tesman's villa in the west end of Christiania.

ACT I

Scene—*A spacious, handsome and tastefully furnished drawing room, decorated in dark colors. In the back a wide doorway with curtains drawn back, leading into a smaller room decorated in the same style as the drawing room. In the right-hand wall of the front room a folding door leading out to the hall. In the opposite wall, on the left, a glass door, also with curtains drawn back. Through the panes can be seen part of a veranda outside and trees covered with autumn foliage. An oval table, with a cover on it and surrounded by chairs, stands well forward. In front, by the wall on the right, a wide stove of dark porcelain, a high-backed armchair, a cushioned footrest and two footstools. A settee with a small round table in front of it fills the upper right-hand corner. In front, on the left, a little way from the wall, a sofa. Further back than the glass door a piano. On either side of the doorway at the back a whatnot with terra-cotta and majolica ornaments. Against the back wall of the inner room a sofa, with a table, and one or two chairs. Over the sofa hangs the portrait of a handsome elderly man in a general's uniform. Over the table a hanging lamp with an opal glass shade. A number of bouquets are arranged about the drawing room in vases and glasses. Others lie upon the tables. The floors in both rooms are covered with thick carpets. Morning light. The sun shines in through the glass door.*

Miss Juliana Tesman, *with her bonnet on and carrying a parasol, comes in from the hall, followed by* Berta, *who carries a bouquet wrapped in paper.* Miss Tesman *is a comely and pleasant-looking lady of about sixty-five. She is nicely but simply dressed in a gray walking costume.* Berta *is a middle-aged woman of plain and rather countrified appearance.*

Miss Tes. [*stops close to the door, listens and says softly*]. Upon my word, I don't believe they are stirring yet!

Berta [*also softly*]. I told you so, miss. Remember how late the steamboat got in last night. And then, when they got home!—good lord, what a lot the young mistress had to unpack before she could get to bed.

Miss Tes. Well, well—let them have their sleep out. But let us see that they get a good breath of the fresh morning air when they do appear. [*She goes to the glass door and throws it open.*]

BERTA [*beside the table, at a loss what to do with the bouquet in her hand*]. I declare, there isn't a bit of room left. I think I'll put it down here, miss. [*She places it on the piano.*]

MISS TES. So you've got a new mistress now, my dear Berta. Heaven knows it was a wrench to me to part with you.

BERTA [*on the point of weeping*]. And do you think it wasn't hard for me too, miss? After all the blessed years I've been with you and Miss Rina.

MISS TES. We must make the best of it, Berta. There was nothing else to be done. George can't do without you, you see—he absolutely can't. He has had you to look after him ever since he was a little boy.

BERTA. Ah, but, Miss Julia, I can't help thinking of Miss Rina lying helpless at home there, poor thing. And with only that new girl too! She'll never learn to take proper care of an invalid.

MISS TES. Oh, I shall manage to train her. And of course, you know, I shall take most of it upon myself. You needn't be uneasy about my poor sister, my dear Berta.

BERTA. Well, but there's another thing, miss. I'm so mortally afraid I shan't be able to suit the young mistress.

MISS TES. Oh well—just at first there may be one or two things——

BERTA. Most like she'll be terrible grand in her ways.

MISS TES. Well, you can't wonder at that—General Gabler's daughter! Think of the sort of life she was accustomed to in her father's time. Don't you remember how we used to see her riding down the road along with the general? In that long black habit—and with feathers in her hat?

BERTA. Yes indeed—I remember well enough! But, good lord, I should never have dreamt in those days that she and Master George would make a match of it.

MISS TES. Nor I. But by the bye, Berta—while I think of it: in future you mustn't say Master George. You must say Doctor Tesman.

BERTA. Yes, the young mistress spoke of that too—last night—the moment they set foot in the house. Is it true then, miss?

MISS TES. Yes, indeed it is. Only think, Berta—some foreign university has made him a doctor—while he has been abroad, you understand. I hadn't heard a word about it until he told me himself upon the pier.

BERTA. Well, well, he's clever enough for anything, he is. But I didn't think he'd have gone in for doctoring people too.

MISS TES. No, no, it's not that sort of doctor he is. [*Nods significantly.*] But let me tell you, we may have to call him something still grander before long.

BERTA. You don't say so! What can that be, miss?

MISS TES. [*smiling*]. H'm—wouldn't you like to know! [*With emotion.*] Ah dear, dear—if my poor brother could only look up from his grave now and see what his little boy has grown into! [*Looks around.*] But bless me, Berta—why have you done this? Taken the chintz covers off all the furniture?

BERTA. The mistress told me to. She

can't abide covers on the chairs, she says.

Miss Tes. Are they going to make this their everyday sitting room then?

Berta. Yes, that's what I understood—from the mistress. Master George—the doctor—he said nothing.

[George Tesman *comes from the right into the inner room, humming to himself and carrying an unstrapped empty portmanteau. He is a middle-sized, young-looking man of thirty-three, rather stout, with a round, open cheerful face, fair hair and beard. He wears spectacles and is somewhat carelessly dressed in comfortable indoor clothes.*]

Miss Tes. Good morning, good morning, George.

Tes. [*in the doorway between the rooms*]. Aunt Julia! Dear Aunt Julia! [*Goes up to her and shakes hands warmly.*] Come all this way—so early! Eh?

Miss Tes. Why, of course I had to come and see how you were getting on.

Tes. In spite of your having had no proper night's rest?

Miss Tes. Oh, that makes no difference to me.

Tes. Well, I suppose you got home all right from the pier? Eh?

Miss Tes. Yes, quite safely, thank goodness. Judge Brack was good enough to see me right to my door.

Tes. We were so sorry we couldn't give you a seat in the carriage. But you saw what a pile of boxes Hedda had to bring with her.

Miss Tes. Yes, she had certainly plenty of boxes.

Berta [*to* Tesman]. Shall I go in and see if there's anything I can do for the mistress?

Tes. No, thank you, Berta—you needn't. She said she would ring if she wanted anything.

Berta [*going toward the right*]. Very well.

Tes. But look here—take this portmanteau with you.

Berta [*taking it*]. I'll put it in the attic. [*She goes out by the hall door.*]

Tes. Fancy, Auntie—I had the whole of that portmanteau chock-full of copies of documents. You wouldn't believe how much I have picked up from all the archives I have been examining—curious old details that no one has had any idea of——

Miss Tes. Yes, you don't seem to have wasted your time on your wedding trip, George.

Tes. No, that I haven't. But do take off your bonnet, Auntie. Look here! Let me untie the strings—eh?

Miss Tes. [*while he does so*]. Well, well—this is just as if you were still at home with us.

Tes. [*with the bonnet in his hand, looks at it from all sides*]. Why, what a gorgeous bonnet you've been investing in!

Miss Tes. I bought it on Hedda's account!

Tes. On Hedda's account? Eh?

Miss Tes. Yes, so that Hedda needn't be ashamed of me if we happened to go out together.

Tes. [*patting her cheek*]. You always think of everything, Aunt Julia. [*Lays the bonnet on a chair beside the table.*] And now, look here—suppose we sit comfortably on the sofa and have a little chat till Hedda comes. [*They seat themselves. She places her parasol in the corner of the sofa.*]

Miss Tes. [*takes both his hands and looks at him*]. What a delight it is to have you again, as large as life, before my very eyes, George! My George—my poor brother's own boy!

TES. And it's a delight for me, too, to see you again, Aunt Julia! You who have been father and mother in one to me.

MISS TES. Oh yes, I know you will always keep a place in your heart for your old aunts.

TES. And what about Aunt Rina? No improvement—eh?

MISS TES. Oh no—we can scarcely look for any improvement in her case, poor thing. There she lies, helpless, as she has lain for all these years. But heaven grant I may not lose her yet awhile! For if I did, I don't know what I should make of my life, George—especially now that I haven't you to look after any more.

TES. [*patting her back*]. There, there, there!

MISS TES. [*suddenly changing her tone*]. And to think that here you are a married man, George! And that you should be the one to carry off Hedda Gabler—the beautiful Hedda Gabler! Only think of it—she that was so beset with admirers!

TES. [*hums a little and smiles complacently*]. Yes, I fancy I have several good friends about town who would like to stand in my shoes—eh?

MISS TES. And then this fine long wedding tour you have had! More than five—nearly six months——

TES. Well, for me it has been a sort of tour of research as well. I have had to do so much grubbing among old records—and to read no end of books too, Auntie.

MISS TES. Oh yes, I suppose so. [*More confidentially and lowering her voice a little.*] But listen now, George—have you nothing—nothing special to tell me?

TES. As to our journey?

MISS TES. Yes.

TES. No, I don't know of anything except what I have told you in my letters. I had a doctor's degree conferred on me—but that I told you yesterday.

MISS TES. Yes, yes, you did. But what I mean is—haven't you any—any—expectations?

TES. Expectations?

MISS TES. Why, you know, George—I'm your old auntie!

TES. Why, of course I have expectations.

MISS TES. Ah!

TES. I have every expectation of being a professor one of these days.

MISS TES. Oh yes, a professor——

TES. Indeed, I may say I am certain of it. But my dear auntie—you know all about that already!

MISS TES. [*laughing to herself*]. Yes, of course I do. You are right there. [*Changing the subject.*] But we were talking about your journey. It must have cost a great deal of money, George.

TES. Well, you see—my handsome traveling scholarship went a good way.

MISS TES. But I can't understand how you can have made it go far enough for two.

TES. No, that's not so easy to understand—eh?

MISS TES. And especially traveling with a lady—they tell me that makes it ever so much more expensive.

TES. Yes, of course—it makes it a little more expensive. But Hedda had to have this trip, Auntie! She really had to. Nothing else would have done.

MISS TES. No, no, I suppose not. A wedding tour seems to be quite indispensable nowadays. But tell me now—

have you gone thoroughly over the house yet?

TES. Yes, you may be sure I have. I have been afoot ever since daylight.

MISS TES. And what do you think of it all?

TES. I'm delighted! Quite delighted! Only I can't think what we are to do with the two empty rooms between this inner parlor and Hedda's bedroom.

MISS TES. [*laughing*]. Oh, my dear George, I daresay you may find some use for them—in the course of time.

TES. Why, of course you are quite right, Aunt Julia! You mean as my library increases—eh?

MISS TES. Yes, quite so, my dear boy. It was your library I was thinking of.

TES. I am specially pleased on Hedda's account. Often and often, before we were engaged, she said that she would never care to live anywhere but in Secretary Falk's villa.

MISS TES. Yes, it was lucky that this very house should come into the market just after you had started.

TES. Yes, Aunt Julia, the luck was on our side, wasn't it- eh?

MISS TES. But the expense, my dear George! You will find it very expensive, all this.

TES. [*looks at her a little cast down*]. Yes, I suppose I shall, Aunt!

MISS TES. Oh, frightfully!

TES. How much do you think? In round numbers? Eh?

MISS TES. Oh, I can't even guess until all the accounts come in.

TES. Well, fortunately Judge Brack has secured the most favorable terms for me—so he said in a letter to Hedda.

MISS TES. Yes, don't be uneasy, my dear boy. Besides, I have given security for the furniture and all the carpets.

TES. Security? You? My dear aunt Julia—what sort of security could you give?

MISS TES. I have given a mortgage on our annuity.

TES. [*jumps up*]. What! on your—and Aunt Rina's annuity!

MISS TES. Yes, I knew of no other plan, you see.

TES. [*placing himself before her*]. Have you gone out of your senses, Auntie? Your annuity—it's all that you and Aunt Rina have to live upon.

MISS TES. Well, well, don't get so excited about it. It's only a matter of form, you know—Judge Brack assured me of that. It was he that was kind enough to arrange the whole affair for me. A mere matter of form, he said.

TES. Yes, that may be all very well. But nevertheless——

MISS TES. You will have your own salary to depend upon now. And, good heavens, even if we did have to pay up a little—to eke things out a bit at the start——! Why, it would be nothing but a pleasure to us.

TES. Oh, Auntie—will you never be tired of making sacrifices for me!

MISS TES. [*rises and lays her hands on his shoulders*]. Have I had any other happiness in this world except to smooth your way for you, my dear boy? You who have had neither father nor mother to depend on. And now we have reached the goal, George! Things have looked black enough for us sometimes; but, thank heaven, now you have nothing to fear.

TES. Yes, it is really marvelous how everything has turned out for the best.

MISS TES. And the people who opposed you—who wanted to bar the way for you—now you have them at your feet. They have fallen, George. Your most dangerous rival—his fall was the worst. And now he has to lie on the bed he has made for himself—poor misguided creature.

TES. Have you heard anything of Eilert? Since I went away, I mean.

MISS TES. Only that he is said to have published a new book.

TES. What! Eilert Lövborg! Recently—eh?

MISS TES. Yes, so they say. Heaven knows whether it can be worth anything! Ah, when your new book appears—that will be another story, George! What is it to be about?

TES. It will deal with the domestic industries of Brabant during the Middle Ages.

MISS TES. Fancy—to be able to write on such a subject as that!

TES. However, it may be some time before the book is ready. I have all these collections to arrange first, you see.

MISS TES. Yes, collecting and arranging—no one can beat you at that. There you are my poor brother's own son.

TES. I am looking forward eagerly to setting to work at it, especially now that I have my own delightful home to work in.

MISS TES. And, most of all, now that you have got the wife of your heart, my dear George.

TES. [*embracing her*]. Oh yes, yes, Aunt Julia. Hedda—she is the best part of all! [*Looks toward the doorway.*] I believe I hear her coming—eh?

[HEDDA *enters from the left through the inner room. She is a woman of nine-and-twenty. Her face and figure show refinement and distinction. Her complexion is pale and opaque. Her steel-gray eyes express a cold, unruffled repose. Her hair is of an agreeable medium brown but not particularly abundant. She is dressed in a tasteful, somewhat loose-fitting morning gown.*]

MISS TES. [*going to meet* HEDDA]. Good morning, my dear Hedda! Good morning, and a hearty welcome.

HEDDA [*holds out her hand*]. Good morning, dear Miss Tesman! So early a call! That is kind of you.

MISS TES. [*with some embarrassment*]. Well—has the bride slept well in her new home?

HEDDA. Oh yes, thanks. Passably.

TES. [*laughing*]. Passably! Come, that's good, Hedda! You were sleeping like a stone when I got up.

HEDDA. Fortunately. Of course one has always to accustom one's self to new surroundings, Miss Tesman—little by little. [*Looking toward the left.*] Oh—there the servant has gone and opened the veranda door and let in a whole flood of sunshine.

MISS TES. [*going toward the door*]. Well, then, we will shut it.

HEDDA. No, no, not that! Tesman, please draw the curtains. That will give a softer light.

TES. [*at the door*]. All right—all right. There now, Hedda, now you have both shade and fresh air.

HEDDA. Yes, fresh air we certainly must have, with all these stacks of flowers—— But—won't you sit down, Miss Tesman?

MISS TES. No, thank you. Now that I have seen that everything is all right here—thank heaven!—I must be getting home again. My sister is lying longing for me, poor thing.

Tes. Give her my very best love, Auntie, and say I shall look in and see her later in the day.

Miss Tes. Yes, yes, I'll be sure to tell her. But by-the-bye, George—[*feeling in her dress pocket*]—I have —for you here——

Tes. What is it, Auntie? Eh?

Miss Tes. [*produces a flat parcel wrapped in newspaper and hands it to him*]. Look here, my dear boy.

Tes. [*opening the parcel*]. Well, I declare! Have you really saved them for me, Aunt Julia! Hedda! isn't this touching—eh?

Hedda [*beside the whatnot on the right*]. Well, what is it?

Tes. My old morning shoes! My slippers.

Hedda. Indeed. I remember you often spoke of them while we were abroad.

Tes. Yes, I missed them terribly. [*Goes up to her.*] Now you shall see them, Hedda!

Hedda [*going toward the stove*]. Thanks, I really don't care about it.

Tes. [*following her*]. Only think—ill as she was, Aunt Rina embroidered these for me. Oh, you can't think how many associations cling to them.

Hedda [*at the table*]. Scarcely for me.

Miss Tes. Of course not for Hedda, George.

Tes. Well, but now that she belongs to the family, I thought—

Hedda [*interrupting*]. We shall never get on with this servant, Tesman.

Miss Tes. Not get on with Berta?

Tes. Why, dear, what puts that in your head? Eh?

Hedda [*pointing*]. Look there! She has left her old bonnet lying about on a chair.

Tes. [*in consternation drops the slippers on the floor*]. Why, Hedda——

Hedda. Just fancy if anyone should come in and see it!

Tes. But, Hedda—that's Aunt Julia's bonnet.

Hedda. Is it!

Miss Tes. [*taking up the bonnet*]. Yes, indeed it's mine. And, what's more, it's not old, Madame Hedda.

Hedda. I really did not look closely at it, Miss Tesman.

Miss Tes. [*trying on the bonnet*]. Let me tell you it's the first time I have worn it—the very first time.

Tes. And a very nice bonnet it is too—quite a beauty!

Miss Tes. Oh, it's no such great things, George. [*Looks around her.*] My parasol——? Ah, here. [*Takes it.*] For this is mine too [*mutters*]—not Berta's.

Tes. A new bonnet and a new parasol! Only think, Hedda!

Hedda. Very handsome indeed.

Tes. Yes, isn't it? Eh? But, Auntie, take a good look at Hedda before you go! See how handsome she is!

Miss Tes. Oh, my dear boy, there's nothing new in that. Hedda was always lovely. [*She nods and goes toward the right.*]

Tes. [*following*]. Yes, but have you noticed what splendid condition she is in? How she has filled out on the journey?

Hedda [*crossing the room*]. Oh, do be quiet!

Miss Tes. [*who has stopped and turned*]. Filled out?

Tes. Of course you don't notice it so much now that she has that dress on. But I, who can see——

HEDDA [*at the glass door, impatiently*]. Oh, you can't see anything.

TES. It must be the mountain air in the Tyrol——

HEDDA [*curtly interrupting*]. I am exactly as I was when I started.

TES. So you insist, but I'm quite certain you are not. Don't you agree with me, Auntie?

MISS TES. [*who has been gazing at her with folded hands*]. Hedda is lovely—lovely—lovely. [*Goes up to her, takes her head between both hands, draws it downward and kisses her hair.*] God bless and preserve Hedda Tesman—for George's sake.

HEDDA [*gently freeing herself*]. Oh! Let me go.

MISS TES. [*in quiet emotion*]. I shall not let a day pass without coming to see you.

TES. No, you won't, will you, Auntie? Eh?

MISS TES. Good-by—good-by! [*She goes out by the hall door.* TESMAN *accompanies her. The door remains half open.* TESMAN *can be heard repeating his message to Aunt Rina and his thanks for the slippers. In the meantime* HEDDA *walks about the room raising her arms and clenching her hands as if in desperation. Then she flings back the curtains from the glass door and stands there looking out. Presently* TESMAN *returns and closes the door behind him.*]

TES. [*picks up the slippers from the floor*]. What are you looking at, Hedda?

HEDDA [*once more calm and mistress of herself*]. I am only looking at the leaves. They are so yellow—so withered.

TES. [*wraps up the slippers and lays them on the table*]. Well, you see, we are well into September now.

HEDDA [*again restless*]. Yes, to think of it! Already in—in September.

TES. Don't you think Aunt Julia's manner was strange, dear? Almost solemn? Can you imagine what was the matter with her? Eh?

HEDDA. I scarcely know her, you see. Is she often like that?

TES. No, not as she was today.

HEDDA [*leaving the glass door*]. Do you think she was annoyed about the bonnet?

TES. Oh, scarcely at all. Perhaps a little, just at the moment——

HEDDA. But what an idea, to pitch her bonnet about in the drawing room! No one does that sort of thing.

TES. Well, you may be sure Aunt Julia won't do it again.

HEDDA. In any case, I shall manage to make my peace with her.

TES. Yes, my dear, good Hedda, if you only would.

HEDDA. When you call this afternoon you might invite her to spend the evening here.

TES. Yes, that I will. And there's one thing more you could do that would delight her heart.

HEDDA. What is it?

TES. If you could only prevail on yourself to say *du* to her. For my sake, Hedda? Eh?

HEDDA. No, no, Tesman—you really mustn't ask that of me. I have told you so already. I shall try to call her "Aunt," and you must be satisfied with that.

TES. Well, well. Only I think now that you belong to the family, you——

HEDDA. H'm—I can't in the least see why. [*She goes up toward the middle doorway.*]

TES. [*after a pause*]. Is there anything the matter with you, Hedda? Eh?

HEDDA. I'm only looking at my old piano. It doesn't go at all well with all the other things.

TES. The first time I draw my salary we'll see about exchanging it.

HEDDA. No, no—no exchanging. I don't want to part with it. Suppose we put it there in the inner room and then get another here in its place. When it's convenient, I mean.

TES. [*a little taken aback*]. Yes—of course we could do that.

HEDDA [*takes up the bouquet from the piano*]. These flowers were not here last night when we arrived.

TES. Aunt Julia must have brought them for you.

HEDDA [*examining the bouquet*]. A visiting card. [*Takes it out and reads*] "Shall return later in the day." Can you guess whose card it is?

TES. No. Whose? Eh?

HEDDA. The name is Mrs Elvsted.

TES. Is it really? Sheriff Elvsted's wife? Miss Rysing that was.

HEDDA. Exactly. The girl with the irritating hair, that she was always showing off. An old flame of yours I've been told.

TES. [*laughing*]. Oh, that didn't last long, and it was before I knew you, Hedda. But fancy her being in town!

HEDDA. It's odd that she should call upon us. I have scarcely seen her since we left school.

TES. I haven't seen her either for—heaven knows how long. I wonder how she can endure to live in such an out-of-the-way hole—eh?

HEDDA [*after a moment's thought says suddenly*]. Tell me, Tesman—isn't it somewhere near there that he—that—Eilert Lövborg is living?

TES. Yes, he is somewhere in that part of the country.

[BERTA *enters by the hall door.*]

BERTA. That lady, ma'am, that brought some flowers a little while ago, is here again. [*Pointing.*] The flowers you have in your hand, ma'am.

HEDDA. Ah, is she? Well, please show her in.

[BERTA *opens the door for* MRS ELVSTED *and goes out herself.* MRS ELVSTED *is a woman of fragile figure, with pretty, soft features. Her eyes are light blue, large, round and somewhat prominent, with a startled, inquiring expression. Her hair is remarkably light, almost flaxen, and unusually abundant and wavy. She is a couple of years younger than* HEDDA. *She wears a dark visiting dress, tasteful but not quite in the latest fashion.*]

HEDDA [*receives her warmly*]. How do you do, my dear Mrs Elvsted? It's delightful to see you again.

MRS ELVS. [*nervously struggling for self-control*]. Yes, it's a very long time since we met.

TES. [*gives her his hand*]. And we too—eh?

HEDDA. Thanks for your lovely flowers——

MRS ELVS. Oh, not at all. I would have come straight here yesterday afternoon, but I heard that you were away.

TES. Have you just come to town? Eh?

MRS ELVS. I arrived yesterday, about midday. Oh, I was quite in despair when I heard that you were not at home.

HEDDA. In despair! How so?

TES. Why, my dear Mrs Rysing—I mean Mrs Elvsted —

HEDDA. I hope that you are not in any trouble?

MRS ELVS. Yes, I am. And I don't know another living creature here that I can turn to.

HEDDA [*laying the bouquet on the table*]. Come—let us sit here on the sofa.

MRS ELVS. Oh, I am too restless to sit down.

HEDDA. Oh no, you're not. Come here. [*She draws* MRS ELVS. *down upon the sofa and sits at her side.*]

TES. Well? What is it, Mrs Elvsted?

HEDDA. Has anything particular happened to you at home?

MRS ELVS. Yes—and no. Oh—I am so anxious that you should not misunderstand me.

HEDDA. Then your best plan is to tell us the whole story, Mrs Elvsted.

TES. I suppose that's what you have come for—eh?

MRS ELVS. Yes, yes—of course it is. Well then, I must tell you—if you don't already know—that Eilert Lövborg is in town too.

HEDDA. Lövborg!

TES. What! Has Eilert Lövborg come back? Fancy that, Hedda!

HEDDA. Well, well—I hear it.

MRS ELVS. He has been here a week already. Just fancy—a whole week! In this terrible town, alone! With so many temptations on all sides.

HEDDA. But my dear Mrs Elvsted—how does he concern you so much?

MRS ELVS. [*looks at her with a startled air and says rapidly*]. He was the children's tutor.

HEDDA. Your children's?

MRS ELVS. My husband's. I have none.

HEDDA. Your stepchildren's, then?

MRS ELVS. Yes.

TES. [*somewhat hesitantly*]. Then was he—I don't know how to express it—was he—regular enough in his habits to be fit for the post? Eh?

MRS ELVS. For the last two years his conduct has been irreproachable.

TES. Has it, indeed? Fancy that, Hedda!

HEDDA. I hear it.

MRS ELVS. Perfectly irreproachable, I assure you! In every respect. But all the same—now that I know he is here—in this great town—and with a large sum of money in his hands—I can't help being in mortal fear for him.

TES. Why did he not remain where he was? With you and your husband? Eh?

MRS ELVS. After his book was published he was too restless and unsettled to remain with us.

TES. Yes; by-the-bye, Aunt Julia told me he had published a new book.

MRS ELVS. Yes, a big book, dealing with the march of civilization—in broad outline, as it were. It came out about a fortnight ago. And since it has sold so well and been so much read—and made such a sensation——

TES. Has it, indeed? It must be something he has had lying by since his better days.

MRS ELVS. Long ago, you mean?

TES. Yes.

MRS ELVS. No, he has written it all since he has been with us—within the last year.

TES. Isn't that good news, Hedda? Think of that.

MRS ELVS. Ah yes, if only it would last!

HEDDA. Have you seen him here in town?

MRS ELVS. No, not yet. I have had the greatest difficulty in finding out his address. But this morning I discovered it at last.

HEDDA [*looks searchingly at her*]. Do you know, it seems to me a little odd of your husband—h'm——

MRS ELVS. [*starting nervously*]. Of my husband! What?

HEDDA. That he should send you to town on such an errand—that he does not come himself and look after his friend.

MRS ELVS. Oh no, no—my husband has no time. And besides, I—I have some shopping to do.

HEDDA [*with a slight smile*]. Ah, that is a different matter.

MRS ELVS. [*rising quickly and uneasily*]. And now I beg and implore you, Mr Tesman—receive Eilert Lövborg kindly if he comes to you! And that he is sure to do. You see, you were such great friends in the old days. And then you are interested in the same studies—the same branch of science—so far as I can understand.

TES. We used to be, at any rate.

MRS ELVS. That is why I beg so earnestly that you—you too—will keep a sharp eye upon him. Oh, you will promise me that, Mr Tesman—won't you?

TES. With the greatest of pleasure, Mrs Rysing——

HEDDA. Elvsted.

TES. I assure you that I shall do all I possibly can for Eilert. You may rely upon me.

MRS ELVS. Oh, how very, very kind of you! [*Presses his hands.*] Thanks, thanks, thanks! [*Frightened.*] You see, my husband is very fond of him!

HEDDA [*rising*]. You ought to write to him, Tesman. Perhaps he may not care to come to you of his own accord.

TES. Well, perhaps it would be the right thing to do, Hedda. Eh?

HEDDA. And the sooner the better. Why not at once?

MRS ELVS. [*imploringly*]. Oh, if you only would!

TES. I'll write this moment. Have you his address, Mrs—Mrs Elvsted?

MRS ELVS. Yes. [*Takes a slip of paper from her pocket and hands it to him.*] Here it is.

TES. Good, good. Then I'll go in—— [*Looks about him.*] By-the-bye, my slippers? Oh, here. [*Takes the packet and is about to go.*]

HEDDA. Be sure to write him a cordial, friendly letter. And a good long one too.

TES. Yes, I will.

MRS ELVS. But please, please don't say a word to show that I have suggested it.

TES. No, how could you think I would? Eh? [*He goes out to the right through the inner room.*]

HEDDA [*goes up to* MRS ELVS., *smiles and says in a low voice*]. There. We have killed two birds with one stone.

MRS ELVS. What do you mean?

HEDDA. Could you not see that I wanted him to go?

MRS ELVS. Yes, to write the letter——

HEDDA. And that I might speak to you alone?

MRS ELVS. [*confused*]. About the same thing?

HEDDA. Precisely.

MRS ELVS. [*apprehensively*]. But there is nothing more, Mrs Tesman! Absolutely nothing!

HEDDA. Oh yes, but there is. There is a great deal more—I can see that. Sit here—and we'll have a cosy, confidential chat. [*She forces* MRS ELVS. *to sit in the easy chair beside the stove and seats herself on one of the footstools.*]

Mrs Elvs. [*anxiously looking at her watch*]. But, my dear Mrs Tesman—I was really on the point of going.

Hedda. Oh, you can't be in such a hurry. Well? Now tell me something about your life at home.

Mrs Elvs. Oh, that is just what I care least to speak about.

Hedda. But to me, dear——? Why, weren't we school fellows?

Mrs Elvs. Yes, but you were in the class above me. Oh, how dreadfully afraid of you I was then!

Hedda. Afraid of me?

Mrs Elvs. *Yes*, dreadfully. For when we met on the stairs you used always to pull my hair.

Hedda. Did I really?

Mrs Elvs. Yes, and once you said you would burn it off my head.

Hedda. Oh, that was all nonsense, of course.

Mrs Elvs. Yes, but I was so silly in those days. And since then, too—we have drifted so far—far apart from each other. Our circles have been so entirely different.

Hedda. Well then, we must try to drift together again. Now listen! At school we said *du* to each other and we called each other by our Christian names——

Mrs Elvs. No, I am sure you must be mistaken.

Hedda. No, not at all! I can remember quite distinctly. So now we are going to renew our old friendship. [*Draws the footstool closer to* Mrs Elvs.] There now! [*Kisses her cheek.*] You must say *du* to me and call me Hedda.

Mrs Elvs. [*presses and pats her hands*]. Oh, how good and kind you are! I am not used to such kindness.

Hedda. There, there, there! And I shall say *du* to you, as in the old days, and call you my dear Thora.

Mrs Elvs. My name is Thea.

Hedda. Why, of course! I meant Thea. [*Looks at her compassionately.*] So you are not accustomed to goodness and kindness, Thea? Not in your own home?

Mrs Elvs. Oh, if I only had a home! But I haven't any; I have never had a home.

Hedda [*looks at her for a moment*]. I almost suspected as much.

Mrs Elvs. [*gazing helplessly before her*]. Yes—yes—yes.

Hedda. I don't quite remember—was it not as housekeeper that you first went to Mr Elvsted's?

Mrs Elvs. I really went as governess. But his wife—his late wife—was an invalid and rarely left her room. So I had to look after the housekeeping as well.

Hedda. And then—at last—you became mistress of the house.

Mrs Elvs. [*sadly*]. Yes, I did.

Hedda. Let me see—about how long ago was that?

Mrs Elvs. My marriage?

Hedda. Yes.

Mrs Elvs. Five years ago.

Hedda. To be sure, it must be that.

Mrs Elvs. Oh, those five years! Or at all events the last two or three of them! Oh, if you could only imagine——

Hedda [*giving her a little slap on the hand*]. De? Fie, Thea!

Mrs Elvs. Yes, yes, I will try——Well, if—you could only imagine and understand——

Hedda [*lightly*]. Eilert Lövborg has been in your neighborhood about three years, hasn't he?

MRS ELVS. [*looks at her doubtfully*]. Eilert Lövborg? Yes—he has.

HEDDA. Had you known him before, in town here?

MRS ELVS. Scarcely at all. I mean—I knew him by name, of course.

HEDDA. But you saw a good deal of him in the country?

MRS ELVS. Yes, he came to us every day. You see, he gave the children lessons; for in the long run I couldn't manage it all myself.

HEDDA. No, that's clear. And your husband——? I suppose he is often away from home?

MRS ELVS. Yes. Being sheriff, you know, he has to travel about a good deal in his district.

HEDDA [*leaning against the arm of the chair*]. Thea—my poor, sweet Thea—now you must tell me everything—exactly as it stands.

MRS ELVS. Well then, you must question me.

HEDDA. What sort of man is your husband, Thea? I mean—you know—in everyday life. Is he kind to you?

MRS ELVS. [*evasively*]. I am sure he means well in everything.

HEDDA. I should think he must be altogether too old for you. There is at least twenty years' difference between you, is there not?

MRS ELVS. [*irritably*]. Yes, that is true too. Everything about him is repellent to me! We have not a thought in common. We have no single point of sympathy—he and I.

HEDDA. But is he not fond of you all the same? In his own way?

MRS ELVS. Oh, I really don't know. I think he regards me simply as a useful property. And then it doesn't cost much to keep me. I am not expensive.

HEDDA. That is stupid of you.

MRS ELVS. [*shakes her head*]. It cannot be otherwise—not with him. I don't think he really cares for anyone but himself—and perhaps a little for the children.

HEDDA. And for Eilert Lövborg, Thea.

MRS ELVS. [*looking at her*]. For Eilert Lövborg? What put that into your head?

HEDDA. Well, my dear—I should say when he sends you after him all the way to town——[*Smiling almost imperceptibly.*] And besides, you said so yourself to Tesman.

MRS ELVS. [*with a little nervous twitch*]. Did I? Yes, I suppose I did. [*Vehemently but not loudly.*] No--I may just as well make a clean breast of it at once! For it must all come out in any case.

HEDDA. Why, my dear Thea——

MRS ELVS. Well, to make a long story short: My husband did not know that I was coming.

HEDDA. What! Your husband didn't know it!

MRS ELVS. No, of course not. For that matter, he was away from home himself—he was traveling. Oh, I could bear it no longer, Hedda! I couldn't indeed—so utterly alone as I should have been in future.

HEDDA. Well? And then?

MRS ELVS. So I put together some of my things—what I needed most—as quietly as possible. And then I left the house.

HEDDA. Without a word?

MRS ELVS. Yes—and took the train straight to town.

HEDDA. Why, my dear, good Thea—to think of you daring to do it!

MRS ELVS. [*rises and moves about the room*]. What else could I possibly do?

HEDDA. But what do you think your husband will say when you go home again?

MRS ELVS. [*at the table, looks at her*]. Back to him?

HEDDA. Of course.

MRS ELVS. I shall never go back to him again.

HEDDA [*rising and going toward her*]. Then you have left your home —for good and all?

MRS ELVS. Yes. There was nothing else to be done.

HEDDA. But then—to take flight so openly.

MRS ELVS. Oh, it's impossible to keep things of that sort secret.

HEDDA. But what do you think people will say of you, Thea?

MRS ELVS. They may say what they like for aught *I* care. [*Seats herself wearily and sadly on the sofa.*] I have done nothing but what I had to do.

HEDDA [*after a short silence*]. And what are your plans now? What do you think of doing?

MRS ELVS. I don't know yet. I only know this, that I must live here, where Eilert Lövborg is—if I am to live at all.

HEDDA [*takes a chair from the table, seats herself beside her and strokes her hands*]. My dear Thea— how did this—this friendship—between you and Eilert Lövborg come about?

MRS ELVS. Oh, it grew up gradually. I gained a sort of influence over him.

HEDDA. Indeed?

MRS ELVS. He gave up his old habits. Not because I asked him to, for I never dared do that. But of course he saw how repulsive they were to me, and so he dropped them.

HEDDA [*concealing an involuntary smile of scorn*]. Then you have reclaimed him—as the saying goes—my little Thea.

MRS ELVS. So he says himself, at any rate. And he, on his side, has made a real human being of me— taught me to think and to understand so many things.

HEDDA. Did he give you lessons too, then?

MRS ELVS. No, not exactly lessons. But he talked to me—talked about such an infinity of things. And then came the lovely, happy time when I began to share in his work—when he allowed me to help him!

HEDDA. Oh, he did, did he?

MRS ELVS. Yes! He never wrote anything without my assistance.

HEDDA. You were two good comrades, in fact?

MRS ELVS. [*eagerly*]. Comrades! Yes, fancy, Hedda—that is the very word he used! Oh, I ought to feel perfectly happy, and yet I cannot, for I don't know how long it will last.

HEDDA. Are you no surer of him than that?

MRS ELVS. [*gloomily*]. A woman's shadow stands between Eilert Lövborg and me.

HEDDA [*looks at her anxiously*]. Who can that be?

MRS ELVS. I don't know. Someone he knew in his—in his past. Someone he has never been able wholly to forget.

HEDDA. What has he told you— about this?

MRS ELVS. He has only once—quite vaguely—alluded to it.

HEDDA. Well! And what did he say?

MRS ELVS. He said that when they parted she threatened to shoot him with a pistol.

HEDDA [*with cool composure*]. Oh, nonsense! No one does that sort of thing here.

MRS ELVS. No. And that is why I think it must have been that red-haired singing woman whom he once——

HEDDA. Yes, very likely.

MRS ELVS. For I remember they used to say of her that she carried loaded firearms.

HEDDA. Oh—then of course it must have been she.

MRS ELVS. [*wringing her hands*]. And now just fancy. Hedda—I hear that this singing woman—that she is in town again! Oh, I don't know what to do.

HEDDA [*glancing toward the inner room*]. Hush! Here comes Tesman. [*Rises and whispers.*] Thea—all this must remain between you and me.

MRS ELVS. [*springing up*]. Oh yes, yes! for heaven's sake!

[GEORGE TESMAN, *with a letter in his hand, comes from the right through the inner room.*]

TES. There now—the epistle is finished.

HEDDA. That's right. And now Mrs Elvsted is just going. Wait a moment —I'll go with you to the garden gate.

TES. Do you think Berta could post the letter, Hedda dear?

HEDDA [*takes it*]. I will tell her to.

[BERTA *enters from the hall.*]

BERTA. Judge Brack wishes to know if Mrs Tesman will receive him.

HEDDA. Yes, ask Judge Brack to come in. And look here—put this letter in the post.

BERTA [*taking the letter*]. Yes, ma'am. [*She opens the door for* JUDGE BRACK *and goes out herself.* BRACK *is a man of forty-five, thick-set but well built and elastic in his movements. His face is roundish with an aristocratic profile. His hair is short, still almost black and carefully dressed. His eyes are lively and sparkling, his eyebrows thick. His mustaches are also thick with short-cut ends. He wears a well-cut walking suit, a little too youthful for his age. He uses an eyeglass which he now and then lets drop.*]

BRACK [*with his hat in his hand, bowing*]. May one venture to call so early in the day?

HEDDA. Of course one may.

TES. [*presses his hand*]. You are welcome at any time. [*Introducing him.*] Judge Brack—Miss Rysing——

HEDDA. Oh!

BRACK [*bowing*]. Ah—delighted!

HEDDA [*looks at him and laughs*]. It's nice to have a look at you by daylight, Judge!

BRACK. Do you find me—altered?

HEDDA. A little younger, I think.

BRACK. Thank you so much.

TES. But what do you think of Hedda—eh? Doesn't she look flourishing? She has actually——

HEDDA. Oh, do leave me alone. You haven't thanked Judge Brack for all the trouble he has taken——

BRACK. Oh, nonsense—it was a pleasure to me.

HEDDA. Yes, you are a friend indeed. But here stands Thea all impatience to be off—so au revoir, Judge. I shall be back again presently. [*Mutual salutations.* MRS ELVSTED *and* HEDDA *go out by the hall door.*]

BRACK. Well, is you wife tolerably satisfied?

TES. Yes, we can't thank you sufficiently. Of course she talks of a little rearrangement here and there, and one or two things are still wanting. We shall have to buy some additional trifles.

BRACK. Indeed!

TES. But we won't trouble you about these things. Hedda says she herself will look after what is wanting. Shan't we sit down? Eh?

BRACK. Thanks, for a moment. [*Seats himself beside the table.*] There is something I wanted to speak to you about, my dear Tesman.

TES. Indeed? Ah, I understand! [*Seating himself.*] I suppose it's the serious part of the frolic that is coming now. Eh?

BRACK. Oh, the money question is not so very pressing; though, for that matter, I wish we had gone a little more economically to work.

TES. But that would never have done, you know! Think of Hedda, my dear fellow! You, who know her so well—— I couldn't possibly ask her to put up with a shabby style of living!

BRACK. No, no—that is just the difficulty.

TES. And then—fortunately—it can't be long before I receive my appointment.

BRACK. Well, you see—such things are often apt to hang fire for a time.

TES. Have you heard anything definite? Eh?

BRACK. Nothing exactly definite—— [*Interrupting himself.*] But by-the-bye—I have one piece of news for you.

TES. Well?

BRACK. Your old friend Eilert Lövborg has returned to town.

TES. I know that already.

BRACK. Indeed! How did you learn it?

TES. From the lady who went out with Hedda.

BRACK. Really? What was her name? I didn't quite catch it.

TES. Mrs Elvsted.

BRACK. Aha—Sheriff Elvsted's wife? Of course—he has been living up in their regions.

TES. And fancy—I'm delighted to hear that he is quite a reformed character!

BRACK. So they say.

TES. And then he has published a new book—eh?

BRACK. Yes, indeed he has.

TES. And I hear it has made some sensation!

BRACK. Quite an unusual sensation.

TES. Fancy—isn't that good news! A man of such extraordinary talents —I felt so grieved to think that he had gone irretrievably to ruin.

BRACK. That was what everybody thought.

TES. But I cannot imagine what he will take to now! How in the world will he be able to make his living? Eh?

[*During the last words* HEDDA *has entered by the hall door.*]

HEDDA [*to* BRACK, *laughing with a touch of scorn*]. Tesman is forever worrying about how people are to make their living.

TES. Well, you see, dear—we were talking about poor Eilert Lövborg.

HEDDA [*glancing at him rapidly*]. Oh, indeed? [*Seats herself in the armchair beside the stove and asks indifferently*] What is the matter with him?

TES. Well—no doubt he has run through all his property long ago, and he can scarcely write a new book every year—eh? So I really can't see what is to become of him.

BRACK. Perhaps I can give you some information on that point.

TES. Indeed!

BRACK. You must remember that his relations have a good deal of influence.

TES. Oh, his relations, unfortunately, have entirely washed their hands of him.

BRACK. At one time they called him the hope of the family.

TES. At one time, yes! But he has put an end to all that.

HEDDA. Who knows? [*With a slight smile.*] I hear they have reclaimed him up at Sheriff Elvsted's.

BRACK. And then this book that he has published——

TES. Well, well, I hope to goodness they may find something for him to do. I have just written to him. I asked him to come and see us this evening, Hedda dear.

BRACK. But, my dear fellow, you are booked for my bachelors' party this evening. You promised on the pier last night.

HEDDA. Had you forgotten, Tesman?

TES. Yes, I had utterly forgotten.

BRACK. But it doesn't matter, for you may be sure he won't come.

TES. What makes you think that? Eh?

BRACK [*with a little hesitation, rising and resting his hands on the back of his chair*]. My dear Tesman—and you too, Mrs Tesman—I think I ought not to keep you in the dark about something that—that——

TES. That concerns Eilert?

BRACK. Both you and him.

TES. Well, my dear judge, out with it.

BRACK. You must be prepared to find your appointment deferred longer than you desired or expected.

TES. [*jumping up uneasily*]. Is there some hitch about it? Eh?

BRACK. The nomination may perhaps be made conditional on the result of a competition——

TES. Competition! Think of that, Hedda!

HEDDA [*leans farther back in the chair*]. Aha—aah!

TES. But who can my competitor be? Surely not——?

BRACK. Yes, precisely—Eilert Lövborg.

TES. [*clasping his hands*]. No, no—it's quite inconceivable! Quite impossible! Eh?

BRACK. H'm—that is what it may come to, all the same.

TES. Well, but, Judge Brack—it would show the most incredible lack of consideration for me. [*Gesticulates with his arms.*] For—just think—I'm a married man. We have been married on the strength of these prospects, Hedda and I, and run deep into debt and borrowed money from Aunt Julia too. Good heavens, they had as good as promised me the appointment. Eh?

BRACK. Well, well, well—no doubt you will get it in the end; only after a contest.

HEDDA [*immovable in her armchair*]. Fancy, Tesman, there will be a sort of sporting interest in that.

TES. Why, my dearest Hedda, how can you be so indifferent about it?

HEDDA [*as before*]. I am not at all indifferent. I am most eager to see who wins.

BRACK. In any case, Mrs Tesman, it is best that you should know how matters stand. I mean—before you set about the little purchases I hear you are threatening.

HEDDA. This can make no difference.

BRACK. Indeed! Then I have no more to say. Good-by! [*To* TES.] I shall look in on my way back from my afternoon walk and take you home with me.

TES. Oh yes, yes—your news has quite upset me.

HEDDA [*reclining, holds out her hand*]. Good-by, Judge, and be sure you call in the afternoon.

BRACK. Many thanks. Good-by, good-by!

TES. [*accompanying him to the door*]. Good-by, my dear judge! You must really excuse me. [JUDGE BRACK *goes out by the hall door.*]

TES. [*crosses the room*]. Oh, Hedda—one should never rush into adventures. Eh?

HEDDA [*looks at him smilingly*]. Do you do that?

TES. Yes, dear—there is no denying—it was adventurous to go and marry and set up house upon mere expectations.

HEDDA. Perhaps you are right there.

TES. Well—at all events, we have our delightful home, Hedda! Fancy, the home we both dreamed of—the home we were in love with, I may almost say. Eh?

HEDDA [*rising slowly and wearily*]. It was part of our compact that we were to go into society—to keep open house.

TES. Yes, if you only knew how I had been looking forward to it! Fancy—to see you as hostess—in a select circle? Eh? Well, well, well—for the present we shall have to get on without society, Hedda—only to invite Aunt Julia now and then. Oh, I intended you to lead such an utterly different life, dear!

HEDDA. Of course I cannot have my man in livery just yet.

TES. Oh no, unfortunately. It would be out of the question for us to keep a footman, you know.

HEDDA. And the saddle horse I was to have had——

TES. [*aghast*]. The saddle horse!

HEDDA. I suppose I must not think of that now.

TES. Good heavens, no! That's as clear as daylight.

HEDDA [*goes up the room*]. Well, I shall have one thing at least to kill time with in the meanwhile.

TES. [*beaming*]. Oh, thank heaven for that! What is it, Hedda? Eh?

HEDDA [*in the middle doorway, looks at him with covert scorn*]. My pistols, George.

TES. [*in alarm*]. Your pistols!

HEDDA [*with cold eyes*]. General Gabler's pistols. [*She goes out through the inner room to the left.*]

TES. [*rushes up to the middle doorway and calls after her*]. No, for heaven's sake, Hedda darling—don't touch those dangerous things! For my sake, Hedda! Eh?

ACT II

SCENE—*The room at the* TESMANS' *as in the first act, except that the piano has been removed and an elegant little writing table with bookshelves put in its place. A smaller table stands near the sofa on the left. Most of the bouquets have been taken away.* MRS ELVSTED'S *bouquet is upon the large table in front. It is afternoon.*

HEDDA, *dressed to receive callers, is alone in the room. She stands by the open glass door loading a revolver.*

The fellow to it lies in an open pistol case on the writing table.

HEDDA [*looks down the garden and calls*]. So you are here again, Judge!

BRACK [*is heard calling from a distance*]. As you see, Mrs Tesman!

HEDDA [*raises the pistol and points*]. Now I'll shoot you, Judge Brack!

BRACK [*calling unseen*]. No, no, no! Don't stand aiming at me!

HEDDA. This is what comes of sneaking in by the back way. [*She fires.*]

BRACK [*nearer*]. Are you out of your senses!

HEDDA. Dear me—did I happen to hit you?

BRACK [*still outside*]. I wish you would let these pranks alone!

HEDDA. Come in then, Judge.

[BRACK, *dressed as though for a men's party, enters by the glass door. He carries a light overcoat over his arm.*]

BRACK. What the deuce—haven't you tired of that sport yet? What are you shooting at?

HEDDA. Oh, I am only firing in the air.

BRACK [*gently takes the pistol out of her hand*]. Allow me, madam! [*Looks at it.*] Ah—I know this pistol well! [*Looks around.*] Where is the case? Ah, here it is. [*Lays the pistol in it and shuts it.*] Now we won't play at that game any more today.

HEDDA. Then what in heaven's name would you have me do with myself?

BRACK. Have you had no visitors?

HEDDA [*closing the glass door*]. Not one. I suppose all our set are still out of town.

BRACK. And is Tesman not at home either?

HEDDA [*at the writing table, putting the pistol case in a drawer which she shuts*]. No. He rushed off to his aunt's directly after lunch; he didn't expect you so early.

BRACK. H'm—how stupid of me not to have thought of that!

HEDDA [*turning her head to look at him*]. Why stupid?

BRACK. Because if I had thought of it I should have come a little—earlier.

HEDDA [*crossing the room*]. Then you would have found no one to receive you, for I have been in my room changing my dress ever since lunch.

BRACK. And is there no sort of little chink that we could hold a parley through?

HEDDA. You have forgotten to arrange one.

BRACK. That was another piece of stupidity.

HEDDA. Well, we must just settle down here—and wait. Tesman is not likely to be back for some time yet.

BRACK. Never mind; I shall not be impatient.

[HEDDA *seats herself in the corner of the sofa.* BRACK *lays his overcoat over the back of the nearest chair and sits down but keeps his hat in his hand. A short silence. They look at each other.*]

HEDDA. Well?

BRACK [*in the same tone*]. Well?

HEDDA. I spoke first.

BRACK [*bending a little forward*]. Come, let us have a cosy little chat, Mrs Hedda.

HEDDA [*leaning further back in the sofa*]. Does it not seem like a whole eternity since our last talk? Of course I don't count those few words yesterday evening and this morning.

BRACK. You mean since our last confidential talk? Our last tête-à-tête?

HEDDA. Well, yes—since you put it so.

BRACK. Not a day has passed but I have wished that you were home again.

HEDDA. And I have done nothing but wish the same thing.

BRACK. You? Really, Mrs Hedda? And I thought you had been enjoying your tour so much!

HEDDA. Oh yes, you may be sure of that!

BRACK. But Tesman's letters spoke of nothing but happiness.

HEDDA. Oh, Tesman! You see, he thinks nothing so delightful as grubbing in libraries and making copies of old parchments, or whatever you call them.

BRACK [*with a spice of malice*]. Well, that is his vocation in life—or part of it at any rate.

HEDDA. Yes, of course; and no doubt when it's your vocation—— But *I!* Oh, my dear Mr Brack, how mortally bored I have been.

BRACK [*sympathetically*]. Do you really say so? In downright earnest?

HEDDA. Yes, you can surely understand it! To go for six whole months without meeting a soul that knew anything of our circle or could talk about the things we are interested in.

BRACK. Yes, yes—I too should feel that a deprivation.

HEDDA. And then, what I found most intolerable of all——

BRACK. Well?

HEDDA. —was being everlastingly in the company of—one and the same person.

BRACK [*with a nod of assent*]. Morning, noon and night, yes—at all possible times and seasons.

HEDDA. I said "everlastingly."

BRACK. Just so. But I should have thought with our excellent Tesman one could——

HEDDA. Tesman is—a specialist, my dear judge.

BRACK. Undeniably.

HEDDA. And specialists are not at all amusing to travel with. Not in the long run at any rate.

BRACK. Not even—the specialist one happens to love?

HEDDA. Faugh—don't use that sickening word!

BRACK [*taken aback*]. What do you say, Mrs Hedda?

HEDDA [*half laughing, half irritated*]. You should just try it! To hear of nothing but the history of civilization morning, noon and night——

BRACK. Everlastingly.

HEDDA. Yes, yes, yes! And then all this about the domestic industry of the Middle Ages! That's the most disgusting part of it!

BRACK [*looks searchingly at her*]. But tell me—in that case how am I to understand your——? H'm——

HEDDA. My accepting George Tesman, you mean?

BRACK. Well, let us put it so.

HEDDA. Good heavens, do you see anything so wonderful in that?

BRACK. Yes and no—Mrs Hedda.

HEDDA. I had positively danced myself tired, my dear judge. My day was done. [*With a slight shudder.*] Oh no —I won't say that, nor think it either!

BRACK. You have assuredly no reason to.

HEDDA. Oh, reasons—— [*Watching him closely.*] And George Tesman—after all, you must admit that he is correctness itself.

BRACK. His correctness and respectability are beyond all question.

HEDDA. And I don't see anything absolutely ridiculous about him. Do you?

BRACK. Ridiculous? N - no — I shouldn't exactly say so.

HEDDA. Well—and his powers of research, at all events, are untiring. I see no reason why he should not one day come to the front after all.

BRACK [*looks at her hesitatingly*]. I thought that you, like everyone else, expected him to attain the highest distinction.

HEDDA [*with an expression of fatigue*]. Yes, so I did. And then—since he was bent, at all hazards, on being allowed to provide for me—I really don't know why I should not have accepted his offer?

BRACK. No—if you look at it in that light.

HEDDA. It was more than my other adorers were prepared to do for me, my dear judge.

BRACK [*laughing*]. Well, I can't answer for all the rest; but as for myself, you know quite well that I have always entertained a—a certain respect for the marriage tie—for marriage as an institution, Mrs Hedda.

HEDDA [*jestingly*]. Oh, I assure you I have never cherished any hopes with respect to you.

BRACK. All I require is a pleasant and intimate interior, where I can make myself useful in every way and am free to come and go as—as a trusted friend

HEDDA. Of the master of the house, do you mean?

BRACK [*bowing*]. Frankly—of the mistress first of all; but of course of the master, too, in the second place. Such a triangular friendship—if I may call it so—is really a great convenience for all parties, let me tell you.

HEDDA. Yes, I have many a time longed for someone to make a third on our travels. Oh—those railway-carriage tête-à-têtes!

BRACK. Fortunately your wedding journey is over now.

HEDDA [*shaking her head*]. Not by a long—long way. I have only arrived at a station on the line.

BRACK. Well, then the passengers jump out and move about a little, Mrs Hedda.

HEDDA. I never jump out.

BRACK. Really?

HEDDA. No—because there is always someone standing by to——

BRACK [*laughing*]. To look at your ankles, do you mean?

HEDDA. Precisely.

BRACK. Well, but, dear me——

HEDDA [*with a gesture of repulsion*]. I won't have it. I would rather keep my seat where I happen to be—and continue the tête-à-tête.

BRACK. But suppose a third person were to jump in and join the couple.

HEDDA. Ah that is quite another matter!

BRACK. A trusted, sympathetic friend——

HEDDA. —with a fund of conversation on all sorts of lively topics——

BRACK. —and not the least bit of a specialist!

HEDDA [*with an audible sigh*]. Yes, that would be a relief indeed.

BRACK [*hears the front door open and glances in that direction*]. The triangle is completed.

HEDDA [*half aloud*]. And on goes the train.

[GEORGE TESMAN, *in a gray walking suit with a soft felt hat, enters from the hall. He has a number of un-*

bound books under his arm and in his pockets.]

TES. [*goes up to the table beside the corner settee*]. Ouf—what a load for a warm day—all these books. [*Lays them on the table.*] I'm positively perspiring, Hedda. Hallo—are you there already, my dear judge? Eh? Berta didn't tell me.

BRACK [*rising*]. I came in through the garden.

HEDDA. What books have you got there?

TES.[*stands looking them through*]. Some new books on my special subjects—quite indispensable to me.

HEDDA. Your special subjects?

BRACK. Yes, books on his special subjects, Mrs Tesman. [BRACK *and* HEDDA *exchange a confidential smile.*]

HEDDA. Do you need still more books on your special subjects?

TES. Yes, my dear Hedda, one can never have too many of them. Of course one must keep up with all that is written and published.

HEDDA. Yes, I suppose one must.

TES. [*searching among his books*]. And look here—I have got hold of Eilert Lövborg's new book too. [*Offering it to her.*] Perhaps you would like to glance through it, Hedda? Eh?

HEDDA. No, thank you. Or rather—afterwards perhaps.

TES. I looked into it a little on the way home.

BRACK. What do you think of it—as a specialist?

TES. I think it shows quite remarkable soundness of judgment. He never wrote like that before. [*Putting the books together.*] Now I shall take all these into my study. I'm longing to cut the leaves! And then I must change my clothes. [*To* BRACK.] I suppose we needn't start just yet? Eh?

BRACK. Oh, dear no—there is not the slightest hurry.

TES. Well then, I will take my time. [*Is going with his books but stops in the doorway and turns.*] By-the-bye, Hedda—Aunt Julia is not coming this evening.

HEDDA. Not coming? Is it that affair of the bonnet that keeps her away?

TES. Oh, not at all. How could you think such a thing of Aunt Julia? Just fancy! The fact is, Aunt Rina is very ill.

HEDDA. She always is.

TES. Yes, but today she is much worse than usual, poor dear.

HEDDA. Oh, then it's only natural that her sister should remain with her. I must bear my disappointment.

TES. And you can't imagine, dear, how delighted Aunt Julia seemed to be—because you had come home looking so flourishing!

HEDDA [*half aloud, rising*]. Oh, those everlasting aunts!

TES. What?

HEDDA [*going to the glass door*]. Nothing.

TES. Oh, all right. [*He goes through the inner room, out to the right.*]

BRACK. What bonnet were you talking about?

HEDDA. Oh, it was a little episode with Miss Tesman this morning. She had lain down her bonnet on the chair there—[*looks at him and smiles*]—and I pretended to think it was the servant's.

BRACK [*shaking his head*]. Now my dear Mrs Hedda, how could you do such a thing? To that excellent old lady too!

HEDDA [*nervously crossing the*

room]. Well, you see—these impulses come over me all of a sudden, and I cannot resist them. [*Throws herself down in the easy chair by the stove.*] Oh, I don't know how to explain it.

Brack [*behind the easy chair*]. You are not really happy—that is the bottom of it.

Hedda [*looking straight before her*]. I know of no reason why I should be—happy. Perhaps you can give me one?

Brack. Well—amongst other things, because you have got exactly the home you had set your heart on.

Hedda [*looks up at him and laughs*]. Do you too believe in that legend?

Brack. Is there nothing in it, then?

Hedda. Oh yes, there is something in it.

Brack. Well?

Hedda. There is this in it, that I made use of Tesman to see me home from evening parties last summer——

Brack. I, unfortunately, had to go quite a different way.

Hedda. That's true. I know you were going a different way last summer.

Brack [*laughing*]. Oh! fie, Mrs Hedda! Well, then—you and Tesman——?

Hedda. Well, we happened to pass here one evening; Tesman, poor fellow, was writhing in the agony of having to find conversation; so I took pity on the learned man——

Brack [*smiles doubtfully*]. You took pity? H'm——

Hedda. Yes, I really did. And so—to help him out of his torment—I happened to say, in pure thoughtlessness, that I should like to live in this villa.

Brack. No more than that?

Hedda. Not that evening.

Brack. But afterward——

Hedda. Yes, my thoughtlessness had consequences, my dear judge.

Brack. Unfortunately that too often happens, Mrs Hedda.

Hedda. Thanks! So you see it was this enthusiasm for Secretary Falk's villa that first constituted a bond of sympathy between George Tesman and me. From that came our engagement and our marriage and our wedding journey and all the rest of it. Well, well, my dear judge—as you make your bed so you must lie, I could almost say.

Brack. This is exquisite! And you really cared not a rap about it all the time?

Hedda. No, heaven knows I didn't.

Brack. But now? Now that we have made it so homelike for you?

Hedda. Uh—the rooms all seem to smell of lavender and dried love leaves. But perhaps it's Aunt Julia that has brought that scent with her.

Brack [*laughing*]. No, I think it must be a legacy from the late Mrs Secretary Falk.

Hedda. Yes, there is an odor of mortality about it. It reminds me of a bouquet—the day after the ball. [*Clasps her hands behind her head, leans back in her chair and looks at him.*] Oh, my dear judge—you cannot imagine how horribly I shall bore myself here.

Brack. Why should not you too find some sort of vocation in life, Mrs Hedda?

Hedda. A vocation—that should attract me?

Brack. If possible, of course.

Hedda. Heaven knows what sort of a vocation that could be. I often wonder whether—— [*Breaking off.*] But that would never do either.

BRACK. Who can tell? Let me hear what it is.

HEDDA. Whether I might not get Tesman to go into politics, I mean.

BRACK [*laughing*]. Tesman? No, really now, political life is not the thing for him—not at all in his line.

HEDDA. No, I daresay not. But if I could get him into it all the same?

BRACK. Why—what satisfaction could you find in that? If he is not fitted for that sort of thing, why should you want to drive him into it?

HEDDA. Because I am bored, I tell you! [*After a pause.*] So you think it quite out of the question that Tesman should ever get into the ministry?

BRACK. H'm—you see, my dear Mrs Hedda—to get into the ministry he would have to be a tolerably rich man.

HEDDA [*rising impatiently*]. Yes, there we have it! It is this genteel poverty I have managed to drop into! [*Crosses the room.*] That is what makes life so pitiable! So utterly ludicrous! For that's what it is.

BRACK. Now I should say the fault lay elsewhere.

HEDDA. Where, then?

BRACK. You have never gone through any really stimulating experience.

HEDDA. Anything serious, you mean?

BRACK. Yes, you may call it so. But now you may perhaps have one in store.

HEDDA [*tossing her head*]. Oh, you're thinking of the annoyances about this wretched professorship! But that must be Tesman's own affair. I assure you I shall not waste a thought upon it.

BRACK. No, no, I daresay not. But suppose now that what people call—in elegant language—a solemn responsibility were to come upon you? [*Smiling.*] A new responsibility, Mrs Hedda?

HEDDA [*angrily*]. Be quiet! Nothing of that sort will ever happen!

BRACK [*warily*]. We will speak of this again a year hence—at the very outside.

HEDDA [*curtly*]. I have no turn for anything of the sort, Judge Brack. No responsibilities for me!

BRACK. Are you so unlike the generality of women as to have no turn for duties which——

HEDDA [*beside the glass door*]. Oh, be quiet, I tell you! I often think there is only one thing in the world I have any turn for.

BRACK [*drawing near to her*]. And what is that, if I may ask?

HEDDA [*stands looking out*]. Boring myself to death. Now you know it. [*Turns, looks toward the inner room and laughs.*] Yes, as I thought! Here comes the professor.

BRACK [*softly, in a tone of warning*]. Come, come, come, Mrs Hedda!

[GEORGE TESMAN, *dressed for the party, with his gloves and hat in his hand, enters from the right through the inner room.*]

TES. Hedda, has no message come from Eilert Lövborg? Eh?

HEDDA. No.

TES. Then you'll see he'll be here presently.

BRACK. Do you really think he'll come?

TES. Yes, I am almost sure of it. For what you were telling us this morning must have been a mere floating rumor.

BRACK. You think so?

TES. At any rate, Aunt Julia said she did not believe for a moment that he would ever stand in my way again. Fancy that!

BRACK. Well then, that's all right.

TES. [*placing his hat and gloves on a chair on the right*]. Yes, but you must really let me wait for him as long as possible.

BRACK. We have plenty of time yet. None of my guests will arrive before seven or half-past.

TES. Then meanwhile we can keep Hedda company and see what happens. Eh?

HEDDA [*placing* BRACK's *hat and overcoat upon the corner settee*]. And at the worst Mr Lövborg can remain here with me.

BRACK [*offering to take his things*]. Oh, allow me, Mrs Tesman! What do you mean by "at the worst"?

HEDDA. If he won't go with you and Tesman.

TES. [*looks dubiously at her*]. But, Hedda dear—do you think it would quite do for him to remain with you? Eh? Remember, Aunt Julia can't come.

HEDDA. No, but Mrs Elvsted is coming. We three can have a cup of tea together.

TES. Oh yes, that will be all right.

BRACK [*smiling*]. And that would perhaps be the safest plan for him.

HEDDA. Why so?

BRACK. Well, you know, Mrs Tesman, how you used to gird at my little bachelor parties. You declared they were adapted only for men of the strictest principles.

HEDDA. But no doubt Mr Lövborg's principles are strict enough now. A converted sinner—— [BERTA *appears at the hall door.*]

BERTA. There's a gentleman asking if you are at home, ma'am.

HEDDA. Well, show him in.

TES. [*softly*]. I'm sure it is he! Fancy that!

[EILERT LÖVBORG *enters from the hall. He is slim and lean, of the same age as* TESMAN *but looks older and somewhat worn out. His hair and beard are of a blackish brown, his face long and pale but with patches of color on the cheekbones. He is dressed in a well-cut black visiting suit, quite new. He has dark gloves and a silk hat. He stops near the door and makes a rapid bow, seeming somewhat embarrassed.*]

TES. [*goes up to him and shakes him warmly by the hand*]. Well, my dear Eilert—so at last we meet again!

LÖV. [*speaks in a subdued voice*]. Thanks for your letter, Tesman. [*Approaching* HEDDA.] Will you too shake hands with me, Mrs Tesman?

HEDDA [*taking his hand*]. I am glad to see you, Mr Lövborg. [*With a motion of her hand.*] I don't know whether you two gentlemen——

LÖV. [*bowing slightly*]. Judge Brack, I think.

BRACK [*doing likewise*]. Oh yes—in the old days——

TES. [*to* LÖVBORG, *with his hands on his shoulders*]. And now you must make yourself entirely at home, Eilert! Mustn't he, Hedda? For I hear you are going to settle in town again. Eh?

LÖV. Yes, I am.

TES. Quite right, quite right. Let me tell you, I have got hold of your new book but I haven't had time to read it yet.

LÖV. You may spare yourself the trouble.

TES. Why so?

LÖV. Because there is very little in it.

TES. Just fancy—how can you say so?

BRACK. But it has been very much praised, I hear.

LÖV. That was what I wanted; so I put nothing into the book but what everyone would agree with.

TES. Well, but, my dear Eilert——

BRACK. Very wise of you.

LÖV. For now I mean to win myself a position again—to make a fresh start.

TES. [*a little embarrassed*]. Ah, that is what you wish to do? Eh?

LÖV. [*smiling, lays down his hat and draws a packet, wrapped in paper, from his coat pocket*]. But when this one appears, George Tesman, you will have to read it. For this is the real book—the book I have put my true self into.

TES. Indeed? And what is it?

LÖV. It is the continuation.

TES. The continuation? Of what?

LÖV. Of the book.

TES. Of the new book?

LÖV. Of course.

TES. Why, my dear Eilert—does it not come down to our own days?

LÖV. Yes, it does; and this one deals with the future.

TES. With the future! But, good heavens, we know nothing of the future!

LÖV. No, but there is a thing or two to be said about it all the same. [*Opens the packet.*] Look here——

TES. Why, that's not your handwriting.

LÖV. I dictated it. [*Turning over the pages.*] It falls into two sections. The first deals with the civilizing forces of the future. And here is the second—[*running through the pages toward the end*]—forecasting the probable line of development.

TES. How odd now! I should never have thought of writing anything of that sort.

HEDDA [*at the glass door, drumming on the pane*]. H'm—I daresay not.

LÖV. [*replacing the manuscript in its paper and laying the packet on the table*]. I brought it thinking I might read you a little of it this evening.

TES. That was very good of you, Eilert. But this evening——? [*Looking at* BRACK.] I don't quite see how we can manage it.

LÖV. Well then, some other time. There is no hurry.

BRACK. I must tell you, Mr Lövborg—there is a little gathering at my house this evening—mainly in honor of Tesman, you know.

LÖV. [*looking for his hat*]. Oh—then I won't detain you.

BRACK. No, but listen—will you not do me the favor of joining us?

LÖV. [*curtly and decidedly*]. No, I can't—thank you very much.

BRACK. Oh, nonsense—do! We shall be quite a select little circle. And I assure you we shall have a "lively time," as Mrs Hed—as Mrs Tesman says.

LÖV. I have no doubt of it. But nevertheless——

BRACK. And then you might bring your manuscript with you and read it to Tesman at my house. I could give you a room to yourselves.

TES. Yes, think of that, Eilert—why shouldn't you? Eh?

HEDDA [*interposing*]. But, Tesman, if Mr Lövborg would really rather not! I am sure Mr Lövborg is much more inclined to remain here and have supper with me.

LÖV. [*looking at her*]. With you, Mrs Tesman?

HEDDA. And with Mrs Elvsted.

Löv. Ah! [*Lightly.*] I saw her for a moment this morning.

Hedda. Did you? Well, she is coming this evening. So you see you are almost bound to remain, Mr Lövborg, or she will have no one to see her home.

Löv. That's true. Many thanks, Mrs Tesman—in that case I will remain.

Hedda. Then I have one or two orders to give the servant. [*She goes to the hall door and rings.* Berta *enters.* Hedda *talks to her in a whisper and points toward the inner room.* Berta *nods and goes out again.*]

Tes. [*at the same time to* Lövborg]. Tell me, Eilert—is it this new subject—the future—that you are going to lecture about?

Löv. Yes.

Tes. They told me at the book seller's that you are going to deliver a course of lectures this autumn.

Löv. That is my intention. I hope you won't take it ill, Tesman.

Tes. Oh no, not in the least! But——

Löv. I can quite understand that it must be disagreeable to you.

Tes. [*cast down*]. Oh, I can't expect you, out of consideration for me, to——

Löv. But I shall wait till you have received your appointment.

Tes. Will you wait? Yes, but—are you not going to compete with me? Eh?

Löv. No; it is only the moral victory I care for.

Tes. Why, bless me—then Aunt Julia was right after all! Oh yes—I knew it! Hedda! Just fancy—Eilert Lövborg is not going to stand in our way!

Hedda [*curtly*]. Our way? Pray leave me out of the question. [*She goes up toward the inner room where* Berta *is placing a tray with decanters and glasses on the table.* Hedda *nods approval and comes forward again.* Berta *goes out.*]

Tes. [*at the same time*]. And you, Judge Brack—what do you say to this? Eh?

Brack. Well, I say that a moral victory—h'm—may be all very fine——

Tes. Yes, certainly. But all the same——

Hedda [*looking at* Tesman *with a cold smile*]. You stand there looking as if you were thunderstruck.

Tes. Yes—so I am—I almost think ——

Brack. Don't you see, Mrs Tesman, a thunderstorm has just passed over?

Hedda [*pointing toward the inner room*]. Will you not take a glass of cold punch, gentlemen?

Brack [*looking at his watch*]. A stirrup cup? Yes, it wouldn't come amiss.

Tes. A capital idea, Hedda! Just the thing! Now that the weight has been taken off my mind——

Hedda. Will you not join them, Mr Lövborg?

Löv. [*with a gesture of refusal*]. No, thank you. Nothing for me.

Brack. Why, bless me—cold punch is surely not poison.

Löv. Perhaps not for everyone.

Hedda. I will keep Mr Lövborg company in the meantime.

Tes. Yes, yes, Hedda dear, do. [*He and* Brack *go into the inner room, seat themselves, drink punch, smoke cigarettes and carry on a lively conversation during what follows.* Eilert Lövborg *remains beside the stove.* Hedda *goes to the writing table.*]

Hedda [*raising her voice a little*]. Do you care to look at some photographs, Mr Lövborg? You know Tesman and I made a tour in the Tyrol on our way home. [*She takes up an album and places it on the table beside the sofa, in the further corner of which she seats herself.* EILERT LÖVBORG *approaches, stops and looks at her. Then he takes a chair and seats himself at her left, with his back toward the inner room.*]

HEDDA [*opening the album*]. Do you see this range of mountains, Mr Lövborg? It's the Ortler group. Tesman has written the name underneath. Here it is: "The Ortler group near Meran."

LÖV. [*who has never taken his eyes off her, says softly and slowly*]. Hedda —Gabler!

HEDDA [*glancing hastily at him*]. Ah! Hush!

LÖV. [*repeats softly*]. Hedda Gabler!

HEDDA [*looking at the album*]. That was my name in the old days—when we two knew each other.

LÖV. And I must teach myself never to say Hedda Gabler again—never, as long as I live.

HEDDA [*still turning over the pages*]. Yes, you must. And I think you ought to practice in time. The sooner the better, I should say.

LÖV. [*in a tone of indignation*]. Hedda Gabler married? And married to—George Tesman!

HEDDA. Yes—so the world goes.

LÖV. Oh, Hedda, Hedda—how could you throw yourself away!

HEDDA [*looks sharply at him*]. What? I can't allow this!

LÖV. What do you mean? [TESMAN *comes into the room and goes toward the sofa.*]

HEDDA [*hears him coming and says in an indifferent tone*]. And this is a view from the Val d'Ampezzo, Mr Lövborg. Just look at these peaks! [*Looks affectionately up at* TESMAN.] What's the name of these curious peaks, dear?

TES. Let me see. Oh, those are the Dolomites.

HEDDA. Yes, that's it! Those are the Dolomites, Mr Lövborg.

TES. Hedda dear, I only wanted to ask whether I shouldn't bring you a little punch after all? For yourself at any rate—eh?

HEDDA. Yes, do, please; and perhaps a few biscuits.

TES. No cigarettes?

HEDDA. No.

TES. Very well. [*He goes into the inner room and out to the right.* BRACK *sits in the inner room and keeps an eye from time to time on* HEDDA *and* LÖVBORG.]

LÖV. [*softly, as before*]. Answer me, Hedda—how could you go and do this?

HEDDA [*apparently absorbed in the album*]. If you continue to say *du* to me I won't talk to you.

LÖV. May I not say *du* when we are alone?

HEDDA. No. You may think it, but you mustn't say it.

LÖV. Ah, I understand. It is an offense against George Tesman, whom you—love.

HEDDA [*glances at him and smiles*]. Love? What an idea!

LÖV. You don't love him, then!

HEDDA. But I won't hear of any sort of unfaithfulness! Remember that.

LÖV. Hedda—answer me one thing —

HEDDA. Hush!

[TESMAN *enters with a small tray from the inner room.*]

TES. Here you are! Isn't this tempting? [*He puts the tray on the table.*]

HEDDA. Why do you bring it yourself?

TES. [*filling the glasses*]. Because I think it's such fun to wait upon you, Hedda.

HEDDA. But you have poured out two glasses. Mr Lövborg said he wouldn't have any.

TES. No, but Mrs Elvsted will soon be here, won't she?

HEDDA. Yes, by-the-bye—Mrs Elvsted.

TES. Had you forgotten her? Eh?

HEDDA. We were so absorbed in these photographs. [*Shows him a picture.*] Do you remember this little village?

TES. Oh, it's that one just below the Brenner Pass. It was there we passed the night——

HEDDA. —and met that lively party of tourists.

TES. Yes, that was the place. Fancy—if we could only have had you with us, Eilert! Eh? [*He returns to the inner room and sits beside* BRACK.]

LÖV. Answer me this one thing, Hedda.

HEDDA. Well?

LÖV. Was there no love in your friendship for me either? Not a spark—not a tinge of love in it?

HEDDA. I wonder if there was? To me it seems as though we were two good comrades—two thoroughly intimate friends. [*Smilingly.*] You especially were frankness itself.

LÖV. It was you that made me so.

HEDDA. As I look back upon it all I think there was really something beautiful, something fascinating—something daring—in—in that secret intimacy—that comradeship which no living creature so much as dreamed of.

LÖV. Yes, yes, Hedda! Was there not? When I used to come to your father's in the afternoon—and the general sat over at the window reading his papers—with his back toward us——

HEDDA. And we two on the corner sofa——

LÖV. Always with the same illustrated paper before us——

HEDDA. For want of an album, yes.

LÖV. Yes, Hedda, and when I made my confessions to you—told you about myself, things that at that time no one else knew! There I would sit and tell you of my escapades—my days and nights of devilment. Oh, Hedda—what was the power in you that forced me to confess these things?

HEDDA. Do you think it was any power in me?

LÖV. How else can I explain it? And all those—those roundabout questions you used to put to me——

HEDDA. Which you understood so particularly well——

LÖV. How could you sit and question me like that? Question me quite frankly——

HEDDA. In roundabout terms, please observe.

LÖV. Yes, but frankly nevertheless. Cross-question me about—all that sort of thing?

HEDDA. And how could you answer, Mr Lövborg?

LÖV. Yes, that is just what I can't understand—in looking back upon it. But tell me now, Hedda—was there not love at the bottom of our friendship? On your side did you not feel as though you might purge my stains away if I made you my confessor? Was it not so?

HEDDA. No, not quite.

Löv. What was your motive, then?

HEDDA. Do you think it quite incomprehensible that a young girl—when it can be done—without anyone knowing——

Löv. Well?

HEDDA. —should be glad to have a peep, now and then, into a world which——

Löv. Which——?

HEDDA. —which she is forbidden to know anything about?

Löv. So that was it?

HEDDA. Partly. Partly—I almost think.

Löv. Comradeship in the thirst for life. But why should not that, at any rate, have continued?

HEDDA. The fault was yours.

Löv. It was you that broke with me.

HEDDA. Yes, when our friendship threatened to develop into something more serious. Shame upon you, Eilert Lövborg! How could you think of wronging your—your frank comrade?

Löv. [*clenching his hands*]. Oh, why did you not carry out your threat? Why did you not shoot me down?

HEDDA. Because I have such a dread of scandal.

Löv. Yes, Hedda, you are a coward at heart.

HEDDA. A terrible coward. [*Changing her tone.*] But it was a lucky thing for you. And now you have found ample consolation at the Elvsteds'.

Löv. I know what Thea has confided to you.

HEDDA. And perhaps you have confided to her something about us?

Löv. Not a word. She is too stupid to understand anything of that sort.

HEDDA. Stupid?

Löv. She is stupid about matters of that sort.

HEDDA. And I am cowardly. [*Bends over toward him, without looking him in the face, and says more softly.*] But now I will confide something to you.

Löv. [*eagerly*]. Well?

HEDDA. The fact that I dared not shoot you down——

Löv. Yes!

HEDDA. —that was not my most arrant cowardice—that evening.

Löv. [*looks at her a moment, understands and whispers passionately*]. Oh, Hedda! Hedda Gabler! Now I begin to see a hidden reason beneath our comradeship! You and I! After all, then, it was your craving for life——

HEDDA [*softly, with a sharp glance*]. Take care! Believe nothing of the sort!

[*Twilight has begun to fall. The hall door is opened from without by* BERTA.]

HEDDA. [*closes the album with a bang and calls smilingly*]. Ah, at last! My darling Thea—come along!

[MRS ELVSTED *enters from the hall. She is in evening dress. The door is closed behind her.*]

HEDDA [*on the sofa, stretches out her arms toward her*]. My sweet Thea—you can't think how I have been longing for you!

[MRS ELVSTED, *in passing, exchanges slight salutations with the gentlemen in the inner room, then goes up to the table and gives* HEDDA *her hands.* EILERT LÖVBORG *has risen. He and* MRS ELVSTED *greet each other with a silent nod.*]

MRS ELVS. Ought I go in and talk to your husband for a moment?

HEDDA. Oh, not at all. Leave those

two alone. They will soon be going.

MRS ELVS. Are they going out?

HEDDA. Yes, to a supper party.

MRS ELVS. [*quickly, to* LÖVBORG]. Not you?

LÖV. No.

HEDDA. Mr Lövborg remains with us.

MRS ELVS. [*takes a chair and is about to seat herself at his side*]. Oh, how nice it is here!

HEDDA. No, thank you, my little Thea! Not there! You'll be good enough to come over here to me. I will sit between you.

MRS ELVS. Yes, just as you please. [*She goes round the table and seats herself on the sofa on* HEDDA'S *right.* LÖVBORG *reseats himself on his chair.*]

LÖV. [*after a short pause, to* HEDDA]. Is not she lovely to look at?

HEDDA [*lightly stroking her hair*]. Only to look at?

LÖV. Yes. For we two–she and I–we are two real comrades. We have absolute faith in each other; so we can sit and talk with perfect frankness—

HEDDA. Not roundabout, Mr Lövborg?

LÖV. Well——

MRS ELVS. [*softly clinging close to* HEDDA]. Oh, how happy I am, Hedda; for, only think, he says I have inspired him too.

HEDDA [*looks at her with a smile*]. Ah! Does he say that, dear?

LÖV. And then she is so brave, Mrs Tesman!

MRS ELVS. Good heavens–am I brave?

LÖV. Exceedingly–where your comrade is concerned.

HEDDA. Ah yes–courage! If one only had that!

LÖV. What then? What do you mean?

HEDDA. Then life would perhaps be livable after all. [*With a sudden change of tone.*] But now, my dearest Thea, you really must have a glass of cold punch.

MRS ELVS. No, thanks–I never take anything of that kind.

HEDDA. Well then, you, Mr Lövborg.

LÖV. Nor I, thank you.

MRS ELVS. No, he doesn't either.

HEDDA [*looks fixedly at him*]. But if I say you shall?

LÖV. It would be no use.

HEDDA [*laughing*]. Then I, poor creature, have no sort of power over you?

LÖV. Not in that respect.

HEDDA. But seriously, I think you ought to–for your own sake.

MRS ELVS. Why, Hedda!

LÖV. How so?

HEDDA. Or rather on account of other people.

LÖV. Indeed?

HEDDA. Otherwise people might be apt to suspect that–in your heart of hearts–you did not feel quite secure –quite confident of yourself.

MRS ELVS. [*softly*]. Oh! please, Hedda——

LÖV. People may suspect what they like–for the present.

MRS ELVS. [*joyfully*]. Yes, let them!

HEDDA. I saw it plainly in Judge Brack's face a moment ago.

LÖV. What did you see?

HEDDA. His contemptuous smile when you dared not go with them into the inner room.

LÖV. Dared not? Of course I preferred to stop here and talk to you.

MRS ELVS. What could be more natural, Hedda?

HEDDA. But the judge could not guess that. And I saw, too, the way he smiled and glanced at Tesman when you dared not accept his invitation to this wretched little supper party of his.

Löv. Dared not? Do you say I dared not?

Hedda. I don't say so. But that was how Judge Brack understood it.

Löv. Well, let him.

Hedda. Then you are not going with them?

Löv. I will stay here with you and Thea.

Mrs Elvs. Yes, Hedda—how can you doubt that?

Hedda [*smiles and nods approvingly to* Lövborg]. Firm as a rock! Faithful to your principles now and forever! Ah, that is how a man should be! [*Turns to* Mrs Elvsted *and caresses her.*] Well now, what did I tell you when you came to us this morning in such a state of distraction——

Löv. [*surprised*]. Distraction!

Mrs Elvs. [*terrified*]. Hedda—oh, Hedda!

Hedda. You can see for yourself, you haven't the slightest reason to be in such mortal terror—— [*Interrupting herself.*] There! Now we can all three enjoy ourselves!

Löv. [*who has given a start*]. Ah—what is all this, Mrs Tesman?

Mrs Elvs. Oh, my God, Hedda! What are you saying? What are you doing?

Hedda. Don't get excited! That horrid Judge Brack is sitting watching you.

Löv. So she was in mortal terror! On my account!

Mrs Elvs. [*softly and piteously*]. Oh, Hedda—now you have ruined everything!

Löv. [*looks fixedly at her for a moment. His face is distorted*]. So that was my comrade's frank confidence in me?

Mrs Elvs. [*imploringly*]. Oh, my dearest friend—only let me tell you——

Löv. [*takes one of the glasses of punch, raises it to his lips and says in a low, husky voice*]. Your health, Thea! [*He empties the glass, puts it down and takes the second.*]

Mrs Elvs. [*softly*]. Oh, Hedda, Hedda—how could you do this?

Hedda. *I* do it? I? Are you crazy?

Löv. Here's to your health too, Mrs Tesman. Thanks for the truth. Hurrah for the truth! [*He empties the glass and is about to refill it.*]

Hedda [*lays her hand on his arm*]. Come, come—no more for the present. Remember you are going out to supper.

Mrs Elvs. No, no, no!

Hedda. Hush! They are sitting watching you.

Löv. [*putting down the glass*]. Now, Thea—tell me the truth——

Mrs Elvs. Yes.

Löv. Did your husband know that you had come after me?

Mrs Elvs. [*wringing her hands*]. Oh, Hedda—do you hear what he is asking?

Löv. Was it arranged between you and him that you were to come to town and look after me? Perhaps it was the sheriff himself that urged you to come? Aha, my dear—no doubt he wanted my help in his office! Or was it at the card table that he missed me?

Mrs Elvs. [*softly, in agony*]. Oh, Lövborg, Lövborg!

Löv. [*seizes a glass and is on the point of filling it*]. Here's a glass for the old sheriff too!

Hedda [*preventing him*]. No more

just now. Remember you have to read your manuscript to Tesman.

LÖV. [*calmly, putting down the glass*]. It was stupid of me, all this, Thea—to take it in this way, I mean. Don't be angry with me, my dear, dear comrade. You shall see—both you and the others—that if I was fallen once—now I have risen again! Thanks to you, Thea.

MRS ELVS. [*radiant with joy*]. Oh, heaven be praised!

[BRACK *has in the meantime looked at his watch. He and* TESMAN *rise and come into the drawing room.*]

BRACK [*takes his hat and overcoat*]. Well, Mrs Tesman, our time has come.

HEDDA. I suppose it has.

LÖV. [*rising*]. Mine too, Judge Brack.

MRS ELVS. [*softly and imploringly*]. Oh, Lövborg, don't do it!

HEDDA [*pinching her arm*]. They can hear you!

MRS ELVS. [*with a suppressed shriek*]. Ow!

LÖV. [*to* BRACK]. You were good enough to invite me.

BRACK. Well, are you coming after all?

LÖV. Yes, many thanks.

BRACK. I'm delighted.

LÖV. [*to* TESMAN, *putting the parcel of MS in his pocket*]. I should like to show you one or two things before I send it to the printers.

TES. Fancy—that will be delightful. But, Hedda dear, how is Mrs Elvsted to get home? Eh?

HEDDA. Oh, that can be managed somehow.

LÖV. [*looking toward the ladies*]. Mrs Elvsted? Of course I'll come again and fetch her. [*Approaching.*] At ten or thereabouts, Mrs Tesman? Will that do?

HEDDA. Certainly. That will do capitally.

TES. Well then, that's all right. But you must not expect me so early, Hedda.

HEDDA. Oh, you may stop as long—as long as ever you please.

MRS ELVS. [*trying to conceal her anxiety*]. Well then, Mr Lövborg—I shall remain here until you come.

LÖV. [*with his hat in his hands*]. Pray do, Mrs Elvsted.

BRACK. And now off goes the excursion train, gentlemen! I hope we shall have a lively time, as a certain fair lady puts it.

HEDDA. Ah, if only the fair lady could be present unseen!

BRACK. Why unseen?

HEDDA. In order to hear a little of your liveliness at first hand, Judge Brack.

BRACK [*laughingly*]. I should not advise the fair lady to try it.

TES. [*also laughing*]. Come, you're a nice one, Hedda! Fancy that!

BRACK. Well, good-by, good-by, ladies.

LÖV. [*bowing*]. About ten o'clock then.

[BRACK, LÖVBORG *and* TESMAN *go out by the hall door. At the same time* BERTA *enters from the inner room with a lighted lamp which she places on the dining-room table; she goes out by the way she came.*]

MRS ELVS. [*who has risen and is wandering restlessly about the room*]. Hedda—Hedda—what will come of all this?

HEDDA. At ten o'clock—he will be here. I can see him already—with vine leaves in his hair—flushed and fearless——

MRS ELVS. Oh, I hope he may.

HEDDA. And then, you see—then he

will have regained control over himself. Then he will be a free man for all his days.

MRS ELVS. Oh God!—If he would only come as you see him now!

HEDDA. He will come as I see him—so and not otherwise! [*Rises and approaches* THEA.] You may doubt him as long as you please; I believe in him. And now we will try——

MRS ELVS. You have some hidden motive in this, Hedda!

HEDDA. Yes, I have. I want for once in my life to have power to mold a human destiny.

MRS ELVS. Have you not the power?

HEDDA. I have not—and have never had it.

MRS ELVS. Not your husband's?

HEDDA. Do you think that is worth the trouble? Oh, if you could only understand how poor I am. And fate has made you so rich! [*Clasps her passionately in her arms.*] I think I must burn your hair off after all.

MRS ELVS. Let me go! Let me go! I am afraid of you, Hedda!

BERTA [*in the middle doorway*]. Tea is laid in the dining room, ma'am.

HEDDA. Very well. We are coming.

MRS ELVS. No, no, no! I would rather go home alone! At once!

HEDDA. Nonsense! First you shall have a cup of tea, you little stupid. And then—at ten o'clock—Eilert Lövborg will be here—with vine leaves in his hair. [*She drags* MRS ELVSTED *almost by force toward the middle doorway.*]

ACT III

SCENE—*The room at the* TESMANS'. *The curtains are drawn over the middle doorway and also over the glass door. The lamp, half turned down and with a shade over it, is burning on the table. In the stove, the door of which stands open, there has been a fire which is now nearly burnt out.*

MRS ELVSTED, *wrapped in a large shawl and with her feet upon a footrest, sits close to the stove, sunk back in the armchair.* HEDDA, *fully dressed, lies sleeping upon the sofa with a sofa blanket over her.*

MRS ELVS. [*after a pause suddenly sits up in her chair and listens eagerly. Then she sinks back again wearily, moaning to herself*]. Not yet! Oh God—oh God—not yet!

[BERTA *slips in by the hall door. She has a letter in her hand.*]

MRS ELVS. [*turns and whispers eagerly*]. Well—has anyone come?

BERTA [*softly*]. Yes, a girl has brought this letter.

MRS ELVS. [*quickly, holding out her hand*]. A letter! Give it to me!

BERTA. No, it's for Doctor Tesman, ma'am.

MRS ELVS. Oh, indeed.

BERTA. It was Miss Tesman's servant that brought it. I'll lay it here on the table.

MRS ELVS. Yes, do.

BERTA [*laying down the letter*]. I think I had better put out the lamp. It's smoking.

MRS ELVS. Yes, put it out. It must soon be daylight now.

BERTA [*putting out the lamp*]. It is daylight already, ma'am.

MRS ELVS. Yes, broad day! And no one come back yet!

BERTA. Lord bless you, ma'am—I guessed how it would be.

MRS ELVS. You guessed.

BERTA. Yes, when I saw that a certain person had come back to town—

and that he went off with them. For we've heard enough about that gentleman before now.

MRS ELVS. Don't speak so loud. You will waken Mrs Tesman.

BERTA [*looks toward the sofa and sighs*]. No, no—let her sleep, poor thing. Shan't I put some wood on the fire?

MRS ELVS. Thanks, not for me.

BERTA. Oh, very well. [*She goes softly out by the hall door.*]

HEDDA [*is awakened by the shutting of the door and looks up*]. What's that?

MRS ELVS. It was only the servant.

HEDDA [*looking about her*]. Oh, we're here! Yes, now I remember. [*Sits erect upon the sofa, stretches herself and rubs her eyes.*] What o'clock is it, Thea?

MRS ELVS. [*looks at her watch*]. It's past seven.

HEDDA. When did Tesman come home?

MRS ELVS. He has not come.

HEDDA. Not come home yet?

MRS ELVS. [*rising*]. No one has come.

HEDDA. Think of our watching and waiting here till four in the morning——

MRS ELVS. [*wringing her hands*]. And how I watched and waited for him!

HEDDA [*yawns and says with her hand before her mouth*]. Well, well—we might have spared ourselves the trouble.

MRS ELVS. Did you get a little sleep?

HEDDA. Oh yes, I believe I have slept pretty well. Have you not?

MRS ELVS. Not for a moment. I couldn't, Hedda!—not to save my life.

HEDDA [*rises and goes toward her*]. There—there—there! There's nothing to be so alarmed about. I understand quite well what has happened.

MRS ELVS. Well, what do you think? Won't you tell me?

HEDDA. Why, of course it has been a very late affair at Judge Brack's——

MRS ELVS. Yes, yes, that is clear enough. But all the same——

HEDDA. And then, you see, Tesman hasn't cared to come home and ring us up in the middle of the night. [*Laughing.*] Perhaps he wasn't inclined to show himself either—immediately after a jollification.

MRS ELVS. But in that case—where can he have gone?

HEDDA. Of course he has gone to his aunt's and slept there. They have his old room ready for him.

MRS ELVS. No, he can't be with them, for a letter has just come for him from Miss Tesman. There it lies.

HEDDA. Indeed? [*Looks at the address.*] Why, yes, it's addressed in Aunt Julia's own hand. Well then, he has remained at Judge Brack's. And as for Eilert Lövborg—he is sitting, with vine leaves in his hair, reading his manuscript.

MRS ELVS. Oh, Hedda, you are just saying things you don't believe a bit.

HEDDA. You really are a little blockhead, Thea.

MRS ELVS. Oh yes, I suppose I am.

HEDDA. And how mortally tired you look.

MRS ELVS. Yes, I am mortally tired.

HEDDA. Well then, you must do as I tell you. You must go into my room and lie down for a little while.

MRS ELVS. Oh no, no—I shouldn't be able to sleep.

HEDDA. I am sure you would.

MRS ELVS. Well, but your husband is certain to come soon now, and then I want to know at once.

HEDDA. I shall take care to let you know when he comes.

MRS ELVS. Do you promise me, Hedda?

HEDDA. Yes, rely upon me. Just you go in and have a sleep in the meantime.

MRS ELVS. Thanks; then I'll try to. [*She goes off through the inner room.*]

[HEDDA *goes up to the glass door and draws back the curtains. The broad daylight streams into the room. Then she takes a little hand glass from the writing table, looks at herself in it and arranges her hair. Next she goes to the hall door and presses the bell button.* BERTA *presently appears at the hall door.*]

BERTA. Did you want anything, ma'am?

HEDDA. Yes; you must put some more wood in the stove. I am shivering.

BERTA. Bless me—I'll make up the fire at once. [*She rakes the embers together and lays a piece of wood upon them, then stops and listens.*] That was a ring at the front door, ma'am.

HEDDA. Then go to the door. I will look after the fire.

BERTA. It'll soon burn up. [*She goes out by the hall door.*]

[HEDDA *kneels on the footrest and lays some more pieces of wood in the stove. After a short pause* GEORGE TESMAN *enters from the hall. He looks tired and rather serious. He steals on tiptoe toward the middle doorway and is about to slip through the curtains.*]

HEDDA [*at the stove, without looking up*]. Good morning.

TES. [*turns*]. Hedda! [*Approaching her.*] Good heavens—are you up so early? Eh?

HEDDA. Yes, I am up very early this morning.

TES. And I never doubted you were still sound asleep! Fancy that, Hedda!

HEDDA. Don't speak so loud. Mrs Elvsted is resting in my room.

TES. Has Mrs Elvsted been here all night?

HEDDA. Yes, since no one came to fetch her.

TES. Ah, to be sure.

HEDDA [*closes the door of the stove and rises*]. Well, did you enjoy yourself at Judge Brack's?

TES. Have you been anxious about me? Eh?

HEDDA. No, I should never think of being anxious. But I asked if you had enjoyed yourself.

TES. Oh yes—for once in a way. Especially the beginning of the evening, for then Eilert read me part of his book. We arrived more than an hour too early—fancy that! And Brack had all sorts of arrangements to make—so Eilert read to me.

HEDDA [*seating herself by the table on the right*]. Well? Tell me, then——

TES. [*sitting on a footstool near the stove*]. Oh! Hedda, you can't conceive what a book that is going to be! I believe it is one of the most remarkable things that has ever been written. Fancy that!

HEDDA. Yes, yes; I don't care about that——

TES. I must make a confession to you, Hedda. When he had finished reading—a horrid feeling came over me.

HEDDA. A horrid feeling?

TES. I felt jealous of Eilert for having had it in him to write such a book.

Only think, Hedda!

HEDDA. Yes, yes, I am thinking!

TES. And then how pitiful to think that he—with all his gifts—should be irreclaimable after all.

HEDDA. I suppose you mean that he has more courage than the rest?

TES. No, not at all—I mean that he is incapable of taking his pleasures in moderation.

HEDDA. And what came of it all—in the end?

TES. Well, to tell the truth, I think it might best be described as an orgy, Hedda.

HEDDA. Had he vine leaves in his hair?

TES. Vine leaves? No, I saw nothing of the sort. But he made a long, rambling speech in honor of the woman who had inspired him in his work—that was the phrase he used.

HEDDA. Did he name her?

TES. No, he didn't; but I can't help thinking he meant Mrs Elvsted. You may be sure he did.

HEDDA. Well—where did you part from him?

TES. On the way to town. We broke up—the last of us at any rate—all together, and Brack came with us to get a breath of fresh air. And then, you see, we agreed to take Eilert home; for he had had far more than was good for him.

HEDDA. I daresay.

TES. But now comes the strange part of it, Hedda; or, I should rather say, the melancholy part of it. I declare I am almost ashamed—on Eilert's account—to tell you——

HEDDA. Oh, go on.

TES. Well, as we were getting near town, you see, I happened to drop a little behind the others. Only for a minute or two—fancy that!

HEDDA. Yes, yes, yes, but——?

TES. And then, as I hurried after them—what do you think I found by the wayside? Eh?

HEDDA. Oh, how should I know!

TES. You mustn't speak of it to a soul, Hedda! Do you hear! Promise me, for Eilert's sake. [*Draws a parcel, wrapped in paper, from his coat pocket.*] Fancy, dear—I found this.

HEDDA. Is not that the parcel he had with him yesterday?

TES. Yes, it is the whole of his precious, irreplaceable manuscript! And he had gone and lost it and knew nothing about it. Only fancy, Hedda. So deplorably——

HEDDA. But why did you not give him back the parcel at once?

TES. I didn't dare to—in the state he was then in——

HEDDA. Did you not tell any of the others that you had found it?

TES. Oh, far from it! You can surely understand that for Eilert's sake I wouldn't do that.

HEDDA. So no one knows that Eilert Lövborg's manuscript is in your possession?

TES. No. And no one must know it.

HEDDA. Then what did you say to him afterward?

TES. I didn't talk to him again at all, for when we got in among the streets he and two or three of the others gave us the slip and disappeared. Fancy that!

HEDDA. Indeed! They must have taken him home then.

TES. Yes, so it would appear. And Brack, too, left us.

HEDDA. And what have you been doing with yourself since?

TES. Well, I and some of the others went home with one of the party, a jolly fellow, and took our morning coffee with him; or perhaps I should rather call it our night coffee—eh? But now, when I have rested a little and given Eilert, poor fellow, time to have his sleep out, I must take this back to him.

HEDDA [*holds out her hand for the packet*]. No—don't give it to him! Not in such a hurry, I mean. Let me read it first.

TES. No, my dearest Hedda, I mustn't, I really mustn't.

HEDDA. You must not?

TES. No—for you can imagine what a state of despair he will be in when he awakens and misses the manuscript. He has no copy of it, you must know! He told me so.

HEDDA [*looking searchingly at him*]. Can such a thing not be reproduced? Written over again?

TES. No, I don't think that would be possible. For the inspiration, you see——

HEDDA. Yes, yes—I suppose it depends on that. [*Lightly.*] But by-the-bye—here is a letter for you.

TES. Fancy!

HEDDA [*handing it to him.*] It came early this morning.

TES. It's from Aunt Julia! What can it be? [*He lays the packet on the other footstool, opens the letter, runs his eye through it and jumps up.*] Oh, Hedda—she says that poor Aunt Rina is dying!

HEDDA. Well, we were prepared for that.

TES. And that if I want to see her again I must make haste. I'll run in to them at once.

HEDDA [*suppressing a smile.*] Will you run?

TES. Oh, dearest Hedda—if you could only make up your mind to come with me! Just think!

HEDDA [*rises and says wearily, repelling the idea*]. No, no, don't ask me. I will not look upon sickness and death. I loathe all sorts of ugliness.

TES. Well, well then—— [*Bustling around.*] My hat—my overcoat? Oh, in the hall—— I do hope I mayn't come too late, Hedda! Eh?

HEDDA. Oh, if you run——

BERTA. Judge Brack is at the door and wishes to know if he may come in.

TES. At this time! No, I can't possibly see him.

HEDDA. But I can. [*To* BERTA.] Ask Judge Brack to come in. [BERTA *goes out.*]

HEDDA [*quickly whispering*]. The parcel, Tesman! [*She snatches it up from the stool.*]

TES. Yes, give it to me!

HEDDA. No, no, I will keep it till you come back. [*She goes to the writing table and places it in the bookcase.* TESMAN *stands in a flurry of haste and cannot get his gloves on.*]

[JUDGE BRACK *enters from the hall.*]

HEDDA [*nodding to him*]. You are an early bird, I must say.

BRACK. Yes, don't you think so? [*To* TESMAN.] Are you on the move too?

TES. Yes, I must rush off to my aunts'. Fancy—the invalid one is lying at death's door, poor creature.

BRACK. Dear me, is she, indeed? Then on no account let me detain you. At such a critical moment —

TES. Yes, I must really rush—— Good-by! Good-by! [*He hastens out by the hall door.*]

HEDDA [*approaching*]. You seem to have made a particularly lively night of it at your rooms, Judge Brack.

BRACK. I assure you I have not had my clothes off, Mrs Hedda.

HEDDA. Not you either?

BRACK. No, as you may see. But what has Tesman been telling you of the night's adventures?

HEDDA. Oh, some tiresome story. Only that they went and had coffee somewhere or other.

BRACK. I have heard about that coffee party already. Eilert Lövborg was not with them, I fancy?

HEDDA. No, they had taken him home before that.

BRACK. Tesman too?

HEDDA. No, but some of the others, he said.

BRACK [*smiling*]. George Tesman is really an ingenuous creature, Mrs Hedda.

HEDDA. Yes, heaven knows he is. Then is there something behind all this?

BRACK. Yes, perhaps there may be.

HEDDA. Well then, sit down, my dear judge, and tell your story in comfort. [*She seats herself to the left of the table.* BRACK *sits near her, at the long side of the table.*]

HEDDA. Now then?

BRACK. I had special reasons for keeping track of my guests—or rather of some of my guests—last night.

HEDDA. Of Eilert Lövborg among the rest, perhaps?

BRACK. Frankly, yes.

HEDDA. Now you make me really curious.

BRACK. Do you know where he and one or two of the others finished the night, Mrs Hedda?

HEDDA. If it is not quite unmentionable, tell me.

BRACK. Oh no, it's not at all unmentionable. Well, they put in an appearance at a particularly animated soiree.

HEDDA. Of the lively kind?

BRACK. Of the very liveliest.

HEDDA. Tell me more of this, Judge Brack.

BRACK. Lövborg, as well as the others, had been invited in advance. I knew all about it. But he had declined the invitation; for now, as you know, he has become a new man.

HEDDA. Up at the Elvsteds', yes. But he went after all, then?

BRACK. Well, you see, Mrs Hedda—unhappily the spirit moved him at my rooms last evening——

HEDDA. Yes, I hear he found inspiration.

BRACK. Pretty violent inspiration. Well, I fancy that altered his purpose; for we menfolk are unfortunately not always so firm in our principles as we ought to be.

HEDDA. Oh, I am sure you are an exception, Judge Brack. But as to Lövborg?

BRACK. To make a long story short—he landed at last in Mademoiselle Diana's rooms.

HEDDA. Mademoiselle Diana's?

BRACK. It was Mademoiselle Diana that was giving the soiree to a select circle of her admirers and her lady friends.

HEDDA. Is she a red-haired woman?

BRACK. Precisely.

HEDDA. A sort of a—singer?

BRACK. Oh yes—in her leisure moments. And, moreover, a mighty huntress—of men—Mrs Hedda. You have no doubt heard of her. Eilert Lövborg was one of her most enthusiastic protectors—in the days of his glory.

HEDDA. And how did all this end?

BRACK. Far from amicably, it appears. After a most tender meeting they seem to have come to blows——

HEDDA. Lövborg and she?

BRACK. Yes. He accused her or her

friends of having robbed him. He declared that his pocketbook had disappeared—and other things as well. In short he seems to have made a furious disturbance.

HEDDA. And what came of it all?

BRACK. It came to a general scrimmage in which the ladies as well as the gentlemen took part. Fortunately the police at last appeared on the scene.

HEDDA. The police too?

BRACK. Yes. I fancy it will prove a costly frolic for Eilert Lövborg, crazy being that he is.

HEDDA. How so?

BRACK. He seems to have made a violent resistance—to have hit one of the constables on the head and torn the coat off his back. So they had to march him off to the police station with the rest.

HEDDA. How have you learnt all this?

BRACK. From the police themselves.

HEDDA [*gazing straight before her*]. So that is what happened. Then he had no vine leaves in his hair?

BRACK. Vine leaves, Mrs Hedda?

HEDDA [*changing her tone*]. But tell me now, Judge—what is your real reason for tracking out Eilert Lövborg's movements so carefully?

BRACK. In the first place, it could not be entirely indifferent to me if it should appear in the police court that he came straight from my house.

HEDDA. Will the matter come into court then?

BRACK. Of course. However, I should scarcely have troubled so much about that. But I thought that as a friend of the family it was my duty to supply you and Tesman with a full account of his nocturnal exploits.

HEDDA. Why so, Judge Brack?

BRACK. Why, because I have a shrewd suspicion that he intends to use you as a sort of blind.

HEDDA. Oh, how can you think such a thing!

BRACK. Good heavens, Mrs Hedda —we have eyes in our head. Mark my words! This Mrs Elvsted will be in no hurry to leave town again.

HEDDA. Well, even if there should be anything between them, I suppose there are plenty of other places where they could meet.

BRACK. Not a single home. Henceforth, as before, every respectable house will be closed against Eilert Lövborg.

HEDDA. And so ought mine to be, you mean?

BRACK. Yes. I confess it would be more than painful to me if this personage were to be made free of your house. How superfluous, how intrusive he would be if he were to force his way into——

HEDDA. —into the triangle?

BRACK. Precisely. It would simply mean that I should find myself homeless.

HEDDA [*looks at him with a smile*]. So you want to be the one cock in the basket—that is your aim.

BRACK [*nods slowly and lowers his voice*]. Yes, that is my aim. And for that I will fight—with every weapon I can command.

HEDDA [*her smile vanishing*]. I see you are a dangerous person—when it comes to the point.

BRACK. Do you think so?

HEDDA. I am beginning to think so. And I am exceedingly glad to think—that you have no sort of hold over me.

BRACK [*laughing equivocally*]. Well, well, Mrs Hedda—perhaps you are right there. If I had, who knows what I might be capable of?

HEDDA. Come, come now, Judge Brack. That sounds almost like a threat.

BRACK [*rising*]. Oh, not at all! The triangle, you know, ought, if possible, to be spontaneously constructed.

HEDDA. There I agree with you.

BRACK. Well, now I have said all I had to say, and I had better be getting back to town. Good-by, Mrs Hedda. [*He goes toward the glass door.*]

HEDDA [*rising*]. Are you going through the garden?

BRACK. Yes, it's a short cut for me.

HEDDA. And then it is a back way too.

BRACK. Quite so. I have no objection to back ways. They may be piquant enough at times.

HEDDA. When there is ball practice going on, you mean?

BRACK [*in the doorway, laughing to her*]. Oh, people don't shoot their tame poultry, I fancy.

HEDDA [*also laughing*]. Oh no, when there is only one cock in the basket—— [*They exchange laughing nods of farewell. He goes. She closes the door behind him.*]

[HEDDA, *who has become quite serious, stands for a moment looking out. Presently she goes and peeps through the curtain over the middle doorway. Then she goes to the writing table, takes* LÖVBORG'S *packet out of the bookcase and is on the point of looking through its contents.* BERTA *is heard speaking loudly in the hall.* HEDDA *turns and listens. Then she hastily locks up the packet in the drawer and lays the key on the inkstand.*]

[EILERT LÖVBORG, *with his greatcoat on and his hat in his hand, tears open the hall door. He looks somewhat confused and irritated.*]

LÖV. [*looking toward the hall*]. And I tell you I must and will come in! There! [*He closes the door, turns and sees* HEDDA, *at once regains his self-control and bows.*]

HEDDA [*at the writing table*]. Well, Mr Lövborg, this is rather a late hour to call for Thea.

LÖV. You mean rather an early hour to call on you. Pray pardon me.

HEDDA. How do you know that she is still here?

LÖV. They told me at her lodgings that she had been out all night.

HEDDA [*going to the oval table*]. Did you notice anything about the people of the house when they said that?

LÖV. [*looks inquiringly at her*]. Notice anything about them?

HEDDA. I mean, did they seem to think it odd?

LÖV. [*suddenly understanding*]. Oh yes, of course! I am dragging her down with me! However, I didn't notice anything. I suppose Tesman is not up yet?

HEDDA. No–I think not.

LÖV. When did he come home?

HEDDA. Very late.

LÖV. Did he tell you anything?

HEDDA. Yes, I gathered that you had had an exceedingly jolly evening at Judge Brack's.

LÖV. Nothing more?

HEDDA. I don't think so. However, I was so dreadfully sleepy——

[MRS ELVSTED *enters through the curtains of the middle doorway.*]

MRS ELVS. [*going toward him*]. Ah, Lövborg! At last!

LÖV. Yes, at last. And too late!

MRS ELVS. [*looks anxiously at him*]. What is too late?

Löv. Everything is too late now. It is all over with me.

Mrs Elvs. Oh no, no—don't say that!

Löv. You will say the same when you hear——

Mrs Elvs. I won't hear anything!

Hedda. Perhaps you would prefer to talk to her alone! If so, I will leave you.

Löv. No, stay—you too. I beg you to stay.

Mrs Elvs. Yes, but I won't hear anything, I tell you.

Löv. It is not last night's adventures that I want to talk about.

Mrs Elvs. What is it then?

Löv. I want to say that now our ways must part.

Mrs Elvs. Part!

Hedda [*involuntarily*]. I knew it!

Löv. You can be of no more service to me, Thea.

Mrs Elvs. How can you stand there and say that! No more service to you! Am I not to help you now, as before? Are we not to go on working together?

Löv. Henceforward I shall do no work.

Mrs Elvs. [*despairingly*]. Then what am I to do with my life?

Löv. You must try to live your life as if you had never known me.

Mrs Elvs. But you know I cannot do that!

Löv. Try if you cannot, Thea. You must go home again.

Mrs Elvs. [*in vehement protest*]. Never in this world! Where you are, there will I be also! I will not let myself be driven away like this! I will remain here! I will be with you when the book appears.

Hedda [*half aloud, in suspense*]. Ah yes—the book!

Löv. [*looks at her*]. My book and Thea's, for that is what it is.

Mrs Elvs. Yes, I feel that it is. And that is why I have a right to be with you when it appears! I will see with my own eyes how respect and honor pour in upon you afresh. And the happiness—the happiness—oh, I must share it with you!

Löv. Thea—our book will never appear.

Hedda. Ah!

Mrs Elvs. Never appear!

Löv. Can never appear.

Mrs Elvs. [*in agonized foreboding*]. Lövborg—what have you done with the manuscript?

Hedda [*looks anxiously at him*]. Yes, the manuscript?

Mrs Elvs. Where is it?

Löv. Oh! Thea—don't ask me about it!

Mrs Elvs. Yes, yes, I will know. I demand to be told at once.

Löv. The manuscript—— Well then —I have torn the manuscript into a thousand pieces.

Mrs Elvs. [*shrieks*]. Oh no, no!

Hedda [*involuntarily*]. But that's not——

Löv. [*looks at her*]. Not true, you think?

Hedda [*collecting herself*]. Oh well, of course—since you say so. But it sounded so improbable.

Löv. It is true, all the same.

Mrs Elvs. [*wringing her hands*]. Oh God!—oh God! Hedda—torn his own work to pieces!

Löv. I have torn my own life to pieces. So why should I not tear my lifework too?

Mrs Elvs. And you did this last night?

Löv. Yes, I tell you! Tore it into a thousand pieces and scattered them on the fiord—far out. There there is cool sea water at any rate—let them drift upon it—drift with the current and the wind. And then presently they will sink—deeper and deeper—as I shall, Thea.

Mrs Elvs. Do you know, Lövborg, that what you have done with the book—I shall think of it to my dying day as though you had killed a little child.

Löv. Yes, you are right. It is a sort of child murder.

Mrs Elvs. How could you then! Did not the child belong to me too?

Hedda [*almost inaudibly*]. Ah, the child——

Mrs Elvs. [*breathing heavily*]. It is all over then. Well, well, now I will go, Hedda.

Hedda. But you are not going away from town?

Mrs Elvs. Oh, I don't know what I shall do. I see nothing but darkness before me. [*She goes out by the hall door.*]

Hedda [*stands waiting for a moment*]. So you are not going to see her home, Mr Lövborg?

Löv. I? Through the streets? Would you have people see her walking with me?

Hedda. Of course I don't know what else may have happened last night. But is it so utterly irretrievable?

Löv. It will not end with last night —I know that perfectly well. And the thing is that now I have no taste for that sort of life either. I won't begin it anew. She has broken my courage and my power of braving life out.

Hedda [*looking straight before her*]. So that pretty little fool has had her fingers in a man's destiny. [*Looks at him.*] But all the same, how could you treat her so heartlessly?

Löv. Oh, don't say that it was heartless!

Hedda. To go and destroy what has filled her whole soul for months and years! You do not call that heartless!

Löv. To you I can tell the truth, Hedda.

Hedda. The truth?

Löv. First promise me—give me your word—that what I now confide to you Thea shall never know.

Hedda. I give you my word.

Löv. Good. Then let me tell you that what I said just now was untrue.

Hedda. About the manuscript?

Löv. Yes. I have not torn it to pieces —nor thrown it into the fiord.

Hedda. No, n—— But—where is it then?

Löv. I have destroyed it none the less—utterly destroyed it, Hedda! Thea said that what I had done seemed to her like a child murder.

Hedda. Yes, so she said.

Löv. But to kill this child—that is not the worst thing a father can do to it.

Hedda. Not the worst?

Löv. No. I wanted to spare Thea from hearing the worst.

Hedda. Then what is the worst?

Löv. Suppose now, Hedda, that a man—in the small hours of the morning—came home to his child's mother after a night of riot and debauchery and said: "Listen—I have been here and there—in this place and in that. And I have taken our child with me —to this place and to that. And I have lost the child—utterly lost it. The devil knows into what hands it may have fallen—who may have had their clutches on it."

Hedda. Well—but when all is said

and done, you know—that was only a book.

Löv. Thea's pure soul was in that book.

Hedda. Yes, so I understand.

Löv. And you can understand, too, that for her and me together no future is possible.

Hedda. What path do you mean to take then?

Löv. None. I will only try to make an end of it all—the sooner the better.

Hedda. I don't understand. [*A step nearer to him.*] Eilert Lövborg—listen to me. Will you not try to—to do it beautifully?

Löv. Beautifully? [*Smiling.*] With vine leaves in my hair, as you used to dream in the old days?

Hedda. No, no. I have lost my faith in the vine leaves. But beautifully, nevertheless! For once in a way! Good-by! You must go now—and do not come here any more.

Löv. Good-by, Mrs Tesman. And give George Tesman my love. [*He is on the point of going.*]

Hedda. No, wait! I must give you a memento to take with you. [*She goes to the writing table and opens the drawer and the pistol case, then returns to* Löv. *with one of the pistols.*]

Löv. [*looks at her*]. This? Is this the memento?

Hedda [*nodding slowly*]. Do you recognize it? It was aimed at you once.

Löv. You should have used it then.

Hedda. Take it—and do you use it now.

Löv. [*puts the pistol in his breast pocket*]. Thanks!

Hedda. And beautifully, Eilert Lövborg. Promise me that!

Löv. Good-by, Hedda Gabler. [*He goes out by the hall door.*]

[Hedda *listens for a moment at the door. Then she goes up to the writing table, takes out the packet of manuscript, peeps under the cover, draws a few of the sheets half out and looks at them. Next she goes over and seats herself in the armchair beside the stove, with the packet in her lap. Presently she opens the stove door and then the packet.*]

Hedda [*throws one of the quires into the fire and whispers to herself*]. Now I am burning your child, Thea! Burning it, curlylocks! [*Throwing one or two more quires into the stove.*] Your child and Eilert Lövborg's. [*Throws the rest in.*] I am burning—I am burning your child.

ACT IV

Scene—*The same rooms at the* Tesmans'. *It is evening. The drawing room is in darkness. The back room is lighted by the hanging lamp over the table. The curtains over the glass door are drawn close.*

Hedda, *dressed in black, walks to and fro in the dark room. Then she goes into the back room and disappears for a moment to the left. She is heard to strike a few chords on the piano. Presently she comes in sight again and returns to the drawing room.*

Berta *enters from the right, through the inner room, with a lighted lamp, which she places on the table in front of the corner settee in the drawing room. Her eyes are red with weeping, and she has black ribbons in her cap. She goes quietly and circum spectly out to the right.*

HEDDA *goes up to the glass door, lifts the curtain a little aside and looks out into the darkness.*

Shortly afterward MISS TESMAN, *in mourning, with a bonnet and veil on, comes in from the hall.* HEDDA *goes toward her and holds out her hand.*

MISS TES. Yes, Hedda, here I am, in mourning and forlorn; for now my poor sister has at last found peace.

HEDDA. I have heard the news already, as you see. Tesman sent me a card.

MISS TES. Yes, he promised me he would. But nevertheless I thought that to Hedda—here in the house of life—I ought myself to bring the tidings of death.

HEDDA. That was very kind of you.

MISS TES. Ah, Rina ought not to have left us just now. This is not the time for Hedda's house to be a house of mourning.

HEDDA [*changing the subject*]. She died quite peacefully, did she not, Miss Tesman?

MISS TES. Oh, her end was so calm, so beautiful. And then she had the unspeakable happiness of seeing George once more—and bidding him good-by. Has he come home yet?

HEDDA. No. He wrote that he might be detained. But won't you sit down?

MISS TES. No, thank you, my dear, dear Hedda. I should like to, but I have so much to do. I must prepare my dear one for her rest as well as I can. She shall go to her grave looking her best.

HEDDA. Can I not help you in any way?

MISS TES. Oh, you must not think of it! Hedda Tesman must have no hand in such mournful work. Nor let her thoughts dwell on it either—not at this time.

HEDDA. One is not always mistress of one's thoughts.

MISS TES. [*continuing*]. Ah yes, it is the way of the world. At home we shall be sewing a shroud, and here there will soon be sewing too, I suppose—but of another sort, thank God!

[GEORGE TESMAN *enters by the hall door.*]

HEDDA. Ah, you have come at last!

TES. You here, Aunt Julia? With Hedda? Fancy that!

MISS TES. I was just going, my dear boy. Well, have you done all you promised?

TES. No; I'm really afraid I have forgotten half of it. I must come to you again tomorrow. Today my brain is all in a whirl. I can't keep my thoughts together.

MISS TES. Why, my dear George, you mustn't take it in this way.

TES. Mustn't? How do you mean?

MISS TES. Even in your sorrow you must rejoice, as I do—rejoice that she is at rest.

TES. Oh yes, yes—you are thinking of Aunt Rina.

HEDDA. You will feel lonely now, Miss Tesman.

MISS TES. Just at first, yes. But that will not last very long, I hope. I daresay I shall soon find an occupant for poor Rina's little room.

TES. Indeed? Who do you think will take it? Eh?

MISS TES. Oh, there's always some poor invalid or other in want of nursing, unfortunately.

HEDDA. Would you really take such a burden upon you again?

MISS TES. A burden! Heaven forgive you, child—it has been no burden to me.

HEDDA. But suppose you had a total stranger on your hands——

MISS TES. Oh, one soon makes friends with sick folk, and it's such an absolute necessity for me to have someone to live for. Well, heaven be praised, there may soon be something in this house, too, to keep an old aunt busy.

HEDDA. Oh, don't trouble about anything here.

TES. Yes, just fancy what a nice time we three might have together if——

HEDDA. If——?

TES. [*uneasily*]. Oh, nothing. It will all come right. Let us hope so—eh?

MISS TES. Well, well, I daresay you two want to talk to each other. [*Smiling.*] And perhaps Hedda may have something to tell you too, George. Good-by! I must go home to Rina. [*Turning at the door.*] How strange it is to think that now Rina is with me and with my poor brother as well!

TES. Yes, fancy that, Aunt Julia. Eh?

[MISS TESMAN *goes out by the hall door.*]

HEDDA [*follows* TESMAN *coldly and searchingly with her eyes*]. I almost believe your aunt Rina's death affects you more than it does your aunt Julia.

TES. Oh, it's not that alone. It's Eilert I am so terribly uneasy about.

HEDDA [*quickly*]. Is there anything new about him?

TES. I looked in at his rooms this afternoon, intending to tell him the manuscript was in safe keeping.

HEDDA. Well, did you not find him?

TES. No. He wasn't at home. But afterward I met Mrs Elvsted, and she told me that he had been here early this morning.

HEDDA. Yes, directly after you had gone.

TES. And he said that he had torn his manuscript to pieces—eh?

HEDDA. Yes, so he declared.

TES. Why, good heavens, he must have been completely out of his mind! And I suppose you thought it best not to give it back to him, Hedda?

HEDDA. No, he did not get it.

TES. But of course you told him that we had it?

HEDDA. No. [*Quickly.*] Did you tell Mrs Elvsted?

TES. No; I thought I had better not. But you ought to have told him. Fancy if, in desperation, he should go and do himself some injury! Let me have the manuscript, Hedda. I will take it to him at once. Where is it?

HEDDA [*cold and immovable, leaning on the armchair*]. I have not got it.

TES. Have not got it? What in the world do you mean?

HEDDA. I have burned it—every line of it.

TES. [*with a violent movement of terror*]. Burned! Burned Eilert's manuscript!

HEDDA. Don't scream so. The servant might hear you.

TES. Burned! Why, good God! No, no, no! It's impossible!

HEDDA. It is so, nevertheless.

TES. Do you know what you have done, Hedda? It's unlawful appropriation of lost property. Fancy that! Just ask Judge Brack, and he'll tell you what it is.

HEDDA. I advise you not to speak of it—either to Judge Brack or to anyone else.

TES. But how could you do anything so unheard of? What put it into your head? What possessed you? Answer me that—eh?

HEDDA [*suppressing an almost imperceptible smile*]. I did it for your sake, George.

TES. For my sake!

HEDDA. This morning, when you told me about what he had read to you——

TES. Yes, yes—what then?

HEDDA. You acknowledged that you envied him his work.

TES. Oh, of course I didn't mean that literally.

HEDDA. No matter—I could not bear the idea that anyone should throw you into the shade.

TES. [*in an outburst of mingled doubt and joy*]. Hedda! Oh, is this true? But—but—I never knew you to show your love like that before. Fancy that!

HEDDA. Well, I may as well tell you that—just at this time—— [*Impatiently breaking off.*] No, no; you can ask Aunt Julia. She will tell you fast enough.

TES Oh, I almost think I understand you, Hedda! [*Clasps his hands together.*] Great heavens! Do you really mean it! Eh?

HEDDA. Don't shout so. The servant might hear.

TES. [*laughing in irrepressible glee*]. The servant! Why, how absurd you are, Hedda. It's only my old Berta. Why, I'll tell Berta myself.

HEDDA [*clenching her hands together in desperation*]. Oh, it is killing me—it is killing me, all this!

TES. What is, Hedda? Eh?

HEDDA [*coldly, controlling herself*]. All this—absurdity—George.

TES. Absurdity! Do you see anything absurd in my being overjoyed at the news? But after all—perhaps I had better not say anything to Berta.

HEDDA. Oh—why not that too?

TES. No, no, not yet! But I must certainly tell Aunt Julia. And then that you have begun to call me George too! Fancy that! Oh, Aunt Julia will be so happy—so happy!

HEDDA. When she hears that I have burned Eilert Lövborg's manuscript—for your sake?

TES. No, by the bye—that affair of the manuscript—of course nobody must know about that. But that you love me so much, Hedda—Aunt Julia must really share my joy in that! I wonder, now, whether this sort of thing is usual in young wives? Eh?

HEDDA. I think you had better ask Aunt Julia that question too.

TES. I will indeed, some time or other. [*Looks uneasy and downcast again.*] And yet the manuscript—the manuscript! Good God! It is terrible to think what will become of poor Eilert now.

[MRS ELVSTED, *dressed as in the first act, with hat and cloak, enters by the hall door.*]

MRS ELVS. [*greets them hurriedly and says in evident agitation*]. Oh, dear Hedda, forgive my coming again.

HEDDA. What is the matter with you, Thea?

TES. Something about Eilert Lövborg again—eh?

MRS ELVS. Yes! I am dreadfully afraid some misfortune has happened to him.

HEDDA [*seizes her arm*]. Ah—do you think so?

TES. Why, good lord—what makes you think that, Mrs Elvsted?

MRS ELVS. I heard them talking of

him at my boardinghouse—just as I came in. Oh, the most incredible rumors are afloat about him today.

TES. Yes, fancy, so I heard too! And I can bear witness that he went straight home to bed last night. Fancy that!

HEDDA. Well, what did they say at the boardinghouse?

MRS ELVS. Oh, I couldn't make out anything clearly. Either they knew nothing definite or else—— They stopped talking when they saw me, and I did not dare to ask.

TES. [*moving about uneasily*]. We must hope—we must hope that you misunderstood them, Mrs Elvsted.

MRS ELVS. No, no; I am sure it was of him they were talking. And I heard something about the hospital or——

TES. The hospital?

HEDDA. No—surely that cannot be!

MRS ELVS. Oh, I was in such mortal terror! I went to his lodgings and asked for him there.

HEDDA. You could make up your mind to that, Thea!

MRS ELVS. What else could I do? I really could bear the suspense no longer.

TES. But you didn't find him either —eh?

MRS ELVS. No. And the people knew nothing about him. He hadn't been home since yesterday afternoon, they said.

TES. Yesterday! Fancy, how could they say that?

MRS ELVS. Oh, I am sure something terrible must have happened to him.

TES. Hedda dear how would it be if I were to go and make inquiries?

HEDDA. No, no—don't you mix yourself up in this affair.

[JUDGE BRACK, *with his hat in his hand, enters by the hall door, which* BERTA *opens and closes behind him. He looks grave and bows in silence.*]

TES. Oh, is that you, my dear judge? Eh?

BRACK. Yes. It was imperative I should see you this evening.

TES. I can see you have heard the news about Aunt Rina.

BRACK. Yes, that among other things.

TES. Isn't it sad—eh?

BRACK. Well, my dear Tesman, that depends on how you look at it.

TES. [*looks doubtfully at him*]. Has anything else happened?

BRACK. Yes.

HEDDA [*in suspense*]. Anything sad, Judge Brack?

BRACK. That, too, depends on how you look at it, Mrs Tesman.

MRS ELVS. [*unable to restrain her anxiety*]. Oh! It is something about Eilert Lövborg!

BRACK [*with a glance at her*]. What makes you think that, madam? Perhaps you have already heard something?

MRS ELVS. [*in confusion*]. No, nothing at all, but——

TES. Oh, for heaven's sake, tell us!

BRACK [*shrugging his shoulders*]. Well, I regret to say Eilert Lövborg has been taken to the hospital. He is lying at the point of death.

MRS ELVS. [*shrieks*]. Oh God! Oh God!

TES. To the hospital! And at the point of death!

HEDDA [*involuntarily*]. So soon then——

MRS ELVS. [*wailing*]. And we parted in anger, Hedda!

HEDDA [*whispers*]. Thea—Thea—be careful!

MRS ELVS. [*not heeding her*]. I

must go to him! I must see him alive!

Brack. It is useless, madam. No one will be admitted.

Mrs Elvs. Oh, at least tell me what has happened to him. What is it?

Tes. You don't mean to say that he has himself—— Eh?

Hedda. Yes, I am sure he has.

Tes. Hedda, how can you——?

Brack [*keeping his eyes fixed upon her*]. Unfortunately you have guessed quite correctly, Mrs Tesman.

Mrs Elvs. Oh, how horrible!

Tes. Himself, then! Fancy that!

Hedda. Shot himself!

Brack. Rightly guessed again, Mrs Tesman.

Mrs Elvs. [*with an effort at self-control*]. When did it happen, Mr Brack?

Brack. This afternoon between three and four.

Tes. But, good lord, where did he do it? Eh?

Brack [*with some hesitation*]. Where? Well—I suppose at his lodgings.

Mrs Elvs. No, that cannot be; for I was there between six and seven.

Brack. Well then, somewhere else. I don't know exactly. I only know that he was found. He had shot himself—in the breast.

Mrs Elvs. Oh, how terrible! That he should die like that!

Hedda [*to* Brack]. Was it in the breast?

Brack. Yes—as I told you.

Hedda. Not in the temple?

Brack. In the breast, Mrs Tesman.

Hedda. Well, well—the breast is a good place too.

Brack. How do you mean, Mrs Tesman?

Hedda [*evasively*]. Oh, nothing—nothing.

Tes. And the wound is dangerous, you say—eh?

Brack. Absolutely mortal. The end has probably come by this time.

Mrs Elvs. Yes, yes, I feel it. The end! The end! Oh, Hedda!

Tes. But tell me, how have you learned all this?

Brack [*curtly*]. Through one of the police. A man I had some business with.

Hedda [*in a clear voice*]. At last a deed worth doing!

Tes. [*terrified*]. Good heavens, Hedda! What are you saying?

Hedda. I say there is beauty in this.

Brack. H'm, Mrs Tesman——

Tes. Beauty! Fancy that!

Mrs Elvs. Oh, Hedda, how can you talk of beauty in such an act!

Hedda. Eilert Lövborg has himself made up his account with life. He has had the courage to do—the one right thing.

Mrs Elvs. No, you must never think that was how it happened! It must have been in delirium that he did it.

Tes. In despair!

Hedda. That he did not. I am certain of that.

Mrs Elvs. Yes, yes! In delirium! Just as when he tore up our manuscript.

Brack [*starting*]. The manuscript? Has he torn that up?

Mrs Elvs. Yes, last night.

Tes. [*whispers softly*]. Oh, Hedda, we shall never get over this.

Brack. H'm, very extraordinary.

Tes. [*moving about the room*]. To think of Eilert going out of the world in this way! And not leaving behind him the book that would have immortalized his name——

MRS ELVS. Oh, if only it could be put together again!

TES. Yes, if it only could! I don't know what I would not give——

MRS ELVS. Perhaps it can, Mr Tesman.

TES. What do you mean?

MRS ELVS. [*searches in the pocket of her dress*]. Look here. I have kept all the loose notes he used to dictate from.

HEDDA [*a step forward*]. Ah!

TES. You have kept them, Mrs Elvsted! Eh?

MRS ELVS. Yes, I have them here. I put them in my pocket when I left home. Here they still are.

TES. Oh, do let me see them!

MRS ELVS. [*hands him a bundle of papers*]. But they are in such disorder —all mixed up.

TES. Fancy if we could make something out of them after all! Perhaps if we two put our heads together——

MRS ELVS. Oh yes, at least let us try.

TES. We will manage it! We must! I will dedicate my life to this task.

HEDDA. You, George? Your life?

TES. Yes, or rather all the time I can spare. My own collections must wait in the meantime. Hedda—you understand, eh? I owe this to Eilert's memory.

HEDDA. Perhaps.

TES. And so, my dear Mrs Elvsted, we will give our whole minds to it. There is no use in brooding over what can't be undone—eh? We must try to control our grief as much as possible, and——

MRS ELVS. Yes, yes, Mr Tesman, I will do the best I can.

TES. Well then, come here. I can't rest until we have looked through the notes. Where shall we sit? Here? No, in there, in the back room. Excuse me, my dear judge. Come with me, Mrs Elvsted.

MRS ELVS. Oh, if only it were possible! [TESMAN *and* MRS ELVSTED *go into the back room. She takes off her hat and cloak. They both sit at the table under the hanging lamp and are soon deep in an eager examination of the papers.* HEDDA *crosses to the stove and sits in the armchair. Presently* BRACK *goes up to her.*]

HEDDA [*in a low voice*]. Oh, what sense of freedom it gives me, this act of Eilert Lövborg's.

BRACK. Freedom, Mrs Hedda? Well, of course, it is a release for him——

HEDDA. I mean for me. It gives me a sense of freedom to know that a deed of deliberate courage is still possible in this world—a deed of spontaneous beauty.

BRACK [*smiling*]. H'm—my dear Mrs Hedda——

HEDDA. Oh, I know what you are going to say. For you are a kind of specialist too, like—you know!

BRACK [*looking hard at her*]. Eilert Lövborg was more to you than perhaps you are willing to admit to yourself. Am I wrong?

HEDDA. I don't answer such questions. I only know Eilert Lövborg has had the courage to live his life after his own fashion. And then—the last great act, with its beauty! Ah! That he should have the will and the strength to turn away from the banquet of life—so early.

BRACK. I am sorry, Mrs Hedda, but I fear I must dispel an amiable illusion.

HEDDA. Illusion?

BRACK. Which could not have lasted long in any case.

HEDDA. What do you mean?

Brack. Eilert Lövborg did not shoot himself voluntarily.

Hedda. Not voluntarily?

Brack. No. The thing did not happen exactly as I told it.

Hedda [*in suspense*]. Have you concealed something? What is it?

Brack. For poor Mrs Elvsted's sake I idealized the facts a little.

Hedda. What are the facts?

Brack. First, that he is already dead.

Hedda. At the hospital?

Brack. Yes—without regaining consciousness.

Hedda. What more have you concealed?

Brack. This—the event did not happen at his lodgings.

Hedda. Oh, that can make no difference.

Brack. Perhaps it may. For I must tell you—Eilert Lövborg was found shot in—in Mademoiselle Diana's boudoir.

Hedda [*makes a motion as if to rise but sinks back again*]. That is impossible, Judge Brack! He cannot have been there again today.

Brack. He was there this afternoon. He went there, he said, to demand the return of something which they had taken from him. Talked wildly about a lost child——

Hedda. Ah—so that was why——

Brack. I thought probably he meant his manuscript, but now I hear he destroyed that himself. So I suppose it must have been his pocketbook.

Hedda. Yes, no doubt. And there—there he was found?

Brack. Yes, there. With a pistol in his breast pocket, discharged. The ball had lodged in a vital part.

Hedda. In the breast—yes.

Brack. No—in the bowels.

Hedda [*looks up at him with an expression of loathing*]. That too! Oh, what curse is it that makes everything I touch turn ludicrous and mean?

Brack. There is one point more, Mrs Hedda—another disagreeable feature in the affair.

Hedda. And what is that?

Brack. The pistol he carried——

Hedda [*breathless*]. Well? What of it?

Brack. He must have stolen it.

Hedda [*leaps up*]. Stolen it! That is not true! He did not steal it!

Brack. No other explanation is possible. He must have stolen it—— Hush!

[Tesman *and* Mrs Elvsted *have risen from the table in the back room and come into the drawing room.*]

Tes. [*with the papers in both his hands*]. Hedda dear, it is almost impossible to see under that lamp. Think of that!

Hedda. Yes, I am thinking.

Tes. Would you mind our sitting at your writing table—eh?

Hedda. If you like. [*Quickly.*] No, wait! Let me clear it first.

Tes. Oh, you needn't trouble, Hedda. There is plenty of room.

Hedda. No, no; let me clear it, I say! I will take these things in and put them on the piano. There! [*She has drawn out an object, covered with sheet music, from under the bookcase, places several other pieces of music upon it and carries the whole into the inner room to the left.* Tesman *lays the scraps of paper on the writing table and moves the lamp there from the corner table.* Hedda *returns.*]

Hedda [*behind* Mrs Elvsted's *chair, gently ruffling her hair*]. Well, my sweet Thea, how goes it with Eilert Lövborg's monument?

MRS ELVS. [*looks dispiritedly up at her*]. Oh, it will be terribly hard to put in order.

TES. We must manage it. I am determined. And arranging other people's papers is just the work for me.

[HEDDA *goes over to the stove and seats herself on one of the footstools.* BRACK *stands over her, leaning on the armchair.*]

HEDDA [*whispers*]. What did you say about the pistol?

BRACK [*softly*]. That he must have stolen it.

HEDDA. Why stolen it?

BRACK. Because every other explanation ought to be impossible, Mrs Hedda.

HEDDA. Indeed?

BRACK [*glances at her*]. Of course Eilert Lövborg was here this morning. Was he not?

HEDDA. Yes.

BRACK. Were you alone with him?

HEDDA. Part of the time.

BRACK. Did you not leave the room whilst he was here?

HEDDA. No.

BRACK. Try to recollect. Were you not out of the room a moment?

HEDDA. Yes, perhaps just a moment —out in the hall.

BRACK. And where was your pistol case during that time?

HEDDA. I had it locked up in——

BRACK. Well, Mrs Hedda?

HEDDA. The case stood there on the writing table.

BRACK. Have you looked since to see whether both the pistols are there?

HEDDA. No.

BRACK. Well, you need not. I saw the pistol found in Lövborg's pocket, and I knew it at once as the one I had seen yesterday—and before too.

HEDDA. Have you it with you?

BRACK. No, the police have it.

HEDDA. What will the police do with it?

BRACK. Search till they find the owner.

HEDDA. Do you think they will succeed?

BRACK [*bends over her and whispers*]. No, Hedda Gabler—not so long as I say nothing.

HEDDA [*looks frightened at him*]. And if you do not say nothing—what then?

BRACK [*shrugs his shoulders*]. There is always the possibility that the pistol was stolen.

HEDDA [*firmly*]. Death rather than that.

BRACK [*smiling*]. People say such things—but they don't do them.

HEDDA [*without replying*]. And supposing the pistol was stolen and the owner is discovered? What then?

BRACK. Well, Hedda—then comes the scandal.

HEDDA. The scandal!

BRACK. Yes, the scandal—of which you are mortally afraid. You will, of course, be brought before the court—both you and Mademoiselle Diana. She will have to explain how the thing happened—whether it was an accidental shot or murder. Did the pistol go off as he was trying to take it out of his pocket to threaten her with? Or did she tear the pistol out of his hand, shoot him and push it back into his pocket? That would be quite like her, for she is an able-bodied young person, this same Mademoiselle Diana.

HEDDA. But *I* have nothing to do with all this repulsive business.

BRACK. No. But you will have to answer the question: Why did you give Eilert Lövborg the pistol? And what conclusions will people draw from the fact that you did give it to him?

HEDDA [*lets her head sink*]. That is true. I did not think of that.

BRACK. Well, fortunately there is no danger so long as I say nothing.

HEDDA [*looks up at him*]. So I am in your power, Judge Brack. You have me at your beck and call from this time forward.

BRACK [*whispers softly*]. Dearest Hedda—believe me—I shall not abuse my advantage.

HEDDA. I am in your power none the less. Subject to your will and your demands. A slave, a slave then! [*Rises impetuously.*] No, I cannot endure the thought of that! Never!

BRACK [*looks half mockingly at her*]. People generally get used to the inevitable.

HEDDA [*returns his look*]. Yes, perhaps. [*She crosses to the writing table. Suppressing an involuntary smile, she imitates* TESMAN's *intonations.*] Well? Are you getting on, George? Eh?

TES. Heaven knows, dear. In any case it will be the work of months.

HEDDA [*as before*]. Fancy that! [*Passes her hands softly through* MRS ELVSTED's *hair.*] Doesn't it seem strange to you, Thea? Here are you sitting with Tesman—just as you used to sit with Eilert Lövborg?

MRS ELVS. Ah, if I could only inspire your husband in the same way.

HEDDA. Oh, that will come too—in time.

TES. Yes, do you know, Hedda—I really think I begin to feel something of the sort. But won't you go and sit with Brack again?

HEDDA. Is there nothing I can do to help you two?

TES. No, nothing in the world. [*Turning his head.*] I trust to you to keep Hedda company, my dear Brack.

BRACK [*with a glance at* HEDDA]. With the very greatest of pleasure.

HEDDA. Thanks. But I am tired this evening. I will go in and lie down a little on the sofa.

TES. Yes, do, dear—eh?

[HEDDA *goes into the back room and draws the curtains. A short pause. Suddenly she is heard playing a wild dance on the piano.*]

MRS ELVS. [*starts from her chair*]. Oh—what is that?

TES. [*runs to the doorway*]. Why, my dearest Hedda—don't play dance music tonight! Just think of Aunt Rina! And of Eilert too!

HEDDA [*puts her head out between the curtains*]. And of Aunt Julia. And of all the rest of them. After this I will be quiet. [*Closes the curtains again.*]

TES. [*at the writing table*]. It's not good for her to see us at this distressing work. I'll tell you what, Mrs Elvsted—you shall take the empty room at Aunt Julia's, and then I will come over in the evenings and we can sit and work there—eh?

HEDDA [*in the inner room*]. I hear what you are saying, Tesman. But how am *I* to get through the evenings out here?

TES. [*turning over the papers*]. Oh, I daresay Judge Brack will be so kind as to look in now and then, even though I am out.

BRACK [*in the armchair, calls out gaily*]. Every blessed evening, with all the pleasure in life, Mrs Tesman! We shall get on capitally together, we two!

HEDDA [*speaking loud and clear*]. Yes, don't you flatter yourself we will, Judge Brack? Now that you are the one cock in the basket—— [*A shot is heard within.* TESMAN, MRS ELVSTED *and* BRACK *leap to their feet.*]

TES. Oh, now she is playing with those pistols again. [*He throws back the curtains and runs in, followed by* MRS ELVSTED. HEDDA *lies stretched on the sofa, lifeless. Confusion and cries.* BERTA *enters in alarm from the right.*]

TES. [*shrieks to* BRACK]. Shot herself! Shot herself in the temple! Fancy that!

BRACK [*half fainting in the arm-chair*]. Good God!—people don't do such things.

GHOSTS

PERSONS OF THE PLAY

MRS ALVING, *a widow.*
OSWALD ALVING, *her son, an artist.*
MANDERS, *the pastor of the parish.*
ENGSTRAND, *a carpenter.*
REGINA ENGSTRAND, *his daughter, in Mrs Alving's service.*

The action takes place at Mrs Alving's house on one of the larger fiords of western Norway.

ACT I

SCENE—*A large room looking upon a garden. A door in the left-hand wall and two in the right. In the middle of the room a round table with chairs set about it and books, magazines and newspapers upon it. In the foreground on the left a window, by which is a small sofa with a worktable in front of it. At the back the room opens into a conservatory rather smaller than the room. From the right-hand side of this a door leads to the garden. Through the large panes of glass that form the outer wall of the conservatory a gloomy fiord landscape can be discerned, half obscured by steady rain.*

ENGSTRAND *is standing close up to the garden door. His left leg is slightly deformed, and he wears a boot with a clump of wood under the sole.* REGINA, *with an empty garden syringe in her hand, is trying to prevent his coming in.*

REG. [*below her breath*]. What is it you want? Stay where you are. The rain is dripping off you.

ENG. God's good rain, my girl.

REG. The devil's own rain, that's what it is!

ENG. Lord, how you talk, Regina. [*Takes a few limping steps forward.*] What I wanted to tell you was this——

REG. Don't clump about like that, stupid! The young master is lying asleep upstairs.

ENG. Asleep still? In the middle of the day?

REG. Well, it's no business of yours.

ENG. I was out on a spree last night——

REG. I don't doubt it.

ENG. Yes, we are poor weak mortals, my girl——

REG. We are indeed.

ENG. —and the temptations of the world are manifold, you know—but, for all that, here I was at my work at half-past five this morning.

REG. Yes, yes, but make yourself scarce now. I am not going to stand here as if I had a rendezvous with you.

ENG. As if you had a what?

REG. I am not going to have anyone find you here; so now you know, and you can go.

ENG. [*coming a few steps nearer*]. Not a bit of it! Not before we have had a little chat. This afternoon I shall have finished my job down at the schoolhouse, and I shall be off home to town by tonight's boat.

REG. [*mutters*]. Pleasant journey to you!

ENG. Thanks, my girl. Tomorrow is the opening of the orphanage, and I expect there will be a fine kickup here and plenty of good strong drink, don't you know. And no one shall say of Jacob Engstrand that he can't hold off when temptation comes in his way.

REG. Oho!

ENG. Yes, because there will be a lot of fine folk here tomorrow. Parson Manders is expected from town too.

REG. What is more, he's coming today.

ENG. There you are! And I'm going to be precious careful he doesn't have anything to say against me, do you see?

REG. Oh, that's your game, is it?

ENG. What do you mean?

REG. [*with a significant look at him*]. What is it you want to humbug Mr Manders out of this time?

ENG. Sh! Sh! Are you crazy? Do you suppose *I* would want to humbug Mr Manders? No, no—Mr Manders has always been too kind a friend for me to do that. But what I wanted to talk to you about was my going back home tonight.

REG. The sooner you go, the better I shall be pleased.

ENG. Yes, only I want to take you with me, Regina.

REG. [*open-mouthed*]. You want to take me—— What did you say?

ENG. I want to take you home with me, I said.

REG. [*contemptuously*]. You will never get me home with you.

ENG. Ah, we shall see about that.

REG. Yes, you can be quite certain we *shall* see about that. I, who have been brought up by a lady like Mrs Alving? I, who have been treated almost as if I were her own child? Do you suppose I am going home with *you*—to such a house as yours? Not likely!

ENG. What the devil do you mean? Are you setting yourself up against your father, you hussy?

REG. [*mutters without looking at him*]. You have often told me I was none of yours.

ENG. Bah! Why do you want to pay any attention to that?

REG. Haven't you many and many a time abused me and called me a——? For shame!

ENG. I'll swear I never used such an ugly word.

REG. Oh, it doesn't matter what word you used.

ENG. Besides, that was only when I was a bit fuddled—hm! Temptations are manifold in this world, Regina.

REG. Ugh!

ENG. And it was when your mother was in a nasty temper. I had to find some way of getting my knife into her, my girl. She was always so precious genteel. [*Mimicking her.*] "Let go, Jacob! Let me be! Please to remember that I was three years with the Alvings at Rosenvold, and they were people who went to court!" [*Laughs.*] Bless my soul, she never could forget that Captain Alving got a court appointment while she was in service here.

REG. Poor Mother—you worried her into her grave pretty soon.

ENG. [*shrugging his shoulders*]. Of course, of course; I have got to take the blame for everything.

REG. [*beneath her breath, as she turns away*]. Ugh—that leg too!

ENG. What are you saying, my girl?

REG. *Pied de mouton.*

ENG. Is that English?

Reg. Yes.

Eng. You have had a good education out here, and no mistake; and it may stand you in good stead now, Regina.

Reg. [*after a short silence*]. And what was it you wanted me to come to town for?

Eng. Need you ask why a father wants his only child? Ain't I a poor lonely widower?

Reg. Oh, don't come to me with that tale. Why do you want me to go?

Eng. Well, I must tell you I am thinking of taking up a new line now.

Reg. [*whistles*]. You have tried that so often—but it has always proved a fool's errand.

Eng. Ah, but this time you will just see, Regina! Strike me dead if——

Reg. [*stamping her foot*]. Stop swearing!

Eng. Sh! Sh!—you're quite right, my girl, quite right! What I wanted to say was only this, that I have put by a tidy penny out of what I have made by working at this new orphanage up here.

Reg. Have you? All the better for you.

Eng. What is there for a man to spend his money on out here in the country?

Reg. Well, what then?

Eng. Well, you see, I thought of putting the money into something that would pay. I thought of some kind of an eating house for seafaring folk——

Reg. Heavens!

Eng. Oh, a high-class eating house, of course—not a pigsty for common sailors. Damn it, no; it would be a place ships' captains and first mates would come to; really good sort of people, you know.

Reg. And what should I——

Eng. You would help there. But only to make a show, you know. You wouldn't find it hard work, I promise you, my girl. You should do exactly as you like.

Reg. Oh yes, quite so!

Eng. But we must have some women in the house; that is as clear as daylight. Because in the evening we must make the place a little attractive—some singing and dancing and that sort of thing. Remember they are seafolk—wayfarers of the waters of life! [*Coming nearer to her.*] Now don't be a fool and stand in your own way, Regina. What good are you going to do here? Will this education that your mistress has paid for be of any use? You are to look after the children in the new home, I hear. Is that the sort of work for you? Are you so frightfully anxious to go and wear out your health and strength for the sake of these dirty brats?

Reg. No; if things were to go as I want them to, then—— Well, it may happen; who knows? It may happen!

Eng. What may happen?

Reg. Never you mind. Is it much that you have put by up here?

Eng. Taking it all round, I should say about forty or fifty pounds.

Reg. That's not so bad.

Eng. It's enough to make a start with, my girl.

Reg. Don't you mean to give me any of the money?

Eng. No, I'm hanged if I do.

Reg. Don't you mean to send me as much as a dress length of stuff just for once?

Eng. Come and live in the town with me and you will have plenty of dresses.

Reg. Pooh! I can get that much for myself if I have a mind to.

ENG. But it's far better to have a father's guiding hand, Regina. Just now I can get a nice house in Little Harbour Street. They don't want much money down for it–and we could make it like a sort of seaman's home, don't you know.

REG. But I have no intention of living with you! I have nothing whatever to do with you. So now be off!

ENG. You wouldn't be living with me long, my girl. No such luck–not if you knew how to play your cards. Such a fine wench as you have grown this last year or two——

REG. Well?

ENG. It wouldn't be very long before some first mate came along–or perhaps a captain.

REG. I don't mean to marry a man of that sort. Sailors have no *savoir-vivre.*

ENG. What haven't they got?

REG. I know what sailors are, I tell you. They aren't the sort of people to marry.

ENG. Well, don't bother about marrying them. You can make it pay just as well. [*More confidentially.*] That fellow–the Englishman–the one with the yacht–he gave seventy pounds, he did; and she wasn't a bit prettier than you.

REG. [*advancing toward him*]. Get out!

ENG. [*stepping back*]. Here! here! –you're not going to hit me, I suppose?

REG. Yes! If you talk like that of Mother, I will hit you. Get out, I tell you! [*Pushes him up to the garden door.*] And don't bang the doors. Young Mr Alving——

ENG. Is asleep–I know. It's funny how anxious you are about young Mr Alving. [*In a lower tone.*] Oho! Is it possible that it is *he* that——

REG. Get out, and be quick about it! Your wits are wandering, my good man. No, don't go that way; Mr Manders is just coming along. Be off down the kitchen stairs.

ENG. [*moving toward the right*]. Yes, yes–all right. But have a bit of a chat with him that's coming along. He's the chap to tell you what a child owes to its father. For I am your father anyway, you know. I can prove it by the register. [*He goes out through the farther door which* REGINA *has opened. She shuts it after him, looks hastily at herself in the mirror, fans herself with her handkerchief and sets her collar straight, then busies herself with the flowers.* MANDERS *enters the conservatory through the garden door. He wears an overcoat, carries an umbrella and has a small traveling bag slung over his shoulder on a strap.*]

MAN. Good morning, Miss Engstrand.

REG. [*turning round with a look of pleased surprise*]. Oh, Mr Manders, good morning. The boat is in then?

MAN. Just in. [*Comes into the room.*] It is most tiresome, this rain every day.

REG. [*following him in*]. It's a splendid rain for the farmers, Mr Manders.

MAN. Yes, you are quite right. We townfolk think so little about that. [*Begins to take off his overcoat.*]

REG. Oh, let me help you. That's it. Why, how wet it is! I will hang it up in the hall. Give me your umbrella too; I will leave it open so that it will dry. [*She goes out with the things by the farther door on the right.* MANDERS *lays his bag and his hat down on a chair.* REGINA *re-enters.*]

MAN. Ah, it's very pleasant to get indoors. Well, is everything going on well here?

REG. Yes, thanks.

MAN. Properly busy though, I expect, getting ready for tomorrow?

REG. Oh yes, there is plenty to do.

MAN. And Mrs Alving is at home, I hope?

REG. Yes, she is. She has just gone upstairs to take the young master his chocolate.

MAN. Tell me—I heard down at the pier that Oswald had come back.

REG. Yes, he came the day before yesterday. We didn't expect him till today.

MAN. Strong and well, I hope?

REG. Yes, thank you, well enough. But dreadfully tired after his journey. He came straight from Paris without a stop—I mean he came all the way without breaking his journey. I fancy he is having a sleep now, so we must talk a little bit more quietly if you don't mind.

MAN. All right, we will be very quiet.

REG. [*while she moves an armchair up to the table*]. Please sit down, Mr Manders, and make yourself at home. [*He sits down; she puts a footstool under his feet.*] There! Is that comfortable?

MAN. Thank you, thank you. That is most comfortable. [*Looks at her.*] I'll tell you what, Miss Engstrand, I certainly think you have grown since I saw you last.

REG. Do you think so? Mrs Alving says, too, that I have developed.

MAN. Developed? Well, perhaps a little—just suitably. [*A short pause.*]

REG. Shall I tell Mrs Alving you are here?

MAN. Thanks, there is no hurry, my dear child. Now tell me, Regina my dear, how has your father been getting on here?

REG. Thank you, Mr Manders, he is getting on pretty well.

MAN. He came to see me the last time he was in town.

REG. Did he? He is always so glad when he can have a chat with you.

MAN. And I suppose you have seen him pretty regularly every day?

REG. I? Oh yes, I do—whenever I have time, that is to say.

MAN. Your father has not a very strong character, Miss Engstrand. He sadly needs a guiding hand.

REG. Yes, I can quite believe that.

MAN. He needs someone with him that he can cling to, someone whose judgment he can rely on. He acknowledged that freely himself the last time he came up to see me.

REG. Yes, he has said something of the same sort to me. But I don't know whether Mrs Alving could do without me—most of all just now, when we have the new orphanage to see about. And I should be dreadfully unwilling to leave Mrs Alving too; she has always been so good to me.

MAN. But a daughter's duty, my good child—— Naturally we should have to get your mistress's consent first.

REG. Still I don't know whether it would be quite the thing, at my age, to keep house for a single man.

MAN. What! My dear Miss Engstrand, it is your own father we are speaking of!

REG. Yes, I daresay, but still Now if it were in a good house and with a real gentleman——

MAN. But, my dear Regina——

REG. —one whom I could feel an affection for and really feel in the position of a daughter to——

MAN. Come, come—my dear good child——

REG. —I should like very much to live in town. Out here it is terribly lonely, and you know yourself, Mr Manders, what it is to be alone in the world. And, though I say it, I really am both capable and willing. Don't you know any place that would be suitable for me, Mr Manders?

MAN. I? No, indeed I don't.

REG. But, dear Mr Manders—at any rate don't forget me, in case——

MAN. [*getting up*]. No, I won't forget you, Miss Engstrand.

REG. Because, if I——

MAN. Perhaps you will be so kind as to let Mrs Alving know I am here?

REG. I will fetch her at once, Mr Manders. [*Goes out to the left.* MANDERS *walks up and down the room once or twice, stands for a moment at the farther end of the room with his hands behind his back and looks out into the garden. Then he comes back to the table, takes up a book and looks at the title page, gives a start and looks at some of the others.*]

MAN. Hm! Really!

[MRS ALVING *comes in by the door on the left. She is followed by* REGINA, *who goes out again at once through the nearer door on the right.*]

MRS ALV. [*holding out her hand*]. I am very glad to see you, Mr Manders.

MAN. How do you do, Mrs Alving. Here I am, as I promised.

MRS ALV. Always punctual!

MAN. Indeed, I was hard put to it to get away. What with vestry meetings and committees——

MRS ALV. It was all the kinder of you to come in such good time; we can settle our business before dinner. But where is your luggage?

MAN. [*quickly*]. My things are down at the village shop. I am going to sleep there tonight.

MRS ALV. [*repressing a smile*]. Can't I really persuade you to stay the night here this time?

MAN. No, no; many thanks all the same; I will put up there, as usual. It is so handy for getting on board the boat again.

MRS ALV. Of course you shall do as you please. But it seems to me quite another thing, now we are two old people——

MAN. Ha! Ha! You will have your jokes! And it's natural you should be in high spirits today—first of all there is the great event tomorrow, and also you have got Oswald home.

MRS ALV. Yes, am I not a lucky woman! It is more than two years since he was home last, and he has promised to stay the whole winter with me.

MAN. Has he really? That is very nice and filial of him, because there must be many more attractions in his life in Rome or in Paris, I should think.

MRS ALV. Yes, but he has his mother here, you see. Bless the dear boy, he has got a corner in his heart for his mother still.

MAN. Oh, it would be very sad if absence and preoccupation with such a thing as art were to dull the natural affections.

MRS ALV. It would, indeed. But there is no fear of that with him, I am glad to say. I am quite curious to see if you recognize him again. He will be down directly; he is just lying down for a little on the sofa upstairs. But do sit down, my dear friend.

MAN. Thank you. You are sure I

am not disturbing you?

Mrs Alv. Of course not. [*She sits down at the table.*]

Man. Good. Then I will show you—— [*He goes to the chair where his bag is lying and takes a packet of papers from it, then sits down at the opposite side of the table and looks for a clear space to put the papers down.*] Now first of all, here is—— [*Breaks off.*] Tell me, Mrs Alving, what are these books doing here?

Mrs Alv. These books? I am reading them.

Man. Do you read this sort of thing?

Mrs Alv. Certainly I do.

Man. Do you feel any the better or the happier for reading books of this kind?

Mrs Alv. I think it makes me, as it were, more self-reliant.

Man. That is remarkable! But why?

Mrs Alv. Well, they give me an explanation or a confirmation of lots of different ideas that have come into my own mind. But what surprises me, Mr Manders, is that, properly speaking, there is nothing at all new in these books. There is nothing more in them than what most people think and believe. The only thing is that most people either take no account of it or won't admit it to themselves.

Man. But, good heavens, do you seriously think that most people——?

Mrs Alv. Yes, indeed I do.

Man. But not here in the country at any rate? Not here amongst people like ourselves?

Mrs Alv. Yes, amongst people like ourselves too.

Man. Well, really, I must say!

Mrs Alv. But what is the particular objection that you have to these books?

Man. What objection? You surely don't suppose that I take any particular interest in such productions?

Mrs Alv. In fact, you don't know anything about what you are denouncing?

Man. I have read quite enough about these books to disapprove of them.

Mrs Alv. Yes, but your own opinion——

Man. My dear Mrs Alving, there are many occasions in life when one has to rely on the opinion of others. That is the way in this world, and it is quite right that it should be so. What would become of society otherwise?

Mrs Alv. Well, you may be right.

Man. Apart from that, naturally I don't deny that literature of this kind may have a considerable attraction. And I cannot blame you, either, for wishing to make yourself acquainted with the intellectual tendencies which I am told are at work in the wider world in which you have allowed your son to wander for so long. But——

Mrs Alv. But——?

Man. [*lowering his voice*]. But one doesn't talk about it, Mrs Alving. One certainly is not called upon to account to everyone for what one reads or thinks in the privacy of one's own room.

Mrs Alv. Certainly not. I quite agree with you.

Man. Just think of the consideration you owe to this orphanage, which you decided to build at a time when your thoughts on such subjects were very different from what they are now—as far as I am able to judge.

Mrs Alv. Yes, I freely admit that. But it was about the orphanage——

MAN. It was about the orphanage we were going to talk; quite so. Well—walk warily, dear Mrs Alving! And now let us turn to the business in hand. [*Opens an envelope and takes out some papers.*] You see these?

MRS ALV. The deeds?

MAN. Yes, the whole lot—and everything in order. I can tell you it has been no easy matter to get them in time. I had positively to put pressure on the authorities; they are almost painfully conscientious when it is a question of settling property. But here they are at last. [*Turns over the papers.*] Here is the deed of conveyance of that part of the Rosenvold estate known as the Solvik property, together with the buildings newly erected thereon—the school, the masters' houses and the chapel. And here is the legal sanction for the statutes of the institution. Here you see—[*reads*] —"Statutes for the Captain Alving Orphanage."

MRS ALV. [*after a long look at the papers*]. That seems all in order.

MAN. I thought "Captain" was the better title to use, rather than your husband's court title of "Chamberlain." "Captain" seems less ostentatious.

MRS ALV. Yes, yes; just as you think best.

MAN. And here is the certificate for the investment of the capital in the bank, the interest being earmarked for the current expenses of the orphanage.

MRS ALV. Many thanks, but I think it will be most convenient if you will kindly take charge of them.

MAN. With pleasure. I think it will be best to leave the money in the bank for the present. The interest is not very high, it is true; four per cent at six months' call. Later on, if we can find some good mortgage—of course it must be a first mortgage and on unexceptionable security—we can consider the matter further.

MRS ALV. Yes, yes, my dear Mr Manders, you know best about all that.

MAN. I will keep my eye on it anyway. But there is one thing in connection with it that I have often meant to ask you about.

MRS ALV. What is that?

MAN. Shall we insure the buildings or not?

MRS ALV. Of course we must insure them.

MAN. Ah, but wait a moment, dear lady. Let us look into the matter a little more closely.

MRS ALV. Everything of mine is insured—the house and its contents, my livestock—everything.

MAN. Naturally. They are your own property. I do exactly the same, of course. But this, you see, is quite a different case. The orphanage is, so to speak, dedicated to higher uses.

MRS ALV. Certainly, but——

MAN. As far as I am personally concerned, I can conscientiously say that I don't see the smallest objection to our insuring ourselves against all risks.

MRS ALV. That is certainly what I think.

MAN. But what about the opinion of the people hereabouts?

MRS ALV. Their opinion?

MAN. Is there any considerable body of opinion here—opinion of some account, I mean—that might take exception to it?

MRS ALV. What, exactly, do you mean by opinion of some account?

MAN. Well, I was thinking particularly of persons of such independent and influential position that one could hardly refuse to attach weight to their opinion.

Mrs Alv. There are a certain number of such people here who might perhaps take exception to it if we——

Man. That's just it, you see. In town there are lots of them. All my fellow clergymen's congregations, for instance! It would be so extremely easy for them to interpret it as meaning that neither you nor I had a proper reliance on Divine protection.

Mrs Alv. But as far as you are concerned, my dear friend, you have at all events the consciousness that——

Man. Yes, I know, I know; my own mind is quite easy about it, it is true. But we should not be able to prevent a wrong and injurious interpretation of our action. And that sort of thing, moreover, might very easily end in exercising a hampering influence on the work of the orphanage.

Mrs Alv. Oh well, if that is likely to be the effect of it——

Man. Nor can I entirely overlook the difficult–indeed, I may say painful–position I might possibly be placed in. In the best circles in town the matter of this orphanage is attracting a great deal of attention. Indeed, the orphanage is to some extent built for the benefit of the town too, and it is to be hoped that it may result in the lowering of our poor rate by a considerable amount. But as I have been your adviser in the matter and have taken charge of the business side of it, I should be afraid that it would be I that spiteful persons would attack first of all.

Mrs Alv. Yes, you ought not to expose yourself to that.

Man. Not to mention the attacks that would undoubtedly be made upon me in certain newspapers and reviews.

Mrs Alv. Say no more about it, dear Mr Manders; that quite decides it.

Man. Then you don't wish it to be insured?

Mrs Alv. No, we will give up the idea.

Man. [*leaning back in his chair*]. But suppose, now, that some accident happened–one can never tell–would you be prepared to make good the damage?

Mrs Alv. No; I tell you quite plainly I would not do so under any circumstances.

Man. Still, you know, Mrs Alving –after all, it is a serious responsibility that we are taking upon ourselves.

Mrs Alv. But do you think we can do otherwise?

Man. No, that's just it. We really can't do otherwise. We ought not to expose ourselves to a mistaken judgment, and we have no right to do anything that will scandalize the community.

Mrs Alv. You ought not to, as a clergyman, at any rate.

Man. And, what is more, I certainly think that we may count upon our enterprise being attended by good fortune–indeed, that it will be under a special protection.

Mrs Alv. Let us hope so, Mr Manders.

Man. Then we will leave it alone?

Mrs Alv. Certainly.

Man. Very good. As you wish. [*Makes a note.*] No insurance then.

Mrs Alv. It's a funny thing that you should just have happened to speak about that today——

Man. I have often meant to ask you about it.

Mrs Alv. –because yesterday we

very nearly had a fire up there.

MAN. Do you mean it!

MRS ALV. Oh, as a matter of fact it was nothing of any consequence. Some shavings in the carpenter's shop caught fire.

MAN. Where Engstrand works?

MRS ALV. Yes. They say he is often so careless with matches.

MAN. He has so many things on his mind, poor fellow—so many anxieties. Heaven be thanked, I am told he is really making an effort to live a blameless life.

MRS ALV. Really? Who told you so?

MAN. He assured me himself that it is so. He's a good workman too.

MRS ALV. Oh yes, when he is sober.

MAN. Ah, that sad weakness of his! But the pain in his poor leg often drives him to it, he tells me. The last time he was in town I was really quite touched by him. He came to my house and thanked me so gratefully for getting him work here, where he could have the chance of being with Regina.

MRS ALV. He doesn't see very much of her.

MAN. But he assured me that he saw her every day.

MRS ALV. Oh well, perhaps he does.

MAN. He feels so strongly that he needs someone who can keep a hold on him when temptations assail him. That is the most winning thing about Jacob Engstrand; he comes to one like a helpless child and accuses himself and confesses his frailty. The last time he came and had a talk with me—— Suppose now, Mrs Alving, that it were really a necessity of his existence to have Regina at home with him again——

MRS ALV. [*standing up suddenly*]. Regina!

MAN. —you ought not to set yourself against him.

MRS ALV. Indeed, I set myself very definitely against that. And besides, you know Regina is to have a post in the orphanage.

MAN. But consider, after all he is her father——

MRS ALV. I know best what sort of a father he has been to her. No, she shall never go to him with my consent.

MAN. [*getting up*]. My dear lady, don't judge so hastily. It is very sad how you misjudge poor Engstrand. One would really think you were afraid——

MRS ALV. [*more calmly*]. That is not the question. I have taken Regina into my charge, and in my charge she remains. [*Listens.*] Hush, dear Mr Manders, don't say any more about it. [*Her face brightens with pleasure.*] Listen! Oswald is coming downstairs. We will only think about him now.

[OSWALD ALVING, *in a light overcoat, hat in hand and smoking a big meerschaum pipe, comes in by the door on the left.*]

OSW. [*standing in the doorway*]. Oh, I beg your pardon, I thought you were in the office. [*Comes in.*] Good morning, Mr Manders.

MAN. [*staring at him*]. Well! It's most extraordinary——

MRS ALV. Yes, what do you think of him, Mr Manders?

MAN. I—I—no, can it possibly be——

OSW. Yes, it really is the prodigal son, Mr Manders.

MAN. Oh, my dear young friend——

OSW. Well, the son come home then.

MRS ALV. Oswald is thinking of the

time when you were so opposed to the idea of his being a painter.

MAN. We are only fallible, and many steps seem to us hazardous at first that afterward—— [*Grasps his hand.*] Welcome, welcome! Really, my dear Oswald—may I still call you Oswald?

OSW. What else would you think of calling me?

MAN. Thank you. What I mean, my dear Oswald, is that you must not imagine that I have any unqualified disapproval of the artist's life. I admit that there are many who, even in that career, can keep the inner man free from harm.

OSW. Let us hope so.

MRS ALV. [*beaming with pleasure*]. I know one who has kept both the inner and the outer man free from harm. Just take a look at him, Mr Manders.

OSW. [*walks across the room*]. Yes, yes, Mother dear, of course.

MAN. Undoubtedly—no one can deny it. And I hear you have begun to make a name for yourself. I have often seen mention of you in the papers—and extremely favorable mention too. Although I must admit latterly I have not seen your name so often.

OSW. [*going toward the conservatory*]. I haven't done so much painting just lately.

MRS ALV. An artist must take a rest sometimes, like other people.

MAN. Of course, of course. At those times the artist is preparing and strengthening himself for a greater effort.

OSW. Yes. Mother, will dinner soon be ready?

MRS ALV. In half an hour. He has a fine appetite, thank goodness.

MAN. And a liking for tobacco too.

OSW. I found father's pipe in the room upstairs and——

MAN. Ah, that is what it was!

MRS ALV. What?

MAN. When Oswald came in at that door with the pipe in his mouth I thought for the moment it was his father in the flesh.

OSW. Really?

MRS ALV. How can you say so! Oswald takes after me.

MAN. Yes, but there is an expression about the corners of his mouth—something about the lips—that reminds me so exactly of Mr Alving—especially when he smokes.

MRS ALV. I don't think so at all. To my mind Oswald has much more of a clergyman's mouth.

MAN. Well, yes—a good many of my colleagues in the church have a similar expression.

MRS ALV. But put your pipe down, my dear boy. I don't allow any smoking in here.

OSW. [*puts down his pipe*]. All right; I only wanted to try it because I smoked it once when I was a child.

MRS ALV. You?

OSW. Yes; it was when I was quite a little chap. And I can remember going upstairs to Father's room one evening when he was in very good spirits.

MRS ALV. Oh, you can't remember anything about those days.

OSW. Yes, I remember plainly that he took me on his knee and let me smoke his pipe. "Smoke, my boy," he said, "have a good smoke, boy!" And I smoked as hard as I could until I felt I was turning quite pale and the perspiration was standing in great drops on my forehead. Then he laughed—such a hearty laugh——

MAN. It was an extremely odd thing to do.

MRS ALV. Dear Mr Manders, Oswald only dreamt it.

OSW. No indeed, Mother, it was no dream. Because—don't you remember?—you came into the room and carried me off to the nursery, where I was sick, and I saw that you were crying. Did Father often play such tricks?

MAN. In his young days he was full of fun.

OSW. And, for all that, he did so much with his life—so much that was good and useful, I mean—short as his life was.

MAN. Yes, my dear Oswald Alving, you have inherited the name of a man who undoubtedly was both energetic and worthy. Let us hope it will be a spur to your energies.

OSW. It ought to be, certainly.

MAN. In any case it was nice of you to come home for the day that is to honor his memory.

OSW. I could do no less for my father.

MRS ALV. And to let me keep him so long here—that's the nicest part of what he has done.

MAN. Yes, I hear you are going to spend the winter at home.

OSW. I am here for an indefinite time, Mr Manders. Oh, it's good to be at home again!

MRS ALV. [*beaming*]. Yes, isn't it?

MAN. [*looking sympathetically at him*]. You went out into the world very young, my dear Oswald.

OSW. I did. Sometimes I wonder if I wasn't too young.

MRS ALV. Not a bit of it. It is the best thing for an active boy, and especially for an only child. It's a pity when they are kept at home with their parents and get spoilt.

MAN. That is a very debatable question, Mrs Alving. A child's own home is, and always must be, his proper place.

OSW. There I agree entirely with Mr Manders.

MAN. Take the case of your own son. Oh yes, we can talk about it before him. What has the result been in his case? He is six or seven and twenty and has never yet had the opportunity of learning what a well-regulated home means.

OSW. Excuse me, Mr Manders, you are quite wrong there.

MAN. Indeed? I imagined that your life abroad had practically been spent entirely in artistic circles.

OSW. So it has.

MAN. And chiefly amongst the younger artists.

OSW. Certainly.

MAN. But I imagined that those gentry, as a rule, had not the means necessary for family life and the support of a home.

OSW. There are a considerable number of them who have not the means to marry, Mr Manders.

MAN. That is exactly my point.

OSW. But they can have a home of their own all the same; a good many of them have. And they are very well-regulated and very comfortable homes too.

[MRS ALVING, *who has listened to him attentively, nods assent but says nothing.*]

MAN. Oh, but I am not talking of bachelor establishments. By a home I mean family life—the life a man lives with his wife and children.

OSW. Exactly, or with his children and his children's mother.

MAN. [*starts and clasps his hands*]. Good heavens!

OSW. What is the matter?

MAN. Lives with–with–his children's mother!

OSW. Well, would you rather he should repudiate his children's mother?

MAN. Then what you are speaking of are those unprincipled conditions known as irregular unions!

OSW. I have never noticed anything particularly unprincipled about these people's lives.

MAN. But do you mean to say that it is possible for a man of any sort of bringing up and a young woman to reconcile themselves to such a way of living–and to make no secret of it either?

OSW. What else are they to do? A poor artist and a poor girl–it costs a good deal to get married. What else are they to do?

MAN. What are they to do? Well, Mr Alving, I will tell you what they ought to do. They ought to keep away from each other from the very beginning–that is what they ought to do!

OSW. That advice wouldn't have much effect upon hot-blooded young folk who are in love.

MRS ALV. No, indeed it wouldn't.

MAN. [*persistently*]. And to think that the authorities tolerate such things! That they are allowed to go on openly! [*Turns to* MRS ALVING.] Had I so little reason, then, to be sadly concerned about your son? In circles where open immorality is rampant–where, one may say, it is honored——

OSW. Let me tell you this, Mr Manders. I have been a constant Sunday guest at one or two of these "irregular" households——

MAN. On Sunday too!

OSW. Yes, that is the day of leisure. But never have I heard one objectionable word there; still less have I ever seen anything that could be called immoral. No; but do you know when and where I *have* met with immorality in artists' circles?

MAN. No, thank heaven, I don't!

OSW. Well, then, I shall have the pleasure of telling you. I have met with it when some one or other of your model husbands and fathers have come out there to have a bit of a look round on their own account and have done the artists the honor of looking them up in their humble quarters. Then we had a chance of learning something, I can tell you. These gentlemen were able to instruct us about places and things that we had never so much as dreamt of.

MAN. What? Do you want me to believe that honorable men when they get away from home will——

OSW. Have you never, when these same honorable men come home again, heard them deliver themselves on the subject of the prevalence of immorality abroad?

MAN. Yes, of course, but——

MRS ALV. I have heard them too.

OSW. Well, you can take their word for it, unhesitatingly. Some of them are experts in the matter. [*Putting his hands to his head.*] To think that the glorious freedom of the beautiful life over there should be so besmirched!

MRS ALV. You mustn't get too heated, Oswald; you gain nothing by that.

OSW. No, you are quite right, Mother. Besides, it isn't good for me. It's because I am so infernally tired, you know. I will go out and take a turn before dinner. I beg your pardon, Mr Manders. It is impossible for you to realize the feeling, but it takes me that way. [*Goes out by the farther door on the right.*]

MRS ALV. My poor boy!

MAN. You may well say so. This is what it has brought him to! [MRS ALVING *looks at him but does not speak.*] He called himself the prodigal son. It's only too true, alas—only too true! [MRS ALVING *looks steadily at him.*] And what do you say to all this?

MRS ALV. I say that Oswald was right in every single word he said.

MAN. Right? Right? To hold such principles as that?

MRS ALV. In my loneliness here I have come to just the same opinions as he, Mr Manders. But I have never presumed to venture upon such topics in conversation. Now there is no need; my boy shall speak for me.

MAN. You deserve the deepest pity, Mrs Alving. It is my duty to say an earnest word to you. It is no longer your businessman and adviser, no longer your old friend and your dead husband's old friend, that stands before you now. It is your priest that stands before you, just as he did once at the most critical moment of your life.

MRS ALV. And what is it that my priest has to say to me?

MAN. First of all I must stir your memory. The moment is well chosen. Tomorrow is the tenth anniversary of your husband's death; tomorrow the memorial to the departed will be unveiled; tomorrow I shall speak to the whole assembly that will be met together. But today I want to speak to you alone.

MRS ALV. Very well, Mr Manders, speak!

MAN. Have you forgotten that after barely a year of married life you were standing at the very edge of a precipice?—that you forsook your house and home?—that you ran away from your husband—yes, Mrs Alving, ran away, ran away—and refused to return to him in spite of his requests and entreaties?

MRS ALV. Have you forgotten how unspeakably unhappy I was during that first year?

MAN. To crave for happiness in this world is simply to be possessed by a spirit of revolt. What right have we to happiness? No! we must do our duty, Mrs Alving. And your duty was to cleave to the man you had chosen and to whom you were bound by a sacred bond.

MRS ALV. You know quite well what sort of a life my husband was living at that time—what excesses he was guilty of.

MAN. I know only too well what rumor used to say of him, and I should be the last person to approve of his conduct as a young man, supposing that rumor spoke the truth. But it is not a wife's part to be her husband's judge. You should have considered it your bounden duty humbly to have borne the cross that a higher will had laid upon you. But instead of that you rebelliously cast off your cross, you deserted the man whose stumbling footsteps you should have supported, you did what was bound to imperil your good name and reputation and came very near to imperiling the reputation of others into the bargain.

MRS ALV. Of others? Of one other, you mean.

MAN. It was the height of imprudence, your seeking refuge with me.

MRS ALV. With our priest? With our intimate friend?

MAN. All the more on that account. You should thank God that I possessed the necessary strength of mind—that I was able to turn you from your outrageous intention and that it was vouchsafed to me to succeed in leading you back into the path of duty and back to your lawful husband.

MRS ALV. Yes, Mr Manders, that certainly was your doing.

MAN. I was but the humble instrument of a higher power. And is it not true that my having been able to bring you again under the yoke of duty and obedience sowed the seeds of a rich blessing on all the rest of your life? Did things not turn out as I foretold to you? Did not your husband turn from straying in the wrong path, as a man should? Did he not, after all, live a life of love and good report with you all his days? Did he not become a benefactor to the neighborhood? Did he not so raise you up to his level so that by degrees you became his fellow worker in all his undertakings?—and a noble fellow worker too, I know, Mrs Alving; that praise I will give you. But now I come to the second serious false step in your life.

MRS ALV. What do you mean?

MAN. Just as once you forsook your duty as a wife so, since then, you have forsaken your duty as a mother.

MRS ALV. Oh!

MAN. You have been overmastered all your life by a disastrous spirit of willfulness. All your impulses have led you toward what is undisciplined and lawless. You have never been willing to submit to any restraint. Anything in life that has seemed irksome to you you have thrown aside recklessly and unscrupulously, as if it were a burden that you were free to rid yourself of if you would. It did not please you to be a wife any longer, and so you left your husband. Your duties as a mother were irksome to you, so you sent your child away among strangers.

MRS ALV. Yes, that is true; I did that.

MAN. And that is why you have become a stranger to him.

MRS ALV. No, no, I am not that!

MAN. You are; you must be. And what sort of a son is it that you have got back? Think over it seriously, Mrs Alving. You erred grievously in your husband's case—you acknowledge as much by erecting this memorial to him. Now you are bound to acknowledge how much you have erred in your son's case; possibly there may still be time to reclaim him from the paths of wickedness. Turn over a new leaf and set yourself to reform what there may still be that is capable of reformation in him. Because [*with uplifted forefinger*] in very truth, Mrs Alving, you are a guilty mother! That is what I have thought it my duty to say to you.

[*A short silence.*]

MRS ALV. [*speaking slowly and with self-control*]. You have had your say, Mr Manders, and tomorrow you will be making a public speech in memory of my husband. I shall not speak tomorrow. But now I wish to speak to you for a little, just as you have been speaking to me.

MAN. By all means; no doubt you wish to bring forward some excuses for your behavior.

MRS ALV. No. I only want to tell you something.

MAN. Well?

MRS ALV. In all that you said just now about me and my husband and about our life together after you had, as you put it, led me back into the path of duty—there was nothing that you knew at first hand. From that moment you never again set foot in our house—you who had been our daily companion before that.

MAN. Remember that you and your husband moved out of town immediately afterward.

MRS ALV. Yes, and you never once came out here to see us in my husband's lifetime. It was only the business in connection with the orphanage that obliged you to come and see me.

MAN. [*in a low and uncertain voice*]. Helen—if that is a reproach, I can only beg you to consider——

MRS ALV. —the respect you owed to your calling?—yes. All the more as I was a wife who had tried to run away from her husband. One can never be too careful to have nothing to do with such reckless women.

MAN. My dear—Mrs Alving, you are exaggerating dreadfully.

MRS ALV. Yes, yes—very well. What I mean is this, that when you condemn my conduct as a wife you have nothing more to go upon than ordinary public opinion.

MAN. I admit it. What then?

MRS ALV. Well—now, Mr Manders, now I am going to tell you the truth. I had sworn to myself that you should know it one day—you and you only!

MAN. And what may the truth be?

MRS ALV. The truth is this, that my husband died just as great a profligate as he had been all his life.

MAN. [*feeling for a chair*]. What are you saying?

MRS ALV. After nineteen years of married life, just as profligate—in his desires, at all events—as he was before you married us.

MAN. And can you talk of his youthful indiscretions—his irregularities—his excesses, if you like—as a profligate life!

MRS ALV. That was what the doctor who attended him called it.

MAN. I don't understand what you mean.

MRS ALV. It is not necessary you should.

MAN. It makes my brain reel. To think that your marriage—all the years of wedded life you spent with your husband—were nothing but a hidden abyss of misery.

MRS ALV. That and nothing else. Now you know.

MAN. This—this bewilders me. I can't understand it! I can't grasp it! How in the world was it possible? How could such a state of things remain concealed?

MRS ALV. That was just what I had to fight for incessantly, day after day. When Oswald was born I thought I saw a slight improvement. But it didn't last long. And after that I had to fight doubly hard—fight a desperate fight so that no one should know what sort of a man my child's father was. You know quite well what an attractive manner he had; it seemed as if people could believe nothing but good of him. He was one of those men whose mode of life seems to have no effect upon their reputations. But at last, Mr Manders—you must hear this too—at last something happened more abominable than everything else.

MAN. More abominable than what you have told me!

MRS ALV. I had borne with it all, though I knew only too well what he indulged in in secret, when he was out of the house. But when it came to the point of scandal coming within our four walls——

MAN. Can you mean it! Here?

MRS ALV. Yes, here in our own home. It was in there [*pointing to the nearer door on the right*] in the dining room that I got the first hint of it. I had something to do in there and the door was standing ajar. I heard our maid come up from the garden with water for the flowers in the conservatory.

MAN. Well?

MRS ALV. Shortly afterward I heard my husband come in too. I heard him say something to her in a low voice. And then I heard—[*with a short laugh*]—oh, it rings in my ears still, with its mixture of what was heartbreaking and what was so ridiculous—I heard my own servant whisper: "Let me go, Mr Alving! Let me be!"

MAN. What unseemly levity on his part! But surely nothing more than levity, Mrs Alving, believe me.

MRS ALV. I soon knew what to believe. My husband had his will of the girl—and that intimacy had consequences, Mr Manders.

MAN. [*as if turned to stone*]. And all that in this house! In this house!

MRS ALV. I have suffered a good deal in this house. To keep him at home in the evening—and at night—I have had to play the part of boon companion in his secret drinking bouts in his room up there. I have had to sit there alone with him, have had to hobnob and drink with him, have had to listen to his ribald senseless talk, have had to fight with brute force to get him to bed——

MAN. [*trembling*]. And you were able to endure all this!

MRS ALV. I had my little boy and endured it for his sake. But when the crowning insult came—when my own servant—then I made up my mind that there should be an end of it. I took the upper hand in the house absolutely—both with him and all the others. I had a weapon to use against him, you see; he didn't dare to speak. It was then that Oswald was sent away. He was about seven then and was beginning to notice things and ask questions, as children will. I could endure all that, my friend. It seemed to me that the child would be poisoned if he breathed the air of this polluted house. That was why I sent him away. And now you understand, too, why he never set foot here as long as his father was alive. No one knows what it meant to me.

MAN. You have indeed had a pitiable experience.

MRS ALV. I could never have gone through with it if I had not had my work. Indeed, I can boast that I have worked. All the increase in the value of the property, all the improvements, all the useful arrangements that my husband got the honor and glory of—do you suppose that he troubled himself about any of them? He who used to lie the whole day on the sofa reading old Official Lists! No, you may as well know that too. It was I that kept him up to the mark when he had his lucid intervals; it was I that had to bear the whole burden of it when he began his excesses again or took to whining about his miserable condition.

MAN. And this is the man you are building a memorial to!

MRS ALV. There you see the power of an uneasy conscience.

MAN. An uneasy conscience? What do you mean?

MRS ALV. I had always before me the fear that it was impossible that the truth should not come out and be believed. That is why the orphanage is to exist, to silence all rumors and clear away all doubt.

MAN. You certainly have not fallen short of the mark in that, Mrs Alving.

MRS ALV. I had another very good reason. I did not wish Oswald, my own son, to inherit a penny that belonged to his father.

MAN. Then it is with Mr Alving's property——

MRS ALV. Yes. The sums of money that, year after year, I have given toward this orphanage make up the amount of property–I have reckoned it carefully–which in the old days made Lieutenant Alving a catch.

MAN. I understand.

MRS ALV. That was my purchase money. I don't wish it to pass into Oswald's hands. My son shall have everything from me, I am determined.

[OSWALD *comes in by the farther door on the right. He has left his hat and coat outside.*]

MRS ALV. Back again, my own dear boy?

OSW. Yes, and what can one do outside in this everlasting rain? I hear dinner is nearly ready. That's good!

[REGINA *comes in from the dining room, carrying a parcel.*]

REG. This parcel has come for you, ma'am. [*Gives it to her.*]

MRS ALV. [*glancing at* MANDERS]. The ode to be sung tomorrow, I expect.

MAN. Hm!

REG. And dinner is ready.

MRS ALV. Good. We will come in a moment. I will just——[*Begins to open the parcel.*]

REG. [*to* OSWALD]. Will you drink white or red wine, sir?

OSW. Both, Miss Engstrand.

REG. *Bien*–very good, Mr Alving. [*Goes into the dining room.*]

OSW. I may as well help you to uncork it. [*Follows her into the dining room, leaving the door ajar after him.*]

MRS ALV. Yes, I thought so. Here is the ode, Mr Manders.

MAN. [*clasping his hands*]. How shall I ever have the courage tomorrow to speak the address that——

MRS ALV. Oh, you will get through it.

MAN. [*in a low voice, fearing to be heard in the dining room*]. Yes, we must raise no suspicions.

MRS ALV. [*quietly but firmly*]. No; and then this long, dreadful comedy will be at an end. After tomorrow I shall feel as if my dead husband had never lived in this house. There will be no one else here then but my boy and his mother.

[*From the dining room is heard the noise of a chair falling; then* REGINA'S *voice is heard in a loud whisper:* "Oswald! Are you mad? Let me go!"]

MRS ALV. [*starting in horror*]. Oh! [*She stares wildly at the half-open door.* OSWALD *is heard coughing and humming, then the sound of a bottle being uncorked.*]

MAN. [*in an agitated manner*]. What's the matter? What is it, Mrs Alving?

MRS ALV. [*hoarsely*]. Ghosts. The

couple in the conservatory—over again.

Man. What are you saying! Regina——? Is she——?

Mrs Alv. Yes. Come. Not a word! [*Grips* Manders *by the arm and walks unsteadily with him into the dining room.*]

ACT II

The same scene. The landscape is still obscured by mist. Manders *and* Mrs Alving *come in from the dining room.*

Mrs Alv. [*calls into the dining room from the doorway*]. Aren't you coming in here, Oswald?

Osw. No, thanks; I think I will go out for a bit.

Mrs Alv. Yes, do; the weather is clearing a little. [*She shuts the dining-room door, then goes to the hall door and calls.*] Regina!

Reg. [*from without*]. Yes, ma'am?

Mrs Alv. Go down into the laundry and help with the garlands.

Reg. Yes, ma'am.

[Mrs Alving *satisfies herself that she has gone, then shuts the door.*]

Man. I suppose he can't hear us?

Mrs Alv. Not when the door is shut. Besides, he is going out.

Man. I am still quite bewildered. I don't know how I managed to swallow a mouthful of your excellent dinner.

Mrs Alv. [*walking up and down and trying to control her agitation*]. Nor I. But what are we to do?

Man. Yes, what are we to do? Upon my word, I don't know; I am so completely unaccustomed to things of this kind.

Mrs Alv. I am convinced that nothing serious has happened yet.

Man. Heaven forbid! But it is most unseemly behavior, for all that.

Mrs Alv. It is nothing more than a foolish jest of Oswald's, you may be sure.

Man. Well, of course, as I said, I am quite inexperienced in such matters; but it certainly seems to me——

Mrs Alv. Out of the house she shall go—and at once. That part of it is as clear as daylight.

Man. Yes. That is quite clear.

Mrs Alv. But where is she to go? We should not be justified in——

Man. Where to? Home to her father, of course.

Mrs Alv. To whom, did you say?

Man. To her—— No, of course Engstrand isn't—— But, great heavens, Mrs Alving, how is such a thing possible? You surely may have been mistaken in spite of everything.

Mrs Alv. There was no chance of mistake, more's the pity. Joanna was obliged to confess it to me—and my husband couldn't deny it. So there was nothing else to do but to hush it up.

Man. No, that was the only thing to do.

Mrs Alv. The girl was sent away at once and was given a tolerably liberal sum to hold her tongue. She looked after the rest herself when she got to town. She renewed an old acquaintance with the carpenter Engstrand; gave him a hint, I suppose, of how much money she had got and told him some fairy tale about a foreigner who had been here in his yacht in the summer. So she and Engstrand were married in a great hurry. Why, you married them yourself!

Man. I can't understand it. I remember clearly Engstrand's coming to arrange about the marriage. He was full of contrition and accused himself bitterly for the light conduct he and his fiancée had been guilty of.

MRS ALV. Of course he had to take the blame on himself.

MAN. But the deceitfulness of it! And with me too! I positively would not have believed it of Jacob Engstrand. I shall most certainly give him a serious talking to. And the immorality of such a marriage! Simply for the sake of the money! What sum was it that the girl had?

MRS ALV. It was seventy pounds.

MAN. Just think of it—for a paltry seventy pounds to let yourself be bound in marriage to a fallen woman!

MRS ALV. What about myself then? I let myself be bound in marriage to a fallen man.

MAN. Heaven forgive you! what are you saying? A fallen man?

MRS ALV. Do you suppose my husband was any purer when I went with him to the altar than Joanna was when Engstrand agreed to marry her?

MAN. The two cases are as different as day from night.

MRS ALV. Not so very different after all. It is true there was a great difference in the price paid, between a paltry seventy pounds and a whole fortune.

MAN. How can you compare such totally different things! I presume you consulted your own heart—and your relations.

MRS ALV. [*looking away from him*]. I thought you understood where what you call my heart had strayed to at that time.

MAN. [*in a constrained voice*]. If I had understood anything of the kind, I would not have been a daily guest in your husband's house.

MRS ALV. Well, at any rate this much is certain, that I didn't consult myself in the matter at all.

MAN. Still you consulted those nearest to you, as was only right—your mother, your two aunts.

MRS ALV. Yes, that is true. The three of them settled the whole matter for me. It seems incredible to me now, how clearly they made out that it would be sheer folly to reject such an offer. If my mother could only see what all that fine prospect has led to!

MAN. No one can be responsible for the result of it. Anyway, there is this to be said, that the match was made in complete conformity with law and order.

MRS ALV. [*going to the window*]. Oh, law and order! I often think it is that that is at the bottom of all the misery in the world.

MAN. Mrs Alving, it is very wicked of you to say that.

MRS ALV. That may be so, but I don't attach importance to those obligations and considerations any longer. I cannot! I must struggle for my freedom.

MAN. What do you mean?

MRS ALV. [*tapping on the window-panes*]. I ought never to have concealed what sort of a life my husband led. But I had not the courage to do otherwise then—for my own sake either. I was too much of a coward.

MAN. A coward?

MRS ALV. If others had known anything of what happened, they would have said: "Poor man, it is natural enough that he should go astray when he has a wife that has run away from him."

MAN. They would have had a certain amount of justification for saying so.

Mrs Alv. [*looking fixedly at him*]. If I had been the woman I ought, I would have taken Oswald into my confidence and said to him: "Listen, my son, your father was a dissolute man——"

Man. Miserable woman.

Mrs Alv. —and I would have told him all I have told you, from beginning to end.

Man. I am shocked at you, Mrs Alving.

Mrs Alv. I know. I know quite well! I am shocked at myself when I think of it. [*Comes away from the window.*] I am coward enough for that.

Man. Can you call it cowardice that you simply did your duty? Have you forgotten that a child should love and honor his father and mother?

Mrs Alv. Don't let us talk in such general terms. Suppose we say: "Ought Oswald to love and honor Mr Alving?"

Man. You are a mother—isn't there a voice in your heart that forbids you to shatter your son's ideals?

Mrs Alv. And what about the truth?

Man. What about his ideals?

Mrs Alv. Oh—ideals, ideals—— If only I were not such a coward as I am!

Man. Do not spurn ideals, Mrs Alving—they have a way of avenging themselves cruelly. Take Oswald's own case now. He hasn't many ideals, more's the pity. But this much I have seen, that his father is something of an ideal to him.

Mrs Alv. You are right there.

Man. And his conception of his father is what you inspired and encouraged by your letters.

Mrs Alv. Yes, I was swayed by duty and consideration for others; that was why I lied to my son year in and year out. Oh, what a coward—what a coward I have been!

Man. You have built up a happy illusion in your son's mind, Mrs Alving—and that is a thing you certainly ought not to undervalue.

Mrs Alv. Ah, who knows if that is such a desirable thing after all! But, anyway, I don't intend to put up with any goings on with Regina. I am not going to let him get the poor girl into trouble.

Man. Good heavens, no—that would be a frightful thing!

Mrs Alv. If only I knew whether he meant it seriously and whether it would mean happiness for him——

Man. In what way? I don't understand.

Mrs Alv. But that is impossible. Regina is not equal to it, unfortunately.

Man. I don't understand. What do you mean?

Mrs Alv. If I were not such a miserable coward, I would say to him: "Marry her or make any arrangement you like with her—only let there be no deceit in the matter."

Man. Heaven forgive you! Are you actually suggesting anything so abominable, so unheard of, as a marriage between them!

Mrs Alv. Unheard of, do you call it? Tell me honestly, Mr Manders, don't you suppose there are plenty of married couples out here in the country that are just as nearly related as they are?

Man. I am sure I don't understand you.

Mrs Alv. Indeed, you do.

Man. I suppose you are thinking

of cases where possibly—— It is only too true, unfortunately, that family life is not always as stainless as it should be. But as for the sort of thing you hint at—well, it's impossible to tell, at all events with any certainty. Here, on the other hand—for you, a mother, to be willing to allow your——

MRS ALV. But I am not willing to allow it. I would not allow it for anything in the world; that is just what I was saying.

MAN. No, because you are a coward, as you put it. But supposing you were not a coward! Great heavens—such a revolting union!

MRS ALV. Well, for the matter of that, we are all descended from a union of that description, so we are told. And who was it that was responsible for this state of things, Mr Manders?

MAN. I can't discuss such questions with you, Mrs Alving; you are by no means in the right frame of mind for that. But for you to dare to say that it is cowardly of you——

MRS ALV. I will tell you what I mean by that. I am frightened and timid because I am obsessed by the presence of ghosts that I never can get rid of.

MAN. The presence of what?

MRS ALV. Ghosts. When I heard Regina and Oswald in there it was just like seeing ghosts before my eyes. I am half inclined to think we are all ghosts, Mr Manders. It is not only what we have inherited from our fathers and mothers that exists again in us, but all sorts of old dead ideas and all kinds of old dead beliefs and things of that kind. They are not actually alive in us, but there they are dormant, all the same, and we can never be rid of them. Whenever I take up a newspaper and read it I fancy I see ghosts creeping between the lines. There must be ghosts all over the world. They must be as countless as the grains of the sands, it seems to me. And we are so miserably afraid of the light, all of us.

MAN. Ah!—there we have the outcome of your reading. Fine fruit it has borne—this abominable, subversive, free-thinking literature!

MRS ALV. You are wrong there, my friend. You are the one who made me begin to think, and I owe you my best thanks for it.

MAN. I!

MRS ALV. Yes, by forcing me to submit to what you called my duty and my obligations, by praising as right and just what my whole soul revolted against as it would against something abominable. That was what led me to examine your teachings critically. I only wanted to unravel one point in them, but as soon as I had got that unraveled the whole fabric came to pieces. And then I realized that it was only machine made.

MAN. [*softly and with emotion*]. Is that all I accomplished by the hardest struggle of my life?

MRS ALV. Call it rather the most ignominious defeat of your life.

MAN. It was the greatest victory of my life, Helen; victory over myself.

MRS ALV. It was a wrong done to both of us.

MAN. A wrong?—wrong for me to entreat you, as a wife, to go back to your lawful husband when you came to me half distracted and crying: "Here I am, take me!" Was that a wrong?

MRS ALV. I think it was.

MAN. We two do not understand one another.

MRS ALV. Not now, at all events.

MAN. Never—even in my most secret thoughts—have I for a moment regarded you as anything but the wife of another.

MRS ALV. Do you believe what you say?

MAN. Helen!

MRS ALV. One so easily forgets one's own feelings.

MAN. Not I. I am the same as I always was.

MRS ALV. Yes, yes—don't let us talk any more about the old days. You are buried up to your eyes now in committees and all sorts of business, and I am here, fighting with ghosts both without and within me.

MAN. I can at all events help you to get the better of those without you. After all that I have been horrified to hear from you today I cannot conscientiously allow a young defenseless girl to remain in your house.

MRS ALV. Don't you think it would be best if we could get her settled? by some suitable marriage, I mean.

MAN. Undoubtedly. I think in any case it would have been desirable for her. Regina is at an age now that—well, I don't know much about these things, but——

MRS ALV. Regina developed very early.

MAN. Yes, didn't she? I fancy I remember thinking she was remarkably well developed, bodily, at the time I prepared her for confirmation. But for the time being she must in any case go home. Under her father's care —no, but of course Engstrand is not—— To think that he, of all men, could so conceal the truth from me!

[*A knock is heard at the hall door.*]

MRS ALV. Who can that be? Come in!

[ENGSTRAND, *dressed in his Sunday clothes, appears in the doorway.*]

ENG. I humbly beg pardon, but——

MAN. Aha! Hm!

MRS ALV. Oh, it's you, Engstrand!

ENG. There were none of the maids about, so I took the great liberty of knocking.

MRS ALV. That's all right. Come in. Do you want to speak to me?

ENG. [*coming in*]. No, thank you very much, ma'am. It was Mr Manders I wanted to speak to for a moment.

MAN. [*walking up and down*]. Hm! —do you? You want to speak to me, do you?

ENG. Yes sir, I wanted so very much to——

MAN. [*stopping in front of him*]. Well, may I ask what it is you want?

ENG. It's this way, Mr Manders. We are being paid off now. And many thanks to you, Mrs Alving. And now the work is quite finished I thought it would be so nice and suitable if all of us, who have worked so honestly together all this time, were to finish up with a few prayers this evening.

MAN. Prayers? Up at the orphanage?

ENG. Yes sir, but if it isn't agreeable to you, then——

MAN. Oh, certainly—but—hm!

ENG. I have made a practice of saying a few prayers there myself each evening.

MRS ALV. Have you?

ENG. Yes, ma'am, now and then—just as a little edification, so to speak. But I am only a poor common man and haven't rightly the gift, alas—and so I thought that as Mr Manders happened to be here, perhaps——

MAN. Look here, Engstrand. First of all I must ask you a question. Are you in a proper frame of mind for such a thing? Is your conscience free and untroubled?

ENG. Heaven have mercy on me a sinner! My conscience isn't worth our speaking about, Mr Manders.

MAN. But it is just what we must speak about. What do you say to my question?

ENG. My conscience? Well—it's uneasy sometimes, of course.

MAN. Ah, you admit that, at all events. Now will you tell me, without any concealment—what is your relationship to Regina?

MRS ALV. [*hastily*]. Mr Manders!

MAN. [*calming her*]. Leave it to me!

ENG. With Regina? Good lord, how you frightened me! [*Looks at* MRS ALVING.] There is nothing wrong with Regina, is there?

MAN. Let us hope not. What I want to know is, what is your relationship to her? You pass as her father, don't you?

ENG. [*unsteadily*]. Well—hm!—you know, sir, what happened between me and my poor Joanna.

MAN. No more distortion of the truth! Your late wife made a full confession to Mrs Alving before she left her service.

ENG. What!—do you mean to say—— Did she do that after all?

MAN. You see it has all come out, Engstrand.

ENG. Do you mean to say that she, who gave me her promise and solemn oath——

MAN. Did she take an oath?

ENG. Well, no—she only gave me her word, but as seriously as a woman could.

MAN. And all these years you have been hiding the truth from me—from me, who have had such complete and absolute faith in you.

ENG. I am sorry to say I have, sir.

MAN. Did I deserve that from you, Engstrand? Haven't I been always ready to help you in word and deed as far as lay in my power? Answer me! Is it not so?

ENG. Indeed, there's many a time I should have been very badly off without you, sir.

MAN. And this is the way you repay me—by causing me to make false entries in the church registers and afterward keeping back from me for years the information which you owed it both to me and to your sense of the truth to divulge. Your conduct has been absolutely inexcusable, Engstrand, and from today everything is at end between us.

ENG. [*with a sigh*]. Yes, I can see that's what it means.

MAN. Yes, because how can you possibly justify what you did?

ENG. Was the poor girl to go and increase her load of shame by talking about it? Just suppose, sir, for a moment, that your reverence was in the same predicament as my poor Joanna——

MAN. I!

ENG. Good lord, sir, I don't mean the same predicament. I mean, suppose there were something your reverence were ashamed of in the eyes of the world, so to speak. We men oughtn't to judge a poor woman too hardly, Mr Manders.

MAN. But I am not doing so at all. It is you I am blaming.

ENG. Will your reverence grant me leave to ask you a small question?

MAN. Ask away.

ENG. Shouldn't you say it was right for a man to raise up the fallen?

MAN. Of course it is.

ENG. And isn't a man bound to keep his word of honor?

MAN. Certainly he is, but——

ENG. At the time when Joanna had her misfortune with this Englishman —or maybe he was an American or a Russian, as they call 'em—well, sir, then she came to town. Poor thing, she had refused me once or twice before; she only had eyes for good-looking men in those days, and I had this crooked leg then. Your reverence will remember how I had ventured up into a dancing saloon where seafaring men were reveling in drunkenness and intoxication, as they say. And when I tried to exhort them to turn from their evil ways——

MRS ALV. [*coughs from the window*]. Ahem!

MAN. I know, Engstrand, I know—the rough brutes threw you downstairs. You have told me about that incident before. The affliction to your leg is a credit to you.

ENG. I don't want to claim credit for it, your reverence. But what I wanted to tell you was that she came then and confided in me with tears and gnashing of teeth. I can tell you, sir, it went to my heart to hear her.

MAN. Did it, indeed, Engstrand? Well, what then?

ENG. Well, then I said to her: "The American is roaming about on the high seas, he is. And you, Joanna," I said, "you have committed a sin and are a fallen woman. But here stands Jacob Engstrand," I said, "on two strong legs"—of course that was only speaking in a kind of metaphor, as it were, your reverence.

MAN. I quite understand. Go on.

ENG. Well, sir, that was how I rescued her and made her my lawful wife, so that no one should know how recklessly she had carried on with the stranger.

MAN. That was all very kindly done. The only thing I cannot justify was your bringing yourself to accept the money.

ENG. Money? I? Not a farthing.

MAN. [*to* MRS ALVING, *in a questioning tone*]. But——

ENG. Ah yes!—wait a bit; I remember now. Joanna did have a trifle of money, you are quite right. But I didn't want to know anything about that. "Fie," I said, "on the mammon of unrighteousness, it's the price of your sin; as for this tainted gold"—or notes, or whatever it was—"we will throw it back in the American's face," I said. But he had gone away and disappeared on the stormy seas, your reverence.

MAN. Was that how it was, my good fellow?

ENG. It was, sir. So then Joanna and I decided that the money should go toward the child's bringing up, and that's what became of it; and I can give a faithful account of every single penny of it.

MAN. This alters the complexion of the affair very considerably.

ENG. That's how it was, your reverence. And I make bold to say that I have been a good father to Regina—as far as was in my power—for I am a poor erring mortal, alas!

MAN. There, there, my dear Engstrand——

ENG. Yes, I do make bold to say that I brought up the child and made my poor Joanna a loving and careful husband, as the Bible says we ought. But it never occurred to me to go to your reverence and claim credit for it or boast about it because I had done one good deed in this world. No; when Jacob Engstrand does a thing like that he holds his tongue about it. Unfortunately it doesn't often happen, I know that only too well. And whenever I do come to see your reverence I never seem to have anything but trouble and wickedness to talk about. Because, as I said just now—and I say it again—conscience can be very hard on us sometimes.

MAN. Give me your hand, Jacob Engstrand.

ENG. Oh, sir, I don't like——

MAN. No nonsense. [*Grasps his hand.*] That's it!

ENG. And may I make bold humbly to beg your reverence's pardon.

MAN. You? On the contrary, it is for me to beg your pardon.

ENG. Oh no, sir.

MAN. Yes, certainly it is, and I do it with my whole heart. Forgive me for having so much misjudged you. And I assure you that if I can do anything for you to prove my sincere regret and my good will toward you——

ENG. Do you mean it, sir?

MAN. It would give me the greatest pleasure.

ENG. As a matter of fact, sir, you could do it now. I am thinking of using the honest money I have put away out of my wages up here in establishing a sort of sailors' home in the town.

MRS ALV. You?

ENG. Yes, to be a sort of refuge, as it were. There are such manifold temptations lying in wait for sailormen when they are roaming about on shore. But my idea is that in this house of mine they should have a sort of parental care looking after them.

MAN. What do you say to that, Mrs Alving?

ENG. I haven't much to begin such a work with, I know; but Heaven might prosper it, and if I found any helping hand stretched out to me, then——

MAN. Quite so; we will talk over the matter further. Your project attracts me enormously. But in the meantime go back to the orphanage and put everything tidy and light the lights, so that the occasion may seem a little solemn. And then we will spend a little edifying time together, my dear Engstrand, for now I am sure you are in a suitable frame of mind.

ENG. I believe I am, sir, truly. Good-by, then, Mrs Alving, and thank you for all your kindness and take good care of Regina for me. [*Wipes a tear from his eye.*] Poor Joanna's child—it is an extraordinary thing, but she seems to have grown into my life and to hold me by the heartstrings. That's how I feel about it, truly. [*Bows and goes out.*]

MAN. Now then, what do you think of him, Mrs Alving? That was quite another explanation that he gave us.

MRS ALV. It was, indeed.

MAN. There, you see how exceedingly careful we ought to be in condemning our fellow men. But at the same time it gives one genuine pleasure to find that one was mistaken. Don't you think so?

MRS ALV. What I think is that you are, and always will remain, a big baby, Mr Manders.

MAN. I?

MRS ALV. [*laying her hands on his shoulders*]. And I think that I should like very much to give you a good hug.

MAN. [*drawing back hastily*]. No,

no, good gracious! What an idea!

MRS ALV. [*with a smile*]. Oh, you needn't be afraid of me.

MAN. [*standing by the table*]. You choose such an extravagant way of expressing yourself sometimes. Now I must get these papers together and put them in my bag. [*Does so.*] That's it. And now good-by for the present. Keep your eyes open when Oswald comes back. I will come back and see you again presently.

[*He takes his hat and goes out by the hall door.* MRS ALVING *sighs, glances out of the window, puts one or two things tidy in the room and turns to go into the dining room. She stops in the doorway with a stifled cry.*]

MRS ALV. Oswald, are you still sitting at table!

OSW. [*from the dining room*]. I am only finishing my cigar.

MRS ALV. I thought you had gone out for a little turn.

OSW. [*from within the room*]. In weather like this? [*A glass is heard clinking.* MRS ALVING *leaves the door open and sits down with her knitting on the couch by the window.*] Wasn't that Mr Manders that went out just now?

MRS ALV. Yes, he has gone over to the orphanage.

OSW. Oh. [*The clink of a bottle on a glass is heard again.*]

MRS ALV. [*with an uneasy expression*]. Oswald dear, you should be careful with that liqueur. It is strong.

OSW. It's a good protective against the damp.

MRS ALV. Wouldn't you rather come in here?

OSW. You know you don't like smoking in there.

MRS ALV. You may smoke a cigar in here, certainly.

OSW. All right; I will come in then. Just one drop more. There! [*Comes in smoking a cigar and shuts the door after him. A short silence.*] Where has the parson gone?

MRS ALV. I told you he had gone over to the orphanage.

OSW. Oh, so you did.

MRS. ALV. You shouldn't sit so long at table, Oswald.

OSW. [*holding his cigar behind his back*]. But it's so nice and cosy, Mother dear. [*Caresses her with one hand.*] Think what it means to me—to have come home, to sit at my mother's own table, in my mother's own room, and to enjoy the charming meals she gives me.

MRS ALV. My dear, dear boy!

OSW. [*a little impatiently, as he walks up and down smoking*]. And what else is there for me to do here? I have no occupation.

MRS ALV. No occupation?

OSW. Not in this ghastly weather, when there isn't a blink of sunshine all day long. [*Walks up and down the floor.*] Not to be able to work, it's——

MRS ALV. I don't believe you were wise to come home.

OSW. Yes, Mother; I had to.

MRS ALV. Because I would ten times rather give up the happiness of having you with me sooner than that you should——

OSW. [*standing still by the table*]. Tell me, Mother—is it really such a great happiness for you to have me at home?

MRS ALV. Can you ask?

OSW. [*crumpling up a newspaper*]. I should have thought it would have been pretty much the same to you whether I were here or away.

MRS ALV. Have you the heart to say that to your mother, Oswald?

OSW. But you have been quite happy living without me so far.

MRS ALV. Yes, I have lived without you—that is true.

[*A silence. The dusk falls by degrees.* OSWALD *walks restlessly up and down. He has laid aside his cigar.*]

OSW. [*stopping beside* MRS ALVING]. Mother, may I sit on the couch beside you?

MRS ALV. Of course, my dear boy.

OSW. [*sitting down*]. Now I must tell you something, Mother.

MRS ALV. [*anxiously*]. What?

OSW. [*staring in front of him*]. I can't bear it any longer.

MRS ALV. Bear what? What do you mean?

OSW. [*as before*]. I couldn't bring myself to write to you about it, and since I have been at home——

MRS ALV. [*catching him by the arm*]. Oswald, what is it?

OSW. Both yesterday and today I have tried to push my thoughts away from me—to free myself from them. But I can't.

MRS ALV. [*getting up*]. You must speak plainly, Oswald!

OSW. [*drawing her down to her seat again*]. Sit still, and I will try and tell you. I have made a great deal of the fatigue I felt after my journey——

MRS ALV. Well, what of that?

OSW. But that isn't what is the matter. It is no ordinary fatigue.

MRS ALV. [*trying to get up*]. You are not ill, Oswald!

OSW. [*pulling her down again*]. Sit still, Mother. Do take it quietly. I am not exactly ill—not ill in the usual sense. [*Takes his head in his hands.*] Mother, it's my mind that has broken down—gone to pieces—I shall never be able to work any more! [*Buries his face in his hands and throws himself at her knees in an outburst of sobs.*]

MRS ALV. [*pale and trembling*]. Oswald! Look at me! No, no, it isn't true!

OSW. [*looking up with a distracted expression*]. Never to be able to work any more! Never—never! A living death! Mother, can you imagine anything so horrible!

MRS ALV. My poor unhappy boy! How has this terrible thing happened?

OSW. [*sitting up again*]. That is just what I cannot possibly understand. I have never lived recklessly in any sense. You must believe that of me, Mother! I have never done that.

MRS ALV. I haven't a doubt of it, Oswald.

OSW. And yet this comes upon me all the same—this terrible disaster!

MRS ALV. Oh, but it will all come right again, my dear precious boy. It is nothing but overwork. Believe me, that is so.

OSW. [*dully*]. I thought so too, at first; but it isn't so.

MRS ALV. Tell me all about it.

OSW. Yes, I will.

MRS ALV. When did you first feel anything?

OSW. It was just after I had been home last time and had got back to Paris. I began to feel the most violent pains in my head—mostly at the back, I think. It was as if a tight band of iron was pressing on me from my neck upward.

MRS ALV. And then?

OSW. At first I thought it was nothing but the headaches I always used to be so much troubled with while I was growing.

MRS ALV. Yes, yes——

OSW. But it wasn't; I soon saw that.

I couldn't work any longer. I would try and start some big new picture, but it seemed as if all my faculties had forsaken me, as if all my strength were paralyzed. I couldn't manage to collect my thoughts; my head seemed to swim—everything went round and round. It was a horrible feeling! At last I sent for a doctor—and from him I learned the truth.

MRS ALV. In what way, do you mean?

OSW. He was one of the best doctors there. He made me describe what I felt and then he began to ask me a whole heap of questions which seemed to me to have nothing to do with the matter. I couldn't see what he was driving at——

MRS ALV. Well?

OSW. At last he said: "You have had the canker of disease in you practically from your birth"—the actual word he used was *vermoulu*.

MRS ALV. [*anxiously*]. What did he mean by that?

OSW. I couldn't understand either—and I asked him for a clearer explanation. And then the old cynic said—— [*Clenching his fist.*] Oh!

MRS ALV. What did he say?

OSW. He said: "The sins of the fathers are visited on the children."

MRS ALV. [*getting up slowly*]. The sins of the fathers!

OSW. I nearly struck him in the face.

MRS ALV. [*walking across the room*]. The sins of the fathers!

OSW. [*smiling sadly*]. Yes, just imagine! Naturally I assured him that what he thought was impossible. But do you think he paid any heed to me? No, he persisted in his opinion; and it was only when I got out your letters and translated to him all the passages that referred to my father——

MRS ALV. Well, and then?

OSW. Well, then of course he had to admit that he was on the wrong tack; and then I learned the truth—the incomprehensible truth! I ought to have had nothing to do with the joyous happy life I had lived with my comrades. It had been too much for my strength. So it was my own fault!

MRS ALV. No, no, Oswald! Don't believe that!

OSW. There was no other explanation of it possible, he said. That is the most horrible part of it. My whole life incurably ruined—just because of my own imprudence. All that I wanted to do in the world—not to dare to think of it any more—not to be *able* to think of it! Oh! if only I could live my life over again—if only I could undo what I have done! [*Throws himself on his face on the couch.* MRS ALVING *wrings her hands and walks up and down silently fighting with herself.* OSWALD *looks up after a while, raising himself on his elbows.*] If only it had been something I had inherited—something I could not help. But instead of that to have disgracefully, stupidly, thoughtlessly thrown away one's happiness, one's health, everything in the world—one's future, one's life——

MRS ALV. No, no, my darling boy; that is impossible! [*Bending over him.*] Things are not so desperate as you think.

OSW. Ah, you don't know—— [*Springs up.*] And to think, Mother, that I should bring all this sorrow upon you! Many a time I have almost wished and hoped that you really did not care so very much for me.

MRS ALV. I, Oswald? My only son! All that I have in the world! The only thing I care about!

Osw. [*taking hold of her hands and kissing them*]. Yes, yes, I know that is so. When I am at home I know that is true. And that is one of the hardest parts of it to me. But now you know all about it, and now we won't talk any more about it today. I can't stand thinking about it long at a time. [*Walks across the room.*] Let me have something to drink, Mother.

Mrs Alv. To drink? What do you want?

Osw. Oh, anything you like. I suppose you have got some punch in the house?

Mrs Alv. Yes, but my dear Oswald——

Osw. Don't tell me I mustn't, Mother. Do be nice! I must have something to drown these gnawing thoughts. [*Goes into the conservatory.*] And how—how gloomy it is here! [Mrs Alving *rings the bell.*] And this incessant rain. It may go on week after week—a whole month. Never a ray of sunshine. I don't remember ever having seen the sun shine once when I have been at home.

Mrs Alv. Oswald—you are thinking of going away from me!

Osw. Hm! [*Sighs deeply.*] I am not thinking about anything. I *can't* think about anything! [*In a low voice.*] I have to let that alone.

Reg. [*coming from the dining room*]. Did you ring, ma'am?

Mrs Alv. Yes, let us have the lamp in.

Reg. In a moment, ma'am; it is all ready lit. [*Goes out.*]

Mrs Alv. [*going up to* Oswald]. Oswald, don't keep anything back from me.

Osw. I don't, Mother. [*Goes to the table.*] It seems to me I have told you a good lot.

[Regina *brings the lamp and puts it upon the table.*]

Mrs Alv. Regina, you might bring us a small bottle of champagne.

Reg. Yes, ma'am. [*Goes out.*]

Osw. [*taking hold of his mother's face*]. That's right. I knew my mother wouldn't let her son go thirsty.

Mrs Alv. My poor dear boy, how could I refuse you anything now?

Osw. [*eagerly*]. Is that true, Mother? Do you mean it?

Mrs Alv. Mean what?

Osw. That you couldn't deny me anything?

Mrs Alv. My dear Oswald——

Osw. Hush!

[Regina *brings in a tray with a small bottle of champagne and two glasses, which she puts on the table.*]

Reg. Shall I open the bottle?

Osw. No, thank you. I will do it.

[Regina *goes out.*]

Mrs Alv. [*sitting down at the table*]. What did you mean when you asked if I could refuse you nothing?

Osw. [*busy opening the bottle*]. Let us have a glass first—or two. [*He draws the cork, fills one glass and is going to fill the other.*]

Mrs Alv. [*holding her hand over the second glass*]. No, thanks—not for me.

Osw. Oh well, for me then! [*He empties his glass, fills it again and empties it, then sits down at the table.*]

Mrs Alv. [*expectantly*]. Now tell me.

Osw. [*without looking at her*]. Tell me this; I thought you and Mr Manders seemed so strange—so quiet—at dinner.

Mrs Alv. Did you notice that?

Osw. Yes. Ahem! [*After a short pause.*] Tell me—what do you think of Regina?

MRS ALV. What do I think of her?

OSW. Yes, isn't she splendid?

MRS ALV. Dear Oswald, you don't know her as well as I do.

OSW. What of that?

MRS ALV. Regina was too long at home, unfortunately. I ought to have taken her under my charge sooner.

OSW. Yes, but isn't she splendid to look at, Mother? [*Fills his glass.*]

MRS ALV. Regina has many serious faults.

OSW. Yes, but what of that? [*Drinks.*]

MRS ALV. But I am fond of her all the same, and I have made myself responsible for her. I wouldn't for the world she should come to any harm.

OSW. [*jumping up*]. Mother, Regina is my only hope of salvation!

MRS ALV. [*getting up*]. What do you mean?

OSW. I can't go on bearing all this agony of mind alone.

MRS ALV. Haven't you your mother to help you bear it?

OSW. Yes, I thought so; that was why I came home to you. But it is no use; I see that it isn't. I cannot spend my life here.

MRS ALV. Oswald!

OSW. I must live a different sort of life, Mother; so I shall have to go away from you. I don't want you watching it.

MRS ALV. My unhappy boy! But, Oswald, as long as you are ill like this

OSW. If it was only a matter of feeling ill, I would stay with you, Mother. You are the best friend I have in the world.

MRS ALV. Yes, I am that, Oswald, am I not?

OSW. [*walking restlessly about*]. But all this torment–the regret, the remorse–and the deadly fear. Oh–this horrible fear!

MRS ALV. [*following him*]. Fear? Fear of what? What do you mean?

OSW. Oh, don't ask me any more about it. I don't know what it is. I can't put it into words. [MRS ALVING *crosses the room and rings the bell.*] What do you want?

MRS ALV. I want my boy to be happy, that's what I want. He mustn't brood over anything. [*To* REGINA, *who has come to the door.*] More champagne–a large bottle.

OSW. Mother!

MRS ALV. Do you think we country people don't know how to live?

OSW. Isn't she splendid to look at? What a figure! And the picture of health!

MRS ALV. [*sitting down at the table*]. Sit down, Oswald, and let us have a quiet talk.

OSW. [*sitting down*]. You don't know, Mother, that I owe Regina a little reparation.

MRS ALV. You!

OSW. Oh, it was only a little thoughtlessness–call it what you like. Something quite innocent anyway. The last time I was home——

MRS ALV. Yes?

OSW. –she used often to ask me questions about Paris, and I told her one thing and another about the life there. And I remember saying one day: "Wouldn't you like to go there yourself?"

MRS ALV. Well?

OSW. I saw her blush, and she said: "Yes, I should like to very much." "All right," I said, "I daresay it might be managed"–or something of that sort.

MRS ALV. And then?

Osw. I naturally had forgotten all about it, but the day before yesterday I happened to ask her if she was glad I was to be so long at home——

Mrs Alv. Well?

Osw. —and she looked so queerly at me and asked: "But what is to become of my trip to Paris?"

Mrs Alv. Her trip!

Osw. And then I got it out of her that she had taken the thing seriously and had been thinking about me all the time and had set herself to learn French——

Mrs Alv. So that was why——

Osw. Mother—when I saw this fine, splendid, handsome girl standing there in front of me—I had never paid any attention to her before then—but now, when she stood there as if with open arms, ready for me to take her to myself——

Mrs Alv. Oswald!

Osw. —then I realized that my salvation lay in her, for I saw the joy of life in her.

Mrs Alv. [*starting back*]. The joy of life? Is there salvation in that?

Reg. [*coming from the dining room with a bottle of champagne*]. Excuse me for being so long, but I had to go to the cellar. [*Puts the bottle down on the table.*]

Osw. Bring another glass too.

Reg. [*looking at him in astonishment*]. The mistress's glass is there, sir.

Osw. Yes, but fetch one for yourself, Regina. [Regina *starts and gives a quick shy glance at* Mrs Alving.] Well?

Reg. [*in a low and hesitating voice*]. Do you wish me to, ma'am?

Mrs Alv. Fetch the glass, Regina.

[Regina *goes into the dining room.*]

Osw. [*looking after her*]. Have you noticed how well she walks?—so firmly and confidently!

Mrs Alv. It cannot be, Oswald.

Osw. It is settled! You must see that. It is no use forbidding it. [Regina *comes in with a glass which she holds in her hand.*] Sit down, Regina. [Regina *looks questioningly at* Mrs Alving.]

Mrs Alv. Sit down. [Regina *sits down on a chair near the dining-room door, still holding the glass in her hand.*] Oswald, what was it you were saying about the joy of life?

Osw. Ah, Mother—the joy of life! You don't know very much about that at home here. I shall never realize it here.

Mrs Alv. Not even when you are with me?

Osw. Never at home. But you can't understand that.

Mrs Alv. Yes, indeed I almost think I do understand you—now.

Osw. That—and the joy of work. They are really the same thing at bottom. But you don't know anything about that either.

Mrs Alv. Perhaps you are right. Tell me some more about it, Oswald.

Osw. Well, all I mean is that here people are brought up to believe that work is a curse and a punishment for sin and that life is a state of wretchedness and that the sooner we can get out of it the better.

Mrs Alv. A vale of tears, yes. And we quite conscientiously make it so.

Osw. But the people over there will have none of that. There is no one there who really believes doctrines of that kind any longer. Over there the mere fact of being alive is thought to be a matter for exultant happiness. Mother, have you noticed that everything I have painted has turned upon the joy of life?—always upon the joy of life, unfailingly. There is light there and sunshine and a holiday feeling—and people's faces beaming with happiness. That is why I am afraid to stay at home here with you.

MRS ALV. Afraid? What are you afraid of here with me?

OSW. I am afraid that all these feelings that are so strong in me would degenerate into something ugly here.

MRS ALV. [*looking steadily at him*]. Do you think that is what would happen?

OSW. I am certain it would. Even if one lived the same life at home here as over there—it would never really be the same life.

MRS. ALV. [*who has listened anxiously to him, gets up with a thoughtful expression and says*]. Now I see clearly how it all happened.

OSW. What do you see?

MRS ALV. I see it now for the first time. And now I can speak.

OSW. [*getting up*]. Mother, I don't understand you.

REG. [*who has got up also*]. Perhaps I had better go.

MRS ALV. No, stay here. Now I can speak. Now, my son, you shall know the whole truth. Oswald! Regina!

OSW. Hush!—here is the parson. [MANDERS *comes in by the hall door.*]

MAN. Well, my friends, we have been spending an edifying time over there.

OSW. So have we.

MAN. Engstrand must have help with his sailors' home. Regina must go home with him and give him her assistance.

REG. No, thank you, Mr Manders.

MAN. [*perceiving her for the first time*]. What? You in here?—and with a wineglass in your hand!

REG. [*putting down the glass hastily*]. I beg your pardon!

OSW. Regina is going away with me, Mr Manders.

MAN. Going away! With you!

OSW. Yes, as my wife—if she insists on that.

MAN. But, good heavens!

REG. It is not my fault, Mr Manders.

OSW. Or else she stays here if I stay.

REG. [*involuntarily*]. Here!

MAN. I am amazed at you, Mrs Alving.

MRS ALV. Neither of those things will happen, for now I can speak openly.

MAN. But you won't do that! No, no, no!

MRS ALV. Yes, I can and will. And without destroying anyone's ideals.

OSW. Mother, what is it that is being concealed from me?

REG. [*listening*]. Mrs Alving! Listen! They are shouting outside. [*Goes into the conservatory and looks out.*]

OSW. [*going to the window on the left*]. What can be the matter? Where does that glare come from?

REG. [*calls out*]. The orphanage is on fire!

MRS ALV. [*going to the window*]. On fire?

MAN. On fire? Impossible! I was there just a moment ago.

OSW. Where is my hat? Oh, never mind that. Father's orphanage— [*Runs out through the garden door.*]

MRS ALV. My shawl, Regina! The whole place is in flames.

MAN. How terrible! Mrs Alving, that fire is a judgment on this house of sin!

Mrs Alv. Quite so. Come, Regina. [*She and* Regina *hurry out.*]

Man. [*clasping his hands*]. And no insurance! [*Follows them out.*]

ACT III

The same scene. All the doors are standing open. The lamp is still burning on the table. It is dark outside, except for a faint glimmer of light seen through the windows at the back. Mrs Alving, *with a shawl over her head, is standing in the conservatory looking out.* Regina, *also wrapped in a shawl, is standing a little behind her.*

Mrs Alv. Everything burned—down to the ground.

Reg. It is burning still in the basement.

Mrs Alv. I can't think why Oswald doesn't come back. There is no chance of saving anything.

Reg. Shall I go and take his hat to him?

Mrs Alv. Hasn't he even got his hat?

Reg. [*pointing to the hall*]. No, there it is, hanging up.

Mrs Alv. Never mind. He is sure to come back soon. I will go and see what he is doing. [*Goes out by the garden door.* Manders *comes in from the hall.*]

Man. Isn't Mrs Alving here?

Reg. She has just this moment gone down into the garden.

Man. I have never spent such a terrible night in my life.

Reg. Isn't it a shocking misfortune, sir?

Man. Oh, don't speak about it. I scarcely dare to think about it.

Reg. But how can it have happened?

Man. Don't ask me, Miss Engstrand! How should I know? Are you going to suggest too—— Isn't it enough that your father——

Reg. What has he done?

Man. He has nearly driven me crazy.

Eng. [*coming in from the hall*]. Mr Manders!

Man. [*turning round with a start*]. Have you even followed me here?

Eng. Yes, God help us all! Great heavens! What a dreadful thing, your reverence!

Man. [*walking up and down*]. Oh dear, oh dear!

Reg. What do you mean?

Eng. Our little prayer meeting was the cause of it all, don't you see? [*Aside to* Regina.] Now we've got the old fool, my girl. [*Aloud.*] And to think it is my fault that Mr Manders should be the cause of such a thing!

Man. I assure you, Engstrand——

Eng. But there was no one else carrying a light there except you, sir.

Man. [*standing still*]. Yes, so you say. But I have no clear recollection of having had a light in my hand.

Eng. But I saw quite distinctly your reverence take a candle and snuff it with your fingers and throw away the burning bit of wick among the shavings.

Man. Did you see that?

Eng. Yes, distinctly.

Man. I can't understand it at all. It is never my habit to snuff a candle with my fingers.

Eng. Yes, it wasn't like you to do that, sir. But who would have thought it could be such a dangerous thing to do?

Man. [*walking restlessly backward and forward*]. Oh, don't ask me!

Eng. [*following him about*]. And

you hadn't insured it either, had you, sir?

MAN. No, no, no; you heard me say so.

ENG. You hadn't insured it–and then went and set light to the whole place! Good lord, what bad luck!

MAN. [*wiping the perspiration from his forehead*]. You may well say so, Engstrand.

ENG. And that it should happen to a charitable institution that would have been of service both to the town and the country, so to speak! The newspapers won't be very kind to your reverence, I expect.

MAN. No, that is just what I am thinking of. It is almost the worst part of the whole thing. The spiteful attacks and accusations–it is horrible to think of!

MRS ALV. [*coming in from the garden*]. I can't get him away from the fire.

MAN. Oh, there you are, Mrs Alving.

MRS ALV. You will escape having to make your inaugural address now, at all events, Mr Manders.

MAN. Oh, I would so gladly have——

MRS ALV. [*in a dull voice*]. It is just as well it has happened. This orphanage would never have come to any good.

MAN. Don't you think so?

MRS ALV. Do you?

MAN. But it is, nonetheless, an extraordinary piece of ill luck.

MRS ALV. We will discuss it simply as a business matter. Are you waiting for Mr Manders, Engstrand?

ENG. [*at the hall door*]. Yes, I am.

MRS ALV. Sit down then, while you are waiting.

ENG. Thank you, I would rather stand.

MRS ALV. [*to* MANDERS]. I suppose you are going by the boat?

MAN. Yes. It goes in about an hour.

MRS ALV. Please take all the documents back with you. I don't want to hear another word about the matter. I have something else to think about now.

MAN. Mrs Alving——

MRS ALV. Later on I will send you a power of attorney to deal with it exactly as you please.

MAN. I shall be most happy to undertake that. I am afraid the original intention of the bequest will have to be entirely altered now.

MRS ALV. Of course.

MAN. Provisionally, I should suggest this way of disposing of it. Make over the Slovik property to the parish. The land is undoubtedly not without a certain value; it will always be useful for some purpose or another. And as for the interest on the remaining capital that is on deposit in the bank, possibly I might make suitable use of that in support of some undertaking that promises to be of use to the town.

MRS ALV. Do exactly as you please. The whole thing is a matter of indifference to me now.

ENG. You will think of my sailors' home, Mr Manders?

MAN. Yes, certainly; that is a suggestion. But we must consider the matter carefully.

ENG. [*aside*]. Consider!–devil take it! Oh lord!

MAN. [*signing*]. And unfortunately I can't tell how much longer I may have anything to do with the matter –whether public opinion may not force me to retire from it altogether. That depends entirely upon the result of the inquiry into the cause of the fire.

MRS ALV. What do you say?

MAN. And one cannot in any way reckon upon the result beforehand.

ENG. [*going nearer to him*]. Yes, indeed one can; because here stand I, Jacob Engstrand.

MAN. Quite so, but——

ENG. [*lowering his voice*]. And Jacob Engstrand isn't the man to desert a worthy benefactor in the hour of need, as the saying is.

MAN. Yes, but, my dear fellow, how——

ENG. You might say Jacob Engstrand is an angel of salvation, so to speak, your reverence.

MAN. No, no, I couldn't possibly accept that.

ENG. That's how it will be, all the same. I know someone who has taken the blame for someone else on his shoulders before now, I do.

MAN. Jacob! [*Grasps his hand.*] You are one in a thousand! You shall have assistance in the matter of your sailors' home, you may rely upon that.

[ENGSTRAND *tries to thank him but is prevented by emotion.*]

MAN. [*hanging his wallet over his shoulder*]. Now we must be off. We will travel together.

ENG. [*by the dining-room door, says aside to* REGINA]. Come with me, you hussy! You shall be as cozy as the yolk in an egg!

REG. [*tossing her head*]. *Merci!* [*She goes out into the hall and brings back* MANDERS' *luggage.*]

MAN. Good-by, Mrs Alving! And may the spirit of order and of what is lawful speedily enter into this house.

MRS ALV. Good-by, Mr Manders. [*She goes into the conservatory as she sees* OSWALD *coming in by the garden door.*]

ENG. [*as he and* REGINA *are helping* MANDERS *on with his coat*]. Good-by, my child. And if anything should happen to you, you know where Jacob Engstrand is to be found. [*Lowering his voice.*] Little Harbour Street, ahem! [*To* MRS ALVING *and* OSWALD.] And my house for poor seafaring men shall be called the "Alving Home," it shall. And if I can carry out my own ideas about it I shall make bold to hope that it may be worthy of bearing the late Mr Alving's name.

MAN. [*at the door*]. Ahem—ahem! Come along, my dear Engstrand. Good-by—good-by! [*He and* ENGSTRAND *go out by the hall door.*]

OSW. [*going to the table*]. What house was he speaking about?

MRS ALV. I believe it is some sort of a home that he and Mr Manders want to start.

OSW. It will be burned up just like this one.

MRS ALV. What makes you think that?

OSW. Everything will be burned up; nothing will be left that is in memory of my father. Here am I being burned up too.

[REGINA *looks at him in alarm.*]

MRS ALV. Oswald! You should not have stayed so long over there, my poor boy.

OSW. [*sitting down at the table*]. I almost believe you are right.

MRS ALV. Let me dry your face, Oswald; you are all wet. [*Wipes his face with her handkerchief.*]

OSW. [*looking straight before him with no expression in his eyes*]. Thank you, Mother.

MRS ALV. And aren't you tired, Oswald? Don't you want to go to sleep?

OSW. [*uneasily*]. No, no—not to

sleep! I never sleep; I only pretend to. [*Gloomily.*] That will come soon enough.

Mrs Alv. [*looking at him anxiously*]. Anyhow, you are really ill, my darling boy.

Reg. [*intently*]. Is Mr Alving ill?

Osw. [*impatiently*]. And do shut all the doors! This deadly fear——

Mrs Alv. Shut the doors, Regina. [Regina *shuts the doors and remains standing by the hall door.* Mrs Alving *takes off her shawl;* Regina *does the same.* Mrs Alving *draws up a chair near to* Oswald's *and sits down beside him.*] That's it! Now I will sit beside you.

Osw. Yes, do. And Regina must stay in here too. Regina must always be near me. You must give me a helping hand, you know, Regina. Won't you do that?

Reg. I don't understand——

Mrs Alv. A helping hand?

Osw. Yes—when there is need for it.

Mrs Alv. Oswald, have you not your mother to give you a helping hand?

Osw. You? [*Smiles.*] No, Mother, you will never give me the kind of helping hand I mean. [*Laughs grimly.*] You! Ha, ha! [*Looks gravely at her.*] After all, you have the best right. [*Impetuously.*] Why don't you call me by my Christian name, Regina? Why don't you say Oswald?

Reg. [*in a low voice*] I did not think Mrs Alving would like it.

Mrs Alv. It will not be long before you have the right to do it. Sit down here now beside us too. [Regina *sits down quietly and hesitatingly at the other side of the table.*] And now, my poor tortured boy, I am going to take the burden off your mind——

Osw. You, Mother?

Mrs Alv. —all that you call remorse and regret and self-reproach.

Osw. And you think you can do that?

Mrs Alv. Yes, now I can, Oswald. A little while ago you were talking about the joy of life and what you said seemed to shed a new light upon everything in my whole life.

Osw. [*shaking his head*]. I don't in the least understand what you mean.

Mrs Alv. You should have known your father in his young days in the army. He was full of the joy of life, I can tell you.

Osw. Yes, I know.

Mrs Alv. It gave me a holiday feeling only to look at him, full of irrepressible energy and exuberant spirits.

Osw. What then?

Mrs Alv. Well, then this boy, full of the joy of life—for he was just like a boy then—had to make his home in a second-rate town which had none of the joy of life to offer him but only dissipations. He had to come out here and live an aimless life; he had only an official post. He had no work worth devoting his whole mind to; he had nothing more than official routine to attend to. He had not a single companion capable of appreciating what the joy of life meant; nothing but idlers and tipplers——

Osw. Mother!

Mrs Alv. And so the inevitable happened!

Osw. What was the inevitable?

Mrs Alv. You said yourself this evening what would happen in your case if you stayed at home.

Osw. Do you mean by that that Father——

MRS ALV. Your poor father never found any outlet for the overmastering joy of life that was in him. And I brought no holiday spirit into his home either.

OSW. You didn't either?

MRS ALV. I had been taught about duty and the sort of thing that I believed in so long here. Everything seemed to turn upon duty—my duty or his duty—and I am afraid I made your poor father's home unbearable to him, Oswald.

OSW. Why did you never say anything about it to me in your letters?

MRS ALV. I never looked at it as a thing I could speak of to you, who were his son.

OSW. What way did you look at it, then?

MRS ALV. I only saw the one fact, that your father was a lost man before ever you were born.

OSW. [*in a choking voice*]. Ah! [*He gets up and goes to the window.*]

MRS ALV. And then I had the one thought in my mind, day and night, that Regina in fact had as good a right in this house—as my own boy had.

OSW. [*turns round suddenly*]. Regina?

REG. [*gets up and asks in choking tones*]. I?

MRS ALV. Yes, now you both know it.

OSW. Regina!

REG. [*to herself*]. So Mother was one of that sort too.

MRS ALV. Your mother had many good qualities, Regina.

REG. Yes, but she was one of that sort too, all the same. I have even thought so myself sometimes, but—— Then, if you please, Mrs Alving, may I have permission to leave at once?

MRS ALV. Do you really wish to, Regina?

REG. Yes indeed, I certainly wish to.

MRS ALV. Of course you shall do as you like, but——

OSW. [*going up to* REGINA]. Leave now? This is your home.

REG. *Merci*, Mr Alving—oh, of course I may say Oswald now, but that is not the way I thought it would become allowable.

MRS ALV. Regina, I have not been open with you.

REG. No, I can't say you have! If I had known Oswald was ill—— And now that there can never be anything serious between us—— No, I really can't stay here in the country and wear myself out looking after invalids.

OSW. Not even for the sake of one who has so near a claim on you?

REG. No, indeed I can't. A poor girl must make some use of her youth, otherwise she may easily find herself out in the cold before she knows where she is. And I have got the joy of life in me too, Mrs Alving!

MRS ALV. Yes, unfortunately; but don't throw yourself away, Regina.

REG. Oh, what's going to happen will happen. If Oswald takes after his father, it is just as likely I take after my mother, I expect. May I ask, Mrs Alving, whether Mr Manders knows this about me?

MRS ALV. Mr Manders knows everything.

REG. [*putting on her shawl*]. Oh well, then, the best thing I can do is to get away by the boat as soon as I can. Mr Manders is such a nice gentleman to deal with, and it certainly seems to me that I have just as much right to some of that money as he—

as that horrid carpenter.

MRS ALV. You are quite welcome to it, Regina.

REG. [*looking at her fixedly*]. You might as well have brought me up like a gentleman's daughter; it would have been more suitable. [*Tosses her head.*] Oh well—never mind! [*With a bitter glance at the unopened bottle.*] I daresay someday I shall be drinking champagne with gentlefolk after all.

MRS ALV. If ever you need a home, Regina, come to me.

REG. No, thank you, Mrs Alving. Mr Manders takes an interest in me, I know. And if things should go very badly with me, I know one house at any rate where I shall feel at home.

MRS ALV. Where is that?

REG. In the "Alving Home."

MRS ALV. Regina—I can see quite well—you are going to your ruin!

REG. Pooh!—good-by. [*She bows to them and goes out through the hall.*]

OSW. [*standing by the window and looking out*]. Has she gone?

MRS ALV. Yes.

OSW. [*muttering to himself*]. I think it's all wrong.

MRS ALV. [*going up to him from behind and putting her hands on his shoulders*]. Oswald, my dear boy—has it been a great shock to you?

OSW. [*turning his face toward her*]. All this about Father, do you mean?

MRS ALV. Yes, about your unhappy father. I am so afraid it may have been too much for you.

OSW. What makes you think that? Naturally it has taken me entirely by surprise; but, after all, I don't know that it matters much to me.

MRS ALV. [*drawing back her hands*]. Doesn't matter!—that your father's life was such a terrible failure!

OSW. Of course I can feel sympathy for him, just as I would for anyone else, but——

MRS ALV. No more than that! For your own father!

OSW. [*impatiently*]. Father—Father! I never knew anything of my father. I don't remember anything else about him except that he once made me sick.

MRS ALV. It is dreadful to think of! But surely a child should feel some affection for his father, whatever happens?

OSW. When the child has nothing to thank his father for? When he has never known him? Do you really cling to that antiquated superstition—you who are so broadminded in other things?

MRS ALV. You call it nothing but a superstition!

OSW. Yes, and you can see that for yourself quite well, Mother. It is one of those beliefs that are put into circulation in the world and——

MRS ALV. Ghosts of beliefs!

OSW. [*walking across the room*]. Yes, you might call them ghosts.

MRS ALV. [*with an outburst of feeling*]. Oswald—then you don't love me either!

OSW. You I know, at any rate——

MRS ALV. You know me, yes; but is that all?

OSW. And I know how fond you are of me, and I ought to be grateful to you for that. Besides, you can be so tremendously useful to me now that I am ill.

MRS ALV. Yes, can't I, Oswald! I could almost bless your illness, as it has driven you home to me. For I see quite well that you are not my very own yet; you must be won.

Osw. [*impatiently*]. Yes, yes, yes; all that is just a way of talking. You must remember I am a sick man, Mother. I can't concern myself much with anyone else; I have enough to do, thinking about myself.

Mrs Alv. [*gently*]. I will be very good and patient.

Osw. And cheerful too, Mother!

Mrs Alv. Yes, my dear boy, you are quite right. [*Goes up to him.*] Now have I taken away all your remorse and self-reproach?

Osw. Yes, you have done that. But who will take away the fear?

Mrs Alv. The fear?

Osw. [*crossing the room*]. Regina would have done it for one kind word.

Mrs Alv. I don't understand you. What fear do you mean—and what has Regina to do with it?

Osw. Is it very late, Mother?

Mrs Alv. It is early morning. [*Looks out through the conservatory windows.*] The dawn is breaking already on the heights. And the sky is clear, Oswald. In a little while you will see the sun.

Osw. I am glad of that. After all, there may be many things yet for me to be glad of and to live for——

Mrs Alv. I should hope so!

Osw. —even if I am not able to work.

Mrs Alv. You will soon find you are able to work again now, my dear boy. You have no longer all those painful depressing thoughts to brood over.

Osw. No, it is a good thing that you have been able to rid me of those fancies. If only, now, I could overcome this one thing. [*Sits down on the couch.*] Let us have a little chat, Mother.

Mrs Alv. Yes, let us. [*Pushes an armchair near to the couch and sits down beside him.*]

Osw. The sun is rising—and you know all about it; so I don't feel the fear any longer.

Mrs Alv. I know all about what?

Osw. [*without listening to her*]. Mother, isn't it the case that you said this evening there was nothing in the world you would not do for me if I asked you?

Mrs Alv. Yes, certainly I said so.

Osw. And will you be as good as your word, Mother?

Mrs Alv. You may rely upon that, my own dear boy. I have nothing else to live for but you.

Osw. Yes, yes; well, listen to me, Mother. You are very strong-minded, I know. I want you to sit quite quiet when you hear what I am going to tell you.

Mrs Alv. But what is this dreadful thing?

Osw. You mustn't scream. Do you hear? Will you promise me that? We are going to sit and talk it over quite quietly. Will you promise me that, Mother?

Mrs Alv. Yes, yes, I promise—only tell me what it is.

Osw. Well, then, you must know that this fatigue of mine—and my not being able to think about my work—all that is not really the illness itself.

Mrs Alv. What is the illness itself?

Osw. What I am suffering from is hereditary; it—[*touches his forehead and speaks very quietly*]—it lies here.

Mrs Alv. [*almost speechless*]. Oswald! No—no!

Osw. Don't scream; I can't stand it. Yes, I tell you, it lies here, waiting.

And any time, any moment, it may break out.

MRS ALV. How horrible!

OSW. Do keep quiet. That is the state I am in.

MRS ALV. [*springing up*]. It isn't true, Oswald! It is impossible! It can't be that!

OSW. I had one attack while I was abroad. It passed off quickly. But when I learned the condition I had been in then this dreadful haunting fear took possession of me.

MRS ALV. That was the fear then——

OSW. Yes, it is so indescribably horrible, you know. If only it had been an ordinary mortal disease—— I am not so much afraid of dying; though of course I should like to live as long as I can.

MRS ALV. Yes, yes, Oswald, you must!

OSW. But this is so appallingly horrible. To become like a helpless child again—to have to be fed, to have to be—— Oh, it's unspeakable!

MRS ALV. My child has his mother to tend him.

OSW. [*jumping up*]. No, never; that is just what I won't endure! I dare not think what it would mean to linger on like that for years—to get old and gray like that. And you might die before I did. [*Sits down in* MRS ALVING's *chair.*] Because it doesn't necessarily have a fatal end quickly, the doctor said. He called it a kind of softening of the brain—or something of that sort. [*Smiles mournfully.*] I think that expression sounds so nice. It always makes me think of cherry-colored velvet curtains—something that is soft to stroke.

MRS ALV. [*with a scream*]. Oswald!

OSW. [*jumps up and walks about the room*]. And now you have taken Regina from me! If I had only had her. She would have given me a helping hand, I know.

MRS ALV. [*going up to him*]. What do you mean, my darling boy? Is there any help in the world I would not be willing to give you?

OSW. When I had recovered from the attack I had abroad the doctor told me that when it recurred—and it will recur—there would be no more hope.

MRS ALV. And he was heartless enough to——

OSW. I insisted on knowing. I told him I had arrangements to make. [*Smiles cunningly.*] And so I had. [*Takes a small box from his inner breast pocket.*] Mother, do you see this?

MRS ALV. What is it?

OSW. Morphia powders.

MRS ALV. [*looking at him in terror*]. Oswald—my boy!

OSW. I have twelve of them saved up.

MRS ALV. [*snatching at it*]. Give me the box, Oswald!

OSW. Not yet, Mother. [*Puts it back in his pocket.*]

MRS ALV. I shall never get over this!

OSW. You must. If I had had Regina here now, I would have told her quietly how things stand with me—and asked her to give me this last helping hand. She would have helped me, I am certain.

MRS ALV. Never!

OSW. If this horrible thing had come upon me and she had seen me lying helpless, like a baby, past help, past saving, past hope—with no chance of recovering——

MRS ALV. Never in the world

would Regina have done it.

Osw. Regina would have done it. Regina was so splendidly lighthearted. And she would very soon have tired of looking after an invalid like me.

Mrs Alv. Then thank heaven Regina is not here!

Osw. Well, now you have got to give me that helping hand, Mother.

Mrs Alv. [*with a loud scream*]. I!

Osw. Who has a better right than you?

Mrs Alv. I! Your mother!

Osw. Just for that reason.

Mrs Alv. I, who gave you your life!

Osw. I never asked you for life. And what kind of a life was it that you gave me? I don't want it! You shall take it back!

Mrs Alv. Help! Help! [*Runs into the hall.*]

Osw. [*following her*]. Don't leave me! Where are you going?

Mrs Alv. [*in the hall*]. To fetch the doctor to you, Oswald! Let me out!

Osw. [*going into the hall*]. You shan't go out. And no one shall come in. [*Turns the key in the lock.*]

Mrs Alv. [*coming in again*]. Oswald! Oswald!—my child!

Osw. [*following her*]. Have you a mother's heart—and can bear to see me suffering this unspeakable terror?

Mrs Alv. [*controlling herself after a moment's silence*]. There is my hand on it.

Osw. Will you?

Mrs Alv. If it becomes necessary. But it shan't become necessary. No, no—it is impossible it should!

Osw. Let us hope so. And let us live together as long as we can. Thank you, Mother. [*He sits down in the armchair which* Mrs Alving *had moved beside the couch. Day is breaking; the lamp is still burning on the table.*]

Mrs Alv. [*coming cautiously nearer*]. Do you feel calmer now?

Osw. Yes.

Mrs Alv. [*bending over him*]. It has only been a dreadful fancy of yours, Oswald. Nothing but fancy. All this upset has been bad for you. But now you will get some rest, at home with your own mother, my darling boy. You shall have everything you want, just as you did when you were a little child. There now. The attack is over. You see how easily it passed off! I knew it would. And look, Oswald, what a lovely day we are going to have! Brilliant sunshine. Now you will be able to see your home properly. [*She goes to the table and puts out the lamp. It is sunrise. The glaciers and peaks in the distance are seen bathed in bright morning light.*]

Osw. [*who has been sitting motionless in the armchair, with his back to the scene outside, suddenly says*]. Mother, give me the sun.

Mrs Alv. [*standing at the table and looking at him in amazement*]. What do you say?

Osw. [*repeats in a dull, toneless voice*]. The sun—the sun.

Mrs Alv. [*going up to him*]. Oswald, what is the matter with you? [Oswald *seems to shrink up in the chair; all his muscles relax; his face loses its expression and his eyes stare stupidly.* Mrs Alving *is trembling with terror.*] What is it? [*Screams.*] Oswald! What is the matter with you? [*Throws herself on her knees beside him and shakes him.*] Oswald! Oswald! Look at me! Don't you know me?

Osw. [*in an expressionless voice as before*]. The sun—the sun.

Mrs Alv. [*jumps up despairingly, beats her head with her hands and screams*]. I can't bear it! [*Whispers as though paralyzed with fear.*] I can't bear it! Never! [*Suddenly.*] Where has he got it? [*Passes her hand quickly over his coat.*] Here! [*Draws back a little way and cries.*] No, no, no!—Yes!—no, no! [*She stands a few steps from him, her hands thrust into her hair, and stares at him in speechless terror.*]

Osw. [*sitting motionless as before*]. The sun—the sun.

AN ENEMY OF THE PEOPLE

PERSONS OF THE PLAY

Dr Thomas Stockmann, *medical officer of the Municipal Baths.*

Mrs Stockmann, *his wife.*

Petra, *their daughter, a teacher.*

Ejlif and Morten, *their sons (aged thirteen and ten respectively).*

Peter Stockmann, *the doctor's elder brother; mayor of the town and chief constable, chairman of the Baths Committee, etc., etc.*

Morten Kiil, *a tanner (Mrs Stockmann's adoptive father).*

Hovstad, *editor of the* People's Messenger.

Billing, *subeditor.*

Captain Horster.

Aslaksen, *a printer.*

Men of various conditions and occupations, some few women and a troop of schoolboys—the audience at a public meeting.

The action takes place in a coast town in southern Norway.

ACT I

Scene—Dr Stockmann's *sitting room. It is evening. The room is plainly but neatly appointed and furnished. In the right-hand wall are two doors; the farther leads out to the hall, the nearer to the doctor's study. In the left-hand wall, opposite the door leading to the hall, is a door leading to the other rooms occupied by the family. In the middle of the same wall stands the stove and, further forward, a couch with a looking glass hanging over it and an oval table in front of it. On the table a lighted lamp with a lamp shade. At the back of the room an open door leads to the dining room.* Billing *is seen sitting at the dining table, on which a lamp is burning. He has a napkin tucked under his chin, and* Mrs Stockmann *is standing by the table handing him a large plateful of roast beef. The other places at the table are empty and the table somewhat in disorder, a meal having evidently recently been finished.*

Mrs Sto. You see, if you come an hour late, Mr Billing, you have to put up with cold meat.

Bill. [*as he eats*]. It is uncommonly good, thank you—remarkably good.

Mrs Sto. My husband makes such a point of having his meals punctually, you know.

Bill. That doesn't affect me a bit. Indeed, I almost think I enjoy a meal all the better when I can sit down and eat all by myself and undisturbed.

Mrs Sto. Oh well, as long as you are enjoying it—— [*Turns to the hall door, listening.*] I expect that is Mr Hovstad coming too.

Bill. Very likely.

[Peter Stockmann *comes in. He wears an overcoat and his official hat and carries a stick.*]

Peter. Good evening, Katherine.

Mrs Sto. [*coming forward into the sitting room*]. Ah, good evening—is it you? How good of you to come up and see us!

Peter. I happened to be passing, and so——[*looks into the dining room.*] But you have company with you, I see.

Mrs Sto. [*a little embarrassed*]. Oh no—it was quite by chance he came in. [*Hurriedly.*] Won't you come in and have something too?

Peter. I! No, thank you. Good gracious—hot meat at night! Not with my digestion.

Mrs Sto. Oh, but just once in a way——

Peter. No, no, my dear lady; I stick to my tea and bread and butter. It is much more wholesome in the long run—and a little more economical too.

Mrs Sto. [*smiling*]. Now you mustn't think that Thomas and I are spendthrifts.

Peter. Not you, my dear; I would never think that of you. [*Points to the doctor's study.*] Is he not at home?

Mrs Sto. No, he went out for a little turn after supper—he and the boys.

Peter. I doubt if that is a wise thing to do. [*Listens.*] I fancy I hear him coming now.

Mrs Sto. No, I don't think it is he. [*A knock is heard at the door.*] Come in! [Hovstad *comes in from the hall.*] Oh, it is you, Mr Hovstad!

Hov. Yes; I hope you will forgive me, but I was delayed at the printer's. Good evening, Mr Mayor.

Peter [*bowing a little distantly*]. Good evening. You have come on business, no doubt.

Hov. Partly. It's about an article for the paper.

Peter. So I imagined. I hear my brother has become a prolific contributor to the *People's Messenger*.

Hov. Yes, he is good enough to write in the *People's Messenger* when he has any home truths to tell.

Mrs Sto. [*to* Hovstad]. But won't you——? [*Points to the dining room.*]

Peter. Quite so, quite so. I don't blame him in the least, as a writer, for addressing himself to the quarters where he will find the readiest sympathy. And, besides that, I personally have no reason to bear any ill will to your paper, Mr Hovstad.

Hov. I quite agree with you.

Peter. Taking one thing with another, there is an excellent spirit of toleration in the town—an admirable municipal spirit. And it all springs from the fact of our having a great common interest to unite us—an interest that is in an equally high degree the concern of every right-minded citizen.

Hov. The Baths, yes.

Peter. Exactly—our fine, new, handsome Baths. Mark my words, Mr Hovstad—the Baths will become the focus of our municipal life! Not a doubt of it!

Mrs Sto. That is just what Thomas says.

PETER. Think how extraordinarily the place has developed within the last year or two! Money has been flowing in, and there is some life and some business doing in the town. Houses and landed property are rising in value every day.

HOV. And unemployment is diminishing.

PETER. Yes, that is another thing. The burden of the poor rates has been lightened, to the great relief of the propertied classes; and that relief will be even greater if only we get a really good summer this year and lots of visitors—plenty of invalids who will make the Baths talked about.

HOV. And there is a good prospect of that, I hear.

PETER. It looks very promising. Inquiries about apartments and that sort of thing are reaching us every day.

HOV. Well, the doctor's article will come in very suitably.

PETER. Has he been writing something just lately?

HOV. This is something he wrote in the winter, a recommendation of the Baths—an account of the excellent sanitary conditions here. But I held the article over, temporarily.

PETER. Ah—some little difficulty about it, I suppose?

HOV. No, not at all; I thought it would be better to wait till the spring, because it is just at this time that people begin to think seriously about their summer quarters.

PETER. Quite right; you were perfectly right, Mr Hovstad.

HOV. Yes, Thomas is really indefatigable when it is a question of the Baths.

PETER. Well—remember, he is the medical officer of the Baths.

HOV. Yes, and what is more, they owe their existence to him.

PETER. To him? Indeed! It is true I have heard from time to time that some people are of that opinion. At the same time I must say I imagined that I took a modest part in the enterprise.

MRS STO. Yes, that is what Thomas is always saying.

HOV. But who denies it, Mr Stockmann? You set the thing going and made a practical concern of it; we all know that. I only meant that the idea of it came first from the doctor.

PETER. Oh, ideas—yes! My brother has had plenty of them in his time—unfortunately. But when it is a question of putting an idea into practical shape you have to apply to a man of different mettle, Mr Hovstad. And I certainly should have thought that in this house at least——

MRS STO. My dear Peter——

HOV. How can you think that——

MRS STO. Won't you go in and have something, Mr Hovstad? My husband is sure to be back directly.

HOV. Thank you, perhaps just a morsel. [*Goes into the dining room.*]

PETER [*lowering his voice a little*]. It is a curious thing that these farmers' sons never seem to lose their want of tact.

MRS STO. Surely it is not worth bothering about! Cannot you and Thomas share the credit as brothers?

PETER. I should have thought so, but apparently some people are not satisfied with a share.

MRS STO. What nonsense! You and Thomas get on so capitally together. [*Listens.*] There he is at last, I think. [*Goes out and opens the door leading to the hall.*]

DR STO. [*laughing and talking out-*

side]. Look here—here is another guest for you, Katherine. Isn't that jolly! Come in, Captain Horster; hang your coat up on this peg. Ah, you don't wear an overcoat. Just think, Katherine; I met him in the street and could hardly persuade him to come up! [Captain Horster *comes into the room and greets* Mrs Stockmann. *He is followed by* Dr Stockmann.] Come along in, boys. They are ravenously hungry again, you know. Come along, Captain Horster; you must have a slice of beef. [*Pushes* Horster *into the dining room.* Ejlif *and* Morten *go in after them.*]

Mrs Sto. But, Thomas, don't you see——

Dr Sto. [*turning in the doorway*]. Oh, is it you, Peter? [*Shakes hands with him.*] Now that is very delightful.

Peter. Unfortunately I must go in a moment.

Dr Sto. Rubbish! There is some toddy just coming in. You haven't forgotten the toddy, Katherine?

Mrs Sto. Of course not, the water is boiling now. [*Goes into the dining room.*]

Peter. Toddy too!

Dr Sto. Yes; sit down and we will have it comfortably.

Peter. Thanks, I never care about an evening's drinking.

Dr Sto. But this isn't an evening's drinking.

Peter. It seems to me—— [*Looks toward the dining room.*] It is extraordinary how they can put away all that food.

Dr Sto. [*rubbing his hands*]. Yes, isn't it splendid to see young people eat? They have always got an appetite, you know! That's as it should be. Lots of food—to build up their strength! They are the people who are going to stir up the fermenting forces of the future, Peter.

Peter. May I ask what they will find here to "stir up," as you put it?

Dr Sto. Ah, you must ask the young people that—when the time comes. We shan't be able to see it, of course. That stands to reason—two old fogies like us——

Peter. Really, really! I must say that is an extremely odd expression to——

Dr Sto. Oh, you mustn't take me too literally, Peter. I am so heartily happy and contented, you know. I think it is such an extraordinary piece of good fortune to be in the middle of all this growing, germinating life. It is a splendid time to live in! It is as if a whole new world were being created around one.

Peter. Do you really think so?

Dr Sto. Ah, naturally you can't appreciate it as keenly as I. You have lived all your life in these surroundings and your impressions have got blunted. But I, who have been buried all these years in my little corner up north, almost without ever seeing a stranger who might bring new ideas with him—well, in my case it has just the same effect as if I had been transported into the middle of a crowded city.

Peter. Oh, a city!

Dr Sto. I know, I know; it is all cramped enough here, compared with many other places. But there is life here, there is promise—there are innumerable things to work for and fight for, and that is the main thing. [*Calls.*] Katherine, hasn't the postman been here?

Mrs Sto. [*from the dining room*]. No.

DR STO. And then to be comfortably off, Peter! That is something one learns to value when one has been on the brink of starvation as we have.

PETER. Oh, surely——

DR STO. Indeed, I can assure you we have often been very hard put to it up there. And now to be able to live like a lord! Today, for instance, we had roast beef for dinner—and, what is more, for supper too. Won't you come and have a little bit? Or let me show it you at any rate? Come here.

PETER. No, no—not for worlds!

DR STO. Well, but just come here then. Do you see we have got a table cover?

PETER. Yes, I noticed it.

DR STO. And we have got a lampshade too. Do you see? All out of Katherine's savings! It makes the room so cozy. Don't you think so? Just stand here for a moment—no, no, not there—just here, that's it! Look now, when you get the light on it altogether—I really think it looks very nice, doesn't it?

PETER. Oh, if you can afford luxuries of this kind——

DR STO. Yes, I can afford it now. Katherine tells me I earn almost as much as we spend.

PETER. Almost—yes!

DR STO. But a scientific man must live in a little bit of style. I am quite sure an ordinary civil servant spends more in a year than I do.

PETER. I daresay. A civil servant—a man in a well-paid position——

DR STO. Well, any ordinary merchant then! A man in that position spends two or three times as much as——

PETER. It just depends on circumstances.

DR STO. At all events I assure you I don't waste money unprofitably. But I can't find it in my heart to deny myself the pleasure of entertaining my friends. I need that sort of thing, you know. I have lived for so long shut out of it all that it is a necessity of life to me to mix with young, eager, ambitious men, men of liberal and active minds; and that describes every one of those fellows who are enjoying their supper in there. I wish you knew more of Hovstad.

PETER. By the way, Hovstad was telling me he was going to print another article of yours.

DR STO. An article of mine?

PETER. Yes, about the Baths. An article you wrote in the winter.

DR STO. Oh, that one! No, I don't intend that to appear just for the present.

PETER. Why not? It seems to me that this would be the most opportune moment.

DR STO. Yes, very likely—under normal conditions. [*Crosses the room.*]

PETER [*following him with his eyes*]. Is there anything abnormal about the present conditions?

DR STO. [*standing still*]. To tell you the truth, Peter, I can't say just at this moment—at all events not tonight. There may be much that is very abnormal about the present conditions—and it is possible there may be nothing abnormal about them at all. It is quite possible it may be merely my imagination.

PETER. I must say it all sounds most mysterious. Is there something going on that I am to be kept in ignorance of? I should have imagined that I, as chairman of the governing body of the Baths——

Dr Sto. And I should have imagined that I— Oh, come, don't let us fly out at one another, Peter.

Peter. Heaven forbid! I am not in the habit of flying out at people, as you call it. But I am entitled to request most emphatically that all arrangements shall be made in a businesslike manner, through the proper channels, and shall be dealt with by the legally constituted authorities. I can allow no going behind our backs by any roundabout means.

Dr Sto. Have I ever at any time tried to go behind your backs?

Peter. You have an ingrained tendency to take your own way at all events, and that is almost equally inadmissible in a well-ordered community. The individual ought undoubtedly to acquiesce in subordinating himself to the community —or, to speak more accurately, to the authorities who have the care of the community's welfare.

Dr Sto. Very likely. But what the deuce has all this got to do with me?

Peter. That is exactly what you never appear to be willing to learn, my dear Thomas. But, mark my words, someday you will have to suffer for it—sooner or later. Now I have told you. Good-by.

Dr Sto. Have you taken leave of your senses? You are on the wrong scent altogether.

Peter. I am not usually that. You must excuse me now if I— [*Calls into the dining room.*] Good night, Katherine. Good night, gentlemen. [*Goes out.*]

Mrs Sto. [*coming from the dining room*]. Has he gone?

Dr Sto. Yes, and in such a bad temper.

Mrs Sto. But, dear Thomas, what have you been doing to him again?

Dr Sto. Nothing at all. And, anyhow, he can't oblige me to make my report before the proper time.

Mrs Sto. What have you got to make a report to him about?

Dr Sto. Hm! Leave that to me, Katherine. . . . It is an extraordinary thing that the postman doesn't come.

[Hovstad, Billing *and* Horster *have got up from the table and come into the sitting room.* Ejlif *and* Morten *come in after them.*]

Bill. [*stretching himself*]. Ah!—one feels a new man after a meal like that.

Hov. The mayor wasn't in a very sweet temper tonight, then.

Dr Sto. It is his stomach; he has a wretched digestion.

Hov. I rather think it was us two of the *People's Messenger* that he couldn't digest.

Mrs Sto. I thought you came out of it pretty well with him.

Hov. Oh yes, but it isn't anything more than a sort of truce.

Bill. That is just what it is! That word sums up the situation.

Dr Sto. We must remember that Peter is a lonely man, poor chap. He has no home comforts of any kind; nothing but everlasting business. And all that infernal weak-tea wash that he pours into himself! Now then, my boys, bring chairs up to the table. Aren't we going to have that toddy, Katherine?

Mrs Sto. [*going into the dining room*]. I am just getting it.

Dr Sto. Sit down here on the couch beside me, Captain Horster. We so seldom see you. Please sit down, my friends.

[*They sit down at the table.* Mrs Stockmann *brings a tray, with a spirit lamp, glasses, bottles, etc., upon it.*]

MRS STO. There you are! This is arrack and this is rum and this one is the brandy. Now everyone must help himself.

DR STO. [*taking a glass*]. We will. [*They all mix themselves some toddy.*] And let us have the cigars. Ejlif, you know where the box is. And you, Morten, can fetch my pipe. [*The two boys go into the room on the right.*] I have a suspicion that Ejlif pockets a cigar now and then!—but I take no notice of it. [*Calls out.*] And my smoking cap too, Morten. Katherine, you can tell him where I left it. Ah, he has got it. [*The boys bring the various things.*] Now, my friends. I stick to my pipe, you know. This one has seen plenty of bad weather with me up north. [*Touches glasses with them.*] Your good health! Ah, it is good to be sitting snug and warm here.

MRS STO. [*who sits knitting*]. Do you sail soon, Captain Horster?

HORS. I expect to be ready to sail next week.

MRS STO. I suppose you are going to America?

HORS. Yes, that is the plan.

MRS STO. Then you won't be able to take part in the coming election.

HORS. Is there going to be an election?

BILL. Didn't you know?

HORS. No, I don't mix myself up with those things.

BILL. But do you not take an interest in public affairs?

HORS. No, I don't know anything about politics.

BILL. All the same, one ought to vote at any rate.

HORS. Even if one doesn't know anything about what is going on?

BILL. Doesn't know! What do you mean by that? A community is like a ship; everyone ought to be prepared to take the helm.

HORS. Maybe that is all very well on shore, but on board ship it wouldn't work.

HOV. It is astonishing how little most sailors care about what goes on on shore.

BILL. Very extraordinary.

DR STO. Sailors are like birds of passage: they feel equally at home in any latitude. And that is only an additional reason for our being all the more keen, Hovstad. Is there to be anything of public interest in tomorrow's *Messenger?*

HOV. Nothing about municipal affairs. But the day after tomorrow I was thinking of printing your article——

DR STO. Ah, devil take it—my article! Look here, that must wait a bit.

HOV. Really? We had just got convenient space for it, and I thought it was just the opportune moment——

DR STO. Yes, yes, very likely you are right; but it must wait all the same. I will explain to you later.

[PETRA *comes in from the hall in hat and cloak and with a bundle of exercise books under her arm.*]

PETRA. Good evening.

DR STO. Good evening, Petra; come along.

[*Mutual greetings;* PETRA *takes off her things and puts them down on a chair by the door.*]

PETRA. And you have all been sitting here enjoying yourselves while I have been out slaving!

DR STO. Well, come and enjoy yourself too!

BILL. May I mix a glass for you?

PETRA [*coming to the table*]. Thanks, I would rather do it; you always mix it too strong. But I forgot, Father—I have a letter for you. [*Goes to the chair where she has laid her things.*]

DR STO. A letter? From whom?

PETRA [*looking in her coat pocket*]. The postman gave it to me just as I was going out.

DR STO. [*getting up and going to her.*] And you only give it to me now!

PETRA. I really had not time to run up again. There it is!

DR STO. [*seizing the letter*]. Let's see, let's see, child! [*Looks at the address.*] Yes, that's all right!

MRS STO. Is it the one you have been expecting so anxiously, Thomas?

DR STO. Yes, it is. I must go to my room now and—— Where shall I get a light, Katherine? Is there no lamp in my room again?

MRS STO. Yes, your lamp is already lit on your desk.

DR STO. Good, good. Excuse me for a moment. [*Goes into his study.*]

PETRA. What do you suppose it is, Mother?

MRS STO. I don't know; for the last day or two he has always been asking if the postman has not been.

BILL. Probably some country patient.

PETRA. Poor old Dad!—he will overwork himself soon. [*Mixes a glass for herself.*] There, that will taste good!

HOV. Have you been teaching in the evening school again today?

PETRA [*sipping from her glass*]. Two hours.

BILL. And four hours of school in the morning——

PETRA. Five hours.

MRS STO. And you have still got exercises to correct, I see.

PETRA. A whole heap, yes.

HORS. You are pretty full up with work too, it seems to me.

PETRA. Yes—but that is good. One is so delightfully tired after it.

BILL. Do you like that?

PETRA. Yes, because one sleeps so well then.

MOR. You must be dreadfully wicked, Petra.

PETRA. Wicked?

MOR. Yes, because you work so much. Mr Rörlund says work is a punishment for our sins.

EJL. Pooh, what a duffer you are to believe a thing like that!

MRS STO. Come, come, Ejlif!

BILL [*laughing*]. That's capital!

HOV. Don't you want to work as hard as that, Morten?

MOR. No, indeed I don't.

HOV. What do you want to be then?

MOR. I should like best to be a Viking.

EJL. You would have to be a pagan then.

MOR. Well, I could become a pagan, couldn't I?

BILL. I agree with you, Morten! My sentiments exactly.

MRS STO. [*signaling to him*]. I am sure that is not true, Mr Billing.

BILL. Yes, I swear it is! I am a pagan and I am proud of it. Believe me, before long we shall all be pagans.

MOR. And then shall be allowed to do anything we like?

BILL. Well, you see, Morten——

MRS STO. You must go to your room now, boys; I am sure you have some lessons to learn for tomorrow.

EJL. I should like so much to stay a little longer.

MRS STO. No, no; away you go, both of you.

[*The boys say good night and go*

into the room on the left.]

HOV. Do you really think it can do the boys any harm to hear such things?

MRS STO. I don't know, but I don't like it.

PETRA. But you know, Mother, I think you really are wrong about it.

MRS STO. Maybe, but I don't like it —not in our own home.

PETRA. There is so much falsehood both at home and at school. At home one must not speak, and at school we have to stand and tell lies to the children.

HORS. Tell lies?

PETRA. Yes, don't you suppose we have to teach them all sorts of things that we don't believe?

BILL. That is perfectly true.

PETRA. If only I had the means I would start a school of my own, and it would be conducted on very different lines.

BILL. Oh, bother the means!

HORS. Well, if you are thinking of that, Miss Stockmann, I shall be delighted to provide you with a schoolroom. The great big old house my father left me is standing almost empty; there is an immense dining room downstairs——

PETRA [*laughing*]. Thank you very much, but I am afraid nothing will come of it.

HOV. No, Miss Petra is much more likely to take to journalism, I expect. By the way, have you had time to do anything with that English story you promised to translate for us?

PETRA. No, not yet; but you shall have it in good time.

[DR STOCKMANN *comes in from his room with an open letter in his hand.*]

DR STO. [*waving the letter*]. Well, now the town will have something new to talk about, I can tell you!

BILL. Something new?

MRS STO. What is this?

DR STO. A great discovery, Katherine.

HOV. Really?

MRS STO. A discovery of yours?

DR STO. A discovery of mine. [*Walks up and down.*] Just let them come saying, as usual, that it is all fancy and a crazy man's imagination! But they will be careful what they say this time, I can tell you!

PETRA. But, Father, tell us what it is.

DR STO. Yes, yes—only give me time, and you shall know all about it. If only I had Peter here now! It just shows how we men can go about forming our judgments when in reality we are as blind as any moles.

HOV. What are you driving at, Doctor?

DR STO. [*standing still by the table*]. Isn't it the universal opinion that our town is a healthy spot?

HOV. Certainly.

DR STO. Quite an unusually healthy spot, in fact—a place that deserves to be recommended in the warmest possible manner either for invalids or for people who are well.

MRS STO. Yes, but my dear Thomas——

DR STO. And we have been recommending it and praising it—I have written and written, both in the *Messenger* and in pamphlets——

HOV. Well, what then?

DR STO. And the Baths—we have called them the "main artery of the town's lifeblood," the "nerve center of our town," and the devil knows what else.

BILL. "The town's pulsating heart" was the expression I once used on an important occasion.

Dr Sto. Quite so. Well, do you know what they really are, these great, splendid, much-praised Baths that have cost so much money—do you know what they are?

Hov. No, what are they?

Mrs Sto. Yes, what are they?

Dr Sto. The whole place is a pest-house!

Petra. The baths, Father?

Mrs Sto. [*at the same time*]. Our Baths!

Hov. But, Doctor——

Bill. Absolutely incredible!

Dr Sto. The whole Bath establishment is a whited, poisoned sepulcher, I tell you—the gravest possible danger to the public health! All the nastiness up at Mölledal, all that stinking filth, is infecting the water in the conduit pipes leading to the reservoir, and the same cursed, filthy poison oozes out on the shore too.

Hors. Where the bathing place is?

Dr Sto. Just there.

Hov. How do you come to be so certain of all this, Doctor?

Dr Sto. I have investigated the matter most conscientiously. For a long time past I have suspected something of the kind. Last year we had some very strange cases of illness among the visitors—typhoid cases and cases of gastric fever——

Mrs Sto. Yes, that is quite true.

Dr Sto. At the time we supposed the visitors had been infected before they came; but later on, in the winter, I began to have a different opinion, and so I set myself to examine the water as well as I could.

Mrs Sto. Then that is what you have been so busy with?

Dr Sto. Indeed, I have been busy, Katherine. But here I had none of the necessary scientific apparatus; so I sent samples, both of the drinking water and of the sea water, up to the university to have an accurate analysis made by a chemist.

Hov. And have you got that?

Dr Sto. [*showing him the letter*]. Here it is! It proves the presence of decomposed organic matter in the water—it is full of infusoria. The water is absolutely dangerous to use, either internally or externally.

Mrs Sto. What a mercy you discovered it in time.

Dr Sto. You may well say so.

Hov. And what do you propose to do now, Doctor?

Dr Sto. To see the matter put right—naturally.

Hov. Can that be done?

Dr Sto. It must be done. Otherwise the Baths will be absolutely useless and wasted. But we need not anticipate that; I have a very clear idea what we shall have to do.

Mrs Sto. But why have you kept this all so secret, dear?

Dr Sto. Do you suppose I was going to run about the town gossiping about it before I had absolute proof? No, thank you. I am not such a fool.

Petra. Still you might have told us.

Dr Sto. Not a living soul. But tomorrow you may run round to the old Badger——

Mrs Sto. Oh, Thomas! Thomas!

Dr Sto. Well, to your grandfather then. The old boy will have something to be astonished at! I know he thinks I am cracked—and there are lots of other people think so too, I have noticed. But now these good folks shall see—they shall just see! [*Walks about, rubbing his hands.*] There will be a nice upset in the town, Katherine; you can't imagine what it will be. All the conduit pipes will have to be relaid.

Hov. [*getting up*]. All the conduit pipes?

Dr Sto. Yes, of course. The intake is too low down; it will have to be lifted to a position much higher up.

Petra. Then you were right after all.

Dr Sto. Ah, you remember, Petra —I wrote opposing the plans before the work was begun. But at that time no one would listen to me. Well, I am going to let them have it now! Of course I have prepared a report for the Baths Committee; I have had it ready for a week and was only waiting for this to come. [*Shows the letter.*] Now it shall go off at once. [*Goes into his room and comes back with some papers.*] Look at that! Four closely written sheets!—and the letter shall go with them. Give me a bit of paper, Katherine—something to wrap them up in. That will do! Now give it to—to—[*stamps his foot*]—what the deuce is her name?—give it to the maid and tell her to take it at once to the mayor.

[Mrs Stockmann *takes the packet and goes out through the dining room.*]

Petra. What do you think Uncle Peter will say, Father?

Dr Sto. What is there for him to say? I should think he would be very glad that such an important truth has been brought to light.

Hov. Will you let me print a short note about your discovery in the *Messenger?*

Dr Sto. I shall be very much obliged if you will.

Hov. It is very desirable that the public should be informed of it without delay.

Dr Sto. Certainly.

Mrs Sto. [*coming back*]. She has just gone with it.

Bill. Upon my soul, Doctor, you are going to be the foremost man in the town.

Dr Sto. [*walking about happily*]. Nonsense! As a matter of fact, I have done nothing more than my duty. I have only made a lucky find—that's all. Still, all the same——

Bill. Hovstad, don't you think the town ought to give Doctor Stockmann some sort of testimonial?

Hov. I will suggest it, anyway.

Bill. And I will speak to Aslaksen about it.

Dr Sto. No, my good friends, don't let us have any of that nonsense. I won't hear of anything of the kind. And if the Baths Committee should think of voting me an increase of salary, I will not accept it. Do you hear, Katherine?—I won't accept it.

Mrs Sto. You are quite right, Thomas.

Petra [*lifting her glass*]. Your health, Father!

Hov. *and* Bill. Your health, Doctor! Good health!

Hors. [*touches glasses with* Dr. Stockmann]. I hope it will bring you nothing but good luck.

Dr Sto. Thank you, thank you, my dear fellows! I feel tremendously happy! It is a splendid thing for a man to be able to feel that he has done a service to his native town and to his fellow citizens. Hurrah, Katherine! [*He puts his arms round her and whirls her round and round while she protests with laughing cries. They all laugh, clap their hands and cheer the doctor. The boys put their heads in at the door to see what is going on.*]

ACT II

Scene—*The same. The door into the dining room is shut. It is morning.* Mrs Stockmann, *with a sealed letter in her hand, comes in from the dining room, goes to the door of the doctor's study and peeps in.*

Mrs Sto. Are you in, Thomas?

Dr Sto. [*from within his room*]. Yes, I have just come in. [*Comes into the room.*] What is it?

Mrs Sto. A letter from your brother.

Dr Sto. Aha, let us see! [*Opens the letter and reads.*] "I return herewith the manuscript you sent me——" [*Reads on in a low murmur.*] Hm!

Mrs Sto. What does he say?

Dr Sto. [*putting the paper in his pocket*]. Oh, he only writes that he will come up here himself about midday.

Mrs Sto. Well, try and remember to be at home this time.

Dr Sto. That will be all right; I have got through all my morning visits.

Mrs Sto. I am extremely curious to know how he takes it.

Dr Sto. You will see he won't like its having been I, and not he, that made the discovery.

Mrs Sto. Aren't you a little nervous about that?

Dr Sto. Oh, he really will be pleased enough, you know. But at the same time Peter is so confoundedly afraid of anyone's doing any service to the town except himself.

Mrs Sto. I will tell you what, Thomas—you should be good-natured and share the credit of this with him. Couldn't you make out that it was he who set you on the scent of this discovery?

Dr Sto. I am quite willing. If only I can get the thing set right. I——

[Morten Kiil *puts his head in through the door leading from the hall, looks round in an inquiring manner and chuckles.*]

Morten Kiil. [*slyly*]. Is it—is it true?

Mrs Sto. [*going to the door*]. Father!—is it you?

Dr Sto. Ah, Mr Kiil—good morning, good morning!

Mrs Sto. But come along in.

Morten Kiil. If it is true, I will; if not, I am off.

Dr Sto. If what is true?

Morten Kiil. This tale about the water supply. Is it true?

Dr Sto. Certainly it is true. But how did you come to hear it?

Morten Kiil. [*coming in*]. Petra ran in on her way to the school——

Dr Sto. Did she?

Morten Kiil. Yes, and she declares that—— I thought she was only making a fool of me, but it isn't like Petra to do that.

Dr Sto. Of course not. How could you imagine such a thing!

Morten Kiil. Oh well, it is better never to trust anybody; you may find you have been made a fool of before you know where you are. But it is really true all the same?

Dr Sto. You can depend upon it that it is true. Won't you sit down? [*Settles him on the couch.*] Isn't it a real bit of luck for the town?

Morten Kiil [*suppressing his laughter*]. A bit of luck for the town?

Dr Sto. Yes, that I made the discovery in good time.

Morten Kiil [*as before*]. Yes, yes, yes! But I should never have thought you the sort of man to pull your own brother's leg like this!

DR STO. Pull his leg?

MRS STO. Really, Father dear——

MORTEN KIIL [*resting his hands and his chin on the handle of his stick and winking slying at the doctor*]. Let me see, what was the story? Some kind of beast that had got into the water pipes, wasn't it?

DR STO. Infusoria—yes.

MORTEN KIIL. And a lot of these beasts had got in, according to Petra—a tremendous lot.

DR STO. Certainly; hundreds of thousands of them, probably.

MORTEN KIIL. But no one can see them—isn't that so?

DR STO. Yes, you can't see them.

MORTEN KIIL [*with a quiet chuckle*]. Damme—it's the finest story I have ever heard!

DR STO. What do you mean?

MORTEN KIIL. But you will never get the mayor to believe a thing like that.

DR STO. We shall see.

MORTEN KIIL. Do you think he will be fool enough to?

DR STO. I hope the whole town will be fools enough.

MORTEN KIIL. The whole town! Well, it wouldn't be a bad thing. It would just serve them right and teach them a lesson. They think themselves so much cleverer than we old fellows. They hounded me out of the council; they did, I tell you—they hounded me out. Now they shall pay for it. You pull their legs too, Thomas!

DR STO. Really, I——

MORTEN KIIL. You pull their legs! [*Gets up.*] If you can work it so that the mayor and his friends all swallow the same bait, I will give ten pounds to a charity—like a shot!

DR STO. That is very kind of you.

MORTEN KIIL. Yes, I haven't got much money to throw away, I can tell you; but if you can work this, I will give five pounds to a charity at Christmas.

[HOVSTAD *comes in by the hall door.*]

HOV. Good morning! [*Stops.*] Oh, I beg your pardon.

DR STO. Not at all; come in.

MORTEN KIIL [*with another chuckle*]. Oho!—is he in this too?

HOV. What do you mean?

DR STO. Certainly he is.

MORTEN KIIL. I might have known it! It must get into the papers. You know how to do it, Thomas! Set your wits to work. Now I must go.

DR STO. Won't you stay a little while?

MORTEN KIIL. No, I must be off now. You keep up this game for all it is worth; you won't repent it, I'm damned if you will! [*He goes out;* MRS STOCKMANN *follows him into the hall.*]

DR STO. [*laughing*]. Just imagine—the old chap doesn't believe a word of all this about the water supply.

HOV. Oh, that was it then?

DR STO. Yes, that was what we were talking about. Perhaps it is the same thing that brings you here?

HOV. Yes, it is. Can you spare me a few minutes, Doctor?

DR STO. As long as you like, my dear fellow.

HOV. Have you heard from the mayor yet?

DR STO. Not yet. He is coming here later.

HOV. I have given the matter a great deal of thought since last night.

DR STO. Well?

HOV. From your point of view, as a doctor and a man of science, this affair of the water supply is an isolated matter. I mean, you do not realize that it involves a great many other things.

Dr Sto. How do you mean? Let us sit down, my dear fellow. No, sit here on the couch. [Hovstad *sits down on the couch,* Dr Stockmann *on a chair on the other side of the table.*] Now then. You mean that——

Hov. You said yesterday that the pollution of the water was due to impurities in the soil.

Dr Sto. Yes, unquestionably it is due to that poisonous morass up at Mölledal.

Hov. Begging your pardon, Doctor, I fancy it is due to quite another morass altogether.

Dr Sto. What morass?

Hov. The morass that the whole life of our town is built on and is rotting in.

Dr Sto. What the deuce are you driving at, Hovstad?

Hov. The whole of the town's interests have, little by little, got into the hands of a pack of officials.

Dr Sto. Oh, come!—they are not all officials.

Hov. No, but those that are not officials are at any rate the officials' friends and adherents; it is the wealthy folk, the old families in the town, that have got us entirely in their hands.

Dr Sto. Yes, but after all they are men of ability and knowledge.

Hov. Did they show any ability or knowledge when they laid the conduit pipes where they are now?

Dr Sto. No, of course that was a great piece of stupidity on their part. But that is going to be set right now.

Hov. Do you think that will be all such plain sailing?

Dr Sto. Plain sailing or no, it has got to be done anyway.

Hov. Yes, provided the press takes up the question.

Dr Sto. I don't think that will be necessary, my dear fellow; I am certain my brother——

Hov. Excuse me, Doctor; I feel bound to tell you I am inclined to take the matter up.

Dr Sto. In the paper?

Hov. Yes. When I took over the *People's Messenger* my idea was to break up this ring of self-opinionated old fossils who had got hold of all the influence.

Dr Sto. But you know you told me yourself what the result had been; you nearly ruined your paper.

Hov. Yes, at the time we were obliged to climb down a peg or two, it is quite true, because there was a danger of the whole project of the Baths coming to nothing if they failed us. But now the scheme has been carried through, and we can dispense with these grand gentlemen.

Dr Sto. Dispense with them, yes; but we owe them a great debt of gratitude.

Hov. That shall be recognized ungrudgingly. But a journalist of my democratic tendencies cannot let such an opportunity as this slip. The bubble of official infallibility must be pricked. This superstition must be destroyed like any other.

Dr Sto. I am wholeheartedly with you in that, Mr Hovstad; if it is a superstition, away with it!

Hov. I should be very reluctant to bring the mayor into it, because he is your brother. But I am sure you will agree with me that truth should be the first consideration.

Dr Sto. That goes without saying.

[*With sudden emphasis.*] Yes, but—but——

Hov. You must not misjudge me. I am neither more self-interested nor more ambitious than most men.

Dr Sto. My dear fellow—who suggests anything of the kind?

Hov. I am of humble origin, as you know, and that has given me opportunities of knowing what is the most crying need in the humbler ranks of life. It is that they should be allowed some part in the direction of public affairs, Doctor. That is what will develop their faculties and intelligence and self-respect——

Dr Sto. I quite appreciate that.

Hov. Yes—and in my opinion a journalist incurs a heavy responsibility if he neglects a favorable opportunity of emancipating the masses—the humble and oppressed. I know well enough that in exalted circles I shall be called an agitator and all that sort of thing, but they may call me what they like. If only my conscience doesn't reproach me, then——

Dr Sto. Quite right. Quite right, Mr Hovstad. But all the same—devil take it! [*A knock is heard at the door.*] Come in!

[Aslaksen *appears at the door. He is poorly but decently dressed in black, with a slightly crumpled white neckcloth; he wears gloves and has a felt hat in his hand.*]

Asl. [*bowing*]. Excuse my taking the liberty, Doctor——

Dr Sto. [*getting up*]. Ah, it is you, Aslaksen!

Asl. Yes, Doctor.

Hov. [*standing up*]. Is it me you want, Aslaksen?

Asl. No, I didn't know I should find you here. No, it was the doctor I——

Dr Sto. I am quite at your service. What is it?

Asl. Is what I heard from Mr Billing true, sir—that you mean to improve our water supply?

Dr Sto. Yes, for the Baths.

Asl. Quite so, I understand. Well, I have come to say that I will back that up by every means in my power.

Hov. [*to the doctor*]. You see!

Dr Sto. I shall be very grateful to you, but——

Asl. Because it may be no bad thing to have us small tradesmen at your back. We form, as it were, a compact majority in the town—if we choose. And it is always a good thing to have the majority with you, Doctor.

Dr Sto. That is undeniably true, but I confess I don't see why such unusual precautions should be necessary in this case. It seems to me that such a plain, straightforward thing——

Asl. Oh, it may be very desirable all the same. I know our local authorities so well; officials are not generally very ready to act on proposals that come from other people. That is why I think it would not be at all amiss if we made a little demonstration.

Hov. That's right.

Dr Sto. Demonstration, did you say? What on earth are you going to make a demonstration about?

Asl. We shall proceed with the greatest moderation, Doctor. Moderation is always my aim; it is the greatest virtue in a citizen—at least I think so.

Dr Sto. It is well known to be a characteristic of yours, Mr Aslaksen.

Asl. Yes, I think I may pride myself on that. And this matter of the water supply is of the greatest importance to us small tradesmen. The Baths promise to be a regular gold mine for the town. We shall all make our living out of them, especially those of us who are householders. That is why we will back up the project as strongly as possible. And as I am at present chairman of the Householders' Association——

DR STO. Yes?

ASL. And, what is more, local secretary of the Temperance Society—— You know, sir, I suppose, that I am a worker in the temperance cause?

DR STO. Of course, of course.

ASL. Well, you can understand that I come into contact with a great many people. And as I have the reputation of a temperate and law-abiding citizen—like yourself, Doctor—I have a certain influence in the town, a little bit of power, if I may be allowed to say so.

DR STO. I know that quite well, Mr Aslaksen.

ASL. So you see it would be an easy matter for me to set on foot some testimonial, if necessary.

DR STO. A testimonial?

ASL. Yes, some kind of an address of thanks from the townsmen for your share in a matter of such importance to the community. I need scarcely say that it would have to be drawn up with the greatest regard to moderation, so as not to offend the authorities—who, after all, have the reins in their hands. If we pay strict attention to that, no one can take it amiss, I should think!

HOV. Well, and even supposing they didn't like it——

ASL. No, no, no; there must be no discourtesy to the authorities, Mr Hovstad. It is no use falling foul of those upon whom our welfare so closely depends. I have done that in my time, and no good ever comes of it. But no one can take exception to a reasonable and frank expression of a citizen's views.

DR STO. [*shaking him by the hand*]. I can't tell you, dear Mr Aslaksen, how extremely pleased I am to find such hearty support among my fellow citizens. I am delighted—delighted! Now you will take a small glass of sherry, eh?

ASL. No, thank you; I never drink alcohol of that kind.

DR STO. Well, what do you say to a glass of beer then?

ASL. Nor that either, thank you, Doctor. I never drink anything as early as this. I am going into town now to talk over with one or two householders and prepare the ground.

DR STO. It is tremendously kind of you, Mr Aslaksen, but I really cannot understand the necessity for all these precautions. It seems to me that the thing should go of itself.

ASL. The authorities are somewhat slow to move, Doctor. Far be it from me to seem to blame them——

HOV. We are going to stir them up in the paper tomorrow, Aslaksen.

ASL. But not violently, I trust, Mr Hovstad. Proceed with moderation, or you will do nothing with them. You may take my advice; I have gathered my experience in the school of life. Well, I must say good-by, Doctor. You know now that we small tradesmen are at your back at all events, like a solid wall. You have the compact majority on your side, Doctor.

DR STO. I am very much obliged, dear Mr Aslaksen. [*Shakes hands with him.*] Good-by, good-by.

ASL. Are you going my way,

toward the printing office, Mr Hovstad?

Hov. I will come later; I have something to settle up first.

Asl. Very well. [*Bows and goes out;* Stockmann *follows him into the hall.*]

Hov. [*as* Stockmann *comes in again*]. Well, what do you think of that, Doctor? Don't you think it is high time we stirred a little life into all this slackness and vacillation and cowardice?

Dr Sto. Are you referring to Aslaksen?

Hov. Yes, I am. He is one of those who are floundering in a bog—decent enough fellow though he may be otherwise. And most of the people here are in just the same case—seesawing and edging first to one side and then to the other, so overcome with caution and scruple that they never dare to take any decided step.

Dr Sto. Yes, but Aslaksen seemed to me so thoroughly well intentioned.

Hov. There is one thing I esteem higher than that, and that is for a man to be self-reliant and sure of himself.

Dr Sto. I think you are perfectly right there.

Hov. That is why I want to seize this opportunity and try if I cannot manage to put a little virility into these well-intentioned people for once. The idol of Authority must be shattered in this town. This gross and inexcusable blunder about the water supply must be brought home to the mind of every municipal voter.

Dr Sto. Very well; if you are of opinion that it is for the good of the community, so be it. But not until I have had a talk with my brother.

Hov. Anyway, I will get a leading article ready, and if the mayor refuses to take the matter up——

Dr Sto. How can you suppose such a thing possible?

Hov. It is conceivable. And in that case——

Dr Sto. In that case I promise you —— Look here, in that case you may print my report—every word of it.

Hov. May I? Have I your word for it?

Dr Sto. [*giving him the MS*]. Here it is; take it with you. It can do no harm for you to read it through, and you can give it me back later on.

Hov. Good, good! That is what I will do. And now good-by, Doctor.

Dr Sto. Good-by, good-by. You will see everything will run quite smoothly, Mr Hovstad—quite smoothly.

Hov. Hm!—we shall see. [*Bows and goes out.*]

Dr Sto. [*opens the dining-room door and looks in*]. Katherine! Oh, you are back, Petra?

Petra [*coming in*]. Yes, I have just come from the school.

Mrs Sto. [*coming in*]. Has he not been here yet?

Dr Sto. Peter? No. But I have had a long talk with Hovstad. He is quite excited about my discovery. I find it has a much wider bearing than I at first imagined. And he has put his paper at my disposal if necessity should arise.

Mrs Sto. Do you think it will?

Dr Sto. Not for a moment. But at all events it makes me feel proud to know that I have the liberal-minded independent press on my side. Yes, and—just imagine—I have had a visit from the chairman of the Householders' Association!

Mrs Sto. Oh! What did he want?

DR STO. To offer me his support too. They will support me in a body if it should be necessary. Katherine—do you know what I have got behind me?

MRS STO. Behind you? No, what have you got behind you?

DR STO. The compact majority.

MRS STO. Really? Is that a good thing for you, Thomas?

DR STO. I should think it was a good thing. [*Walks up and down rubbing his hands.*] By Jove, it's a fine thing to feel this bond of brotherhood between oneself and one's fellow citizens!

PETRA. And to be able to do so much that is good and useful, Father!

DR STO. And for one's own native town into the bargain, my child!

MRS STO. That was a ring at the bell

DR STO. It must be he then. [*A knock is heard at the door.*] Come in!

PETER [*comes in from the hall*]. Good morning.

DR STO. Glad to see you, Peter!

MRS STO. Good morning, Peter. How are you?

PETER. So-so, thank you. [*To* DR STOCKMANN.] I received from you yesterday, after office hours, a report dealing with the condition of the water at the Baths.

DR STO. Yes. Have you read it?

PETER. Yes, I have.

DR STO. And what have you to say to it?

PETER [*with a sidelong glance*]. Hm!

MRS STO. Come along, Petra. [*She and* PETRA *go into the room on the left.*]

PETER [*after a pause*]. Was it necessary to make all these investigations behind my back?

DR STO. Yes, because until I was absolutely certain about it——

PETER. Then you mean that you are absolutely certain now?

DR STO. Surely you are convinced of that.

PETER. Is it your intention to bring this document before the Baths Committee as a sort of official communication?

DR STO. Certainly. Something must be done in the matter—and that quickly.

PETER. As usual, you employ violent expressions in your report. You say, among other things, that what we offer visitors in our Baths is a permanent supply of poison.

DR STO. Well, can you describe it any other way, Peter? Just think—water that is poisonous, whether you drink it or bathe in it! And this we offer to the poor sick folk who come to us trustfully and pay us at an exorbitant rate to be made well again!

PETER. And your reasoning leads you to this conclusion, that we must build a sewer to draw off the alleged impurities from Mölledal and must relay the water conduits.

DR STO. Yes. Do you see any other way out of it? I don't.

PETER. I made a pretext this morning to go and see the town engineer and, as if only half seriously, broached the subject of these proposals as a thing we might perhaps have to take under consideration sometime later on.

DR STO. Sometime later on!

PETER. He smiled at what he considered to be my extravagance, naturally. Have you taken the trouble to consider what your proposed alterations would cost? According to the information I obtained, the expenses would probably mount up to fifteen or twenty thousand pounds.

Dr Sto. Would it cost so much?

Peter. Yes, and the worst part of it would be that the work would take at least two years.

Dr Sto. Two years? Two whole years?

Peter. At least. And what are we to do with the Baths in the meantime? Close them? Indeed, we should be obliged to. And do you suppose anyone would come near the place after it had got about that the water was dangerous?

Dr Sto. Yes, but, Peter, that is what it is.

Peter. And all this at this juncture—just as the Baths are beginning to be known. There are other towns in the neighborhood with qualifications to attract visitors for bathing purposes. Don't you suppose they would immediately strain every nerve to divert the entire stream of strangers to themselves? Unquestionably they would, and then where should we be? We should probably have to abandon the whole thing, which has cost us so much money—and then you would have ruined your native town.

Dr Sto. I—should have ruined——

Peter. It is simply and solely through the Baths that the town has before it any future worth mentioning. You know that just as well as I.

Dr Sto. But what do you think ought to be done then?

Peter. Your report has not convinced me that the condition of the water at the Baths is as bad as you represent it to be.

Dr Sto. I tell you it is even worse! —or at all events it will be in summer, when the warm weather comes.

Peter. As I said, I believe you exaggerate the matter considerably. A capable physician ought to know what measures to take—he ought to be capable of preventing injurious influences or of remedying them if they become obviously persistent.

Dr Sto. Well? What more?

Peter. The water supply for the Baths is now an established fact, and in consequence must be treated as such. But probably the committee, at its discretion, will not be disinclined to consider the question of how far it might be possible to introduce certain improvements consistently with a reasonable expenditure.

Dr Sto. And do you suppose that I will have anything to do with such a piece of trickery as that?

Peter. Trickery!

Dr Sto. Yes, it would be a trick—a fraud, a lie, a downright crime toward the public, toward the whole community!

Peter. I have not, as I remarked before, been able to convince myself that there is actually any imminent danger.

Dr Sto. You have! It is impossible that you should not be convinced. I know I have represented the facts absolutely truthfully and fairly. And you know it very well, Peter, only you won't acknowledge it. It was owing to your action that both the Baths and the water conduits were built where they are, and that is what you won't acknowledge—that damnable blunder of yours. Pooh!—do you suppose I don't see through you?

Peter. And even if that were true? If I perhaps guard my reputation somewhat anxiously, it is in the interests of the town. Without moral authority I am powerless to direct public affairs as seems, to my judgment, to be best for the common good. And on that account—and for various other reasons too—it appears to me to be a matter of importance that your report should not be delivered to the committee. In the interests of the public you must withhold it. Then later on I will raise the question and we will do our best privately; but nothing of this unfortunate affair—not a single word of it—must come to the ears of the public.

Dr Sto. I am afraid you will not be able to prevent that now, my dear Peter.

Peter. It must and shall be prevented.

Dr Sto. It is no use, I tell you. There are too many people that know about it.

Peter. That know about it? Who? Surely you don't mean those fellows on the *People's Messenger?*

Dr Sto. Yes, they know. The liberal-minded independent press is going to see that you do your duty.

Peter [*after a short pause*]. You are an extraordinarily independent man, Thomas. Have you given no thought to the consequences this may have for yourself?

Dr Sto. Consequences? For me?

Peter. For you and yours, yes.

Dr Sto. What the deuce do you mean?

Peter. I believe I have always behaved in a brotherly way to you—have always been ready to oblige or to help you?

Dr Sto. Yes, you have, and I am grateful to you for it.

Peter. There is no need. Indeed, to some extent I was forced to do so—for my own sake. I always hoped that if I helped to improve your financial position I should be able to keep some check on you.

Dr Sto. What! Then it was only for your own sake——

Peter. Up to a certain point, yes. It is painful for a man in an official position to have his nearest relative compromising himself time after time.

Dr Sto. And do you consider that I do that?

Peter. Yes, unfortunately, you do, without even being aware of it. You have a restless, pugnacious, rebellious disposition. And then there is that disastrous propensity of yours to want to write about every sort of possible and impossible thing. The moment an idea comes into your head you must needs go and write a newspaper article or a whole pamphlet about it.

Dr Sto. Well, but is it not the duty of a citizen to let the public share in any new ideas he may have?

Peter. Oh, the public doesn't require any new ideas. The public is best served by the good old-established ideas it already has.

Dr Sto. And that is your honest opinion?

Peter. Yes, and for once I must talk frankly to you. Hitherto I have tried to avoid doing so because I know how irritable you are, but now I must tell you the truth, Thomas. You have no conception what an amount of harm you do yourself by your impetuosity. You complain of the authorities, you even complain of the government—you are always pulling them to pieces; you insist that you have been neglected and persecuted. But what else can such a cantankerous man as you expect?

Dr Sto. What next? Cantankerous, am I?

Peter. Yes, Thomas, you are an extremely cantankerous man to work with—I know that to my cost. You disregard everything that you ought to have consideration for. You seem completely to forget that it is me you have to thank for your appointment here as medical officer to the Baths.

Dr Sto. I was entitled to it as a matter of course! I and nobody else! I was the first person to see that the town could be made into a flourishing watering place, and I was the only one who saw it at that time. I had to fight single-handed in support of the idea for many years, and I wrote and wrote——

Peter. Undoubtedly. But things were not ripe for the scheme then—though of course you could not judge of that in your out-of-the-way corner up north. But as soon as the opportune moment came I—and the others—took the matter into our hands——

Dr Sto. Yes, and made this mess of all my beautiful plan. It is pretty obvious now what clever fellows you were!

Peter. To my mind the whole thing only seems to mean that you are seeking another outlet for your combativeness. You want to pick a quarrel with your superiors—an old habit of yours. You cannot put up with any authority over you. You look askance at anyone who occupies a superior official position; you regard him as a personal enemy, and then any stick is good enough to beat him with. But now I have called your attention to the fact that the town's interests are at stake—and, incidentally, my own too. And therefore I must tell you, Thomas, that you will find me inexorable with regard to what I am about to require you to do.

Dr Sto. And what is that?

Peter. As you have been so indiscreet as to speak of this delicate matter to outsiders, despite the fact that you ought to have treated it as entirely official and confidential, it is obviously impossible to hush it up now. All sorts of rumors will get about directly, and everybody who has a grudge against us will take care to embellish these rumors. So it will be necessary for you to refute them publicly.

Dr Sto. I! How? I don't understand.

Peter. What we shall expect is that, after making further investigations, you will come to the conclusion that the matter is not by any means as dangerous or as critical as you imagined in the first instance.

Dr Sto. Oho!—so that is what you expect!

Peter. And, what is more, we shall expect you to make public profession of your confidence in the committee and in their readiness to consider fully and conscientiously what steps may be necessary to remedy any possible defects.

Dr Sto. But you will never be able to do that by patching and tinkering at it—never! Take my word for it, Peter; I mean what I say, as deliberately and emphatically as possible.

Peter. As an officer under the committee you have no right to any individual opinion.

Dr Sto. [*amazed*]. No right?

Peter. In your official capacity, no. As a private person it is quite another matter. But as a subordinate member of the staff of the Baths you have no right to express any opinion which runs contrary to that of your superiors.

Dr Sto. This is too much! I, a doctor, a man of science, have no right to——

Peter. The matter in hand is not simply a scientific one. It is a complicated matter and has its economic as well as its technical side.

Dr Sto. I don't care what it is! I intend to be free to express my opinion on any subject under the sun.

Peter. As you please—but not on any subject concerning the Baths. That we forbid.

Dr Sto. [*shouting*]. You forbid! You! A pack of——

Peter. *I* forbid it—I, your chief; and if I forbid it, you have to obey.

Dr Sto. [*controlling himself*]. Peter—if you were not my brother——

Petra [*throwing open the door*]. Father, you shan't stand this!

Mrs Sto. [*coming in after her*]. Petra, Petra!

Peter. Oh, so you have been eavesdropping.

Mrs Sto. You were talking so loud we couldn't help——

Petra. Yes, I was listening.

Peter. Well, after all, I am very glad.

Dr Sto. [*going up to him*]. You were saying something about forbidding and obeying?

Peter. You obliged me to take that tone with you.

Dr Sto. And so I am to give myself the lie publicly?

Peter. We consider it absolutely necessary that you should make some public statement as I have asked for.

Dr Sto. And if I do not—obey?

Peter. Then we shall publish a statement ourselves to reassure the public.

Dr Sto. Very well, but in that case I shall use my pen against you. I stick to what I have said; I will show that I am right and that you are wrong. And what will you do then?

Peter. Then I shall not be able to prevent your being dismissed.

Dr Sto. What?

Petra. Father—dismissed!

Mrs Sto. Dismissed!

Peter. Dismissed from the staff of the Baths. I shall be obliged to propose that you shall immediately be given notice and shall not be allowed any further participation in the Baths' affairs.

Dr Sto. You would dare to do that!

Peter. It is you that are playing the daring game.

Petra. Uncle, that is a shameful way to treat a man like Father!

Mrs Sto. Do hold your tongue, Petra!

Peter [*looking at* Petra]. Oh, so we volunteer our opinions already, do we? Of course. [*To* Mrs Stockmann.] Katherine, I imagine you are the most sensible person in this house. Use any influence you may have over your husband and make him see what this will entail for his family as well as——

Dr Sto. My family is my own concern and nobody else's!

Peter. —for his own family, as I was saying, as well as for the town he lives in.

Dr Sto. It is I who have the real good of the town at heart! I want to lay bare the defects that sooner or later must come to the light of day. I will show whether I love my native town.

Peter. You, who in your blind obstinacy want to cut off the most important source of the town's welfare?

Dr Sto. The source is poisoned, man! Are you mad? We are making our living by retailing filth and corruption! The whole of our flourishing municipal life derives its sustenance from a lie!

Peter. All imagination—or something even worse. The man who can throw out such offensive insinuations about his native town must be an enemy to our community.

Dr Sto. [*going up to him*]. Do you dare to——

Mrs Sto. [*throwing herself between them*]. Thomas!

Petra [*catching her father by the arm*]. Don't lose your temper, Father!

Peter. I will not expose myself to violence. Now you have had a warning, so reflect on what you owe to yourself and your family. Good-by. [*Goes out.*]

Dr Sto. [*walking up and down*]. Am I to put up with such treatment as this? In my own house, Katherine! What do you think of that?

Mrs Sto. Indeed, it is both shameful and absurd, Thomas.

Petra. If only I could give Uncle a piece of my mind.

Dr Sto. It is my own fault. I ought to have flown out at him long ago!—shown my teeth!—bitten! To hear him call me an enemy to our community! Me! I shall not take that lying down, upon my soul!

Mrs Sto. But, dear Thomas, your brother has power on his side.

Dr Sto. Yes, but I have right on mine, I tell you.

Mrs Sto. Oh yes, right—right. What is the use of having right on your side if you have not got might?

Petra. Oh, Mother!—how can you say such a thing?

Dr Sto. Do you imagine that in a free country it is no use having right on your side? You are absurd, Katherine. Besides, haven't I got the liberal-minded independent press to lead the way and the compact majority behind me? That is might enough, I should think!

Mrs Sto. But, good heavens, Thomas, you don't mean to——

Dr Sto. Don't mean to what?

Mrs Sto. To set yourself up in opposition to your brother.

Dr Sto. In God's name, what else do you suppose I should do but take my stand on right and truth?

Petra. Yes, I was just going to say that.

Mrs Sto. But it won't do you any earthly good. If they won't do it, they won't.

Dr Sto. Oho, Katherine! Just give me time and you will see how I will carry the war into their camp.

Mrs Sto. Yes, you carry the war into their camp and you get your dismissal—that is what you will do.

Dr Sto. In any case I shall have done my duty toward the public—toward the community. I, who am called its enemy!

Mrs Sto. But toward your family, Thomas? Toward your own home? Do you think that is doing your duty toward those you have to provide for?

Petra. Ah, don't think always first of us, Mother.

Mrs Sto. Oh, it is easy for you to talk; you are able to shift for yourself if need be. But remember the boys, Thomas, and think a little, too, of yourself and of me.

Dr Sto. I think you are out of your senses, Katherine! If I were to be such a miserable coward as to go on my knees to Peter and his damned crew, do you suppose I should ever know an hour's peace of mind all my life afterward?

MRS STO. I don't know anything about that, but God preserve us from the peace of mind we shall have, all the same, if you go on defying him! You will find yourself again without the means of subsistence, with no income to count upon. I should think we had had enough of that in the old days. Remember that, Thomas; think what that means.

DR STO. [*collecting himself with a struggle and clenching his fists*]. And this is what this slavery can bring upon a free, honorable man! Isn't it horrible, Katherine?

MRS STO. Yes, it is sinful to treat you so, it is perfectly true. But, good heavens, one has to put up with so much injustice in this world. There are the boys, Thomas! Look at them! What is to become of them? Oh no, no, you can never have the heart——

[EJLIF *and* MORTEN *have come in while she was speaking, with their school books in their hands.*]

DR STO. The boys! [*Recovers himself suddenly.*] No, even if the whole world goes to pieces, I will never bow my neck to this yoke! [*Goes toward his room.*]

MRS STO. [*following him*]. Thomas—what are you going to do?

DR STO. [*at his door*]. I mean to have the right to look my sons in the face when they are grown men. [*Goes into his room.*]

MRS STO. [*bursting into tears*]. God help us all!

PETRA. Father is splendid! He will not give in.

[*The boys look on in amazement;* PETRA *signs to them not to speak.*]

ACT III

SCENE—*The editorial office of the* People's Messenger. *The entrance door is on the left-hand side of the back wall; on the right-hand side is another door with glass panels through which the printing room can be seen. Another door in the right-hand wall. In the middle of the room is a large table covered with papers, newspapers and books. In the foreground on the left a window, before which stand a desk and a high stool. There are a couple of easy chairs by the table and other chairs standing along the wall. The room is dingy and uncomfortable; the furniture is old, the chairs stained and torn. In the printing room the compositors are seen at work and a printer is working a hand press.* HOVSTAD *is sitting at the desk writing.* BILLING *comes in from the right with* DR STOCKMANN's *manuscript in his hand.*

BILL. Well, I must say!

HOV. [*still writing*]. Have you read it through?

BILL. [*laying the MS on the desk*]. Yes, indeed I have.

HOV. Don't you think the doctor hits them pretty hard?

BILL. Hard? Bless my soul, he's crushing! Every word falls like—how shall I put it?—like the blow of a sledge hammer.

HOV. Yes, but they are not the people to throw up the sponge at the first blow.

BILL. That is true, and for that reason we must strike blow upon blow until the whole of this aristocracy tumbles to pieces. As I sat in there reading this I almost seemed to see a revolution in being.

HOV. [*turning round*]. Hush! Speak

so that Aslaksen cannot hear you.

BILL. [*lowering his voice*]. Aslaksen is a chickenhearted chap, a coward; there is nothing of the man in him. But this time you will insist on your own way, won't you? You will put the doctor's article in?

HOV. Yes, and if the mayor doesn't like it——

BILL. That will be the devil of a nuisance.

HOV. Well, fortunately we can turn the situation to good account whatever happens. If the mayor will not fall in with the doctor's project, he will have all the small tradesmen down on him—the whole of the Householders' Association and the rest of them. And if he does fall in with it, he will fall out with the whole crowd of large shareholders in the Baths, who up to now have been his most valuable supporters.

BILL. Yes, because they will certainly have to fork out a pretty penny.

HOV. Yes, you may be sure they will. And in this way the ring will be broken up, you see, and then in every issue of the paper we will enlighten the public on the mayor's incapability on one point and another and make it clear that all the positions of trust in the town, the whole control of municipal affairs, ought to be put in the hands of the Liberals.

BILL. That is perfectly true! I see it coming—I see it coming; we are on the threshold of a revolution!

[*A knock is heard at the door.*]

HOV. Hush! [*Calls out.*] Come in! [DR STOCKMANN *comes in by the street door.* HOVSTAD *goes to meet him.*] Ah, it is you, Doctor! Well?

DR STO. You may set to work and print it, Mr Hovstad!

HOV. Has it come to that then?

BILL. Hurrah!

DR STO. Yes, print away. Undoubtedly it has come to that. Now they must take what they get. There is going to be a fight in the town, Mr Billing!

BILL. War to the knife, I hope! We will get our knives to their throats, Doctor!

DR STO. This article is only a beginning. I have already got four or five more sketched out in my head. Where is Aslaksen?

BILL. [*calls into the printing room*]. Aslaksen, just come here for a minute!

HOV. Four or five more articles, did you say? On the same subject?

DR STO. No—far from it, my dear fellow. No, they are about quite another matter. But they all spring from the question of the water supply and the drainage. One thing leads to another, you know. It is like beginning to pull down an old house, exactly.

BILL. Upon my soul, it's true; you find you are not done till you have pulled all the old rubbish down.

ASL. [*coming in*]. Pulled down? You are not thinking of pulling down the Baths, surely, Doctor?

HOV. Far from it; don't be afraid.

DR STO. No, we meant something quite different. Well, what do you think of my article, Mr Hovstad?

HOV. I think it is simply a masterpiece.

DR STO. Do you really think so? Well, I am very pleased, very pleased.

HOV. It is so clear and intelligible. One need have no special knowledge to understand the bearing of it. You will have every enlightened man on your side.

ASL. And every prudent man too, I

hope.

BILL. The prudent and the imprudent—almost the whole town.

ASL. In that case we may venture to print it.

DR STO. I should think so!

HOV. We will put it in tomorrow morning.

DR STO. Of course—you must not lose a single day. What I wanted to ask you, Mr Aslaksen, was if you would supervise the printing of it yourself.

ASL. With pleasure.

DR STO. Take care of it as if it were a treasure! No misprints—every word is important. I will look in again a little later; perhaps you will be able to let me see a proof. I can't tell you how eager I am to see it in print and see it burst upon the public——

BILL. Burst upon them—yes, like a flash of lightning!

DR STO. —and to have it submitted to the judgment of my intelligent fellow townsmen. You cannot imagine what I have gone through today. I have been threatened first with one thing and then with another; they have tried to rob me of my most elementary rights as a man——

BILL. What! Your rights as a man!

DR STO. —they have tried to degrade me, to make a coward of me, to force me to put personal interests before my most sacred convictions.

BILL. That is too much—I'm damned if it isn't.

HOV. Oh, you mustn't be surprised at anything from that quarter.

DR STO. Well, they will get the worst of it with me; they may assure themselves of that. I shall consider the *People's Messenger* my sheet anchor now, and every single day I will bombard them with one article after another, like bombshells——

ASL. Yes, but——

BILL. Hurrah!—it is war, it is war!

DR STO. I shall smite them to the ground—I shall crush them—I shall break down all their defenses before the eyes of the honest public! That is what I shall do!

ASL. Yes, but in moderation, Doctor —proceed with moderation.

BILL. Not a bit of it, not a bit of it! Don't spare the dynamite!

DR STO. Because it is not merely a question of water supply and drains now, you know. No—it is the whole of our social life that we have got to purify and disinfect.

BILL. Spoken like a deliverer!

DR STO. All the incapables must be turned out, you understand—and that in every walk of life! Endless vistas have opened themselves to my mind's eye today. I cannot see it all quite clearly yet, but I shall in time. Young and vigorous standard-bearers—those are what we need and must seek, my friends; we must have new men in command at all our outposts.

BILL. Hear, hear!

DR STO. We only need to stand by one another, and it will all be perfectly easy. The revolution will be launched like a ship that runs smoothly off the stocks. Don't you think so?

HOV. For my part I think we have now a prospect of getting the municipal authority into the hands where it should lie.

ASL. And if only we proceed with moderation, I cannot imagine that there will be any risk.

DR STO. Who the devil cares whether there is any risk or not! What I am doing I am doing in the name of truth and for the sake of my conscience.

Hov. You are a man who deserves to be supported, Doctor.

Asl. Yes, there is no denying that the doctor is a true friend to the town—a real friend to the community, that he is.

Bill. Take my word for it, Aslaksen, Doctor Stockmann is a friend of the people.

Asl. I fancy the Householders' Association will make use of that expression before long.

Dr Sto. [*affected, grasps their hands*]. Thank you, thank you, my dear staunch friends. It is very refreshing to me to hear you say that; my brother called me something quite different. By Jove, he shall have it back, with interest! But now I must be off to see a poor devil. I will come back, as I said. Keep a very careful eye on the manuscript, Aslaksen, and don't for worlds leave out any of my notes of exclamation! Rather put one or two more in! Capital, capital! Well, good-by for the present—good-by, good-by!

[*They show him to the door and bow him out.*]

Hov. He may prove an invaluably useful man to us.

Asl. Yes, so long as he confines himself to this matter of the Baths. But if he goes farther afield, I don't think it would be advisable to follow him.

Hov. Hm!—that all depends.

Bill. You are so infernally timid, Aslaksen!

Asl. Timid? Yes, when it is a question of the local authorities I am timid, Mr Billing; it is a lesson I have learned in the school of experience, let me tell you. But try me in higher politics, in matters that concern the government itself, and then see if I am timid.

Bill. No, you aren't, I admit. But this is simply contradicting yourself.

Asl. I am a man with a conscience, and that is the whole matter. If you attack the government, you don't do the community any harm anyway; those fellows pay no attention to attacks, you see—they go on just as they are in spite of them. But *local* authorities are different; they *can* be turned out, and then perhaps you may get an ignorant lot into office who may do irreparable harm to the householders and everybody else.

Hov. But what of the education of citizens by self-government—don't you attach any importance to that?

Asl. When a man has interests of his own to protect he cannot think of everything, Mr Hovstad.

Hov. Then I hope I shall never have interests of my own to protect!

Bill. Hear, hear!

Asl. [*with a smile*]. Hm! [*Points to the desk.*] Mr Sheriff Stensgaard was your predecessor at that editorial desk.

Bill. [*spitting*]. Bah! That turncoat.

Hov. I am not a weathercock—and never will be.

Asl. A politician should never be too certain of anything, Mr Hovstad. And as for you, Mr Billing, I should think it is time for you to be taking in a reef or two in your sails, seeing that you are applying for the post of secretary to the Bench.

Bill. I!

Hov. Are you, Billing?

Bill. Well, yes—but you must clearly understand I am doing it only to annoy the bigwigs.

Asl. Anyhow, it is no business of mine. But if I am to be accused of timidity and of inconsistency in my principles, this is what I want to point out: my political past is an open book. I have never changed, except perhaps to become a little more moderate, you see. My heart is still with the people, but I don't deny that my reason has a certain bias toward the authorities—the local ones, I mean. [*Goes into the printing room.*]

BILL. Oughtn't we to try and get rid of him, Hovstad?

HOV. Do you know anyone else who will advance the money for our paper and printing bill?

BILL. It is an infernal nuisance that we don't possess some capital to trade on.

HOV. [*sitting down at his desk*]. Yes, if we only had that, then——

BILL. Suppose you were to apply to Doctor Stockmann?

HOV. [*turning over some papers*]. What is the use? He has got nothing.

BILL. No, but he has got a warm man in the background, old Morten Kiil—"the Badger," as they call him.

HOV. [*writing*]. Are you so sure *he* has got anything?

BILL. Good lord, of course he has! And some of it must come to the Stockmanns. Most probably he will do something for the children at all events.

HOV. [*turning half round*]. Are you counting on that?

BILL. Counting on it? Of course I am not counting on anything.

HOV. That is right. And I should not count on the secretaryship to the Bench either, if I were you; for I can assure you—you won't get it.

BILL. Do you think I am not quite aware of that? My object is precisely *not* to get it. A slight of that kind stimulates a man's fighting power—it is like getting a supply of fresh bile—and I am sure one needs that badly enough in a hole-and-corner place like this, where it is so seldom anything happens to stir one up.

HOV. [*writing*]. Quite so, quite so.

BILL. Ah, I shall be heard of yet! Now I shall go and write the appeal to the Householders' Association. [*Goes into the room on the right.*]

HOV. [*sitting at his desk, biting his penholder, says slowly*]. Hm!—that's it, is it? [*A knock is heard.*] Come in! [PETRA *comes in by the outer door.* HOVSTAD *gets up.*] What, you!—here?

PETRA. Yes, you must forgive me.

HOV. [*pulling a chair forward*]. Won't you sit down?

PETRA. No, thank you; I must go again in a moment.

HOV. Have you come with a message from your father, by any chance?

PETRA. No, I have come on my own account. [*Takes a book out of her coat pocket.*] Here is the English story.

HOV. Why have you brought it back?

PETRA. Because I am not going to translate it.

HOV. But you promised me faithfully——

PETRA. Yes, but then I had not read it. I don't suppose you have read it either?

HOV. No, you know quite well I don't understand English; but——

PETRA. Quite so. That is why I wanted to tell you that you must find something else. [*Lays the book on the table.*] You can't use this for the *People's Messenger.*

HOV. Why not?

PETRA. Because it conflicts with all your opinions.

HOV. Oh, for that matter——

PETRA. You don't understand me. The burden of this story is that there is a supernatural power that looks after the so-called good people in this world and makes everything happen for the best in their case—while all the so-called bad people are punished.

HOV. Well, but that is all right. That is just what our readers want.

PETRA. And are you going to be the one to give it to them? For myself, I do not believe a word of it. You know quite well that things do not happen so in reality.

HOV. You are perfectly right, but an editor cannot always act as he would prefer. He is often obliged to bow to the wishes of the public in unimportant matters. Politics are the most important thing in life—for a newspaper anyway; and if I want to carry my public with me on the path that leads to liberty and progress, I must not frighten them away. If they find a moral tale of this sort in the serial at the bottom of the page, they will be all the more ready to read what is printed above it; they feel more secure, as it were.

PETRA. For shame! You would never go and set a snare like that for your readers; you are not a spider!

HOV. [*smiling*]. Thank you for having such a good opinion of me. No; as a matter of fact, that is Billing's idea and not mine.

PETRA. Billing's!

HOV. Yes; anyway, he propounded that theory here one day. And it is Billing who is so anxious to have that story in the paper; I don't know anything about the book.

PETRA. But how can Billing, with his emancipated views——

HOV. Oh, Billing is a many-sided man. He is applying for the post of secretary to the Bench too, I hear.

PETRA. I don't believe it, Mr Hovstad. How could he possibly bring himself to do such a thing?

HOV. Ah, you must ask him that.

PETRA. I should never have thought it of him.

HOV. [*looking more closely at her*]. No? Does it really surprise you so much?

PETRA. Yes. Or perhaps not altogether. Really, I don't quite know——

HOV. We journalists are not much worth, Miss Stockmann.

PETRA. Do you really mean that?

HOV. I think so sometimes.

PETRA. Yes, in the ordinary affairs of everyday life, perhaps; I can understand that. But now, when you have taken a weighty matter in hand——

HOV. This matter of your father's, you mean?

PETRA. Exactly. It seems to me that now you must feel you are a man worth more than most.

HOV. Yes, today I do feel something of that sort.

PETRA. Of course you do, don't you? It is a splendid vocation you have chosen—to smooth the way for the march of unappreciated truths and new and courageous lines of thought. If it were nothing more than because you stand fearlessly in the open and take up the cause of an injured man——

HOV. Especially when that injured man is—ahem!—I don't rightly know how to——

PETRA. When that man is so upright and so honest, you mean?

HOV. [*more gently*]. Especially when he is your father, I meant.

PETRA [*suddenly checked*]. *That?*

HOV. Yes, Petra—Miss Petra.

PETRA. Is it *that* that is first and foremost with you? Not the matter itself? Not the truth? Not my father's big generous heart?

Hov. Certainly—of course—that too.

Petra. No, thank you; you have betrayed yourself, Mr Hovstad, and now I shall never trust you again in anything.

Hov. Can you really take it so amiss in me that it is mostly for your sake——

Petra. What I am angry with you for is for not having been honest with my father. You talked to him as if the truth and the good of the community were what lay nearest to your heart. You have made fools of both my father and me. You are not the man you made yourself out to be. And that I shall never forgive you—never!

Hov. You ought not to speak so bitterly, Miss Petra—least of all now.

Petra. Why not now especially?

Hov. Because your father cannot do without my help.

Petra [*looking him up and down*]. Are you that sort of man too? For shame!

Hov. No, no, I am not. This came upon me so unexpectedly—you must believe that.

Petra. I know what to believe. Good-by.

Asl. [*coming from the printing room hurriedly and with an air of mystery*]. Damnation, Hovstad! [*Sees* Petra.] Oh, this is awkward.

Petra. There is the book; you must give it to someone else. [*Goes toward the door.*]

Hov. [*following her*]. But, Miss Stockmann——

Petra. Good-by. [*Goes out.*]

Asl. I say—Mr Hovstad——

Hov. Well, well! What is it?

Asl. The mayor is outside in the printing room.

Hov. The mayor, did you say?

Asl. Yes, he wants to speak to you. He came in by the back door—didn't want to be seen, you understand.

Hov. What can he want? Wait a bit—I will go myself. [*Goes to the door of the printing room, opens it, bows and invites* Peter Stockmann *in.*] Just see, Aslaksen, that no one——

Asl. Quite so. [*Goes into the printing room.*]

Peter. You did not expect to see me here, Mr Hovstad?

Hov. No, I confess I did not.

Peter [*looking round*]. You are very snug in here—very nice indeed.

Hov. Oh——

Peter. And here I come, without any notice, to take up your time!

Hov. By all means, Mr Mayor. I am at your service. But let me relieve you of your—— [*Takes* Stockmann's *hat and stick and puts them on a chair.*] Won't you sit down?

Peter [*sitting down by the table*]. Thank you. [Hovstad *sits down.*] I have had an extremely annoying experience today, Mr Hovstad.

Hov. Really? Ah well, I expect with all the various business you have to attend to——

Peter. The medical officer of the Baths is responsible for what happened today.

Hov. Indeed? The doctor?

Peter. He has addressed a kind of report to the Baths Committee on the subject of certain supposed defects in the Baths.

Hov. Has he, indeed?

Peter. Yes—has he not told you? I thought he said——

Hov. Ah yes—it is true he did mention something about——

Asl. [*coming from the printing

room]. I ought to have that copy——

Hov. [*angrily*]. Ahem!—there it is on the desk.

Asl. [*taking it*]. Right.

Peter. But look there—that is the thing I was speaking of!

Asl. Yes, that is the doctor's article, Mr Mayor.

Hov. Oh, is *that* what you were speaking about?

Peter. Yes, that is it. What do you think of it?

Hov. Oh, I am only a layman—and I have only taken a very cursory glance at it.

Peter. But you are going to print it?

Hov. I cannot very well refuse a distinguished man.

Asl. I have nothing to do with editing the paper, Mr Mayor.

Peter. I understand.

Asl. I merely print what is put into my hands.

Peter. Quite so.

Asl. And so I must—— [*Moves off toward the printing room.*]

Peter. No, but wait a moment, Mr Aslaksen. You will allow me, Mr Hovstad?

Hov. If you please, Mr Mayor.

Peter. You are a discreet and thoughtful man, Mr Aslaksen.

Asl. I am delighted to hear you think so, sir.

Peter. And a man of very considerable influence.

Asl. Chiefly among the small tradesmen, sir.

Peter. The small taxpayers are the majority—here as everywhere else.

Asl. That is true.

Peter. And I have no doubt you know the general trend of opinion among them, don't you?

Asl. Yes, I think I may say I do, Mr Mayor.

Peter. Yes. Well, since there is such a praiseworthy spirit of self-sacrifice among the less wealthy citizens of our town——

Asl. What?

Hov. Self-sacrifice?

Peter. It is pleasing evidence of a public-spirited feeling, extremely pleasing evidence. I might almost say I hardly expected it. But you have a closer knowledge of public opinion than I.

Asl. But, Mr Mayor——

Peter. And indeed it is no small sacrifice that the town is going to make.

Hov. The town?

Asl. But I don't understand. Is it the Baths?

Peter. At a provisional estimate the alterations that the medical officer asserts to be desirable will cost somewhere about twenty thousand pounds.

Asl. That is a lot of money, but——

Peter. Of course it will be necessary to raise a municipal loan.

Hov. [*getting up*]. Surely you never mean that the town must pay?

Asl. Do you mean that it must come out of the municipal funds?—out of the ill-filled pockets of the small tradesmen?

Peter. Well, my dear Mr Aslaksen, where else is the money to come from?

Asl. The gentlemen who own the Baths ought to provide that.

Peter. The proprietors of the Baths are not in a position to incur any further expense.

Asl. Is that absolutely certain, Mr Mayor?

Peter. I have satisfied myself that it is so. If the town wants these very extensive alterations, it will have to pay for them.

ASL. But, damn it all—I beg your pardon—this is quite another matter, Mr Hovstad!

HOV. It is, indeed.

PETER. The most fatal part of it is that we shall be obliged to shut the Baths for a couple of years.

HOV. Shut them? Shut them altogether?

ASL. For two years?

PETER. Yes, the work will take as long as that—at least.

ASL. I'm damned if we will stand that, Mr Mayor! What are we householders to live upon in the meantime?

PETER. Unfortunately that is an extremely difficult question to answer, Mr Aslaksen. But what would you have us do? Do you suppose we shall have a single visitor in the town if we go about proclaiming that our water is polluted, that we are living over a plague spot, that the entire town——

ASL. And the whole thing is merely imagination?

PETER. With the best will in the world I have not been able to come to any other conclusion.

ASL. Well, then, I must say it is absolutely unjustifiable of Doctor Stockmann—I beg your pardon, Mr Mayor—

PETER. What you say is lamentably true, Mr Aslaksen. My brother has unfortunately always been a headstrong man.

ASL. After this do you mean to give him your support, Mr Hovstad?

HOV. Can you suppose for a moment that I——

PETER. I have drawn up a short résumé of the situation as it appears from a reasonable man's point of view. In it I have indicated how certain possible defects might suitably be remedied without outrunning the resources of the Baths Committee.

HOV. Have you got it with you, Mr Mayor?

PETER [*fumbling in his pocket*]. Yes, I brought it with me in case you should——

ASL. Good lord, there he is!

PETER. Who? My brother?

HOV. Where? Where?

ASL. He has just gone through the printing room.

PETER. How unlucky! I don't want to meet him here, and I had still several things to speak to you about.

HOV. [*pointing to the door on the right*]. Go in there for the present.

PETER. But——

HOV. You will find only Billing in there.

ASL. Quick, quick, Mr Mayor—he is just coming.

PETER. Yes, very well; but see that you get rid of him quickly. [*Goes out through the door on the right, which* ASLAKSEN *opens for him and shuts after him.*]

HOV. Pretend to be doing something, Aslaksen. [*Sits down and writes.* ASLAKSEN *begins foraging among a heap of newspapers that are lying on a chair.*]

DR STO. [*coming in from the printing room*]. Here I am again. [*Puts down his hat and stick.*]

HOV. [*writing*]. Already, Doctor? Hurry up with what we were speaking about, Aslaksen. We are very pressed for time today.

DR STO. [*to* ASLAKSEN]. No proof for me to see yet, I hear.

ASL. [*without turning round*]. You couldn't expect it yet, Doctor.

DR STO. No, no; but I am impatient, as you can understand. I shall not know a moment's peace of mind till I see it in print.

Hov. Hm! It will take a good while yet, won't it, Aslaksen?

Asl. Yes, I am almost afraid it will.

Dr Sto. All right, my dear friends, I will come back. I do not mind coming back twice if necessary. A matter of such great importance—the welfare of the town at stake—it is no time to shirk trouble. [*Is just going but stops and comes back.*] Look here—there is one thing more I want to speak to you about.

Hov. Excuse me, but could it not wait till some other time?

Dr Sto. I can tell you in half-a-dozen words. It is only this. When my article is read tomorrow and it is realized that I have been quietly working the whole winter for the welfare of the town——

Hov. Yes, but, Doctor——

Dr Sto. I know what you are going to say. You don't see how on earth it was any more than my duty—my obvious duty as a citizen. Of course it wasn't; I know that as well as you. But my fellow citizens, you know—— Good lord, think of all the good souls who think so highly of me!

Asl. Yes, our townsfolk have had a very high opinion of you so far, Doctor.

Dr Sto. Yes, and that is just why I am afraid they—— Well, this is the point: when this reaches them, especially the poorer classes, and sounds in their ears like a summons to take the town's affairs into their own hands for the future——

Hov. [*getting up*]. Ahem! Doctor, I won't conceal from you the fact——

Dr Sto. Ah! I knew there was something in the wind! But I won't hear a word of it. If anything of that sort is being set on foot——

Hov. Of what sort?

Dr Sto. Well, whatever it is—whether it is a demonstration in my honor or a banquet or a subscription list for some presentation to me—whatever it is, you must promise me solemnly and faithfully to put a stop to it. You too, Mr Aslaksen; do you understand?

Hov. You must forgive me, Doctor, but sooner or later we must tell you the plain truth——

[*He is interrupted by the entrance of* Mrs Stockmann, *who comes in from the street door.*]

Mrs Sto. [*seeing her husband*]. Just as I thought!

Hov. [*going toward her*]. You too, Mrs Stockmann?

Dr Sto. What on earth do *you* want here, Katherine?

Mrs Sto. I should think you know very well what I want.

Hov. Won't you sit down? Or perhaps——

Mrs Sto. No, thank you; don't trouble. And you must not be offended at my coming to fetch my husband; I am the mother of three children, you know.

Dr Sto. Nonsense!—we know all about that.

Mrs Sto. Well, one would not give you credit for much thought for your wife and children today; if you had had that, you would not have gone and dragged us all into misfortune.

Dr Sto. Are you out of your senses, Katherine? Because a man has a wife and children is he not to be allowed to proclaim the truth?—is he not to be allowed to be an actively useful citizen?—is he not to be allowed to do a service to his native town?

Mrs Sto. Yes, Thomas—in reason.

Asl. Just what I say. Moderation in everything.

Mrs Sto. And that is why you wrong us, Mr Hovstad, in enticing my husband away from his home and making a dupe of him in all this.

Hov. I certainly am making a dupe of no one.

Dr Sto. Making a dupe of me! Do you suppose *I* should allow myself to be duped!

Mrs Sto. It is just what you do. I know quite well you have more brains than anyone in the town, but you are extremely easily duped, Thomas. [*To* Hovstad.] Please to realize that he loses his post at the Baths if you print what he has written.

Asl. What!

Hov. Look here, Doctor——

Dr Sto. [*laughing*]. Ha-ha!—just let them try! No, no—they will take good care not to. I have got the compact majority behind me, let me tell you!

Mrs Sto. Yes, that is just the worst of it—your having any such horrid thing behind you.

Dr Sto. Rubbish, Katherine! Go home and look after your house and leave me to look after the community. How can you be so afraid when I am so confident and happy? [*Walks up and down rubbing his hands.*] Truth and the people will win the fight, you may be certain! I see the whole of the broad-minded middle class marching like a victorious army! [*Stops beside a chair.*] What the deuce is that lying there!

Asl. Good lord!

Hov. Ahem!

Dr Sto. Here we have the topmost pinnacle of authority! [*Takes the mayor's official hat carefully between his finger tips and holds it up in the air.*]

Mrs Sto. The mayor's hat!

Dr Sto. And here is the staff of office too. How in the name of all that's wonderful——

Hov. Well, you see——

Dr Sto. Oh, I understand. He has been here trying to talk it over. Ha-ha!—he made rather a mistake there! And as soon as he caught sight of me in the printing room—— [*Bursts out laughing.*] Did he run away, Mr Aslaksen?

Asl. [*hurriedly*]. Yes, he ran away, Doctor.

Dr Sto. Ran away without his stick or his—— Fiddlesticks! Peter doesn't run away and leave his belongings behind him. But what the deuce have you done with him? Ah!—in there, of course. Now you shall see, Katherine!

Mrs Sto. Thomas—please don't!

Asl. Don't be rash, Doctor.

[Dr Stockmann *has put on the mayor's hat and taken his stick in his hand. He goes up to the door, opens it and stands with his hand to his hat at the salute.* Peter Stockmann *comes in red with anger.* Billing *follows him.*]

Peter. What does this tomfoolery mean?

Dr Sto. Be respectful, my good Peter. I am the chief authority in the town now. [*Walks up and down.*]

Mrs Sto. [*almost in tears*]. Really, Thomas!

Peter [*following him about*]. Give me my hat and stick.

Dr Sto. [*in the same tone as before*]. If you are chief constable, let me tell you that I am the mayor—I am the master of the whole town, please understand!

Peter. Take off my hat, I tell you. Remember it is part of an official uniform.

Dr Sto. Pooh! Do you think the

newly awakened lionhearted people are going to be frightened by an official hat? There is going to be a revolution in the town tomorrow, let me tell you. You thought you could turn me out, but now I shall turn you out—turn you out of all your various offices. Do you think I cannot? Listen to me. I have triumphant social forces behind me. Hovstad and Billing will thunder in the *People's Messenger*, and Aslaksen will take the field at the head of the whole Householders' Association.

ASL. That I won't, Doctor.

DR STO. Of course you will.

PETER. Ah!—may I ask then if Mr Hovstad intends to join this agitation?

HOV. No, Mr Mayor.

ASL. No, Mr Hovstad is not such a fool as to go and ruin his paper and himself for the sake of an imaginary grievance.

DR STO. [*looking round him*]. What does this mean?

HOV. You have represented your case in a false light, Doctor, and therefore I am unable to give you my support.

BILL. And after what the mayor was so kind as to tell me just now I——

DR STO. A false light! Leave that part of it to me. Only print my article; I am quite capable of defending it.

HOV. I am not going to print it. I cannot and will not and dare not print it.

DR STO. You dare not? What nonsense! You are the editor, and an editor controls his paper, I suppose!

ASL. No, it is the subscribers, Doctor.

PETER. Fortunately, yes.

ASL. It is public opinion—the enlightened public—householders and people of that kind; they control the newspapers.

DR STO. [*composedly*]. And I have all these influences against me?

ASL. Yes, you have. It would mean the absolute ruin of the community if your article were to appear.

DR STO. Indeed.

PETER. My hat and stick, if you please. [DR STOCKMANN *takes off the hat and lays it on the table with the stick.* PETER STOCKMANN *takes them up.*] Your authority as mayor has come to an untimely end.

DR STO. We have not got to the end yet. [*To* HOVSTAD.] Then it is quite impossible for you to print my article in the *People's Messenger?*

HOV. Quite impossible—out of regard for your family as well.

MRS STO. You need not concern yourself about his family, thank you, Mr Hovstad.

PETER [*taking a paper from his pocket*]. It will be sufficient, for the guidance of the public, if this appears. It is an official statement. May I trouble you?

HOV. [*taking the paper*]. Certainly; I will see that it is printed.

DR STO. But not mine. Do you imagine that you can silence me and stifle the truth? You will not find it so easy as you suppose. Mr Aslaksen, kindly take my manuscript at once and print it as a pamphlet—at my expense. I will have four hundred copies—no, five—six hundred.

ASL. If you offered me its weight in gold, I could not lend my press for any such purpose, Doctor. It would be flying in the face of public opinion. You will not get it printed anywhere in the town.

DR STO. Then give it me back.

HOV. [*giving him the MS*]. Here it is.

DR STO. [*taking his hat and stick*]. It shall be made public all the same. I will read it out at a mass meeting of the townspeople. All my fellow citizens shall hear the voice of truth!

PETER. You will not find any public body in the town that will give you the use of their hall for such a purpose.

ASL. Not a single one, I am certain.

BILL. No, I'm damned if you will find one.

MRS STO. But this is too shameful! Why should everyone turn against you like that?

DR STO. [*angrily*]. I will tell you why. It is because all the men in this town are old women—like you; they all think of nothing but their families and never of the community itself.

MRS STO. [*putting her arm into his*]. Then I will show them that an—an old woman can be a man for once. I am going to stand by you, Thomas!

DR STO. Bravely said, Katherine! It shall be made public—as I am a living soul! If I can't hire a hall, I shall hire a drum and parade the town with it and read it at every street corner.

PETER. You are surely not such an arrant fool as that!

DR STO. Yes, I am.

ASL. You won't find a single man in the whole town to go with you, Doctor Stockmann.

BILL. No, I'm damned if you will.

MRS STO. Don't give in, Thomas. I will tell the boys to go with you.

DR STO. That is a splendid idea!

MRS STO. Morten will be delighted, and Ejlif will do whatever he does.

DR STO. Yes, and Petra!—and you too, Katherine!

MRS STO. No, I won't do that; but I will stand at the window and watch you, that's what I will do.

DR STO. [*puts his arms around her and kisses her*]. Thank you, my dear! Now you and I are going to try a fall, my fine gentlemen! I am going to see whether a pack of cowards can succeed in gagging a patriot who wants to purify society! [*He and his wife go out by the street door.*]

PETER [*shaking his head seriously*]. Now he has sent *her* out of her senses too.

ACT IV

SCENE—*A big old-fashioned room in* CAPTAIN HORSTER'S *house. At the back folding doors, which are standing open, lead to an anteroom. Three windows in the left-hand wall. In the middle of the opposite wall a platform has been erected. On this is a small table with two candles, a water bottle and glass and a bell. The room is lit by lamps placed between the windows. In the foreground on the left there is a table with candles and a chair. To the right is a door and some chairs standing near it. The room is nearly filled with a crowd of townspeople of all sorts, a few women and schoolboys being amongst them. People are still streaming in from the back, and the room is soon filled.*

1ST CITIZEN [*meeting another*]. Hullo, Lamstad! You here too?

2ND CITIZEN. I go to every public meeting, I do.

3RD CITIZEN. Brought your whistle too, I expect!

2ND CITIZEN. I should think so. Haven't you?

3RD CITIZEN. Rather! And old

Evansen said he was going to bring a cow horn, he did.

2ND CITIZEN. Good old Evensen! [*Laughter among the crowd.*]

5TH CITIZEN [*coming up to them*]. I say, tell me what is going on here tonight.

2ND CITIZEN. Doctor Stockmann is going to deliver an address attacking the mayor.

4TH CITIZEN. But the mayor is his brother.

1ST CITIZEN. That doesn't matter; Doctor Stockmann's not the chap to be afraid.

3RD CITIZEN. But he is in the wrong; it said so in the *People's Messenger.*

2ND CITIZEN. Yes, I expect he must be in the wrong this time, because neither the Householders' Association nor the Citizens' Club would lend him their hall for his meeting.

1ST CITIZEN. He couldn't even get the loan of the hall at the Baths.

2ND CITIZEN. No, I should think not.

A MAN IN ANOTHER PART OF THE CROWD. I say—who are we to back up in this?

ANOTHER MAN BESIDE HIM. Watch Aslaksen and do as he does.

BILL. [*pushing his way through the crowd with a writing case under his arm*]. Excuse me, gentlemen—do you mind letting me through? I am reporting for the *People's Messenger.* Thank you very much! [*He sits down at the table on the left.*]

A WORKMAN. Who was that?

SECOND WORKMAN. Don't you know him? It's Billing, who writes for Aslaksen's paper.

[CAPTAIN HORSTER *brings in* MRS STOCKMANN *and* PETRA *through the door on the right.* EJLIF *and* MORTEN *follow them in.*]

HORS. I thought you might all sit here; you can slip out easily from here if things get too lively.

MRS STO. Do you think there will be a disturbance?

HORS. One can never tell—with such a crowd. But sit down and don't be uneasy.

MRS STO. [*sitting down*]. It was extremely kind of you to offer my husband the room.

HORS. Well, if nobody else would —

PETRA [*who has sat down beside her mother*]. And it was a plucky thing to do, Captain Horster.

HORS. Oh, it is not such a great matter as all that.

[HOVSTAD *and* ASLAKSEN *make their way through the crowd.*]

ASL. [*going up to* HORSTER]. Has the doctor not come yet?

HORS. He is waiting in the next room.

[*Movement in the crowd by the door at the back.*]

HOV. Look—here comes the mayor!

BILL. Yes, I'm damned if he hasn't come after all!

[PETER STOCKMANN *makes his way gradually through the crowd, bows courteously and takes up a position by the wall on the left. Shortly afterward* DR STOCKMANN *comes in by the right-hand door. He is dressed in a black frock coat with a white tie. There is a little feeble applause, which is hushed down. Silence is obtained.*]

DR STO. [*in an undertone*]. How do you feel, Katherine?

MRS STO. All right, thank you. [*Lowering her voice.*] Be sure not to lose your temper, Thomas.

DR STO. Oh, I know how to control myself. [*Looks at his watch, steps onto the platform and bows.*] It is a quarter past—so I will begin. [*Takes *his MS out of his pocket.*]

ASL. I think we ought to elect a chairman first.

DR STO. No, it is quite unnecessary.

SOME OF THE CROWD. Yes—yes!

PETER. I certainly think too that we ought to have a chairman.

DR STO. But I have called this meeting to deliver a lecture, Peter.

PETER. Doctor Stockmann's lecture may possibly lead to a considerable conflict of opinion.

VOICES IN THE CROWD. A chairman! A chairman!

HOV. The general wish of the meeting seems to be that a chairman should be elected.

DR STO. [*restraining himself*]. Very well—let the meeting have its way.

ASL. Will the mayor be good enough to undertake the task?

THREE MEN [*clapping their hands*]. Bravo! Bravo!

PETER. For various reasons, which you will easily understand, I must beg to be excused. But fortunately we have amongst us a man who I think will be acceptable to you all. I refer to the president of the Householders' Association, Mr Aslaksen.

SEVERAL VOICES. Yes—Aslaksen! Bravo, Aslaksen!

[DR STOCKMANN *takes up his MS and walks up and down the platform.*]

ASL. Since my fellow citizens choose to entrust me with this duty I cannot refuse. [*Loud applause.* ASLAKSEN *mounts the platform.*]

BILL. [*writing*]. "Mr Aslaksen was elected with enthusiasm."

ASL. And now, as I am in this position, I should like to say a few brief words. I am a quiet and peaceable man who believes in discreet moderation and—and—in moderate discretion. All my friends can bear witness to that.

SEVERAL VOICES. That's right! That's right, Aslaksen!

ASL. I have learned in the school of life and experience that moderation is the most valuable virtue a citizen can possess——

PETER. Hear, hear!

ASL. And moreover that discretion and moderation are what enable a man to be of most service to the community. I would therefore suggest to our esteemed fellow citizen, who has called this meeting, that he should strive to keep strictly within the bounds of moderation.

A MAN BY THE DOOR. Three cheers for the Moderation Society!

A VOICE. Shame!

SEVERAL VOICES. Sh! Sh!

ASL. No interruptions, gentlemen, please! Does anyone wish to make any remarks?

PETER. Mr Chairman.

ASL. The mayor will address the meeting.

PETER. In consideration of the close relationship in which, as you all know, I stand to the present medical officer of the Baths, I should have preferred not to speak this evening. But my official position with regard to the Baths and my solicitude for the vital interests of the town compel me to bring forward a motion. I venture to presume that there is not a single one of our citizens present who considers it desirable that unreliable and exaggerated accounts of the sanitary condition of the Baths and the town should be spread abroad.

SEVERAL VOICES. No, no! Certainly not! We protest against it!

PETER. Therefore I should like to propose that the meeting should not permit the medical officer either to read or comment on his proposed lecture.

DR STO. [*impatiently*]. Not permit — What the devil—

MRS STO. [*coughing*]. Ahem!—ahem!

DR. STO. [*collecting himself*]. Very well. Go ahead!

PETER. In my communication to the *People's Messenger* I have put the essential facts before the public in such a way that every fair-minded citizen can easily form his own opinion. From it you will see that the main result of the medical officer's proposals—apart from their constituting a vote of censure on the leading men of the town—would be to saddle the ratepayers with an unnecessary expenditure of at least some thousands of pounds. [*Sounds of disapproval among the audience and some catcalls.*]

ASL. [*ringing his bell*]. Silence, please, gentlemen! I beg to support the mayor's motion. I quite agree with him that there is something behind this agitation started by the doctor. He talks about the Baths, but it is a revolution he is aiming at—he wants to get the administration of the town put into new hands. No one doubts the honesty of the doctor's intentions—no one will suggest that there can be any two opinions as to that. I myself am a believer in self-government for the people, provided it does not fall too heavily on the ratepayers. But that would be the case here, and that is why I will see Doctor Stockmann damned—I beg your pardon—before I go with him in the matter. You can pay too dearly for a thing sometimes; that is my opinion. [*Loud applause on all sides.*]

HOV. I, too, feel called upon to explain my position. Doctor Stockmann's agitation appeared to be gaining a certain amount of sympathy at first, so I supported it as impartially as I could. But presently we had reason to suspect that we had allowed ourselves to be misled by misrepresentation of the state of affairs—

DR STO. Misrepresentation!

HOV. Well, let us say a not entirely trustworthy representation. The mayor's statement has proved that. I hope no one here has any doubts as to my liberal principles; the attitude of the *People's Messenger* toward important political questions is well known to everyone. But the advice of experienced and thoughtful men has convinced me that in purely local matters a newspaper ought to proceed with a certain caution.

ASL. I entirely agree with the speaker.

HOV. And, in the matter before us, it is now an undoubted fact that Doctor Stockmann has public opinion against him. Now what is an editor's first and most obvious duty, gentlemen? Is it not to work in harmony with his readers? Has he not received a sort of tacit mandate to work persistently and assiduously for the welfare of those whose opinions he represents? Or is it possible I am mistaken in that?

VOICES FROM THE CROWD. No, no! You are quite right!

HOV. It has cost me a severe struggle to break with a man in whose house I have been lately a frequent guest—a man who till today has been able to pride himself on the undivided good will of his fellow citizens—a man whose only, or at all events whose essential, failing is that he is swayed by his heart rather than his head.

A Few Scattered Voices. That is true! Bravo, Stockmann!

Hov. But my duty to the community obliged me to break with him. And there is another consideration that impels me to oppose him and, as far as possible, to arrest him on the perilous course he has adopted; that is, consideration for his family——

Dr Sto. Please stick to the water supply and drainage!

Hov. —consideration, I repeat, for his wife and his children for whom he has made no provision.

Mor. Is that us, Mother?

Mrs Sto. Hush!

Asl. I will now put the mayor's proposition to the vote.

Dr Sto. There is no necessity! Tonight I have no intention of dealing with all that filth down at the Baths. No; I have something quite different to say to you.

Peter [*aside*]. What is coming now?

A Drunken Man [*by the entrance door*]. I am a ratepayer! And therefore I have a right to speak too! And my entire—firm—inconceivable opinion is——

A Number of Voices. Be quiet, at the back there!

Others. He is drunk! Turn him out! [*They turn him out.*]

Dr Sto. Am I allowed to speak?

Asl. [*ringing his bell*]. Doctor Stockmann will address the meeting.

Dr Sto. I should like to have seen anyone, a few days ago, dare to attempt to silence me as has been done tonight! I would have defended my sacred rights as a man like a lion! But now it is all one to me; I have something of even weightier importance to say to you. [*The crowd presses nearer to him,* Morten Kiil *conspicuous among them.*]

Dr Sto. [*continuing*]. I have thought and pondered a great deal these last few days—pondered over such a variety of things that in the end my head seemed too full to hold them——

Peter [*with a cough*]. Ahem!

Dr Sto. —but I got them clear in my mind at last, and then I saw the whole situation lucidly. And that is why I am standing here tonight. I have a great revelation to make to you, my fellow citizens! I will impart to you a discovery of a far wider scope than the trifling matter that our water supply is poisoned and our medicinal Baths are standing on pestiferous soil.

A Number of Voices [*shouting*]. Don't talk about the Baths! We won't hear you! None of that!

Dr Sto. I have already told you that what I want to speak about is the great discovery I have made lately—the discovery that all the sources of our *moral* life are poisoned and that the whole fabric of our civic community is founded on the pestiferous soil of falsehood.

Voices of Disconcerted Citizens. What is that he says?

Peter. Such an insinuation!

Asl. [*with his hand on his bell*]. I call upon the speaker to moderate his language.

Dr Sto. I have always loved my native town as a man only can love the home of his youthful days. I was not old when I went away from here, and exile, longing and memories cast as it were an additional halo over both the town and its inhabitants. [*Some clapping and applause.*] And there I stayed, for many years, in a horrible hole far away up north. When I came into contact with some of the people that lived scattered about among the rocks I often thought it would of been more service to the poor half-starved creatures if a veterinary doctor had been sent up there instead of a man like me. [*Murmurs among the crowd.*]

BILL. [*laying down his pen*]. I'm damned if I have ever heard——

HOV. It is an insult to a respectable population!

DR STO. Wait a bit! I do not think anyone will charge me with having forgotten my native town up there. I was like one of the eider ducks brooding on its nest, and what I hatched was—the plans for these Baths. [*Applause and protests.*] And then when fate at last decreed for me the great happiness of coming home again—I assure you, gentlemen, I thought I had nothing more in the world to wish for. Or rather there was one thing I wished for—eagerly, untiringly, ardently—and that was to be able to be of service to my native town and the good of the community.

PETER [*looking at the ceiling*]. You chose a strange way of doing it—ahem!

DR STO. And so, with my eyes blinded to the real facts, I reveled in happiness. But yesterday morning—no, to be precise, it was yesterday afternoon—the eyes of my mind were opened wide, and the first thing I realized was the colossal stupidity of the authorities. [*Uproar, shouts and laughter.* MRS STOCKMANN *coughs persistently.*]

PETER. Mr Chairman!

ASL. [*ringing his bell*]. By virtue of my authority——

DR STO. It is a petty thing to catch me up on a word, Mr Aslaksen. What I mean is only that I got scent of the unbelievable piggishness our leading men had been responsible for down at the Baths. I can't stand leading men at any price! I have had enough of such people in my time. They are like billy goats in a young plantation; they do mischief everywhere. They stand in a free man's way whichever way he turns, and what I should like best would be to see them exterminated like any other vermin. [*Uproar.*]

PETER. Mr Chairman, can we allow such expressions to pass?

ASL. [*with his hand on his bell*]. Doctor——

DR STO. I cannot understand how it is that I have only now acquired a clear conception of what these gentry are, when I had almost daily before my eyes in this town such an excellent specimen of them—my brother Peter—slow-witted and hidebound in prejudice—— [*Laughter, uproar and hisses.* MRS STOCKMANN *sits coughing assiduously.* ASLAKSEN *rings his bell violently.*]

THE DRUNKEN MAN [*who has got in again*]. Is it me he is talking about? My name's Petersen, all right—but devil take me if I——

ANGRY VOICES. Turn out that drunken man! Turn him out. [*He is turned out again.*]

PETER. Who was that person?

1ST CITIZEN. I don't know who he is, Mr Mayor.

2ND CITIZEN. He doesn't belong here.

3RD CITIZEN. I expect he is a navvy from over at—— [*the rest is inaudible.*]

ASL. He had obviously had too

much beer. Proceed, Doctor, but please strive to be moderate in your language.

Dr Sto. Very well, gentlemen, I will say no more about our leading men. And if anyone imagines, from what I have just said, that my object is to attack these people this evening, he is wrong–absolutely wide of the mark. For I cherish the comforting conviction that these parasites–all these venerable relics of a dying school of thought–are most admirably paving the way for their own extinction; they need no doctor's help to hasten their end. Nor is it folk of that kind who constitute the most pressing danger to the community. It is not they who are most instrumental in poisoning the sources of our moral life and directing the ground on which we stand. It is not they who are the most dangerous enemies of truth and freedom amongst us.

Shouts from all Sides. Who, then? Who is it? Name! Name!

Dr Sto. You may depend upon it, I shall name them! That is precisely the great discovery I made yesterday. [*Raises his voice.*] The most dangerous enemy to truth and freedom amongst us is the compact majority–yes, the damned compact Liberal majority–that is it! Now you know. [*Tremendous uproar. Most of the crowd are shouting, stamping and hissing. Some of the older men among them exchange stolen glances and seem to be enjoying themselves.* Mrs Stockmann *gets up, looking anxious.* Ejlif *and* Morten *advance threateningly upon some schoolboys who are playing pranks.* Aslaksen *rings his bell and begs for silence.* Hovstad *and* Billing *both talk at once but are inaudible. At last quiet is restored.*]

Asl. As chairman I call upon the speaker to withdraw the ill-considered expressions he has just used.

Dr Sto. Never, Mr Aslaksen! It is the majority in our community that denies me my freedom and seeks to prevent my speaking the truth.

Hov. The majority always has right on its side.

Bill. And truth too, by God!

Dr Sto. The majority *never* has right on its side. Never, I say! That is one of these social lies against which an independent intelligent man must wage war. Who is it that constitute the majority of the population in a country? Is it the clever folk or the stupid? I don't imagine you will dispute the fact that at present the stupid people are in an absolutely overwhelming majority all the world over. But, good lord!–you can never pretend that it is right that the stupid folk should govern the clever ones! [*Uproar and cries.*] Oh yes–you can shout me down, I know! but you cannot answer me. The majority has *might* on its side–unfortunately; but *right* it has *not.* I am in the right–I and a few other scattered individuals. The minority is always in the right. [*Renewed uproar.*]

Hov. Aha!–so Doctor Stockmann has become an aristocrat since the day before yesterday!

Dr Sto. I have already said that I don't intend to waste a word on the puny, narrow-chested, short-winded crew whom we are leaving astern. Pulsating life no longer concerns itself with them. I am thinking of the few, the scattered few amongst us, who have absorbed new and vigorous truths. Such men stand, as it were, at the outposts, so far ahead that the compact majority has not yet been able to come up with them; and there they are fighting for truths that are too newly born into the world of consciousness to have any considerable number of people on their side as yet.

Hov. So the doctor is a revolutionary now!

Dr Sto. Good heavens—of course I am, Mr Hovstad! I propose to raise a revolution against the lie that the majority has the monopoly of the truth. What sort of truths are they that the majority usually supports? They are truths that are of such advanced age that they are beginning to break up. And if a truth is as old as that, it is also in a fair way to become a lie, gentlemen. [*Laughter and mocking cries.*] Yes, believe me or not, as you like; but truths are by no means as long lived as Methuselah—as some folk imagine. A normally constituted truth lives, let us say, as a rule, seventeen or eighteen or at most twenty years; seldom longer. But truths as aged as that are always worn frightfully thin, and nevertheless it is only then that the majority recognizes them and recommends them to the community as wholesome moral nourishment. There is no great nutritive value in that sort of fare, I can assure you; and, as a doctor, I ought to know. These "majority truths" are like last year's cured meat—like rancid, tainted ham; and they are the origin of the moral scurvy that is rampant in our communities.

Asl. It appears to me that the speaker is wandering a long way from his subject.

Peter. I quite agree with the chairman.

Dr Sto. Have you gone clean out of your senses, Peter? I am sticking as closely to my subject as I can; for my subject is precisely this, that it is the masses, the majority—this infernal compact majority—that poisons the sources of our moral life and infects the ground we stand on.

Hov. And all this because the great, broad-minded majority of the people is prudent enough to show deference only to well-ascertained and well-approved truths?

Dr Sto. Ah, my good Mr Hovstad, don't talk nonsense about well-ascertained truths! The truths of which the masses now approve are the very truths that the fighters at the outposts held to in the days of our grandfathers. We fighters at the outposts nowadays no longer approve of them; and I do not believe there is any other well-ascertained truth except this, that no community can live a healthy life if it is nourished only on such old marrowless truths.

Hov. But instead of standing there using vague generalities it would be interesting if you would tell us what these old marrowless truths are that we are nourished on. [*Applause from many quarters.*]

Dr Sto. Oh, I could give you a whole string of such abominations; but to begin with I will confine myself to one well-approved truth, which at bottom is a foul lie but upon which, nevertheless, Mr Hovstad and the *People's Messenger* and all the *Messenger's* supporters are nourished.

Hov. And that is——?

Dr Sto. That is the doctrine you have inherited from your forefathers and proclaim thoughtlessly far and wide—the doctrine that the public, the crowd, the masses, are the essential part of the population—that they constitute the people—that the common folk, the ignorant and incomplete element in the community, have the same right to pronounce judgment and to approve, to direct and to govern as the isolated, intellectually superior personalities in it.

BILL. Well, damn me if ever I——

HOV. [*at the same time, shouting out*]. Fellow citizens, take good note of that!

A NUMBER OF VOICES [*angrily*]. Oho!—we are not the people! Only the superior folk are to govern, are they!

A WORKMAN. Turn the fellow out for talking such rubbish!

ANOTHER. Out with him!

ANOTHER [*calling out*]. Blow your horn, Evensen! [*A horn is blown loudly amidst hisses and an angry uproar.*]

DR STO. [*when the noise has somewhat abated*]. Be reasonable! Can't you stand hearing the voice of truth for once? I don't in the least expect you to agree with me all at once, but I must say I did expect Mr Hovstad to admit I was right when he had recovered his composure a little. He claims to be a freethinker.

VOICES [*in murmurs of astonishment*]. Freethinker, did he say? Is Hovstad a freethinker?

HOV. [*shouting*]. Prove it, Doctor Stockmann! When have I said so in print?

DR STO. [*reflecting*]. No, confound it, you are right!—you have never had the courage to. Well, I won't put you in a hole, Mr Hovstad. Let us say it is I that am the freethinker then. I am going to prove to you, scientifically, that the *People's Messenger* leads you by the nose in a shameful manner when it tells you that you—that the common people, the crowd, the masses—are the real essence of the people. That is only a newspaper lie, I tell you! The common people are nothing more than the raw material of which a people is made. [*Groans, laughter and uproar.*] Well, isn't that the case? Isn't there an enormous difference between a well-bred and an ill-bred strain of animals? Take, for instance, a common barn-door hen. What sort of eating do you get from a shriveled up old scrag of a fowl like that? Not much, do you? And what sort of eggs does it lay? A fairly good crow or a raven can lay pretty nearly as good an egg. But take a well-bred Spanish or Japanese hen or a good pheasant or a turkey—then you will see the difference. Or take the case of dogs, with whom we humans are on such intimate terms. Think first of an ordinary common cur—I mean one of the horrible, coarse-haired, lowbred curs that do nothing but run about the streets and befoul the walls of the houses. Compare one of these curs with a poodle whose sires for many generations have been bred in a gentleman's house, where they have had the best of food and had the opportunity of hearing soft voices and music. Do you not think that the poodle's brain is developed to quite a different degree from that of the cur? Of course it is. It is puppies of well-bred poodles like that that showmen train to do incredibly clever tricks—things that a common cur could never learn to do even if it stood on its head. [*Uproar and mocking cries.*]

A CITIZEN [*calls out*]. Are you going to make out we are dogs now?

ANOTHER CITIZEN. We are not animals, Doctor!

DR STO. Yes, but, bless my soul, we *are*, my friend! It is true we are the finest animals anyone could wish for; but, even amongst us, exceptionally fine animals are rare. There is a tremendous difference between poodle-men and cur-men. And the amusing part of it is that Mr Hovstad quite agrees with me as long as it is a question of four-footed animals.

HOV. Yes, it is true enough as far as they are concerned.

DR STO. Very well. But as soon as I extend the principle and apply it to two-legged animals Mr Hovstad stops short. He no longer dares to think independently or to pursue his ideas to their logical conclusion, so he turns the whole theory upside down and proclaims in the *People's Messenger* that it is the barn-door hens and street curs that are the finest specimens in the menagerie. But that is always the way as long as a man retains the traces of common origin and has not worked his way up to intellectual distinction.

HOV. I lay no claim to any sort of distinction. I am the son of humble countryfolk, and I am proud that the stock I come from is rooted deep among the common people he insults.

VOICES. Bravo, Hovstad! Bravo! Bravo!

DR STO. The kind of common people I mean are not only to be found low down in the social scale; they crawl and swarm all around us—even in the highest social positions. You have only to look at your own fine, distinguished mayor! My brother Peter is every bit as plebeian as anyone that walks in two shoes—— [*Laughter and hisses.*]

PETER. I protest against personal allusions of this kind.

DR STO. [*imperturbably*]. —and that, not because he is, like myself, descended from some old rascal of a pirate from Pomerania or thereabouts—because that is who we are descended from——

PETER. An absurd legend. I deny it!

DR STO. —but because he thinks what his superiors think and holds the same opinions as they. People who do that are, intellectually speaking, common people; and that is why my magnificent brother Peter is in reality so very far from any distinction—and consequently also so far from being liberal-minded.

PETER. Mr Chairman!

HOV. So it is only the distinguished men that are liberal-minded in this country? We are learning something quite new! [*Laughter.*]

DR STO. Yes, that is part of my new discovery too. And another part of it is that broad-mindedness is almost precisely the same thing as morality. That is why I maintain that it is absolutely inexcusable in the *People's Messenger* to proclaim, day in and day out, the false doctrine that it is the masses, the crowd, the compact majority, that have the monopoly of broad-mindedness and morality—and that vice and corruption and every kind of intellectual depravity are the result of culture just as the filth that is draining into our Baths is the result of the tanneries up at Mölledal! [*Uproar and interruptions.* DR STOCKMANN *is undisturbed and goes on, carried away by his ardor, with a smile.*] And yet this same *People's Messenger* can go on preaching that the masses ought to be elevated to higher conditions of life! But, bless my soul, if the *Messenger's* teaching is to be depended upon, this very raising up the masses would mean nothing more or less than setting them straightway upon the paths of depravity! Happily the theory that culture demoralizes is only an old falsehood that our forefathers believed in and we have inherited. No, it is ignorance, poverty, ugly conditions of life, that do the devil's work! In a house which does not get aired and swept every day—my wife Katherine maintains that the floor ought to be scrubbed as well, but that is a debatable question—in such a house, let me tell you, people will lose within two or three years the power of thinking or acting in a moral manner. Lack of oxygen weakens the conscience. And there must be a plentiful lack of oxygen in very many houses in this town, I should think, judging from the fact that the whole compact majority can be unconscientious enough to wish to build the town's prosperity on a quagmire of falsehood and deceit.

ASL. We cannot allow such a grave accusation to be flung at a citizen community.

A CITIZEN. I move that the chairman direct the speaker to sit down.

VOICES [*angrily*]. Hear, hear! Quite right! Make him sit down!

DR STO. [*losing his self-control*]. Then I will go and shout the truth at every street corner! I will write it in other towns' newspapers! The whole country shall know what is going on here.

HOV. It almost seems as if Doctor Stockmann's intentions were to ruin the town.

DR STO. Yes, my native town is so dear to me that I would rather ruin it than see it flourishing upon a lie.

ASL. This is really serious. [*Uproar and catcalls.* MRS STOCKMANN *coughs but to no purpose; her husband does not listen to her any longer.*]

HOV. [*shouting above the din*]. A man must be a public enemy to wish to ruin a whole community!

DR STO. [*with growing fervor*]. What does the destruction of a community matter, I tell you! All who live by lies ought to be exterminated like vermin! You will end by infecting the whole country; you will bring about such a state of things that the whole country will deserve to be ruined. And if things come to that pass, I shall say from the bottom of my heart: Let the whole country perish, let all these people be exterminated!

VOICES FROM THE CROWD. That is talking like an out-and-out enemy of the people!

BILL. There sounded the voice of the people, by all that's holy!

THE WHOLE CROWD [*shouting*]. Yes, yes! He is an enemy of the people! He hates his country! He hates his own people!

ASL. Both as a citizen and as an individual I am profoundly disturbed by what we have had to listen to. Doctor Stockmann has shown himself in a light I should never have dreamed of. I am unhappily obliged to subscribe to the opinion which I have just heard my estimable fellow citizens utter, and I propose that we should give expression to that opinion in a resolution. I propose a resolution as follows: "This meeting declares that it considers Doctor Thomas Stockmann, medical officer of the Baths, to be an enemy of the people." [*A storm of cheers and applause. A number of men surround the doctor and hiss him.* MRS STOCKMANN *and* PETRA *have got up from their seats.* MORTEN *and* EJLIF *are fighting the other schoolboys for hissing; some of their elders separate them.*]

DR STO. [*to the men who are hissing him*]. Oh, you fools! I tell you that——

ASL. [*ringing his bell*]. We cannot hear you now, Doctor. A formal vote is about to be taken; but, out of regard for personal feelings, it shall be by ballot and not verbal. Have you any clean paper, Mr Billing?

BILL. I have both blue and white here.

ASL. [*going to him*]. That will do nicely; we shall get on more quickly that way. Cut it up into small strips —yes, that's it. [*To the meeting.*] Blue means no; white means yes. I will come round myself and collect votes.

[PETER STOCKMANN *leaves the hall.* ASLAKSEN *and one or two others go around the room with the slips of paper in their hats.*]

1ST CITIZEN [*to* HOVSTAD]. I say, what has come to the doctor? What are we to think of it?

HOV. Oh, you know how headstrong he is.

2ND CITIZEN [*to* BILLING]. Billing, you go to their house—have you ever noticed if the fellow drinks?

BILL. Well, I'm hanged if I know what to say. There are always spirits on the table when you go.

3RD CITIZEN. I rather think he goes quite off his head sometimes.

1ST CITIZEN. I wonder if there is any madness in his family?

BILL. I shouldn't wonder if there were.

4TH CITIZEN. No, it is nothing more than sheer malice; he wants to get even with somebody for something or other.

BILL. Well, certainly he suggested a rise in his salary on one occasion lately and did not get it.

THE CITIZENS [*together*]. Ah!—then it is easy to understand how it is!

THE DRUNKEN MAN [*who has got amongst the audience again*]. I want a blue one, I do! And I want a white one too!

VOICES. It's that drunken chap again! Turn him out!

MORTEN KIIL [*going up to* DR STOCKMANN]. Well, Stockmann, do you see what these monkey tricks of yours lead to?

DR STO. I have done my duty.

MORTEN KIIL. What was that you said about the tanneries at Mölledal?

DR STO. You heard well enough. I said they were the source of all the filth.

MORTEN KIIL. My tannery too?

DR STO. Unfortunately your tannery is by far the worst.

MORTEN KIIL. Are you going to put that in the papers?

DR STO. I shall conceal nothing.

MORTEN KIIL. That may cost you dear, Stockmann. [*Goes out.*]

A STOUT MAN [*going up to* CAPTAIN HORSTER *without taking any notice of the ladies*]. Well, Captain, so you lend your house to enemies of the people?

HORS. I imagine I can do what I like with my own possessions, Mr Vik.

THE STOUT MAN. Then you can have no objection to my doing the same with mine.

HORS. What do you mean, sir?

THE STOUT MAN. You shall hear from me in the morning. [*Turns his back on him and moves off.*]

PETRA. Was that not your owner, Captain Horster?

HORS. Yes, that was Mr Vik the shipowner.

ASL. [*with the voting papers in his hands, gets up onto the platform and rings his bell*]. Gentlemen, allow me to announce the result. By the votes of everyone here except one person——

A YOUNG MAN. That is the drunk chap!

ASL. By the votes of everyone here except a tipsy man this meeting of citizens declares Doctor Thomas Stockmann to be an enemy of the people. [*Shouts and applause.*] Three cheers for our ancient and honorable citizen community! [*Renewed applause.*] Three cheers for our able and energetic mayor, who has so loyally suppressed the promptings of family feeling! [*Cheers.*] The meeting is dissolved. [*Gets down.*]

BILL. Three cheers for the chairman!

THE WHOLE CROWD. Three cheers for Aslaksen! Hurrah!

DR STO. My hat and coat, Petra! Captain, have you room on your ship for passengers to the New World?

HORS. For you and yours we will make room, Doctor.

DR STO. [*as* PETRA *helps him into his coat*]. Good. Come, Katherine! Come, boys!

MRS STO. [*in an undertone*]. Thomas dear, let us go out by the back way.

DR STO. No back ways for me, Katherine. [*Raising his voice.*] You will hear more of this enemy of the people before he shakes the dust off his shoes upon you! I am not so forgiving as a certain Person; I do not say: "I forgive you, for ye know not what ye do."

ASL. [*shouting*]. That is a blasphemous comparison, Doctor Stockmann!

BILL. It is, by God. It's dreadful for an earnest man to listen to.

A COARSE VOICE. Threatens us now, does he!

OTHER VOICES [*excitedly*]. Let's go and break his windows! Duck him in the fiord!

ANOTHER VOICE. Blow your horn, Evensen! Pip, pip!

[*Hornblowing, hisses and wild cries.* DR STOCKMANN *goes out through the hall with his family,* HORSTER *elbowing a way for them.*]

THE WHOLE CROWD [*howling after as they go*]. Enemy of the people! Enemy of the people!

BILL. [*as he puts his papers together*]. Well, I'm damned if I go and drink toddy with the Stockmanns tonight!

[*The crowd press toward the exit. The uproar continues outside; shouts of* "Enemy of the people!" *are heard from without.*]

ACT V

SCENE—DR STOCKMANN'S *study. Bookcases and cabinets containing specimens line the walls. At the back is a door leading to the hall; in the foreground on the left a door leading to the sitting room. In the right-hand wall are two windows, of which all the panes are broken. The doctor's desk, littered with books and papers, stands in the middle of the room, which is in disorder. It is morning.* DR STOCKMANN, *in dressing gown, slippers and a smoking cap, is bending down and raking with an um-*

brella under one of the cabinets. After a little while he rakes out a stone.

Dr Sto. [*calling through the open sitting-room door*]. Katherine, I have found another one.

Mrs Sto. [*from the sitting room*]. Oh, you will find a lot more yet, I expect.

Dr Sto. [*adding the stone to a heap of others on the table*]. I shall treasure these stones as relics. Ejlif and Morten shall look at them every day, and when they are grown up they shall inherit them as heirlooms. [*Rakes about under a bookcase.*] Hasn't—what the deuce is her name?—the girl, you know—hasn't she been to fetch the glazier yet?

Mrs Sto. [*coming in*]. Yes, but he said he didn't know if he would be able to come today.

Dr Sto. You will see he won't dare to come.

Mrs Sto. Well, that is just what Randine thought—that he didn't dare to on account of the neighbors. [*Calls into the sitting room.*] What is it you want, Randine? Give it to me. [*Goes in and comes out again directly.*] Here is a letter for you, Thomas.

Dr Sto. Let me see it. [*Opens and reads it.*] Ah!—of course.

Mrs Sto. Who is it from?

Dr Sto. From the landlord. Notice to quit.

Mrs Sto. Is it possible? Such a nice man——

Dr Sto. [*looking at the letter*]. Doesn't like doing it but dares not do otherwise—on account of his fellow citizens—out of regard for public opinion. Is in a dependent position—dare not offend certain influential men——

Mrs Sto. There, you see, Thomas!

Dr Sto. Yes, yes, I see well enough; the whole lot of them in the town are cowards; not a man among them dares do anything for fear of the others. [*Throws the letter onto the table.*] But it doesn't matter to us, Katherine. We are going to sail away to the New World and——

Mrs Sto. But, Thomas, are you sure we are well advised to take this step?

Dr Sto. Are you suggesting that I should stay here, where they have pilloried me as an enemy of the people—branded me—broken my windows! And just look here, Katherine—they have torn a great rent in my black trousers too!

Mrs Sto. Oh dear!—and they are the best pair you have got!

Dr Sto. You should never wear your best trousers when you go out to fight for freedom and truth. It is not that I care so much about the trousers, you know; you can always sew them up again for me. But that the common herd should dare to make this attack on me, as if they were my equals—that is what I cannot, for the life of me, swallow!

Mrs Sto. There is no doubt they have behaved very ill to you, Thomas; but is that sufficient reason for our leaving our native country for good and all?

Dr Sto. If we went to another town, do you suppose we should not find the common people just as insolent as they are here? Depend upon it, there is not much to choose between them. Oh well, let the curs snap—that is not the worst part of it. The worst is that from one end of this country to the other every man is the slave of his party. Although, as far as that goes, I daresay it is not much better in the free West either;

the compact majority and liberal public opinion and all that infernal old bag of tricks are probably rampant there too. But there things are done on a larger scale, you see. They may kill you, but they won't put you to death by slow torture. They don't squeeze a free man's soul in a vise, as they do here. And, if need be, one can live in solitude. [*Walks up and down.*] If only I knew where there was a virgin forest or a small South Sea island for sale cheap——

Mrs Sto. But think of the boys, Thomas.

Dr Sto. [*standing still*]. What a strange woman you are, Katherine! Would you prefer to have the boys grow up in a society like this? You saw for yourself last night that half the population are out of their minds; and if the other half have not lost their senses, it is because they are mere brutes, with no sense to lose.

Mrs Sto. But, Thomas dear, the imprudent things you said had something to do with it, you know.

Dr Sto. Well, isn't what I said perfectly true? Don't they turn every idea topsy-turvy? Don't they make a regular hotchpotch of right and wrong? Don't they say that the things I know are true are lies? The craziest part of it all is the fact of these "liberals," men of full age, going about in crowds imagining that they are the broad-minded party! Did you ever hear anything like it, Katherine?

Mrs Sto. Yes, yes, it's mad enough of them, certainly; but——[Petra *comes in from the sitting room.*] Back from school already?

Petra. Yes. I have been given notice of dismissal.

Mrs Sto. Dismissal?

Dr Sto. You too?

Petra. Mrs Busk gave me my notice, so I thought it was best to go at once.

Dr Sto. You were perfectly right too!

Mrs Sto. Who would have thought Mrs Busk was a woman like that!

Petra. Mrs Busk isn't a bit like that, Mother; I saw quite plainly how it hurt her to do it. But she didn't dare do otherwise, she said; and so I got my notice.

Dr Sto. [*laughing and rubbing his hands*]. She didn't dare do otherwise either! It's delicious!

Mrs Sto. Well, after the dreadful scenes last night——

Petra. It was not only that. Just listen to this, Father!

Dr Sto. Well?

Petra. Mrs Busk showed me no less than three letters she received this morning——

Dr Sto. Anonymous, I suppose?

Petra. Yes.

Dr Sto. Yes, because they didn't dare to risk signing their names, Katherine!

Petra. And two of them were to the effect that a man who has been our guest here was declaring last night at the club that my views on various subjects are extremely emancipated——

Dr Sto. You did not deny that, I hope?

Petra. No, you know I wouldn't. Mrs Busk's own views are tolerably emancipated when we are alone together, but now that this report about me is being spread she dare not keep me on any longer.

Mrs Sto. And someone who had been a guest of ours! That shows you the return you get for your hospitality, Thomas!

DR STO. We won't live in such a disgusting hole any longer. Pack up as quickly as you can, Katherine; the sooner we can get away, the better.

MRS STO. Be quiet—I think I hear someone in the hall. See who it is, Petra.

PETRA [*opening the door*]. Oh, it's you, Captain Horster! Do come in.

HORS. [*coming in*]. Good morning. I thought I would just come in and see how you were.

DR STO. [*shaking his hand*]. Thanks; that is really kind of you.

MRS STO. And thank you, too, for helping us through the crowd, Captain Horster.

PETRA. How did you manage to get home again?

HORS. Oh, somehow or other. I am fairly strong, and there is more sound than fury about these folk.

DR STO. Yes, isn't their swinish cowardice astonishing? Look here, I will show you something! There are all the stones they have thrown through my windows. Just look at them! I'm hanged if there are more than two decently large bits of hard stone in the whole heap; the rest are nothing but gravel—wretched little things. And yet they stood out there bawling and swearing that they would do me some violence, but as for *doing* anything—you don't see much of that in this town.

HORS. Just as well for you this time, Doctor!

DR STO. True enough. But it makes one angry all the same; because if someday it should be a question of a national fight in real earnest, you will see that public opinion will be in favor of taking to one's heels and the compact majority will turn tail like a flock of sheep, Captain Horster. That is what is so mournful to think of; it gives me so much concern that—— No, devil take it, it is ridiculous to care about it! They have called me an enemy of the people, so an enemy of the people let me be!

MRS STO. You will never be that, Thomas.

DR STO. Don't swear to that, Katherine. To be called an ugly name may have the same effect as a pin scratch in the lung. And that hateful name—I can't get quit of it. It is sticking here in the pit of my stomach, eating into me like a corrosive acid. And no magnesia will remove it.

PETRA. Bah!—you should only laugh at them, Father.

HORS. They will change their minds someday, Doctor.

MRS STO. Yes, Thomas, as sure as you are standing here.

DR STO. Perhaps, when it is too late. Much good may it do them! They may wallow in their filth then and rue the day when they drove a patriot into exile. When do you sail, Captain Horster?

HORS. Hm!—that was just what I had come to speak about.

DR STO. Why, has anything gone wrong with the ship?

HORS. No, but what has happened is that I am not to sail in it.

PETRA. Do you mean that you have been dismissed from your command?

HORS. [*smiling*]. Yes, that's just it.

PETRA. You too.

MRS STO. There, you see, Thomas!

DR STO. And that for the truth's sake! Oh, if I had thought such a thing possible——

HORS. You mustn't take it to heart; I shall be sure to find a job with some shipowner or other, elsewhere.

DR STO. And that is this man Vik

—a wealthy man, independent of everyone and everything! Shame on him!

HORS. He is quite an excellent fellow otherwise; he told me himself he would willingly have kept me on if only he had dared.

DR STO. But he didn't dare? No, of course not.

HORS. It is not such an easy matter, he said, for a party man——

DR STO. The worthy man spoke the truth. A party is like a sausage machine; it mashes up all sorts of heads together into the same mincemeat—fatheads and blockheads, all in one mash!

MRS STO. Come, come, Thomas dear!

PETRA [*to* HORSTER]. If only you had not come home with us, things might not have come to this pass.

HORS. I do not regret it.

PETRA [*holding out her hand to him*]. Thank you for that!

HORS. [*to* DR STOCKMANN]. And so what I came to say was that if you are determined to go away I have thought of another plan——

DR STO. That's splendid!—if only we can get away at once.

MRS STO. Hush!—wasn't that someone knocking?

PETRA. That is Uncle, surely.

DR STO. Aha! [*Calls out.*] Come in!

MRS STO. Dear Thomas, promise me definitely—

[PETER STOCKMANN *comes in from the hall.*]

PETER. Oh, you are engaged. In that case I will——

DR STO. No, no, come in.

PETER. But I wanted to speak to you alone.

MRS STO. We will go into the sitting room in the meanwhile.

HORS. And I will look in again later.

DR STO. No, go in there with them, Captain Horster; I want to hear more about——

HORS. Very well, I will wait then. [*He follows* MRS STOCKMANN *and* PETRA *into the sitting room.*]

DR STO. I daresay you find it rather draughty here today. Put your hat on.

PETER. Thank you, if I may. [*Does so.*] I think I caught cold last night; I stood and shivered——

DR STO. Really? I found it warm enough.

PETER. I regret that it was not in my power to prevent those excesses last night.

DR STO. Have you anything particular to say to me besides that?

PETER [*taking a big letter from his pocket*]. I have this document for you from the Baths Committee.

DR STO. My dismissal?

PETER. Yes, dating from today. [*Lays the letter on the table.*] It gives us pain to do it; but, to speak frankly, we dared not do otherwise on account of public opinion.

DR STO. [*smiling*]. Dared not? I seem to have heard that word before, today.

PETER. I must beg you to understand your position clearly. For the future you must not count on any practice whatever in the town.

DR STO. Devil take the practice! But why are you so sure of that?

PETER. The Householders' Association is circulating a list from house to house. All right-minded citizens are being called upon to give up employing you, and I can assure you that not a single head of a family will risk refusing his signature. They simply dare not.

Dr Sto. No, no; I don't doubt it. But what then?

Peter. If I might advise you, it would be best to leave the place for a little while.

Dr Sto. Yes, the propriety of leaving the place *has* occurred to me.

Peter. Good. And then, when you have had six months to think things over, if, after mature consideration, you can persuade yourself to write a few words of regret, acknowledging your error——

Dr Sto. I might have my appointment restored to me, do you mean?

Peter. Perhaps. It is not at all impossible.

Dr Sto. But what about public opinion then? Surely you would not dare to do it on account of public feeling.

Peter. Public opinion is an extremely mutable thing. And, to be quite candid with you, it is a matter of great importance to us to have some admission of that sort from you in writing.

Dr Sto. Oh, that's what you are after, is it! I will just trouble you to remember what I said to you lately about foxy tricks of that sort!

Peter. Your position was quite different then. At that time you had reason to suppose you had the whole town at your back.

Dr Sto. Yes, and now I feel I have the whole town *on* my back. [*Flaring up.*] I would not do it if I had the devil and his dam on my back! Never—never, I tell you!

Peter. A man with a family has no right to behave as you do. You have no right to do it, Thomas.

Dr Sto. I have no right! There is only one single thing in the world a free man has no right to do. Do you know what that is?

Peter. No.

Dr Sto. Of course you don't, but I will tell you. A free man has no right to soil himself with filth; he has no right to behave in a way that would justify his spitting in his own face.

Peter. This sort of thing sounds extremely plausible, of course; and if there were no other explanation for your obstinacy—— But as it happens that there is——

Dr Sto. What do you mean?

Peter. You understand very well what I mean. But, as your brother and as a man of discretion, I advise you not to build too much upon expectations and prospects that may so very easily fail you.

Dr Sto. What in the world is all this about?

Peter. Do you really ask me to believe that you are ignorant of the terms of Mr Kiil's will?

Dr Sto. I know that the small amount he possesses is to go to an institution for indigent old workpeople. How does that concern me?

Peter. In the first place, it is by no means a small amount that is in question. Mr Kiil is a fairly wealthy man.

Dr Sto. I had no notion of that!

Peter. Hm!—hadn't you really? Then I suppose you had no notion, either, that a considerable portion of his wealth will come to your children, you and your wife having a liferent of the capital. Has he never told you so?

Dr Sto. Never, on my honor! Quite the reverse; he has consistently done nothing but fume at being so unconscionably heavily taxed. But are you perfectly certain of this, Peter?

Peter. I have it from an absolutely

reliable source.

Dr Sto. Then, thank God, Katherine is provided for—and the children too! I must tell her this at once. [*Calls out.*] Katherine, Katherine!

Peter [*restraining him*]. Hush, don't say a word yet!

Mrs Sto. [*opening the door*]. What is the matter?

Dr Sto. Oh, nothing, nothing; you can go back. [*She shuts the door.* Dr Stockmann *walks up and down in his excitement.*] Provided for! Just think of it, we are all provided for! And for life! What a blessed feeling it is to know one is provided for!

Peter. Yes, but that is just exactly what you are not. Mr Kiil can alter his will any day he likes.

Dr Sto. But he won't do that, my dear Peter. The Badger is much too delighted at my attack on you and your wise friends.

Peter [*starts and looks intently at him*]. Ah, that throws a light on various things.

Dr Sto. What things?

Peter. I see that the whole thing was a combined maneuver on your part and his. These violent, reckless attacks that you have made against the leading men of the town, under the pretense that it was in the name of truth——

Dr Sto. What about them?

Peter. I see that they were nothing else than the stipulated price for that vindictive old man's will.

Dr Sto. [*almost speechless*]. Peter—you are the most disgusting plebeian I have ever met in all my life.

Peter. All is over between us. Your dismissal is irrevocable—we have a weapon against you now. [*Goes out.*]

Dr Sto. For shame! For shame! [*Calls out.*] Katherine, you must have the floor scrubbed after him! Let—what's her name?—devil take it, the girl who has always got soot on her nose——

Mrs Sto. [*in the sitting room*]. Hush, Thomas, be quiet!

Petra [*coming to the door*]. Father, Grandfather is here, asking if he may speak to you alone.

Dr Sto. Certainly he may. [*Going to the door.*] Come in, Mr Kiil. [Morten Kiil *comes in.* Dr Stockmann *shuts the door after him.*] What can I do for you? Won't you sit down?

Morten Kiil. I won't sit. [*Looks around.*] You look very comfortable here today, Thomas.

Dr Sto. Yes, don't we!

Morten Kiil. Very comfortable—plenty of fresh air. I should think you have got enough today of that oxygen you were talking about yesterday. Your conscience must be in splendid order today, I should think.

Dr Sto. It is.

Morten Kiil. So I should think. [*Taps his chest.*] Do you know what I have got here?

Dr Sto. A good conscience too, I hope.

Morten Kiil. Bah! No, it is something better than that. [*He takes a thick pocketbook from his breast pocket, opens it and displays a packet of papers.*]

Dr Sto. [*looking at him in astonishment*]. Shares in the Baths?

Morten Kiil. They were not difficult to get today.

Dr Sto. And you have been buying——

Morten Kiil. As many as I could pay for.

Dr Sto. But, my dear Mr Kiil—consider the state of the Baths' affairs!

Morten Kiil. If you behave like a reasonable man, you can soon set the Baths on their feet again.

Dr Sto. Well, you can see for yourself that I have done all I can, but—— They are all mad in this town!

Morten Kiil. You said yesterday that the worst of this pollution came from my tannery. If that is true, then my grandfather and my father before me and I myself, for many years past, have been poisoning the town like three destroying angels. Do you think I am going to sit quiet under that reproach?

Dr Sto. Unfortunately I am afraid you will have to.

Morten Kiil. No, thank you. I am jealous of my name and reputation. They call me "the Badger," I am told. A badger is a kind of pig, I believe; but I am not going to give them the right to call me that. I mean to live and die a clean man.

Dr Sto. And how are you going to set about it?

Morten Kiil. You shall cleanse me, Thomas.

Dr Sto. I!

Morten Kiil. Do you know what money I have bought these shares with? No, of course you can't know—but I will tell you. It is the money that Katherine and Petra and the boys will have when I am gone. Because I have been able to save a little bit after all, you know.

Dr Sto. [*flaring up*]. And you have gone and taken Katherine's money for *this!*

Morten Kiil. Yes, the whole of the money is invested in the Baths now. And now I just want to see whether you are quite stark, staring mad, Thomas! If you still make out that these animals and other nasty things of that sort come from my tannery, it will be exactly as if you were to flay broad strips of skin from Katherine's body and Petra's and the boys'; and no decent man would do that—unless he were mad.

Dr Sto. [*walking up and down*]. Yes, but I *am* mad; I *am* mad!

Morten Kiil. You cannot be so absurdly mad as all that when it is a question of your wife and children.

Dr Sto. [*standing still in front of him*]. Why couldn't you consult me about it before you went and bought all that trash?

Morten Kiil. What is done cannot be undone.

Dr Sto. [*walks about uneasily*]. If only I were not so certain about it! But I am absolutely convinced that I am right.

Morten Kiil [*weighing the pocket-book in his hand*]. If you stick to your mad idea, this won't be worth much, you know. [*Puts the pocket-book in his pocket.*]

Dr Sto. But, hang it all! it might be possible for science to discover some prophylactic, I should think—or some antidote of some kind——

Morten Kiil. To kill these animals, do you mean?

Dr Sto. Yes, or to make them innocuous.

Morten Kiil. Couldn't you try some ratsbane?

Dr Sto. Don't talk nonsense! They all say it is only imagination, you know. Well, let it go at that! Let them have their own way about it! Haven't the ignorant, narrow-minded curs reviled me as an enemy of the people?—and haven't they been ready to tear the clothes off my back too?

Morten Kiil. And broken all your windows to pieces!

Dr Sto. And then there is my duty to my family. I must talk it over with Katherine; she is great on those things.

Morten Kiil. That is right; be guided by a reasonable woman's advice.

Dr Sto. [*advancing toward him*]. To think you could do such a preposterous thing! Risking Katherine's money in this way and putting me in such a horribly painful dilemma! When I look at you I think I see the devil himself.

Morten Kiil. Then I had better go. But I must have an answer from you before two o'clock—yes or no. If it is no, the shares go to a charity, and that this very day.

Dr Sto. And what does Katherine get?

Morten Kiil. Not a halfpenny. [*The door leading to the hall opens, and* Hovstad *and* Aslaksen *make their appearance.*] Look at those two!

Dr Sto. [*staring at them*]. What the devil!—have *you* actually the face to come into my house?

Hov. Certainly.

Asl. We have something to say to you, you see.

Morten Kiil [*in a whisper*]. Yes or no—before two o'clock.

Asl. [*glancing at* Hovstad]. Aha! [Morten Kiil *goes out.*]

Dr Sto. Well, what do you want with me? Be brief.

Hov. I can quite understand that you are annoyed with us for our attitude at the meeting yesterday.

Dr Sto. Attitude, do you call it? Yes, it was a charming attitude! I call it weak, womanish—damnably shameful!

Hov. Call it what you like, we could not do otherwise.

Dr Sto. You *dared* not do otherwise—isn't that it?

Hov. Well, if you like to put it that way.

Asl. But why did you not let us have word of it beforehand?—just a hint to Mr Hovstad or to me?

Dr Sto. A hint? Of what?

Asl. Of what was behind it all.

Dr Sto. I don't understand you in the least.

Asl. [*with a confidential nod*]. Oh yes, you do, Doctor Stockmann.

Hov. It is no good making a mystery of it any longer.

Dr Sto. [*looking first at one of them and then at the other*]. What the devil do you both mean?

Asl. May I ask if your father-in-law is not going round the town buying up all the shares in the Baths?

Dr Sto. Yes, he has been buying Bath shares today; but——

Asl. It would have been more prudent to get someone else to do it—someone less nearly related to you.

Hov. And you should not have let your name appear in the affair. There was no need for anyone to know that the attack on the Baths came from you. You ought to have consulted me, Doctor Stockmann.

Dr Sto. [*looks in front of him; then a light seems to dawn on him and he says in amazement*]. Are such things conceivable? Are such things possible?

Asl. [*with a smile*]. Evidently they are. But it is better to use a little finesse, you know.

Hov. And it is much better to have several persons in a thing of that sort, because the responsibility of each individual is lessened when there are others with him.

Dr Sto. [*composedly*]. Come to

the point, gentlemen. What do you want?

Asl. Perhaps Mr Hovstad had better——

Hov. No, you tell him, Aslaksen.

Asl. Well, the fact is that now we know the bearings of the whole affair we think we might venture to put the *People's Messenger* at your disposal.

Dr Sto. Do you dare do that now? What about public opinion? Are you not afraid of a storm breaking upon our heads?

Hov. We will try to weather it.

Asl. And you must be ready to go off quickly on a new tack, Doctor. As soon as your invective has done its work——

Dr Sto. Do you mean as soon as my father-in-law and I have got hold of the shares at a low figure?

Hov. Your reasons for wishing to get the control of the Baths are mainly scientific, I take it.

Dr Sto. Of course; it was for scientific reasons that I persuaded the old Badger to stand in with me in the matter. So we will tinker at the conduit pipes a little and dig up a little bit of the shore, and it shan't cost the town a sixpence. That will be all right—eh?

Hov. I think so—if you have the *People's Messenger* behind you.

Asl. The press is a power in a free community, Doctor.

Dr Sto. Quite so. And so is public opinion. And you, Mr Aslaksen—I suppose you will be answerable for the Householders' Association?

Asl. Yes, and for the Temperance Society. You may rely on that.

Dr Sto. But, gentlemen—I really am ashamed to ask the question—but what return do you——

Hov. We should prefer to help you without any return whatever, believe me. But the *People's Messenger* is in rather a shaky condition; it doesn't go really well, and I should be very unwilling to suspend the paper now, when there is so much work to do here in the political way.

Dr Sto. Quite so; that would be a great trial to such a friend of the people as you are. [*Flares up.*] But I am an enemy of the people, remember! [*Walks about the room.*] Where have I put my stick? Where the devil is my stick?

Hov. What's that?

Asl. Surely you never mean——

Dr Sto. [*standing still*]. And suppose I don't give you a single penny of all I get out of it? Money is not very easy to get out of us rich folk, please to remember!

Hov. And you please to remember that this affair of the shares can be represented in two ways!

Dr Sto. Yes, and you are just the man to do it. If I don't come to the rescue of the *People's Messenger*, you will certainly take an evil view of the affair; you will hunt me down, I can well imagine—pursue me—try to throttle me as a dog does a hare.

Hov. It is a natural law; every animal must fight for its own livelihood.

Asl. And get its food where it can, you know.

Dr Sto. [*walking about the room*]. Then you go and look for yours in the gutter, because I am going to show you which is the strongest animal of us three. [*Finds an umbrella and brandishes it above his head.*] Ah, now!

Hov. You are surely not going to use violence!

Asl. Take care what you are doing

with that umbrella.

Dr Sto. Out of the window with you, Mr Hovstad!

Hov. [*edging to the door*]. Are you quite mad!

Dr Sto. Out of the window, Mr Aslaksen! Jump, I tell you! You will have to do it sooner or later.

Asl. [*running round the writing table*]. Moderation, Doctor–I am a delicate man–I can stand so little—— [*Calls out.*] Help, help!

[Mrs Stockmann, Petra *and* Horster *come in from the sitting room.*]

Mrs Sto. Good gracious, Thomas! What is happening?

Dr Sto. [*brandishing the umbrella*]. Jump out, I tell you! Out into the gutter!

Hov. An assault on an unoffending man! I call you to witness, Captain Horster. [*Hurries out through the hall.*]

Asl. [*irresolutely*]. If I only knew the way about here—— [*Steals out through the sitting room.*]

Mrs Sto. [*holding her husband back*]. Control yourself, Thomas!

Dr Sto. [*throwing down the umbrella*]. Upon my soul, they have escaped after all.

Mrs Sto. What did they want you to do?

Dr Sto. I will tell you later on; I have something else to think about now. [*Goes to the table and writes something on a calling card.*] Look there, Katherine; what is written there?

Mrs Sto. Three big No's; what does that mean?

Dr Sto. I will tell you that too, later on. [*Holds out the card to* Petra.] There, Petra; tell sooty-face to run over to the Badger's with that as quickly as she can. Hurry up!

[Petra *takes the card and goes out to the hall.*]

Dr Sto. Well, I think I have had a visit from every one of the devil's messengers today! But now I am going to sharpen my pen till they can feel its point; I shall dip it in venom and gall; I shall hurl my inkpot at their heads!

Mrs Sto. Yes, but we are going away, you know, Thomas.

[Petra *comes back.*]

Dr Sto. Well?

Petra. She has gone with it.

Dr Sto. Good. . . . Going away, did you say? No, I'll be hanged if we are going away! We are going to stay where we are, Katherine!

Petra. Stay here?

Mrs Sto. Here, in the town?

Dr Sto. Yes, here. This is the field of battle–this is where the fight will be. This is where I shall triumph! As soon as I have had my trousers sewn up I shall go out and look for another house. We must have a roof over our heads for the winter.

Hors. That you shall have in my house.

Dr Sto. Can I?

Hors. Yes, quite well. I have plenty of room, and I am almost never at home.

Mrs Sto. How good of you, Captain Horster!

Petra. Thank you!

Dr Sto. [*grasping his hand*]. Thank you, thank you! That is one trouble over! Now I can set to work in earnest at once. There is an endless amount of things to look through here, Katherine! Luckily I shall have all my time at my disposal, because I have been dismissed from the Baths, you know.

Mrs Sto. [*with a sigh*]. Oh yes, I

expected that.

DR STO. And they want to take my practice away from me too. Let them! I have got the poor people to fall back upon anyway—those that don't pay anything; and, after all, they need me most too. But, by Jove, they will have to listen to me; I shall preach to them in season and out of season, as it says somewhere.

MRS STO. But, dear Thomas, I should have thought events had showed you what use it is to preach.

DR STO. You are really ridiculous, Katherine. Do you want me to let myself be beaten off the field by public opinion and the compact majority and all that devilry? No, thank you! And what I want to do is so simple and clear and straightforward. I only want to drum into the heads of these curs the fact that the Liberals are the most insidious enemies of freedom—that party programs strangle every young and vigorous truth—that considerations of expediency turn morality and justice upside down—and that they will end by making life here unbearable. Don't you think, Captain Horster, that I ought to be able to make people understand that?

HORS. Very likely; I don't know much about such things myself.

DR STO. Well, look here—I will explain! It is the party leaders that must be exterminated. A party leader is like a wolf, you see—like a voracious wolf. He requires a certain number of smaller victims to prey upon every year if he is to live. Just look at Hovstad and Aslaksen! How many smaller victims have they not put an end to—or at any rate maimed and mangled until they are fit for nothing except to be householders or subscribers to the *People's Messenger!* [*Sits down on the edge of the table.*] Come here, Katherine—look how beautifully the sun shines today! And this lovely spring air I am drinking in!

MRS STO. Yes, if only we could live on sunshine and spring air, Thomas.

DR STO. Oh, you will have to pinch and save a bit—then we shall get along. That gives me very little concern. What is much worse is that I know of no one who is liberal-minded and high-minded enough to venture to take up my work after me.

PETRA. Don't think about that, Father; you have plenty of time before you. Hullo, here are the boys already!

[EJLIF *and* MORTEN *come in from the sitting room.*]

MRS STO. Have you got a holiday?

MOR. No, but we were fighting with the other boys between lessons——

EJL. That isn't true; it was the other boys were fighting with us.

MOR. Well, and then Mr Rörlund said we had better stay at home for a day or two.

DR STO. [*snapping his fingers and getting up from the table*]. I have it! I have it, by Jove! You shall never set foot in the school again!

THE BOYS. No more school!

MRS STO. But, Thomas——

DR STO. Never, I say. I will educate you myself; that is to say, you shan't learn a blessed thing——

MOR. Hooray!

DR STO. —but I will make liberal-minded and high minded men of you. You must help me with that, Petra.

PETRA. Yes, Father, you may be sure I will.

Dr Sto. And my school shall be in the room where they insulted me and called me an enemy of the people. But we are too few as we are; I must have at least twelve boys to begin with.

Mrs Sto. You will certainly never get them in this town.

Dr Sto. We shall. [*To the boys.*] Don't you know any street urchins—regular ragamuffins?

Mor. Yes, Father, I know lots!

Dr Sto. That's capital! Bring me some specimens of them. I am going to experiment with curs just for once; there may be some exceptional heads amongst them.

Mor. And what are we going to do when you have made liberal-minded and high-minded men of us?

Dr Sto. Then you shall drive all the wolves out of the country, my boys!

[Ejlif *looks rather doubtful about it;* Morten *jumps about crying* "Hurrah!"]

Mrs Sto. Let us hope it won't be the wolves that will drive you out of the country, Thomas.

Dr Sto. Are you out of your mind, Katherine? Drive me out! Now—when I am the strongest man in the town!

Mrs Sto. The strongest—now?

Dr Sto. Yes, and I will go so far as to say that now I am the strongest man in the whole world.

Mor. I say!

Dr Sto. [*lowering his voice*]. Hush! You mustn't say anything about it yet, but I have made a great discovery.

Mrs Sto. Another one?

Dr Sto. Yes. [*Gathers them round him and says confidentially.*] It is this, let me tell you—that the strongest man in the world is he who stands most alone.

Mrs Sto. [*smiling and shaking her head*]. Oh, Thomas, Thomas!

Petra [*encouragingly, as she grasps her father's hands*]. Father!

A DOLL'S HOUSE

PERSONS OF THE PLAY

TORVALD HELMER.
NORA, *his wife*.
DR RANK.
MRS LINDE.
NILS KROGSTAD.
HELMER'S THREE YOUNG CHILDREN.
ANNE, *their nurse*.
A HOUSEMAID.
A PORTER.
The action takes place in Helmer's house.

ACT I

SCENE—*A room furnished comfortably and tastefully but not extravagantly. At the back a door to the right leads to the entrance hall; another to the left leads to Helmer's study. Between the doors stands a piano. In the middle of the left-hand wall is a door and beyond a window. Near the window are a round table, armchairs and a small sofa. In the right-hand wall, at the farther end, another door; and on the same side, nearer the footlights, a stove, two easy chairs and a rocking chair; between the stove and the door a small table. Engravings on the walls; a cabinet with china and other small objects; a small bookcase with well-bound books. The floors are carpeted, and a fire burns in the stove. It is winter.*

A bell rings in the hall; shortly afterward the door is heard to open. Enter NORA, *humming a tune and in high spirits. She is in outdoor dress and carries a number of parcels; these she lays on the table to the right. She leaves the outer door open after her, and through it is seen a* PORTER *who is carrying a Christmas tree and a basket, which he gives to the* MAID *who has opened the door.*

NORA. Hide the Christmas tree carefully, Helen. Be sure the children do not see it till this evening, when it is dressed. [*To the* PORTER, *taking out her purse.*] How much?

POR. Sixpence.

NORA. There is a shilling. No, keep the change. [*The* PORTER *thanks her and goes out.* NORA *shuts the door. She is laughing to herself as she takes off her hat and coat. She takes a packet of macaroons from her pocket and eats one or two, then goes cautiously to her husband's door and listens.*] Yes, he is in. [*Still humming, she goes to the table on the right.*]

HEL. [*calls out from his room*]. Is that my little lark twittering out there?

NORA [*busy opening some of the parcels*]. Yes, it is!

HEL. Is it my little squirrel bustling about?

NORA. Yes!

HEL. When did my squirrel come home?

NORA. Just now. [*Puts the bag of macaroons into her pocket and wipes her mouth.*] Come in here, Torvald, and see what I have bought.

HEL. Don't disturb me. [*A little later he opens the door and looks into the room, pen in hand.*] Bought, did you say? All these things? Has my little spendthrift been wasting money again?

NORA. Yes, but, Torvald, this year we really can let ourselves go a little. This is the first Christmas that we have not needed to economize.

HEL. Still, you know, we can't spend money recklessly.

NORA. Yes, Torvald, we may be a wee bit more reckless now, mayn't we? Just a tiny wee bit! You are going to have a big salary and earn lots and lots of money.

HEL. Yes, after the new year; but then it will be a whole quarter before the salary is due.

NORA. Pooh! We can borrow till then.

HEL. Nora! [*Goes up to her and takes her playfully by the ear.*] The same little featherhead! Suppose, now, that I borrowed fifty pounds today and you spent it all in the Christmas week and then on New Year's Eve a slate fell on my head and killed me and——

NORA [*putting her hands over his mouth*]. Oh! don't say such horrid things.

HEL. Still, suppose that happened,—what then?

NORA. If that were to happen, I don't suppose I should care whether I owed money or not.

HEL. Yes, but what about the people who had lent it?

NORA. They? Who would bother about them? I should not know who they were.

HEL. That is like a woman! But seriously, Nora, you know what I think about that. No debt, no borrowing. There can be no freedom or beauty about a home life that depends on borrowing and debt. We two have kept bravely on the straight road so far, and we will go on the same way for the short time longer that there need be any struggle.

NORA [*moving toward the stove*]. As you please, Torvald.

HEL. [*following her*]. Come, come, my little skylark must not droop her wings. What is this! Is my little squirrel out of temper? [*Taking out his purse.*] Nora, what do you think I have got here?

NORA [*turning round quickly*]. Money!

HEL. There you are. [*Gives her some money.*] Do you think I don't know what a lot is wanted for housekeeping at Christmas time?

NORA [*counting*]. Ten shillings—a pound—two pounds! Thank you, thank you, Torvald; that will keep me going for a long time.

HEL. Indeed it must.

NORA. Yes, yes, it will. But come here and let me show you what I have bought. And all so cheap! Look, here is a new suit for Ivar and a sword, and a horse and a trumpet for Bob, and a doll and dolly's bedstead for Emmy—they are very plain, but anyway she will soon break them in pieces. And here are dress lengths and handkerchiefs for the maids; old Anne ought really to have something better.

HEL. And what is in this parcel?

NORA [*crying out*]. No, no! You mustn't see that till this evening.

HEL. Very well. But now tell me, you extravagant little person, what would you like for yourself?

NORA. For myself? Oh, I am sure I don't want anything.

HEL. Yes, but you must. Tell me something reasonable that you would particularly like to have.

NORA. No, I really can't think of anything—unless, Torvald——

HEL. Well?

NORA [*playing with his coat buttons and without raising her eyes to his*]. If you really want to give me something, you might—you might——

HEL. Well, out with it!

NORA [*speaking quickly*]. You might give me money, Torvald. Only just as much as you can afford; and then one of these days I will buy something with it.

HEL. But, Nora——

NORA. Oh, do! dear Torvald; please, please do! Then I will wrap it up in beautiful gilt paper and hang it on the Christmas tree. Wouldn't that be fun?

HEL. What are little people called that are always wasting money?

NORA. Spendthrifts—I know. Let us do as I suggest, Torvald, and then I shall have time to think what I am most in want of. That is a very sensible plan, isn't it?

HEL. [*smiling*]. Indeed it is—that is to say, if you were really to save out of the money I give you and then really buy something for yourself. But if you spend it all on the housekeeping and any number of unnecessary things, then I merely have to pay up again.

NORA. Oh, but, Torvald——

HEL. You can't deny it, my dear little Nora. [*Puts his arm around her waist.*] It's a sweet little spendthrift, but she uses up a deal of money. One would hardly believe how expensive such little persons are!

NORA. It's a shame to say that. I do really save all I can.

HEL. [*laughing*]. That's very true—all you can. But you can't save anything!

NORA [*smiling quietly and happily*]. You haven't any idea how many expenses we skylarks and squirrels have, Torvald.

HEL. You are an odd little soul. Very like your father. You always find some new way of wheedling money out of me, and as soon as you have got it it seems to melt in your hands. You never know where it has gone. Still, one must take you as you are. It is in the blood; for indeed it is true that you can inherit these things, Nora.

NORA. Ah, I wish I had inherited many of Papa's qualities.

HEL. And I would not wish you to be anything but just what you are, my sweet little skylark. But, do you know, it strikes me that you are looking rather—what shall I say?—rather uneasy today.

NORA. Do I?

HEL. You do, really. Look straight at me.

NORA [*looks at him*]. Well?

HEL. [*wagging his finger at her*]. Hasn't Miss Sweet Tooth been breaking rules in town today?

NORA. No; what makes you think that?

HEL. Hasn't she paid a visit to the confectioner's?

NORA. No, I assure you, Torvald——

HEL. Not been nibbling sweets?

NORA. No, certainly not.

HEL. Not even taken a bite at a macaroon or two?

NORA. No, Torvald, I assure you, really——

HEL. There, there, of course I was only joking.

NORA [*going to the table on the right*]. I should not think of going against your wishes.

HEL. No, I am sure of that; besides, you gave me your word. [*Going up to her.*] Keep your little Christmas secrets to yourself, my darling. They will all be revealed tonight when the Christmas tree is lit, no doubt.

NORA. Did you remember to invite Doctor Rank?

HEL. No. But there is no need; as a matter of course he will come to dinner with us. However, I will ask him when he comes in this morning. I have ordered some good wine. Nora, you can't think how I am looking forward to this evening.

NORA. So am I! And how the children will enjoy themselves, Torvald!

HEL. It is splendid to feel that one has a perfectly safe appointment and a big enough income. It's delightful to think of, isn't it?

NORA. It's wonderful!

HEL. Do you remember last Christmas? For a full three weeks beforehand you shut yourself up every evening till long after midnight, making ornaments for the Christmas tree and all the other fine things that were to be a surprise to us. It was the dullest three weeks I ever spent!

NORA. I didn't find it dull.

HEL. [*smiling*]. But there was precious little result, Nora.

NORA. Oh, you shouldn't tease me about that again. How could I help the cat's going in and tearing everything to pieces?

HEL. Of course you couldn't, poor little girl. You had the best of intentions to please us all, and that's the main thing. But it is a good thing that our hard times are over.

NORA. Yes, it is really wonderful.

HEL. This time I needn't sit here and be dull all alone and you needn't ruin your dear eyes and your pretty little hands——

NORA [*clapping her hands*]. No, Torvald, I needn't any longer, need I! It's wonderfully lovely to hear you say so! [*Taking his arm.*] Now I will tell you how I have been thinking we ought to arrange things, Torvald. As soon as Christmas is over—— [*A bell rings in the hall.*] There's the bell. [*She tidies the room a little.*] There's someone at the door. What a nuisance!

HEL. If it is a caller, remember I am not at home.

MAID [*in the doorway*]. A lady to see you, ma'am—a stranger.

NORA. Ask her to come in.

MAID [*to* HELMAR]. The doctor came at the same time, sir.

HEL. Did he go straight into my room?

MAID. Yes sir.

[HEL. *goes into his room. The* MAID *ushers in* MRS LINDE, *who is in traveling dress, and shuts the door.*]

MRS L. [*in a dejected and timid voice*]. How do you do, Nora?

NORA [*doubtfully*]. How do you do——

MRS L. You don't recognize me, I suppose.

NORA. No, I don't know—yes, to be sure, I seem to—— [*Suddenly.*] Yes! Christine! Is it really you?

MRS L. Yes, it is I.

NORA. Christine! To think of my not recognizing you! And yet how could I? [*In a gentle voice.*] How you have altered, Christine!

MRS L. Yes, I have indeed. In nine, ten long years——

NORA. Is it so long since we met? I suppose it is. The last eight years have been a happy time for me, I can tell you. And so now you have come into the town and have taken this long journey in winter—that was plucky of you.

MRS L. I arrived by steamer this morning.

NORA. To have some fun at Christmas time, of course. How delightful! We will have such fun together! But take off your things. You are not cold, I hope. [*Helps her.*] Now we will sit down by the stove and be cozy. No, take this armchair; I will sit here in the rocking chair. [*Takes her hands.*] Now you look like your old self again; it was only the first moment—— You are a little paler, Christine, and perhaps a little thinner.

MRS L. And much, much older, Nora.

NORA. Perhaps a little older; very, very little; certainly not much. [*Stops suddenly and speaks seriously.*] What a thoughtless creature I am, chattering away like this. My poor, dear Christine, do forgive me.

MRS L. What do you mean, Nora?

NORA [*gently*]. Poor Christine, you are a widow.

MRS L. Yes; it is three years ago now.

NORA. Yes, I knew; I saw it in the papers. I assure you, Christine, I meant ever so often to write to you at the time, but I always put it off and something always prevented me.

MRS L. I quite understand, dear.

NORA. It was very bad of me, Christine. Poor thing, how you must have suffered. And he left you nothing?

MRS L. No.

NORA. And no children?

MRS L. No.

NORA. Nothing at all, then?

MRS L. Not even any sorrow or grief to live upon.

NORA [*looking incredulously at her*]. But, Christine, is that possible?

MRS L. [*smiles sadly and strokes her hair*]. It sometimes happens, Nora.

NORA. So you are quite alone. How dreadfully sad that must be. I have three lovely children. You can't see them just now, for they are out with their nurse. But now you must tell me all about it.

MRS L. No, no; I want to hear about you.

NORA. No, you must begin. I mustn't be selfish today; today I must only think of your affairs. But there is one thing I must tell you. Do you know we have just had a great piece of good luck?

MRS L. No, what is it?

NORA. Just fancy, my husband has been made manager of the bank!

MRS L. Your husband? What good luck!

NORA. Yes, tremendous! A barrister's profession is such an uncertain thing, especially if he won't undertake unsavory cases; and naturally Torvald has never been willing to do that, and I quite agree with him. You may imagine how pleased we are! He is to take up his work in the bank at the new year, and then he will have a big salary and lots of commissions. For the future we can live quite differently—we can do just as we like. I feel so relieved and so happy, Christine! It will be splendid to have heaps of money and not need to have any anxiety, won't it?

MRS L. Yes, anyhow I think it would be delightful to have what one needs.

NORA. No, not only what one needs but heaps and heaps of money.

MRS L. [*smiling*]. Nora, Nora, haven't you learned sense yet? In our schooldays you were a great spendthrift.

NORA [*laughing*]. Yes, that is what Torvald says now. [*Wags her finger at her.*] But "Nora, Nora" is not so silly as you think. We have not been in a position for me to waste money. We have both had to work.

MRS L. You too?

NORA. Yes; odds and ends, needlework, crochet work, embroidery and that kind of thing. [*Dropping her voice.*] And other things as well. You know Torvald left his office when we were married? There was no prospect of promotion there, and he had to try and earn more than before. But during the first year he overworked himself dreadfully. You see, he had to make money every way he could; and he worked early and late; but he couldn't stand it and fell dreadfully ill, and the doctors said it was necessary for him to go south.

MRS L. You spent a whole year in Italy, didn't you?

NORA. Yes. It was no easy matter to get away, I can tell you. It was just after Ivar was born, but naturally we had to go. It was a wonderfully beautiful journey, and it saved Torvald's life. But it cost a tremendous lot of money, Christine.

MRS L. So I should think.

NORA. It cost about two hundred and fifty pounds. That's a lot, isn't it?

MRS L. Yes, and in emergencies like that it is lucky to have the money.

NORA. I ought to tell you that we had it from Papa.

MRS L. Oh, I see. It was just about that time that he died, wasn't it?

NORA. Yes; and, just think of it, I couldn't go and nurse him. I was expecting little Ivar's birth every day and I had my poor sick Torvald to look after. My dear, kind father—I never saw him again, Christine. That was the saddest time I have known since our marriage.

MRS L. I know how fond you were of him. And then you went off to Italy?

NORA. Yes; you see, we had money then, and the doctors insisted on our going, so we started a month later.

MRS L. And your husband came back quite well?

NORA. As sound as a bell!

MRS L. But—the doctor?

NORA. What doctor?

MRS L. I thought your maid said the gentleman who arrived here just as I did was the doctor.

NORA. Yes, that was Doctor Rank but he doesn't come here professionally. He is our greatest friend and comes in at least once every day. No, Torvald has not had an hour's illness since then, and our children are strong and healthy and so am I. [*Jumps up and claps her hands.*] Christine! Christine! It's good to be alive and happy! But how horrid of me; I am talking of nothing but my own affairs. [*Sits on a stool near her and rests her arms on her knees.*] You mustn't be angry with me. Tell me, is it really true that you did not love your husband? Why did you marry him?

MRS L. My mother was alive then and was bedridden and helpless, and I had to provide for my two younger brothers; so I did not think I was justified in refusing his offer.

NORA. No, perhaps you were quite right. He was rich at that time, then?

MRS L. I believe he was quite well off. But his business was a precarious one, and when he died it all went to pieces and there was nothing left.

NORA. And then?

MRS L. Well, I had to turn my hand to anything I could find—first a small shop, then a small school and so on. The last three years have seemed like one long working day, with no rest. Now it is at an end, Nora. My poor mother needs me no more, for she is gone; and the boys do not need me either; they have got situations and can shift for themselves.

NORA. What a relief you must feel it.

MRS L. No indeed; I only feel my life unspeakably empty. No one to live for any more. [*Gets up restlessly.*] That was why I could not stand the life in my little backwater any longer. I hope it may be easier here to find something which will busy me and occupy my thoughts. If only I could have the good luck to get some regular work—office work of some kind——

NORA. But, Christine, that is so frightfully tiring, and you look tired out now. You had far better go away to some watering place.

MRS L. [*walking to the window*]. I have no father to give me money for a journey, Nora.

NORA [*rising*]. Oh, don't be angry with me.

MRS L. [*going up to her*]. It is you that must not be angry with me, dear. The worst of a position like mine is that it makes one so bitter. No one to work for and yet obliged to be always on the lookout for chances. One must live, and so one becomes selfish. When you told me of the happy turn your fortunes have taken—you will hardly believe it—I was delighted not so much on your account as on my own.

NORA. How do you mean? Oh, I understand. You mean that perhaps Torvald could get you something to do.

MRS L. Yes, that was what I was thinking of.

NORA. He must, Christine. Just leave it to me; I will broach the subject very cleverly—I will think of something that will please him very much. It will make me so happy to be of some use to you.

MRS L. How kind you are, Nora, to be so anxious to help me! It is doubly kind in you, for you know so little of the burdens and troubles of life.

NORA. I? I know so little of them?

MRS L. [*smiling*]. My dear! Small household cares and that sort of thing! You are a child, Nora.

NORA [*tosses her head and crosses the stage*]. You ought not to be so superior.

MRS L. No?

NORA. You are just like the others. They all think that I am incapable of anything really serious——

MRS L. Come, come.

NORA. —that I have gone through nothing in this world of cares.

MRS L. But, my dear Nora, you have just told me all your troubles.

NORA. Pooh!—those were trifles. [*Lowering her voice.*] I have not told you the important thing.

MRS L. The important thing? What do you mean?

NORA. You look down upon me altogether, Christine—but you ought not to. You are proud, aren't you, of having worked so hard and so long for your mother?

Mrs L. Indeed, I don't look down on anyone. But it is true that I am both proud and glad to think that I was privileged to make the end of my mother's life almost free from care.

Nora. And you are proud to think of what you have done for your brothers.

Mrs L. I think I have the right to be.

Nora. I think so too. But now listen to this; I too have something to be proud and glad of.

Mrs L. I have no doubt you have. But what do you refer to?

Nora. Speak low. Suppose Torvald were to hear! He mustn't on any account–no one in the world must know, Christine, except you.

Mrs L. But what is it?

Nora. Come here. [*Pulls her down on the sofa beside her.*] Now I will show you that I too have something to be proud and glad of. It was I who saved Torvald's life.

Mrs L. "Saved"? How?

Nora. I told you about our trip to Italy. Torvald would never have recovered if he had not gone there.

Mrs L. Yes, but your father gave you the necessary funds.

Nora [*smiling*]. Yes, that is what Torvald and the others think, but——

Mrs L. But—

Nora. Papa didn't give us a shilling. It was I who procured the money.

Mrs L. You? All that large sum?

Nora. Two hundred and fifty pounds. What do you think of that?

Mrs L. But, Nora, how could you possibly do it? Did you win a prize in the lottery?

Nora [*contemptuously*]. In the lottery? There would have been no credit in that.

Mrs L. But where did you get it from, then?

Nora [*humming and smiling with an air of mystery*]. Hm, hm! Aha!

Mrs L. Because you couldn't have borrowed it.

Nora. Couldn't I? Why not?

Mrs L. No, a wife cannot borrow without her husband's consent.

Nora [*tossing her head*]. Oh, if it is a wife who has any head for business–a wife who has the wit to be a little bit clever——

Mrs L. I don't understand it at all, Nora.

Nora. There is no need you should. I never said I had borrowed the money. I may have got it some other way. [*Lies back on the sofa.*] Perhaps I got it from some other admirers. When anyone is as attractive as I am——

Mrs L. You are a mad creature.

Nora. Now you know you're full of curiosity, Christine.

Mrs L. Listen to me, Nora dear. Haven't you been a little bit imprudent?

Nora [*sits up straight*]. Is it imprudent to save your husband's life?

Mrs L. It seems to me imprudent, without his knowledge, to——

Nora. But it was absolutely necessary that he should not know! My goodness, can't you understand that? It was necessary he should have no idea what a dangerous condition he was in. It was to me that the doctors came and said that his life was in danger and that the only thing to save him was to live in the south. Do you suppose I didn't try, first of all, to get what I wanted as if it were for myself? I told him how much I should love to travel abroad like other young wives; I tried tears and entreaties with him; I told him that he ought to remember the condition I was in and that he ought to be kind and indulgent to me; I even hinted that he might raise a loan. That nearly made him angry, Christine. He said I was thoughtless and that it was his duty as my husband not to indulge me in my whims and caprices—as I believe he called them. Very well, I thought, you must be saved—and that was how I came to devise a way out of the difficulty.

Mrs L. And did your husband never get to know from your father that the money had not come from him?

Nora. No, never. Papa died just at that time. I had meant to let him into the secret and beg him never to reveal it. But he was so ill then—alas, there never was any need to tell him.

Mrs L. And since then have you never told your secret to your husband?

Nora. Good heavens, no! How could you think so? A man who has such strong opinions about these things! And besides, how painful and humiliating it would be for Torvald, with his manly independence, to know that he owed me anything! It would upset our mutual relations altogether; our beautiful happy home would no longer be what it is now.

Mrs L. Do you mean never to tell him about it?

Nora [*meditatively and with a half-smile*]. Yes—someday, perhaps, after many years, when I am no longer as nice looking as I am now. Don't laugh at me! I mean, of course, when Torvald is no longer as devoted to me as he is now; when my dancing and dressing-up and reciting have palled on him; then it may be a good thing to have something in reserve—— [*Breaking off.*] What nonsense! That time will never come. Now what do you think of my great secret, Christine? Do you still think I am of no use? I can tell you, too, that this affair has caused me a lot of worry. It has been by no means easy for me to meet my engagements punctually. I may tell you that there is something that is called, in business, quarterly interest and another thing called payment in installments, and it is always so dreadfully difficult to manage them. I have had to save a little here and there, where I could, you understand. I have not been able to put aside much from my housekeeping money, for Torvald must have a good table. I couldn't let my children be shabbily dressed; I have felt obliged to use up all he gave me for them, the sweet little darlings!

Mrs L. So it has all had to come out of your own necessaries of life, poor Nora?

Nora. Of course. Besides, I was the one responsible for it. Whenever Torvald has given me money for new dresses and such things I have never spent more than half of it; I have always bought the simplest and cheapest things. Thank heaven any clothes look well on me, and so Torvald has never noticed it. But it was often very hard on me, Christine—because it is delightful to be really well dressed, isn't it?

Mrs L. Quite so.

Nora. Well, then I have found other ways of earning money. Last winter I was lucky enough to get a lot of copying to do, so I locked myself up and sat writing every evening until quite late at night. Many a time I was desperately tired, but all the same it was a tremendous pleasure to sit there working and earning money. It was like being a man.

MRS L. How much have you been able to pay off in that way?

NORA. I can't tell you exactly. You see, it is very difficult to keep an account of a business matter of that kind. I only know that I have paid every penny that I could scrape together. Many a time I was at my wits' end. [*Smiles.*] Then I used to sit here and imagine that a rich old gentleman had fallen in love with me——

MRS L. What! Who was it?

NORA. Be quiet!—that he had died and that when his will was opened it contained, written in big letters, the instruction: "The lovely Mrs Nora Helmer is to have all I possess paid over to her at once in cash."

MRS L. But, my dear Nora—who could the man be?

NORA. Good gracious, can't you understand? There was no old gentleman at all; it was only something that I used to sit here and imagine, when I couldn't think of any way of procuring money. But it's all the same now; the tiresome old person can stay where he is as far as I am concerned; I don't care about him or his will either, for I am free from care now. [*Jumps up.*] My goodness, it's delightful to think of, Christine! Free from care! To be able to be free from care, quite free from care; to be able to play and romp with the children; to be able to keep the house beautifully and have everything just as Torvald likes it! And, think of it, soon the spring will come and the big blue sky! Perhaps we shall be able to take a little trip—perhaps I shall see the sea again! Oh, it's a wonderful thing to be alive and be happy. [*A bell is heard in the hall.*]

MRS L. [*rising*]. There is the bell; perhaps I had better go.

NORA. No, don't go; no one will come in here; it is sure to be for Torvald.

SERVANT [*at the hall door*]. Excuse me, ma'am—there is a gentleman to see the master, and as the doctor is with him——

NORA. Who is it?

KROG. [*at the door*]. It is I, Mrs Helmer. [MRS LINDE *starts, trembles and turns to the window.*]

NORA [*takes a step toward him and speaks in a strained, low voice*]. You? What is it? What do you want to see my husband about?

KROG. Bank business—in a way. I have a small post in the bank, and I hear your husband is to be our chief now.

NORA. Then it is——

KROG. Nothing but dry business matters, Mrs Helmer; absolutely nothing else.

NORA. Be so good as to go into the study then. [*She bows indifferently to him and shuts the door into the hall, then comes back and makes up the fire in the stove.*]

MRS L. Nora—who was that man?

NORA. A lawyer of the name of Krogstad.

MRS L. Then it really was he.

NORA. Do you know the man?

MRS L. I used to—many years ago. At one time he was a solicitor's clerk in our town.

NORA. Yes, he was.

MRS L. He is greatly altered.

NORA. He made a very unhappy marriage.

MRS L. He is a widower now, isn't he?

NORA. With several children. There now, it is burning up. [*Shuts the door of the stove and moves the rocking chair aside.*]

MRS L. They say he carries on various kinds of business.

NORA. Really! Perhaps he does; I don't know anything about it. But don't let us think of business; it is so tiresome.

DR RANK [*comes out of* HELMER'S *study. Before he shuts the door he calls to him*]. No, my dear fellow, I won't disturb you; I would rather go in to your wife for a little while. [*Shuts the door and sees* MRS LINDE.] I beg your pardon; I am afraid I am disturbing you too.

NORA. No, not at all. [*Introducing him.*] Doctor Rank, Mrs Linde.

RANK. I have often heard Mrs Linde's name mentioned here. I think I passed you on the stairs when I arrived, Mrs Linde?

MRS L. Yes, I go up very slowly; I can't manage stairs well.

RANK. Ah! Some slight internal weakness?

MRS L. No, the fact is I have been overworking myself.

RANK. Nothing more than that? Then I suppose you have come to town to amuse yourself with our entertainments?

MRS L. I have come to look for work.

RANK. Is that a good cure for overwork?

MRS L. One must live, Doctor Rank.

RANK. Yes, the general opinion seems to be that it is necessary.

NORA. Look here, Doctor Rank—you know you want to live.

RANK. Certainly. However wretched I may feel, I want to prolong the agony as long as possible. All my patients are like that. And so are those who are morally diseased; one of them, and a bad case too, is at this very moment with Helmer——

MRS L. [*sadly*]. Ah!

NORA. Whom do you mean?

RANK. A lawyer of the name of Krogstad, a fellow you don't know at all. He suffers from a diseased moral character, Mrs Helmer, but even he began talking of its being highly important that he should live.

NORA. Did he? What did he want to speak to Torvald about?

RANK. I have no idea; I only heard that it was something about the bank.

NORA. I didn't know this—what's his name?—Krogstad had anything to do with the bank.

RANK. Yes, he has some sort of appointment there. [*To* MRS LINDE.] I don't know whether you find also in your part of the world that there are certain people who go zealously snuffing about to smell out moral corruption and, as soon as they have found some, put the person concerned into some lucrative position where they can keep their eye on him. Healthy natures are left out in the cold.

MRS L. Still I think the sick are those who most need taking care of.

RANK. [*shrugging his shoulders*]. Yes, there you are. That is the sentiment that is turning society into a sick house.

[NORA, *who has been absorbed in her thoughts, breaks out into smothered laughter and claps her hands.*]

RANK. Why do you laugh at that? Have you any notion what society really is?

Nora. What do I care about tiresome society? I am laughing at something quite different, something extremely amusing. Tell me, Doctor Rank, are all the people who are employed in the bank dependent on Torvald now?

Rank. Is that what you find so extremely amusing?

Nora [*smiling and humming*]. That's my affair! [*Walking about the room.*] It's perfectly glorious to think that we have—that Torvald has so much power over so many people. [*Takes the packet from her pocket.*] Doctor Rank, what do you say to a macaroon?

Rank. What, macaroons? I thought they were forbidden here.

Nora. Yes, but these are some Christine gave me.

Mrs L. What! I?

Nora. Oh well, don't be alarmed! You couldn't know that Torvald had forbidden them. I must tell you that he is afraid they will spoil my teeth. But, bah!—once in a way—— That's so, isn't it, Doctor Rank? By your leave! [*Puts a macaroon into his mouth.*] You must have one too, Christine. And I shall have one, just a little one—or at most two. [*Walking about.*] I am tremendously happy. There is just one thing in the world now that I should dearly love to do.

Rank. Well, what is that?

Nora. It's something I should dearly love to say if Torvald could hear me.

Rank. Well, why can't you say it?

Nora. No, I daren't; it's so shocking.

Mrs L. Shocking?

Rank. Well, I should not advise you to say it. Still, with us you might. What is it you would so much like to say if Torvald could hear you?

Nora. I should just love to say—Well, I'm damned!

Rank. Are you mad?

Mrs L. Nora dear!

Rank. Say it, here he is!

Nora [*hiding the packet*]. Hush! Hush! Hush!

[Helmer *comes out of his room with his coat over his arm and his hat in his hand.*]

Nora. Well, Torvald dear, have you got rid of him?

Hel. Yes, he has just gone.

Nora. Let me introduce you—this is Christine, who has come to town.

Hel. Christine? Excuse me, but I don't know——

Nora. Mrs Linde, dear; Christine Linde.

Hel. Of course. A school friend of my wife's, I presume?

Mrs L. Yes, we have known each other since then.

Nora. And just think, she has taken a long journey in order to see you.

Hel. What do you mean?

Mrs L. No, really, I——

Nora. Christine is tremendously clever at bookkeeping, and she is frightfully anxious to work under some clever man, so as to perfect herself——

Hel. Very sensible, Mrs Linde.

Nora. And when she heard you had been appointed manager of the bank—the news was telegraphed, you know—she traveled here as quick as she could. Torvald, I am sure you will be able to do something for Christine, for my sake, won't you?

Hel. Well, it is not altogether impossible. I presume you are a widow, Mrs Linde?

Mrs L. Yes.

HEL. And have had some experience of bookkeeping?

MRS L. Yes, a fair amount.

HEL. Ah well, it's very likely I may be able to find something for you.

NORA [*clapping her hands*]. What did I tell you?

HEL. You have just come at a fortunate moment, Mrs Linde.

MRS L. How am I to thank you?

HEL. There is no need. [*Puts on his coat.*] But today you must excuse me——

RANK. Wait a minute; I will come with you. [*Brings his fur coat from the hall and warms it at the fire.*]

NORA. Don't be long away, Torvald dear.

HEL. About an hour, not more.

NORA. Are you going too, Christine?

MRS L. [*putting on her cloak*]. Yes, I must go and look for a room.

HEL. Oh well, then, we can walk down the street together.

NORA [*helping her*]. What a pity it is we are so short of space here; I am afraid it is impossible for us——

MRS L. Please don't think of it! Good-by, Nora dear, and many thanks.

NORA. Good-by for the present. Of course you will come back this evening. And you too, Doctor Rank. What do you say? If you are well enough? Oh, you must be! Wrap yourself up well. [*They go to the door all talking together. Children's voices are heard on the staircase.*]

NORA. There they are. There they are! [*She runs to open the door. The* NURSE *comes in with the children.*] Come in! Come in! [*Stoops and kisses them.*] Oh, you sweet blessings! Look at them, Christine! Aren't they darlings?

RANK. Don't let us stand here in the draught.

HEL. Come along, Mrs Linde; the place will only be bearable for a mother now!

[RANK, HELMER *and* MRS LINDE *go downstairs. The* NURSE *comes forward with the children;* NORA *shuts the hall door.*]

NORA. How fresh and well you look! Such red cheeks!—like apples and roses. [*The children all talk at once while she speaks to them.*] Have you had great fun? That's splendid! What, you pulled both Emmy and Bob along on the sledge? Both at once? That *was* good. You are a clever boy, Ivar. Let me take her for a little, Anne. My sweet little baby doll! [*Takes the baby from the* MAID *and dances it up and down.*] Yes, yes, Mother will dance with Bob too. What! Have you been snowballing? I wish I had been there too! No, no, I will take their things off, Anne; please let me do it, it is such fun. Go in now, you look half frozen. There is some hot coffee for you on the stove.

[*The* NURSE *goes into the room on the left.* NORA *takes off the children's things and throws them about while they all talk to her at once.*]

NORA. *Really!* Did a big dog run after you? But it didn't bite you? No, dogs don't bite nice little dolly children. You mustn't look at the parcels, Ivar. What are they? Ah, I daresay you would like to know. No, no—it's something nasty! Come, let us have a game! What shall we play at? Hide and seek? Yes, we'll play hide and seek. Bob shall hide first. Must I hide? Very well, I'll hide first. [*She and the children laugh and shout and romp in and out of the room; at last*

NORA *hides under the table; the children rush in and look for her but do not see her; they hear her smothered laughter, run to the table, lift up the cloth and find her. Shouts of laughter. She crawls forward and pretends to frighten them. Fresh laughter. Meanwhile there has been a knock at the hall door but none of them has noticed it. The door is half opened and* KROGSTAD *appears. He waits a little; the game goes on.*]

KROG. Excuse me, Mrs Helmer.

NORA [*with a stifled cry turns round and gets up onto her knees*]. Ah! What do you want?

KROG. Excuse me, the outer door was ajar; I suppose someone forgot to shut it.

NORA [*rising*]. My husband is out, Mr Krogstad.

KROG. I know that.

NORA. What do you want here then?

KROG. A word with you.

NORA. With me? [*To the children, gently.*] Go in to Nurse. What? No, the strange man won't do Mother any harm. When he has gone we will have another game. [*She takes the children into the room on the left and shuts the door after them.*] You want to speak to me?

KROG. Yes, I do.

NORA. Today? It is not the first of the month yet.

KROG. No, it is Christmas Eve, and it will depend on yourself what sort of a Christmas you will spend.

NORA. What do you want? Today it is absolutely impossible for me——

KROG. We won't talk about that till later on. This is something different. I presume you can give me a moment?

NORA. Yes—yes, I can—although——

KROG. Good. I was in Olsen's Restaurant and saw your husband going down the street——

NORA. Yes?

KROG. With a lady.

NORA. What then?

KROG. May I make so bold as to ask if it was a Mrs Linde?

NORA. It was.

KROG. Just arrived in town?

NORA. Yes, today.

KROG. She is a great friend of yours, isn't she?

NORA. She is. But I don't see——

KROG. I knew her too, once upon a time.

NORA. I am aware of that.

KROG. Are you? So you know all about it; I thought as much. Then I can ask you, without beating about the bush—is Mrs Linde to have an appointment in the bank?

NORA. What right have you to question me, Mr Krogstad? You, one of my husband's subordinates! But since you ask, you shall know. Yes, Mrs Linde *is* to have an appointment. And it was I who pleaded her cause, Mr Krogstad, let me tell you that.

KROG. I was right in what I thought then.

NORA [*walking up and down the stage*]. Sometimes one has a tiny little bit of influence, I should hope. Because one is a woman it does not necessarily follow that—— When anyone is in a subordinate position, Mr Krogstad, they should really be careful to avoid offending anyone who—who——

KROG. Who has influence?

NORA. Exactly.

KROG. [*changing his tone*]. Mrs Helmer, you will be so good as to use your influence on my behalf.

NORA. What? What do you mean?

KROG. You will be so kind as to see

that I am allowed to keep my subordinate position in the bank.

NORA. What do you mean by that? Who proposes to take your post away from you?

KROG. Oh, there is no necessity to keep up the pretense of ignorance. I can quite understand that your friend is not very anxious to expose herself to the chance of rubbing shoulders with me, and I quite understand, too, whom I have to thank for being turned off.

NORA. But I assure you——

KROG. Very likely; but, to come to the point, the time has come when I should advise you to use your influence to prevent that.

NORA. But, Mr Krogstad, I *have* no influence.

KROG. Haven't you? I thought you said yourself just now——

NORA. Naturally I did not mean you to put that construction on it. I! What should make you think I have any influence of that kind with my husband?

KROG. Oh, I have known your husband from our student days. I don't suppose he is any more unassailable than other husbands.

NORA. If you speak slightingly of my husband, I shall turn you out of the house.

KROG. You are bold, Mrs Helmer.

NORA. I am not afraid of you any longer. As soon as the New Year comes I shall in a very short time be free of the whole thing.

KROG. [*controlling himself*]. Listen to me, Mrs Helmer. If necessary, I am prepared to fight for my small post in the bank as if I were fighting for my life.

NORA. So it seems.

KROG. It is not only for the sake of the money; indeed, that weighs least with me in the matter. There is another reason—well, I may as well tell you. My position is this. I daresay you know, like everybody else, that once, many years ago, I was guilty of an indiscretion.

NORA. I think I have heard something of the kind.

KROG. The matter never came into court, but every way seemed to be closed to me after that. So I took to the business that you know of. I had to do something; and, honestly, I don't think I've been one of the worst. But now I must cut myself free from all that. My sons are growing up; for their sake I must try and win back as much respect as I can in the town. This post in the bank was like the first step up for me—and now your husband is going to kick me downstairs again into the mud.

NORA. But you must believe me, Mr Krogstad; it is not in my power to help you at all.

KROG. Then it is because you haven't the will, but I have means to compel you.

NORA. You don't mean that you will tell my husband that I owe you money?

KROG. Hm! Suppose I were to tell him?

NORA. It would be perfectly infamous of you. [*Sobbing.*] To think of his learning my secret, which has been my joy and pride, in such an ugly, clumsy way—that he should learn it from you! And it would put me in a horribly disagreeable position.

KROG. Only disagreeable?

NORA. [*impetuously*]. Well, do it then!—and it will be the worse for you. My husband will see for himself what a blackguard you are, and you certainly won't keep your post then.

Krog. I asked you if it was only a disagreeable scene at home that you were afraid of?

Nora. If my husband does get to know of it, of course he will at once pay you what is still owing, and we shall have nothing more to do with you.

Krog. [*coming a step nearer*]. Listen to me, Mrs Helmer. Either you have a very bad memory or you know very little of business. I shall be obliged to remind you of a few details.

Nora. What do you mean?

Krog. When your husband was ill you came to me to borrow two hundred and fifty pounds.

Nora. I didn't know anyone else to go to.

Krog. I promised to get you that amount——

Nora. Yes, and you did so.

Krog. I promised to get you that amount on certain conditions. Your mind was so taken up with your husband's illness and you were so anxious to get the money for your journey that you seem to have paid no attention to the conditions of our bargain. Therefore it will not be amiss if I remind you of them. Now I promised to get the money on the security of a bond which I drew up.

Nora. Yes, and which I signed.

Krog. Good. But below your signature there were a few lines constituting your father a surety for the money; those lines your father should have signed.

Nora. Should? He did sign them.

Krog. I had left the date blank; that is to say your father should himself have inserted the date on which he signed the paper. Do you remember that?

Nora. Yes, I think I remember.

Krog. Then I gave you the bond to send by post to your father. Is that not so?

Nora. Yes.

Krog. And you naturally did so at once, because five or six days afterward you brought me the bond with your father's signature. And then I gave you the money.

Nora. Well, haven't I been paying it off regularly?

Krog. Fairly so, yes. But—to come back to the matter in hand—that must have been a very trying time for you, Mrs Helmer?

Nora. It was, indeed.

Krog. Your father was very ill, wasn't he?

Nora. He was very near his end.

Krog. And died soon afterward?

Nora. Yes.

Krog. Tell me, Mrs Helmer, can you by any chance remember what day your father died?—on what day of the month, I mean.

Nora. Papa died on the twenty-ninth of September.

Krog. That is correct; I have ascertained it for myself. And, as that is so, there is a discrepancy [*taking a paper from his pocket*] which I cannot account for.

Nora. What discrepancy? I don't know——

Krog. The discrepancy consists, Mrs Helmer, in the fact that your father signed this bond three days after his death.

Nora. What do you mean? I don't understand.

Krog. Your father died on the twenty-ninth of September. But look here; your father has dated his signature the second of October. It is a discrepancy, isn't it? [NORA *is silent.*] Can you explain it to me? [NORA *is still silent.*] It is a remarkable thing, too, that the words "second of October," as well as the year, are not written in your father's handwriting but in one that I think I know. Well, of course it can be explained; your father may have forgotten to date his signature and someone else may have dated it haphazard before they knew of his death. There is no harm in that. It all depends on the signature of the name, and *that* is genuine, I suppose, Mrs Helmer? It was your father himself who signed his name here?

NORA [*after a short pause, throws her head up and looks defiantly at him*]. No, it was not. It was I that wrote Papa's name.

KROG. Are you aware that is a dangerous confession?

NORA. In what way? You shall have your money soon.

KROG. Let me ask you a question: why did you not send the paper to your father?

NORA. It was impossible; Papa was so ill. If I had asked him for his signature, I should have had to tell him what the money was to be used for; and when he was so ill himself I couldn't tell him that my husband's life was in danger—it was impossible.

KROG. It would have been better for you if you had given up your trip abroad.

NORA. No, that was impossible. That trip was to save my husband's life; I couldn't give that up.

KROG. But did it never occur to you that you were committing a fraud on me?

NORA. I couldn't take that into account; I didn't trouble myself about you at all. I couldn't bear you because you put so many heartless difficulties in my way although you knew what a dangerous condition my husband was in.

KROG. Mrs Helmer, you evidently do not realize clearly what it is that you have been guilty of. But I can assure you that my one false step, which lost me all my reputation, was nothing more or nothing worse than what you have done.

NORA. You? Do you ask me to believe that you were brave enough to run a risk to save your wife's life?

KROG. The law cares nothing about motives.

NORA. Then it must be a very foolish law.

KROG. Foolish or not, it is the law by which you will be judged if I produce this paper in court.

NORA. I don't believe it. Is a daughter not to be allowed to spare her dying father anxiety and care? Is a wife not to be allowed to save her husband's life? I don't know much about law, but I am certain that there must be laws permitting such things as that. Have you no knowledge of such laws—you who are a lawyer? You must be a very poor lawyer, Mr Krogstad.

KROG. Maybe. But matters of business—such business as you and I have had together—do you think I don't understand that? Very well. Do as you please. But let me tell you this—if I lose my position a second time, you shall lose yours with me. [*He bows and goes out through the hall.*]

NORA [*appears buried in thought for a short time, then tosses her head*]. Nonsense! Trying to frighten me like that! I am not so silly as he thinks. [*Begins to busy herself putting the children's things in order.*] And yet—— No, it's impossible! I did it for love's sake.

THE CHILDREN [*in the doorway on the left*]. Mother, the stranger man has gone out through the gate.

NORA. Yes, dears, I know. But don't tell anyone about the stranger man. Do you hear? Not even Papa.

CHILDREN. No, Mother; but will you come and play again?

NORA. No, no—not now.

CHILDREN. But, Mother, you promised us.

NORA. Yes, but I can't now. Run away in; I have such a lot to do. Run away in, my sweet little darlings. [*She gets them into the room by degrees and shuts the door on them, then sits down on the sofa, takes up a piece of needlework and sews a few stitches but soon stops.*] No! [*Throws down the work, gets up, goes to the hall door and calls out.*] Helen! bring the tree in. [*Goes to the table on the left, opens a drawer and stops again.*] No, no! It is quite impossible!

MAID [*coming in with the tree*]. Where shall I put it, ma'am?

NORA. Here, in the middle of the floor.

MAID. Shall I get you anything else?

NORA. No, thank you. I have all I want.

[*Exit* MAID.]

NORA [*begins dressing the tree*]. A candle here—and flowers here — The horrible man! It's all nonsense—there's nothing wrong. The tree shall be splendid! I will do everything I can think of to please you, Torvald! I will sing for you, dance for you—— [HELMER *comes in with some papers under his arm.*] Oh, are you back already?

HEL. Yes. Has anyone been here?

NORA. Here? No.

HEL. That is strange. I saw Krogstad going out of the gate.

NORA. Did you? Oh yes, I forgot, Krogstad was here for a moment.

HEL. Nora, I can see from your manner that he has been here begging you to say a good word for him.

NORA. Yes.

HEL. And you were to appear to do it of your own accord; you were to conceal from me the fact of his having been here; didn't he beg that of you too?

NORA. Yes, Torvald, but——

HEL. Nora, Nora, and you would be a party to that sort of thing? To have any talk with a man like that and give him any sort of promise? And to tell me a lie into the bargain?

NORA. A lie?

HEL. Didn't you tell me no one had been here? [*Shakes his finger at her.*] My little songbird must never do that again. A songbird must have a clean beak to chirp with—no false notes! [*Puts his arm around her waist.*] That is so, isn't it? Yes, I am sure it is. [*Lets her go.*] We will say no more about it. [*Sits down by the stove.*] How warm and snug it is here! [*Turns over his papers.*]

NORA [*after a short pause during which she busies herself with the Christmas tree*]. Torvald!

HEL. Yes.

NORA. I am looking forward tremendously to the fancy-dress ball at the Stenborgs' the day after tomorrow.

HEL. And I am tremendously curious to see what you are going to surprise me with.

NORA. It was very silly of me to want to do that.

HEL. What do you mean?

NORA. I can't hit upon anything that will do; everything I think of seems so silly and insignificant.

HEL. Does my little Nora acknowledge that at last?

NORA [*standing behind his chair with her arms on the back of it*]. Are you very busy, Torvald?

HEL. Well——

NORA. What are all those papers?

HEL. Bank business.

NORA. Already?

HEL. I have got authority from the retiring manager to undertake the necessary changes in the staff and in the rearrangement of the work, and I must make use of the Christmas week for that, so as to have everything in order for the new year.

NORA. Then that was why this poor Krogstad——

HEL. Hm!

NORA [*leans against the back of his chair and strokes his hair*]. If you hadn't been so busy, I should have asked you a tremendously big favor, Torvald.

HEL. What is that? Tell me.

NORA. There is no one has such good taste as you. And I do so want to look nice at the fancy-dress ball. Torvald, couldn't you take me in hand and decide what I shall go as and what sort of a dress I shall wear?

HEL. Aha! So my obstinate little woman is obliged to get someone to come to her rescue?

NORA. Yes, Torvald, I can't get along a bit without your help.

HEL. Very well, I will think it over; we shall manage to hit upon something.

NORA. That is nice of you. [*Goes to the Christmas tree. A short pause.*] How pretty the red flowers look! But tell me, was it really something very bad that this Krogstad was guilty of?

HEL. He forged someone's name. Have you any idea what that means?

NORA. Isn't it possible that he was driven to do it by necessity?

HEL. Yes; or, as in so many cases, by imprudence. I am not so heartless as to condemn a man altogether because of a single false step of that kind.

NORA. No, you wouldn't, would you, Torvald?

HEL. Many a man has been able to retrieve his character if he has openly confessed his fault and taken his punishment.

NORA. Punishment?

HEL. But Krogstad did nothing of that sort; he got himself out of it by a cunning trick, and that is why he has gone under altogether.

NORA. But do you think it would——

HEL. Just think how a guilty man like that has to lie and play the hypocrite with everyone, how he has to wear a mask in the presence of those near and dear to him, even before his own wife and children. And about the children—that is the most terrible part of it all, Nora.

NORA. How?

HEL. Because such an atmosphere of lies infects and poisons the whole life of a home. Each breath the children take in such a house is full of the germs of evil.

NORA [*coming nearer him*]. Are you sure of that?

HEL. My dear, I have often seen it in the course of my life as a lawyer. Almost everyone who has gone to the bad early in life has had a deceitful mother.

NORA. Why do you only say—mother?

HEL. It seems most commonly to be the mother's influence, though naturally a bad father's would have the same result. Every lawyer is familiar with the fact. This Krogstad, now, has been persistently poisoning his own children with lies and dissimulation; that is why I say he has lost all moral character. [*Holds out his hands to her.*] That is why my sweet little Nora must promise me not to plead his cause. Give me your hand on it. Come, come, what is this? Give me your hand. There now, that's settled. I assure you it would be quite impossible for me to work with him; I literally feel physically ill when I am in the company of such people.

NORA [*takes her hand out of his and goes to the opposite side of the Christmas tree*]. How hot it is in here, and I have such a lot to do.

HEL. [*getting up and putting his papers in order*]. Yes, and I must try and read through some of these before dinner, and I must think about your costume too. And it is just possible I may have something ready in gold paper to hang up on the tree. [*Puts his hand on her head.*] My precious little singing bird! [*He goes into his room and shuts the door after him.*]

NORA [*after a pause, whispers*]. No, no—it isn't true. It's impossible; it must be impossible.

[*The* NURSE *opens the door on the left.*]

NURSE. The little ones are begging so hard to be allowed to come in to Mamma.

NORA. No, no, no! Don't let them come in to me! You stay with them, Anne.

NURSE. Very well, ma'am. [*Shuts the door.*]

NORA [*pale with terror*]. Deprave my little children? Poison my home? [*A short pause. Then she tosses her head.*] It's not true. It can't possibly be true.

ACT II

THE SAME SCENE—*The Christmas tree is in the corner by the piano, stripped of its ornaments and with burned-down candle ends on its disheveled branches.* NORA'S *cloak and hat are lying on the sofa. She is alone in the room, walking about uneasily. She stops by the sofa and takes up her cloak.*

NORA [*drops the cloak*]. Someone is coming now. [*Goes to the door and listens.*] No—it is no one. Of course no one will come today, Christmas Day—nor tomorrow either. But perhaps—— [*Opens the door and looks out.*] No, nothing in the letter box; it is quite empty. [*Comes forward.*] What rubbish! Of course he can't be in earnest about it. Such a thing couldn't happen; it is impossible—I have three little children.

[*Enter the* NURSE *from the room on the left, carrying a big cardboard box.*]

NURSE. At last I have found the box with the fancy dress.

NORA. Thanks; put it on the table.

NURSE [*in doing so*]. But it is very much in want of mending.

NORA. I should like to tear it into a hundred thousand pieces.

NURSE. What an idea! It can easily be put in order—just a little patience.

NORA. Yes, I will go and get Mrs Linde to come and help me with it.

NURSE. What, out again? In this horrible weather? You will catch cold, ma'am, and make yourself ill.

NORA. Well, worse than that might happen. How are the children?

NURSE. The poor little souls are playing with their Christmas presents, but——

NORA. Do they ask much for me?

NURSE. You see, they are so accustomed to having their mamma with them.

NORA. Yes—but, Nurse, I shall not be able to be so much with them now as I was before.

NURSE. Oh well, young children easily get accustomed to anything.

NORA. Do you think so? Do you think they would forget their mother if she went away altogether?

NURSE. Good heavens!—went away altogether?

NORA. Nurse, I want you to tell me something I have often wondered about—how could you have the heart to put your own child out among strangers?

NURSE. I was obliged to if I wanted to be little Nora's nurse.

NORA. Yes, but how could you be willing to do it?

NURSE. What, when I was going to get such a good place by it? A poor girl who has got into trouble should be glad to. Besides, that wicked man didn't do a single thing for me.

NORA. But I suppose your daughter has quite forgotten you.

NURSE. No, indeed she hasn't. She wrote to me when she was confirmed and when she was married.

NORA [*putting her arms round her neck*]. Dear old Anne, you were a good mother to me when I was little.

NURSE. Little Nora, poor dear, had no other mother but me.

NORA. And if my little ones had no other mother, I am sure you would—— What nonsense I am talking! [*Opens the box.*] Go in to them. Now I must—— You will see tomorrow how charming I shall look.

NURSE. I am sure there will be no one at the ball so charming as you, ma'am. [*Goes into the room on the left.*]

NORA [*begins to unpack the box but soon pushes it away from her*]. If only I dared go out. If only no one would come. If only I could be sure nothing would happen here in the meantime. Stuff and nonsense! No one will come. Only I mustn't think about it. I will brush my muff. What lovely, lovely gloves! Out of my thoughts, out of my thoughts! One, two, three, four, five, six—— [*Screams.*] Ah! there is someone coming. [*Makes a movement toward the door but stands irresolute.*]

[*Enter* MRS LINDE *from the hall, where she has taken off her cloak and hat.*]

NORA. Oh, it's you, Christine. There is no one else out there, is there? How good of you to come!

MRS L. I heard you were up asking for me.

NORA. Yes, I was passing by. As a matter of fact, it is something you could help me with. Let us sit down here on the sofa. Look here. Tomorrow evening there is to be a fancy-dress ball at the Stenborgs', who live above us, and Torvald wants me to go as a Neapolitan fishergirl and dance the tarantella that I learnt at Capri.

MRS L. I see; you are going to keep up the character.

NORA. Yes, Torvald wants me to. Look, here is the dress; Torvald had it made for me there, but now it is all so torn, and I haven't any idea——

Mrs L. We will easily put that right. It is only some of the trimming come unsewn here and there. Needle and thread? Now then, that's all we want.

Mrs L. [*sewing*]. So you are going to be dressed up tomorrow, Nora. I will tell you what–I shall come in for a moment and see you in your fine feathers. But I have completely forgotten to thank you for a delightful evening yesterday.

Nora [*gets up and crosses the stage*]. Well, I don't think yesterday was as pleasant as usual. You ought to have come down to town a little earlier, Christine. Certainly Torvald does understand how to make a house dainty and attractive.

Mrs L. And so do you, it seems to me; you are not your father's daughter for nothing. But tell me, is Doctor Rank always as depressed as he was yesterday?

Nora. No; yesterday it was very noticeable. I must tell you that he suffers from a very dangerous disease. He has consumption of the spine, poor creature. His father was a horrible man who committed all sorts of excesses, and that is why his son was sickly from childhood, do you understand?

Mrs L. [*dropping her sewing*]. But, my dearest Nora, how do you know anything about such things?

Nora [*walking about*]. Pooh! When you have three children you get visits now and then from–from married women who know something of medical matters, and they talk about one thing and another.

Mrs L. [*goes on sewing. A short silence*]. Does Doctor Rank come here every day?

Nora. Every day regularly. He is Torvald's most intimate friend and a friend of mine too. He is just like one of the family.

Mrs L. But tell me this–is he perfectly sincere? I mean, isn't he the kind of man that is very anxious to make himself agreeable?

Nora. Not in the least. What makes you think that?

Mrs L. When you introduced him to me yesterday he declared he had often heard my name mentioned in this house, but afterward I noticed that your husband hadn't the slightest idea who I was. So how could Doctor Rank——

Nora. That is quite right, Christine. Torvald is so absurdly fond of me that he wants me absolutely to himself, as he says. At first he used to seem almost jealous if I mentioned any of the dear folks at home, so naturally I gave up doing so. But I often talk about such things with Doctor Rank because he likes hearing about them.

Mrs L. Listen to me, Nora. You are still very like a child in many things, and I am older than you in many ways and have a little more experience. Let me tell you this–you ought to make an end of it with Doctor Rank.

Nora. What ought I to make an end of?

Mrs L. Of two things, I think. Yesterday you talked some nonsense about a rich admirer who was to leave you money——

Nora. An admirer who doesn't exist, unfortunately! But what then?

Mrs L. Is Doctor Rank a man of means?

Nora. Yes, he is.

MRS L. And has no one to provide for?

NORA. No, no one; but——

MRS L. And comes here every day?

NORA. Yes, I told you so.

MRS L. But how can this well-bred man be so tactless?

NORA. I don't understand you at all.

MRS L. Don't prevaricate, Nora. Do you suppose I don't guess who lent you the two hundred and fifty pounds?

NORA. Are you out of your senses? How can you think of such a thing! A friend of ours, who comes here every day! Do you realize what a horribly painful position that would be?

MRS L. Then it really isn't he?

NORA. No, certainly not. It would never have entered into my head for a moment. Besides, he had no money to lend then; he came into his money afterward.

MRS L. Well, I think that was lucky for you, my dear Nora.

NORA. No, it would never have come into my head to ask Doctor Rank. Although I am quite sure that if I had asked him——

MRS L. But of course you won't.

NORA. Of course not. I have no reason to think it could possibly be necessary. But I am quite sure that if I told Doctor Rank——

MRS L. Behind your husband's back?

NORA. I must make an end of it with the other one, and that will be behind his back too. I *must* make an end of it with him.

MRS L. Yes, that is what I told you yesterday, but——

NORA [*walking up and down*]. A man can put a thing like that straight much easier than a woman.

MRS L. One's husband, yes.

NORA. Nonsense! [*Standing still.*] When you pay off a debt you get your bond back, don't you?

MRS L. Yes, as a matter of course.

NORA. And can tear it into a hundred thousand pieces and burn it up—the nasty dirty paper!

MRS L. [*looks hard at her, lays down her sewing and gets up slowly*]. Nora, you are concealing something from me.

NORA. Do I look as if I were?

MRS L. Something has happened to you since yesterday morning. Nora, what is it?

NORA [*going nearer to her*]. Christine! [*Listens.*] Hush! There's Torvald come home. Do you mind going in to the children for the present? Torvald can't bear to see dressmaking going on. Let Anne help you.

MRS L. [*gathering some of the things together*]. Certainly—but I am not going away from here till we have had it out with one another. [*She goes into the room on the left as Helmer comes in from the hall.*]

NORA [*going up to* HELMER]. I have wanted you so much, Torvald dear.

HEL. Was that the dressmaker?

NORA. No, it was Christine; she is helping me to put my dress in order. You will see I shall look quite smart.

HEL. Wasn't that a happy thought of mine, now?

NORA. Splendid! But don't you think it is nice of me, too, to do as you wish?

HEL. Nice?—because you do as your husband wishes? Well, well, you little rogue, I am sure you did not mean it in that way. But I am not going to disturb you; you will want to be trying on your dress, I expect.

Nora. I suppose you are going to work.

Hel. Yes. [*Shows her a bundle of papers.*] Look at that. I have just been in to the bank. [*Turns to go into his room.*]

Nora. Torvald.

Hel. Yes.

Nora. If your little squirrel were to ask you for something very, very prettily——

Hel. What then?

Nora. Would you do it?

Hel. I should like to hear what it is first.

Nora. Your squirrel would run about and do all her tricks if you would be nice and do what she wants.

Hel. Speak plainly.

Nora. Your skylark would chirp, chirp about in every room, with her song rising and falling——

Hel. Well, my skylark does that anyhow.

Nora. I would play the fairy and dance for you in the moonlight, Torvald.

Hel. Nora–you surely don't mean that request you made of me this morning?

Nora [*going near him*]. Yes, Torvald, I beg you so earnestly——

Hel. Have you really the courage to open up that question again?

Nora. Yes, dear, you *must* do as I ask; you *must* let Krogstad keep his post in the bank.

Hel. My dear Nora, it is his post that I have arranged Mrs Linde shall have.

Nora. Yes, you have been awfully kind about that, but you could just as well dismiss some other clerk instead of Krogstad.

Hel. This is simply incredible obstinacy! Because you chose to give him a thoughtless promise that you would speak for him I am expected to——

Nora. That isn't the reason, Torvald. It is for your own sake. This fellow writes in the most scurrilous newspapers; you have told me so yourself. He can do you an unspeakable amount of harm. I am frightened to death of him.

Hel. Ah, I understand; it is recollections of the past that scare you.

Nora. What do you mean?

Hel. Naturally you are thinking of your father.

Nora. Yes–yes, of course. Just recall to your mind what these malicious creatures wrote in the papers about Papa and how horribly they slandered him. I believe they would have procured his dismissal if the Department had not sent you over to inquire into it and if you had not been so kindly disposed and helpful to him.

Hel. My little Nora, there is an important difference between your father and me. Your father's reputation as a public official was not above suspicion. Mine is, and I hope it will continue to be so as long as I hold my office.

Nora. You never can tell what mischief these men may contrive. We ought to be so well off, so snug and happy here in our peaceful home, and have no cares–you and I and the children, Torvald! That is why I beg you so earnestly——

Hel. And it is just by interceding for him that you make it impossible for me to keep him. It is already known at the bank that I mean to dismiss Krogstad. Is it to get about now that the new manager has changed his mind at his wife's bidding?

NORA. And what if it did?

HEL. Of course!—if only this obstinate little person can get her way! Do you suppose I am going to make myself ridiculous before my whole staff, to let people think I am a man to be swayed by all sorts of outside influence? I should very soon feel the consequences of it, I can tell you! And besides, there is one thing that makes it quite impossible for me to have Krogstad in the bank as long as I am manager.

NORA. Whatever is that?

HEL. His moral failings I might perhaps have overlooked if necessary——

NORA. Yes, you could—couldn't you?

HEL. And I hear he is a good worker too. But I knew him when we were boys. It was one of those rash friendships that so often prove an incubus in afterlife. I may as well tell you plainly, we were once on very intimate terms with one another. But this tactless fellow lays no restraint on himself when other people are present. On the contrary, he thinks it gives him the right to adopt a familiar tone with me, and every minute it is "I say, Helmer, old fellow!" and that sort of thing. I assure you it is extremely painful for me. He would make my position in the bank intolerable.

NORA. Torvald, I don't believe you mean that.

HEL. Don't you? Why not?

NORA. Because it is such a narrow-minded way of looking at things.

HEL. What are you saying? Narrow-minded? Do you think I am narrow-minded?

NORA. No, just the opposite, dear—and it is exactly for that reason——

HEL. It's the same thing. You say my point of view is narrow-minded, so I must be so too. Narrow-minded! Very well—I must put an end to this. [*Goes to the hall door and calls.*] Helen!

NORA. What are you going to do?

HEL. [*looking among his papers*]. Settle it. [*Enter* MAID.] Look here; take this letter and go downstairs with it at once. Find a messenger and tell him to deliver it and be quick. The address is on it, and here is the money.

MAID. Very well, sir. [*Exit with the letter.*]

HEL. [*putting his papers together*]. Now then, little Miss Obstinate.

NORA [*breathlessly*]. Torvald—what was that letter?

HEL. Krogstad's dismissal.

NORA. Call her back, Torvald! There is still time. Oh, Torvald, call her back! Do it for my sake—for your own sake—for the children's sake! Do you hear me, Torvald? Call her back! You don't know what that letter can bring upon us.

HEL. It's too late.

NORA. Yes, it's too late.

HEL. My dear Nora, I can forgive the anxiety you are in, although really it is an insult to me. It is, indeed. Isn't it an insult to think that I should be afraid of a starving quill driver's vengeance? But I forgive you nevertheless, because it is such eloquent witness to your great love for me. [*Takes her in his arms.*] And that is as it should be, my own darling Nora. Come what will, you may be sure I shall have both courage and strength if they be needed. You will see I am man enough to take everything upon myself.

NORA [*in a horror-stricken voice*]. What do you mean by that?

HEL. Everything, I say.

NORA [*recovering herself*]. You will never have to do that.

HEL. That's right. Well, we will share it, Nora, as man and wife should. That is how it shall be. [*Caressing her.*] Are you content now? There! there!—not these frightened dove's eyes! The whole thing is only the wildest fancy! Now you must go and play through the tarantella and practice with your tambourine. I shall go into the inner office and shut the door, and I shall hear nothing; you can make as much noise as you please. [*Turns back at the door.*] And when Rank comes tell him where he will find me. [*Nods to her, takes his papers and goes into his room and shuts the door after him.*]

NORA [*bewildered with anxiety, stands as if rooted to the spot and whispers*]. He was capable of doing it. He will do it. He will do it in spite of everything. No, not that! Never, never! Anything rather than that! Oh, for some help, some way out of it! [*The doorbell rings.*] Doctor Rank! Anything rather than that—anything, whatever it is! [*She puts her hands over her face, pulls herself together, goes to the door and opens it.* RANK *is standing without, hanging up his coat. During the following dialogue it begins to grow dark.*]

NORA. Good day, Doctor Rank. I knew your ring. But you mustn't go in to Torvald now; I think he is busy with something.

RANK. And you?

NORA [*brings him in and shuts the door after him*]. Oh, you know very well I always have time for you.

RANK. Thank you. I shall make use of as much of it as I can.

NORA. What do you mean by that? As much of it as you can?

RANK. Well, does that alarm you?

NORA. It was such a strange way of putting it. Is anything likely to happen?

RANK. Nothing but what I have long been prepared for. But I certainly didn't expect it to happen so soon.

NORA [*gripping him by the arm*]. What have you found out? Doctor Rank, you must tell me.

RANK [*sitting down by the stove*]. It is all up with me. And it can't be helped.

NORA [*with a sigh of relief*]. Is it about yourself?

RANK. Who else? It is no use lying to one's self. I am the most wretched of all my patients, Mrs Helmer. Lately I have been taking stock of my internal economy. Bankrupt! Probably within a month I shall lie rotting in the churchyard.

NORA. What an ugly thing to say!

RANK. The thing itself is cursedly ugly, and the worst of it is that I shall have to face so much more that is ugly before that. I shall only make one more examination of myself; when I have done that I shall know pretty certainly when it will be that the horrors of dissolution will begin. There is something I want to tell you. Helmer's refined nature gives him an unconquerable disgust at everything that is ugly; I won't have him in my sickroom.

NORA. Oh, but, Doctor Rank——

RANK. I won't have him there. Not on any account. I bar my door to him. As soon as I am quite certain that the worst has come I shall send you my card with a black cross on it, and then you will know that the loathsome end has begun.

NORA. You are quite absurd today. And I wanted you so much to be in a really good humor.

RANK. With death stalking beside me? To have to pay this penalty for another man's sin! Is there any justice in that? And in every single family, in one way or another, some such inexorable retribution is being exacted.

NORA [*putting her hands over her ears*]. Rubbish! Do talk of something cheerful.

RANK. Oh, it's a mere laughing matter, the whole thing. My poor innocent spine has to suffer for my father's youthful amusements.

NORA [*sitting at the table on the left*]. I suppose you mean that he was too partial to asparagus and pâté de foie gras, don't you?

RANK. Yes, and to truffles.

NORA. Truffles, yes. And oysters too, I suppose?

RANK. Oysters, of course; that goes without saying.

NORA. And heaps of port and champagne. It is sad that all these nice things should take their revenge on our bones.

RANK. Especially that they should revenge themselves on the unlucky bones of those who have not had the satisfaction of enjoying them.

NORA. Yes, that's the saddest part of it all.

RANK [*with a searching look at her*]. Hm!

NORA [*after a short pause*]. Why did you smile?

RANK. No, it was you that laughed.

NORA. No, it was you that smiled, Doctor Rank!

RANK [*rising*]. You are a greater rascal than I thought.

NORA. I am in a silly mood today.

RANK. So it seems.

NORA [*putting her hands on his shoulders*]. Dear, dear Doctor Rank, death mustn't take you away from Torvald and me.

RANK. It is a loss you would easily recover from. Those who are gone are soon forgotten.

NORA [*looking at him anxiously*]. Do you believe that?

RANK. People form new ties, and then——

NORA. Who will form new ties?

RANK. Both you and Helmer, when I am gone. You yourself are already on the highroad to it, I think. What did that Mrs Linde want here last night?

NORA. Oho! You don't mean to say that you are jealous of poor Christine?

RANK. Yes, I am. She will be my successor in this house. When I am done for, this woman will——

NORA. Hush! Don't speak so loud. She is in that room.

RANK. Today again. There, you see.

NORA. She has only come to sew my dress for me. Bless my soul, how unreasonable you are! [*Sits down on the sofa.*] Be nice now, Doctor Rank, and tomorrow you will see how beautifully I shall dance, and you can imagine I am doing it all for you—and for Torvald too, of course. [*Takes various things out of the box.*] Doctor Rank, come and sit down here, and I will show you something.

RANK [*sitting down*]. What is it?

NORA. Just look at those!

RANK. Silk stockings.

NORA. Flesh colored. Aren't they lovely? It is so dark here now, but tomorrow— No, no, no! You must only look at the feet. Oh well, you may have leave to look at the legs too.

RANK. Hm!

NORA. Why are you looking so critical? Don't you think they will fit me?

RANK. I have no means of forming an opinion about that.

NORA [*looks at him for a moment*]. For shame! [*Hits him lightly on the ear with the stockings.*] That's to punish you. [*Folds them up again.*]

RANK. And what other nice things am I to be allowed to see?

NORA. Not a single thing more, for being so naughty. [*She looks among the things, humming to herself.*]

RANK [*after a short silence*]. When I am sitting here talking to you as intimately as this I cannot imagine for a moment what would have become of me if I had never come into this house.

NORA [*smiling*]. I believe you do feel thoroughly at home with us.

RANK [*in a lower voice, looking straight in front of him*]. And to be obliged to leave it all—

NORA. Nonsense, you are not going to leave it.

RANK [*as before*]. And not be able to leave behind one the slightest token of one's gratitude, scarcely even a fleeting regret—nothing but an empty place which the firstcomer can fill as well as any other.

NORA. And if I asked you now for a— No!

RANK. For what?

NORA. For a big proof of your friendship—

RANK. Yes, yes!

NORA. I mean a tremendously big favor—

RANK. Would you really make me so happy for once?

NORA. Ah, but you don't know what it is yet.

RANK. No—but tell me.

NORA. I really can't, Doctor Rank. It is something out of all reason; it means advice and help and a favor—

RANK. The bigger a thing it is, the better. I can't conceive what it is you mean. Do tell me. Haven't I your confidence?

NORA. More than anyone else. I know you are my truest and best friend, and so I will tell you what it is. Well, Doctor Rank, it is something you must help me to prevent. You know how devotedly, how inexpressibly deeply Torvald loves me; he would never for a moment hesitate to give his life for me.

RANK [*leaning toward her*]. Nora —do you think he is the only one—

NORA [*with a slight start*]. The only one—?

RANK. The only one who would gladly give his life for your sake.

NORA [*sadly*]. Is that it?

RANK. I was determined you should know it before I went away, and there will never be a better opportunity than this. Now you know it, Nora. And now you know, too, that you can trust me as you would trust no one else.

NORA [*rises deliberately and quietly*]. Let me pass.

RANK [*makes room for her to pass him but sits still*]. Nora!

NORA [*at the hall door*]. Helen, bring in the lamp. [*Goes over to the stove.*] Dear Doctor Rank, that was really horrid of you.

RANK. To have loved you as much

as anyone else does? Was that horrid?

NORA. No, but to go and tell me so. There was really no need——

RANK. What do you mean? Did you know? [MAID *enters with lamp, puts it down on the table and goes out.*] Nora—Mrs Helmer—tell me, had you any idea of this?

NORA. Oh, how do I know whether I had or whether I hadn't? I really can't tell you. To think you could be so clumsy, Doctor Rank! We were getting on so nicely.

RANK. Well, at all events you know that you can command me body and soul. So won't you speak out?

NORA [*looking at him*]. After what happened?

RANK. I beg you to let me know what it is.

NORA. I can't tell you anything now.

RANK. Yes, yes. You mustn't punish me in that way. Let me have permission to do for you whatever a man may do.

NORA. You can do nothing for me now. Besides, I really don't need any help at all. You will find that the whole thing is merely fancy on my part. It really is so—of course it is! [*Sits down in the rocking chair and looks at him with a smile.*] You are a nice sort of man, Doctor Rank! Don't you feel ashamed of yourself now the lamp has come?

RANK. Not a bit. But perhaps I had better go—forever?

NORA. No indeed, you shall not. Of course you must come here just as before. You know very well Torvald can't do without you.

RANK. Yes, but you?

NORA. Oh, I am always tremendously pleased when you come.

RANK. It is just that that put me on the wrong track. You are a riddle to me. I have often thought that you would almost as soon be in my company as in Helmer's.

NORA. Yes—you see, there are some people one loves best and others whom one would almost always rather have as companions.

RANK. Yes, there is something in that.

NORA. When I was at home of course I loved Papa best. But I always thought it tremendous fun if I could steal down into the maids' room, because they never moralized at all and talked to each other about such entertaining things.

RANK. I see—it is *their* place I have taken.

NORA [*jumping up and going to him*]. Oh, dear, nice Doctor Rank, I never meant that at all. But surely you can understand that being with Torvald is a little like being with Papa——

[*Enter* MAID *from the hall.*]

MAID. If you please, ma'am. [*Whispers and hands her a card.*]

NORA [*glancing at the card*]. Oh! [*Puts it in her pocket.*]

RANK. Is there anything wrong?

NORA. No, no, not in the least. It is only something—it is my new dress——

RANK. What? Your dress is lying there.

NORA. Oh yes, that one; but this is another. I ordered it. Torvald mustn't know about it.

RANK. Oho! Then that was the great secret.

NORA. Of course. Just go in to him; he is sitting in the inner room. Keep him as long as——

RANK. Make your mind easy; I won't let him escape. [*Goes into* HELMER'S *room.*]

Nora [*to the* Maid]. And he is tanding waiting in the kitchen?

Maid. Yes; he came up the back tairs.

Nora. But didn't you tell him no ne was in?

Maid. Yes, but it was no good.

Nora. He won't go away?

Maid. No; he says he won't until he as seen you, ma'am.

Nora. Well, let him come in—but uietly. Helen, you mustn't say anyhing about it to anyone. It is a surrise for my husband.

Maid. Yes, ma'am, I quite undertand. [*Exit.*]

Nora. This dreadful thing is going o happen! It will happen in spite of ne! No, no, no, it can't happen—it han't happen! [*She bolts the door of* Ielmer's *room. The* Maid *opens the all door for* Krogstad *and shuts it fter him. He is wearing a fur coat, igh boots and a fur cap.*]

Nora [*advancing toward him*]. peak low—my husband is at home.

Krog. No matter about that.

Nora. What do you want of me?

Krog. An explanation of something.

Nora. Make haste then. What is it?

Krog. You know, I suppose, that I ave got my dismissal.

Nora. I couldn't prevent it, Mr rogstad. I fought as hard as I could n your side, but it was no good.

Krog. Does your husband love you little then? He knows what I can xpose you to, and yet he ventures——

Nora. How can you suppose that e has any knowledge of the sort?

Krog. I didn't suppose so at all. It ould not be the least like our dear 'orvald Helmer to show so much ourage——

Nora. Mr Krogstad, a little respect or my husband, please.

Krog. Certainly—all the respect he deserves. But since you have kept the matter so carefully to yourself, I make bold to suppose that you have a little clearer idea than you had yesterday of what it actually is that you have done?

Nora. More than you could ever teach me.

Krog. Yes, such a bad lawyer as I am.

Nora. What is it you want of me?

Krog. Only to see how you were, Mrs Helmer. I have been thinking about you all day long. A mere cashier, a quill driver, a—well, a man like me—even he has a little of what is called feeling, you know.

Nora. Show it then; think of my little children.

Krog. Have you and your husband thought of mine? But never mind about that. I only wanted to tell you that you need not take this matter too seriously. In the first place there will be no accusation made on my part.

Nora. No, of course not; I was sure of that.

Krog. The whole thing can be arranged amicably; there is no reason why anyone should know anything about it. It will remain a secret between us three.

Nora. My husband must never get to know anything about it.

Krog. How will you be able to prevent it? Am I to understand that you can pay the balance that is owing?

Nora. No, not just at present.

Krog. Or perhaps that you have some expedient for raising the money soon?

Nora. No expedient that I mean to make use of.

Krog. Well, in any case it would

have been of no use to you now. If you stood there with ever so much money in your hand, I would never part with your bond.

NORA. Tell me what purpose you mean to put it to.

KROG. I shall only preserve it—keep it in my possession. No one who is not concerned in the matter shall have the slightest hint of it. So that if the thought of it has driven you to any desperate resolution——

NORA. It has.

KROG. If you had it in your mind to run away from your home——

NORA. I had.

KROG. Or even something worse——

NORA. How could you know that?

KROG. Give up the idea.

NORA. How did you know I had thought of *that?*

KROG. Most of us think of that at first. I did too—but I hadn't the courage.

NORA [*faintly*]. No more than I.

KROG. [*in a tone of relief*]. No, that's it, isn't it—you hadn't the courage either?

NORA. No, I haven't—I haven't.

KROG. Besides, it would have been a great piece of folly. Once the first storm at home is over—— I have a letter for your husband in my pocket.

NORA. Telling him everything?

KROG. In as lenient a manner as I possibly could.

NORA [*quickly*]. He mustn't get the letter. Tear it up. I will find some means of getting money.

KROG. Excuse me, Mrs Helmer, but I think I told you just now——

NORA. I am not speaking of what I owe you. Tell me what sum you are asking my husband for, and I will get the money.

KROG. I am not asking your hus band for a penny.

NORA. What do you want then?

KROG. I will tell you. I want t rehabilitate myself, Mrs Helmer; want to get on, and in that your hus band must help me. For the last yea and a half I have not had a hand i anything dishonorable, and all tha time I have been struggling in mos restricted circumstances. I was con tent to work my way up step b step. Now I am turned out, and I an not going to be satisfied with merel being taken into favor again. I wan to get on, I tell you. I want to ge into the bank again, in a higher posi tion. Your husband must make a plac for me——

NORA. That he will never do!

KROG. He will; I know him; he dar not protest. And as soon as I am i there again with him then you wi see! Within a year I shall be th manager's right hand. It will be Ni Krogstad and not Torvald Helme who manages the bank.

NORA. That's a thing you will neve see!

KROG. Do you mean that yo will——

NORA. I have courage enough fc it now.

KROG. Oh, you can't frighten m A fine, spoilt lady like you——

NORA. You will see, you will se

KROG. Under the ice, perhaps Down into the cold, coal-blac water? And then, in the spring, t float up to the surface, all horrib and unrecognizable, with your ha fallen out——

NORA. You can't frighten me.

KROG. Nor you me. People don do such things, Mrs Helmer. Beside what use would it be? I should hav im completely in my power all the ame.

NORA. Afterward? When I am no onger——

KROG. Have you forgotten that it s I who have the keeping of your eputation? [NORA *stands speechlessly ooking at him.*] Well, now, I have warned you. Do not do anything oolish. When Helmer has had my etter I shall expect a message from im. And be sure you remember that t is your husband himself who has orced me into such ways as this gain. I will never forgive him for hat. Good-by, Mrs Helmer. [*Exit hrough the hall.*]

NORA [*goes to the hall door, opens t slightly and listens*]. He is going. He is not putting the letter in the ox. Oh no, no! that's impossible! *Opens the door by degrees.*] What s that? He is standing outside. He is ot going downstairs. Is he hesitat-ng? Can he—— [*A letter drops in the ox; then* KROGSTAD'S *footsteps are eard, till they die away as he goes ownstairs.* NORA *utters a stifled cry nd runs across the room to the table y the sofa. A short pause.*]

NORA. In the letter box. [*Steals cross to the hall door.*] There it lies -Torvald, Torvald, there is no hope or us now!

[MRS LINDE *comes in from the oom on the left, carrying the dress.*]

MRS L. There, I can't see anything ore to mend now. Would you like o try it on?

NORA [*in a hoarse whisper*]. Chris-ine, come here.

MRS L. [*throwing the dress down n the sofa*]. What is the matter with ou? You look so agitated!

NORA. Come here. Do you see that etter? There, look—you can see it through the glass in the letter box.

MRS L. Yes, I see it.

NORA. That letter is from Krogstad.

MRS L. Nora—it was Krogstad who lent you the money!

NORA. Yes, and now Torvald will know all about it.

MRS L. Believe me, Nora, that's the best thing for both of you.

NORA. You don't know all. I forged a name.

MRS L. Good heavens!

NORA. I only want to say this to you, Christine—you must be my witness.

MRS L. Your witness? What do you mean? What am I to——

NORA. If I should go out of my mind—and it might easily happen——

MRS L. Nora!

NORA. Or if anything else should happen to me—anything, for instance, that might prevent my being here——

MRS L. Nora! Nora! you are quite out of your mind.

NORA. And if it should happen that there were someone who wanted to take all the responsibility, all the blame, you understand——

MRS L. Yes, yes—but how can you suppose——

NORA. Then you must be my witness, that is not true, Christine. I am not out of my mind at all; I am in my right senses now, and I tell you no one else has known anything about it; I, and I alone, did the whole thing. Remember that.

MRS L. I will, indeed. But I don't understand all this.

NORA. How should you understand it? A wonderful thing is going to happen.

MRS L. A wonderful thing?

NORA. Yes, a wonderful thing! But

it is so terrible. Christine, it *mustn't* happen, not for all the world.

Mrs L. I will go at once and see Krogstad.

Nora. Don't go to him; he will do you some harm.

Mrs L. There was a time when he would gladly do anything for my sake.

Nora. He?

Mrs L. Where does he live?

Nora. How should I know? Yes— [*feeling in her pocket*]—here is his card. But the letter, the letter!

Hel. [*calls from his room, knocking at the door*]. Nora!

Nora [*cries out anxiously*]. Oh, what's that? What do you want?

Hel. Don't be so frightened. We are not coming in; you have locked the door. Are you trying on your dress?

Nora. Yes, that's it. I look so nice, Torvald.

Mrs L. [*who has read the card*]. I see he lives at the corner here.

Nora. Yes, but it's no use. It is hopeless. The letter is lying there in the box.

Mrs L. And your husband keeps the key?

Nora. Yes, always.

Mrs L. Krogstad must ask for his letter back unread, he must find some pretense——

Nora. But it is just at this time that Torvald generally——

Mrs L. You must delay him. Go in to him in the meantime. I will come back as soon as I can. [*She goes out hurriedly through the hall door.*]

Nora [*goes to* Helmer's *door, opens it and peeps in*]. Torvald!

Hel. [*from the inner room*]. Well? May I venture at last to come into my own room again? Come along, Rank, now you will see—— [*Halting in the doorway.*] But what is this?

Nora. What is what, dear?

Hel. Rank led me to expect a splendid transformation.

Rank [*in the doorway*]. I understood so, but evidently I was mistaken.

Nora. Yes, nobody is to have the chance of admiring me in my dress until tomorrow.

Hel. But, my dear Nora, you look so worn out. Have you been practicing too much?

Nora. No, I have not practiced at all.

Hel. But you will need to——

Nora. Yes, indeed I shall, Torvald. But I can't get on a bit without you to help me; I have absolutely forgotten the whole thing.

Hel. Oh, we will soon work it up again.

Nora. Yes, help me, Torvald. Promise that you will! I am so nervous about it—all the people—— You must give yourself up to me entirely this evening. Not the tiniest bit of business—you mustn't even take a pen in your hand. Will you promise, Torvald dear?

Hel. I promise. This evening I will be wholly and absolutely at your service, you helpless little mortal. Ah, by the way, first of all I will just— [*Goes toward the hall door.*]

Nora. What are you going to do there?

Hel. Only see if any letters have come.

Nora. No, no! Don't do that, Torvald!

Hel. Why not?

Nora. Torvald, please don't. There is nothing there.

Hel. Well, let me look. [*Turns to*

go to the letter box. NORA, *at the piano, plays the first bars of the tarantella.* HELMER *stops in the doorway.*] Aha!

NORA. I can't dance tomorrow if I don't practice with you.

HEL. [*going up to her*]. Are you really so afraid of it, dear?

NORA. Yes, so dreadfully afraid of it. Let me practice at once; there is time now, before we go to dinner. Sit down and play for me, Torvald dear; criticize me and correct me as you play.

HEL. With great pleasure, if you wish me to. [*Sits down at the piano.*]

NORA [*takes out of the box a tambourine and a long variegated shawl. She hastily drapes the shawl round her. Then she springs to the front of the stage and calls out*]. Now play for me! I am going to dance!

[HELMER *plays and* NORA *dances.* RANK *stands by the piano behind* HELMER *and looks on.*]

HEL. [*as he plays*]. Slower, slower!

NORA. I can't do it any other way.

HEL. Not so violently, Nora!

NORA. This is the way.

HEL. [*stops playing*]. No, no–that is not a bit right.

NORA [*laughing and swinging the tambourine*]. Didn't I tell you so?

RANK. Let me play for her.

HEL. [*getting up*]. Yes, do. I can correct her better then.

[RANK *sits down at the piano and plays.* NORA *dances more and more wildly.* HELMER *has taken up a position by the stove and during her dance gives her frequent instructions. She does not seem to hear him; her hair comes down and falls over her shoulders; she pays no attention to it but goes on dancing. Enter* MRS LINDE.]

MRS L. [*standing as if spellbound in the doorway*]. Oh!

NORA [*as she dances*]. Such fun, Christine!

HEL. My dear darling Nora, you are dancing as if your life depended on it.

NORA. So it does.

HEL. Stop, Rank; this is sheer madness. Stop, I tell you! [RANK *stops playing, and* NORA *suddenly stands still.* HELMER *goes up to her.*] I could never have believed it. You have forgotten everything I taught you.

NORA [*throwing away the tambourine*]. There, you see.

HEL. You will want a lot of coaching.

NORA. Yes, you see how much I need it. You must coach me up to the last minute. Promise me that, Torvald!

HEL. You can depend on me.

NORA. You must not think of anything but me, either today or tomorrow; you mustn't open a single letter –not even open the letter box––

HEL. Ah, you are still afraid of that fellow—

NORA. Yes, indeed I am.

HEL. Nora, I can tell from your looks that there is a letter from him lying there.

NORA. I don't know; I think there is; but you must not read anything of that kind now. Nothing horrid must come between us till this is all over.

RANK [*whispers to* HELMER]. You mustn't contradict her.

HEL. [*taking her in his arms*]. The child shall have her way. But tomorrow night, after you have danced––

NORA. Then you will be free. [*The* MAID *appears in the doorway to the right.*]

MAID. Dinner is served, ma'am.

NORA. We will have champagne, Helen.

MAID. Very good, ma'am. [*Exit.*]

HEL. Hullo!—are we going to have a banquet?

NORA. Yes, a champagne banquet till the small hours. [*Calls out.*] And a few macaroons, Helen—lots, just for once!

HEL. Come, come, don't be so wild and nervous. Be my own little skylark, as you used.

NORA. Yes, dear, I will. But go in now, and you too, Doctor Rank. Christine, you must help me to do up my hair.

RANK [*whispers to* HELMER *as they go out*]. I suppose there is nothing—she is not expecting anything?

HEL. Far from it, my dear fellow; it is simply nothing more than this childish nervousness I was telling you of. [*They go into the right-hand room.*]

NORA. Well!

MRS L. Gone out of town.

NORA. I could tell from your face.

MRS L. He is coming home tomorrow evening. I wrote a note for him.

NORA. You should have let it alone; you must prevent nothing. After all, it is splendid to be waiting for a wonderful thing to happen.

MRS L. What is it that you are waiting for?

NORA. Oh, you wouldn't understand. Go in to them, I will come in a moment. [MRS LINDE *goes into the dining room.* NORA *stands still for a little while, as if to compose herself. Then she looks at her watch.*] Five o'clock. Seven hours till midnight; and then four-and-twenty hours till the next midnight. Then the tarantella will be over. Twenty-four and seven? Thirty-one hours to live.

HEL. [*from the doorway on the right*]. Where's my little skylark?

NORA [*going to him with her arms outstretched*]. Here she is!

ACT III

THE SAME SCENE—*The table has been placed in the middle of the stage with chairs round it. A lamp is burning on the table. The door into the hall stands open. Dance music is heard in the room above.* MRS LINDE *is sitting at the table idly turning over the leaves of a book; she tries to read but does not seem able to collect her thoughts. Every now and then she listens intently for a sound at the outer door.*

MRS L. [*looking at her watch*]. Not yet—and the time is nearly up. If only he does not—— [*Listens again.*] Ah, there he is. [*Goes into the hall and opens the outer door carefully. Light footsteps are heard on the stairs. She whispers.*] Come in. There is no one here.

KROG. [*in the doorway*]. I found note from you at home. What does this mean?

MRS L. It is absolutely necessary that I should have a talk with you.

KROG. Really? And it is absolutely necessary that it should be here?

MRS L. It is impossible where I live there is no private entrance to my rooms. Come in; we are quite alone. The maid is asleep, and the Helmers are at the dance upstairs.

KROG. [*coming into the room*]. Are the Helmers really at a dance tonight?

MRS L. Yes, why not?

KROG. Certainly—why not?

MRS L. Now, Nils, let us have a talk.

KROG. Can we two have anything to talk about?

MRS L. We have a great deal to talk about.

KROG. I shouldn't have thought so.

MRS L. No, you have never properly understood me.

KROG. Was there anything else to understand except what was obvious to all the world—a heartless woman jilts a man when a more lucrative chance turns up?

MRS L. Do you believe I am as absolutely heartless as all that? And do you believe it with a light heart?

KROG. Didn't you?

MRS L. Nils, did you really think that?

KROG. If it were as you say, why did you write to me as you did at the time?

MRS L. I could do nothing else. As I had to break with you, it was my duty also to put an end to all that you felt for me.

KROG. [*wringing his hands*]. So that was it. And all this—only for the sake of money!

MRS L. You mustn't forget that I had a helpless mother and two little brothers. We couldn't wait for you, Nils; your prospects seemed hopeless then.

KROG. That may be so, but you had no right to throw me over for anyone else's sake.

MRS L. Indeed, I don't know. Many a time did I ask myself if I had the right to do it.

KROG. [*more gently*]. When I lost you it was as if all the solid ground went from under my feet. Look at me now—I am a shipwrecked man clinging to a bit of wreckage.

MRS L. But help may be near.

KROG. It *was* near, but then you came and stood in my way.

MRS L. Unintentionally, Nils. It was only today that I learned it was your place I was going to take in the bank.

KROG. I believe you, if you say so. But now that you know it, are you not going to give it up to me?

MRS L. No, because that would not benefit you in the least.

KROG. Oh, benefit, benefit—I would have done it whether or no.

MRS L. I have learned to act prudently. Life and hard, bitter necessity have taught me that.

KROG. And life has taught me not to believe in fine speeches.

MRS L. Then life has taught you something very reasonable. But deeds you must believe in.

KROG. What do you mean by that?

MRS L. You said you were like a shipwrecked man clinging to some wreckage.

KROG. I had good reason to say so.

MRS L. Well, I am like a shipwrecked woman clinging to some wreckage—no one to mourn for, no one to care for.

KROG. It was your own choice.

MRS L. There was no other choice —then.

KROG. Well, what now?

MRS L. Nils, how would it be if we two shipwrecked people could join forces?

KROG. What are you saying?

MRS L. Two on the same piece of wreckage would stand a better chance than each on their own.

KROG. Christine!

MRS L. What do you suppose brought me to town?

Krog. Do you mean that you gave me a thought?

Mrs L. I could not endure life without work. All my life, as long as I can remember, I have worked, and it has been my greatest and only pleasure. But now I am quite alone in the world—my life is so dreadfully empty and I feel so forsaken. There is not the least pleasure in working for one's self. Nils, give me someone and something to work for.

Krog. I don't trust that. It is nothing but a woman's overstrained sense of generosity that prompts you to make such an offer of yourself.

Mrs L. Have you ever noticed anything of the sort in me?

Krog. Could you really do it? Tell me—do you know all about my past life?

Mrs L. Yes.

Krog. And do you know what they think of me here?

Mrs L. You seemed to me to imply that with me you might have been quite another man.

Krog. I am certain of it.

Mrs L. Is it too late now?

Krog. Christine, are you saying this deliberately? Yes, I am sure you are. I see it in your face. Have you really the courage, then——

Mrs L. I want to be a mother to someone, and your children need a mother. We two need each other. Nils, I have faith in your real character—I can dare anything with you.

Krog. [*grasps her hands*]. Thanks, thanks, Christine! Now I shall find a way to clear myself in the eyes of the world. Ah, but I forgot——

Mrs L. [*listening*]. Hush! The tarantella! Go, go!

Krog. Why? What is it?

Mrs L. Do you hear them up there? When that is over we may expect them back.

Krog. Yes, yes—I will go. But it is all no use. Of course you are not aware what steps I have taken in the matter of the Helmers.

Mrs L. Yes, I know all about that.

Krog. And in spite of that have you the courage to——

Mrs L. I understand very well to what lengths a man like you might be driven by despair.

Krog. If I could only undo what I have done!

Mrs L. You cannot. Your letter is lying in the letter box now.

Krog. Are you sure of that?

Mrs L. Quite sure, but——

Krog. [*with a searching look at her*]. Is that what it all means?—that you want to save your friend at any cost? Tell me frankly. Is that it?

Mrs L. Nils, a woman who has once sold herself for another's sake doesn't do it a second time.

Krog. I will ask for my letter back.

Mrs L. No, no.

Krog. Yes, of course I will. I will wait here till Helmer comes; I will tell him he must give me my letter back—that it only concerns my dismissal—that he is not to read it——

Mrs L. No, Nils, you must not recall your letter.

Krog. But, tell me, wasn't it for that very purpose that you asked me to meet you here?

Mrs L. In my first moment of fright it was. But twenty-four hours have elapsed since then, and in that time I have witnessed incredible things in this house. Helmer must know all about it. This unhappy secret must be disclosed; they must have a complete understanding between them, which is impossible with all this concealment and falsehood going on.

KROG. Very well, if you will take the responsibility. But there is one thing I can do in any case, and I shall do it at once.

MRS L. [*listening*]. You must be quick and go! The dance is over; we are not safe a moment longer.

KROG. I will wait for you below.

MRS L. Yes, do. You must see me back to my door.

KROG. I have never had such an amazing piece of good fortune in my life! [*Goes out through the outer door. The door between the room and the hall remains open.*]

MRS L. [*tidying up the room and laying her hat and cloak ready*]. What a difference! What a difference! Someone to work for and live for—a home to bring comfort into. That I will do, indeed. I wish they would be quick and come. [*Listens.*] Ah, there they are now. I must put on my things. [*Takes up her hat and cloak.* HELMER'S *and* NORA'S *voices are heard outside; a key is turned, and* HELMER *brings* NORA *almost by force into the hall. She is in an Italian costume with a large black shawl round her; he is in evening dress and a black domino which is flying open.*]

NORA [*hanging back in the doorway and struggling with him*]. No, no, no!—don't take me in. I want to go upstairs again; I don't want to leave so early.

HEL. But, my dearest Nora—

NORA. Please, Torvald dear—please, *please*—only an hour more.

HEL. Not a single minute, my sweet Nora. You know that was our agreement. Come along into the room; you are catching cold standing there. [*He brings her gently into the room in spite of her resistance.*]

MRS L. Good evening.

NORA. Christine!

HEL. You here so late, Mrs Linde?

MRS L. Yes, you must excuse me; I was so anxious to see Nora in her dress.

NORA. Have you been sitting here waiting for me?

MRS L. Yes; unfortunately I came too late—you had already gone upstairs—and I thought I couldn't go away again without having seen you.

HEL. [*taking off* NORA'S *shawl*]. Yes, take a good look at her. I think she is worth looking at. Isn't she charming, Mrs Linde?

MRS L. Yes, indeed she is.

HEL. Doesn't she look remarkably pretty? Everyone thought so at the dance. But she is terribly self-willed, this sweet little person. What are we to do with her? You will hardly believe that I had almost to bring her away by force.

NORA. Torvald, you will repent not having let me stay, even if it were only for half an hour.

HEL. Listen to her, Mrs Linde! She had danced her tarantella, and it had been a tremendous success, as it deserved—although possibly the performance was a trifle too realistic—a little more so, I mean, than was strictly compatible with the limitations of art. But never mind about that! The chief thing is, she had made a success—she had made a tremendous success. Do you think I was going to let her remain there after that and spoil the effect? No indeed! I took my charming little Capri maiden—my capricious little Capri maiden, I should say—on my arm, took one quick turn round the room, a curtsey on either side, and, as they say in novels, the beautiful apparition disappeared. An exit ought always to be effective, Mrs Linde; but that is what I cannot make Nora understand. Pooh! this room is hot. [*Throws his domino on a chair and opens the door of his room.*] Hullo! it's all dark in here. Oh, of course—excuse me. [*He goes in and lights some candles.*]

NORA [*in a hurried and breathless whisper*]. Well?

MRS L. [*in a low voice*]. I have had a talk with him.

NORA. Yes, and——

MRS L. Nora, you must tell your husband all about it.

NORA [*in an expressionless voice*]. I knew it.

MRS L. You have nothing to be afraid of as far as Krogstad is concerned, but you must tell him.

NORA. I won't tell him.

MRS L. Then the letter will.

NORA. Thank you, Christine. Now I know what I must do. Hush!

HEL. [*coming in again*]. Well, Mrs Linde, have you admired her?

MRS L. Yes, and now I will say good night.

HEL. What, already? Is this yours, this knitting?

MRS L. [*taking it*]. Yes, thank you. I had very nearly forgotten it.

HEL. So you knit?

MRS L. Of course.

HEL. Do you know, you ought to embroider.

MRS L. Really? Why?

HEL. Yes, it's far more becoming. Let me show you. You hold the embroidery thus in your left hand and use the needle with the right—like this—with a long easy sweep. Do you see?

MRS L. Yes, perhaps——

HEL. Yes, but in the case of knitting—that can never be anything but ungraceful; look here—the arms close together, the knitting needles going up and down—it has a sort of Chinese effect. . . . That was really excellent champagne they gave us.

MRS L. Well—good night, Nora, and don't be self-willed any more.

HEL. That's right, Mrs Linde.

MRS L. Good night, Mr Helmer.

HEL. [*accompanying her to the door*]. Good night, good night. I hope you will get home all right. I should be very happy to—— But you haven't any great distance to go. Good night, good night. [*She goes out; he shuts the door after her and comes in again.*] Ah!—at last we have got rid of her. She is a frightful bore, that woman.

NORA. Aren't you very tired, Torvald?

HEL. No, not in the least.

NORA. Nor sleepy?

HEL. Not a bit. On the contrary I feel extraordinarily lively. And you —you really look both tired and sleepy.

NORA. Yes, I am very tired. I want to go to sleep at once.

HEL. There, you see it was quite right of me not to let you stay there any longer.

NORA. Everything you do is quite right, Torvald.

HEL. [*kissing her on the forehead*]. Now my little skylark is speaking reasonably. Did you notice what good spirits Rank was in this evening?

NORA. Really? Was he? I didn't speak to him at all.

HEL. And I very little, but I have not for a long time seen him in such good form. [*Looks for a while at her and then goes nearer to her.*] It is delightful to be at home by ourselves again, to be all alone with you—you fascinating, charming little darling!

NORA. Don't look at me like that, Torvald.

HEL. Why shouldn't I look at my dearest treasure?—at all the beauty that is mine, all my very own?

NORA [*going to the other side of the table*]. You mustn't say things like that to me tonight.

HEL. [*following her*]. You have still got the tarantella in your blood, I see. And it makes you more captivating than ever. Listen—the guests are beginning to go now. [*In a lower voice.*] Nora—soon the whole house will be quiet.

NORA. Yes, I hope so.

HEL. Yes, my own darling Nora. Do you know that when I am out at a party with you like this why I speak so little to you, keep away from you and only send a stolen glance in your direction now and then?—do you know why I do that? It is because I make believe to myself that we are secretly in love and you are my secretly promised bride and that no one suspects there is anything between us.

NORA. Yes, yes—I know very well your thoughts are with me all the time.

HEL. And when we are leaving and I am putting the shawl over your beautiful young shoulders—on your lovely neck—then I imagine that you are my young bride and that we have just come from our wedding and I am bringing you, for the first time, into our home—to be alone with you for the first time—quite alone with my shy little darling! All this evening I have longed for nothing but you. When I watched the seductive figures of the tarantella my blood was on fire; I could endure it no longer, and that was why I brought you down so early——

NORA. Go away, Torvald! You must let me go. I won't——

HEL. What's that? You're joking, my little Nora! You won't—you won't? Am I not your husband? [*A knock is heard at the outer door.*]

NORA [*starting*]. Did you hear——

HEL. [*going into the hall*]. Who is it?

RANK [*outside*]. It is I. May I come in for a moment?

HEL. [*in a fretful whisper*]. Oh, what does he want now? [*Aloud.*] Wait a minute. [*Unlocks the door.*] Come, that's kind of you not to pass by our door.

RANK. I thought I heard your voice, and I felt as if I should like to look in. [*With a swift glance round.*] Ah yes!—these dear familiar rooms. You are very happy and cosy in here, you two.

HEL. It seems to me that you looked after yourself pretty well upstairs too.

RANK. Excellently. Why shouldn't I? Why shouldn't one enjoy everything in this world?—at any rate as much as one can and as long as one can. The wine was capital——

HEL. Especially the champagne.

RANK. So you noticed that too? It is almost incredible how much I managed to put away!

NORA. Torvald drank a great deal of champagne tonight too.

RANK. Did he?

NORA. Yes, and he is always in such good spirits afterward.

RANK. Well, why should one not enjoy a merry evening after a well-spent day?

HEL. Well spent? I am afraid I

can't take credit for that.

Rank [*clapping him on the back*]. But I can, you know!

Hel. Exactly.

Nora. Doctor Rank, you must have been occupied with some scientific investigation today.

Hel. Just listen!—little Nora talking about scientific investigations!

Nora. And may I congratulate you on the result?

Rank. Indeed you may.

Nora. Was it favorable, then?

Rank. The best possible, for both doctor and patient—certainty.

Nora [*quickly and searchingly*]. Certainty?

Rank. Absolute certainty. So wasn't I entitled to make a merry evening of it after that?

Nora. Yes, you certainly were, Doctor Rank.

Hel. I think so too, so long as you don't have to pay for it in the morning.

Rank. Oh well, one can't have anything in this life without paying for it.

Nora. Doctor Rank—are you fond of fancy-dress balls?

Rank. Yes, if there is a fine lot of pretty costumes.

Nora. Tell me—what shall we two wear at the next?

Hel. Little featherbrain!—are you thinking of the next already?

Rank. We two? Yes, I can tell you. You shall go as a good fairy——

Hel. Yes, but what do you suggest as an appropriate costume for that?

Rank. Let your wife go dressed just as she is in everyday life.

Hel. That was really very prettily turned. But can't you tell us what you will be?

Rank. Yes, my dear friend, I have quite made up my mind about that.

Hel. Well?

Rank. At the next fancy-dress ball I shall be invisible.

Hel. That's a good joke!

Rank. There is a big black hat—have you ever heard of hats that make you invisible? If you put one on, no one can see you.

Hel. [*suppressing a smile*]. Yes, you are quite right.

Rank. But I am clean forgetting what I came for. Helmer, give me a cigar—one of the dark Havanas.

Hel. With the greatest pleasure. [*Offers him his case.*]

Rank [*takes a cigar and cuts off the end*]. Thanks.

Nora [*striking a match*]. Let me give you a light.

Rank. Thank you. [*She holds the match for him to light his cigar.*] And now good-by!

Hel. Good-by, good-by, dear old man!

Nora. Sleep well, Doctor Rank.

Rank. Thank you for that wish.

Nora. Wish me the same.

Rank. You? Well, if you want me to sleep well! And thanks for the light. [*He nods to them both and goes out.*]

Hel. [*in a subdued voice*]. He has drunk more than he ought.

Nora [*absently*]. Maybe. [Helmer *takes a bunch of keys out of his pocket and goes into the hall.*] Torvald. What are you going to do there?

Hel. Empty the letter box; it is quite full; there will be no room to put the newspaper in tomorrow morning.

Nora. Are you going to work tonight?

Hel. You know quite well I'm not. What is this? Someone has been at the lock.

Nora. At the lock?

Hel. Yes, someone has. What can it mean? I should never have thought the maid—— Here is a broken hairpin. Nora, it is one of yours.

Nora [*quickly*]. Then it must have been the children.

Hel. Then you must get them out of those ways. There, at last I have got it open. [*Takes out the contents of the letter box and calls to the kitchen.*] Helen! Helen, put out the light over the front door. [*Goes back into the room and shuts the door into the hall. He holds out his hand full of letters.*] Look at that—look what a heap of them there are. [*Turning them over.*] What on earth is that?

Nora [*at the window*]. The letter—— No! Torvald, no!

Hel. Two cards—of Ranks.

Nora. Of Doctor Rank's?

Hel. [*looking at them*]. Doctor Rank. They were on the top. He must have put them in when he went out.

Nora. Is there anything written on them?

Hel. There is a black cross over the name. Look there—what an uncomfortable idea! It looks as if he were announcing his own death.

Nora. It is just what he is doing.

Hel. What? Do you know anything about it? Has he said anything to you?

Nora. Yes. He told me that when the cards came it would be his leave-taking from us. He means to shut himself up and die.

Hel. My poor old friend. Certainly I knew we should not have him very long with us. But so soon! And so he hides himself away like a wounded animal.

Nora. If it has to happen, it is best it should be without a word—don't you think so, Torvald?

Hel. [*walking up and down*]. He had so grown into our lives. I can't think of him as having gone out of them. He, with his sufferings and his loneliness, was like a cloudy background to our sunlit happiness. Well, perhaps it is best so. For him, anyway. [*Standing still.*] And perhaps for us too, Nora. We two are thrown quite upon each other now. [*Puts his arms round her.*] My darling wife, I don't feel as if I could hold you tight enough. Do you know, Nora, I have often wished that you might be threatened by some great danger, so that I might risk my life's blood and everything for your sake.

Nora [*disengages herself and says firmly and decidedly*]. Now you must read your letters, Torvald.

Hel. No, no; not tonight. I want to be with you, my darling wife.

Nora. With the thought of your friend's death——

Hel. You are right; it has affected us both. Something ugly has come between us—the thought of the horrors of death. We must try and rid our minds of that. Until then—we will each go to our own room.

Nora [*hanging on his neck*]. Good night, Torvald—good night!

Hel. [*kissing her on the forehead*]. Good night, my little singing bird. Sleep sound, Nora. Now I will read my letters through. [*He takes his letters and goes into his room, shutting the door after him.*]

Nora [*gropes distractedly about, seizes* Helmer's *domino, throws it about her while she says in quick, hoarse, spasmodic whispers*]. Never to see him again. Never! Never! [*Puts her shawl over her head.*] Never to see my children again either—never again. Never! Never! Ah! the icy black water—the unfathomable depths—if only it were over! He has got it now—now he is reading it. Good-by, Torvald and my children! [*She is about to rush out through the hall when* Helmer *opens his door hurriedly and stands with an open letter in his hand.*]

Hel. Nora!

Nora. Ah!

Hel. What is this? Do you know what is in this letter?

Nora. Yes, I know. Let me go! Let me get out!

Hel. [*holding her back*]. Where are you going?

Nora [*trying to get free*]. You shan't save me, Torvald!

Hel. [*reeling*]. True? Is this true, that I read here? Horrible! No, no—it is impossible that it is true.

Nora. It is true. I have loved you above everything else in the world.

Hel. Oh, don't let us have any silly excuses.

Nora [*taking a step toward him*]. Torvald!

Hel. Miserable creature—what have you done?

Nora. Let me go. You shall not suffer for my sake. You shall not take it upon yourself.

Hel. No tragedy airs, please. [*Locks the hall door.*] Here you shall stay and give me an explanation. Do you understand what you have done? Answer me! Do you understand what you have done?

Nora [*looks steadily at him and says with a growing look of coldness in her face*]. Yes, now I am beginning to understand thoroughly.

Hel. [*walking about the room*]. What a horrible awakening! All these eight years—she who was my joy and pride—a hypocrite, a liar—worse, worse—a criminal! The unutterable ugliness of it all! For shame! For shame! [Nora *is silent and looks steadily at him. He stops in front of her.*] I ought to have suspected that something of the sort would happen. I ought to have foreseen it. All your father's want of principle—be silent!—all your father's want of principle has come out in you. No religion, no morality, no sense of duty—— How I am punished for having winked at what he did! I did it for your sake, and this is how you repay me.

Nora. Yes, that's just it.

Hel. Now you have destroyed all my happiness. You have ruined all my future. It is horrible to think of! I am in the power of an unscrupulous man; he can do what he likes with me, ask anything he likes of me, give me any orders he pleases—I dare not refuse. And I must sink to such miserable depths because of a thoughtless woman!

Nora. When I am out of the way you will be free.

Hel. No fine speeches, please. Your father had always plenty of those ready too. What good would it be to me if you were out of the way, as you say? Not the slightest. He can make the affair known everywhere, and if he does, I may be falsely suspected of having been a party to your criminal action. Very likely people will think I was behind it all—that it was I who prompted you! And I have to thank you for all this—you whom I have cherished during the whole of our married life. Do you understand now what it is you have done for me?

Nora [*coldly and quietly*]. Yes.

Hel. It is so incredible that I can't take it in. But we must come to some-understanding. Take off that shawl. Take it off, I tell you. I must try and appease him in some way or another. The matter must be hushed up at any cost. And as for you and me, it must appear as if everything between us were just as before—but naturally only in the eyes of the world. You will still remain in my house, that is a matter of course. But I shall not allow you to bring up the children; I dare not trust them to you. To think that I should be obliged to say so to one whom I have loved so dearly and whom I still —— No, that is all over. From this moment happiness is not the question; all that concerns us is to save the remains, the fragments, the appearance——

[*A ring is heard at the front door-bell.*]

Hel. [*with a start*]. What is that? So late! Can the worst—can he—— Hide yourself, Nora. Say you are ill.

[Nora *stands motionless.* Helmer *goes and unlocks the hall door.*]

Maid [*half dressed, comes to the door*]. A letter for the mistress.

Hel. Give it to me. [*Takes the letter and shuts the door.*] Yes, it is from him. You shall not have it; I will read it myself.

Nora. Yes, read it.

Hel. [*standing by the lamp*]. I scarcely have the courage to do it. It may mean ruin for the both of us. No, I must know. [*Tears open the letter, runs his eye over a few lines, looks at a paper enclosed and gives a shout of joy.*] Nora! [*She looks at him questioningly.*] Nora! No, I must read it once again. Yes, it is true! I am saved! Nora, I am saved!

Nora. And I?

Hel. You too, of course; we are both saved, both you and I. Look, he sends you your bond back. He says he regrets and repents—that a happy change in his life—— Never mind what he says! We are saved, Nora! No one can do anything to you. Oh, Nora, Nora—— No, first I must destroy these hateful things. Let me see. [*Takes a look at the bond.*] No, no, I won't look at it. The whole thing shall be nothing but a bad dream to me. [*Tears up the bond and both letters, throws them all into the stove and watches them burn.*] There—now it doesn't exist any longer. He says that since Christmas Eve you—— These must have been three dreadful days for you, Nora.

Nora. I have fought a hard fight these three days.

Hel. And suffered agonies and seen no way out, but—— No, we won't call any of the horrors to mind. We will only shout with joy and keep saying, "It's all over! It's all over!" Listen to me, Nora. You don't seem to realize that it is all over. What is this?—such a cold, set face! My poor little Nora, I quite understand; you don't feel as if you could believe that I have forgiven you. But it is true, Nora, I swear it; I have forgiven you everything. I know that what you did you did out of love for me.

Nora. That is true.

Hel. You have loved me as a wife ought to love her husband. Only you had not sufficient knowledge to judge of the means you used. But do you suppose you are any the less dear to me because you don't understand how to act on your own responsibility? No, no; only lean on me; I will advise and direct you. I should not be a man if this womanly helplessness did not just give you a double attractiveness in my eyes. You must not think any more about the hard things I said in my first moment of consternation, when I thought everything was going to overwhelm me. I have forgiven you, Nora; I swear to you I have forgiven you.

Nora. Thank you for your forgiveness. [*She goes out through the door to the right.*]

Hel. No, don't go. [*Looks in.*] What are you doing in there?

Nora [*from within*]. Taking off my fancy dress.

Hel. [*standing at the open door*]. Yes, do. Try and calm yourself and make your mind easy again, my frightened little singing bird. Be at rest and feel secure; I have broad wings to shelter you under. [*Walks up and down by the door.*] How warm and cosy our home is, Nora. Here is shelter for you; here I will protect you like a hunted dove that I have saved from a hawk's claws; I will bring peace to your poor beating heart. It will come, little by little, Nora, believe me. Tomorrow morning you will look upon it all quite differently; soon everything will be just as it was before. Very soon you won't need me to assure you that I have forgiven you; you will yourself feel the certainty that I have done so. Can you suppose I should ever think of such a thing as repudiating you or even reproaching you? You have no idea what a true man's heart is like, Nora. There is something so indescribably sweet and satisfying, to a man, in the knowledge that he has forgiven his wife—forgiven her freely and with all his heart. It seems as if that had made her, as it were, doubly his own; he has given her a new life, so to speak, and she has in a way become both wife and child to him. So you shall be for me after this, my little scared, helpless darling. Have no anxiety about anything, Nora; only be frank and open with me, and I will serve as will and conscience both to you—— What is this? Not gone to bed? Have you changed your things?

Nora [*in everyday dress*]. Yes, Torvald, I have changed my things now.

Hel. But what for?—so late as this.

Nora. I shall not sleep tonight.

Hel. But, my dear Nora——

Nora [*looking at her watch*]. It is not so very late. Sit down here, Torvald. You and I have much to say to one another. [*She sits down at one side of the table.*]

Hel. Nora—what is this?—this cold set face?

Nora. Sit down. It will take some time; I have a lot to talk over with you.

Hel. [*sits down at the opposite side of the table*]. You alarm me, Nora!—and I don't understand you.

Nora. No, that is just it. You don't understand me, and I have never understood you either—before tonight. No, you mustn't interrupt me. You must simply listen to what I say. Torvald, this is a settling of accounts.

Hel. What do you mean by that?

Nora [*after a short silence*]. Isn't there one thing that strikes you as strange in our sitting here like this?

Hel. What is that?

Nora. We have been married now eight years. Does it not occur to you that this is the first time we two, you and I, husband and wife, have had a serious conversation?

Hel. What do you mean, serious?

Nora. In all these eight years—longer than that—from the very beginning of our acquaintance we have never exchanged a word on any serious subject.

HEL. Was it likely that I would be continually and forever telling you about worries that you could not help me to bear?

NORA. I am not speaking about business matters. I say that we have never sat down in earnest together to try and get at the bottom of anything.

HEL. But, dearest Nora, would it have been any good to you?

NORA. That is just it; you have never understood me. I have been greatly wronged, Torvald—first by Papa and then by you.

HEL. What! By us two—by us two who have loved you better than anyone else in the world?

NORA [*shaking her head*]. You have never loved me. You have only thought it pleasant to be in love with me.

HEL. Nora, what do I hear you saying?

NORA. It is perfectly true, Torvald. When I was at home with Papa he told me his opinion about everything, and so I had the same opinions; and if I differed from him I concealed the fact, because he would not have liked it. He called me his doll child, and he played with me just as I used to play with my dolls. And when I came to live with you——

HEL. What sort of an expression is that to use about our marriage?

NORA [*undisturbed*]. I mean that I was simply transferred from Papa's hands to yours. You arranged everything according to your own taste, and so I got the same tastes as you—or else I pretended to. I am really not quite sure which—I think sometimes the one and sometimes the other. When I look back on it it seems to me as if I have been living here like a poor woman—just from hand to mouth. I have existed merely to perform tricks for you, Torvald. But you would have it so. You and Papa have committed a great sin against me. It is your fault that I have made nothing of my life.

HEL. How unreasonable and how ungrateful you are, Nora! Have you not been happy here?

NORA. No, I have never been happy. I thought I was, but it has never really been so.

HEL. Not—not happy!

NORA. No, only merry. And you have always been so kind to me. But our home has been nothing but a playroom. I have been your doll wife, just as at home I was papa's doll child; and here the children have been my dolls. I thought it great fun when you played with me, just as they thought it great fun when I played with them. That is what our marriage has been, Torvald.

HEL. There is some truth in what you say—exaggerated and strained as your view of it is. But for the future it shall be different. Playtime shall be over and lesson time shall begin.

NORA. Whose lessons? Mine or the children's?

HEL. Both yours and the children's, my darling Nora.

NORA. Alas, Torvald, you are not the man to educate me into being a proper wife for you.

HEL. And you can say that!

NORA. And I—how am I fitted to bring up the children?

HEL. Nora!

NORA. Didn't you say so yourself a little while ago—that you dare not trust me to bring them up?

HEL. In a moment of anger! Why do you pay any heed to that?

NORA. Indeed, you were perfectly right. I am not fit for the task. There is another task I must undertake first. I must try and educate myself—you are not the man to help me in that. I must do that for myself. And that is why I am going to leave you now.

HEL. [*springing up*]. What do you say?

NORA. I must stand quite alone if I am to understand myself and everything about me. It is for that reason that I cannot remain with you any longer.

HEL. Nora, Nora!

NORA. I am going away from here now, at once. I am sure Christine will take me in for the night.

HEL. You are out of your mind! I won't allow it! I forbid you!

NORA. It is no use forbidding me anything any longer. I will take with me what belongs to myself. I will take nothing from you, either now or later.

HEL. What sort of madness is this?

NORA. Tomorrow I shall go home—I mean to my old home. It will be easiest for me to find something to do there.

HEL. You blind, foolish woman!

NORA. I must try and get some sense, Torvald.

HEL. To desert your home, your husband and your children! And you don't consider what people will say!

NORA. I cannot consider that at all. I only know that it is necessary for me.

HEL. It's shocking. This is how you would neglect your most sacred duties.

NORA. What do you consider my most sacred duties?

HEL. Do I need to tell you that? Are they not your duties to your husband and your children?

NORA. I have other duties just as sacred.

HEL. That you have not. What duties could those be?

NORA. Duties to myself.

HEL. Before all else you are a wife and a mother.

NORA. I don't believe that any longer. I believe that before all else I am a reasonable human being just as you are—or, at all events, that I must try and become one. I know quite well, Torvald, that most people would think you right and that views of that kind are to be found in books; but I can no longer content myself with what most people say or with what is found in books. I must think over things for myself and get to understand them.

HEL. Can you understand your place in your own home? Have you not a reliable guide in such matters as that?—have you no religion?

NORA. I am afraid, Torvald, I do not exactly know what religion is.

HEL. What are you saying?

NORA. I know nothing but what the clergyman said when I went to be confirmed. He told us that religion was this and that and the other. When I am away from all this and am alone I will look into that matter too. I will see if what the clergyman said is true, or at all events if it is true for me.

HEL. This is unheard of in a girl of your age! But if religion cannot lead you aright, let me try and awaken your conscience. I suppose you have some moral sense? Or—answer me—am I to think you have none?

NORA. I assure you, Torvald, that is not an easy question to answer. I really don't know. The thing perplexes me altogether. I only know that you and I look at it in quite a different light. I am learning, too, that the law is quite another thing from what I supposed; but I find it impossible to convince myself that the law is right. According to it a woman has no right to spare her old dying father or to save her husband's life. I can't believe that.

HEL. You talk like a child. You don't understand the conditions of the world in which you live.

NORA. No, I don't. But now I am going to try. I am going to see if I can make out who is right, the world or I.

HEL. You are ill, Nora; you are delirious; I almost think you are out of your mind.

NORA. I have never felt my mind so clear and certain as tonight.

HEL. And is it with a clear and certain mind that you forsake your husband and your children?

NORA. Yes, it is.

HEL. Then there is only one possible explanation.

NORA. What is that?

HEL. You do not love me any more.

NORA. No, that is just it.

HEL. Nora!—and you can say that?

NORA. It gives me great pain, Torvald, for you have always been so kind to me, but I cannot help it. I do not love you any more.

HEL. [*regaining his composure*]. Is that a clear and certain conviction too?

NORA. Yes, absolutely clear and certain. That is the reason why I will not stay here any longer.

HEL. And can you tell me what I have done to forfeit your love?

NORA. Yes, indeed I can. It was tonight, when the wonderful thing did not happen; then I saw you were not the man I had thought you.

HEL. Explain yourself better—I don't understand you.

NORA. I have waited so patiently for eight years; for, goodness knows, I knew very well that wonderful things don't happen every day. Then this horrible misfortune came upon me, and then I felt quite certain that the wonderful thing was going to happen at last. When Krogstad's letter was lying out there never for a moment did I imagine that you would consent to accept this man's conditions. I was so absolutely certain that you would say to him: Publish the thing to the whole world. And when that was done——

HEL. Yes, what then?—when I had exposed my wife to shame and disgrace?

NORA. When that was done I was so absolutely certain you would come forward and take everything upon yourself and say: I am the guilty one.

HEL. Nora!

NORA. You mean that I would never have accepted such a sacrifice on your part? No, of course not. But what would my assurances have been worth against yours? That was the wonderful thing which I hoped for and feared, and it was to prevent that that I wanted to kill myself.

HEL. I would gladly work night and day for you, Nora—bear sorrow and want for your sake. But no man would sacrifice his honor for the one he loves.

NORA. It is a thing hundreds of thousands of women have done.

HEL. Oh, you think and talk like a heedless child.

NORA. Maybe. But you neither think nor talk like the man I could bind myself to. As soon as your fear was over—and it was not fear for what threatened me but for what might happen to you—when the whole thing was past, as far as you were concerned it was exactly as if nothing at all had happened. Exactly as before, I was your little skylark, your doll, which you would in the future treat with doubly gentle care because it was so brittle and fragile. [*Getting up.*] Torvald—it was then it dawned upon me that for eight years I had been living here with a strange man and had borne him three children. Oh, I can't bear to think of it! I could tear myself into little bits!

HEL. [*sadly*]. I see, I see. An abyss has opened between us—there is no denying it. But, Nora, would it not be possible to fill it up?

NORA. As I am now, I am no wife for you.

HEL. I have it in me to become a different man.

NORA. Perhaps—if your doll is taken away from you.

HEL. But to part!—to part from you! No, no, Nora; I can't understand that idea.

NORA [*going out to the right*]. That makes it all the more certain that it must be done. [*She comes back with her cloak and hat and a small bag which she puts on a chair by the table.*]

HEL. Nora. Nora, not now! Wait till tomorrow.

NORA [*putting on her cloak*]. I cannot spend the night in a strange man's room.

HEL. But can't we live here like brother and sister?

NORA [*putting on her hat*]. You know very well that would not last long. [*Puts the shawl round her.*] Good-by, Torvald. I won't see the little ones. I know they are in better hands than mine. As I am now, I can be of no use to them.

HEL. But someday, Nora—someday?

NORA. How can I tell? I have no idea what is going to become of me.

HEL. But you are my wife, whatever becomes of you.

NORA. Listen, Torvald. I have heard that when a wife deserts her husband's house, as I am doing now, he is legally freed from all obligations toward her. In any case I set you free from all your obligations. You are not to feel yourself bound in the slightest way, any more than I shall. There must be perfect freedom on both sides. See, here is your ring back. Give me mine.

HEL. That too?

NORA. That too.

HEL. Here it is.

NORA. That's right. Now it is all over. I have put the keys here. The maids know all about everything in the house—better than I do. Tomorrow, after I have left her, Christine will come here and pack up my own things that I brought with me from home. I will have them sent after me.

HEL. All over! All over! Nora, shall you never think of me again?

NORA. I know I shall often think of you and the children and this house.

HEL. May I write to you, Nora?

NORA. No—never. You must not do that.

HEL. But at least let me send you——

NORA. Nothing—nothing.

HEL. Let me help you if you are in want.

NORA. No. I can receive nothing from a stranger.

HEL. Nora—can I never be anything more than a stranger to you?

NORA [*taking her bag*]. Ah, Torvald, the most wonderful thing of all would have to happen.

HEL. Tell me what that would be!

NORA. Both you and I would have to be so changed that— Oh, Torvald, I don't believe any longer in wonderful things happening.

HEL. But I will believe in it. Tell me. So changed that—

NORA. That our life together would be a real wedlock. Good-by. [*She goes out through the hall.*]

HEL. [*sinks down on a chair at the door and buries his face in his hands*]. Nora! Nora! [*Looks round and rises.*] Empty! She is gone. [*A hope flashes across his mind.*] The most wonderful thing of all—?

[*The sound of a door shutting is heard from below.*]

THE LEAGUE OF YOUTH

PERSONS OF THE PLAY

CHAMBERLAIN BRATSBERG, *owner of ironworks.*

ERIK BRATSBERG, *his son, a merchant.*

THORA, *his daughter.*

SELMA, *Erik's wife.*

DR FIELDBO, *physician at the chamberlain's works.*

STENSGARD, *a lawyer.*

MONS MONSEN, *of Stonelee.*

BASTIAN MONSEN, *his son.*

RAGNA, *his daughter.*

HELLE, *student of theology, tutor at Stonelee.*

RINGDAL, *manager of the ironworks.*

ANDERS LUNDESTAD, *landowner.*

DANIEL HEIRE.

MADAM RUNDHOLMEN, *widow of a storekeeper and publican.*

ASLAKSEN, *a printer.*

A MAIDSERVANT AT THE CHAMBERLAIN'S.

A WAITER.

A WAITRESS AT MADAM RUNDHOLMEN'S.

Townspeople, guests at the chamberlain's, etc., etc.

The action takes place in the neighborhood of the ironworks not far from a market town in southern Norway.

ACT 1

SCENE—*The Seventeenth of May. A popular fete in the chamberlain's grounds. Music and dancing in the background. Colored lights among the trees. In the middle, somewhat toward the back, a rostrum. To the right the entrance to a large refreshment tent; before it a table with benches. In the foreground on the left another table, decorated with flowers and surrounded with lounging chairs.*

A crowd of people. LUNDESTAD, *with a committee badge at his buttonhole, stands on the rostrum.* RINGDAL, *also with a committee badge, at the table on the left.*

LUN. Therefore, friends and fellow citizens, I drink to our freedom! As we have inherited it from our fathers, so will we preserve it for ourselves and for our children! Three cheers for the day! Three cheers for the Seventeenth of May!

THE CROWD. Hurrah! Hurrah! Hurrah!

RIN. [*as* LUNDESTAD *descends from the rostrum*]. And one cheer more for old Lundestad!

SOME OF THE CROWD [*hissing*]. Ss! Ss!

MANY VOICES [*drowning the others*]. Hurrah for Lundestad! Long live old Lundestad! Hurrah!

[*The crowd gradually disperses.* MONSEN, *his son* BASTIAN, STENSGARD *and* ASLAKSEN *make their way forward through the throng.*]

MON. 'Pon my soul, it's time he was laid on the shelf!

ASL. It was the local situation he was talking about! Ho-ho!

MON. He has made the same speech year after year as long as I can remember. Come over here.

STEN. No, no, not that way, Mr Monsen. We are quite deserting your daughter.

MON. Oh, Ragna will find us again.

BAS. Young Helle is with her.

STEN. Helle?

MON. Yes, Helle, but [*nudging* STENSGARD *familiarly*] you have me here, and the rest of us. Come on! Here we shall be out of the crowd and can discuss more fully what—— [*Has meanwhile taken a seat beside the table on the left.*]

RIN. [*approaching*]. Excuse me, Mr Monsen—that table is reserved.

STEN. Reserved? For whom?

RIN. For the chamberlain's party.

STEN. Oh, confound the chamberlain's party! There's none of them here.

RIN. We expect them every minute.

STEN. Let them sit somewhere else. [*Takes a chair.*]

LUN. [*laying his hand on the chair*]. No, the table is reserved, and there's an end of it.

MON. [*rising*]. Come, Mr Stensgard; there are just as good seats over there. [*Crosses to the right.*] Waiter! Ha, no waiters either. The committee should have seen to that in time. Oh, Aslaksen, just go in and get us four bottles of champagne. Order the dearest; tell them to put it down to Monsen!

[ASLAKSEN *goes into the tent; the three others seat themselves.*]

LUN. [*goes quietly over to them and addresses* STENSGARD]. I hope you won't take it ill——

MON. Take it ill! Good gracious, no!

LUN. [*still to* STENSGARD]. It's not my doing; it's the committee that decided——

MON. Of course. The committee orders, and we must obey.

LUN. [*as before*]. You see, we are on the chamberlain's own ground here. He has been so kind as to throw open his park.

STEN. We're extremely comfortable here, Mr Lundestad—if only people would leave us in peace—the crowd, I mean.

LUN. [*unruffled*]. Very well, then it's all right. [*Goes toward the back.*]

ASL. [*entering from the tent*]. The waiter is just coming with the wine. [*Sits.*]

MON. A table apart, under special care of the committee! And on our Independence Day of all others!

STEN. But why on earth do you put up with all this, you good people?

MON. The habit of generations, you see.

ASL. You're new to the district, Mr Stensgard. If only you knew a little of the local situation . . .

A WAITER [*brings champagne*]. Was it you that ordered——

ASL. Yes, certainly; open the bottle.

THE WAITER [*pouring out the wine*]. It goes to your account, Mr Monsen?

MON. The whole thing; don't be afraid.

[*The* WAITER *goes.*]

MON. [*clinks glasses with* STENSGARD]. Here's welcome among us, Mr Stensgard! It gives me great pleasure to have made your acquaintance. The newspapers have made us familiar with your name on all sorts of public occasions. You have great gifts of oratory, Mr Stensgard, and a warm heart for the public weal. I trust you will enter with life and vigor into the—h'm, into the——

ASL. The local situation.

MON. Oh yes, the local situation. I drink to that. [*They drink.*]

STEN. Whatever I do, I shall certainly put life and vigor into it.

MON. Bravo! Hear, hear! Another glass in honor of that promise.

STEN. No, stop; I've already——

MON. Oh, nonsense! Another glass, I say—to seal the bond!

[*They clink glasses and drink. During what follows* BASTIAN *keeps on filling the glasses as soon as they are empty.*]

MON. However—since we have got upon the subject—I must tell you that it's not the chamberlain himself that keeps everything under his thumb. No sir—old Lundestad is the man that stands behind and drives the sledge.

STEN. So I am told in many quarters. I can't understand how a Liberal like him——

MON. Lundestad? Do you call Anders Lundestad a Liberal? To be sure, he professed Liberalism in his young days, when he was still at the foot of the ladder. And then he inherited his seat in Parliament from his father. Lord! everything runs in families here.

STEN. Isn't there a way to stop it?

ASL. Yes, damn it all, Mr Stensgard—see if you can't put a stop to them!

STEN. I don't say that I——

ASL. Yes, you! You are just the man. You have the gift of gab and the pen of a ready writer. My paper's at your disposal.

MON. If anything is to be done, it must be done quickly. The preliminary election comes on in three days now.

STEN. And if you were elected, your private affairs would not prevent your accepting the charge?

MON. My private affairs would suffer, of course; but if it appeared that the good of the community demanded the sacrifice——

STEN. Good; that's good. And you have a party already; that I can see clearly.

MON. I flatter myself the majority of the younger, go-ahead generation——

ASL. H'm, h'm! 'Ware spies!

[DANIEL HEIRE *enters from the tent; he peers about shortsightedly and approaches.*]

HEIRE. May I beg for the loan of a spare seat? I want to sit over there.

MON. The benches are fastened here, you see; but won't you take a place at this table?

HEIRE. Here? At this table? Oh yes, with pleasure. [*Sits.*] Dear, dear! Champagne, I believe.

MON. Yes; won't you join us in a glass?

HEIRE. No, thank you! Madam Rundholmen's champagne—— Well, well, just half a glass to keep you company. If only one had a glass now.

MON. Bastian, go and get one.

BAS. Oh, Aslaksen, go and fetch a glass.

[ASLAKSEN *goes into the tent. A pause.*]

HEIRE. Don't let me interrupt you, gentlemen. I wouldn't for the world! Thanks, Aslaksen. [*Bows to* STENSGARD.] Have I the pleasure of addressing our new legal luminary, Mr Stensgard?

MON. Quite right. [*Introducing them.*] Mr Stensgard, Mr Daniel Heire——

BAS. Capitalist.

HEIRE. Ex-capitalist, you should rather say. It's all gone now; slipped through my fingers, so to speak. Not that I'm bankrupt——

MON. Drink, drink, while the froth is on it.

HEIRE. But rascality, you understand–sharp practice and so forth–I say no more. Well, well, I am confident it is only temporary. When I get my outstanding lawsuits and some other little matters off my hands I shall soon be on the track of our aristocratic old Reynard the Fox. Let us drink to that—— You won't, eh?

STEN. I should like to know first who your aristocratic old Reynard the Fox may be.

HEIRE. Hee-hee; you needn't look so uncomfortable, man. You don't suppose I'm alluding to Mr Monsen. No; it's Chamberlain Bratsberg, my dear young friend.

STEN. What! In money matters the chamberlain is surely above reproach.

HEIRE. You think so, young man? H'm; I say no more. [*Draws nearer.*] Twenty years ago I was worth no end of money. My father left me a great fortune. You've heard of my father, I daresay? No? Old Hans Heire? They called him Gold Hans. He was a shipowner; made heaps of money in the blockade time; had his window frames and doorposts gilded; he could afford it–I say no more.

ASL. Didn't he gild his chimney-pots too?

HEIRE. No; that was only a penny-a-liner's lie; invented long before your time, however. But he made the money fly, and so did I in my time. My visit to London, for instance–haven't you heard of my visit to London? I took a prince's retinue with me. And the sums I have lavished on art and science! And on bringing rising talent to the front!

ASL. [*rises*]. Well, good-by, gentlemen.

MON. What? Are you leaving us?

ASL. Yes; I want to stretch my legs a bit. [*Goes.*]

HEIRE [*speaking low*]. He was one of them–just as grateful as the rest, hee-hee! Do you know I kept him a whole year at college?

STEN. Indeed? Has Aslaksen been to college?

HEIRE. Like young Monsen. He made nothing of it; also like–I say no more. Had to give him up, you see; he had already developed his unhappy taste for spirits.

MON. But you've forgotten what you were going to tell Mr Stensgard about the chamberlain.

HEIRE. Oh, it's a complicated business. When my father was in his glory things were going downhill with the old chamberlain–this one's father; he was a chamberlain too.

BAS. Everything runs in families here.

HEIRE. Including the social graces–I say no more. The conversion of the currency, rash speculations, extravagances he launched out into, forced him to sell some of his land.

STEN. And your father bought it?

HEIRE. Bought and paid for it. Well, what then? I come into my property; I make improvements by the thousand——

BAS. Of course.

HEIRE. Your health, my friend! Improvements by the thousand, I say –thinning the woods and so forth. Years pass, and then comes Master Reynard–the present one, I mean–and repudiates the bargain.

STEN. But, my dear Mr Heire, you could surely have snapped your fingers at him.

HEIRE. Not so easily! Some small formalities had been overlooked, he declared! Besides, I happened then to be in temporary difficulties, which afterward became permanent. And what can a man do without capital?

MON. You're right there, by God! And in many ways you can't do very much with capital either. That I know to my cost. Why, even my innocent children——

BAS. [*thumps the table*]. Ugh, Father! If I only had certain people here!

STEN. Your children, you say?

MON. Yes; take Bastian, for example. Perhaps I haven't given him a good education.

HEIRE. A threefold education! First for the university, then for painting and then for—— It's a civil engineer he is now, isn't it?

BAS. Yes, that I am, by the lord!

MON. Yes, that he is; I can produce his bills and his certificates to prove it! But who gets the town business? Who has got the local road-making–especially these last two years? Foreigners, or at any rate strangers–in short, people no one knows anything about!

HEIRE. Yes, it's shameful the way things go on. Whenever there's a post of confidence going it's always the same! Never Monsen–always someone that enjoys the confidence–of the people in power. Well, well, *commune suffragium*, as the Roman law puts it: that means shipwreck in the Common Council, sir. It's a shame! Your health!

MON. Thanks! But to change the subject–how are all your lawsuits getting on?

HEIRE. They are still pending; I can say no more for the present. Next week I shall have to summon the whole town council before the Arbitration Commission.

BAS. Is it true that you once summoned yourself before the Arbitration Commission?

HEIRE. But I didn't put in an appearance.

MON. Ha, ha! You didn't, eh?

HEIRE. I had a sufficient excuse: had to cross the river, and it was unfortunately the very year of Bastian's bridge–plump! down it went, you know——

BAS. Why, confound it all!

HEIRE. Take it coolly, young man! You are not the first that has bent the bow till it breaks. Everything runs in families, you know–I say no more.

MON. Ho! ho! ho! You say no more, eh? Well, drink, then, and say no more! [*To* STENSGARD.] You see, Mr Heire's tongue is licensed to wag as it pleases.

HEIRE. Yes, freedom of speech is the only civic right I really value.

STEN. What a pity the law should restrict it.

HEIRE. Hee-hee! Our legal friend's mouth is watering for a nice action for slander, eh? Make your mind easy, my dear sir! I'm an old hand, let me tell you!

STEN. Especially at slander?

HEIRE. Your pardon, young man! That outburst of indignation does honor to your heart. I beg you to forget an old man's untimely frankness about your absent friends.

STEN. Absent friends?

HEIRE. I have nothing to say against the son, of course—nor against the daughter. And if I happened to cast a passing slur upon the chamberlain's character——

STEN. The chamberlain's? Is it the chamberlain's family you call my friends?

HEIRE. Well, you don't pay visits to your enemies, I presume?

BAS. Visits?

MON. What?

HEIRE. I am letting cats out of bags!

MON. Have you been paying visits at the chamberlain's?

STEN. Nonsense! A misunderstanding——

HEIRE. A most unhappy slip on my part. But how was I to know it was a secret? [*To* MONSEN.] Besides, you mustn't take my expressions too literally. When I say a visit I mean only a sort of formal call.

STEN. I tell you I haven't exchanged a single word with any of that family!

HEIRE. Is it possible? Were you not received the second time either? I know they were "not at home" the first time.

STEN. [*to* MONSEN]. I had a letter to deliver from a friend in Christiania.

HEIRE [*rising*]. I'll be hanged if it isn't positively revolting! Here is a young man at the outset of his career; full of simple-minded confidence, he seeks out the experienced man of the world and knocks at his door; turns to him, who has brought his ship to port, to beg for—I say no more! The man of the world shuts the door in his face—I say no more! [*With indignation.*] Was there ever such shameful insolence!

STEN. Oh, never mind that stupid business.

HEIRE. Not at home! He, who goes about professing that he is always at home to reputable people!

STEN. Does he say that?

HEIRE. A phrase. He's not at home to Mr Monsen either. But I can't think what has made him hate you so much. Yes, hate you, I say; for what do you think I heard yesterday?

STEN. I don't want to know.

HEIRE. Then I say no more. Besides, the expressions didn't surprise me—coming from the chamberlain, I mean. Only I can't understand why he should have added "demagogue."

STEN. Demagogue!

HEIRE. Well, since you insist upon it, I must confess that the chamberlain called you an adventurer and demagogue.

STEN. [*jumps up*]. What!

HEIRE. Adventurer and demagogue —or demagogue and adventurer; I don't know the order.

STEN. And you heard that?

HEIRE. I? If I had been present, Mr Stensgard, you may be sure I should have stood up for you as you deserve.

MON. There, you see what comes of——

STEN. How dare the old scoundrel——

HEIRE. Come! Keep your temper. Very likely it was a mere figure of speech—a harmless little joke, I have no doubt. You can demand an explanation tomorrow, for I suppose you are going to the great dinner party, eh?

STEN. I am going to no dinner party.

HEIRE. Two calls and no invitation!

STEN. Demagogue and adventurer! What can he be thinking of?

MON. Look there! Talk of the devil! Come, Bastian. [*Goes off with* BASTIAN.]

STEN. What did he mean, Mr Heire?

HEIRE. Haven't the ghost of an idea. It pains you? Your hand, young man! Believe me, you have yet many bitter lessons to learn in this life. You are young; you are confiding; you are trustful. It is beautiful; it is even touching; but—but—trustfulness is silver, experience is gold: that's a proverb of my own invention, sir! God bless you! [*Goes.*]

[CHAMBERLAIN BRATSBERG, *his daughter* THORA *and* DR FIELDBO *enter from the left.*]

LUN. [*strikes the bell on the rostrum*]. Silence for Mr Ringdal's speech!

STEN. [*shouts*]. Mr Lundestad, I demand to be heard.

LUN. Afterward.

STEN. No, now! At once!

LUN. You can't speak just now. Silence for Mr Ringdal!

RIN. [*on the rostrum*]. Ladies and gentlemen! We have at this moment the honor of seeing in our midst the man with the warm heart and the open hand—the man whose door is never closed to any reputable citizen—the man who—who—ladies and gentlemen, our honored guest is no lover of long speeches; so, without more words, I call for three cheers for Chamberlain Bratsberg and his family! Long life to them! Hurrah!

THE CROWD. Hurrah! Hurrah! Hurrah!

[*Great enthusiasm; people press around the* CHAMBERLAIN, *who thanks them and shakes hands with those nearest him.*]

STEN. Now may I speak?

LUN. By all means. The platform is at your service.

STEN. [*jumps upon the table*]. I shall choose my own platform.

THE YOUNG MEN [*crowding around him*]. Hurrah!

CHAM. [*to the* DOCTOR]. Who is this obstreperous personage?

FIEL. Mr Stensgard.

CHAM. Oh, it's he, is it?

STEN. Listen to me, my gladhearted brothers and sisters! Hear me, all you who have in your souls—though it may not reach your lips—the exultant song of the day of our freedom! I am a stranger among you——

ASL. No!

STEN. Thanks for that "No!" I take it as the utterance of a longing. A stranger I am, however; but this I swear, that I come among you for your sorrows and your joys, your victories and defeats. If it lay in my power——

ASL. It does, it does!

LUN. No interruptions! You have no right to speak.

STEN. You still less! I abolish the committee! Freedom on the day of freedom, boys!

THE YOUNG MEN. Hurrah for freedom!

STEN. They deny you the right of speech! You hear it—they want to gag you! Away with this tyranny! I won't stand here declaiming to a flock of dumb animals. I will talk, but you shall talk too. We will talk to each other, from the heart!

THE CROWD [*with growing enthusiasm*]. Hurrah!

STEN. We will have no more of these barren, white-chokered festivities! A golden harvest of deeds shall hereafter shoot up from each Seventeenth of May. May! It is the season of bud and blossom. On the first of June I shall have been just two months among you; and in that time what greatness and littleness, what beauty and deformity, have I not seen?

CHAM. What on earth is he talking about, Doctor?

FIEL. Aslaksen says it's the local situation.

STEN. I have seen great and brilliant possibilities among the masses; but I have seen, too, a spirit of corruption brooding over the germs of promise. I have seen ardent and trustful youth rush yearning forth—and I have seen the door shut in its face.

THORA. Oh, heaven!

CHAM. What does he mean by that?

STEN. There hovers in the air an Influence, a Specter from the dead and rotten past, which spreads darkness and oppression where there should be nothing but buoyancy and light. We must lay that Specter; down with it!

THE CROWD. Hurrah! Hurrah for the Seventeenth of May!

THORA. Come away, Father!

CHAM. What does he mean by a specter? Who is he talking about, Doctor?

FIEL. [*quickly*]. Oh, it's about—— [*Whispers a word or two.*]

CHAM. Aha! So that's it!

THORA [*softly to* FIELDBO]. Thanks!

STEN. If no one else will crush the dragon, I will! But you must help, boys!

MANY VOICES. Yes! Yes!

STEN. We are young! The time belongs to us, but we also belong to the time. Our right is our duty! Listen to me! We must form a league. The moneybag has ceased to rule among us!

CHAM. Bravo! [*To the* DOCTOR.] He said the moneybag, so no doubt you're right.

STEN. Yes, boys, we are the wealth of the country, if only there's metal in us. Our will is the ringing gold that shall pass from man to man. War to the knife against whoever shall deny its currency!

THE CROWD. Hurrah!

STEN. A scornful "bravo" has been flung in my teeth——

CHAM. No, no!

STEN. What care I! Thanks and threats alike are powerless over the perfect will. And now, God be with us! For we are going about His work, with youth and faith to help us. Come, then, into the refreshment tent—our league shall be baptized this very hour.

THE CROWD. Hurrah! Carry him! Shoulder high with him! [*He is lifted shoulder high.*]

VOICES. Speak on! More! More!

STEN. Let us hold together, I say! Providence is on the side of the League of Youth. It lies with us to rule the world! [*He is carried into the tent amid wild enthusiasm.*]

MADAM [*wiping her eyes*]. Oh lord, how beautifully he does speak! Don't you feel as if you could kiss him, Mr Heire?

HEIRE. Thank you, I'd rather not.

MADAM. Oh, you! I daresay not.

HEIRE. Perhaps you would like to kiss him, Madam Rundholmen.

MADAM. How horrid you are! [*She goes into the tent;* HEIRE *follows her.*]

CHAM. Specter—dragon—moneybag! It was horribly rude but well deserved!

LUN. [*approaching*]. I'm heartily sorry, Chamberlain.

CHAM. Yes, where was your knowledge of character, Lundestad? Well, well, we are none of us infallible. Good night and thanks for a pleasant evening. [*Turns to* THORA *and the* DOCTOR.] But bless me, I've been positively rude to that fine young fellow.

FIEL. How so?

THORA. His call, you mean?

CHAM. Yes. Lundestad told me he was an adventurer and—and I forget what else. Fortunately I can make up for it.

THORA. How?

CHAM. Come, Thora, let us see to it at once.

FIEL. Oh, do you think it's worth while, Chamberlain?

THORA [*softly*]. Hush!

CHAM. When one has done an injustice one should lose no time in undoing it; that's a plain duty. Good night, Doctor. After all, I've spent an amusing hour, and that's more than I have to thank you for today.

FIEL. Me, Chamberlain?

CHAM. Yes—you and others.

FIEL. May I ask what I——

CHAM. Don't be curious, Doctor. I am never curious. Come, come—no offense—good night!

[*The* CHAMBERLAIN *and* THORA *go out to the left;* FIELDBO *gazes thoughtfully after them.*]

ASL. [*from the tent*]. Hei, waiter! Pen and ink! Things are getting lively, Doctor!

FIEL. What things?

ASL. He's founding the league.

LUN. [*who has quietly drawn near*]. Are many putting down their names?

ASL. We've enrolled about seven-and-thirty, not counting widows and so forth. Pen and ink, I say. No waiters to be found!—that's the fault of the local situation. [*Goes off behind the tent.*]

LUN. Puh! It has been hot today.

FIEL. I'm afraid hotter days will come.

LUN. Do you think the chamberlain was very angry?

FIEL. Oh, not in the least; you could see that, couldn't you? But what do you say to the new league?

LUN. H'm; I say nothing. What is there to be said?

FIEL. It's the beginning of a struggle for power here in the district.

LUN. Well, well, no harm in a fight. He has great gifts, that Stensgard.

FIEL. He is determined to make his way.

LUN. Youth is always determined to make its way. I was, when I was young. But mightn't we look in and see——

HIERE [*from the tent*]. Well, Mr Lundestad, are you going to move the previous question, eh? To head the opposition? Hee-hee! You must make haste!

LUN. Oh, I daresay I shall be in time.

HEIRE. Too late, sir! Unless you want to stand godfather. [*Cheering from the tent.*] They're chanting Amen; the baptism is over.

LUN. I suppose one may be permitted to listen; I shall keep quiet. [*Enters the tent.*]

HEIRE. There goes one of the falling trees! The place will soon look like a wood after a tornado. Won't I chuckle over it!

FIEL. Tell me, Mr Heire, what interest have you in the matter?

HEIRE. Indeed? I am entirely disinterested, Doctor! If I chuckle, it is on behalf of my fellow citizens. There will be life, spirit, go in things. For my own part, I say, as the Grand Turk said of the Emperor of Austria and the King of France—I don't care whether the pig eats the dog or the dog the pig. [*Goes toward the back on the right.*]

THE CROWD [*in the tent*]. Long live Stensgard! Hurrah for the League of Youth! Wine! Punch! Hei, hei! Beer! Hurrah!

BAS. [*comes from the tent*]. God bless you and everyone. [*With tears in his voice.*] Oh, Doctor, I feel so strong this evening; I must do something.

FIEL. What would you like to do?

BAS. I think I'll go down to the dancing room and fight one or two fellows. [*Goes out behind the tent.*]

STEN. [*comes from the tent without his hat and greatly excited*]. My dear Fieldbo, is that you?

FIEL. At your service, Tribune of the People! For I suppose you've been elected?

STEN. Of course, but——

FIEL. And what is to come of it all? What nice little post are you to have? The management of the bank? Or perhaps——

STEN. Oh, don't talk to me like that! I know you don't mean it. You are not so empty and wooden as you like to appear.

FIEL. Empty and wooden, eh?

STEN. Fieldbo! Be my friend as you used to be! We have not understood each other of late. You have wounded and repelled me with your ridicule and irony. Believe me, it was wrong of you. [*Embraces him.*] Oh, my great God! how happy I am.

FIEL. You too? So am I, so am I.

STEN. Yes, I should be the meanest hound on earth if all heaven's bounty didn't make me good and true. How have I deserved it, Fieldbo?

FIEL. There is my hand! This evening I am your friend indeed!

STEN. Thanks! Be faithful and true, as I shall be! Oh, isn't it an unspeakable joy to carry all that multitude away and along with you? How can you help becoming good from mere thankfulness? And how it makes you love all your fellow creatures! I feel as if I could clasp them all in one embrace and weep and beg their forgiveness because God has given me more than he has them.

FIEL. [*quietly*]. Yes, treasures without price may fall to one man's lot. This evening I would not crush an insect.

STEN. You?

FIEL. Never mind. That's apart from the question. I only mean that I understand you.

STEN. What a lovely night! Listen to the music and merriment floating out over the meadows. And how still it is in the valley! I tell you, the man whose life is not reconsecrated in such an hour does not deserve to live on God's earth!

FIEL. Yes; but tell me now: what do you mean to build up of it—tomorrow and through the working days to come?

STEN. To build up? We have to tear down first. Fieldbo, I had once a dream—or did I see it? No, it was a dream, but such a vivid one! I thought the Day of Judgment was come upon the world. I could see the whole curve of the hemisphere. There was no sun, only a livid storm light. A tempest arose; it came rushing from the west and swept everything before it: first withered leaves, then men; but they kept on their feet all the time, and their garments clung fast to them, so that they seemed to be hurried along sitting. At first they looked like townspeople running after their hats in a wind, but when they came nearer they were emperors and kings and it was their crowns and orbs they were chasing and catching at and seemed always on the point of grasping but never grasped. Oh, there were hundreds of them, and none of them understood in the least what was happening; but many bewailed themselves and asked: "Whence can it come, this terrible storm?" Then came the answer: "One Voice spoke, and the storm is the echo of that one Voice."

FIEL. When did you dream that?

STEN. Oh, several years ago.

FIEL. There were probably disturbances somewhere in Europe and you had been reading the newspapers after a heavy supper.

STEN. The same shiver, the same thrill, that then ran down my back, I felt again tonight. Yes. I will be the Voice——

FIEL. Come, my dear Stensgard, pause and reflect. You will be the Voice, you say. Good! But where will you be the Voice? Here in the parish? Or at most here in the country! And who will echo you and raise the storm? Why, people like Monsen and Aslaksen and that fatheaded genius, Mr Bastian. And instead of the flying emperors and kings we shall see old Lundestad rushing about after his lost seat in Parliament. Then what will it all amount to? Just townsfolk in a wind.

STEN. In the beginning, yes. But who knows how far the storm may sweep?

FIEL. Fiddlesticks with you and your storm! And the first thing you go and do is to turn your weapons precisely against all that is worthy and capable among us.

STEN. That is not true.

FIEL. It is not true! Monsen and the Stonelee gang got hold of you the moment you came here, and if you don't shake him off it will be your ruin. Chamberlain Bratsberg is a man of honor. Do you know why the great Monsen hates him? Why, because——

STEN. Not a word more! I won't hear a word against my friends!

FIEL. Look into yourself, Stensgard! Is Mr Mons Monsen really your friend?

STEN. Mr Monsen has most kindly opened his doors to me.

FIEL. To people of the better sort he opens his doors in vain.

STEN. Oh, whom do you call the better sort? A few stuck-up officials! I know all about it. As for me, I have been received at Stonelee with so much appreciation——

FIEL. Appreciation? Yes, unfortunately—there we are at the root of the matter.

STEN. Not at all! I can see with unprejudiced eyes. Mr Monsen has abilities, he has reading and a keen sense for public affairs.

FIEL. Abilities? Oh yes, in a way. Reading too: he takes in the papers and has read your speeches and articles. And his sense for public affairs he has, of course, proved by applauding the said articles and speeches.

STEN. Now, Fieldbo, up come the dregs of your nature again. Can you never shake off that polluting habit of thought? Why must you always assume mean or ridiculous motives for everything? Oh, you are not serious! Now you look good and true. Do you know Ragna?

FIEL. Ragna Monsen? Oh, after a fashion—at second hand.

STEN. Yes, I know she is sometimes at the chamberlain's.

FIEL. In a quiet way, yes. She and Miss Bratsberg are old schoolfellows.

STEN. And what do you think of her?

FIEL. Why, from all I have heard, she seems to be a very good girl.

STEN. Oh, you should see her in her home! She thinks of nothing but her two little sisters. And how devotedly she must have nursed her mother! You know the mother was out of her mind for some years before she died.

FIEL. Yes; I was their doctor at one time. But surely you don't mean that——

STEN. Yes, Fieldbo, I love her truly; to you I can confess it. Oh, I know what you are surprised at. You think it strange that so soon after—of course you know that I was engaged to Christiana?

FIEL. Yes, so I was told.

STEN. The whole thing was a disappointment. I had to break it off; it was best for all parties. Oh, how I suffered in that affair! The torture, the sense of oppression I endured! Now I am out of it all. That was my reason for leaving town.

FIEL. And with regard to Ragna Monsen are you quite sure of yourself?

STEN. Yes, I am indeed.

FIEL. Well, then, in heaven's name, go in and win! It means your life's happiness! Oh, there's so much I could say to you——

STEN. Really? Has she said anything? Has she confided in Miss Bratsberg?

FIEL. No, that's not what I mean. But how can you, in the midst of your happiness, go and fuddle yourself in these political orgies?

STEN. Why not? Man is a complex machine—I am, at any rate. Besides, my way to her lies through these very party turmoils.

FIEL. A terribly prosaic way.

STEN. Fieldbo, I am ambitious; you know I am. I must make my way in the world. When I remember that I'm thirty and am still on the first round of the ladder I feel my conscience gnawing at me.

FIEL. Not with its wisdom teeth.

STEN. It's of no use talking to you. You have never felt the spur of ambition. You have dawdled and drifted all your days—first at college, then abroad, now here.

FIEL. Perhaps; but it has been delightful. And no reaction follows like what you feel when you get down from the table after——

STEN. Stop that! I can bear anything but that. You are damping my ardor.

FIEL. Oh, come! If your ardor is so easily damped——

STEN. Stop, I say! What right have you to break in upon my happiness? Do you think I am not sincere?

FIEL. Yes, I am sure you are.

STEN. Well, then, why go and make

me feel suspicious of myself? [*Shouts and cheers from the tent.*] They are drinking my health. An idea that can take such hold upon people—by God, it must have truth in it!

[THORA BRATSBERG, RAGNA MONSEN *and* MR HELLE *enter from the left and cross halfway back.*]

HELLE. Look, Miss Bratsberg, there is Mr Stensgard.

THORA. Then I don't go any further. Good night, Ragna dear.

HELLE *and* MISS MONSEN. Good night, good night. [*They go out to the right.*]

THORA [*advancing*]. I am Miss Bratsberg. I have a letter for you from my father.

STEN. For me?

THORA. Yes, here it is. [*Going.*]

FIEL. May I not see you home?

THORA. No, thank you. I can go alone. Good night. [*Goes out to the left.*]

STEN. [*reading the letter by a Chinese lantern*]. What is this!

FIEL. Well—what has the chamberlain to say to you?

STEN. [*bursts into loud laughter*]. I must say I didn't expect this!

FIEL. Tell me.

STEN. Chamberlain Bratsberg is a pitiful creature.

FIEL. You dare to——

STEN. Pitiful! Pitiful. Tell anyone you please that I said so. Or rather, say nothing about it. [*Puts the letter in his pocket.*] Don't mention this to anyone!

[*The* COMPANY *come out from the tent.*]

MON. Mr President! Where is Mr Stensgard?

THE CROWD. There he is! Hurrah!

LUN. Mr President has forgotten his hat. [*Hands it to him.*]

ASL. Here, have some punch! Here's a whole bowlful!

STEN. Thanks, no more.

MON. And the members of the league will recollect that we meet tomorrow at Stonelee.

STEN. Tomorrow? It wasn't tomorrow, was it?

MON. Yes, certainly; to draw up the manifesto.

STEN. No, I really can't tomorrow —I shall see about it the day after tomorrow. Well, good night, gentlemen; hearty thanks all round and hurrah for the future!

THE CROWD. Hurrah! Let's take him home in triumph!

STEN. Thanks, thanks! But you really mustn't.

ASL. We'll all go with you.

STEN. Very well, come along. Good night, Fieldbo; you're not coming with us?

FIEL. No; but let me tell you, what you said about Chamberlain Bratsberg——

STEN. Hush, hush! It was an exaggeration—I withdraw it! Well, my friends, if you're coming, come; I'll take the lead.

MON. Your arm, Stensgard!

BAS. A song! Strike up! Something thoroughly patriotic!

THE CROWD. A song! A song! Music!

[*A popular air is played and sung. The procession marches out by the back to the right.*]

FIEL. [*to* LUNDESTAD, *who remains behind*]. A gallant procession.

LUN. Yes—and with a gallant leader.

FIEL. And where are you going, Mr Lundestad?

LUN. I? I'm going home to bed. [*He nods and goes off.* DR FIELDBO *remains behind alone.*]

ACT II

SCENE—*A garden room at the chamberlain's, elegantly furnished with a piano, flowers and rare plants. Entrance door at the back. On the left a door leading to the dining room; on the right several glass doors lead out to the garden.*

ASLAKSEN *stands at the entrance door. A* MAIDSERVANT *is carrying some dishes of fruit into the dining room.*

THE MAID. Yes, but I tell you they're still at table; you must call again.

ASL. I'd rather wait, if I may.

THE MAID. Oh yes, if you like. You can sit there for the present. [*She goes into the dining room.* ASLAKSEN *takes a seat near the door. Pause.* DR FIELDBO *enters from the back.*]

FIEL. Ah, good evening, Aslaksen, are you here?

THE MAID [*returning*]. You're late this evening, sir.

FIEL. I was called to see a patient.

THE MAID. The chamberlain and Miss Bratsberg have both been inquiring about you.

FIEL. Indeed?

THE MAID. Yes. Won't you go in at once, sir, or shall I say that——

FIEL. No, no, never mind. I can have a snack afterward; I shall wait here. [*She goes out by the back.*]

THE MAID. Dinner will soon be over.

ASL. [*after a pause*]. How can you resist such a dinner, Doctor?

FIEL. Why, man, it seems to me we get too many good things hereabouts rather than too few.

ASL. There I can't agree with you.

FIEL. H'm, I suppose you are waiting for someone?

ASL. Yes, I am.

FIEL. And are things going tolerably at home? Your wife——

ASL. In bed, as usual; coughing and wasting away.

FIEL. And your second child?

ASL. Oh, he's a cripple for the rest of his days; you know that. That's our luck, you see; what is the use of talking about it?

FIEL. Let me look at you, Aslaksen!

ASL. Well, what do you want to see?

FIEL. You've been drinking today.

ASL. Yes, and yesterday too.

FIEL. Well, yesterday there was some excuse for it, but today——

ASL. What about your friends in there then? Aren't they drinking too?

FIEL. Yes, my dear Aslaksen; but circumstances differ so in this world.

ASL. I didn't choose my circumstances.

FIEL. No, God chose them for you.

ASL. No, he didn't. Daniel Heire chose, when he took me from the printing house and sent me to college. And Chamberlain Bratsberg chose, when he ruined Daniel Heire and sent me back to the printing house.

FIEL. Now you know that's not true. The chamberlain did not ruin Daniel Heire; Daniel Heire ruined himself.

ASL. Perhaps! But how dared Daniel Heire ruin himself in the face of his responsibility toward me? God's partly to blame too. Why should he give me talent and ability? Well, of course I could have turned them to account as a respectable handicraftsman, but then comes that tattling old fool——

FIEL. It's base of you to say that. Daniel Heire acted with the best of intentions.

ASL. What good do his "best intentions" do me? You hear them in there, clinking glasses and drinking healths? Well, I too have sat at that table in my day, dressed in purple and fine linen like the best of them! That was just the thing for me, that was—for me that had read so much and had thirsted so long to have my share in all the good things of life. Well. Smash, crash! down you go—and my fine fortunes fell to pi, as we printers say.

FIEL. But you were not so badly off; you had your trade to fall back upon.

ASL. That's easily said. After getting out of your class you can't get into it again. They took the ground from under my feet and shoved me out on the slippery ice.

FIEL. Well, far be it from me to judge you harshly.

ASL. No, you have no right to. What a queer jumble it is! Daniel Heire and Providence and the chamberlain and destiny and circumstance —and I myself in the middle of it! I've often thought of unraveling it all and writing a book about it, but it's so cursedly entangled that—— [*Glances toward the door on the left.*] Ah! They're rising from table.

[*The party, ladies and gentlemen, pass from the dining room into the garden in lively conversation. Among the guests is* STENSGARD, *with* THORA *on his left arm and* SELMA *on his right.* FIELDBO *and* ASLAKSEN *stand beside the door at the back.*]

STEN. I don't know my way here yet; you must tell me where I am to take you.

SELMA. Out into the air; you must see the garden.

STEN. Oh, that will be delightful. [*They go out by the foremost glass door on the right.*]

FIEL. Why, by all that's wonderful, there's Stensgard!

ASL. It's him I want to speak to. I've had a fine chase after him.

[DANIEL HEIRE *and* ERIK BRATSBERG *enter from the dining room.*]

HEIRE. Hee-hee! Excellent sherry! I've tasted nothing like it since I was in London.

ERIK. Yes, it's good, isn't it? It puts life into you.

HEIRE. Well, well—it's a real pleasure to see one's money so well spent.

ERIK. How so? [*Laughing.*] Oh yes, I see, I see. [*They go into the garden.*]

FIEL. You want to speak to Stensgard, you say?

ASL. Yes.

FIEL. On business?

ASL. Of course; the report of the——

FIEL. Well, then, you must wait out there in the meantime.

ASL. In the passage?

FIEL. In the anteroom. This is scarcely the time or place—but the moment I see Stensgard alone I'll tell him.

ASL. Very well; I'll bide my time. [*Goes out by the back.*]

[CHAMBERLAIN BRATSBERG, LUNDESTAD, RINGDAL *and one or two other gentlemen come out of the dining room.*]

CHAM. [*conversing with* LUNDESTAD]. Violent, you say? Well, perhaps the form wasn't all that could be desired; but there were real gems in the speech, I can assure you.

LUN. Well, if you are satisfied, Chamberlain, I have no right to complain.

CHAM. Why should you? Ah, here's the doctor! Starving, I'll be bound.

FIEL. It doesn't matter, Chamberlain. The servants will attend to me. I feel myself almost at home here, you know.

CHAM. Oh, you do, do you? I wouldn't be in too great a hurry.

FIEL. What? Am I taking too great a liberty? You yourself permitted me to——

CHAM. What I permitted, I permitted. Well, well, make yourself at home and forage for something to eat. [*Slaps him lightly on the shoulder and turns to* LUNDESTAD.] Now here's one you may call an adventurer and—and the other thing I can't remember.

FIEL. Why, Chamberlain!

LUN. No, I assure you——

CHAM. No arguments after dinner; it's bad for the digestion. [*Goes with the guests into the garden.*]

LUN. [*to* FIELDBO]. Did you ever see the chamberlain so strange as he is today?

FIEL. I noticed it yesterday evening.

LUN. He will have it that I called Mr Stensgard an adventurer and something else of that sort.

FIEL. Excuse me; I must go out and talk to the ladies. [*Goes out to the right.*]

LUN. [*to* RINGDAL, *who is arranging a card table*]. How do you account for Mr Stensgard's appearance here today?

RIN. He wasn't on the original list.

LUN. An afterthought then? After his attack on the chamberlain yesterday?

RIN. Yes, can you understand it?

LUN. Oh yes, I suppose I can.

RIN. [*more softly*]. You think the chamberlain is afraid of him?

LUN. I think he is prudent.

[*They go up to the back conversing and so out into the garden. At the same time* SELMA *and* STENSGARD *enter by the foremost door on the right.*]

SEL. Yes, just look—over the tops of the trees you can see the church tower and all the upper part of the town.

STEN. So you can; I shouldn't have thought so.

SEL. Isn't it a beautiful view?

STEN. Great heaven, how beautiful it all is! And you live here all the summer?

SEL. No, not my husband and I; we come and go. We have a big showy house in town.

STEN. Perhaps your family live in town?

SEL. My family? Who are my family?

STEN. Oh, I didn't know——

SEL. We fairy princesses have no family.

STEN. Fairy princesses?

SEL. At most we have a wicked stepmother.

STEN. A witch, yes! So you are a princess!

SEL. Princess of all the sunken palaces, whence you hear the soft music on midsummer nights. Doctor Fieldbo thinks it must be pleasant to be a princess, but I must tell you——

ERIK [*coming from the garden*]. Ah, at last I find the little lady!

SEL. The little lady is telling Mr Stensgard the story of her life.

ERIK. Oh, indeed! And what part does the husband play in the little lady's story?

SEL. The prince, of course. [*To* STENSGARD.] You know the prince always comes and breaks the spell, and then all ends happily and the fairy tale is over.

STEN. Oh, it's too short.

SEL. Perhaps—in a way.

ERIK [*putting his arm around her waist*]. But a new fairy tale grows out of the old one, and in it the princess becomes a queen!

SEL. On the same condition as real princesses?

ERIK. What condition?

SEL. They must go into exile—to a foreign kingdom.

ERIK. A cigar, Mr Stensgard?

STEN. Thank you, not just now.

[DR FIELDBO *and* THORA *enter from the garden.*]

SEL. [*going toward them*]. Is that you, Thora dear? I hope you're not ill.

THORA. I? No.

SEL. Oh, but I'm sure you must be; you seem to be always consulting the doctor of late.

THORA. No, I assure you——

SEL. Nonsense; let me feel your pulse! You are burning. My dear doctor, don't you think the fever will pass over?

FIEL. Everything has its time.

THORA. Would you rather have me freezing?

SEL. No, a medium temperature is the best—ask my husband.

CHAM. [*enters from the garden*]. The whole family gathered in secret conclave? That's not very polite to the guests.

THORA. I am just going, Father dear.

CHAM. Aha, it is you the ladies are paying court to, Mr Stensgard!

THORA [*softly to* FIELDBO]. Remain here! [*She goes into the garden.*]

ERIK [*offers* SELMA *his arm*]. Has Madame any objection?

SEL. Come! [*They go out to the right.*]

CHAM. [*looking after them*]. It's impossible to get those two separated.

FIEL. It would be sinful to try.

CHAM. Fools that we are! How Providence blesses us in spite of ourselves. [*Calls out.*] Thora, Thora, do look after Selma. Get a shawl for her; she'll catch cold. How shortsighted we mortals are, Doctor! Do you know any cure for that disease?

FIEL. The spectacles of experience; through them you will see more clearly a second time.

CHAM. You don't say so! Thanks for the advice. But since you feel yourself at home here, you must really pay a little attention to our guests.

FIEL. Certainly; come, Stensgard, shall we——

CHAM. Oh no, no—there's my old friend Hiere out there.

FIEL. He feels at home here too.

CHAM. Ha, ha, ha! So he does.

FIEL. Well, we two will join forces and do our best. [*Goes into the garden.*]

STEN. You were speaking of Daniel Heire, Chamberlain. I must say I was rather surprised to see him here.

CHAM. Were you? Mr Heire and I are old school and college friends. Besides, we have had a good deal to do with each other in many ways since——

STEN. Yes, Mr Heire was good enough to give his own account of some of these transactions yesterday evening.

CHAM. H'm!

STEN. Had it not been for him, I certainly should not have let myself boil over as I did. But he has a vile tongue in his head.

CHAM. My dear young friend—Mr Heire is my guest; you must not forget that. My house is liberty hall, but my guests must not be discussed to their disadvantage.

STEN. I beg your pardon, I'm sure!

CHAM. Oh, never mind; you belong to the younger generation that's not so punctilious. I, at any rate, owe Mr Heire a great deal.

STEN. Yes, he gave one to understand, but I didn't think——

CHAM. I owe him the best part of our domestic happiness. Mr Stensgard! I owe him my daughter-in-law. Daniel Heire was kind to her in her childhood. She was a youthful prodigy; she gave concerts when she was only ten years old. I daresay you have heard her spoken of—Selma Sjöblom.

STEN. Sjöblom? Yes, of course; her father was Swedish?

CHAM. Yes, a music teacher. He came here many years ago. Musicians, you know, are seldom millionaires; in short, Mr Heire has always had an eye for talent; he was struck with the child and had her sent to Berlin, and then, when her father was dead and Heire's fortunes were on the wane, she returned to Christiania, where she was of course taken up by the best people. That was how my son happened to fall in with her.

STEN. Then in that way Heire has indeed been an instrument for good.

CHAM. We are all instruments, Mr Stensgard; you, like the rest of us; an instrument of wrath, I suppose.

STEN. Oh, don't speak of it, Chamberlain. I am utterly ashamed.

CHAM. Ashamed?

STEN. It was most unbecoming.

CHAM. The form was perhaps open to criticism, but the intention was excellent. And now I want to ask you in future, when you are contemplating any move of the sort, just to come to me and tell me of it openly and without reserve. We all want to act for the best, and it is my duty——

STEN. May I speak frankly to you?

CHAM. Do you think I haven't long realized that matters here have in some ways taken a most undesirable turn? But what was I to do? In the late king's time I lived for the most part in Stockholm. I am old now; and besides, it is not in my nature to take the lead in reforms or to throw myself personally into the turmoil of public affairs. You, Mr Stensgard, have every qualification for them; so let us hold together.

STEN. Thanks, Chamberlain; many, many thanks!

[RINGDAL *and* DANIEL HEIRE *enter from the garden.*]

RIN. And I tell you it must be a misunderstanding.

HEIRE. Indeed? I like that! How should I misunderstand my own ears?

CHAM. Anything new, Heire?

HEIRE. Only that Anders Lundestad is going over to the Stonelee party.

CHAM. Oh, you're joking!

HEIRE. I beg your pardon, my dear sir; I have it from his own lips. Mr Lundestad intends, on account of failing health, to retire from political life; you can draw your own conclusions from that.

STEN. He told you so himself?

HEIRE. Of course he did. He made the momentous announcement to an awe-struck circle down in the garden; hee-hee!

CHAM. Why, my dear Ringdal, what can be the meaning of this?

HEIRE. Oh, it's not difficult to guess.

CHAM. Indeed it is, though. This is a most important affair for the district. Come along, Ringdal; we must find him. [*He and* RINGDAL *go down the garden.*]

FIEL. [*entering by the furthest back*

garden door]. Has the chamberlain gone out?

HEIRE. Sh! The sages are deliberating! Lundestad is going to resign.

FIEL. Oh, impossible.

STEN. Can you understand it?

HEIRE. It's the League of Youth that's beginning to work, Mr Stensgard. Do you know what you should call your league? I'll tell you some other time.

STEN. Do you really think it's our league?

HEIRE. Not the least doubt of it. So we are to have the pleasure of sending our respected friend Mr Mons Monsen to Parliament! I wish he were off already—I'd give him a gift with pleasure—I say no more; hee-hee! [*Goes to the garden.*]

STEN. Tell me, Fieldbo—how do you explain all this?

FIEL. There are other things still more difficult to explain. How come you to be here?

STEN. Like the rest, by invitation.

FIEL. I hear you were invited yesterday evening—after your speech.

STEN. What then?

FIEL. How could you accept?

STEN. What the deuce was I to do? I couldn't insult these good people.

FIEL. Indeed! You couldn't? What about your speech then?

STEN. Nonsense! It was principles I attacked in my speech and not persons.

FIEL. And how do you account for the chamberlain's invitation?

STEN. Why, my dear friend, there can be only one way of accounting for it.

FIEL. Namely, that the chamberlain is afraid of you.

STEN. By heaven, he shall have no reason to be! He is a gentleman.

FIEL. That he is.

STEN. Isn't it touching the way he has taken this? And how lovely Miss Bratsberg looked when she brought me the letter!

FIEL. But look here—they haven't mentioned the scene of yesterday, have they?

STEN. They have far too much tact for that. But I am filled with remorse; I must find an opportunity of apologizing.

FIEL. I strongly advise you not to! You don't know the chamberlain.

STEN. Very well, then; my acts shall speak for me.

FIEL. You will not break with the Stonelee party?

STEN. I shall bring about a reconciliation. I have my league; it's a power already.

FIEL. By the bye, while I remember—we were speaking of Miss Monsen—I advised you to go in and win——

STEN. Oh, there's no hurry.

FIEL. But I have been thinking it over; you had better put that out of your head.

STEN. I believe you are right. If you marry into an underbred family, you marry the whole tribe of them.

FIEL. Yes, and there are other reasons——

STEN. Monsen is an underbred fellow; I see that now.

FIEL. Well, polish is not his strong point.

STEN. No, indeed it's not! He goes and speaks ill of his guests; that's ungentlemanly. His rooms all reek of stale tobacco——

FIEL. My dear fellow, how is it you never noticed the stale tobacco before?

STEN. It's the contrast that does it. I made a false start when I settled here. I fell into the clutches of a clique, and they bewildered me with their clamor. But there shall be an end to that! I won't go and wear my life out as a tool in their hands.

FIEL. But what will you do with your league?

STEN. The league will remain as it is. Its purpose is to counteract noxious influences, and I am just beginning to realize what side the noxious influences come from.

FIEL. But do you think the "Youth" will see it in the same light?

STEN. They shall! Fellows like that should bow before my superior insight.

FIEL. But if they won't?

STEN. Then they can go their own way. You don't suppose I am going to let my life slip into a wrong groove and never reach the goal for the sake of mere blind consistency?

FIEL. What do you call the goal?

STEN. A career that gives scope for my talents and fulfils my aspirations.

FIEL. No vague phrases! What do you mean by your goal?

STEN. Well, to you I can make a clean breast of it. My goal is this: in the course of time to get into Parliament, perhaps into the Ministry, and to marry happily into a family of means and position.

FIEL. And by the help of the chamberlain's social connections you intend to——

STEN. I intend to reach the goal by my own exertions! I must and will reach it, and without help from anyone. It will take time, but never mind! Meanwhile I shall enjoy life here, drinking in beauty and sunshine——

FIEL. Here?

STEN. Yes, here! Here there are fine manners; life moves gracefully here; the very floors seem laid to be trodden only by lacquered shoes. Here the armchairs are deep and the ladies sink exquisitely into them. Here conversation moves lightly and elegantly, like a game at battledore; here no blunders come plumping in to make an awkward silence. Oh, Fieldbo—here I feel for the first time what distinction means! Yes, we have indeed an aristocracy of our own; a little circle; an aristocracy of culture; and to it I will belong. Don't you yourself feel the refining influence of this place? Don't you feel that wealth here loses its grossness? When I think of Monsen's money I seem to see piles of fetid bank notes and greasy mortgages—but here! here it is shimmering silver! And the people are the same. Look at the chamberlain—what a fine highbred old fellow!

FIEL. He is, indeed.

STEN. And the son—alert, straightforward, capable!

FIEL. Certainly.

STEN. And then the daughter-in-law! Isn't she a pearl? Good God, what a rich, what a fascinating nature!

FIEL. Miss Bratsberg has that too.

STEN. But she is less remarkable.

FIEL. Oh, you don't know her—how deep and steadfast and true her nature is.

STEN. But, oh, the daughter-in-law! So frank, almost reckless, and yet so appreciative, so irresistible——

FIEL. Why, I really believe you're in love with her.

STEN. With a married woman? Are you crazy? What good would that do me? No, but I am falling in love—I can feel that plainly. Yes, she is indeed deep and steadfast and true.

FIEL. Who?

STEN. Miss Bratsberg, of course.

FIEL. What? You're not thinking——

STEN. Yes, by heaven, I am!

FIEL. It's quite out of the question.

STEN. Ho-ho! Will rules the world, my dear fellow! We shall see if it doesn't.

FIEL. Why, this is the merest extravagance! Yesterday it was Miss Monsen——

STEN. Oh, I was too hasty about that; besides, you yourself advised me not to——

FIEL. I advise you most emphatically to dismiss all thought of either of them.

STEN. Indeed! Perhaps you think of throwing the handkerchief to one of them?

FIEL. I? No, I assure you——

STEN. Well, it wouldn't have mattered if you had. If people stand in my way and balk me of my future, why, I stick at nothing.

FIEL. Take care I don't say the same!

STEN. You! What right have you to pose as guardian and protector to Chamberlain Bratsberg's family?

FIEL. I have at least the right of a friend.

STEN. Pooh! That sort of talk won't do with me. Your motive is mere self-interest! It gratifies your petty vanity to imagine yourself cock of the walk in this house, and so I am to be kept outside the pale.

FIEL. That is the best thing that could happen to you. Here you are standing on hollow ground.

STEN. Am I, indeed? Many thanks. I shall manage to prop it up.

FIEL. Try; but I warn you, it will fall through with you first.

STEN. Ho-ho! So you are intriguing against me, are you? I know you now; you are my enemy, the only one I have here.

FIEL. Indeed, I am not.

STEN. Indeed, you are! You have always been so, ever since our school-days. Just look around here and see how everyone appreciates me, stranger as I am. You, on the other hand, you who know me, have never appreciated me. That is the radical weakness of your character—you can never appreciate anyone. What did you do in Christiania but go about from tea party to tea party, spreading yourself out in little witticisms? That sort of thing brings its own punishment! You dull your sense for all that makes life worth living, and presently you get left behind, fit for nothing.

FIEL. Am I fit for nothing?

STEN. Have you ever been fit to appreciate me?

FIEL. What was I to appreciate in you?

STEN. My will, if nothing else. Everyone else appreciates it—the crowd at the fete—Chamberlain Bratsberg and his family——

FIEL. Mr Mons Monsen and his ditto! And by the bye, that reminds me—there's someone out here waiting for you.

STEN. Who?

FIEL. [*going toward the back*]. One who appreciates you. [*Opens the door and calls.*] Aslaksen, come in!

ASL. [*entering*]. Ah, at last!

FIEL. Good-by for the present; I won't intrude upon friends in council. [*Goes into the garden.*]

STEN. What in the devil's name do you want here?

ASL. I must speak to you. You promised me yesterday an account of the founding of the league, and——

STEN. I can't give it to you now.

ASL. Impossible, Mr Stensgard; the paper appears tomorrow morning.

STEN. Nonsense! It has all to be altered. The matter has entered a new phase; new forces have come into play. What I said about Chamberlain Bratsberg must be entirely recast before it can appear.

ASL. Oh, that about the chamberlain, that's in type already.

STEN. Then it must come out again.

ASL. Not to go in?

STEN. I won't have it published in that form. Why stare at me? Do you think I don't know how to manage the affairs of the league?

ASL. Oh, certainly; but you must let me tell you——

STEN. No arguing, Aslaksen; that I can't stand and won't stand!

ASL. Do you know, Mr Stensgard, that you are doing your best to take the bread out of my mouth? Do you know that?

STEN. No, I know nothing of the sort.

ASL. But you are. Last winter, before you came, my paper was looking up. I edited it myself, and I edited it on a principle.

STEN. You?

ASL. Yes, I! I said to myself: it's the great public that supports a paper; now the great public is the bad public—that comes of the local situation—and the bad public will have a bad paper. So, you see, I edited it.

STEN. Badly! Yes, that's undeniable.

ASL. And I prospered by it. But then you came and brought ideas into the district. The paper took on a color, and then Lundestad's supporters all fell away. The subscribers that are left won't pay their subscriptions.

STEN. Ah, but the paper has become a good one.

ASL. I can't live on a good paper. You were to make things lively; you were to grapple with abuses, as you promised yesterday. The bigwigs were to be pilloried; the paper was to be filled with things people were bound to read—and now you leave me in the lurch.

STEN. Ho-ho! You think I am going to keep you supplied with libels!

ASL. Mr Stensgard, you musn't drive me to desperation, or you'll repent it.

STEN. What do you mean?

ASL. I mean that I must make the paper pay in another way. Before you came I made an honest living out of accidents and suicides and other harmless things that often hadn't even happened. But now you have turned everything topsy-turvy; people now want very different fare.

STEN. Just let me tell you this: if you break loose in any way, if you go a single step beyond my orders and try to exploit the movement in your own dirty interests, I'll go to the opposition printer and start a new paper. We can bring your rag to ruin in a fortnight.

ASL. [*pale*]. You wouldn't do that!

STEN. Yes, I would; and I can edit a paper so as to appeal to the great public.

ASL. Then I'll go this instant to Chamberlain Bratsberg.

STEN. What have you to do with him?

ASL. What have you to do with him? Do you think I don't know why you are invited here? It is because he is afraid of you and of what you may do, and you are making capital of that. But if he's afraid of what you may do, he'll be no less afraid of what

I may print; and I will make capital of that!

STEN. Would you dare to? A wretched creature like your——

ASL. I'll soon show you. If your speech is to be kept out of the paper, the chamberlain shall pay me for keeping it out.

STEN. Try it, just try it! You're drunk, fellow!

ASL. Only in moderation. But I'll fight if you try to take my poor crust out of my mouth. Little you know what sort of a home mine is: a bedridden wife, a crippled child——

STEN. Off with you! Do you think I want to be soiled with your squalor? What are your bedridden wives and deformed brats to me? If you stand in my way you shall be on the parish before the year's out.

ASL. I'll wait one day.

STEN. Ah, you're coming to your senses.

ASL. I shall announce to the subscribers in a handbill that, in consequence of an indisposition contracted at the fete, the editor——

STEN. Yes, do so; I daresay later on we shall come to an understanding.

ASL. I trust we may. Remember this, Mr Stensgard: that paper is my own ewe lamb. [*Goes out by the back.*]

LUN. [*at the foremost garden door*]. Ah, Mr Stensgard!

STEN. Ah, Mr Lundestad!

LUN. You here alone? I should like to have a little talk with you.

STEN. With pleasure.

LUN. Let me say that if anyone has told you that I have said anything to your disadvantage, you mustn't believe it.

STEN. To my disadvantage? What do you mean?

LUN. Oh, nothing. You see, there are so many busybodies here that go about doing nothing but setting people by the ears.

STEN. Well, on the whole—I'm afraid our relations are a little strained.

LUN. They are quite natural relations, Mr Stensgard: the relation of the old to the new; it is always so.

STEN. Oh, come, Mr Lundestad, you are not so old as all that.

LUN. I have held my seat ever since 1839. It's time I should be relieved.

STEN. Relieved?

LUN. Times change, you see. New problems arise, and for their solution we want new forces.

STEN. Now, frankly, Mr Lundestad —are you really going to give up your seat to Monsen?

LUN. No, certainly not to Monsen.

STEN. Then I don't understand——

LUN. Suppose, now, I did retire in Monsen's favor: do you think he would be elected?

STEN. It's hard to say. As the preliminary election comes on the day after tomorrow there may scarcely be time to prepare the public mind, but——

LUN. I don't believe he would manage it. The chamberlain's party, my party, would not vote for him. Of course "my party" is a figure of speech; I mean the men of property, the old families, who are settled on their own land and belong to it. They won't have anything to do with Monsen. Monsen is a newcomer; no one really knows anything about Monsen and his affairs. And then he has had to cut down so much to clear a place for himself—to fell both trees and men, you may say.

STEN. Well, then, if you think he has no chance——

LUN. H'm! You are a man of rare gifts, Mr Stensgard. Providence has dealt lavishly with you. But it ought to have given you one thing more.

STEN. And what might that be?

LUN. Tell me–why do you never think of yourself? Why have you no ambition?

STEN. Ambition? I?

LUN. In one word–why not go into Parliament yourself?

STEN. I? You are not serious?

LUN. Why not? You have qualified, I hear. And if you don't seize this opportunity, then someone else will come in; and it may not be so easy to unseat him.

STEN. Great heavens, Mr Lundestad, do you really mean what you say?

LUN. Oh, I don't want to commit you; if you don't care about it——

STEN. Not care about it! Well, I must confess I'm not so utterly devoid of ambition as you suppose. But do you really think it possible?

LUN. Oh, there's nothing impossible about it. I should do my best and so, no doubt, would the chamberlain; he knows your oratorical gifts. You have the young men on your side.

STEN. Mr Lundestad, by heaven, you are my true friend!

LUN. Oh, you don't mean much by that. If you really looked upon me as a friend, you would relieve me of this burden.

STEN. I place myself entirely at your disposal; I will not fail you.

LUN. Then you are really not disinclined to——

STEN. Here's my hand on it!

LUN. Thanks! Believe me, Mr Stensgard, you will not regret it. But now we must go warily to work. We must both of us take care to be on the electoral college–I to propose you as my successor and put you through your facings before the rest——

STEN. If we once get so far, we are safe. In the electoral college you are omnipotent.

LUN. There is a limit to omnipotence. You must of course bring your oratory into play; you must take care to explain away anything that might seem objectionable——

STEN. You don't mean that I am to break with my party?

LUN. Now just look at the thing reasonably. We have on the one hand certain men or families who are in possession of the common civic advantages–I mean property, independence and power. That is the party I belong to. On the other hand we have the mass of our younger fellow citizens who want to share in these advantages. That is your party. But that party you will quite naturally and properly pass out of when you get into power–to say nothing of taking up a solid position as a man of property–for of course that is essential, Mr Stensgard.

STEN. Yes, I believe it is. But the time is short, and such a position is not to be attained in a day.

LUN. That's true, but perhaps the prospect of such a position would be enough.

STEN. The prospect?

LUN. Have you any objection to a good marriage, Mr Stensgard? There are heiresses in the countryside. A man like you with a future before him–a man who can reckon on attaining the highest offices–you needn't fear a repulse if you play your cards neatly.

STEN. Then, for heaven's sake, help me in the game! You open wide vistas to me! All that I have hoped and longed for, and that seemed so dream-like and far away, stands suddenly before me in living reality—to lead the people toward emancipation, to——

LUN. Yes, we must keep our eyes open. I see your ambition is already on the alert. That's well. The rest will come of itself. I shall never forget your readiness to take the burden of office from my shoulders.

[*The whole party gradually enters from the garden. Two maidservants bring in candles and hand round refreshments during the following scene.*]

SEL. [*goes toward the piano at the back left*]. Mr Stensgard, you must join us; we are going to have a game of forfeits.

[*Follows her toward the back, makes arrangements with her, places chairs, etc., etc.*]

STEN. With pleasure; I am just in the mood.

ERIK [*in an undertone*]. What the deuce is this my father is saying, Mr Heire? What speech has Mr Stensgard been making?

HEIRE. Hee-hee! Don't you know about it?

ERIK. No; we townspeople had our dinner and ball at the club. My father declares Mr Stensgard has broken with the Stonelee gang—that he was frightfully rude to Monsen——

HEIRE. To Monsen! No, you must have misunderstood him, my dear sir.

ERIK. Well, there were a whole lot of people about, but I certainly heard——

HEIRE. Wait till tomorrow—I say no more. You'll have the whole story with your coffee, in Aslaksen's paper. [*They separate.*]

CHAM. Well, my dear Lundestad, are you sticking to those crotchets of yours?

LUN. They are no crotchets, Chamberlain; rather than be ousted, one should give way gracefully.

CHAM. Nonsense; who is dreaming of ousting you?

LUN. H'm; I'm an old weather prophet. There has been a change in the wind. Besides, I have my successor ready, Mr Stensgard——

CHAM. Mr Stensgard?

LUN. Wasn't that what you meant? I took it for a hint when you said he was a man we must make friends with and support.

CHAM. I meant in his onslaught upon the corruption that goes on at Stonelee.

LUN. But how could you count so confidently upon his breaking with that crew?

CHAM. He did it openly enough last evening, my dear fellow.

LUN. Last evening?

CHAM. Yes, when he spoke of Monsen's deplorable influence in the district.

LUN. [*open-mouthed*]. Of Monsen's——

CHAM. Of course; that time on the table——

LUN. On the table? Yes?

CHAM. He was frightfully rude. Ha! ha! It was great sport to hear him.

LUN. Great sport, was it?

CHAM. Yes; I own I'm not sorry to see these people a little roughly handled. But now we must back him up, for after such a savage attack——

LUN. As that of yesterday, you mean?

CHAM. Of course.

LUN. Upon the table?

CHAM. Yes, upon the table.

LUN. Against Monsen?

CHAM. Yes, against Monsen and his set. Of course they'll try to have their revenge; you can't blame them.

LUN. [*decidedly*]. Mr Stensgard must be supported—that is clear.

THORA. Father, you must join in the game.

CHAM. Oh, nonsense, child.

THORA. Yes, you must; Selma insists upon it.

CHAM. Very well, I suppose I must give in. [*In an undertone as they go toward the back.*] I'm quite distressed about Lundestad; he is really failing; fancy he didn't in the least understand what Stensgard——

THORA. Oh, come; they've begun the game. [*She drags him into the circle of young people where the game is in full swing.*]

ERIK [*calls from his place*]. Mr Heire, you are appointed forfeit judge.

HEIRE. Hee-hee! It's my first appointment.

STEN. [*also in the circle*]. On account of your legal experience, Mr Heire.

HEIRE. Oh, my amiable young friend, I should be delighted to sentence you all—I say no more!

STEN. [*slips up to* LUNDESTAD, *who stands in front on the left*]. You were speaking to the chamberlain. What about? Was it about me?

LUN. Unfortunately it was—about that affair of yesterday evening.

STEN. [*writhing*]. Oh, confound it all!

LUN. He said you had been frightfully rude.

STEN. Do you think it isn't a torture to me?

LUN. Now is your chance to atone for it.

ERIK [*calls*]. Mr Stensgard, it's your turn.

STEN. Coming! [*Quickly to* LUNDESTAD.] What do you mean?

LUN. Find an opportunity and apologize to the chamberlain.

STEN. By heaven, I will!

SEL. Make haste, make haste!

STEN. I'm coming! Here I am!

[*The game goes on with noise and laughter. Some elderly gentlemen play cards on the right.* LUNDESTAD *takes a seat on the left,* DANIEL HEIRE *near him.*]

HEIRE. That whelp twits me with my legal experience, does he?

LUN. He's rather free with his tongue, that's certain.

HEIRE. And so the whole family goes and fawns upon him. Hee-hee! They're pitifully afraid of him.

LUN. No, there you are wrong, Mr Heire; the chamberlain is not afraid of him.

HEIRE. Not afraid? Do you think I'm blind, my good sir?

LUN. No, but I can trust you to keep the secret? The chamberlain thinks it was Monsen he was attacking.

HEIRE. Monsen? Oh, absurd!

LUN. Fact, Mr Heire! Someone must have got him persuaded that——

HEIRE. And so he goes and asks him to a state dinner party! Deuce take me, if that isn't the best thing I've heard for long.

LUN. Sh, sh! Remember your promise. The chamberlain's your old schoolfellow, and even if he has been hard upon you——

HEIRE. Hee-hee! I'll pay him back with interest!

LUN. Take care! He is powerful. Don't play tricks in the lion's den!

HEIRE. Bratsberg a lion? Pooh, he's a blockhead, sir, and I am not. Oh, won't I get a rare crop of taunts and jibes and innuendoes out of this when once our great suit comes on!

SEL. [*calls from the circle*]. Learned judge, what shall the owner of this forfeit do?

ERIK [*unnoticed, to* HEIRE]. It's Stensgard's! Think of something amusing.

HEIRE. That forfeit? Hee-hee, let me see; he might—yes, he shall make a speech.

SEL. It's Mr Stensgard's forfeit.

ERIK. Mr Stensgard is to make a speech.

STEN. Oh no, spare me that; I came off badly enough last night.

CHAM. Excellently, Mr Stensgard; I know something of public speaking.

LUN. [*to* HEIRE]. If only he doesn't put his foot in it now.

HEIRE. Put his foot in it? Hee-hee! You're a sharp one! That's an inspiration! [*In an undertone to* STENSGARD.] If you came off badly last night, why not put yourself right again tonight?

STEN. [*seized with a sudden idea*]. Lundestad, here is the opportunity!

LUN. [*evasively*]. Play your cards neatly. [*Looks for his hat and slips quietly toward the door.*]

STEN. Yes, I will make a speech!

THE YOUNG LADIES. Bravo! Bravo!

STEN. Fill your glasses, ladies and gentlemen! I am going to make a speech which shall begin with a fable, for here I seem to breathe the finer air of fableland.

ERIK [*to the* LADIES]. Hush! Listen!

[*The* CHAMBERLAIN *takes his glass from the card table on the right, beside which he remains standing.* RINGDAL, FIELDBO *and one or two other gentlemen come in from the garden.*]

STEN. It was in the springtime. There came a young cuckoo flying over the uplands. Now the cuckoo is an adventurer. There was a great bird parliament on the meadow beneath him, and both wild and tame fowl flocked to it. They came tripping out of the henyards; they waddled up from the goose ponds; down from Stonelee hulked a fat capercailzie, flying low and noisily; he settled down and ruffled his feathers and flapped his wings and made himself even broader than he was, and every now and then he crowed, "Krak, krak, krak!" as much as to say: "I'm the gamecock from Stonelee, I am!"

CHAM. Capital! Hear, hear!

STEN. And then there was an old woodpecker. He bustled up and down the tree trunks, pecking with his pointed beak and gorging himself with grubs and everything that turns to gall. To right and left you heard him going: prik, prik, prik!

ERIK. Excuse me, wasn't it a stork or a——

HEIRE. Say no more!

STEN. That was the old woodpecker. But now there came life into the crew, for they found something to cackle evil about. And they flustered together until at last the young cuckoo began to join in the cackling——

FIEL. [unnoticed]. For God's sake, man, be quiet!

STEN. Now it was an eagle they cackled about—an eagle who dwelt in lonely dignity upon a beetling cliff. They were all agreed about him. "He's a bugbear to the neighborhood," croaked a hoarse raven. But the eagle swooped down into their midst, seized the cuckoo and bore him aloft to his eyrie. Heart conquered heart! From that clear summit the adventurer cuckoo looked far and wide over the lowlands; there he found sunshine and peace, and there he learned to judge aright the swarm from the henyards and the clearings——

FIEL. [*loudly*]. Bravo, Bravo! And now some music.

CHAM. Hush! Don't interrupt him.

STEN. Chamberlain Bratsberg, I stand before you, in the presence of everyone, to beg your forgiveness for last night.

CHAM. [falls a step backward]. Mine?

STEN. I thank you for the magnanimous vengeance you have taken for my senseless words. In me you have henceforth a faithful champion. And now, ladies and gentlemen, I drink the health of the eagle on the mountaintop—the health of Chamberlain Bratsberg.

CHAM. [*clutching at the table*]. Thank you, Mr—Mr Stensgard.

THE GUESTS [*for the most part in painful embarrassment*]. The chamberlain! Chamberlain Bratsberg!

CHAM. Ladies and gentlemen! [*Softly.*] Thora!

THORA. Father!

CHAM. Oh, Doctor, Doctor, what have you done?

STEN. [*with his glass in his hand, radiant with self-satisfaction*]. Now to our places again! Hullo, Fieldbo! Come, in the League of Youth! The game's going merrily!

HEIRE [*in front, on the left*]. Yes, on my soul, the game's going merrily!

[LUNDESTAD *slips out by the door in the back.*]

ACT III

SCENE—*An elegant morning room with entrance door in the back. On the left the door of the* CHAMBERLAIN'S *study; further back a door leading to the drawing room. On the right a door leading to* RINGDAL'S *offices; further forward a window.*

THORA *is seated on the sofa, left, weeping. The* CHAMBERLAIN *paces angrily up and down.*

CHAM. Yes, now we have the epilogue—tears and lamentations——

THORA. Oh, that we had never seen that man!

CHAM. What man?

THORA. That wretched Mr Stensgard, of course.

CHAM. You should rather say: "Oh, that we had never seen that wretched doctor."

THORA. Doctor Fieldbo?

CHAM. Yes, Fieldbo, Fieldbo! Wasn't it he that palmed off a parcel of lies upon me?

THORA. No, my dear father, it was I.

CHAM. You? Well, then, both of you! You were his accomplice—behind my back. A nice state of affairs!

THORA. Oh, Father, if you only knew——

CHAM. Oh, I know enough; more than enough, much more!

[DR FIELDBO *enters from the back.*]

FIEL. Good morning, Chamberlain! Good morning, Miss Bratsberg!

CHAM. [*still pacing the room*]. So you are there, are you—bird of evil omen!

FIEL. Yes, it was an unpleasant affair.

CHAM. [*looking out of the window*]. Oh, you think so?

FIEL. You must have noticed how

I kept my eye upon Stensgard all the evening. When I heard there was to be a game of forfeits I thought there was no danger.

CHAM. [*stamping on the floor*]. To be made a laughingstock by such a windbag! What must my guests have thought of me? That I was mean enough to want to buy this—this—— as Lundestad calls him!

FIEL. Yes, but——

THORA [*unnoticed by her father*]. Don't speak.

CHAM. [*after a short pause turns to* FIELDBO]. Tell me frankly, Doctor: am I really denser than the general run of people?

FIEL. How can you ask such a question?

CHAM. Then how did it happen that I was probably the only person there who didn't understand that that confounded speech was meant for me?

FIEL. Shall I tell you why?

CHAM. Certainly.

FIEL. It is because you regard your position in the district differently from other people.

CHAM. I regard my position as my father before me regarded his. No one would ever have ventured to treat him so.

FIEL. Your father died about 1830.

CHAM. Oh yes, many a barrier has broken down since that time. But, after all, it's my own fault. I have mixed myself up too much with these good people. So now I must be content to have my name coupled with Anders Lundestad's!

FIEL. Frankly, I see no disgrace in that.

CHAM. Oh, you know quite well what I mean. Of course I don't plume myself on rank, on titles or anything of that sort. But what I hold in honor and expect others to hold in honor is the integrity handed down in our family from generation to generation. What I mean is that when a man like Lundestad goes into public life he cannot keep his character and his conduct entirely free from stain. But they might leave me in peace; I stand outside their parties.

FIEL. Not so entirely, Chamberlain; at least you were delighted so long as you thought it was Monsen that was attacked.

CHAM. Don't mention that fellow! It is he that has relaxed the moral sense of the district. And now he has gone and turned my son's head, confound him!

THORA. Erik's?

FIEL. Your son's?

CHAM. Yes; what led him to go and set up in business? It leads to nothing.

FIEL. Why, my dear chamberlain, he must live and——

CHAM. Oh, with economy he could quite well live on the money that came to him from his mother.

FIEL. He might perhaps live on it, but what could he live for?

CHAM. For? Well, if he absolutely must have something to live for, hasn't he qualified as a lawyer? He might live for his profession.

FIEL. No, that he couldn't do; it is against his nature. Then there was no official appointment he could well hope for; you have kept the management of your property in your own hands, and your son has no children to educate. Therefore, when he sees tempting examples around him—people who have started from nothing and are worth their half million——

CHAM. Their half million! Oh, come now, let us keep to the hundred thousands. But neither the half million nor the hundred thousands can be scraped together with perfectly clean hands. I don't mean in the eyes of the world—heaven knows it is easy enough to keep within the law—but in respect to one's own conscience. Of course my son cannot descend to anything questionable, so you may be quite sure Mr Erik Bratsberg's financial operations won't bring in any half millions.

[SELMA, *in walking dress, enters from the back.*]

SEL. Good morning! Is Erik not here?

CHAM. Good morning, child! Are you looking for your husband?

SEL. Yes, he said he was coming here. Mr Monsen called upon him early this morning, and then——

CHAM. Monsen? Does Monsen come to your house?

SEL. Now and then; generally on business. Why, my dear Thora, what's the matter?

THORA. Oh, it's nothing.

SEL. No, it's nothing! At home Erik was out of humor, and here—I can see it in your looks—something is wrong. What is it?

CHAM. Nothing you need trouble about, at any rate. You are too dainty to carry burdens, my little Selma. Go into the drawing room for the present. If Erik said he was coming, he will be here soon, no doubt.

SEL. Come, Thora—and be sure you don't let me sit in a draught. [*Embracing her.*] Oh, I could hug the life out of you, my sweet Thora!

[*The two ladies go off to the left.*]

CHAM. So they are hand in glove, are they, the two speculators! They should go into partnership. Monsen and Bratsberg—how nice it would sound! [*A knock at the door in the back.*] Come in!

[STENSGARD *enters.*]

CHAM. [*recoiling a step*]. What is this?

STEN. Yes, here I am again, Chamberlain!

CHAM. So I see.

FIEL. Are you mad, Stensgard?

STEN. You retired early yesterday evening. When Fieldbo had explained to me how matters stood you had already——

CHAM. Excuse me—all explanations are superfluous.

STEN. I understand that; therefore I have not come to make any.

CHAM. Oh, indeed?

STEN. I know I have insulted you.

CHAM. I know that too, and before I have you turned out perhaps you will be good enough to tell me why you are here.

STEN. Because I love your daughter.

FIEL. What!

CHAM. What does he say, Doctor?

STEN. Ah, you can't grasp the idea, Chamberlain. You are an old man; you have nothing to fight for.

CHAM. And you presume to——

STEN. I am here to ask for your daughter's hand, Chamberlain.

CHAM. You—you? Won't you sit down?

STEN. Thanks, I prefer to stand.

CHAM. What do you say to this, Doctor?

STEN. Oh, Fieldbo is on my side; he is my friend, the only true friend I have.

FIEL. No, no, man! Never in this world if you——

CHAM. Perhaps it was with this view that Doctor Fieldbo secured his friend's introduction into my house?

STEN. You know me only by my

exploits of yesterday and the day before. That is not enough. Besides, I am not the same man today that I was then. My intercourse with you and yours has fallen like a spring shower upon my spirit, making it put forth new blossoms in a single night! You must not hurl me back into my sordid past. Till now I have never been at home with the beautiful in life; it has always been beyond my reach.

CHAM. But my daughter?

STEN. Oh, I shall win her.

CHAM. Indeed? H'm!

STEN. Yes, for I have will on my side. Remember what you told me yesterday. You were opposed to your son's marriage—and see how it has turned out! You must put on the glasses of experience, as Fieldbo said——

CHAM. Ah! That was what you meant?

FIEL. Not in the least! My dear chamberlain, let me speak to him alone.

STEN. Nonsense; I have nothing to speak to you about. Now pray be reasonable, Chamberlain! A family like yours needs new alliances, or its brains stagnate.

CHAM. Oh, this is too much!

STEN. Now, now, don't be angry! These high and mighty airs are unworthy of you—of course you know they are all nonsense at bottom. You'll value me when you come to know me. Yes, yes, you shall value me—both you and your daughter! I will make her——

CHAM. What do you think of this, Doctor?

FIEL. I think it's madness.

STEN. Yes, it would be in you; but I, you see—I have a mission to fulfill on God's beautiful earth.

CHAM. Mr Stensgard, there is the door!

STEN. You show me——

CHAM. The door!

STEN. Don't do that!

CHAM. Out with you! You are an adventurer, an—a—confound my memory! You're a——

STEN. What am I?

CHAM. You are—that other thing—it's on the tip of my tongue——

STEN. Beware how you block my career.

CHAM. Beware? Of what?

STEN. I will attack you in the papers, persecute you, libel you, do all I can to undermine your reputation. You shall shriek under the lash. You shall seem to see spirits in the air raining blows upon you. You shall huddle together in dread, you shall try to creep into shelter——

CHAM. Creep into shelter yourself—in a madhouse; that's the place for you!

STEN. Ha-ha; that is a cheap retort, but you know no better, Mr Bratsberg! I tell you the wrath of the Lord is in me. It is his will you are opposing. He has destined me for the light—beware how you cast a shadow! Well, I see I shall make no way with you today, but that matters nothing. I only ask you to speak to your daughter—to prepare her—to give her the opportunity of choosing! Reflect and look around you. Where can you expect to find a son-in-law among these plodding dunces? Fieldbo says she is deep and steadfast and true. So now you know how matters stand. Good-by, Chamberlain—I leave you to choose between my friendship and my enmity. Good-by! [*Goes out by the back.*]

CHAM. So it has come to this! They dare to treat me thus in my own house!

FIEL. Stensgard dares; no one else would.

CHAM. He today, others tomorrow.

FIEL. Let them come; I shall keep them off; I would go through fire for you.

CHAM. Yes, you who have caused all the mischief! H'm, that Stensgard is the most impudent scoundrel I have ever known! And yet there is something I like about him.

FIEL. He has possibilities.

CHAM. He has openness, Doctor Fieldbo! He doesn't go playing his game behind one's back, like some other people; hee-hee!

FIEL. It's not worth disputing about. Only be firm, Chamberlain; no and no again to Stensgard!

CHAM. Oh, keep your advice to yourself! You may rely upon it that neither he nor anyone else——

RIN. [*enters by the door on the right*]. Excuse me, Chamberlain; one word—— [*Whispers.*]

CHAM. What? In your room?

RIN. He came in by the back way and begs you to see him.

CHAM. H'm. Oh, Doctor, just go into the drawing room for a moment; there's someone here who—— But don't say a word to Selma of Mr Stensgard and his visit. She must be kept outside all this business. As for my daughter, I should prefer that you should say nothing to her either.

[FIELDBO *goes into the drawing room.* RINGDAL *has in the meantime gone back to his office, whence* MONSEN *presently enters.*]

MON. [*at the door*]. I beg ten thousand pardons, sir.

CHAM. Oh, come in, come in!

MON. I trust your family is in good health?

CHAM. Thank you. Is there anything you want?

MON. I can't quite put it that way. Thank heaven I'm one of those that have got pretty nearly all they can want.

CHAM. Oh, indeed? That is a good deal to say.

MON. But I've had to work for it, Chamberlain. Oh, I know you regard my work with no very friendly eye.

CHAM. I cannot suppose that your work is in any way affected by my way of regarding it.

MON. Who knows? I'm thinking of gradually withdrawing from business.

CHAM. Really?

MON. The luck has been on my side. I've gone ahead as far as I care to, so now I think it's about time to slack off a little.

CHAM. Well, I congratulate both you—and other people.

MON. And if I could at the same time do you a service, Chamberlain——

CHAM. Me?

MON. When the Langerud woods were put up to auction five years ago you made a bid for them.

CHAM. Yes, but you outbid me, and they were knocked down to you.

MON. You can have them now, with the sawmills and all appurtenances.

CHAM. After all your sinful cutting and hacking!

MON. Oh, they're valuable still; and with your method of working, in a few years——

CHAM. Thank you; unfortunately I must decline the proposal.

MON. There's a great deal of money in it, Chamberlain. As for me—I may tell you I have a great speculation on hand; the stakes are large; I mean there's a big haul to be made—a hundred thousand or so.

CHAM. That is no trifle.

MON. Ha, ha, ha! A nice round sum to add to the pile. But when you're going into a great battle you need reserve forces, as the saying goes. There's not much ready money about; the names that are worth anything are rather used up.

CHAM. Yes, certain people have taken care of that.

MON. It's a case of you scratch me, I scratch you. Well, Chamberlain, is it to be a bargain? You shall have the woods at your own figure.

CHAM. I will not have them at any figure, Mr Monsen.

MON. Well, one good offer deserves another. Will you help me, sir?

CHAM. What do you mean?

MON. Of course I'll give good security. I have plenty of property. Look here—these papers—just let me explain my position to you.

CHAM. [*waving the papers aside*]. Is it pecuniary aid you want?

MON. Not ready money, oh no! But your support, Chamberlain.

CHAM. And you come to me with such a proposal as this?

MON. Yes, precisely to you. I know you've often let bygones be bygones when a man was in real straits.

CHAM. Well, in a way I must thank you for your good opinion—especially at a time like this; but nevertheless——

MON. Won't you tell me, Chamberlain, what sets you against me?

CHAM. Oh, what's the use?

MON. It might lead to a better understanding between us. I've never stood in your way that I know of.

CHAM. You think not? Then let me tell you of one case in which you have stood in my way. I founded the Ironworks Savings Bank for the benefit of my employees and others. But then you must needs set up as a banker; people take their savings to you——

MON. I give higher interest.

CHAM. Yes, but you charge higher interest on loans.

MON. But I don't make so many difficulties about security and so forth.

CHAM. That is just the mischief of it, for now we have people making bargains to the tune of ten or twenty thousand dollars though neither of the parties has so much as a brass farthing. That is what sets me against you, Mr Monsen. And there is another thing, too, that touches me still more nearly. Do you think it was with my good will that my son flung himself into all these wild speculations?

MON. But how can I help that?

CHAM. It was your example that infected him, as it did the others. Why could you not stick to your last?

MON. Remain a lumberman, like my father?

CHAM. Was it a disgrace to be in my employment? Your father made his bread honorably.

MON. Yes, until he'd almost worked his life out and at last went over the waterfall with his raft. Do you know anything of life in that class, Chamberlain? Have you ever realized what the men have to endure who toil for you deep in the forests and along the river reaches while you sit comfortably at home and fatten on the profits? Can you blame such a man for struggling to rise in the world? I had had a little more schooling than my father; perhaps I had more brains too——

CHAM. Very likely. But by what means have you risen in the world? You began by selling brandy. Then you bought up doubtful debts and enforced them mercilessly—and so you got on and on. How many people have you not ruined to push yourself forward!

MON. That's the course of business: one up, another down.

CHAM. But there are different methods of business. I know of respectable families you have brought to the workhouse.

MON. Daniel Heire is not very far from the workhouse.

CHAM. I understand you, but I can justify my conduct before God and man! When the country was in distress, after the separation from Denmark, my father made sacrifices beyond his means. Thus part of our property came into the hands of the entire family. What was the result? The people who lived upon the property suffered under Daniel Heire's incompetent management. He cut down timber to the injury, I may even say to the ruin, of the district. Was it not my obvious duty to put a stop to it if I was able? And it happened that I was able; I had the law on my side.

MON. I, too, have always had the law on my side.

CHAM. But what about your sense of right, your conscience, if you have such a thing? And how you have broken down all social order! How you have impaired the respect that should attach to wealth! People never think of wealth! People never think of asking nowadays how such and such a fortune was made or how long it has been in such and such a family; they only ask: how much is so-and-so worth?—and they esteem him accordingly. Now I suffer by all this; I find myself regarded as a sort of associate of yours; people speak of us in one breath, because we are the two largest proprietors in the neighborhood. This state of things I cannot long endure.

MON. This state of things shall come to an end, sir; I will give up business. I beg of you, I implore you, to help me!

CHAM. I will not.

MON. I'll pay you what you like.

CHAM. And you dare to——

MON. If not for my sake, then for your son's!

CHAM. My son's!

MON. Yes, he's in it. I reckon he stands to win some twenty thousand dollars.

CHAM. Stands to win?

MON. Yes.

CHAM. Then, good God, who stands to lose all this money?

MON. How do you mean?

CHAM. If my son wins, someone or other must lose!

MON. It's a good stroke of business; I'm not in a position to say more. But I need a solid name; only just your endorsement——

CHAM. Endorsement! On a bill?

MON. Only for ten or fifteen thousand dollars.

CHAM. Do you suppose for a moment that—— My name! In such an affair! My name? As surety, no doubt?

MON. A mere matter of form.

CHAM. A matter of swindling! My name! Not upon any consideration.

I have never put my name on other men's paper.

MON. Never? That's an exaggeration.

CHAM. It is the literal truth.

MON. No, not literal; I've seen it with my own eyes.

CHAM. What have you seen?

MON. Your name—on one bill at least.

CHAM. You have never seen it!

MON. I have! On a bill for two thousand dollars. Think again.

CHAM. Not for two thousand nor ten thousand. On my word of honor, never!

MON. Then it's a forgery.

CHAM. Forgery? Forgery? Where did you see it? In whose hands?

MON. That I won't tell you.

CHAM. Ha-ha! We shall soon find that out.

MON. Listen to me!

CHAM. Silence! It has come to this then! Forgery! They must mix me up in their abominations! No wonder, then, that people bracket me with the rest of you.

MON. Chamberlain—for your own sake and for the sake of others——

CHAM. Off with you! Out of my sight! It is you that are at the root of it all! Yes, you are! Woe unto him from whom offenses come. Your home life is scandalous. What sort of society do you get about you? Persons from Christiania and elsewhere, who think only of eating and drinking and do not care in what company they gorge themselves. Silence! There is worse behind. You have had scandals with your own maidservants. You drove your wife out of her mind by your ill-treatment and debauchery.

MON. Come, this is going too far! You shall pay for these words.

CHAM. Oh, to the deuce with your threats! What harm can you do to me? Me? You asked what I had to say against you. Well, I have said it. Now you know why I have kept you out of decent society.

MON. Yes, and now I'll drag your decent society down——

CHAM. That way!

MON. I know my way, Chamberlain! [*Goes out by the back.*]

CHAM. [*opens the door on the right and calls*]. Ringdal, Ringdal—come here!

RIN. What is it, sir?

CHAM. [*calls into the drawing room*]. Doctor, come this way! Now, Ringdal, now you shall see my prophecies fulfilled.

FIEL. [*entering*]. What can I do for you, Chamberlain?

RIN. What prophecies, sir?

CHAM. What do you say to this, Doctor? You have always accused me of exaggerating when I said that Monsen was corrupting the neighborhood.

FIEL. Well, what then?

CHAM. What do you think? There are forgeries going about.

RIN. Forgeries?

CHAM. Yes, forgeries! And whose name do you think they have forged? Why, mine!

FIEL. Who in the world can have done it?

CHAM. How can I tell? I don't know all the scoundrels in the district. But we shall soon find out. Doctor, do me a service. The papers must have come into the hands either of the Savings Bank or the Ironworks Bank. Drive up to Lundestad; he is the director who knows most about things.

FIEL. Certainly; at once.

RIN. Lundestad is here at the works today; there's a meeting of the school committee.

CHAM. So much the better. Find him; bring him here.

FIEL. I'll go at once. [*Goes out at the back.*]

CHAM. And you, Ringdal, make inquiries at the ironworks. As soon as we have got to the bottom of the matter we'll lay an information. No mercy to the scoundrels!

RIN. Very good, sir. Bless me, who'd have thought of such a thing? [*Goes out at the right.*]

[*The* CHAMBERLAIN *paces the room once or twice and is then about to go into his study. At that instant* ERIK BRATSBERG *enters from the back.*]

ERIK. My dear father!

CHAM. Oh, are you there?

ERIK. I want so much to speak to you.

CHAM. H'm; I'm not much in the humor for speaking to anyone. What is it?

ERIK. You know I have never mixed you up in my affairs, Father.

CHAM. No, that is an honor I should certainly have declined.

ERIK. But now I am forced to——

CHAM. What are you forced to do?

ERIK. Father, you must help me!

CHAM. With money! You may be very sure that——

ERIK. Only this once! I swear I'll never again—— The fact is, I am under certain engagements to Monsen of Stonelee.

CHAM. I know that. You have a brilliant speculation on hand.

ERIK. A speculation? We? No! Who told you so?

CHAM. Monsen himself.

ERIK. Has Monsen been here?

CHAM. He has just gone. I showed him the door.

ERIK. If you don't help me, Father, I am ruined.

CHAM. You?

ERIK. Yes. Monsen has advanced me money. I had to pay terribly dear for it, and now the bills have fallen due.

CHAM. There we have it! What did I tell you?

ERIK. Yes, yes; it's too late now.

CHAM. Ruined! In two years! But how could you expect anything else? What had you to do among these charlatans that go about dazzling people's eyes with wealth that never existed! They were no company for you. Among people of that sort you must meet cunning with cunning, or you'll go to the wall; you have learned that now.

ERIK. Father, will you save me or will you not?

CHAM. No; for the last time, no. I will not.

ERIK. My honor is at stake.

CHAM. Oh, let us have no big phrases! There's no honor involved in commercial success nowadays. Go home and make up your accounts, pay every man his due and have done with it, the sooner the better.

ERIK. Oh, you don't know—— It's only that I am ruined!

[SELMA *and* THORA *enter from the drawing room.*]

SEL. Is that Erik's voice? Good heavens, what is the matter?

CHAM. Nothing. Go into the drawing room again.

SEL. No, I won't go. I will know. Erik, what is it? Tell me!

ERIK. It's only that I am ruined!

THORA. Ruined!

CHAM. There, you see!

SEL. What is ruined?

ERIK. Everything.

SEL. Do you mean you have lost your money?

ERIK. Money, house and everything!

SEL. Is that what you call everything?

ERIK. Let us go, Selma. You are all I have left me. We must bear it together.

SEL. The blow? Bear it together? [*With a cry.*] Do you think I am fit for that now?

CHAM. For heaven's sake!

ERIK. What do you mean?

THORA. Oh, Selma, take care!

SEL. No, I won't take care! I cannot go on lying and shamming any longer! I must speak the truth. I will not "bear" anything!

CHAM. What are you saying?

SEL. Oh, how cruel you have been to me! Shamefully—all of you! It was my part always to accept—never to give. I have been like a pauper among you. You never came and demanded a sacrifice of me; I was not fit to bear anything! I hate you! I loathe you!

ERIK. What can this mean?

CHAM. She is ill; she is out of her mind.

SEL. How I have thirsted for a single drop of your troubles, your anxieties! But when I begged for it you only laughed me off. You have dressed me up like a doll; you have played with me as you would play with a child. How I yearned for a large and high and strenuous part in life! Now you come to me, Erik, now that you have nothing else left. But I will not be treated simply as a last resource. I will have nothing to do with your troubles now. I won't stay with you! I will rather play and sing in the streets! Let me be! Let me be! [*She rushes out by the back.*]

CHAM. Thora, was there any meaning in all that, or——

THORA. Oh yes, there was meaning in it, if only I had seen it sooner. [*Goes out by the back.*]

ERIK. No! All else I can lose, but not her! Selma, Selma! [*Follows* THORA *and* SELMA.]

RIN. [*enters from the right*]. Chamberlain!

CHAM. Well, what is it?

RIN. I have been to the bank.

CHAM. The bank? Oh yes, about the bill.

RIN. It's all right; they have never had any bill endorsed by you.

[FIELDBO *and* LUNDESTAD *enter by the back.*]

FIEL. False alarm, Chamberlain!

CHAM. Indeed? Not at the Savings Bank either?

LUN. Certainly not. During all the years I've been a director I have never once seen your name; except, of course, on your son's bill.

CHAM. My son's bill?

LUN. Yes, the bill you accepted for him early this spring.

CHAM. My son? My son? Do you dare to tell me——

LUN. Why, bless me, just think a moment; the bill for two thousand dollars drawn by your son——

CHAM. [*groping for a chair*]. Oh, my God!

FIEL. For heaven's sake!

RIN. It's not possible that——

CHAM. [*who has sunk down on a chair*]. Quietly, quietly! Drawn by my son, you say? Accepted by me? For two thousand dollars?

FIEL. [*to* LUNDESTAD]. And this bill is in the Savings Bank?

LUN. Not now; it was redeemed

last week by Monsen.

CHAM. By Monsen?

RIN. Monsen may still be at the works; I'll go——

CHAM. Stop here!

[DANIEL HEIRE *enters from the back.*]

HEIRE. Good morning, gentlemen! Good morning, Chamberlain! Thank you so much for the delightful evening we spent yesterday. What do you think I've just heard?

RIN. Excuse me; we are busy.

HEIRE. So are other people, I can tell you; our friend from Stonelee, for example.

CHAM. Monsen?

HEIRE. Hee-hee; it's a pretty story! The electioneering intrigues are in full swing. And what do you think is the last idea? They are going to bribe you, Chamberlain!

LUN. To bribe——

HEIRE. Deuce take me, if it isn't the most impudent thing I ever heard of! I just looked in at Madam Rundholmen's to have a glass of bitters. There sat Messieurs Monsen and Stensgard drinking port—filthy stuff! I wouldn't touch it, but they might have had the decency to offer me a glass all the same. However, Monsen turned to me and said, "What do you bet that Chamberlain Bratsberg won't go with our party at the preliminary election tomorrow?" "Indeed," said I, "how's that to be managed?" "Oh," he said, "this bill will persuade him."

FIEL. Bill?

LUN. At the election?

CHAM. Well? What then?

HEIRE. Oh, I know no more. They said something about two thousand dollars. That's the figure they rate a gentleman's conscience at! Oh, it's abominable, I say!

CHAM. A bill for two thousand dollars?

RIN. And Monsen has it?

HEIRE. No, he handed it over to Stensgard.

LUN. Indeed!

FIEL. To Stensgard?

CHAM. Are you sure of that?

HEIRE. Quite certain. "You can make what use you please of it," he said. But I don't understand——

LUN. I want to speak to you, Mr Heire—and you too, Ringdal.

[*The three converse in a whisper at the back.*]

FIEL. Chamberlain!

CHAM. Well?

FIEL. Your son's bill is genuine, of course?

CHAM. One would suppose so.

FIEL. Of course. But now if the forged bill were to turn up?

CHAM. I will lay no information.

FIEL. Naturally not—but you must do more.

CHAM. [*rising*]. I can do no more.

FIEL. Yes, for heaven's sake, you can and must. You must save the poor fellow.

CHAM. In what way?

FIEL. Quite simply: by acknowledging the signature.

CHAM. Then you think, Doctor, that we stick at nothing in our family?

FIEL. I am trying to think for the best, Chamberlain.

CHAM. And do you believe for a moment that I can tell a lie?—that I can play into the hands of forgers?

FIEL. And do you realize what will be the consequences if you do not?

CHAM. The offender must settle that with the law. [*He goes out to the left.*]

ACT IV

SCENE—*A public room in* MADAM RUNDHOLMEN'S *hotel. Entrance door in the back, a smaller door on either side. A window on the right; before it a table with writing materials; further back, in the middle of the room, another table.*

MADAM [*within, on the left, heard talking loudly*]. Oh, let them go about their business! Tell them they've come here to vote and not to drink. If they won't wait, they can do the other thing.

STEN. [*enters by the back*]. Good morning! H'm, h'm, Madam Rundholmen! [*Goes to the door on the left and knocks.*] Good morning, Madam Rundholmen!

MADAM [*within*]. Oh! Who's there?

STEN. It is I—Stensgard. May I come in?

MADAM. No indeed, you mustn't! No! I'm not dressed.

STEN. What? Are you so late to-day?

MADAM. Oh, I can tell you I've been up since all hours; but one must look a little decent, you know. [*Peeps out with a kerchief over her head.*] Well, what is it? No, you really mustn't look at me, Mr Stensgard. Oh, there's someone else! [*Disappears, slamming the door to.*]

ASL. [*enters from the back with a bundle of papers*]. Good morning, Mr Stensgard.

STEN. Well, is it in?

ASL. Yes, here it is. Look—"The Independence Day Celebrations From Our Special Correspondent." Here's the founding of the league on the other side and your speech up here. I've leaded all the abuse.

STEN. It seems to me it's all leaded.

ASL. Pretty nearly.

STEN. And the extra number was of course distributed yesterday?

ASL. Of course; all over the district, both to subscribers and others. Would you like to see it? [*Hands him a copy.*]

STEN. [*running his eye over the paper*]. "Our respected member, Mr Lundestad, proposes to resign . . . long and faithful service . . . in the words of the poet: 'Rest, patriot, it is thy due!' " H'm! "The association founded on Independence Day: the League of Youth. . . . Mr Stensgard, the guiding intelligence of the league . . . timely reforms, credit on easier terms." Ah, that's very good. Has the polling begun?

ASL. It's in full swing. The whole league is on the spot—both voters and others.

STEN. Oh, deuce take the others—between ourselves, of course. Well, you go down and talk to the waverers.

ASL. All right.

STEN. You can tell them that I am pretty much at one with Lundestad.

ASL. Trust to me; I know the local situation.

STEN. One thing more: just to oblige me, Aslaksen, don't drink to-day.

ASL. Oh, what do you mean?

STEN. We'll have a jolly evening when it's all over, but remember what you, as well as I, have at stake: your paper. Come now, my good fellow, let me see that you can——

ASL. There, that's enough now; I'm old enough to look after myself. [*Goes out to the right.*]

MADAM [*enters from the left, elaborately dressed*]. Now, Mr Stensgard,

I'm at your service. Is it anything of importance?

STEN. No, only that I want you to be good enough to let me know when Mr Monsen comes.

MADAM. He won't be here today.

STEN. Not today?

MADAM. No; he drove past here at four this morning! He's always driving about nowadays. What's more, he came in and roused me out of bed—he wanted to borrow money, you must know.

STEN. Monsen did?

MADAM. Yes. He's a tremendous man to get through money, is Monsen. I hope things may turn out all right for him. And I say the same to you, for I hear you're going into Parliament.

STEN. I? Nonsense! Who told you so?

MADAM. Oh, some of Mr Lundestad's people.

DANIEL HEIRE [*enters from the back*]. Good morning! I'm not in the way, am I?

MADAM. Gracious, no!

HEIRE. Good God, how resplendent! Can it be for me that you've got yourself up like this?

MADAM. Of course. It's for you bachelors we get ourselves up, isn't it?

HEIRE. For marrying men, Madam Rundholmen, for marrying men! Unfortunately my lawsuits take up all my time.

MADAM. Oh, nonsense; you've always plenty of time to get married.

HEIRE. No, deuce take me if I have! Marriage is a thing you've got to give your whole mind to. Well, well—if you can't have me, you must put up with somebody else. For you ought to marry again.

MADAM. Now, do you know, I'm sometimes of the same opinion.

HEIRE. Naturally; when once one has tasted the joys of matrimony—— Of course poor Rundholmen was one in a thousand.

MADAM. Well, I won't go so far as that; he was a bit rough and rather too fond of his glass, but a husband's always a husband.

HEIRE. Very true, Madam Rundholmen; a husband's a husband and a widow's a widow——

MADAM. And business is business. Oh, when I think of all I've got to attend to I don't know whether I'm on my heels or my head. Everyone wants to buy, but when it comes to paying I've got to go in for summonses and executions and lord knows what. Upon my word, I'll soon have to engage a lawyer all to myself.

HEIRE. I'll tell you what, Madam Rundholmen, you should retain Mr Stensgard; he's a bachelor.

MADAM. Oh, how you do talk! I won't listen to a word more. [*Goes out to the right.*]

HEIRE. A substantial woman, sir! Comfortable and well preserved, no children up to date, money well invested. Education too; she's widely read, sir.

STEN. Widely read, eh?

HEIRE. Hee-hee; she ought to be; she had charge of Alm's circulating library for a couple of years. But your head's full of other things today, I daresay.

STEN. Not at all; I don't even know that I shall vote. Who are you going to vote for, Mr Heire?

HEIRE. Haven't got a vote, sir. There was only one kennel that would qualify in the market, and that you bought.

STEN. If you're at a loss for a lodging, I'll give it up to you.

HEIRE. Hee-hee, you're joking. Ah, youth, youth! What a pleasant humor it has! But now I must be off and have a look at the menagerie. I'm told your whole league is afoot. [*Sees* FIELDBO, *who enters from the back.*] Here's the doctor too! I suppose you have come on a scientific mission?

FIEL. A scientific mission?

HEIRE. Yes, to study the epidemic; you've heard of the virulent *rabies agitatoria* that has broken out? God be with you, my dear young friends. [*Goes out to the right.*]

STEN. Tell me quickly—have you seen the chamberlain today?

FIEL. Yes.

STEN. And what did he say?

FIEL. What did he say?

STEN. Yes, you know I have written to him.

FIEL. Have you? What did you write?

STEN. That I am still of the same mind about his daughter, that I want to talk the matter over with him and that I propose to call on him tomorrow.

FIEL. If I were you I should at least defer my visit. It is the chamberlain's birthday tomorrow; a crowd of people will be there.

STEN. That's all right; the more the better. I hold big cards in my hand, let me tell you.

FIEL. And perhaps you have bluffed a little with your big cards.

STEN. How do you mean?

FIEL. I mean you have perhaps embellished your declaration of love with a few little threats or so?

STEN. Fieldbo, you have seen the letter!

FIEL. No, I assure you.

STEN. Well, then, frankly—I have threatened him.

FIEL. Ah! Then I have, in a way, an answer to your letter.

STEN. An answer? Out with it, man!

FIEL. [*shows him a sealed paper*]. Look here—the chamberlain's proxy.

STEN. And who does he vote for?

FIEL. Not for you, at any rate.

STEN. For whom then? For whom?

FIEL. For the sheriff and the provost.

STEN. What! Not even for Lundestad?

FIEL. No. And do you know why? Because Lundestad is going to propose you as his successor.

STEN. He dares to do this!

FIEL. Yes, he does. And he added: "If you see Stensgard, you can tell him how I am voting; it will show him on what footing we stand."

STEN. Good, since he will have it so!

FIEL. Take care; it's danger to tug at an old tower—it may come down on your head.

STEN. Oh, I have learned wisdom in these two days.

FIEL. Indeed? You're not so wise but that you let old Lundestad lead you by the nose.

STEN. Do you think I don't understand that he took me up because he thought I had won over the chamberlain and because he wanted to break up our league and keep Monsen out?

FIEL. But now that he knows you haven't won over the chamberlain——

STEN. He has gone too far to draw back, and I've made good use of the time and scattered announcements broadcast. Most of his supporters will abstain from voting; mine are all here.

FIEL. It's a big stride from the preliminary election to the final election.

STEN. Lundestad knows very well that if he fails me in the College of Electors I'll soon agitate him out of the town council.

FIEL. Not a bad calculation. And to succeed in all this you feel that you must strike root here more firmly than you have as yet done?

STEN. Yes, these people always demand material guarantees, community of interests——

FIEL. Just so, and therefore Miss Bratsberg is to be sacrificed?

STEN. Sacrificed? If that were so, I should be no better than a scoundrel. But it will be for her happiness, of that I'm convinced. What now? Fieldbo, why do you look like that? You have some underhand scheme of your own.

FIEL. I?

STEN. Yes, you have! You are intriguing against me behind my back. Why do you do that? Be open with me—will you?

FIEL. Frankly, I won't. You are so dangerous, so unscrupulous—well, so reckless, at any rate, that one dare not be open with you. Whatever you know, you make use of without hesitation. But this I say to you as a friend: put Miss Bratsberg out of your head.

STEN. I cannot. I must extricate myself from these sordid surroundings. I can't go on living in this hugger-mugger way. Here have I got to be hail-fellow-well-met with Dick, Tom and Harry, to whisper in corners with them, to hobnob with them, to laugh at their beery witticisms, to be hand in glove with hobbledehoys and unlicked cubs. How can I keep my love of the people untarnished in the midst of all this? I feel as if all the electricity went out of my words. I have no elbowroom, no fresh air to breathe. Oh, a longing comes over me at times for exquisite women! I want something that brings beauty with it! I lie here in a sort of turbid eddy while out there the clear blue current sweeps past me—— But what can you understand of all this!

LUN. [*enters from the back*]. Ah, here we are. Good morning, gentlemen.

STEN. I have news for you, Mr Lundestad! Do you know who the chamberlain is voting for?

FIEL. Silence! It's dishonorable of you.

STEN. What do I care? He is voting for the sheriff and the provost.

LUN. Oh, that was to be expected. You went and ruined your chances with him—though I implored you to play your cards neatly.

STEN. I shall play them neatly enough—in future.

FIEL. Take care—two can play at that game. [*Goes out to the right.*]

STEN. That fellow has something up his sleeve. Have you any idea what it can be?

LUN. No, I haven't. But by the bye, I see you are flourishing in the paper today.

STEN. I?

LUN. Yes, with a nice little epitaph on me.

STEN. Oh, that's that beast Aslaksen, of course.

LUN. Your attack on the chamberlain is in too.

STEN. I don't know anything about that. If it's to be war between the chamberlain and me, I have sharper weapons.

LUN. Indeed!

STEN. Have you ever seen this bill? Look at it. Is it good?

LUN. Good, you say? This bill here?

STEN. Yes; look closely at it.

HEIRE [*enters from the right*]. Why, what the deuce can be the meaning of—— Ah, how interesting! Do remain as you are, gentlemen, I beg! Do you know what you irresistibly remind me of? Of a summer night in the Far North.

LUN. That's a curious simile.

HEIRE. A very obvious one—the setting and the rising sun together. Delightful, delightful! But, talking of that, what the deuce is the matter outside there? Your fellow citizens are scuttling about like frightened fowls, cracking and crowing and not knowing what perch to settle on.

STEN. Well, it's an occasion of great importance.

HEIRE. Oh, you and your importance! No, it's something quite different, my dear friends. There are whispers of a great failure, a bankruptcy —oh, not political, Mr Lundestad, I don't mean that!

STEN. A bankruptcy?

HEIRE. Hee-hee! That puts life into our legal friend. Yes, a bankruptcy; someone is on his last legs; the ax is laid to the root of the tree—I say no more! Two strange gentlemen have been seen driving past, but where to? To whose address? Do you know anything, Mr Lundestad?

LUN. I know how to hold my tongue, Mr Heire.

HEIRE. Of course, you are a statesman, a diplomatist. But I must be off and find out all I can about it. It's such sport with these heroes of finance; they are like beads on a string —when one slips off, all the rest follow. [*Goes out by the back.*]

STEN. Is there any truth in all this gossip?

LUN. You showed me a bill; I thought I saw young Bratsberg's name upon it.

STEN. The chamberlain's too.

LUN. And you asked me if it was good?

STEN. Yes; just look at it.

LUN. It's perhaps not so good as it might be.

STEN. You see it then?

LUN. What?

STEN. That it is a forgery.

LUN. A forgery? Forged bills are often the safest; people redeem them first.

STEN. But what do you think? Isn't it a forgery?

LUN. I don't much like the look of it.

STEN. How so?

LUN. I'm afraid there are too many of these about, Mr Stensgard.

STEN. What! It's not possible that ——

LUN. If young Mr Bratsberg slips off the string, those nearest him are only too likely to follow.

STEN. [*seizes his arm*]. What do you mean by those nearest him?

LUN. Who can be nearer than father and son?

STEN. Why, good God!

LUN. Remember, I say nothing! It was Daniel Heire that was talking of failure and bankruptcy and——

STEN. This is a thunderbolt to me.

LUN. Oh, many a man that seemed solid enough has gone to the wall before now. Perhaps he's too good-natured, goes and backs bills; ready money isn't always to be had; property has to be sold for an old song——

STEN. And of course this falls on—falls on the children as well.

LUN. Yes, I'm heartily grieved for Miss Bratsberg. She didn't get much from her mother, and heaven knows if even the little she has is secured.

STEN. Oh, now I understand Fieldbo's advice! He's a true friend after all.

LUN. What did Doctor Fieldbo say?

STEN. He was too loyal to say anything, but I understand him all the same. And now I understand you too, Mr Lundestad.

LUN. Have you not understood me before?

STEN. Not thoroughly. I forget the proverb about the rats and the sinking ship.

LUN. That's not a very nice way to put it. But what's the matter with you? You look quite ill. Good God, I haven't gone and blasted your hopes, have I?

STEN. How do you mean?

LUN. Yes, yes—I see it all. Old fool that I am! My dear Mr Stensgard, if you really love the girl, what does it matter whether she is rich or poor?

STEN. Matter? No, of course——

LUN. Good lord, we all know happiness isn't a matter of money.

STEN. Of course not.

LUN. And with industry and determination you'll soon be on your feet again. Don't let poverty frighten you. I know what love is; I went into all that in my young days. A happy home, a faithful woman——! My dear young friend, beware how you take any step that may involve you in lifelong self-reproach.

STEN. But what will become of your plans?

LUN. Oh, they must go as best they can. I couldn't think of demanding the sacrifice of your heart!

STEN. But I will make the sacrifice. Yes, I will show you that I have the strength for it. Think of the longing multitude out there; they claim me with a sort of voiceless pathos. I cannot, I dare not, fail them!

LUN. Yes, but the stake in the district?

STEN. I shall take measures to fulfill the demands of my fellow citizens in that respect, Mr Lundestad. I see a way, a new way, and I will follow it up. I renounce the happiness of toiling in obscurity for the woman I love. I say to my fellow countrymen: "Here I am—take me!"

LUN. [*looks at him in quiet admiration and presses his hand*]. You are indeed a man of rare gifts, Mr Stensgard. [*Goes out to the right.*]

[STENSGARD *paces the room several times, now stopping for a moment at the window, now running his fingers through his hair. Presently* BASTIAN MONSEN *enters from the back.*]

BAS. Here I am, my dear friend.

STEN. Where have you come from?

BAS. From the nation.

STEN. The nation? What does that mean?

BAS. Don't you know what the nation means? It means the people, the common people; those who have nothing and are nothing, those who lie chained——

STEN. What monkey tricks are these, I should like to know?

BAS. Monkey tricks?

STEN. I have noticed lately that you go about mimicking me; you imitate even my clothes and my handwriting. Be kind enough to stop that.

BAS. What do you mean? Don't we

belong to the same party?

STEN. Yes, but I won't put up with this—you make yourself ridiculous.

BAS. By being like you?

STEN. By aping me. Be sensible now, Monsen, and give it up. It's quite disgusting. But look here—can you tell me when your father is coming back?

BAS. I have no idea. I believe he's gone to Christiania; he may not be back for a week or so.

STEN. Indeed? I'm sorry for that. He has a big stroke of business on hand, I hear.

BAS. I have a big stroke of business on hand too. Look here, Stensgard, you must do me a service.

STEN. Willingly. What is it?

BAS. I feel so full of energy. I have to thank you for that; you have stimulated me. I feel I must do something, Stensgard: I want to get married.

STEN. To get married? To whom?

BAS. Sh! Someone in this house.

STEN. Madam Rundholmen?

BAS. Sh! Yes, it's her. Put in a good word for me, do! This sort of thing is just the thing for me. She's in the swim, you know; she's on the best of terms with the chamberlain's people ever since her sister was housekeeper there. If I get her, perhaps I shall get the town contracts too. So that on the whole—damn it, I love her!

STEN. Oh, love, love! Have done with that sickening hypocrisy.

BAS. Hypocrisy!

STEN. Yes; you are lying to yourself, at any rate. You talk in one breath of town contracts and of love. Why not call a spade a spade? There's something sordid about all this; I will have nothing to do with it.

BAS. But listen!

STEN. Do your dirty work yourself, I say! [*To* FIELDBO, *who enters from the right.*] Well, how goes the election?

FIEL. Excellently for you, it appears. I saw Lundestad just now; he said you were getting all the votes.

STEN. Am I, indeed?

FIEL. But what good will they do you? Since you're not a man of property——

STEN. [*between his teeth*]. Isn't it confounded!

FIEL. Well, you can't do two things at once. If you win on the one side, you must be content to lose on the other. Good-by! [*Goes out by the back.*]

BAS. What did he mean by winning and losing?

STEN. I'll tell you afterward. But now, my dear Monsen—to return to what we were talking about—I promised to put in a good word for you.

BAS. You promised? On the contrary, I thought you said——

STEN. Oh, nonsense; you didn't let me explain myself fully. What I meant was that there is something sordid in mixing up your love with town contracts and so forth; it is an offense against all that is noblest in your nature. So, my dear friend, if you really love the girl——

BAS. The widow.

STEN. Yes, yes, it's all the same. I mean when one really loves a woman, that in itself should be a conclusive reason——

BAS. Yes, that's just what I think. So you'll speak for me, will you?

STEN. Yes, with great pleasure—but on one condition.

BAS. What's that?

STEN. Tit for tat, my dear Bastian—you must put in a word for me too.

BAS. I? With whom?

STEN. Have you really not noticed

anything? Yet it's before your very nose.

BAS. You surely don't mean——

STEN. Your sister Ragna? Yes, it is she. Oh, you don't know how I have been moved by the sight of her quiet, self-sacrificing devotion to her home.

BAS. Do you really mean to say so?

STEN. And you, with your penetrating eye, have suspected nothing?

BAS. Yes, at one time I did think—— But now people are talking of your hanging about the chamberlain's.

STEN. Oh, the chamberlain's! Well, Monsen, I'll tell you frankly that for a moment I did hesitate, but thank goodness that is over; now I see my way quite clear before me.

BAS. There's my hand. I'll back you up, you may be sure. And as for Ragna—why, she daren't do anything but what I and Father wish.

STEN. Yes, but your father—that's just what I wanted to say——

BAS. Sh! There—I hear Madam Rundholmen. Now's your chance to speak for me, if she's not too busy; for then she's apt to be snappish. You do your best, my dear fellow, and leave the rest to me. Do you happen to have seen Aslaksen?

STEN. He's probably at the polling booth.

[BASTIAN *goes out by the back as* MADAM RUNDHOLMEN *enters from the right.*]

MADAM. Things are going as smooth as possible, Mr Stensgard; everyone is voting for you.

STEN. That's very odd.

MADAM. Goodness knows what Monsen of Stonelee will say.

STEN. I want a word with you, Madam Rundholmen.

MADAM. Well, what is it?

STEN. Will you listen to me?

MADAM. Lord, yes, that I will.

STEN. Well, then: you were talking just now about being alone in the world——

MADAM. Oh, it was that horrid old Heire.

STEN. You were saying how hard it is for an unprotected widow——

MADAM. Yes indeed; you should just try it, Mr Stensgard!

STEN. But now if there came a fine young man——

MADAM. A fine young man?

STEN. One who had long loved you in secret——

MADAM. Oh, come now, Mr Stensgard, I won't hear any more of your nonsense.

STEN. You must! A young man who, like yourself, finds it hard to be alone in the world——

MADAM. Well, what then? I don't understand you at all.

STEN. If you could make two people happy, Madam Rundholmen—yourself and——

MADAM. And a fine young man?

STEN. Just so; now, answer me.

MADAM. Mr Stensgard, you can't be in earnest.

STEN. You don't suppose I would jest on such a subject? Should you be disposed?

MADAM. Yes, that I am, the Lord knows! Oh, you dear, sweet——

STEN [*recoiling a step*]. What is this?

MADAM. Bother, here comes someone!

[RAGNA MONSEN *enters hastily, and in evident disquietude, from the back.*]

RAGNA. I beg your pardon—isn't my father here?

MADAM. Your father? Yes; no—I—don't know—excuse me——

RAGNA. Where is he?

MADAM. Your father? Oh, he drove past here——

STEN. Toward Christiania.

RAGNA. No; it's impossible.

MADAM. Yes, I know for certain he drove down the road. Oh, my dear Miss Monsen, you can't think how happy I am! Wait a moment—I'll just run to the cellar and fetch up a bottle of the real thing. [*Goes out to the left.*]

STEN. Tell me, Miss Monsen—is it really your father you are looking for?

RAGNA. Yes, of course it is.

STEN. And you didn't know that he had gone away?

RAGNA. Oh, how should I know? They tell me nothing. But to Christiania? That's impossible; they would have met him. Good-by!

STEN. [*intercepts her*]. Ragna! Tell me! Why are you so changed toward me?

RAGNA. I? Let me pass! Let me go!

STEN. No, you shall not go! I believe Providence guided you here at this moment. Oh, why do you shrink from me? You used not to.

RAGNA. Ah, that is all over, thank God!

STEN. But why?

RAGNA. I have learned to know you better; it is well that I learned in time.

STEN. Oh, that is it! People have been lying about me? Perhaps I am to blame too; I have been lost in a maze of perplexities. But that is past now. Oh, the very sight of you makes a better man of me. It is you I care for deeply and truly; it is you I love, Ragna—you and no other!

RAGNA. Let me pass! I am afraid of you.

STEN. Oh, but tomorrow, Ragna—may I come and speak to you tomorrow?

RAGNA. Yes, yes, if you must; only for heaven's sake not today.

STEN. Only not today! Hurrah! I have won; now I am happy!

MADAM [*enters from the left with cake and wine*]. Come now, we must drink a glass for luck.

STEN. For luck in love! Here's to love and happiness! Hurrah for tomorrow! [*He drinks.*]

HELLE [*entering from the right, to* RAGNA]. Have you found him?

RAGNA. No, he is not here. Come, come!

MADAM. Heaven help us, what's the matter?

HELLE. Nothing; only some visitors have arrived at Stonelee.

RAGNA. Thanks for all your kindness, Madam Rundholmen.

MADAM. Oh, have you got visitors on your hands again?

RAGNA. Yes, yes; excuse me; I must go home. Good-by!

STEN. Good-by—till tomorrow!

[RAGNA *and* HELLE *go out by the back.* DANIEL HEIRE *enters from the right.*]

HEIRE. Ha-ha! It's going like a house on fire! They're all cackling Stensgard, Stensgard! They're all plumping for you. Now you should plump for him too, Madam Rundholmen!

MADAM. Hey, that's an idea. Are they all voting for him?

HEIRE. Unanimously. Mr Stensgard enjoys the confidence of the constituency, as the saying is. Old Lundestad is going about with a face like a pickled cucumber. Oh, it's a pleasure to see it all.

MADAM. They shan't regret having voted for him. If I can't vote, I can stand treat. [*Goes out to the left.*]

HEIRE. Ah, you are the man for the widows, Mr Stensgard! I'll tell you what—if you can only get hold of her, you're a made man, sir!

STEN. Get hold of Madam Rundholmen?

HEIRE. Yes, why not? She's a substantial woman in every sense of the word. She'll be mistress of the situation as soon as the Stonelee card castle has come to grief.

STEN. There's nothing wrong at Stonelee, is there?

HEIRE. Isn't there? You have a short memory, my dear sir. Didn't I tell you there were rumors of failure and bankruptcy and——

STEN. Well, what then?

HEIRE. What then? That's just what we want to know. There's a hue and cry after Monsen; two men have come to Stonelee——

STEN. Yes, I know—a couple of visitors.

HEIRE. Uninvited visitors, my dear young friend; there are whispers of the police and infuriated creditors—there's something queer about the accounts, you must know! Talking of that—what paper was that Monsen gave you yesterday?

STEN. Oh, just a paper. Something queer about the accounts, you say? Look here! You know Chamberlain Bratsberg's signature?

HEIRE. Hee-hee! I should rather think I did.

STEN. [*produces the bill*]. Well, look at this.

HEIRE. Give it here—I'm rather shortsighted, you know. [*After examining it.*] That, my dear sir? That's not the chamberlain's hand.

STEN. Not? Then it is——

HEIRE. And it's drawn by Monsen?

STEN. No, by young Mr Bratsberg.

HEIRE. Nonsense! Let me see. [*Looks at the paper and hands it back again.*] You can light your cigar with this.

STEN. What! The drawer's name too?

HEIRE. A forgery, young man; a forgery, as sure as my name's Daniel. You have only to look at it with the keen eye of suspicion——

STEN. But how can that be? Monsen can't have known——

HEIRE. Monsen? No, he knows nothing about either his own paper or other people's. But I'm glad it has come to an end, Mr Stensgard! It's a satisfaction to one's moral sense. Ah, I have often glowed with a noble indignation, if I may say so, at having to stand by and see—I say no more! But the best of it all is that now Monsen is down he'll drag young Bratsberg after him, and the son will bring the father down——

STEN. Yes, so Lundestad said.

HEIRE. But of course there's method even in bankruptcy. You'll see; I am an old hand at prophecy. Monsen will go to prison; young Bratsberg will compound with his creditors; and the chamberlain will be placed under trustees; that's to say, his creditors will present him with an annuity of a couple of thousand dollars. That's how things go, Mr Stensgard; I know it, I know it! What says the classic? *Fiat justitia, pereat mundau*, which means: Fie on what's called justice in this wicked world, sir!

STEN. [*pacing the room*]. One after the other! Both ways barred!

HEIRE. What the deuce——

STEN. And now too! Just at this moment!

ASL. [*enters from the right*]. I

congratulate you, chosen of the people!

STEN. Elected!

ASL. Elected by 117 votes and Lundestad by 53. The rest all nowhere.

HEIRE. Your first step on the path of glory, Mr Stensgard.

ASL. And it shall cost you a bowl of punch.

HEIRE. Well, it's the first step that costs, they say.

ASL. [*goes off to the left, shouting*]. Punch, Madam Rundholmen! A bowl of punch! The chosen of the people stands treat!

[LUNDESTAD, *and after him several* ELECTORS, *enters from the right.*]

HEIRE [*in a tone of condolence to* LUNDESTAD]. Fifty-three! That's the gray-haired patriot's reward!

LUN. [*whispers to* STENSGARD]. Are you firm in your resolve?

STEN. What's the use of being firm when everything is tumbling about your ears?

LUN. Do you think the game is lost?

ASL. [*returning by the left*]. Madam Rundholmen stands treat herself. She says she has the best right to.

STEN. [*struck by an idea*]. Madam Rundholmen!—has the right to——

LUN. What?

STEN. The game is not lost, Mr Lundestad! [*Sits at the right-hand table and writes.*]

LUN. [*in a low voice*]. Oh, Aslaksen—can you get something into your next paper for me?

ASL. Of course I can. Is it libelous?

LUN. No, certainly not!

ASL. Well, never mind; I'll take it all the same.

LUN. It is my political last will and testament; I shall write it tonight.

A MAIDSERVANT [*enters from the left*]. The punch, with Madam Rundholmen's compliments.

ASL. Hurrah! Now there's some life in the local situation. [*He places the punch bowl on the middle table, serves the others and drinks freely himself during the following scene.* BASTIAN MONSEN *has meanwhile entered from the right.*]

BAS. [*softly*]. You won't forget my letter?

ASL. Don't be afraid. [*Taps his breast pocket.*] I have it here.

BAS. You'll deliver it as soon as you can—when you see she's disengaged, you understand?

ASL. I understand. [*Calls.*] Come now, the glasses are filled.

BAS. You shan't do it for nothing, I promise you.

ASL. All right, all right. [*To the servant.*] A lemon, Karen—quick as the wind!

[BASTIAN *retires.*]

STEN. A word, Aslaksen: shall you be passing here tomorrow evening?

ASL. Tomorrow evening? I can if you like.

STEN. Then you might look in and give Madam Rundholmen this letter.

ASL. From you?

STEN. Yes. Put it in your pocket. There now. Tomorrow evening then?

ASL. All right; trust to me.

[*The servant brings the lemon;* STENSGARD *goes toward the window.*]

BAS. Well—have you spoken to Madam Rundholmen?

STEN. Spoken? Oh yes, I said a word or two.

BAS. And what do you think?

STEN. Oh well—we were interrupted. I can't say anything definite.

BAS. I'll take my chance all the same; she's always complaining of her loneliness. My fate shall be sealed within an hour.

STEN. Within an hour?

BAS. [*sees* MADAM RUNDHOLMEN *who enters from the left*]. Sh! Not a word to anyone! [*Goes toward the back.*]

STEN. [*whispers to* ASLAKSEN]. Give me back the letter.

ASL. Do you want it back?

STEN. Yes, at once; I will deliver it myself.

ASL. Very well, here it is.

[STENSGARD *thrusts the letter into his pocket and mixes with the rest.*]

MADAM [*to* BASTIAN]. What do you say to the election, Mr Bastian?

BAS. I'm delighted. Stensgard and I are bosom friends, you know. I shouldn't much be surprised if he got into Parliament.

MADAM. But your father wouldn't much like that.

BAS. Oh, Father has so many irons in the fire. Besides, if Stensgard's elected, it will still be all in the family, I daresay.

MADAM. How so?

BAS. He wants to marry——

MADAM. Lord! Has he said anything?

BAS. Yes, and I've promised to put in a word for him. It'll be all right. I'm sure Ragna likes him.

MADAM. Ragna!

LUN. [*approaching*]. What is interesting you so deeply, Madam Rundholmen?

MADAM. What do you think he says? Why, that Mr Stensgard's making up to——

LUN. Yes, but he won't find the chamberlain so easy to deal with.

BAS. The chamberlain?

LUN. He probably thinks her too good a match for a mere lawyer.

MADAM. Who? Who?

LUN. Why, his daughter, Miss Bratsberg, of course.

BAS. He's surely not making love to Miss Bratsberg?

LUN. Yes, indeed he is.

MADAM. You are quite sure of that?

BAS. And he told me—— Oh, I want to say a word to you.

[LUNDESTAD *and* BASTIAN *go toward the back.*]

MADAM [*approaching* STENSGARD]. You must be on your guard, Mr Stensgard.

STEN. Against whom?

MADAM. Against malicious people who are slandering you.

STEN. Why, let them—so long as one person doesn't believe their slander.

MADAM. And who may that one person be?

STEN. [*slips the letter into her hand*]. Take this; read it when you are alone.

MADAM. Ah, I knew it! [*Goes off to the left.*]

RIN. [*enters from the right*]. Well, I hear you have won a brilliant victory, Mr Stensgard.

STEN. Yes, I have, Mr Ringdal, in spite of your noble chief's endeavors.

RIN. His endeavors? What to do?

STEN. To keep me out.

RIN. Like other people, he has a right to vote as he pleases.

STEN. It's a pity he is not likely to retain that right for long.

RIN. What do you mean?

STEN. I mean, since his affairs are not so straight as they might be——

RIN. His affairs! What affairs! What have you got into your head?

STEN. Oh, you needn't pretend ignorance. Isn't there a storm brewing? —a great crash impending?

RIN. Yes, so I hear on all sides.

STEN. And aren't both the Bratsbergs involved in it?

RIN. My dear sir, are you crazy?

STEN. Oh, you naturally want to keep it dark.

RIN. What good would that be? That sort of thing can't be kept dark.

STEN. Is it not true then?

RIN. Not a word of it, so far as the chamberlain is concerned. How could you believe such nonsense? Who has been humbugging you?

STEN. I won't tell you just yet.

RIN. Well, you needn't, but whoever it was must have had a motive.

STEN. A motive?

RIN. Yes, just think: is there no one who has an interest in keeping you and the chamberlain apart?

STEN. Yes, on my soul, but there is though!

RIN. The chamberlain in reality thinks very highly of you.

STEN. Does he?

RIN. Yes, and that's why people want to make mischief between you. They reckon on your ignorance of the situation, on your impulsiveness and your confiding disposition——

STEN. Oh, the vipers! And Madam Rundholmen has my letter!

RIN. What letter?

STEN. Oh, nothing. But it's not too late. My dear Mr Ringdal, shall you see the chamberlain this evening?

RIN. In all probability.

STEN. Then tell him to think no more of those threats—he will understand; tell him I shall call tomorrow and explain everything.

RIN. You'll call?

STEN. Yes, to prove to him—— Ah, a proof! Look here, Mr Ringdal, will you give the chamberlain this bill from me?

RIN. This bill?

STEN. Yes; it's a matter I can't explain to you, but just you give it to him.

RIN. Upon my word, Mr Stensgard——

STEN. And just add these words from me: This is how I treat those who vote against me!

RIN. I shan't forget. [*Goes out the back.*]

STEN. I say, Mr Heire—how could you go and palm off that story about the chamberlain upon me?

HEIRE. How could I palm it off on you?

STEN. Yes—it's a lie from beginning to end.

HEIRE. No! Is it, indeed? I'm delighted to hear it. Do you hear, Mr Lundestad? It's all a lie about the chamberlain.

LUN. Sh! We were on a false scent; it's nearer at hand.

STEN. How nearer at hand?

LUN. I know nothing for certain, but they talk of Madam Rundholmen——

STEN. What!

HEIRE. Haven't I prophesied it! She has been too much mixed up with our friend at Stonelee.

LUN. He drove off this morning before daylight.

HEIRE. And his family is out hunting for him.

LUN. And the son has been doing all he knows to get his sister provided for.

STEN. Provided for! "Tomorrow" she said; and then her anxiety about her father——

HEIRE. Hee-hee! You'll see he's gone and hanged himself, sir!

ASL. Has anyone hanged himself?

LUN. Mr Heire says Monsen of Stonelee——

MON. [*enters from the back*]. A dozen of champagne!

ASL. AND OTHERS. Monsen!

MON. Yes, Monsen! Champagne Monsen! Money Monsen! Let's have the wine, confound it all!

HEIRE. But, my dear sir——

STEN. Why, where have you dropped from?

MON. I've been doing a stroke of business, sir! Cleared a hundred thousand! Hei! Tomorrow I'll give a thundering dinner at Stonelee. I invite you all. Champagne, I say! I congratulate you, Stensgard! I hear you're elected.

STEN. Yes; I must explain to you——

MON. Pooh! What does it matter to me? Wine, I say! Where is Madam Rundholmen? [*Makes a motion to go out to the left.*]

MAIDSERVANT [*who has just entered, intercepts him*]. No one can see the mistress just now; she's got a letter——

BAS. Oh, damn it all! [*Goes out by the back.*]

STEN. Is she reading it?

SERVANT. Yes, and it seems quite to have upset her.

STEN. Good-by, Mr Monsen; dinner at Stonelee tomorrow?

MON. Yes, tomorrow. Good-by!

STEN. [*whispers*]. Mr Heire, will you do me a service?

HEIRE. Certainly, certainly.

STEN. Then just run me down a little to Madam Rundholmen, indulge in an innuendo or two at my expense. You are so good at that sort of thing.

HEIRE. What the deuce is the meaning of this?

STEN. I have my reasons. It's a joke, you know—a wager with—with someone you have a grudge against.

HEIRE. Aha, I understand. I say no more!

STEN. Don't go too far, you know. Just place me in a more or less equivocal light—make her a little suspicious of me for the moment.

HEIRE. Rely upon me; it will be a real pleasure to me.

STEN. Thanks, thanks in advance. [*Goes toward the table.*] Mr Lundestad, we shall meet tomorrow forenoon at the chamberlain's.

LUN. Have you hopes?

STEN. A threefold hope.

LUN. Threefold? I don't understand.

STEN. You needn't. Henceforth I will be my own counselor. [*Goes out by the back.*]

MON. [*at the punch bowl*]. Another glass, Aslaksen! Where's Bastian?

ASL. He's just gone out. But I have a letter to deliver for him.

MON. Have you?

ASL. To Madam Rundholmen.

MON. Ah, at last!

ASL. But not till tomorrow evening, he said; tomorrow evening, neither sooner nor later. Here's to you!

HEIRE [*to* LUNDESTAD]. What the deuce is all this business between Stensgard and Madam Rundholmen?

LUN. [*whispers*]. He's courting her.

HEIRE. I suspected as much! But he asked me to run him down a bit—to cast a slur on his character——

LUN. And you said you would?

HEIRE. Yes, of course.

LUN. I believe he says of you that your word is as good as your bond—and no better.

HEIRE. Hee-hee—the dear fellow! He shall find out his mistake this time.

MADAM. [*with an open letter in her*

hand, at the door on the left]. Where is Mr Stensgard?

HEIRE. He kissed your chambermaid and went, Madam Rundholmen!

ACT V

SCENE—*Large reception room at the* CHAMBERLAIN'S. *Entrance door at the back. Doors right and left.*

RINGDAL *stands at a table looking through some papers. A knock.*

RIN. Come in.

FIEL. [*from the back*]. Good morning.

RIN. Good morning, Doctor.

FIEL. All well, eh?

RIN. Oh yes, well enough; but——

FIEL. What?

RIN. Of course you've heard the great news?

FIEL. No. What is it?

RIN. Do you mean to say you haven't heard what has happened at Stonelee?

FIEL. No.

RIN. Monsen has absconded.

FIEL. Absconded! Monsen?

RIN. Absconded.

FIEL. Great heavens!

RIN. There were ugly rumors yesterday, but then Monsen turned up again; he managed to throw dust in people's eyes.

FIEL. But the reason? The reason?

RIN. Enormous losses in timber, they say. Several houses in Christiania have stopped payment, and so——

FIEL. And so he has gone off!

RIN. To Sweden, probably. The authorities took possession at Stonelee this morning. Things are being inventoried and sealed up.

FIEL. And the unfortunate children?

RIN. The son seems to have kept clear of the business; at least I hear he puts a bold face on it.

FIEL. But the daughter?

RIN. Sh! The daughter is here.

FIEL. Here?

RIN. The tutor brought her and the two little ones here this morning. Miss Bratsberg is looking after them—quietly, you know.

FIEL. And how does she bear it?

RIN. Oh, pretty well, I fancy. You may guess, after the treatment she has met with at home—— And, besides, I may tell you she is—— Ah, here's the chamberlain.

CHAM. [*from the left*]. So you are there, my dear doctor?

FIEL. Yes, I am pretty early astir. Let me wish you many happy returns of the day, Chamberlain.

CHAM. Oh, as for happiness—— But thank you all the same; I know you mean it kindly.

FIEL. And may I ask, Chamberlain——

CHAM. One word: be good enough to drop that title.

FIEL. What do you mean?

CHAM. I am an ironmaster and nothing more.

FIEL. Why, what strange notion is this?

CHAM. I have renounced my post and my title. I am sending in my resignation today.

FIEL. You should sleep upon that.

CHAM. When His Majesty was graciously pleased to assign me a place in his immediate circle he did so because of the unblemished honor of my family through long generations.

FIEL. Well, what then?

CHAM. My family is disgraced just as much as Mr Monsen's. Of course you have heard about Monsen?

FIEL. Yes, I have.

CHAM. [*to* RINGDAL]. Any further news about him?

RIN. Only that he brings down with him a good many of the younger men.

CHAM. And my son?

RIN. Your son has sent me his balance sheet. He will be able to pay in full, but there will be nothing over.

CHAM. H'm. Then will you get my resignation copied?

RIN. I'll see to it. [*Goes out by the foremost door on the right.*]

FIEL. Have you reflected what you are doing? Things can be arranged without anyone being a bit the wiser.

CHAM. Indeed! Can I make myself ignorant of what has happened?

FIEL. Oh, after all, what has happened? Has he not written to you, acknowledged his fault and begged for your forgiveness? This is the only time he has done anything of the sort; why not simply blot it out?

CHAM. Would you do what my son has done?

FIEL. He won't repeat it; that is the main point.

CHAM. How do you know he will not repeat it?

FIEL. If for no other reason, because of what you yourself told me—the scene with your daughter-in-law. Whatever else comes of it, that will steady him.

CHAM. [*pacing the room*]. My poor Selma! Our peace and happiness gone!

FIEL. There are higher things than peace and happiness. Your happiness has been an illusion. Yes, I must speak frankly to you: in that, as in many other things, you have built on a hollow foundation. You have been shortsighted and overweening, Chamberlain!

CHAM. [*stops short*]. I?

FIEL. Yes, you! You have plumed yourself on your family honor, but when has that honor been tried? Are you sure it would have stood the test?

CHAM. You can spare your sermons, Doctor. Do you think I have not learned a lesson from the events of these days?

FIEL. I daresay you have, but prove it by showing greater tolerance and clearer insight. You reproach your son, but what have you done for him? You have taken care to develop his faculties but not to form his character. You have lectured him on what he owed to the honor of his family, but you have not guided and molded him so that honor became to him an irresistible instinct.

CHAM. Do you think so?

FIEL. I not only think, I know it. But that is generally the way here: people are bent on learning, not on living. And you see what comes of it: you see hundreds of men with great gifts who never seem to be more than half ripe, who are one thing in their ideas and feeling and something quite different in their habits and acts. Just look at Stensgard——

CHAM. Ah, Stensgard now! What do you make of Stensgard?

FIEL. A patchwork. I have known him from childhood. His father was a mere rag of a man, a withered weed, a nobody. He kept a little huckster's shop and eked things out with pawnbroking, or rather his wife did it for him. She was a coarse-grained woman, the most unwomanly I ever knew. She had her husband declared incapable; she had not an ounce of heart in her. And in that home Stensgard passed his childhood. Then he went to the grammar school. "He shall go to college," said his mother; "I'll make a smart solicitor of him." Squalor at home, high pressure at school; soul, temperament, will, talents, all pulling in different ways—what could it lead to but disintegration of character?

CHAM. What could it lead to, eh? I should like to know what is good enough for you. We are to expect nothing of Stensgard, nothing of my son, but we may look to you, I suppose—to you?

FIEL. Yes, to me—precisely. Oh, you needn't laugh; I take no credit to myself, but my lot has been one that begets equilibrium and firmness of character. I was brought up amid the peace and harmony of a modest middle-class home. My mother is a woman of the finest type; in our home we had no desires that outstripped our opportunities, no cravings that were wrecked on the rocks of circumstance; and death did not break in upon our circle, leaving emptiness and longing behind it. We were brought up in the love of beauty, but it informed our whole view of life instead of being a side interest, a thing apart. We were taught to shun excesses, whether of the intellect or of the feelings.

CHAM. Bless me! So that accounts for your being the pink of perfection.

FIEL. I am far from thinking so. I only say that fate has been infinitely kind to me and that I regard its favors in the light of obligations.

CHAM. Very well; but if Stensgard is under no such obligations, it is all the more to his credit that he—

FIEL. What? What is to his credit?

CHAM. You have misjudged him, my good doctor. Look here. What do you say to this?

FIEL. Your son's bill!

CHAM. Yes; he has sent it to me.

FIEL. Of his own accord?

CHAM. Of his own accord and unconditionally. It is fine: it is noble. From this day forth my house is open to him.

FIEL. Think again! For your own sake, for your daughter's——

CHAM. Oh, let me alone! He is better than you in many ways. At any rate he is straightforward, while you are underhand in your dealings.

FIEL. I?

CHAM. Yes, you! You have made yourself the master of this house; you come and go as you please; I consult you about everything—and yet——

FIEL. Well—and yet?

CHAM. And yet there's always something confoundedly close about you; yes, and something—something uppish that I cannot endure!

FIEL. Please explain yourself!

CHAM. I? No, it is you that ought to explain yourself! But now you must take the consequences.

FIEL. We don't understand each other, Chamberlain. I have no bill to give up to you; yet who knows but I may be making greater sacrifice for your sake?

CHAM. Indeed? How so?

FIEL. By holding my tongue.

CHAM. Holding your tongue, indeed! Shall I tell you what I am tempted to do? To forget my manners, use bad language and join the League of Youth. You are a stiff-necked Pharisee, my good doctor, and that sort of thing is out of place in our free society. Look at Stensgard; he is not like that, so he shall come here whenever he likes; he shall—he shall! Oh, what's the use of talking!

You must take the consequences; as you make your bed, so you must lie.

LUN. [*enters from the back*]. My congratulations, Chamberlain! May you long enjoy the respect and——

CHAM. Oh, go to the devil—I'm almost inclined to say! That's all humbug, my dear Lundestad. There's nothing but humbug in this world.

LUN. That is what Mr Monsen's creditors are saying.

CHAM. Ah, about Monsen—didn't it come upon you like a thunderbolt?

LUN. Oh, you have often prophesied it, Chamberlain.

CHAM. H'm, h'm—yes, to be sure I have. I phophesied it only the day before yesterday; he came here trying to get money out of me——

FIEL. It might have saved him.

LUN. Impossible; he was too deep in the mire, and whatever is, is for the best.

CHAM. That is your opinion? Was it for the best, then, that you were beaten at the polls yesterday?

LUN. I wasn't beaten; everything went just as I wanted. Stensgard is not a man to make an enemy of; he has got what we others have to whistle for.

CHAM. I don't quite understand what you mean.

LUN. He has the power of carrying people away with him. And then he has the luck to be unhampered by either character or conviction or social position, so that Liberalism is the easiest thing in the world for him.

CHAM. Well, really, I should have thought we were all Liberals.

LUN. Yes, of course we are Liberals, Chamberlain, not a doubt of it. But the thing is that we are Liberal only on our own behalf, whereas Stensgard's Liberalism extends to other people. That's the novelty of the thing.

CHAM. And you are going over to these subversive ideas?

LUN. I've read in old storybooks about people who could summon up old spirits but could not lay them again.

CHAM. Why, my dear Lundestad, how can a man of your enlightenment——

LUN. I know it's mere popish superstition, Chamberlain. But new ideas are like those spirits; it's not so easy to lay them; the best plan is to compromise with them as best you can.

CHAM. But now that Monsen has fallen and, no doubt, his crew of agitators with him——

LUN. If Monsen's fall had come two or three days ago, things would have been very different.

CHAM. Yes, unfortunately. You have been too hasty.

LUN. Partly out of consideration for you, Chamberlain.

CHAM. For me?

LUN. Our party must keep up its reputation in the eyes of the people. We represent the old, deep-rooted Norse sense of honor. If I had deserted Stensgard—you know he holds a paper——

CHAM. Not now.

LUN. What?

CHAM. Here it is.

LUN. He has given it up to you?

CHAM. Yes. Personally he is a gentleman; so much I must say for him.

LUN. [*thoughtfully*]. Mr Stensgard has rare abilities.

STEN. [*at the back, standing in the doorway*]. May I come in?

CHAM. [*going to meet him*]. I am delighted to see you.

STEN. And will you accept my congratulations?

CHAM. With all my heart.

STEN. Then with all my heart I wish you happiness! And you must forget all the stupid things I have written.

CHAM. I go by deeds, not words, Mr Stensgard.

STEN. How good of you to say so!

CHAM. And henceforth—since you wish it—you must consider yourself at home here.

STEN. May I? May I really?

[*A knock at the door.*]

[*Several leading men of the neighborhood, town councilors, etc., enter. The* CHAMBERLAIN *goes to receive them, accepts their congratulations and converses with them.*]

THORA [*who has meantime entered by the second door on the left*]. Mr Stensgard, let me thank you.

STEN. You, Miss Bratsberg!

THORA. My father has told me how nobly you have acted.

STEN. But——

THORA. Oh, how we have misjudged you!

STEN. Have you?

THORA. It was your own fault—no, no; it was ours. Oh, what would I not do to atone for our error.

STEN. Would you? You yourself? Would you really?

THORA. All of us would, if we only knew——

CHAM. Refreshments for these gentlemen, my child.

THORA. They are just coming. [*She retires toward the door again where a servant at the same moment appears with cake and wine, which are handed around.*]

STEN. Oh, my dear Lundestad! I feel like a conquering god.

LUN. So you must have felt yesterday, I suppose.

STEN. Pooh! This is something quite different; the final triumph, the crown of all! There is a glory, a halo, over my life.

LUN. Oho! Dreams of love!

STEN. Not dreams! Realities, glorious realities!

LUN. So Brother Bastian has brought you the answer?

STEN. Bastian?

LUN. Yes, he gave me a hint yesterday; he had promised to plead your cause with a certain young lady.

STEN. Oh, what nonsense!

LUN. Why make a mystery of it? If you haven't heard already, I can give you the news. You have won the day, Mr Stensgard; I have it from Ringdal.

STEN. What have you from Ringdal?

LUN. Miss Monsen has accepted you.

STEN. What!

LUN. Accepted you, I say.

STEN. Accepted me! And the father has bolted!

LUN. But the daughter hasn't.

STEN. Accepted me! In the midst of all this family trouble! How unwomanly! How repellent to any man with the least delicacy of feeling! But the whole thing is a misunderstanding. I never commissioned Bastian—— How could that idiot—— However, it doesn't matter to me; he must answer for his follies himself.

HEIRE [*enters from the back*]. Hee-hee! Quite a gathering! Of course, of course! We are paying our respects, propitiating the powers that be, as the saying goes. May I too——

CHAM. Thanks, thanks, old friend!

HEIRE. Oh, I protest, my dear sir.

That is too much condescension. [*New guests arrive.*] Ah, here we have the myrmidons of justice—the executive—I say no more. [*Goes over to* STENSGARD.] Ah, my dear fortunate youth, are you here? Your hand! Accept the assurance of an old man's rejoicing.

STEN. At what?

HEIRE. You asked me yesterday to run you down a little to her—you know——

STEN. Yes, yes; what then?

HEIRE. It was a heartfelt pleasure to me to oblige you.

STEN. Well—and what happened then? How did she take it?

HEIRE. Like a loving woman, of course—burst into tears, locked herself into her room and would neither answer nor show herself.

STEN. Ah, thank goodness!

HEIRE. It's barbarous to subject a widow's heart to such cruel tests, to go and gloat over her jealous agonies! But love has cat's eyes—I say no more! For today, as I drove past, there stood Madam Rundholmen, brisk and buxom, at her open window combing her hair. She looked like a mermaid, if you'll allow me to say so. Oh, she's a fine woman!

STEN. Well, and then?

HEIRE. Why, she laughed like one possessed, sir, and waved a letter in the air and called out, "A proposal, Mr Heire! I'm engaged to be married."

STEN. What! Engaged?

HEIRE. My hearty congratulations, young man; I'm inexpressibly pleased to be the first to announce to you——

STEN. It's all rubbish! It's nonsense!

HEIRE. What is nonsense?

STEN. You have misunderstood her, or else she has misunderstood—— Engaged! Preposterous! Now that Monsen's down she'll probably——

HEIRE. Not at all, sir, not at all! Madam Rundholmen has solid legs to stand on.

STEN. No matter! I have quite other intentions. All that about the letter was only a joke—a wager, as I told you. My dear Mr Heire, do oblige me by not saying a word to anyone of this silly affair.

HEIRE. I see, I see! It's to be kept secret; it's to be a romance. Ah, youth, youth; it's nothing if not poetical.

STEN. Yes, yes; mum's the word. You shan't regret it—I'll take up your cases—— Sh! I rely upon you. [*He retires.*]

CHAM. [*who has meanwhile been talking to* LUNDESTAD]. No, Lundestad—that I really cannot believe!

LUN. I assure you, Chamberlain—Daniel Heire told me so himself.

HEIRE. What did I tell you, may I inquire?

CHAM. Did Mr Stensgard show you a bill yesterday?

HEIRE. Yes; by the bye—what on earth was the meaning of all that?

CHAM. I'll tell you afterward. And you told him it was a forgery?

HEIRE. Pooh, a mere innocent jest.

LUN. And you told him both signatures were forged?

HEIRE. Oh yes; why not both while I was about it?

CHAM. So that was it!

LUN. [*to the* CHAMBERLAIN]. And when he heard that——

CHAM. He gave the bill to Ringdal!

LUN. The bill that was useless as a weapon of offense.

CHAM. He shams magnanimity! Makes a fool of me a second time!

Gains admission to my house and makes me welcome him and thank him—this—this——

HEIRE. Why, what are you going on about, my dear sir?

CHAM. I'll tell you all about it afterward. [*Takes* LUNDESTAD *apart.*] And this is the fellow you protect, push forward, help to rise!

LUN. Well, he took you in too!

CHAM. Oh, I should like to——

LUN. [*pointing to* STENSGARD, *who is speaking to* THORA]. Look there! What will people be fancying!

CHAM. I shall soon put a stop to these fancies.

LUN. Too late, Chamberlain; he'll worm himself forward by dint of promises.

CHAM. I, too, can maneuver.

LUN. What will you do?

CHAM. [*goes over to* FIELDBO]. Doctor Fieldbo, will you do me a service?

FIEL. With pleasure.

CHAM. Then turn that fellow out of my house.

FIEL. Stensgard?

CHAM. Yes, the adventurer; I hate his very name; turn him out!

FIEL. But how can I?

CHAM. I give you a free hand.

FIEL. A free hand! Do you mean it?

CHAM. Yes, yes, by all means.

FIEL. Your hand on it, Chamberlain!

CHAM. Here it is.

FIEL. So be it, then; now or never! [*Loudly.*] May I request the attention of the company for a moment?

CHAM. Silence for Doctor Fieldbo!

FIEL. With Chamberlain Bratsberg's consent I have the pleasure of announcing my engagement to his daughter.

[*An outburst of astonishment.* THORA *utters a slight scream. The* CHAMBERLAIN *is on the point of speaking but refrains. Loud talk and congratulations.*]

STEN. Engagement!

HEIRE. With the chamberlain's—— With your—— What does it mean?

LUN. Is the doctor out of his mind?

STEN. But, Chamberlain——

CHAM. What can I do? I am a Liberal. I join the League of Youth!

FIEL. Thanks, thanks—and forgive me!

CHAM. Associations are the order of the day, Mr Stensgard.

THORA. Oh, my dear father!

LUN. Yes, and engagements are the order of the day. I have another to announce.

STEN. A mere invention!

LUN. No, not a bit of it; Miss Monsen is engaged to——

STEN. False, false, I say!

THORA. No, Father, it's true; they are both here.

CHAM. Who? Where?

THORA. Ragna and Mr Helle [*Goes toward the second door on the right.*]

LUN. Mr Helle! Then it's he——

CHAM. Here? [*Goes toward the door.*] Come in, my dear child.

RAGNA [*shrinking back shyly*]. Oh no, no; there are so many people.

CHAM. Don't be bashful; you couldn't help what has happened.

HELLE. She is homeless now, Chamberlain.

RAGNA. Oh, you must help us!

CHAM. I will indeed, and thank you for giving me the opportunity.

HEIRE. You may well say engagements are the order of the day. I have another.

CHAM. What? You? At your age? How rash of you!

HEIRE. Oh! I say no more.

LUN. The game is up, Mr Stensgard.

STEN. Indeed! [*Loudly.*] I have one to add to the list, Mr Heire! I, too, have cast anchor for life.

CHAM. What?

STEN. One is now and then forced to play a double game to conceal one's true intentions. I regard this as permissible when the general weal is at stake. My lifework lies clear before me and is all in all to me. I consecrate my whole energies to this district; I find here a ferment of ideas which I must strive to clarify. But this task cannot be accomplished by a mere adventurer. The men of the district must gather round one of themselves. Therefore I have determined to unite my interests indissolubly with yours—to unite them by a bond of affection. If I have awakened any false hopes, I must plead for forgiveness. I, too, am engaged.

CHAM. You?

FIEL. Engaged?

HEIRE. I can bear witness.

CHAM. But how——

FIEL. Engaged? To whom?

LUN. It surely can't be——

STEN. Yes, my fellow citizens, I am engaged to Madam Rundholmen!

FIEL. To Madam Rundholmen!

CHAM. The storekeeper's widow!

LUN. H'm. Indeed!

CHAM. How could you?

STEN. A maneuver, Mr Bratsberg!

LUN. He has rare abilities!

ASL. [*looks in at the door, back*]. I humbly beg pardon——

CHAM. Oh, come in, Aslaksen! A visit of congratulation, eh?

ASL. Oh, not at all. But I have something very important to say to Mr Stensgard.

STEN. Another time; you can wait.

ASL. No, I must tell you——

STEN. Hold your tongue! What intrusiveness is this? Yes, gentlemen, strange are the ways of destiny. The district and I required a bond that should bind us firmly together, and I found on my path a woman of ripened character who could make a home for me. I have put off the adventurer, gentlemen, and here I stand in your midst as one of yourselves. Take me; I am ready to stand or fall in any post your confidence may assign me.

LUN. You have won.

CHAM. Well, really, I must say—— [*To the* MAID, *who has entered from the back.*] What are you giggling about?

THE SERVANT. Madam Rundholmen——

THE COMPANY. Madam Rundholmen?

CHAM. What about her?

THE SERVANT. Madam Rundholmen is waiting outside with her young man.

THE COMPANY [*to each other*]. Her young man? Madam Rundholmen! How's this?

STEN. What nonsense!

ASL. Yes, I was just telling you——

CHAM. [*at the door*]. Come along! [BASTIAN MONSEN, *with* MADAM RUNDHOLMEN *on his arm, enters from the back. A general movement.*]

MADAM. I hope I am not intruding, sir.

CHAM. Not at all, not at all.

MADAM. But I couldn't resist bringing up my young man to show him to you and Miss Bratsberg.

CHAM. Yes, I hear you are engaged, but——

THORA. We didn't know——

STEN. [*to* ASLAKSEN]. How is all this?

ASL. I had so much in my head yesterday, so much to think about, I mean——

STEN. But I gave her my letter, and——

ASL. No, you gave her Bastian Monsen's; here is yours.

STEN. Bastian's? And here—— [*Glances at the address, crumples the letter together and crams it into his pocket.*] Oh, curse you for a blunderer!

MADAM. Of course I was willing enough. There's no trusting the menfolk, I know; but when you have it in black and white that their intentions are honorable—— Why, there's Mr Stensgard, I declare! Well, Mr Stensgard, won't you congratulate me?

HEIRE [*to* LUNDESTAD]. How hungrily she glares at him!

CHAM. Of course he will, Madam Rundholmen; but won't you congratulate your sister-in-law to be?

MADAM. Who?

THORA. Ragna; she is engaged too.

BAS. Are you, Ragna?

MADAM. Indeed? Yes, Bastian told me there was something in the wind. I wish you both joy, and welcome into the family, Mr Stensgard!

FIEL. No, no; not Stensgard!

CHAM. No, it's Mr Helle. And you may congratulate my daughter too.

MADAM. Ah, so Lundestad was right after ali. I congratulate you, Miss Thora; and you too, Mr Stensgard.

FIEL. You mean Doctor Fieldbo.

MADAM. What?

FIEL. I am the happy man.

MADAM. Well, now, I don't in the least know where I am.

CHAM. And we have just found out where we are.

STEN. I have an appointment——

CHAM. [*aside*]. Lundestad, what was the other word?

LUN. What other?

CHAM. Not adventurer, but the other?

LUN. Demagogue.

STEN. I take my leave.

CHAM. One word–only one word, Mr Stensgard–a word which has long been on the tip of my tongue.

STEN. [*at the door*]. Excuse me; I'm in a hurry.

CHAM. [*following him*]. Demagogue!

STEN. Good-by, good-by! [*Goes out by the back.*]

CHAM. [*coming forward again*]. Now the air is pure again, my friends.

BAS. I hope you don't blame me, sir, for what has happened at home?

CHAM. Everyone must bear his own burden.

BAS. I had really no part in it.

SEL. [*who du·ing the preceding scene has been listening at the second door on the right*]. Father! May he come now?

CHAM. Selma! You plead for him? After what happened two days ago?

SEL. Oh, two days are a long time. I know now that he can go astray.

CHAM. And that pleases you?

SEL. Yes, that he can; but in future I won't let him.

CHAM. Bring him in then.

[SELMA *goes out again to the right.*]

RIN. [*enters by the foremost door on the right*]. Here is your resignation.

CHAM. You can tear it up.

RIN. Tear it up?

CHAM. Yes, Ringdal; I have found

another way. I can make atonement without that; I shall set to work in earnest.

Erik [*enters with* Selma *from the right*]. Can you forgive me?

Cham. [*hands him the bill*]. I can not be less merciful than fate.

Erik. Father! I shall retire this very day from the business you dislike so much.

Cham. No indeed; you must stick to it. But I will stand at your side. [*Loudly.*] News for you, gentlemen! I have entered into partnership with my son.

Several Gentlemen. You, Chamberlain?

Heire. You, my dear sir?

Cham. Yes, it is a useful and honorable calling, or at any rate it can be made so.

Lun. Well, I'll tell you what, Chamberlain–since you are going to set to work for the good of the district, it would be a shame and disgrace if an old soldier like me were to sulk in his tent.

Erik. Ah, what is this?

Lun. I cannot, in fact. After the disappointments in love that have befallen Mr Stensgard today, heaven forbid we should force the poor fellow into the political mill. He must rest and recover; a change of air is what he wants, and I shall see that he gets it.

The Gentlemen [*shaking hands with him enthusiastically*]. Thanks, Lundestad! That's a good fellow! You won't fail us!

Cham. Now this is as it should be; things are settling down again. But whom have we to thank for all this?

Fiel. Come, Aslaksen, you can explain.

Asl. [*alarmed*]. I, Doctor?

Fiel. What about that letter, then?

Asl. It wasn't my fault, I tell you! It was the election and Bastian Monsen and chance and destiny and Madam Rundholmen's punch–and there was I, with the whole responsibility of the press upon me––

Cham. [*approaching*]. What? What's that?

Asl. The press, sir.

Cham. The press! That's just it! Haven't I always said that the press has marvelous influence these days?

Asl. Oh, Chamberlain––

Cham. No false modesty, Mr Aslaksen! I haven't hitherto been in the habit of reading your paper, but henceforth I will. I shall subscribe for ten copies.

Asl. Oh, you can have twenty, Chamberlain!

Cham. Very well, then, let me have twenty. And if you need money, come to me; I mean to support the press.

Rin. What's this I hear? Your daughter engaged?

Cham. Yes; what do you say to that?

Rin. I am delighted! But when was it arranged?

Fiel. [*quickly*]. I'll tell you later.

Cham. Why, it was arranged on the Seventeenth of May.

Fiel. What?

Cham. The day little Miss Ragna was here.

Thora. Father, Father, did you know?

Cham. Yes, my dear, I have known all along.

Fiel. Oh, Chamberlain!

Thora. Who can have––

Cham. Another time I should advise you young ladies not to talk so loud when I am taking my siesta in the bay window.

THORA. You were behind the curtains?

FIEL. Now I understand!

CHAM. Yes, you are the one to keep your own counsel.

FIEL. Would it have been of any use for me to speak earlier?

CHAM. You are right, Fieldbo. These days have taught me a lesson.

THORA [*aside to* FIELDBO]. Yes, you can keep your own counsel. All this about Mr Stensgard—why did you tell me nothing?

FIEL. When a hawk is hovering over the dovecote one watches and shields his little dove—one does not alarm her.

[*They are interrupted by* MADAM RUNDHOLMEN.]

HEIRE [*to the* CHAMBERLAIN]. I am sorry to tell you, Chamberlain, that the settlement of our little legal differences will have to be adjourned indefinitely.

CHAM. Indeed! Why so?

HEIRE. You must know I've accepted a post as society editor on Aslaksen's paper.

CHAM. I am glad to hear it.

HEIRE. And of course you'll understand—with so much business on hand——

MADAM [*to* THORA]. Yes, I can tell you he's cost me many a tear, that bad man. But now I thank the Lord for Bastian. The other was false as the sea foam; and then he's a terrible smoker, Miss Bratsberg, and frightfully particular about his meals.

A SERVANT [*enters from the left*]. Dinner is on the table.

CHAM. Come along, then, all of you. Mr Lundestad, you shall sit beside me, and you too, Mr Aslaksen.

RIN. We shall have a lot of toasts to drink after dinner.

HEIRE. Yes, and perhaps an old man may be allowed to put in a claim for the toast of "absent friends."

LUN. One absent friend will return, Mr Heire.

HEIRE. Stensgard?

LUN. Yes; you'll see, gentlemen! In ten or fifteen years Stensgard will either be in Parliament or in the Ministry—perhaps in both at once.

FIEL. In ten or fifteen years? Perhaps; but then he can scarcely stand at the head of the League of Youth.

HEIRE. Why not?

FIEL. Why, because by that time his youth will be—questionable.

HEIRE. Then he can stand at the head of the Questionable League, sir. That's what Lundestad means. He says, like Napoleon: "It's the questionable people that make politicians"; hee-hee!

FIEL. Well, after all is said and done, our league shall last through young days and questionable days as well, and it shall continue to be the League of Youth. When Stensgard founded his league and was carried shoulder high amid all the enthusiasm of Independence Day he said: "Providence is on the side of the League of Youth." I think even Mr Helle, theologian as he is, will let us apply that saying to ourselves.

CHAM. I think so too, my friends; for truly we have been groping and stumbling in darkness, but good angels guided us.

LUN. Oh, for that matter, I think the angels were only middling.

ASL. Yes; that comes of the local situation, Mr Lundestad.

THE WILD DUCK

PERSONS OF THE PLAY

WERLE, *a merchant.*
GREGERS WERLE, *his son.*
OLD EKDAL.
HIALMAR EKDAL, *his son, a photographer.*
GINA EKDAL, *Hialmer's wife.*
HEDVIG, *their daughter, a girl of fourteen.*
MRS SORBY, *Werle's housekeeper.*
RELLING, *a doctor.*
MOLVIK, *a student of theology.*
GRABERG, *Werle's bookkeeper.*
PETTERSEN, *Werle's servant.*
JENSEN, *a hired waiter.*
A FLABBY GENTLEMAN.
A THIN-HAIRED GENTLEMAN.
A SHORTSIGHTED GENTLEMAN.
SIX OTHER GENTLEMEN, *guests at Werle's dinner party.*
SEVERAL HIRED WAITERS.

The action takes place in the home of Werle and the studio of Hialmar Ekdal.

ACT I

SCENE—*At* WERLE'S *house. A richly and comfortably furnished study; bookcases and upholstered furniture; a writing table, with papers and documents, in the center of the room; lighted lamps with green shades, giving a subdued light. At the back open folding doors with curtains drawn back. Within is seen a large and handsome room, brilliantly lighted with lamps and branching candlesticks. In front, on the right (in the study), a small baize door leads into* WERLE'S *office. On the left, in front, a fireplace with a glowing coal fire and farther back a double door leading into the dining room.*

WERLE'S *servant,* PETTERSEN, *in livery, and* JENSEN, *the hired waiter, in black, are putting the study in order. In the large room two or three other hired waiters are moving about arranging things and lighting more candles. From the dining room the hum of conversation and laughter of many voices are heard; a glass is tapped with a knife; silence follows, and a toast is proposed; shouts of "Bravo!" and then again a buzz of conversation.*

PET. [*lights a lamp on the chimney place and places a shade over it*]. Hark to them, Jensen! Now the old man's on his legs holding a long palaver about Mrs Sorby.

JEN. [*pushing forward an armchair*]. Is it true, what folks say, that they're—very good friends, eh?

PET. Lord knows.

JEN. I've heard tell as he's been a lively customer in his day.

PET. May be.

JEN. And he's giving this spread in honor of his son, they say.

PET. Yes. His son came home yesterday.

JEN. This is the first time I ever heard as Mr Werle had a son.

PET. Oh yes, he has a son right enough. But he's a fixture, as you might say, up at the Höidal works. He's never once come to town all the years I've been in service here.

A WAITER [*in the doorway of the other room*]. Pettersen, here's an old fellow wanting——

PET. [*mutters*]. The devil—who's this now?

[OLD EKDAL *appears from the right, in the inner room. He is dressed in a threadbare overcoat with a high collar; he wears woolen mittens and carries in his hand a stick and a fur cap. Under his arm a brown paper parcel. Dirty red-brown wig and small gray mustache.*]

PET. [*goes toward him*]. Good lord!—what do you want here?

EKD. [*in the doorway*]. Must get into the office, Pettersen.

PET. The office was closed an hour ago, and——

EKD. So they told me at the front door. But Graberg's in there still. Let me slip in this way, Pettersen; there's a good fellow. [*Points toward the baize door.*] It's not the first time I've come this way.

PET. Well, you may pass. [*Opens the door.*] But mind you go out again the proper way, for we've got company.

EKD. I know, I know—h'm! Thanks, Pettersen, good old friend! Thanks! [*Mutters softly.*] Ass! [*He goes into the office;* PETTERSEN *shuts the door after him.*]

JEN. Is he one of the office people?

PET. No, he's only an outside hand that does odd jobs of copying. But he's been a tiptopper in his day, has old Ekdal.

JEN. You can see he's been through a lot.

PET. Yes; he was an army officer, you know.

JEN. You don't say so?

PET. No mistake about it. But then he went into the timber trade or something of the sort. They say he once played Mr Werle a very nasty trick. They were partners in the Höidal works at the time. Oh, I know old Ekdal well, I do. Many a nip of bitters and bottle of ale we two have drunk at Madam Eriksen's.

JEN. He don't look as if he'd much to stand treat with.

PET. Why, bless you, Jensen, it's me that stands treat. I always think there's no harm in being a bit civil to folks that have seen better days.

JEN. Did he go bankrupt then?

PET. Worse than that. He went to prison.

JEN. To prison!

PET. Or perhaps it was the penitentiary. [*Listens.*] Sh! They're leaving the table.

[*The dining-room door is thrown open from within by a couple of waiters.* MRS SORBY *comes out conversing with two gentlemen. Gradually the whole company follows, amongst them* WERLE. *Last come* HIALMAR EKDAL *and* GREGERS WERLE.]

MRS S. [*in passing, to the servant*]. Tell them to serve the coffee in the music room, Pettersen.

PET. Very well, madam.

[*She goes with the two gentlemen into the inner room and thence out to the right.* PETTERSEN *and* JENSEN *go out the same way.*]

A FLABBY GENTLEMAN [*to a* THIN-HAIRED GENTLEMAN]. Whew! What a dinner! It was no joke to do it justice.

THE THIN-HAIRED GENTLEMAN. Oh, with a little good will one can get through a lot in three hours.

THE FLABBY GENTLEMAN. Yes, but afterward, afterward, my dear Chamberlain!

A THIRD GENTLEMAN. I hear the coffee and maraschino are to be served in the music room.

THE FLABBY GENTLEMAN. Bravo! Then perhaps Mrs Sorby will play us something.

THE THIN-HAIRED GENTLEMAN [*in a low voice*]. I hope Mrs Sorby mayn't play us a tune we don't like, one of these days!

THE FLABBY GENTLEMAN. Oh no, not she! Bertha will never turn against her old friends.

[*They laugh and pass into the inner room.*]

WER. [*in a low voice, dejectedly*]. I don't think anybody noticed it, Gregers.

GREG. [*looks at him*]. Noticed what?

WER. Did you not notice it either?

GREG. What do you mean?

WER. We were thirteen at table.

GREG. Indeed? Were there thirteen of us?

WER. [*glances toward* HIALMAR EKDAL]. Our usual party is twelve. [*To the others.*] This way, gentlemen!

[WERLE *and the others, all except* HIALMAR *and* GREGERS, *go out by the back, to the right.*]

HIAL. [*who has overheard the conversation*]. You ought not to have invited me, Gregers.

GREG. What! Not ask my best and only friend to a party supposed to be in my honor?

HIAL. But I don't think your father likes it. You see, I am quite outside his circle.

GREG. So I hear. But I wanted to see you and have a talk with you, and I certainly shan't be staying long. Ah, we two old schoolfellows have drifted apart from each other. It must be sixteen or seventeen years since we met.

HIAL. Is it so long?

GREG. It is indeed. Well, how goes it with you? You look well. You have put on flesh and grown almost stout.

HIAL. Well, "stout" is scarcely the word, but I daresay I look a little more of a man than I used to.

GREG. Yes, you do; your outer man is in first-rate condition.

HIAL. [*in a tone of gloom*]. Ah, but the inner man! That is a very different matter, I can tell you! Of course you know of the terrible catastrophe that has befallen me and mine since last we met.

GREG. [*more softly*]. How are things going with your father now?

HIAL. Don't let us talk of it, old fellow. Of course my poor unhappy father lives with me. He hasn't another soul in the world to care for him. But you can understand that this is a miserable subject for me. Tell me, rather, how you have been getting on up at the works.

GREG. I have had a delightfully lonely time of it—plenty of leisure to think and think about things. Come over here; we may as well make ourselves comfortable. [*He seats himself in an armchair by the fire and draws* HIALMAR *down into another alongside of it.*]

HIAL. [*sentimentally*]. After all, Gregers, I thank you for inviting me to your father's table; for I take it as a sign that you have got over your feeling against me.

GREG. [*surprised*]. How could you imagine I had any feeling against you?

HIAL. You had at first, you know.

GREG. How at first?

HIAL. After the great misfortune. It was natural enough that you should. Your father was within an ace of being drawn into that—well, that terrible business.

GREG. Why should that give me any feeling against you? Who can have put that into your head?

HIAL. I know it did, Gregers; your father told me so himself.

GREG. [*starts*]. My father! Oh, indeed. H'm. Was that why you never let me hear from you?—not a single word.

HIAL. Yes.

GREG. Not even when you made up your mind to become a photographer?

HIAL. Your father said I had better not write to you at all, about anything.

GREG. [*looking straight before him*]. Well, well, perhaps he was right. But tell me now, Hialmar: are you pretty well satisfied with your present position?

HIAL. [*with a little sigh*]. Oh yes, I am; I have really no cause to complain. At first, as you may guess, I felt it a little strange. It was such a totally new state of things for me. But of course my whole circumstances were totally changed. Father's utter, irretrievable ruin—the shame and disgrace of it, Gregers——

GREG. [*affected*]. Yes, yes; I understand.

HIAL. I couldn't think of remaining at college; there wasn't a shilling to spare; on the contrary, there were debts—mainly to your father, I believe——

GREG. H'm.

HIAL. In short, I thought it best to break, once for all, with my old surroundings and associations. It was your father that specially urged me to it, and since he interested himself so much in me——

GREG. My father did?

HIAL. Yes, you surely knew that, didn't you? Where do you suppose I found the money to learn photography and to furnish a studio and make a start? All that costs a pretty penny, I can tell you.

GREG. And my father provided the money?

HIAL. Yes, my dear fellow, didn't you know? I understood him to say he had written to you about it.

GREG. Not a word about his part in the business. He must have forgotten it. Our correspondence has always been purely a business one So it was my father that——

HIAL. Yes, certainly. He didn't wish it to be generally known, but he it was. And of course it was he, too, that put me in a position to marry. Don't you—don't you know about that either?

GREG. No, I haven't heard a word of it. [*Shakes him by the arm.*] But, my dear Hialmar, I can't tell you what pleasure all this gives me—pleasure and self-reproach. I have perhaps done my father injustice after all—in some things. This proves that he has a heart. It shows a sort of compunction——

HIAL. Compunction?

GREG. Yes, yes—whatever you like to call it. Oh, I can't tell you how glad I am to hear this of Father. So you are a married man, Hialmar! That is further than I shall ever get. Well, I hope you are happy in your married life?

HIAL. Yes, thoroughly happy. She is as good and capable a wife as any man could wish for. And she is by no means without culture.

GREG. [*rather surprised*]. No, of course not.

HIAL. You see, life is itself an education. Her daily intercourse with me—— And then we know one or two rather remarkable men who come a good deal about us. I assure you, you would hardly know Gina again.

GREG. Gina?

HIAL. Yes; had you forgotten that her name was Gina?

GREG. Whose name? I haven't the slightest idea——

HIAL. Don't you remember that she used to be in service here?

GREG. [*looks at him*]. Is it Gina Hansen?

HIAL. Yes, of course it is Gina Hansen.

GREG. —who kept house for us during the last year of my mother's illness?

HIAL. Yes, exactly. But, my dear friend, I'm quite sure your father told you that I was married.

GREG. [*who has risen*]. Oh yes, he mentioned it, but not that—— [*Walking about the room.*] Stay—perhaps he did—now that I think of it. My father always writes such short letters. [*Half seats himself on the arm of the chair.*] Now tell me, Hialmar—this is interesting—how did you come to know Gina—your wife?

HIAL. The simplest thing in the world. You know Gina did not stay here long; everything was so much upset at that time, owing to your mother's illness and so forth, that Gina was not equal to it all; so she gave notice and left. That was the year before your mother died—or it may have been the same year.

GREG. It was the same year. I was up at the works then. But afterward?

HIAL. Well, Gina lived at home with her mother, Madam Hansen, an excellent, hard-working woman who kept a little eating house. She had a room to let too, a very nice comfortable room.

GREG. And I suppose you were lucky enough to secure it?

HIAL. Yes; in fact, it was your father that recommended it to me. So it was there, you see, that I really came to know Gina.

GREG. And then you got engaged?

HIAL. Yes. It doesn't take young people long to fall in love—h'm.

GREG. [*rises and moves about a little*]. Tell me: was it after your engagement—was it then that my father—I mean was it then that you began to take up photography?

HIAL. Yes, precisely. I wanted to make a start and to set up house as soon as possible, and your father and I agreed that this photography business was the readiest way. Gina thought so too. Oh, and there was another thing in its favor, by the bye; it happened, luckily, that Gina had learned to retouch.

GREG. That chimed in marvelously.

HIAL. [*pleased, rises*]. Yes, didn't it? Don't you think it was a marvelous piece of luck?

GREG. Oh, unquestionably. My father seems to have been almost a kind of providence to you.

HIAL. [*with emotion*]. He did not forsake his old friend's son in the hour of his need. For he has a heart, you see.

MRS S. [*enters arm in arm with* WERLE]. Nonsense, my dear Mr Werle; you mustn't stop there any longer staring at all the lights. It's very bad for you.

WER. [*lets go her arm and passes his hand over his eyes*]. I daresay you are right.

[PETTERSEN *and* JENSEN *carry round refreshment trays.*]

MRS S. [*to the guests in the other room*]. This way, if you please, gentlemen. Whoever wants a glass of punch must be so good as to come in here.

THE FLABBY GENTLEMAN [*comes up to* MRS SORBY]. Surely it isn't possible that you have suspended our cherished right to smoke?

MRS S. Yes. No smoking here, in Mr Werle's sanctum, Chamberlain.

THE THIN-HAIRED GENTLEMAN. When did you enact these stringent amendments on the cigar law, Mrs Sorby?

MRS S. After the last dinner, Chamberlain, when certain persons permitted themselves to overstep the mark.

THE THIN-HAIRED GENTLEMAN. And may one never overstep the mark a little bit, Madame Bertha? Not the least little bit?

MRS S. Not in any respect whatsoever, Mr Balle.

[*Most of the guests have assembled in the study; servants hand round glasses of punch.*]

WER. [*to* HIALMAR, *who is studying beside a table*]. What are you studying so intently, Ekdal?

HIAL. Only an album, Mr Werle.

THE THIN-HAIRED GENTLEMAN [*who is wandering about*]. Ah, photographs! They are quite in your line, of course.

THE FLABBY GENTLEMAN [*in an armchair*]. Haven't you brought any of your own with you?

HIAL. No, I haven't.

THE FLABBY GENTLEMAN. You ought to have; it's very good for the digestion to sit and look at pictures.

THE THIN-HAIRED GENTLEMAN. And it contributes to the entertainment, you know.

THE SHORTSIGHTED GENTLEMAN. And all contributions are thankfully received.

MRS S. The chamberlains think that when one is invited out to dinner one ought to exert oneself a little in return, Mr Ekdal.

THE FLABBY GENTLEMAN. Where one dines so well, that duty becomes a pleasure.

THE THIN-HAIRED GENTLEMAN. And when it's a case of the struggle for existence, you know——

MRS S. I quite agree with you!

[*They continue the conversation with laughter and joking.*]

GREG. [*softly*]. You must join in, Hialmar.

HIAL. [*writhing*]. What am I to talk about?

THE FLABBY GENTLEMAN. Don't you think, Mr Werle, that Tokay may be considered one of the more wholesome sorts of wine?

WER. [*by the fire*]. I can answer for the Tokay you had today, at any rate; it's one of the very finest seasons. Of course you would notice that.

THE FLABBY GENTLEMAN. Yes, it had a remarkably delicate flavor.

HIAL. [*shyly*]. Is there any difference between the seasons?

THE FLABBY GENTLEMAN [*laughs*]. Come! That's good!

WER. [*smiles*]. It really doesn't pay to set fine wine before you.

THE THIN-HAIRED GENTLEMAN. Tokay is like photographs, Mr Ekdal; they both need sunshine. Am I not right?

HIAL. Yes, light is important, no doubt.

MRS S. And it's exactly the same with the chamberlains—they, too, depend very much on sunshine, as the saying is.

THE THIN-HAIRED GENTLEMAN. Oh, fie! That's a very threadbare sarcasm!

THE SHORTSIGHTED GENTLEMAN. Mrs Sorby is coming out——

THE FLABBY GENTLEMAN. —and at our expense too. [*Holds up his finger reprovingly.*] Oh, Madame Bertha, Madame Bertha!

MRS S. Yes, and there's not the least doubt that the seasons differ greatly. The old vintages are the finest.

THE SHORTSIGHTED GENTLEMAN. Do you reckon me among the old vintages?

MRS S. Oh, far from it.

THE THIN-HAIRED GENTLEMAN. There now! But me, dear Mrs Sorby——

THE FLABBY GENTLEMAN. Yes, and me? What vintage should you say that we belong to?

MRS S. Why, to the sweet vintages, gentlemen. [*She sips a glass of punch. The gentlemen laugh and flirt with her.*]

WER. Mrs Sorby can always find a loophole—when she wants to. Fill your glasses, gentlemen! Pettersen, will you see to it? Gregers, suppose we have a glass together. [GREGERS *does not move.*] Won't you join us, Ekdal? I found no opportunity of drinking with you at table.

[GRABERG, *the bookkeeper, looks in at the baize door.*]

GRAB. Excuse me, sir, but I can't get out.

WER. Have you been locked in again?

GRAB. Yes, and Flakstad has carried off the keys.

WER. Well, you can pass out this way.

GRAB. But there's someone else——

WER. All right; come through, both of you. Don't be afraid.

[GRABERG *and* OLD EKDAL *come out of the office.*]

WER. [*involuntarily*]. Ugh!

[*The laughter and talk among the guests cease.* HIALMAR *starts at the sight of his father, puts down his glass and turns toward the fireplace.*]

EKD. [*does not look up but makes little bows to both sides as he passes, murmuring*]. Beg pardon, come the wrong way. Door locked—door locked. Beg pardon. [*He and* GRABERG *go out by the back, to the right.*]

WER. [*between his teeth*]. That idiot Graberg.

GREG. [*open-mouthed and staring, to* HIALMAR]. Why, surely that wasn't——

THE FLABBY GENTLEMAN. What's the matter? Who was it?

GREG. Oh, nobody; only the bookkeeper and someone with him.

THE SHORTSIGHTED GENTLEMAN [*to*

HIALMAR]. Did you know that man?

HIAL. I don't know—I didn't notice——

THE FLABBY GENTLEMAN. What the deuce has come over everyone? [*He joins another group who are talking softly.*]

MRS S. [*whispers to the servant*]. Give him something to take with him —something good, mind.

PET. [*nods*]. I'll see to it. [*Goes out.*]

GREG. [*softly and with emotion, to* HIALMAR]. So that was really he!

HIAL. Yes.

GREG. And you could stand there and deny that you knew him!

HIAL. [*whispers vehemently*]. But how could I——

GREG. —acknowledge your own father?

HIAL. [*with pain*]. Oh, if you were in my place——

[*The conversation amongst the guests, which has been carried on in a low tone, now swells into constrained joviality.*]

THE THIN-HAIRED GENTLEMAN [*approaching* HIALMAR *and* GREGERS *in a friendly manner*]. Ah! Reviving old college memories, eh? Don't you smoke, Mr Ekdal? May I give you a light? Oh, by the bye, we mustn't——

HIAL. No, thank you, I won't——

THE FLABBY GENTLEMAN. Haven't you a nice little poem you could recite to us, Mr Ekdal? You used to recite so charmingly.

HIALMAR. I am sorry, I can't remember anything.

THE FLABBY GENTLEMAN. Oh, that's a pity. Well, what shall we do, Balle?

[*Both gentlemen move away and pass into the other room.*]

HIAL. [*gloomily*]. Gregers—I am going! When a man has felt the crushing hand of Fate, you see—— Say good-by to your father for me.

GREG. Yes, yes. Are you going straight home?

HIAL. Yes. Why?

GREG. Oh, because I may perhaps look in on you later.

HIAL. No, you mustn't do that. You must not come to my home. Mine is a melancholy abode, Gregers; especially after a splendid banquet like this. We can always arrange to meet somewhere in the town.

MRS S. [*who has quietly approached*]. Are you going, Ekdal?

HIAL. Yes.

MRS S. Remember me to Gina.

HIAL. Thanks.

MRS S. And say I am coming up to see her one of these days.

HIAL. Yes, thank you. [*To* GREGERS.] Stay here; I will slip out unobserved. [*He saunters away, then into the other room and so out to the right.*]

MRS S. [*softly to the* SERVANT, *who has come back*]. Well, did you give the old man something?

PET. Yes; I sent him off with a bottle of cognac.

MRS S. Oh, you might have thought of something better than that.

PET. Oh no, Mrs Sorby; cognac is what he likes best in the world.

THE FLABBY GENTLEMAN [*in the doorway with a sheet of music in his hand*]. Shall we play a duet, Mrs Sorby?

MRS S. Yes, suppose we do.

THE GUESTS. Bravo, bravo!

[*She goes with all the guests through the back room out to the right.* GREGERS *remains standing by the fire.* WERLE *is looking for something on the writing table and appears to wish that* GREGERS *would go; as*

GREGERS *does not move* WERLE *goes toward the door.*]

GREG. Father, won't you stay a moment?

WER. [*stops*]. What is it?

GREG. I must have a word with you.

WER. Can it not wait until we are alone?

GREG. No, it cannot, for perhaps we shall never be alone together.

WER. [*drawing nearer*]. What do you mean by that?

[*During what follows the pianoforte is faintly heard from the distant music room.*]

GREG. How has that family been allowed to go so miserably to the wall?

WER. You mean the Ekdals, I suppose.

GREG. Yes, I mean the Ekdals. Lieutenant Ekdal was once so closely associated with you.

WER. Much too closely; I have felt that to my cost for many a year. It is thanks to him that I—yes *I*—have had a kind of slur cast upon my reputation.

GREG. [*softly*]. Are you sure that he alone was to blame?

WER. Who else do you suppose?

GREG. You and he acted together in that affair of the forests——

WER. But was it not Ekdal that drew the map of the tracts we had bought—that fraudulent map! It was he who felled all that timber illegally on government ground. In fact, the whole management was in his hands. I was quite in the dark as to what Lieutenant Ekdal was doing.

GREG. Lieutenant Ekdal himself seems to have been very much in the dark as to what he was doing.

WER. That may be. But the fact remains that he was found guilty and I acquitted.

GREG. Yes, I know that nothing was proved against you.

WER. Acquittal is acquittal. Why do you rake up these old miseries that turned my hair gray before its time? Is that the sort of thing you have been brooding over up there, all these years? I can assure you, Gregers, here in the town the whole story has been forgotten long ago—as far as *I* am concerned.

GREG. But that unhappy Ekdal family——

WER. What would you have me do for the people? When Ekdal came out of prison he was a broken-down being, past all help. There are people in the world who dive to the bottom the moment they get a couple of slugs in their body and never come to the surface again. You may take my word for it, Gregers, I have done all I could without positively laying myself open to all sorts of suspicion and gossip.

GREG. Suspicion? Oh, I see.

WER. I have given Ekdal copying to do for the office, and I pay him far, far more for it than his work is worth.

GREG. [*without looking at him*]. H'm; that I don't doubt.

WER. You laugh? Do you think I am not telling you the truth? Well, I certainly can't refer you to my books, for I never enter payments of that sort.

GREG. [*smiles coldly*]. No, there are certain payments it is best to keep no account of.

WER. [*taken aback*]. What do you mean by that?

GREG. [*mustering up courage*]. Have you entered what it cost you to have Hialmar Ekdal taught photography?

WER. I? How "entered" it?

GREG. I have learned that it was you who paid for his training. And I have learned, too, that it was you who enabled him to set up house so comfortably.

WER. Well, and yet you talk as though I had done nothing for the Ekdals! I can assure you these people have cost me enough in all conscience.

GREG. Have you entered any of these expenses in your books?

WER. Why do you ask?

GREG. Oh, I have my reasons. Now tell me: when you interested yourself so warmly in your old friend's son—it was just before his marriage, was it not?

WER. Why, deuce take it—after all these years how can I——

GREG. You wrote me a letter about that time—a business letter, of course—and in a postscript you mentioned—quite briefly—that Hialmar Ekdal had married a Miss Hansen.

WER. Yes, that was quite right. That was her name.

GREG. But you did not mention that this Miss Hansen was Gina Hansen—our former housekeeper.

WER. [*with a forced laugh of derision*]. No; to tell the truth, it didn't occur to me that you were so particularly interested in our former housekeeper.

GREG. No more I was. But [*lowers his voice*] there were others in this house who were particularly interested in her.

WER. What do you mean by that? [*Flaring up.*] You are not alluding to me, I hope?

GREG. [*softly but firmly*]. Yes, I am alluding to you.

WER. And you dare—— You presume to—— How can that ungrateful hound—that photographer fellow—how dare he go making such insinuations!

GREG. Hialmar has never breathed a word about this. I don't believe he has the faintest suspicion of such a thing.

WER. Then where have you got it from? Who can have put such notions in your head?

GREG. My poor unhappy mother told me, and that the very last time I saw her.

WER. Your mother! I might have known as much! You and she—you always held together. It was she who turned you against me from the first.

GREG. No, it was all that she had to suffer and submit to, until she broke down and came to such a pitiful end.

WER. Oh, she had nothing to suffer or submit to; not more than most people, at all events. But there's no getting on with morbid, overstrained creatures—that I have learned to my cost. And you could go on nursing such a suspicion—burrowing into all sorts of slanders against your own father! I must say, Gregers, I really think at your age you might find something more useful to do.

GREG. Yes, it is high time.

WER. Then perhaps your mind would be easier than it seems to be now. What can be your object in remaining up at the works year out and year in, drudging away like a common clerk and not drawing a farthing more than the ordinary monthly wage? It is downright folly.

GREG. Ah, if I were only sure of that.

WER. I understand you well enough. You want to be independent; you won't be beholden to me for anything. Well, now there happens to be an opportunity for you to become independent, your own master in everything.

GREG. Indeed? In what way?

WER. When I wrote you insisting on your coming to town at once—h'm——

GREG. Yes, what is it you really want of me? I have been waiting all day to know.

WER. I want to propose that you should enter the firm as partner.

GREG. I! Join your firm? As partner?

WER. Yes. It would not involve our being constantly together. You could take over the business here in town, and I should move up to the works.

GREG. You would?

WER. The fact is, I am not so fit for work as I once was. I am obliged to spare my eyes, Gregers; they have begun to trouble me.

GREG. They have always been weak.

WER. Not as they are now. And besides, circumstances might possibly make it desirable for me to live up there—for a time, at any rate.

GREG. That is certainly quite a new idea to me.

WER. Listen, Gregers, there are many things that stand between us; but we are father and son after all. We ought surely to be able to come to some sort of understanding with each other.

GREG. Outwardly, you mean, of course?

WER. Well, even that would be something. Think it over, Gregers. Don't you think it ought to be possible? Eh?

GREG. [*looking at him coldly*]. There is something behind all this.

WER. How so?

GREG. You want to make use of me in some way.

WER. In such a close relationship as ours the one can always be useful to the other.

GREG. Yes, so people say.

WER. I want very much to have you at home with me for a time. I am a lonely man, Gregers; I have always felt lonely all my life through, but most of all now that I am getting up in years. I feel the need of someone about me——

GREG. You have Mrs Sorby.

WER. Yes, I have her, and she has become, I may say, almost indispensable to me. She is lively and even tempered; she brightens up the house; and that is a very great thing for me.

GREG. Well, then, you have everything as you wish it.

WER. Yes, but I am afraid it can't last. A woman so situated may easily find herself in a false position in the eyes of the world. For that matter, it does a man no good either.

GREG. Oh, when a man gives such dinners as you give he can risk a great deal.

WER. Yes, but how about the woman, Gregers? I fear she won't accept the situation much longer, and even if she did—even if, out of attachment to me, she were to take her chance of gossip and scandal and all that—do you think, Gregers, you with your strong sense of justice——

GREG. [*interrupts him*]. Tell me in one word: are you thinking of marrying her?

WER. Suppose I were thinking of it? What then?

GREG. That's what I say: what then?

WER. Should you be inflexibly opposed to it?

GREG. Not at all. Not by any means.

WER. I was not sure whether your devotion to your mother's memory——

GREG. I am not overstrained.

WER. Well, whatever you may or not be, at all events you have lifted a great weight from my mind. I am extremely pleased that I can reckon on your concurrence in this matter.

GREG. [*looking intently at him*]. Now I see the use you want to put me to.

WER. Use to put you to? What an expression!

GREG. Oh, don't let us be nice in our choice of words—not when we are alone together, at any rate. [*With a short laugh.*] Well, well. So this is what made it absolutely essential that I should come to town in person. For the sake of Mrs Sorby we are to get up a pretense at family life in the house—a tableau of filial affection. That will be something new, indeed.

WER. How dare you speak in that tone!

GREG. Was there ever any family life here? Never since I can remember. But now, forsooth, your plans demand something of the sort. No doubt it will have an excellent effect when it is reported that the son has hastened home, on the wings of filial piety, to the gray-haired father's wedding feast. What will then remain of all the rumors as to the wrongs the poor dead mother had to submit to? Not a vestige. Her son annihilates them at one stroke.

WER. Gregers—I believe there is no one in the world you detest as you do me.

GREG. [*softly*]. I have seen you at too close quarters.

WER. You have seen me with your mother's eyes. [*Lowers his voice a little.*] But you should remember that her eyes were—clouded now and then.

GREG. [*quivering*]. I see what you are hinting at. But who was to blame for mother's unfortunate weakness? Why, you and all those—— The last of them was this woman that you palmed off upon Hialmar Ekdal when you were—— Ugh!

WER. [*shrugs his shoulders*]. Word for word as if it were your mother speaking!

GREG. [*without heeding*]. And there he is now, with his great, confiding childlike mind, compassed about with all this treachery—living under the same roof with such a creature and never dreaming that what he calls his home is built up on a lie! [*Comes a step nearer.*] When I look back upon your past I seem to see a battlefield with shattered lives on every hand.

WER. I begin to think that the chasm that divides us is too wide.

GREG. [*bowing with self-command*]. So I have observed, and therefore I take my hat and go.

WER. You are going? Out of the house?

GREG. Yes. For at last I see my mission in life.

WER. What mission?

GREG. You would only laugh if I told you.

WER. A lonely man doesn't laugh so easily, Gregers.

GREG. [*pointing toward the background*]. Look, Father—the chamberlains are playing blindman's buff with Mrs Sorby. Good night and good by. [*He goes out by the back to the right. Sound of laughter and merriment from the company, who are now visible in the outer room.*]

WER. [*muttering contemptuously after* GREGERS]. Ha! Poor wretch—and he says he is not overstrained!

ACT II

SCENE—HIALMAR EKDAL'S *studio, a good-sized room, evidently in the top story of the building. On the right a sloping roof of large panes of glass half covered by a blue curtain. In the right-hand corner, at the back, the entrance door; farther forward, on the same side, a door leading to the sitting room. Two doors on the opposite side and between them an iron stove. At the back a wide double sliding door. The studio is plainly but comfortably fitted up and furnished. Between the doors on the right, standing out a little from the wall, a sofa with a table and some chairs; on the table a lighted lamp with a shade; beside the stove an old armchair. Photographic instruments and apparatus of different kinds lying about the room. Against the back wall, to the left of the double door, stands a bookcase containing a few books, boxes and bottles of chemicals, instruments, tools and other objects. Photographs and small articles, such as camel's-hair pencils, paper and so forth, lie on the table.*

GINA EKDAL *sits on a chair by the table, sewing.* HEDVIG *is sitting on the sofa, with her hands shading her eyes and her thumbs in her ears, reading a book.*

GINA [*glances once or twice at* HEDVIG, *as if with secret anxiety, then says*]. Hedvig!

[HEDVIG *does not hear.*]

GINA [*repeats more loudly*]. Hedvig!

HED. [*takes away her hands and looks up*]. Yes, Mother?

GINA. Hedvig dear, you mustn't sit reading any longer now.

HED. Oh, Mother, mayn't I read a little more? Just a little bit?

GINA. No, no, you must put away your book now. Father doesn't like it; he never reads himself in the evening.

HED. [*shuts the book*]. No, Father doesn't care much about reading.

GINA [*puts aside her sewing and takes up a lead pencil and a little account book from the table*]. Can you remember how much we paid for the butter today?

HED. It was one crown sixty-five.

GINA. That's right. [*Puts it down.*] It's terrible what a lot of butter we get through in this house. Then there was the smoked sausage and the cheese—let me see [*writes*]—and the ham [*adds up*]. Yes, that makes just——

HED. And then the beer.

GINA. Yes, to be sure. [*Writes.*] How it do mount up! But we can't manage with no less.

HED. And then you and I didn't need anything hot for dinner, as Father was out.

GINA. No, that was so much to the good. And then I took eight crowns fifty for the photographs.

HED. Really! So much as that?

GINA. Exactly eight crowns fifty.

[*Silence.* GINA *takes up her sewing again;* HEDVIG *takes paper and pencil and begins to draw, shading her eyes with her left hand.*]

HED. Isn't it jolly to think that Father is at Mr Werle's big dinner party?

GINA. You know he's not really Mr Werle's guest. It was the son invited him. [*After a pause.*] We have nothing to do with that Mr Werle.

HED. I'm longing for Father to come home. He promised to ask Mrs Sorby for something nice for me.

GINA. Yes, there's plenty of good things going in that house, I can tell you.

HED. [*goes on drawing*]. And I believe I'm a little hungry too.

[OLD EKDAL, *with the paper parcel under his arm and another parcel in his coat pocket, comes in by the entrance door.*]

GINA. How late you are today, Grandfather!

EKD. They had locked the office door. Had to wait in Graberg's room. And then they let me through—h'm.

HED. Did you get some more copying to do, Grandfather?

EKD. This whole packet. Just look.

GINA. That's capital.

HED. And you have another parcel in your pocket.

EKD. Eh? Oh, never mind, that's nothing. [*Puts his stick away in a corner.*] This work will keep me going a long time, Gina. [*Opens one of the sliding doors in the back wall a little.*] Hush! [*Peeps into the room for a moment, then pushes the door carefully to again.*] Hee-hee! They're fast asleep, all the lot of them. And she's gone into the basket herself. Hee-hee!

HED. Are you sure she isn't cold in that basket, Grandfather?

EKD. Not a bit of it! Cold? With all that straw? [*Goes toward the farther door on the left.*] There are matches in here, I suppose.

GINA. The matches is on the drawers.

[EKDAL *goes into his room.*]

HED. It's nice that Grandfather has got all that copying.

GINA. Yes, poor old Father; it means a bit of pocket money for him.

HED. And he won't be able to sit the whole forenoon down at that horrid Madam Eriksen's.

GINA. No more he won't. [*Short silence.*]

HED. Do you suppose they are still at the dinner table?

GINA. Goodness knows; as like as not.

HED. Think of all the delicious things Father is having to eat! I'm certain he'll be in splendid spirits when he comes. Don't you think so, Mother?

GINA. Yes; and if only we could tell him that we'd got the room let——

HED. But we don't need that this evening.

GINA. Oh, we'd be none the worst of it, I can tell you. It's no use to us as it is.

HED. I mean we don't need it this evening, for Father will be in good humor at any rate. It is best to keep the letting of the room for another time.

GINA [*looks across at her*]. You like having some good news to tell Father when he comes home in the evening?

HED. Yes, for then things are pleasanter somehow.

GINA [*thinking to herself*]. Yes, yes, there's something in that.

[OLD EKDAL *comes in again and is going out by the foremost door to the left.*]

GINA [*half turning in her chair*]. Do you want something in the kitchen, Grandfather?

EKD. Yes, yes, I do. Don't you troublc. [*Goes out.*]

GINA. He's not poking away at the fire, is he? [*Waits a moment.*] Hedvig, go and see what he's about.

[EKDAL *comes in again with a small jug of steaming hot water.*]

HED. Have you been getting some hot water, Grandfather?

EKD. Yes, hot water. Want it for something. Want to write, and the ink has got as thick as porridge–h'm.

GINA. But you'd best have your supper first, Grandfather. It's laid in there.

EKD. Can't be bothered with supper, Gina. Very busy, I tell you. No one's to come to my room. No one–h'm. [*He goes into his room;* GINA *and* HEDVIG *look at each other.*]

GINA [*softly*]. Can you imagine where he's got money from?

HED. From Graberg, perhaps.

GINA. Not a bit of it. Graberg always sends the money to me.

HED. Then he must have got a bottle on credit somewhere.

GINA. Poor Grandfather, who'd give him credit?

[HIALMAR EKDAL, *in an overcoat and gray felt hat, comes in from the right.*]

GINA [*throws down her sewing and rises*]. Why, Ekdal, is that you already?

HED. [*at the same time jumping up*]. Fancy your coming so soon, Father!

HIAL. [*taking off his hat.*] Yes, most of the people were coming away.

HED. So early?

HIAL. Yes, it was a dinner party, you know. [*Takes off his overcoat.*]

GINA. Let me help you.

HED. Me too.

[*They draw off his coat;* GINA *hangs it up on the back wall.*]

HED. Were there many people there, Father?

HIAL. Oh no, not many. We had about twelve or fourteen at table.

GINA. And you had some talk with them all?

HIAL. Oh yes, a little; but Gregers took me up most of the time.

GINA. Is Gregers as ugly as ever?

HIAL. Well, he's not very much to look at. Hasn't the old man come home?

HED. Yes, Grandfather is in his room, writing.

HIAL. Did he say anything?

GINA. No, what should he say?

HIAL. Didn't he say anything about —— I heard something about his having been with Graberg. I'll go in and see him for a moment.

GINA. No, no, better not.

HIAL. Why not? Did he say he didn't want me to go in?

GINA. I don't think he wants to see nobody this evening.

HED. [*making signs*]. H'm–h'm!

GINA [*not noticing*]. He has been in to fetch hot water——

HIAL. Aha! Then he's——

GINA. Yes, I suppose so.

HIAL. Oh God! My poor old white-haired father! Well, well, there let him sit and get all the enjoyment he can.

[OLD EKDAL, *in an indoor coat and with a lighted pipe, comes from his room.*]

EKD. Got home? Thought it was you I heard talking.

HIAL. Yes, I have just come.

EKD. You didn't see me, did you?

HIAL. No, but they told me you had passed through–so I thought I would follow you.

EKD. H'm, good of you, Hialmar. Who were they, all those fellows?

HIAL. Oh, all sorts of people. There was Chamberlain Flor and Chamberlain Balle and Chamberlain Kaspersen and Chamberlain—this, that and the other—I don't know who all.

EKD. [*nodding*]. Hear that, Gina! Chamberlains every one of them!

GINA. Yes, I hear as they're terrible genteel in that house nowadays.

HED. Did the chamberlains sing, Father? Or did they read aloud?

HIAL. No, they only talked nonsense. They wanted me to recite something for them, but I knew better than that.

EKD. You weren't to be persuaded, eh?

GINA. Oh, you might have done it.

HIAL. No; one mustn't be at everybody's beck and call. [*Walks about the room.*] That's not my way, at any rate.

EKD. No, no; Hialmar's not to be had for the asking, he isn't.

HIAL. I don't see why I should bother myself to entertain people on the rare occasions when I go into society. Let the others exert themselves. These fellows go from one great dinner table to the next and gorge and guzzle day out and day in. It's for them to bestir themselves and do something in return for all the good feeding they get.

GINA. But you didn't say that?

HIAL. [*humming*]. Ho-ho-ho; faith, I gave them a bit of my mind.

EKD. Not the chamberlains?

HIAL. Oh, why not? [*Lightly.*] After that we had a little discussion about Tokay.

EKD. Tokay! There's a fine wine for you!

HIAL. [*comes to a standstill*]. It may be a fine wine. But of course you know the vintages differ; it all depends on how much sunshine the grapes have had.

GINA. Why, you know everything, Ekdal.

EKD. And did they dispute that?

HIAL. They tried to, but they were requested to observe it was just the same with chamberlains—that with them, too, different batches were of different qualities.

GINA. What things you do think of!

EKD. Hee-hee! So they got that in their pipes too?

HIAL. Right in their teeth.

EKD. Do you hear that, Gina? He said it right in the very teeth of all the chamberlains.

GINA. Fancy! Right in their teeth!

HIAL. Yes, but I don't want it talked about. One doesn't speak of such things. The whole affair passed off quite amicably, of course. They were nice genial fellows; I didn't want to wound them—not I!

EKD. Right in their teeth, though!

HED. [*caressingly*]. How nice it is to see you in a dress coat! It suits you so well, Father.

HIAL. Yes, don't you think so? And this one really fits to perfection. It fits almost as if it had been made for me—a little tight in the armholes, perhaps; help me, Hedvig [*takes off the coat*]. I think I'll put on my jacket. Where is my jacket, Gina?

GINA. Here it is. [*Brings the jacket and helps him.*]

HIAL. That's it! Don't forget to send the coat back to Molvik first thing tomorrow morning.

GINA [*laying it away*]. I'll be sure and see to it.

HIAL. [*stretching himself*]. After all, there's a more homely feeling about this. A free-and-easy indoor costume suits my whole personality better. Don't you think so, Hedvig?

HED. Yes, Father.

HIAL. When I loosen my necktie into a pair of flowing ends—like this —eh?

HED. Yes, and that goes so well with your mustache and the sweep of your curls.

HIAL. I should not call them curls exactly; I should rather say locks.

HED. Yes, they are too big for curls.

HIAL. Locks describes them better.

HED. [*after a pause, twitching his jacket*]. Father!

HIAL. Well, what is it?

HED. Oh, you know very well.

HIAL. No, really I don't.

HED. [*half laughing, half whispering*]. Oh yes, Father; now don't tease me any longer!

HIAL. Why, what do you mean?

HED. [*shaking him*]. Oh, what nonsense! Come, where are they, Father? All the good things you promised me, you know?

HIAL. Oh—if I haven't forgotten all about them!

HED. Now you're only teasing me, Father! Oh, it's too bad of you! Where have you put them?

HIAL. No, I positively forgot to get anything. But wait a little! I have something else for you, Hedvig. [*Goes and searches in the pockets of the coat.*]

HED. [*skipping and clapping her hands*]. Oh, Mother, Mother!

HIAL. [*with a paper*]. Look, here it is.

GINA. There, you see; if you only give him time——

HED. That? Why, that's only a paper.

HIAL. That is the bill of fare, my dear; the whole bill of fare. Here you see "Menu"—that means bill of fare.

HED. Haven't you anything else?

HIAL. I forgot the other things, I tell you. But you may take my word for it, these dainties are very unsatisfying. Sit down at the table and read the bill of fare, and then I'll describe to you how the dishes taste. Here you are, Hedvig.

HED. [*gulping down her tears*]. Thank you. [*She seats herself but does not read;* GINA *makes signs to her;* HIALMAR *notices it.*]

HIAL. [*pacing up and down the room*]. It's monstrous what absurd things the father of a family is expected to think of, and if he forgets the smallest trifle he is treated to sour faces at once. Well, well, one gets used to that too. [*Stops near the stove by the old man's chair.*] Have you peeped in there this evening, Father?

EKD. Yes, to be sure I have. She's gone into the basket.

HIAL. Ah, she has gone into the basket. Then she's beginning to get used to it.

EKD. Yes, just as I prophesied. But you know there are still a few little things——

HIAL. A few improvements, yes.

EKD. They've got to be made, you know.

HIAL. Yes, let us have a talk about the improvements, Father. Come, let us sit on the sofa.

EKD. All right. H'm—think I'll just fill my pipe first. Must clean it out too. H'm. [*He goes into his room.*]

GINA [*smiling to* HIALMAR]. His pipe!

HIAL. Oh yes, yes, Gina; let him alone—the poor shipwrecked old man. Yes, these improvements—we had better get them out of hand tomorrow.

GINA. You'll hardly have time tomorrow, Ekdal.

HED. [*interposing*]. Oh yes, he will, Mother!

GINA. —for remember them prints that has to be retouched; they've sent for them time after time.

HIAL. There now! Those prints again! I shall get them finished all right. Have any new orders come in?

GINA. No, worse luck; tomorrow I have nothing to do but those two sittings, you know.

HIAL. Nothing else? Oh no, if people won't set about things with a will——

GINA. But what more can I do? Don't I advertise in the papers as much as we can afford?

HIAL. Yes, the papers; you see how much good they do. And I suppose no one has been to look at the room either?

GINA. No, not yet.

HIAL. That was only to be expected. If people won't keep their eyes open—— Nothing can be done without a real effort, Gina!

HED. [*going toward him*]. Shall I fetch you the flute, Father?

HIAL. No; no flute for me; *I* want no pleasures in this world. [*Pacing about.*] Yes indeed, I will work tomorrow; you shall see if I don't. You may be sure I shall work as long as my strength holds out.

GINA. But, my dear good Ekdal, I didn't mean it in that way.

HED. Father, mayn't I bring in a bottle of beer?

HIAL. No, certainly not. I require nothing, nothing. [*Comes to a standstill.*] Beer? Was it beer you were talking about?

HED. [*cheerfully*]. Yes, Father; beautiful fresh beer.

HIAL. Well—since you insist upon it, you may bring in a bottle.

GINA. Yes, do; and we'll be nice and cosy.

[HEDVIG *runs toward the kitchen door.*]

HIAL. [*by the stove, stops her, looks at her, puts his arm round her neck and presses her to him*]. Hedvig, Hedvig!

HED. [*with tears of joy*]. My dear, kind father!

HIAL. No, don't call me that. Here have I been feasting at the rich man's table—battening at the groaning board! And I couldn't even——

GINA [*sitting at the table*]. Oh, nonsense, nonsense, Ekdal.

HIAL. It's not nonsense! And yet you mustn't be too hard upon me. You know that I love you for all that.

HED. [*throwing her arms round him*]. And we love you, oh, so dearly, Father!

HIAL. And if I am unreasonable once in a while—why, then—you must remember that I am a man beset by a host of cares. There, there! [*Dries his eyes.*] No beer at such a moment as this. Give me the flute.

[HEDVIG *runs to the bookcase and fetches it.*]

HIAL. Thanks! That's right. With my flute in my hand and you two at my side—ah!

[HEDVIG *seats herself at the table near* GINA; HIALMAR *paces backward and forward, pipes up vigorously and plays a Bohemian peasant dance, but in a slow plaintive tempo and with sentimental expression.*]

HIAL. [*breaking off the melody, holds out his left hand to* GINA *and says with emotion*]. Our roof may be poor and humble, Gina, but it is home. And with all my heart I say: here dwells my happiness. [*He begins to *play again; almost immediately after a knocking is heard at the entrance door.*]

GINA [*rising*]. Hush, Ekdal—I think there's someone at the door.

HIAL. [*laying the flute on the bookcase*]. There! Again!

[GINA *goes and opens the door.*]

GREG. [*in the passage*]. Excuse me——

GINA [*starting back slightly*]. Oh!

GREG. —does not Mr Ekdal, the photographer, live here?

GINA. Yes, he does.

HIAL. [*going toward the door*]. Gregers! You here after all? Well, come in then.

GREG. [*coming in*]. I told you I would come and look you up.

HIAL. But this evening—— Have you left the party?

GREG. I have left both the party and my father's house. Good evening, Mrs Ekdal. I don't know whether you recognize me?

GINA. Oh yes, it's not difficult to know young Mr Werle again.

GREG. No, I am like my mother, and no doubt you remember her.

HIAL. Left your father's house, did you say?

GREG. Yes, I have gone to a hotel.

HIAL. Indeed. Well, since you're here, take off your coat and sit down.

GREG. Thanks. [*He takes off his overcoat. He is now dressed in a plain gray suit of a countrified cut.*]

HIAL. Here on the sofa. Make yourself comfortable.

GREG. [*looking around him*]. So these are your quarters, Hialmar—this is your home.

HIAL. This is the studio, as you see.

GINA. But it's the largest of our rooms, so we generally sit here.

HIAL. We used to live in a better place, but this flat has one great advantage: there are such capital outer rooms——

GINA. And we have a room on the other side of the passage that we can let.

GREG. [*to* HIALMAR]. Ah—so you have lodgers too?

HIAL. No, not yet. They're not so easy to find, you see; you have to keep your eyes open. [*To* HEDVIG.] How about that beer, eh?

[HEDVIG *nods and goes out into the kitchen.*]

GREG. So that is your daughter?

HIAL. Yes, that is Hedvig.

GREG. And she is your only child?

HIAL. Yes, the only one. She is the joy of our lives, and [*lowering his voice*] at the same time our deepest sorrow, Gregers.

GREG. What do you mean?

HIAL. She is in serious danger of losing her eyesight.

GREG. Becoming blind?

HIAL. Yes. Only the first symptoms have appeared as yet, and she may not feel it much for some time. But the doctor has warned us. It is coming inexorably.

GREG. What a terrible misfortune! How do you account for it?

HIAL. [*sighs*]. Hereditary, no doubt.

GREG. [*starting*]. Hereditary?

GINA. Ekdal's mother had weak eyes.

HIAL. Yes, so my father says; I can't remember her.

GREG. Poor child! And how does she take it?

HIAL. Oh, you can imagine we haven't the heart to tell her of it. She dreams of no danger. Gay and careless and chirping like a little bird, she flutters onward into a life of endless night. [*Overcome.*] Oh, it is cruelly hard on me, Gregers.

[HEDVIG *brings a tray with beer and glasses which she sets upon the table.*]

HIAL. [*stroking her hair*]. Thanks, thanks, Hedvig.

[HEDVIG *puts her arm around his neck and whispers in his ear.*]

HIAL. No, no bread and butter just now. [*Looks up.*] But perhaps you would like some, Gregers?

GREG. [*with a gesture of refusal*]. No, no thank you.

HIAL. [*still melancholy*]. Well, you can bring in a little all the same. If you have a crust, that is all I want. And plenty of butter on it, mind.

[HEDVIG *nods gaily and goes out into the kitchen again.*]

GREG. [*who has been following her with his eyes*]. She seems quite strong and healthy otherwise.

GINA. Yes. In other ways there's nothing amiss with her, thank goodness.

GREG. She promises to be very like you, Mrs Ekdal. How old is she now?

GINA. Hedvig is close on fourteen; her birthday is the day after tomorrow.

GREG. She is pretty tall for her age then.

GINA. Yes, she's shot up wonderful this last year.

GREG. It makes one realize one's own age to see these young people growing up. How long is it now since you were married?

GINA. We've been married—let me see—just on fifteen years.

GREG. Is it so long as that?

GINA [*becomes attentive, looks at him*]. Yes, it is indeed.

HIAL. Yes, so it is. Fifteen years, all but a few months. [*Changing his tone.*] They must have been long years for you up at the works, Gregers.

GREG. They seemed long while I was living them; now they are over, I hardly know how the time has gone.

[OLD EKDAL *comes from his room without his pipe but with his old-fashioned uniform cap on his head; his gait is somewhat unsteady.*]

EKD. Come now, Hialmar, let's sit down and have a good talk about this—h'm—what was it again?

HIAL. [*going toward him*]. Father, we have a visitor here—Gregers Werle—I don't know if you remember him.

EKD. [*looking at* GREGERS, *who has risen*]. Werle? Is that the son? What does he want with me?

HIAL. Nothing! It's me he has come to see.

EKD. Oh! Then there's nothing wrong?

HIAL. No, no, of course not.

EKD. [*with a large gesture*]. Not that I'm afraid, you know; but——

GREG. [*goes over to him*]. I bring you a greeting from your old hunting grounds, Lieutenant Ekdal.

EKD. Hunting grounds?

GREG. Yes, up in Höidal, about the works, you know.

EKD. Oh, up there. Yes, I knew all those places well in the old days.

GREG. You were a great sportsman then.

EKD. So I was, I don't deny it. You're looking at my uniform cap. I don't ask anybody's leave to wear it in the house. So long as I don't go out in the streets with it——

[HEDVIG *brings a plate of bread and butter which she puts upon the table.*]

HIAL. Sit down, Father, and have a glass of beer. Help yourself, Gregers.

[EKDAL *mutters and stumbles over*

to the sofa. GREGERS *seats himself on the chair nearest to him,* HIALMAR *on the other side of* GREGERS. GINA *sits a little way from the table, sewing;* HEDVIG *stands beside her father.*]

GREG. Can you remember, Lieutenant Ekdal, how Hialmar and I used to come up and visit you in the summer and at Christmas?

EKD. Did you? No, no, no; I don't remember it. But, sure enough, I've been a tidy bit of sportsman in my day. I've shot bears too. I've shot nine of 'em no less.

GREG. [*looking sympathetically at him*]. And now you never get any shooting?

EKD. Can't say that, sir. Get a shot now and then, perhaps. Of course not in the old way. For the woods, you see—the woods, the woods—— [*Drinks.*] Are the woods fine up there now?

GREG. Not so fine as in your time. They have been thinned out a good deal.

EKD. Thinned? [*More softly and as if afraid.*] It's dangerous work, that. Bad things come of it. The woods revenge themselves.

HIAL. [*filling up his glass*]. Come—a little more, Father.

GREG. How can a man like you—such a man for the open air—live in the midst of a stuffy town, boxed within four walls?

EKD. [*laughs quietly and glances at* HIALMAR]. Oh, it's not so bad here. Not at all so bad.

GREG. But don't you miss all the things that used to be a part of your very being—the cool sweeping breezes, the free life in the woods and on the uplands, among beasts and birds?

EKD. [*smiling*]. Hialmar, shall we let him see it?

HIAL. [*hastily and a little embarrassed*]. Oh no, no, Father; not this evening.

GREG. What does he want to show me?

HIAL. Oh, it's only something—you can see it another time.

GREG. [*continues, to the old man*]. You see, I have been thinking, Lieutenant Ekdal, that you should come up with me to the works; I am sure to be going back soon. No doubt you could get some copying there too. And here you have nothing on earth to interest you—nothing to liven you up.

EKD. [*stares in astonishment at him*]. Have I nothing on earth to——

GREG. Of course you have Hialmar, but then he has his own family. And a man like you, who has always had such a passion for what is free and wild——

EKD. [*thumps the table*]. Hialmar, he shall see it!

HIAL. Oh, do you think it's worth while, Father? It's all dark.

EKD. Nonsense; it's moonlight [*Rises.*] He shall see it, I tell you. Let me pass! Come on and help me, Hialmar.

HED. Oh yes, do, Father!

HIAL. [*rising*]. Very well then.

GREG. [*to* GINA]. What is it?

GINA. Oh, nothing so wonderful after all.

[EKDAL *and* HIALMAR *have gone to the back wall and are each pushing back a side of the sliding door;* HEDVIG *helps the old man;* GREGERS *remains standing by the sofa;* GINA *sits still and sews. Through the open doorway a large, deep irregular garret is seen with odd nooks and corners, a couple of stovepipes running through it from rooms below. There are sky-*

lights through which clear moonbeams shine in on some parts of the great room; others lie in deep shadow.]

EKD. [*to* GREGERS]. You may come close up if you like.

GREG. [*going over to them*]. Why, what is it?

EKD. Look for yourself, h'm.

HIAL. [*somewhat embarrassed*]. This belongs to Father, you understand.

GREG. [*at the door, looks into the garret*]. Why, you keep poultry, Lieutenant Ekdal.

EKD. Should think we did keep poultry. They've gone to roost now. But you should see our fowls by daylight, sir!

HED. And there's a——

EKD. Sh–sh! Don't say anything about it yet.

GREG. And you have pigeons too, I see.

EKD. Oh yes, haven't we just got pigeons! They have their nest boxes up there under the rooftree; for pigeons like to roost high, you see.

HIAL. They aren't all common pigeons.

EKD. Common! Should think not, indeed! We have tumblers and a pair of pouters too. But come here! Can you see that hutch down there by the wall?

GREG. Yes; what do you use it for?

EKD. That's where the rabbits sleep, sir.

GREG. Dear me, so you have rabbits too?

EKD. Yes, you may take my word for it, we have rabbits! He wants to know if we have rabbits, Hialmar! H'm! But now comes the thing, let me tell you! Here we have it! Move away, Hedvig. Stand here; that's right–and now look down there. Don't you see a basket with straw in it?

GREG. Yes. And I can see a fowl lying in the basket.

EKD. H'm–"a fowl"——

GREG. Isn't it a duck?

EKD. [*hurt*]. Why, of course it's a duck.

HIAL. But what kind of a duck, do you think?

HED. It's not just a common duck.

EKD. Sh!

GREG. And it's not a Muscovy duck either.

EKD. No, Mr — Werle; it's not a Muscovy duck, for it's a wild duck!

GREG. Is it really? A wild duck?

EKD. Yes, that's what it is. That "fowl"–as you call it–is the wild duck. It's our wild duck, sir.

HED. My wild duck. It belongs to me.

GREG. And can it live up here in the garret? Does it thrive?

EKD. Of course it has a trough of water to splash about in, you know.

HIAL. Fresh water every other day.

GINA [*turning toward* HIALMAR]. But, my dear Ekdal, it's getting icy cold here.

EKD. H'm, we had better shut up then. It's as well not to disturb their night's rest too. Close up, Hedvig.

[HIALMAR *and* HEDVIG *push the garret doors together.*]

EKD. Another time you shall see her properly. [*Seats himself in the armchair by the stove.*] Oh, they're curious things, these wild ducks, I can tell you.

GREG. How did you manage to catch it, Lieutenant Ekdal?

EKD. *I* didn't catch it. There's a certain man in this town whom we have to thank for it.

GREG. [*starts slightly*]. That man was not my father, was he?

EKD. You've hit it. Your father and no one else. H'm.

HIAL. Strange that you should guess that, Gregers.

GREG. You were telling me that you owed so many things to my father, and so I thought perhaps——

GINA. But we didn't get the duck from Mr Werle himself.

EKD. It's Hakon Werle we have to thank for her, all the same, Gina. [*To* GREGERS.] He was shooting from a boat, you see, and he brought her down. But your father's sight is not very good now. H'm; she was only wounded.

GREG. Ah! She got a couple of slugs in her body, I suppose?

HIAL. Yes, two or three.

HED. She was hit under the wing so that she couldn't fly.

GREG. And I suppose she dived to the bottom, eh?

EKD. [*sleepily, in a thick voice*]. Of course. Always do that, wild ducks do. They shoot to the bottom as deep as they can get, sir—and bite themselves fast in the tangle and seaweed—and all the devil's own mess that grows down there. And they never come up again.

GREG. But your wild duck came up again, Lieutenant Ekdal.

EKD. He had such an amazingly clever dog, your father had. And that dog—he dived in after the duck and fetched her up again.

GREG. [*who has turned to* HIALMAR]. And then she was sent to you here?

HIAL. Not at once; at first your father took her home. But she wouldn't thrive there, so Pettersen was told to put an end to her.

EKD. [*half asleep*]. H'm—yes—Pettersen—that ass——

HIAL. [*speaking more softly*]. That was how we got her, you see; for Father knows Pettersen a little, and when he heard about the wild duck he got him to hand her over to us.

GREG. And now she thrives as well as possible in the garret there?

HIAL. Yes, wonderfully well. She has got fat. You see, she has lived in there so long now that she has forgotten her natural wild life, and it all depends on that.

GREG. You are right there, Hialmar. Be sure you never let her get a glimpse of the sky and the sea. But I mustn't stay any longer; I think your father is asleep.

HIAL. Oh, as for that——

GREG. But by the bye—you said you had a room to let—a spare room?

HIAL. Yes; what then? Do you know of anybody?

GREG. Can *I* have that room?

HIAL. You?

GINA. Oh no, Mr Werle, you——

GREG. May I have the room? If so, I'll take possession first thing tomorrow morning.

HIAL. Yes, with the greatest pleasure.

GINA. But, Mr Werle, I'm sure it's not at all the sort of room for you.

HIAL. Why, Gina! how can you say that?

GINA. Why, because the room's neither large enough nor light enough, and——

GREG. That really doesn't matter, Mrs Ekdal.

HIAL. I call it quite a nice room, and not at all badly furnished either.

GINA. But remember the pair of them underneath.

GREG. What pair?

GINA. Well, there's one as has been a tutor.

HIAL. That's Molvik—Mr Molvik, B.A.

GINA. And then there's a doctor by the name of Relling.

GREG. Relling? I know him a little; he practiced for a time up in Höidal.

GINA. They're a regular rackety pair, they are. As often as not they're out on the loose in the evenings, and then they come home at all hours, and they are not always just——

GREG. One soon gets used to that sort of thing. I daresay I shall be like the wild duck.

GINA. H'm; I think you ought to sleep upon it first, anyway.

GREG. You seem very unwilling to have me in the house, Mrs Ekdal.

GINA. Oh no! What makes you think that?

HIAL. Well, you really behave strangely about it, Gina. [*To* GREGERS.] Then I suppose you intend to remain in the town for the present?

GREG. [*putting on his overcoat*]. Yes, now I intend to remain here.

HIAL. And yet not at your father's? What do you propose to do then?

GREG. Ah, if I only knew that, Hialmar, I shouldn't be so badly off! But when one has the misfortune to be called Gregers!—"Gregers"—and then "Werle" after it; did you ever hear of anything so hideous?

HIAL. Oh, I don't think so at all.

GREG. Ugh! Bah! I feel I should like to spit on the fellow that answers to such a name. But when a man is once for all doomed to be Gregers Werle—in this world—as I am——

HIAL. [*laughs*]. Ha, ha! If you weren't Gregers Werle, what would you like to be?

GREG. If I should choose, I should like best to be a clever dog.

GINA. A dog!

HED. [*involuntarily*]. Oh no!

GREG. Yes, an amazingly clever dog; one that goes to the bottom after wild ducks when they dive and bite themselves fast in tangle and seaweed down among the ooze.

HIAL. Upon my word now, Gregers—I don't in the least know what you are driving at.

GREG. Oh well, you might not be much the wiser if you did. It's understood, then, that I move in early to-morrow morning. [*To* GINA.] I won't give you any trouble; I do everything for myself. [*To* HIALMAR.] We will talk about the rest to-morrow. Good night, Mrs Ekdal. [*Nods to* HEDVIG.] Good night.

GINA. Good night, Mr Werle.

HED. Good night.

HIAL. [*who has lighted a candle*]. Wait a moment; I must show you a light; the stairs are sure to be dark.

[GREGERS *and* HIALMAR *go out by the passage door.*]

GINA [*looking straight before her with her sewing in her lap*]. Wasn't that queer-like talk about wanting to be a dog?

HED. Do you know, Mother—I believe he meant something quite different by that.

GINA. Why, what should he mean?

HED. Oh, I don't know, but it seemed to me he meant something different from what he said—all the time.

GINA. Do you think so? Yes, it was sort of queer.

HIAL. [*comes back*]. The lamp was still burning. [*Puts out the candle and sets it down.*] Ah, now one can get a mouthful of food at last. [*Begins to eat the bread and butter.*] Well, you see, Gina—if only you keep your eyes open——

GINA. How keep your eyes open?

HIAL. Why, haven't we at last had the luck to get the room let? And just think—to a person like Gregers—a good old friend.

GINA. Well, I don't know what to say about it.

HED. Oh, Mother, you'll see; it 'll be such fun!

HIAL. You're very strange. You were so bent upon getting the room let before, and now you don't like it.

GINA. Yes, I do, Ekdal; if it had only been to someone else. But what do you suppose Mr Werle will say?

HIAL. Old Werle? It doesn't concern him.

GINA. But surely you can see that there's something amiss between them again, or the young man wouldn't be leaving home. You know very well those two can't get on with each other.

HIAL. Very likely not, but——

GINA. And now Mr Werle may fancy it's you that has edged him on——

HIAL. Let him fancy so, then! Mr Werle has done a great deal for me; far be it from me to deny it. But that doesn't make me everlastingly dependent upon him.

GINA. But, my dear Ekdal, maybe Grandfather 'll suffer for it. He may lose the little bit of work he gets from Graberg.

HIAL. I could almost say: so much the better! Is it not humiliating for a man like me to see his gray-haired father treated as a pariah? But now I believe the fullness of time is at hand. [*Takes a fresh piece of bread and butter.*] As sure as I have a mission in life, I mean to fulfill it now!

HED. Oh yes, Father, do!

GINA. Hush! Don't wake him!

HIAL. [*more softly*]. I will fulfill it, I say. The day shall come when—— And that is why I say it's a good thing we have let the room, for that makes me more independent. The man who has a mission in life must be independent. [*By the armchair, with emotion.*] Poor old white-haired Father! Rely on your Hialmar. He has broad shoulders—strong shoulders, at any rate. You shall yet wake up some fine day and—— [*To* GINA.] Do you not believe it?

GINA [*rising*]. Yes, of course I do, but in the meantime suppose we see about getting him to bed.

HIAL. Yes, come.

[*They take hold of the old man carefully.*]

ACT III

SCENE—HIALMAR EKDAL'S *studio. It is morning; the daylight shines through the large window in the slanting roof; the curtain is drawn back.*

HIALMAR *is sitting at the table, busy retouching a photograph; several others lie before him. Presently* GINA, *wearing her hat and cloak, enters by the passage door; she has a covered basket on her arm.*

HIAL. Back already, Gina?

GINA. Oh yes, one can't let the grass grow under one's feet. [*Sets her basket on a chair and takes off her things.*]

HIAL. Did you look in at Greger's room?

GINA. Yes, that I did. It's a rare sight, I can tell you; he's made a pretty mess to start off with.

HIAL. How so?

GINA. He was determined to do everything for himself, he said; so he sets to work to light the stove, and what must he do but screw down the damper till the whole room is full of smoke. Ugh! There was a smell fit to——

HIAL. Well, really!

GINA. But that's not the worst of it; for then he thinks he'll put out the fire and goes and empties his water jug into the stove and so makes the whole floor one filthy puddle.

HIAL. How annoying!

GINA. I've got the porter's wife to clear up after him, pig that he is! But the room won't be fit to live in till the afternoon.

HIAL. What's he doing with himself in the meantime?

GINA. He said he was going out for a little while.

HIAL. I looked in upon him too, for a moment—after you had gone.

GINA. So I heard. You've asked him to lunch.

HIAL. Just to a little bit of early lunch, you know. It's his first day—we can hardly do less. You've got something in the house, I suppose?

GINA. I shall have to find something or other.

HIAL. And don't cut it too fine, for I fancy Relling and Molvik are coming up too. I just happened to meet Relling on the stairs, you see; so I had to——

GINA. Oh, are we to have those two as well?

HIAL. Good lord—a couple more or less can't make any difference.

OLD EKDAL [*opens his door and looks in*]. I say. Hialmar—— [*Sees* GINA.] Oh!

GINA. Do you want anything, Grandfather?

EKD. Oh no, it doesn't matter. H'm! [*Retires again.*]

GINA [*takes up the basket*]. Be sure you see that he doesn't go out.

HIAL. All right, all right. And, Gina, a little herring salad wouldn't be a bad idea. Relling and Molvik were out on the loose again last night.

GINA. If only they don't come before I'm ready for them——

HIAL. No, of course they won't; take your own time.

GINA. Very well, and meanwhile you can be working a bit.

HIAL. Well, I am working! I am working as hard as I can!

GINA. Then you'll have that job off your hands, you see. [*She goes out to the kitchen with her basket.* HIALMAR *sits for a time penciling away at the photograph in an indolent and listless manner.*]

EKD. [*peeps in, looks round the studio and says softly*]. Are you busy?

HIAL. Yes, I'm toiling at these wretched pictures.

EKD. Well, well, never mind—since you're so busy—h'm! [*He goes out again; the door stands open.*]

HIAL. [*continues for some time in silence, then he lays down his brush and goes over to the door*]. Are you busy, Father?

EKD. [*in a grumbling tone within*]. If you're busy, I'm busy too. H'm!

HIAL. Oh, very well then. [*Goes to his work again.*]

EKD. [*presently coming to the door again*]. H'm; I say, Hialmar, I'm not so very busy, you know.

HIAL. I thought you were writing.

EKD. Oh, devil take it! Can't Graberg wait a day or two? After all, it's not a matter of life and death.

Hial. No, and you're not his slave either.

Ekd. And about that other business in there——

Hial. Just what I was thinking of. Do you want to go in? Shall I open the door for you?

Ekd. Well, it wouldn't be a bad notion.

Hial. [*rises*]. Then we'd have that off our hands.

Ekd. Yes, exactly. It's got to be ready first thing tomorrow. It is tomorrow, isn't it? H'm?

Hial. Yes, of course it's tomorrow.

[Hialmar *and* Ekdal *push aside each his half of the sliding door. The morning sun is shining in through the skylights; some doves are flying about; others sit cooing upon the perches; the hens are heard clucking now and then further back in the garret.*]

Hial. There; now you can get to work, Father.

Ekd. [*goes in*]. Aren't you coming too?

Hial. Well, really, do you know—I almost think—— [*Sees* Gina *at the kitchen door.*] I? No; I haven't time; I must work—— But now for our new contrivance—— [*He pulls a cord; a curtain slips down inside, the lower part consisting of a piece of old sailcloth, the upper part of a stretched fishing net. The floor of the garret is thus no longer visible.*]

Hial. [*goes to the table*]. So! Now perhaps I can sit in peace for a little while.

Gina. Is he rampaging in there again?

Hial. Would you rather have him slip down to Madam Eriksen's? [*Seats himself.*] Do you want anything? You know you said——

Gina. I only wanted to ask if you think we can lay the table for lunch here?

Hial. Yes; we have no early appointment, I suppose?

Gina. No, I expect no one today except those two sweethearts that are to be taken together.

Hial. Why the deuce couldn't they be taken together another day?

Gina. Don't you know, I told them to come in the afternoon, when you are having your nap.

Hial. Oh, that's capital. Very well, let us have lunch here then.

Gina. All right, but there's no hurry about laying the cloth; you can have the table for a good while yet.

Hial. Do you think I am not sticking at my work? I'm at it as hard as I can!

Gina. Then you'll be free later on, you know. [*Goes out into the kitchen again. Short pause.*]

Ekd. [*in the garret doorway, behind the net*]. Hialmar!

Hial. Well?

Ekd. Afraid we shall have to move the water trough after all.

Hial. What else have I been saying all along?

Ekd. H'm–h'm–h'm. [*Goes away from the door again.* Hialmar *goes on working a little, glances toward the garret and half rises.* Hedvig *comes in from the kitchen.*]

Hial. [*sits down again hurriedly*]. What do you want?

Hed. I only wanted to come in beside you, Father.

Hial. [*after a pause*]. What makes you go prying around like that? Perhaps you are told off to watch me?

Hed. No, no.

HIAL. What is your mother doing out there?

HED. Oh, Mother's in the middle of making the herring salad. [*Goes to the table.*] Isn't there any little thing I could help you with, Father?

HIAL. Oh no. It is right that I should bear the whole burden—so long as my strength holds out. Set your mind at rest, Hedvig; if only your father keeps his health——

HED. Oh no, Father! You mustn't talk in that horrid way. [*She wanders about a little, stops by the doorway and looks into the garret.*]

HIAL. Tell me, what is he doing?

HED. I think he's making a new path to the water trough.

HIAL. He can never manage that by himself! And here am I doomed to sit!

HED. [*goes to him*]. Let me take the brush, Father; I can do it quite well.

HIAL. Oh, nonsense; you will only hurt your eyes.

HED. Not a bit. Give me the brush.

HIAL. [*rising*]. Well, it won't take more than a minute or two.

HED. Pooh, what harm can it do then? [*Takes the brush.*] There! [*Seats herself.*] I can begin upon this one.

HIAL. But mind you don't hurt your eyes! Do you hear? *I* won't be answerable; you do it on your own responsibility—understand that.

HED. [*retouching*]. Yes, yes, I understand.

HIAL. You are quite clever at it, Hedvig. Only a minute or two, you know. [*He slips through by the edge of the curtain into the garret.* HEDVIG *sits at her work.* HIALMAR *and* EKDAL *are heard disputing inside.*]

HIAL. [*appears behind the net*]. I say, Hedvig—give me those pincers that are lying on the shelf. And the chisel. [*Turns away inside.*] Now you shall see, Father. Just let me show you first what I mean!

[HEDVIG *has fetched the required tools from the shelf and hands them to him through the net.*]

HIAL. Ah, thanks. I didn't come a moment too soon. [*Goes back from the curtain again; they are heard carpentering and talking inside.* HEDVIG *stands looking in at them. A moment later there is a knock at the passage door; she does not notice it.*]

GREGERS WERLE [*bareheaded, in indoor dress, enters and stops near the door*]. H'm!

HED. [*turns and goes toward him*]. Good morning. Please come in.

GREG. Thank you. [*Looking toward the garret.*] You seem to have workpeople in the house.

HED. No, it's only Father and Grandfather. I'll tell them you are here.

GREG. No, no, don't do that; I would rather wait a little. [*Seats himself on the sofa.*]

HED. It looks so untidy here—— [*Begins to clear away the photographs.*]

GREG. Oh, don't take them away. Are those prints that have to be finished off?

HED. Yes, they are a few I was helping Father with.

GREG. Please don't let me disturb you.

HED. Oh no. [*She gathers the things to her and sits down to work;* GREGERS *looks at her meanwhile in silence.*]

GREG. Did the wild duck sleep well last night.

HED. Yes, I think so, thanks.

GREG. [*turning toward the garret*].

It looks quite different by day from what it did last night in the moonlight.

HED. Yes, it changes ever so much. It looks different in the morning and in the afternoon, and it's different on rainy days from what it is in fine weather.

GREG. Have you noticed it?

HED. Yes, how could I help it?

GREG. Are you too fond of being in there with the wild duck?

HED. Yes, when I can manage it.

GREG. But I suppose you haven't much spare time; you go to school, no doubt.

HED. No, not now; Father is afraid of my hurting my eyes.

GREG. Oh, then he reads with you himself?

HED. Father has promised to read with me, but he has never had time yet.

GREG. Then is there nobody else to give you a little help?

HED. Yes, there is Mr Molvik, but he is not always exactly—quite——

GREG. Sober?

HED. Yes, I suppose that's it!

GREG. Why, then, you must have any amount of time on your hands. And in there I suppose it is a sort of world by itself?

HED. Oh yes, quite. And there are such lots of wonderful things.

GREG. Indeed?

HED. Yes, there are big cupboards full of books, and a great many of the books have pictures in them.

GREG. Aha!

HED. And there's an old bureau with drawers and flaps and a big clock with figures that go out and in. But the clock isn't going now.

GREG. So time has come to a standstill in there—in the wild duck's domain?

HED. Yes. And then there's an old paintbox and things of that sort, and all the books.

GREG. And you read the books, I suppose?

HED. Oh yes, when I get the chance. Most of them are English, though, and I don't understand English. But then I look at the pictures. There is one great book called *Harrison's History of London.* It must be a hundred years old, and there are such heaps of pictures in it. At the beginning there is Death with an hourglass and a woman. I think that is horrid. But then there are all the other pictures of churches and castles and streets and great ships sailing on the sea.

GREG. But tell me, where did all those wonderful things come from?

HED. Oh, an old sea captain once lived here, and he brought them home with him. They used to call him "The Flying Dutchman." That was curious, because he wasn't a Dutchman at all.

GREG. Was he not?

HED. No. But at last he was drowned at sea, and so he left all those things behind him.

GREG. Tell me now—when you are sitting in there looking at the pictures don't you wish you could travel and see the real world for yourself?

HED. Oh no! I mean always to stay at home and help Father and Mother.

GREG. To retouch photographs?

HED. No, not only that. I should love above everything to learn to engrave pictures like those in the English books.

GREG. H'm. What does your father say to that?

HED. I don't think father likes it; Father is strange about such things. Only think, he talks of my learning basketmaking and straw plaiting! But I don't think that would be much good.

GREG. Oh no, I don't think so either.

HED. But Father was right in saying that if I had learned basketmaking I could have made the new basket for the wild duck.

GREG. So you could; and it was you that ought to have done it, wasn't it?

HED. Yes, for it's my wild duck.

GREG. Of course it is.

HED. Yes, it belongs to me. But I lend it to Father and Grandfather as often as they please.

GREG. Indeed? What do they do with it?

HED. Oh, they look after it and build places for it and so on.

GREG. I see; for no doubt the wild duck is by far the most distinguished inhabitant of the garret?

HED. Yes, indeed she is; for she is a real wild fowl, you know. And then she is so much to be pitied; she has no one to care for, poor thing.

GREG. She has no family, as the rabbits have.

HED. No. The hens too, many of them, were chickens together; but she has been taken right away from all her friends. And then there is so much that is strange about the wild duck. Nobody knows her, and nobody knows where she came from either.

GREG. And she has been down in the depths of the sea.

HED. [*with a quick glance at him, represses a smile and asks*]. Why do you say "depths of the sea"?

GREG. What else should I say?

HED. You could say "the bottom of the sea."

GREG. Oh, mayn't I just as well say the depths of the sea?

HED. Yes, but it sounds so strange to me when other people speak of the depths of the sea.

GREG. Why so? Tell me why?

HED. No, I won't; it's so stupid.

GREG. Oh no, I am sure it's not. Do tell me why you smiled.

HED. Well, this is the reason: whenever I come to realize suddenly—in a flash—what is in there, it always seems to me that the whole room and everything in it should be called "the depths of the sea." But that is so stupid.

GREG. You mustn't say that.

HED. Oh yes, for you know it is only a garret.

GREG. [*looks fixedly at her*]. Are you so sure of that?

HED. [*astonished*]. That it's a garret?

GREG. Are you quite certain of it?

[HEDVIG *is silent and looks at him open-mouthed.* GINA *comes in from the kitchen with the table things.*]

GREG. [*rising*]. I have come in upon you too early.

GINA. Oh, you must be somewhere, and we're nearly ready now anyway. Clear the table, Hedvig.

[HEDVIG *clears away her things; she and* GINA *lay the cloth during what follows.* GREGERS *seats himself in the armchair and turns over an album.*]

GREG. I hear you can retouch, Mrs Ekdal.

GINA [*with a side glance*]. Yes, I can.

GREG. That was exceedingly lucky.

GINA. How—lucky?

GREG. Since Ekdal took to photography, I mean.

HED. Mother can take photographs too.

GINA. Oh yes, I was bound to learn that.

GREG. So it is really you that carry on the business, I suppose?

GINA. Yes, when Ekdal hasn't time himself——

GREG. He is a great deal taken up with his old father, I daresay.

GINA. Yes; and then you can't expect a man like Ekdal to do nothing but take car-de-visits of Dick, Tom and Harry.

GREG. I quite agree with you, but having once gone in for the thing——

GINA. You can surely understand, Mr Werle, that Ekdal's not like one of your common photographers.

GREG. Of course not, but still——

[*A shot is fired within the garret.*]

GREG. [*starting up*]. What's that?

GINA. Ugh! Now they're firing again!

GREG. Have they firearms in there?

HED. They are out shooting.

GREG. What! [*At the door of the garret.*] Are you shooting, Hialmar?

HIAL. [*inside the net*]. Are you there? I didn't know; I was so taken up—— [*To* HEDVIG.] Why did you not let us know? [*Comes into the studio.*]

GREG. Do you go shooting in the garret?

HIAL. [*showing a double-barreled pistol*]. Oh, only with this thing.

GINA. Yes, you and Grandfather will do yourselves a mischief someday with that there pigstol.

HIAL. [*with irritation*]. I believe I have told you that this kind of firearm is called a pistol.

GINA. Oh, that doesn't make it much better that I can see.

GREG. So you have become a sportsman too, Hialmar?

HIAL. Only a little rabbit shooting now and then. Mostly to please Father, you understand.

GINA. Men are strange beings; they must always have something to pervert theirselves with.

HIAL. [*snappishly*]. Just so; we must always have something to divert ourselves with.

GINA. Yes, that's just what I say.

HIAL. H'm. [*To* GREGERS.] You see, the garret is fortunately so situated that no one can hear us shooting. [*Lays the pistol on the top shelf of the bookcase.*] Don't touch the pistol, Hedvig! One of the barrels is loaded; remember that.

GREG. [*looking through the net*]. You have a fowling piece too, I see.

HIAL. That is Father's old gun. It's of no use now. Something has gone wrong with the lock. But it's fun to have it all the same, for we can take it to pieces now and then and clean and grease it and screw it together again. Of course it's mostly Father that fiddle-faddles with all that sort of thing.

HED. [*beside* GREGERS]. Now you can see the wild duck properly.

GREG. I was just looking at her. One of her wings seems to me to droop a bit.

HED. Well, no wonder; her wing was broken, you know.

GREG. And she trails one foot a little. Isn't that so?

HIAL. Perhaps a very little bit.

HED. Yes, it was by that foot the dog took hold of her.

HIAL. But otherwise she hasn't the least thing the matter with her, and that is simply marvelous for a creature that has a charge of shot in her body and has been between a dog's teeth——

GREG. [*with a glance at* HEDVIG]—and that has lain in the depths of the sea so long.

HED. [*smiling*]. Yes.

GINA [*laying the table*]. That blessed wild duck! What a lot of fuss you do make over her.

HIAL. H'm—will lunch soon be ready?

GINA. Yes, directly. Hedvig, you must come and help me now.

[GINA *and* HEDVIG *go out into the kitchen.*]

HIAL. [*in a low voice*]. I think you had better not stand there looking in at Father; he doesn't like it. [GREGERS *moves away from the garret door.*] Besides, I may as well shut up before the others come. [*Claps his hands to drive the fowls back.*] Shh—shh, in with you! [*Draws up the curtain and pulls the doors together.*] All the contrivances are my own invention. It's really quite amusing to have things of this sort to potter with and to put to rights when they get out of order. And it's absolutely necessary too, for Gina objects to having rabbits and fowls in the studio.

GREG. To be sure, and I suppose the studio is your wife's special department?

HIAL. As a rule I leave the everyday details of business to her, for then I can take refuge in the parlor and give my mind to more important things.

GREG. What things may they be, Hialmar?

HIAL. I wonder you have not asked that question sooner. But perhaps you haven't heard of the invention?

GREG. The invention? No.

HIAL. Really? Have you not? Oh no, out there in the wilds——

GREG. So you have invented something, have you?

HIAL. It is not quite completed yet, but I am working at it. You can easily imagine that when I resolved to devote myself to photography it wasn't simply with the idea of taking likenesses of all sorts of commonplace people.

GREG. No; your wife was saying the same thing just now.

HIAL. I swore that if I concentrated my powers to this handicraft I would so exalt it that it should become both an art and a science. And to that end I determined to make this great invention.

GREG. And what is the nature of the invention? What purpose does it serve?

HIAL. Oh, my dear fellow, you mustn't ask for details yet. It takes time, you see. And you must not think that my motive is vanity. It is not for my own sake that I am working. Oh no; it is my life's mission that stands before me night and day.

GREG. What is your life's mission?

HIAL. Do you forget the old man with the silver hair?

GREG. Your poor father? Well, but what can you do for him?

HIAL. I can raise up his self-respect from the dead by restoring the name of Ekdal to honor and dignity.

GREG. Then that is your life's mission?

HIAL. Yes. I will rescue the shipwrecked man. For shipwrecked he was, by the very first blast of the storm. Even while those terrible investigations were going on he was no longer himself. That pistol there—the one we used to shoot rabbits with—has played its part in the tragedy of the house of Ekdal.

Greg. The pistol? Indeed?

Hial. When the sentence of imprisonment was passed—he had the pistol in his hand.

Greg. Had he?

Hial. Yes, but he dared not use it. His courage failed him. So broken, so demoralized was he even then! Oh, can you understand it? He, a soldier; he, who had shot nine bears and who was descended from two lieutenant colonels—one after the other, of course. Can you understand it, Gregers?

Greg. Yes, I understand it well enough.

Hial. I cannot. And once more the pistol played a part in the history of our house. When he had put on the gray clothes and was under lock and key—oh, that was a terrible time for me, I can tell you. I kept the blinds drawn down over both my windows. When I peeped out I saw the sun shining as if nothing had happened. I could not understand it. I saw people going along the street, laughing and talking about indifferent things. I could not understand it. It seemed to me that the whole of existence must be at a standstill—as if under an eclipse.

Greg. I felt that too, when my mother died.

Hial. It was in such an hour that Hialmar Ekdal pointed the pistol at his own breast.

Greg. You, too, thought of——

Hial. Yes.

Greg. But you did not fire?

Hial. No. At the decisive moment I won the victory over myself. I remained in life. But I can assure you it takes some courage to choose life under circumstances like those.

Greg. Well, that depends on how you look at it.

Hial. Yes indeed, it takes courage. But I am glad I was firm, for now I shall soon perfect my invention; and Doctor Relling thinks, as I do myself, that Father may be allowed to wear his uniform again. I will demand that as my sole reward.

Greg. So that is what he meant about his uniform?

Hial. Yes, that is what he most yearns for. You can't think how my heart bleeds for him. Every time we celebrate any little family festival—Gina's and my wedding day or whatever it may be—in comes the old man in the lieutenant's uniform of happier days. But if he only hears a knock at the door—for he daren't show himself to strangers, you know—he hurries back to his room again as fast as his old legs can carry him. Oh, it's heartrending for a son to see such things!

Greg. How long do you think it will take you to finish your invention?

Hial. Come now, you mustn't expect me to enter into particulars like that. An invention is not a thing completely under one's own control. It depends largely on inspiration—on intuition—and it is almost impossible to predict when the inspiration may come.

Greg. But it's advancing?

Hial. Yes, certainly it is advancing. I turn it over in my mind every day; I am full of it. Every afternoon, when I have had my dinner, I shut myself up in the parlor where I can ponder undisturbed. But I can't be goaded to it; it's not a bit of good. Relling says so too.

Greg. And you don't think that all that business in the garret draws you off and distracts you too much?

HIAL. No, no, no; quite the contrary. You mustn't say that. I cannot be everlastingly absorbed in the same laborious train of thought. I must have something alongside of it to fill up the time of waiting. The inspiration, the intuition, you see—when it comes it comes, and there's an end of it.

GREG. My dear Hialmar, I almost think you have something of the wild duck in you.

HIAL. Something of the wild duck? How do you mean?

GREG. You have dived down and bitten yourself fast in the undergrowth.

HIAL. Are you alluding to the well-nigh fatal shot that has broken my father's wing—and mine too?

GREG. Not exactly to that. I don't say that your wing has been broken, but you have strayed into a poisonous marsh, Hialmar; an insidious disease has taken hold of you, and you have sunk down to die in the dark.

HIAL. I? To die in the dark? Look here, Gregers, you must really leave off talking such nonsense.

GREG. Don't be afraid; I shall find a way to help you up again. I, too, have a mission in life now; I found it yesterday.

HIAL. That's all very well, but you will please leave me out of it. I can assure you that—apart from my very natural melancholy, of course—I am as contented as anyone can wish to be.

GREG. Your contentment is an effect of the marsh poison.

HIAL. Now, my dear Gregers, pray do not go on about disease and poison; I am not used to that sort of talk. In my house nobody ever speaks to me about unpleasant things.

GREG. Ah, that I can easily believe.

HIAL. It's not good for me, you see. And there are no marsh poisons here, as you express it. The poor photographer's roof is lowly, I know—and my circumstances are narrow. But I am an inventor, and I am the bread-winner of a family. That exalts me above my mean surroundings. Ah, here comes lunch!

[GINA *and* HEDVIG *bring bottles of ale, a decanter of brandy, glasses, etc. At the same time* RELLING *and* MOLVIK *enter from the passage; they are both without hat or overcoat.* MOLVIK *is dressed in black.*]

GINA [*placing the things upon the table*]. Ah, you two have come in the nick of time.

RELL. Molvik got it into his head that he could smell herring salad, and then there was no holding him. Good morning again, Ekdal.

HIAL. Gregers, let me introduce you to Mr Molvik—Doctor—— Oh, you know Relling, don't you?

GREG. Yes, slightly.

RELL. Oh, Mr Werle junior! Yes, we two have had one or two little skirmishes up at the Höidal works. You've just moved in?

GREG. I moved in this morning.

RELL. Molvik and I live right under you, so you haven't far to go for the doctor and the clergyman if you should need anything in that line.

GREG. Thanks; it's not quite unlikely, for yesterday we were thirteen at table.

HIAL. Oh, come now, don't let us get upon unpleasant subjects again!

RELL. You may make your mind easy, Ekdal; I'll be hanged if the finger of fate points to you.

HIAL. I should hope not, for the sake of my family. But let us sit down now and eat and drink and be merry.

GREG. Shall we not wait for your father?

HIAL. No, his lunch will be taken in to him later. Come along!

[*The men seat themselves at table and eat and drink.* GINA *and* HEDVIG *go in and out and wait upon them.*]

RELL. Molvik was frightfully screwed yesterday, Mrs Ekdal.

GINA. Really? Yesterday again?

RELL. Didn't you hear him when I brought him home last night?

GINA. No, I can't say I did.

RELL. That was a good thing, for Molvik was disgusting last night.

GINA. Is that true, Molvik?

MOLVIK. Let us draw a veil over last night's proceedings. That sort of thing is totally foreign to my better self.

RELL. [*To* GREGERS]. It comes over him like a sort of possession, and then I have to go out on the loose with him. Mr Molvik is demonic, you see.

GREG. Demonic?

RELL. Molvik is demonic, yes.

GREG. H'm.

RELL. And demonic natures are not made to walk straight through the world; they must meander a little now and then. Well, so you still stick up there at those horrible grimy works?

GREG. I have stuck there until now.

RELL. And did you ever manage to collect that claim you went about presenting?

GREG. Claim? [*Understands him.*] Ah, I see.

HIAL. Have you been presenting claims, Gregers?

GREG. Oh, nonsense.

RELL. Faith, but he has, though! He went round to all the cotters' cabins presenting something he called "the claim of the ideal."

GREG. I was young then.

RELL. You're right; you were very young. And as for the claim of the ideal—you never got it honored while *I* was up there.

GREG. Nor since either.

RELL. Ah, then you've learned to knock a little discount off, I expect.

GREG. Never, when I have a true man to deal with.

HIAL. No, I should think not, indeed. A little butter, Gina.

RELL. And a slice of bacon for Molvik.

MOLVIK. Ugh! not bacon!

[*A knock at the garret door.*]

HIAL. Open the door, Hedvig; Father wants to come out.

[HEDVIG *goes over and opens the door a little way;* EKDAL *enters with a fresh rabbitskin; she closes the door after him.*]

EKD. Good morning, gentlemen! Good sport today. Shot a big one.

HIAL. And you've gone and skinned it without waiting for me!

EKD. Salted it too. It's good tender meat, is rabbit; it's sweet; it tastes like sugar. Good appetite to you, gentlemen! [*Goes into his room.*]

MOLVIK [*rising*]. Excuse me—I can't—I must get downstairs immediately——

RELL. Drink some soda water, man!

MOLVIK [*hurrying away*]. Ugh—ugh. [*Goes out by the passage door.*]

RELL. [*to* HIALMAR]. Let us drain a glass to the old hunter.

HIAL. [*clinks glasses with him*]. To the undaunted sportsman who has looked death in the face!

RELL. To the gray-haired—— [*Drinks.*] By the bye, is his hair gray or white?

HIAL. Something between the two,

I fancy; for that matter, he has very few hairs left of any color.

RELL. Well, well, one can get through the world with a wig. After all, you are a happy man, Ekdal; you have your noble mission to labor for——

HIAL. And I do labor, I can tell you.

RELL. And then you have your excellent wife, shuffling quietly in and out in her felt slippers, with that see-saw walk of hers, and making everything cosy and comfortable about you.

HIAL. Yes, Gina [*nods to her*]—you were a good helpmate on the path of life.

GINA. Oh, don't sit there cricketizing me.

RELL. And your Hedvig too, Ekdal!

HIAL. [*affected*]. The child, yes! The child before everything! Hedvig, come here to me. [*Strokes her hair.*] What day is it tomorrow, eh?

HED. [*shaking him*]. Oh no, you're not to say anything, Father.

HIAL. It cuts me to the heart when I think what a poor affair it will be; only a little festivity in the garret.

HED. Oh, but that's just what I like!

RELL. Just you wait till the wonderful invention sees the light, Hedvig!

HIAL. Yes indeed—then you shall see! Hedvig, I have resolved to make your future secure. You shall live in comfort all your days. I will demand something or other—on your behalf. That shall be the poor inventor's sole reward.

HED. [*whispering, with her arms round his neck*]. Oh, you dear, kind father!

RELL. [*to* GREGERS]. Come now, don't you find it pleasant, for once in a way, to sit at a well-spread table in a happy family circle?

HIAL. Ah yes, I really prize these social hours.

GREG. For my part, I don't thrive in marsh vapors.

RELL. Marsh vapors?

HIAL. Oh, don't begin with that stuff again!

GINA. Goodness knows there's no vapors in this house, Mr Werle; I give the place a good airing every blessed day.

GREG. [*leaves the table*]. No airing you can give will drive out the taint I mean.

HIAL. Taint!

GINA. Yes, what do you say to that, Ekdal!

RELL. Excuse me—may it not be you yourself that have brought the taint from those mines up there?

GREG. It is like you to call what I bring into this house a taint.

RELL. [*goes up to him*]. Look here, Mr Werle junior: I have a strong suspicion that you are still carrying about that "claim of the ideal" large as life in your coattail pocket.

GREG. I carry it in my breast.

RELL. Well, wherever you carry it, I advise you not to come dunning us with it here so long as *I* am on the premises.

GREG. And if I do so nonetheless?

RELL. Then you'll go headforemost down the stairs; now I've warned you.

HIAL. [*rising*]. Oh, but, Relling——

GREG. Yes, you may turn me out.

GINA [*interposing between them*]. We can't have that, Relling. But I must say, Mr Werle, it ill becomes you to talk about vapors and taints after all the mess you made with your stove.

[*A knock at the passage door.*]

HED. Mother, there's somebody knocking.

HIAL. There now, we're going to have a whole lot of people!

GINA. I'll go. [*Goes over and opens the door, starts and draws back.*] Oh—oh dear!

[WERLE, *in a fur coat, advances one step into the room.*]

WER. Excuse me, but I think my son is staying here.

GINA [*with a gulp*]. Yes.

HIAL. [*approaching him*]. Won't you do us the honor to——

WER. Thank you, I merely wish to speak to my son.

GREG. What is it? Here I am.

WER. I want a few words with you in your room.

GREG. In my room? Very well. [*About to go.*]

GINA. No, no, your room's not in a fit state.

WER. Well, then, out in the passage here; I want to have a few words with you alone.

HIAL. You can have them here, sir. Come into the parlor, Relling.

[HIALMAR *and* RELLING *go off to the right;* GINA *takes* HEDVIG *with her into the kitchen.*]

GREG. [*after a short pause*]. Well, now we are alone.

WER. From something you let fall last evening, and from your coming to lodge with the Ekdals, I can't help inferring that you intend to make yourself unpleasant to me in one way or another.

GREG. I intend to open Hialmar Ekdal's eyes. He shall see his position as it really is—that is all.

WER. Is that the mission in life you spoke of yesterday?

GREG. Yes. You have left me no other.

WER. Is it I, then, that have crippled your mind, Gregers?

GREG. You have crippled my whole life. I am not thinking of all that about Mother—but it's thanks to you that I am continually haunted and harassed by a guilty conscience.

WER. Indeed! It is your conscience that troubles you, is it?

GREG. I ought to have taken a stand against you when the trap was set for Lieutenant Ekdal. I ought to have cautioned him, for I had a misgiving as to what was in the wind.

WER. Yes, that was the time to have spoken.

GREG. I did not dare to, I was so cowed and spiritless. I was mortally afraid of you—not only then, but long afterward.

WER. You have got over that fear now, it appears.

GREG. Yes, fortunately. The wrong done to old Ekdal, both by me and by others, can never be undone; but Hialmar I can rescue from all the falsehood and deception that are bringing him to ruin.

WER. Do you think that will be doing him a kindness?

GREG. I have not the least doubt of it.

WER. You think our worthy photographer is the sort of man to appreciate such friendly offices?

GREG. Yes, I do.

WER. H'm—we shall see.

GREG. Besides, if I am to go on living, I must try to find some cure for my sick conscience.

WER. It will never be sound. Your conscience has been sickly from childhood. That is a legacy from your mother, Gregers—the only one she left you.

GREG. [*with a scornful half-smile*]. Have you not yet forgiven her for the mistake you made in supposing she would bring you a fortune?

WER. Don't let us wander from the point. Then you hold to your purpose of setting young Ekdal upon what you imagine to be the right scent?

GREG. Yes, that is my fixed resolve.

WER. Well, in that case I might have spared myself this visit, for of course it is useless to ask whether you will return home with me?

GREG. Quite useless.

WER. And I suppose you won't enter the firm either?

GREG. No.

WER. Very good. But as I am thinking of marrying again, your share in the property will fall to you at once.

GREG. [*quickly*]. No, I do not want that.

WER. You don't want it?

GREG. No, I dare not take it, for conscience' sake.

WER. [*after a pause*]. Are you going up to the works again?

GREG. No; I consider myself released from your service.

WER. But what are you going to do?

GREG. Only to fulfill my mission, nothing more.

WER. Well, but afterward? What are you going to live upon?

GREG. I have laid by a little out of my salary.

WER. How long will that last?

GREG. I think it will last my time.

WER. What do you mean?

GREG. I shall answer no more questions.

WER. Good-by, then, Gregers.

GREG. Good-by.

[WERLE *goes.*]

HIAL [*peeping in*]. He's gone, isn't he?

GREG. Yes.

[HIALMAR *and* RELLING *enter; also* GINA *and* HEDVIG *from the kitchen.*]

RELL. That luncheon party was a failure.

GREG. Put on your coat, Hialmar; I want you to come for a long walk with me.

HIAL. With pleasure. What was it your father wanted? Had it anything to do with me?

GREG. Come along. We must have a talk. I'll go and put on my overcoat. [*Goes out by the passage door.*]

GINA. You shouldn't go out with him, Ekdal.

RELL. No, don't you do it. Stay where you are.

HIAL. [*gets his hat and overcoat*]. Oh, nonsense! When a friend of my youth feels impelled to open his mind to me in private——

RELL. But devil take it—don't you see that the fellow's mad, cracked, demented!

GINA. There, what did I tell you! His mother before him had crazy fits like that sometimes.

HIAL. The more need for a friend's watchful eye. [*To* GINA.] Be sure you have dinner ready in good time. Good-by for the present. [*Goes out by the passage door.*]

RELL. It's a thousand pities the fellow didn't go to hell through one of the Höidal mines.

GINA. Good lord! What makes you say that?

RELL. [*muttering*]. Oh, I have my own reasons.

GINA. Do you think young Werle is really mad?

RELL. No, worse luck; he's no madder than most other people. But one disease he has certainly got in his system.

GINA. What is it that's the matter with him?

RELL. Well, I'll tell you, Mrs Ekdal. He is suffering from an acute attack of integrity.

GINA. Integrity?

HED. Is that a kind of disease?

RELL. Yes, it's a national disease, but it only appears sporadically. [*Nods to* GINA.] Thanks for your hospitality. [*He goes out by the passage door.*]

GINA [*moving restlessly to and fro.*] Ugh, that Gregers Werle—he was always a wretched creature.

HED. [*standing by the table and looking searchingly at her*]. I think all this is very strange.

ACT IV

SCENE—HIALMAR EKDAL'S *studio. A photograph has just been taken; a camera with the cloth over it, a pedestal, two chairs, a folding table, etc., are standing out in the room. Afternoon light; the sun is going down; a little later it begins to grow dusk.*

GINA *stands in the passage doorway with a little box and a wet glass plate in her hand and is speaking to somebody outside.*

GINA. Yes, certainly. When I make a promise I keep it. The first dozen shall be ready on Monday. Good afternoon.

[*Someone is heard going downstairs.* GINA *shuts the door, slips the plate into the box and puts it into the covered camera.*]

HED. [*comes in from the kitchen*]. Are they gone?

GINA [*tidying up*]. Yes, thank goodness. I've got rid of them at last.

HED. But can you imagine why Father hasn't come home yet?

GINA. Are you sure he's not down in Relling's room?

HED. No, he's not; I ran down the kitchen stair just now and asked.

GINA. And his dinner standing and getting cold too.

HED. Yes, I can't understand it. Father's always so careful to be home to dinner!

GINA. Oh, he'll be here directly, you'll see.

HED. I wish he would come; everything seems so queer today.

GINA [*calls out*]. There he is!

[HIALMAR EKDAL *comes in at the passage door.*]

HED. [*going to him*]. Father! Oh, what a time we've been waiting for you!

GINA [*glancing sidelong at him*]. You've been out a long time, Ekdal.

HIAL. [*without looking at her*]. Rather long, yes. [*He takes off his overcoat;* GINA *and* HEDVIG *go to help him; he motions them away.*]

GINA. Perhaps you've had dinner with Werle?

HIAL. [*hanging up his coat*]. No.

GINA [*going toward the kitchen door*]. Then I'll bring some in for you.

HIAL. No; let the dinner alone. I want nothing to eat.

HED. [*going nearer to him*]. Are you not well, Father?

HIAL. Well? Oh yes, well enough. We have had a tiring walk, Gregers and I.

GINA. You didn't ought to have gone so far, Ekdal; you're not used to it.

HIAL. H'm; there's many a thing a man must get used to in this world. [*Wanders about the room.*] Has anyone been here whilst I was out?

GINA. Nobody but the two sweethearts.

HIAL. No new orders?

GINA. No, not today.

HED. There will be some tomorrow, Father, you'll see.

HIAL. I hope there will, for tomorrow I am going to set to work in real earnest.

HED. Tomorrow! Don't you remember what day it is tomorrow?

HIAL. Oh yes, by the bye—— Well, the day after, then. Henceforth I mean to do everything myself; I shall take all the work into my own hands.

GINA. Why, what can be the good of that, Ekdal? It'll only make your life a burden to you. I can manage the photography all right, and you can go on working at your invention.

HED. And think of the wild duck, Father, and all the hens and rabbits and——

HIAL. Don't talk to me of all that trash! From tomorrow I will never set foot in the garret again.

HED. Oh, but, Father, you promised that we should have a little party.

HIAL. H'm, true. Well, then, from the day after tomorrow. I should almost like to wring that cursed wild duck's neck!

HED. [*shrieks*]. The wild duck!

GINA. Well, I never!

HED. [*shaking him*]. Oh no, Father; you know it's my wild duck!

HIAL. That is why I don't do it. I haven't the heart to—for your sake, Hedvig. But in my inmost soul I feel that I ought to do it. I ought not to tolerate under my roof a creature that has been through those hands.

GINA. Why, good gracious, even if Grandfather did get it from that poor creature Pettersen——

HED. [*going after him*]. But think of the wild duck—the poor wild duck!

HIAL. [*stops*]. I tell you I will spare it—for your sake. Not a hair of its head shall be—I mean, it shall be spared. There are greater problems than that to be dealt with. But you should go out a little now, Hedvig, as usual; it is getting dusk enough for you now.

HED. No, I don't care about going out now.

HIAL. Yes, do; it seems to me your eyes are blinking a great deal; all these vapors in here are bad for you. The air is heavy under this roof.

HED. Very well then, I'll run down the kitchen stair and go for a little walk. My cloak and hat? Oh, they're in my own room. Father—be sure you don't do the wild duck any harm whilst I'm out.

HIAL. Not a feather of its head shall be touched. [*Draws her to him.*] You and I, Hedvig—we two—— Well, go along.

[HEDVIG *nods to her parents and goes out through the kitchen.*]

HIAL. [*walks about without looking up*]. Gina.

GINA. Yes?

HIAL. From tomorrow—or say from the day after tomorrow—I

should like to keep the household account book myself.

GINA. Do you want to keep the accounts too now?

HIAL. Yes; or to check the receipts at any rate.

GINA. Lord help us; that's soon done.

HIAL. One would hardly think so; at any rate you seem to make the money go a very long way. [*Stops and looks at her.*] How do you manage it?

GINA. It's because me and Hedvig, we need so little.

HIAL. Is it the case that Father is very liberally paid for the copying he does for Mr Werle?

GINA. I don't know as he gets anything out of the way. I don't know the rates for that sort of work.

HIAL. Well, what does he get, about? Let me hear!

GINA. Oh, it varies; I daresay it 'll come to about as much as he costs us, with a little pocket money over.

HIAL. As much as he costs us! And you have never told me this before.

GINA. No, how could I tell you? It pleased you so much to think he got everything from you.

HIAL. And he gets it from Mr Werle.

GINA. Oh well, he has plenty and to spare, he has.

HIAL. Light the lamp for me, please!

GINA [*lighting the lamp*]. And of course we don't know as it's Mr Werle himself; it may be Graberg.

HIAL. Why attempt such an evasion?

GINA. I don't know; I only thought —

HIAL. H'm!

GINA. It wasn't me that got Grandfather that copying. It was Bertha, when she used to come about us.

HIAL. It seems to me your voice is trembling.

GINA [*putting the lamp shade on*]. Is it?

HIAL. And your hands are shaking, are they not?

GINA [*firmly*]. Come right out with it, Ekdal. What has he been saying about me?

HIAL. Is it true—can it be true that—that there was an—an understanding between you and Mr Werle while you were in service there?

GINA. That's not true. Not at that time. Mr Werle did come after me, that's a fact. And his wife thought there was something in it, and then she made such a hocus-pocus and hurly-burly, and she hustled me and bustled me about so that I left her service.

HIAL. But afterward, then?

GINA. Well, then I went home. And Mother—well, she wasn't the woman you took her for, Ekdal; she kept on worrying and worrying at me about one thing and another—for Mr Werle was a widower by that time.

HIAL. Well, and then?

GINA. I suppose you've got to know it. He gave me no peace until he'd had his way.

HIAL. [*striking his hands together*]. And this is the mother of my child! How could you hide this from me?

GINA. Yes, it was wrong of me; I ought certainly to have told you long ago.

HIAL. You should have told me at the very first—then I should have known the sort of woman you were.

GINA. But would you have married me all the same?

HIAL. How can you dream that I would?

GINA. That's just why I didn't dare tell you anything then. For I'd come to care for you so much, you see, and I couldn't go and make myself utterly miserable.

HIAL. [*walks about*]. And this is my Hedvig's mother! And to know that all I see before me [*kicks at chair*]—all that I call my home—I owe to a favored predecessor! Oh, that scoundrel Werle!

GINA. Do you repent of the fourteen—the fifteen years we've lived together?

HIAL. [*placing himself in front of her*]. Have you not every day, every hour, repented of the spider's web of deceit you have spun around me? Answer me that! How could you help writhing with penitence and remorse?

GINA. Oh, my dear Ekdal, I've had all I could do to look after the house and get through the day's work.

HIAL. Then you never think of reviewing your past?

GINA. No; heaven knows I'd almost forgotten those old stories.

HIAL. Oh, this dull, callous contentment! To me there is something revolting about it. Think of it—never so much as a twinge of remorse!

GINA. But tell me, Ekdal—what would have become of you if you hadn't had a wife like me?

HIAL. Like you!

GINA. Yes; for you know I've always been a bit more practical and wide awake than you. Of course I'm a year or two older.

HIAL. What would have become of me!

GINA. You'd got into all sorts of bad ways when first you met me; that you can't deny.

HIAL. "Bad ways," do you call them? Little do you know what a man goes through when he is in grief and despair—especially a man of my fiery temperament.

GINA. Well, well, that may be so. And I've no reason to crow over you neither, for you turned a moral of a husband, that you did, as soon as ever you had a house and home of your own. And now we'd got everything so nice and cosy about us, and me and Hedvig was just thinking we'd soon be able to let ourselves go a bit in the way of both food and clothes.

HIAL. In the swamp of deceit, yes.

GINA. I wish to goodness that detestable thing had never set his foot inside our doors!

HIAL. And I, too, thought my home such a pleasant one. That was a delusion. Where shall I now find the elasticity of spirit to bring my invention into the world of reality? Perhaps it will die with me, and then it will be your past, Gina, that will have killed it.

GINA [*nearly crying*]. You mustn't say such things, Ekdal. Me, that has only wanted to do the best I could for you all my days!

HIAL. I ask you, what becomes of the breadwinner's dream? When I used to lie in there on the sofa and brood over my invention I had a clear enough presentiment that it would sap my vitality to the last drop. I felt even then that the day when I held the patent in my hand—that day—would bring my—release. And then it was my dream that you should live on after me, the dead inventor's well-to-do widow.

GINA [*drying her tears*]. No, you mustn't talk like that, Ekdal. May the

Lord never let me see the day I am left a widow!

HIAL. Oh, the whole dream has vanished. It is all over now. All over!

[GREGERS WERLE *opens the passage door cautiously and looks in.*]

GREG. May I come in?

HIAL. Yes, come in.

GREG. [*comes forward, his face beaming witih satisfaction, and holds out both his hands to them*]. Well, dear friends! [*Looks from one to the other and whispers to* HIALMAR.] Have you not done it yet?

HIAL. [*aloud*]. It is done.

GREG. It is?

HIAL. I have passed through the bitterest moments of my life.

GREG. But also, I trust, the most ennobling.

HIAL. Well, at any rate, we have got through it for the present.

GINA. God forgive you, Mr Werle.

GREG. [*in great surprise*]. But I don't understand this.

HIAL. What don't you understand?

GREG. After so great a crisis—a crisis that is to be the starting point of an entirely new life—of a communion founded on truth and free from all taint of deception——

HIAL. Yes, yes, I know; I know that quite well.

GREG. I confidently expected, when I entered the room, to find the light of transfiguration shining upon me from both husband and wife. And now I see nothing but dullness, oppression, gloom——

GINA. Oh, is that it? [*Takes off the lamp shade.*]

GREG. You will not understand me, Mrs Ekdal. Ah well, you, I suppose, need time to—— But you, Hialmar? Surely you feel a new consecration after the great crisis?

HIAL. Yes, of course I do. That is —in a sort of way.

GREG. For surely nothing in the world can compare with the joy of forgiving one who has erred and raising her up to oneself in love.

HIAL. Do you think a man can so easily throw off the bitter cup I have drained?

GREG. No, not a common man, perhaps. But a man like you——

HIAL. Good God! I know that well enough. But you must keep me up to it, Gregers. It takes time, you know.

GREG. You have much of the wild duck in you, Hialmar.

[RELLING *has come in at the passage door.*]

RELL. Oho! Is the wild duck to the fore again?

HIAL. Yes; Mr Werle's wing-broken victim.

RELL. Mr Werle? So it's him you are talking about?

HIAL. Him and—ourselves.

RELL. [*in an undertone to* GREGERS]. May the devil fly away with you!

HIAL. What is that you are saying?

RELL. Only uttering a heartfelt wish that this quacksalver would take himself off. If he stays here he is quite equal to making an utter mess of life for both of you.

GREG. These two will not make a mess of life, Mr Relling. Of course I won't speak to Hialmar—him we know. But she too, in her innermost heart, has certainly something loyal and sincere——

GINA [*almost crying*]. You might have let me alone for what I was then.

RELL. [*to* GREGERS]. Is it rude to ask what you really want in this house?

GREG. To lay the foundations of a true marriage.

RELL. So you don't think Ekdal's marriage is good enough as it is?

GREG. No doubt it is as good a marriage as most others, worse luck. But a true marriage it has yet to become.

HIAL. You have never had eyes for the claims of the ideal, Relling.

RELL. Rubbish, my boy! But excuse me, Mr Werle; how many—in round numbers—how many true marriages have you seen in the course of your life?

GREG. Scarcely a single one.

RELL. Nor I either.

GREG. But I have seen innumerable marriages of the opposite kind. And it has been my fate to see at close quarters what ruin such a marriage can work in two human souls.

HIAL. A man's whole moral basis may give away beneath his feet; that is the terrible part of it.

RELL. Well, I can't say I've ever been exactly married, so I don't pretend to speak with authority. But this I know, that the child enters into the marriage problem. And you must leave the child in peace.

HIAL. Oh—Hedvig! My poor Hedvig!

RELL. Yes, you must be good enough to keep Hedvig outside of all this. You two are grown-up people; you are free, in God's name, to make what mess and muddle you please of your life. But you must deal cautiously with Hedvig, I tell you; else you may do her a great injury.

HIAL. An injury!

RELL. Yes, or she may do herself an injury—and perhaps others too.

GINA. How can you know that, Relling?

HIAL. Her sight is in no immediate danger, is it?

RELL. I am not talking about her sight. Hedvig is at a critical age. She may be getting all sorts of mischief into her head.

GINA. That's true—I've noticed it already! She's taken to carrying on with the fire out in the kitchen. She calls it playing at house on fire. I'm often scared for fear she really sets fire to the house.

RELL. You see, I thought as much.

GREG. [*to* RELLING]. But how do you account for that?

RELL. [*sullenly*]. Her constitution's changing, sir.

HIAL. So long as the child has me—so long as *I* am above ground—— [*A knock at the door.*]

GINA. Hush, Ekdal, there's someone in the passage. [*Calls out.*] Come in!

[MRS SORBY, *in walking dress, comes in.*]

MRS S. Good evening.

GINA [*going toward her*]. Is it really you, Bertha?

MRS S. Yes, of course it is. But I'm disturbing you, I'm afraid.

HIAL. No, not at all; an emissary from that house——

MRS S. [*to* GINA]. To tell the truth, I hoped your menfolk would be out at this time. I just ran up to have a little chat with you and to say good-by.

GINA. Good-by? Are you going away then?

MRS S. Yes, tomorrow morning—up to Höidal. Mr Werle started this afternoon. [*Lightly to* GREGERS.] He asked me to say good-by for him.

GINA. Only fancy!

HIAL. I say: beware!

GREG. I must explain the situation.

My father and Mrs Sorby are going to be married.

HIAL. Going to be married!

GINA. Oh, Bertha! So it's come to that at last!

RELL. [*his voice quivering a little*]. This is surely not true?

MRS S. Yes, my dear Relling, it's true enough.

RELL. You are going to marry again?

MRS S. Yes, it looks like it. Werle has got a special license, and we are going to be married quietly up at the works.

GREG. Then I must wish you all happiness, like a dutiful stepson.

MRS S. Thank you very much—if you mean what you say. I certainly hope it will lead to happiness, both for Werle and for me.

RELL. You have every reason to hope that. Mr Werle never gets drunk—so far as I know; and I don't suppose he's in the habit of thrashing his wives, like the late lamented horse doctor.

MRS S. Come now, let Sorby rest in peace. He had his good points too.

RELL. Mr Werle has better ones, I have no doubt.

MRS S. He hasn't frittered away all that was good in him, at any rate. The man who does that must take the consequences.

RELL. I shall go out with Molvik this evening.

MRS S. You mustn't do that, Relling. Don't do it—for my sake.

RELL. There's nothing else for it. [*To* HIALMAR.] If you're going with us, come along.

GINA. No, thank you. Ekdal doesn't go in for that sort of dissertation.

HIAL. [*half aloud, in vexation*]. Oh, do hold your tongue!

RELL. Good-by, Mrs— Werle. [*Goes out through the passage door.*]

GREG. [*to* MRS SORBY]. You seem to know Doctor Relling pretty intimately.

MRS S. Yes, we have known each other for many years. At one time it seemed as if things might have gone further between us.

GREG. It was surely lucky for you that they did not.

MRS S. You may well say that. But I have always been wary of acting on impulse. A woman can't afford absolutely to throw herself away.

GREG. Are you not in the least afraid that I may let my father know about this old friendship?

MRS S. Why, of course I have told him all about it myself.

GREG. Indeed?

MRS S. Your father knows every single thing that can, with any truth, be said about me. I have told him all; it was the first thing I did when I saw what was in his mind.

GREG. Then you have been franker than most people, I think.

MRS S. I have always been frank. We women find that the best policy.

HIAL. What do you say to that, Gina?

GINA. Oh, we're not all alike, us women aren't. Some are made one way, some another.

MRS S. Well, for my part, Gina, I believe it's wisest to do as I've done. And Werle has no secrets either, on his side. That's really the great bond between us, you see. Now he can talk to me as openly as a child. He has never had the chance to do that before. Fancy a man like him, full of health and vigor, passing his whole youth and the best years of his life in listening to nothing but penitential sermons! And very often the sermons had for their text the most imaginary offenses—at least so I understand.

GINA. That's true enough.

GREG. If you ladies are going to follow up this topic, I had better withdraw.

MRS S. You can stay as far as that's concerned. I shan't say a word more. But I wanted you to know that I had done nothing secretly or in an underhand way. I may seem to have come in for a great piece of luck, and so I have, in a sense. But after all, I don't think I am getting any more than I am giving. I shall stand by him always, and I can tend and care for him as no one else can, now that he is getting helpless.

HIAL. Getting helpless?

GREG. [*to* MRS SORBY]. Hush, don't speak of that here.

MRS S. There is no disguising it any longer, however much he would like to. He is going blind.

HIAL. [*starts*]. Going blind? That's strange. He, too, going blind!

GINA. Lots of people do.

MRS S. And you can imagine what that means to a businessman. Well, I shall try as well as I can to make my eyes take the place of his. But I mustn't stay any longer; I have heaps of things to do. Oh, by the bye, Ekdal, I was to tell you that if there is anything Werle can do for you, you must just apply to Graberg.

GREG. That offer I am sure Hialmar Ekdal will decline with thanks.

MRS S. Indeed? I don't think he used to be so——

GINA. No, Bertha, Ekdal doesn't need anything from Mr Werle now.

HIAL. [*slowly and with emphasis*]. Will you present my compliments to your future husband and say that I intend very shortly to call upon Mr Graberg——

GREG. What! You don't really mean that?

HIAL. To call upon Mr Graberg, I say, and obtain an account of the sum I owe his principal. I will pay that debt of honor—ha, ha, ha! a debt of honor, let us call it! In any case I will pay the whole with five per cent interest.

GINA. But, my dear Ekdal, God knows we haven't got the money to do it.

HIAL. Be good enough to tell your future husband that I am working assiduously at my invention. Please tell him that what sustains me in this laborious task is the wish to free myself from a torturing burden of debt. That is my reason for proceeding with the invention. The entire profits shall be devoted to releasing me from my pecuniary obligations to your future husband.

MRS S. Something has happened here.

HIAL. Yes, you are right.

MRS S. Well, good-by. I had something else to speak to you about, Gina, but it must keep till another time. Good-by.

[HIALMAR *and* GREGERS *bow silently.* GINA *follows* MRS SORBY *to the door.*]

HIAL. Not beyond the threshold, Gina!

[MRS SORBY *goes;* GINA *shuts the door after her.*]

HIAL. There now, Gregers, I have got that burden of debt off my mind.

GREG. You soon will, at all events.

HIAL. I think my attitude may be called correct.

GREG. You are the man I have always taken you for.

Hial. In certain cases it is impossible to disregard the claim of the ideal. Yes, as the breadwinner of a family, I cannot but writhe and groan under it. I can tell you it is no joke for a man without capital to attempt the repayment of a long-standing obligation over which, so to speak, the dust of oblivion has gathered. But it cannot be helped; the man in me demands his rights.

Greg. [*laying his hand on* Hialmar's *shoulder*]. My dear Hialmar—was it not a good thing I came?

Hial. Yes.

Greg. Are you not glad to have had your true position made clear to you?

Hial [*somewhat impatiently*]. Yes, of course I am. But there is one thing that is revolting to my sense of justice.

Greg. And what is that?

Hial. It is that—— But I don't know whether I ought to express myself so unreservedly about your father.

Greg. Say what you please so far as I am concerned.

Hial. Well, then, is it not exasperating to think that it is not I, but he, who will realize the true marriage?

Greg. How can you say such a thing?

Hial. Because it is clearly the case. Isn't the marriage between your father and Mrs Sorby founded upon complete confidence, upon entire and unreserved candor on both sides? They hide nothing from each other, they keep no secrets in the background; their relation is based, if I may put it so, on mutual confession and absolution.

Greg. Well, what then?

Hial. Well, is not that the whole thing? Did you not yourself say that this was precisely the difficulty that had to be overcome in order to found a true marriage?

Greg. But this is a totally different matter, Hialmar. You surely don't compare either yourself or your wife with those two—— Oh, you understood me well enough.

Hial. Say what you like, there is something in all this that hurts and offends my sense of justice. It really looks as if there were no just Providence to rule the world.

Gina. Oh no, Ekdal; for God's sake don't say such things.

Greg. H'm; don't let us get upon those questions.

Hial. And yet, after all, I cannot but recognize the guiding finger of Fate. He is going blind.

Gina. Oh, you can't be sure of that.

Hial. There is no doubt about it. At all events there ought not to be, for in that very fact lies the righteous retribution. He has hoodwinked a confiding fellow creature in days gone by——

Greg. I fear he has hoodwinked many.

Hial. And now comes inexorable, mysterious Fate and demands Werle's own eyes.

Gina. Oh, how dare you say such dreadful things! You make me quite scared.

Hial. It is profitable, now and then, to plunge deep into the night side of existence.

[Hedvig, *in her hat and cloak, comes in by the passage door. She is pleasurably excited and out of breath.*]

Gina. Are you back already?

Hedvig. Yes, I didn't care to go any farther. It was a good thing, too, for I've just met someone at the door.

HIAL. It must have been that Mrs Sorby.

HED. Yes.

HIAL. [*walks up and down*]. I hope you have seen her for the last time.

[*Silence.* HEDVIG, *discouraged, looks first at one and then at the other, trying to divine their frame of mind.*]

HED. [*approaching, coaxingly*]. Father.

HIAL. Well—what is it, Hedvig?

HED. Mrs Sorby had something with her for me.

HIAL. [*stops*]. For you?

HED. Yes. Something for tomorrow.

GINA. Bertha has always given you some little thing on your birthday.

HIAL. What is it?

HED. Oh, you mustn't see it now. Mother is to give it to me tomorrow morning before I'm up.

HIAL. What is all this hocus-pocus that I am to be in the dark about?

HED. [*quickly*]. Oh no, you may see it if you like. It's a big letter. [*Takes the letter out of her cloak pocket.*]

HIAL. A letter too?

HED. Yes, it is only a letter. The rest will come afterward, I suppose. But fancy—a letter! I've never had a letter before. And there's "Miss" written upon it. [*Reads.*] "Miss Hedvig Ekdal." Only fancy—that's me!

HIAL. Let me see that letter.

HED. [*hands it to him*]. There it is.

HIAL. That is Mr Werle's hand.

GINA. Are you sure of that, Ekdal?

HIAL. Look for yourself.

GINA. Oh, what do I know about suchlike things?

HIAL. Hedvig, may I open the letter—and read it?

HED. Yes, of course you may, if you want to.

GINA. No, not tonight, Ekdal; it's to be kept till tomorrow.

HED. [*softly*]. Oh, can't you let him read it! It's sure to be something good, and then Father will be glad and everything will be nice again.

HIAL. I may open it then?

HED. Yes, do, Father. I'm so anxious to know what it is.

HIAL. Well and good. [*Opens the letter, takes out a paper, reads it through and appears bewildered.*] What is this?

GINA. What does it say?

HED. Oh yes, Father—tell us!

HIAL. Be quiet. [*Reads it through again; he has turned pale but says with self-control.*] It is a deed of gift, Hedvig.

HED. Is it? What sort of gift am I to have?

HIAL. Read for yourself.

[HEDVIG *goes over and reads for a time by the lamp.*]

HIAL. [*half aloud, clenching his hands*]. The eyes! The eyes—and then that letter!

HED. [*leaves off reading*]. Yes, but it seems to me that it's Grandfather that's to have it.

HIAL. [*takes letter from her*]. Gina—can you understand this?

GINA. I know nothing whatever about it; tell me what's the matter.

HIAL. Mr Werle writes to Hedvig that her old grandfather need not trouble himself any longer with the copying but that he can henceforth draw on the office for a hundred crowns a month——

GREG. Aha!

HED. A hundred crowns, Mother! I read that.

GINA. What a good thing for Grandfather!

HIAL. —a hundred crowns a month so long as he needs it—that means, of course, so long as he lives.

GINA. Well, so he's provided for, poor dear.

HIAL. But there is more to come. You didn't read that, Hedvig. Afterward this gift is to pass on to you.

HED. To me! The whole of it?

HIAL. He says that the same amount is assured to you for the whole of your life. Do you hear that, Gina?

GINA. Yes, I hear.

HED. Fancy—all that money for me! [*Shakes him.*] Father, Father, aren't you glad?

HIAL. [*eluding her*]. Glad! [*Walks about.*] Oh, what vistas—what perspectives open up before me! It is Hedvig, Hedvig that he showers these benefactions upon!

GINA. Yes, because it's Hedvig's birthday.

HED. And you'll get it all the same, Father! You know quite well I shall give all the money to you and Mother.

HIAL. To Mother, yes! There we have it.

GREG. Hialmar, this is a trap he is setting for you.

HIAL. Do you think it's another trap?

GREG. When he was here this morning he said: Hialmar Ekdal is not the man you imagine him to be.

HIAL. Not the man——

GREG. That you shall see, he said.

HIAL. He meant you should see that I would let myself be bought off!

HED. Oh, Mother, what does all this mean?

GINA. Go and take off your things.

[HEDVIG *goes out by the kitchen door, half crying.*]

GREG. Yes, Hialmar—now is the time to show who was right, he or I.

HIAL. [*slowly tears the paper across, lays both pieces on the table and says*]. Here is my answer.

GREG. Just what I expected.

HIAL. [*goes over to* GINA, *who stands by the stove and says in a low voice*]. Now please make a clean breast of it. If the connection between you and him was quite over when you—came to care for me, as you call it—why did he place us in a position to marry?

GINA. I suppose he thought as he could come and go in our house.

HIAL. Only that? Was he not afraid of a possible contingency?

GINA. I don't know what you mean.

HIAL. I want to know whether—your child has the right to live under my roof.

GINA [*draws herself up; her eyes flash*]. You ask that!

HIAL. You shall answer me this one question: Does Hedvig belong to me —or——? Well?

GINA [*looking at him with cold defiance*]. I don't know.

HIAL. [*quivering a little*]. You don't know!

GINA. How should *I* know. A creature like me——

HIAL. [*quietly turning away from her*]. Then I have nothing more to do in this house.

GREG. Take care, Hialmar! Think what you are doing!

HIAL. [*puts on his overcoat*]. In this case there is nothing for a man like me to think twice about.

GREG. Yes indeed, there are endless things to be considered. You three must be together if you are to attain the true frame of mind for self-sacrifice and forgiveness.

HIAL. I don't want to attain it. Never, never! My hat! [*Takes his hat.*] My home has fallen into ruins about me. [*Bursts into tears.*] Gregers, I have no child!

HED. [*who has opened the kitchen door*]. What is that you're saying? [*Coming to him.*] Father, Father!

Gina. There, you see!

HIAL. Don't come near me, Hedvig! Keep far away. I cannot bear to see you. Oh! those eyes! Good-by. [*Makes for the door.*]

HED. [*clinging close to him and screaming loudly*]. No! No' Don't leave me!

GINA [*cries out*]. Look at the child, Ekdal! Look at the child!

HIAL. I will not! I cannot! I must get out—away from all this! [*He tears himself away from* HEDVIG *and goes out by the passage door.*]

HED. [*with despairing eyes*]. He is going away from us, Mother! He is going away from us! He will never come back again!

GINA. Don't cry, Hedvig. Father's sure to come back again.

HED. [*throws herself sobbing on the sofa*]. No, no, he'll never come home to us any more.

GREG. Do you believe I meant all for the best, Mrs Ekdal?

GINA. Yes, I daresay you did, but God forgive you all the same.

HED. [*lying on the sofa*]. Oh, this will kill me! What have I done to him? Mother, you must fetch him home again!

GINA. Yes, yes, yes; only be quiet, and I'll go out and look for him. [*Puts on her outdoor things.*] Perhaps he's gone into Relling's. But you mustn't lie there and cry. Promise me!

HED. [*weeping convulsively*]. Yes, I'll stop, I'll stop; if only Father comes back!

GREG. [*to* GINA, *who is going*]. After all, had you not better leave him to fight out his bitter fight to the end?

GINA. Oh, he can do that afterward. First of all we must get the child quieted. [*Goes out by the passage door.*]

HED. [*sits up and dries her tears*]. Now you must tell me what all this means. Why doesn't Father want me any more?

GREG. You mustn't ask that till you are a big girl—quite grown up.

HED. [*sobs*]. But I can't go on being as miserable as this till I'm grown up. I think I know what it is. Perhaps I'm not really Father's child.

GREG. [*uneasily*]. How could that be?

HED. Mother might have found me. And perhaps Father has just got to know it; I've read of such things.

GREG. Well, but if it were so——

HED. I think he might be just as fond of me for all that. Yes, fonder almost. We got the wild duck in a present, you know, and I love it so dearly all the same.

GREG. [*turning the conversation*]. Ah, the wild duck, by the bye! Let us talk about the wild duck a little, Hedvig.

HED. The poor wild duck! He doesn't want to see it any more either. Only think, he wanted to wring its neck!

GREG. Oh, he won't do that.

HED. No, but he said he would like to. And I think it was horrid of Father to say it, for I pray for the wild duck every night and ask that it may be preserved from death and all that is evil.

GREG. [*looking at her*]. Do you say your prayers every night?

HED. Yes.

GREG. Who taught you to do that?

HED. I myself—one time when Father was very ill and had leeches on his neck and said that death was staring him in the face.

GREG. Well?

HED. Then I prayed for him as I lay in bed, and since then I have always kept it up.

GREG. And now you pray for the wild duck too?

HED. I thought it best to bring in the wild duck, for she was so weakly at first.

GREG. Do you pray in the morning too?

HED. No, of course not.

GREG. Why not in the morning as well?

HED. In the morning it's light, you know, and there's nothing in particular to be afraid of.

GREG. And your father was going to wring the neck of the wild duck that you love so dearly?

HED. No; he said he ought to wring its neck but he would spare it for my sake, and that was kind of Father.

GREG. [*coming a little nearer*]. But suppose you were to sacrifice the wild duck of your own free will for his sake?

HED. [*rising*]. The wild duck!

GREG. Suppose you were to make a free-will offering, for his sake, of the dearest treasure you have in the world?

HED. Do you think that would do any good?

GREG. Try it, Hedvig.

HED. [*softly, with flashing eyes.*] Yes, I will try it.

GREG. Have you really the courage for it, do you think?

HED. I'll ask Grandfather to shoot the wild duck for me.

GREG. Yes, do. But not a word to your mother about it.

HED. Why not?

GREG. She doesn't understand us.

HED. The wild duck! I'll try it tomorrow morning.

[GINA *comes in by the passage door.*]

HED. [*going toward her*]. Did you find him, Mother?

GINA. No, but I heard as he had called and taken Relling with him.

GREG. Are you sure of that?

GINA. Yes, the porter's wife said so. Molvik went with them too, she said.

GREG. This evening, when his mind so sorely needs to wrestle in solitude!

GINA [*takes off her things*]. Yes, men are strange creatures, so they are. The Lord only knows where Relling has dragged him to! I ran over to Madam Eriksen's, but they weren't there.

HED. [*struggling to keep back her tears*]. Oh, if he should never come home any more!

GREG. He will come home again. I shall have news to give him tomorrow, and then you shall see how he comes home. You may rely upon that, Hedvig, and sleep in peace. Good night. [*He goes out by the passage door.*]

HED. [*throws herself sobbing on* GINA's *neck*]. Mother, Mother!

GINA [*pats her shoulder and sighs*]. Ah yes, Relling was right, he was. That's what comes of it when crazy creatures go about presenting the claim of the—what-you-may-call-it.

ACT V

SCENE—HIALMAR EKDAL's *studio. Cold gray morning light. Wet snow lies upon the large panes of the sloping roof window.*

GINA *comes from the kitchen with an apron and bib on and carrying a dusting brush and a duster; she goes toward the sitting-room door. At the same moment* HEDVIG *comes hurriedly in from the passage.*

GINA [*stops*]. Well?

HED. Oh, Mother, I almost think he's down at Relling's——

GINA. There, you see!

HED. —because the porter's wife says she could hear that Relling had two people with him when he came home last night.

GINA. That's just what I thought.

HED. But it's no use his being there if he won't come up to us.

GINA. I'll go down and speak to him at all events.

[OLD EKDAL, *in dressing gown and slippers and with a lighted pipe, appears at the door of his room.*]

EKDAL. Hialmar—isn't Hialmar at home?

GINA. No, he's gone out.

EKDAL. So early? And in such a tearing snowstorm? Well, well, just as he pleases; I can take my morning walk alone. [*He slides the garret door aside;* HEDVIG *helps him; he goes in; she closes it after him.*]

HED. [*in an undertone*]. Only think, Mother, when poor Grandfather hears that Father is going to leave us.

GINA. Oh, nonsense; Grandfather mustn't hear anything about it. It was a heaven's mercy he wasn't at home yesterday in all that hurly-burly.

HED. Yes, but——

[GREGERS *comes in by the passage door.*]

GREG. Well, have you any news of him?

GINA. They say he's down at Relling's.

GREG. At Relling's! Has he really been out with those creatures?

GINA. Yes, like enough.

GREG. When he ought to have been yearning for solitude, to collect and clear his thoughts——

GINA. Yes, you may well say so.

[RELLING *enters from the passage.*]

HED. [*going to him*]. Is Father in your room?

GINA [*at the same time*]. Is he there?

RELL. Yes, to be sure he is.

HED. And you never let us know!

RELL. Yes, I'm a brute. But in the first place I had to look after the other brute; I mean our demonic friend, of course; and then I fell so dead asleep that——

GINA. What does Ekdal say today?

RELL. He says nothing whatever.

HED. Doesn't he speak?

RELL. Not a blessed word.

GREG. No, no; I can understand that very well.

GINA. But what's he doing then?

RELL. He's lying on the sofa, snoring.

GINA. Oh, is he? Yes, Ekdal's a rare one to snore.

HED. Asleep? Can he sleep?

RELL. Well, it certainly looks like it.

GREG. No wonder, after the spiritual conflict that has rent him——

GINA. And then he's never been used to gadding about out of doors at night.

HED. Perhaps it's a good thing that he's getting sleep, Mother.

GINA. Of course it is, and we must take care we don't wake him up too early. Thank you, Relling. I must get the house cleaned up a bit now, and then—— Come and help me, Hedvig.

[GINA *and* HEDVIG *go into the sitting room.*]

GREG. [*turning to* RELLING]. What

is your explanation of the spiritual tumult that is now going on in Hialmar Ekdal?

RELL. Devil a bit of a spiritual tumult have I noticed in him.

GREG. What! Not at such a crisis, when his whole life has been placed on a new foundation? How can you think that such an individuality as Hialmar's——

RELL. Oh, individuality—he! If he ever had any tendency to the abnormal developments you call individuality, I can assure you it was rooted out of him while he was still in his teens.

GREG. That would be strange indeed—considering the loving care with which he was brought up.

RELL. By those two high-flown, hysterical maiden aunts, you mean?

GREG. Let me tell you that they were women who never forgot the claim of the ideal—but of course you will only jeer at me again.

RELL. No, I'm in no humor for that. I know all about those ladies, for he has ladled out no end of rhetoric on the subject of his "two soul mothers." But I don't think he has much to thank them for. Ekdal's misfortune is that in his own circle he has always been looked upon as a shining light.

GREG. Not without reason, surely. Look at the depth of his mind!

RELL. I have never discovered it. That his father believed in it I don't so much wonder; the old lieutenant has been an ass all his days.

GREG. He has had a childlike mind all his days; that is what you cannot understand.

RELL. Well, so be it. But then when our dear sweet Hialmar went to college he at once passed for the great light of the future amongst his comrades too! He was handsome, the rascal—red and white—a shopgirl's dream of manly beauty; and with his superficially emotional temperament and his sympathetic voice and his talent for declaiming other people's verses and other people's thought's——

GREG. [*indignantly*]. Is it Hialmar Ekdal you are talking about in this strain?

RELL. Yes, with your permission; I am simply giving you an inside view of the idol you are groveling before.

GREG. I should hardly have thought I was quite stone-blind.

RELL. Yes, you are—or not far from it. You are a sick man too, you see.

GREG. You are right there.

RELL. Yes. Yours is a complicated case. First of all there is that plaguy integrity fever, and then—what's worse—you are always in a delirium of hero worship; you must always have something to adore, outside yourself.

GREG. Yes, I must certainly seek it outside myself.

RELL. But you make such shocking mistakes about every new phoenix you think you have discovered. Here again you have come to a cotter's cabin with your claim of the ideal, and the people of the house are insolvent.

GREG. If you don't think better than that of Hialmar Ekdal, what pleasure can you find in being everlastingly with him?

RELL. Well, you see, I'm supposed to be a sort of a doctor—save the mark! I can't but give a hand to the poor sick folk who live under the same roof with me.

GREG. Oh, indeed! Hialmar Ekdal is sick too, is he?

RELL. Most people are, worse luck.

GREG. And what remedy are you applying in Hialmar's case?

RELL. My usual one. I am cultivating the life illusion in him.

GREG. Life–illusion? I didn't catch what you said.

RELL. Yes, I said illusion. For illusion, you know, is the stimulating principle.

GREG. May I ask with what illusion Hialmar is inoculated?

RELL. No, thank you; I don't betray professional secrets to quacksalvers. You would probably go and muddle his case still more than you have already. But my method is infallible. I have applied it to Molvik as well. I have made him "demonic." That's the blister I have to put on his neck.

GREG. Is he not really demonic then?

RELL. What the devil do you mean by demonic? It's only a piece of gibberish I've invented to keep up a spark of life in him. But for that, the poor harmless creature would have succumbed to self-contempt and despair many a long year ago. And then the old lieutenant! But he has hit upon his own cure, you see.

GREG. Lieutenant Ekdal? What of him?

RELL. Just think of the old bear hunter shutting himself up in that dark garret to shoot rabbits! I tell you there is not a happier sportsman in the world than that old man pottering about in there among all that rubbish. The four or five withered Christmas trees he has saved up are the same to him as the whole great fresh Höidal forest; the cock and the hens are big game birds in the fir tops, and the rabbits that flop about the garret floor are the bears he has to battle with—the mighty hunter of the mountains!

GREG. Poor unfortunate old man! Yes, he has indeed had to narrow the ideals of his youth.

RELL. While I think of it, Mr Werle junior—don't use that foreign word: ideals. We have the excellent native word: lies.

GREG. Do you think the two things are related?

RELL. Yes, just about as closely as typhus and putrid fever.

GREG. Doctor Relling, I shall not give up the struggle until I have rescued Hialmar from your clutches!

RELL. So much the worse for him. Rob the average man of his life illusion and you rob him of his happiness at the same stroke. [*To* HEDVIG, *who comes in from the sitting room.*] Well, little wild-duck mother. I'm just going down to see whether Papa is still lying meditating upon that wonderful invention of his. [*Goes out by passage door.*]

GREG. [*approaches* HEDVIG]. I can see by your face that you have not yet done it.

HED. What? Oh, that about the wild duck! No.

GREG. I suppose your courage failed when the time came?

HED. No, that wasn't it. But when I awoke this morning and remembered what he had been talking about it seemed so strange.

GREG. Strange?

HED. Yes, I don't know—— Yesterday evening, at the moment, I thought there was something so delightful about it; but since I have slept and thought of it again, it somehow doesn't seem worth while.

GREG. Ah, I thought you could not

have grown up quite unharmed in this house.

HED. I don't care about that, if only Father would come up——

GREG. Oh, if only your eyes had been opened to that which gives life its value—if you possessed the true, joyous, fearless spirit of sacrifice you would soon see how he would come up to you. But I believe in you still, Hedvig. [*He goes out by the passage door.* HEDVIG *wanders about the room for a time; she is on the point of going into the kitchen when a knock is heard at the garret door.* HEDVIG *goes over and opens it a little; old* EKDAL *comes out; she pushes the door to again.*]

EKD. H'm, it's not much fun to take one's morning walk alone.

HED. Wouldn't you like to go shooting, Grandfather?

EKD. It's not the weather for it today. It's so dark there you can scarcely see where you're going.

HED. Do you never want to shoot anything besides the rabbits?

EKD. Do you think the rabbits aren't good enough?

HED. Yes, but what about the wild duck?

EKD. Ho-ho! Are you afraid I shall shoot your wild duck? Never in the world. Never!

HED. No, I suppose you couldn't; they say it's very difficult to shoot wild ducks.

EKD. Couldn't! Should rather think I could.

HED. How would you set about it, Grandfather? I don't mean with my wild duck, but with others.

EKD. I should take care to shoot them in the breast, you know; that's the surest place. And then you must shoot against the feathers, you see—not the way of the feathers.

HED. Do they die then, Grandfather?

EKD. Yes they die right enough—when you shoot properly. Well, I must go and brush up a bit. H'm—understand—h'm. [*Goes into his room.*]

[HEDVIG *waits a little, glances toward the sitting-room door, goes over to the bookcase, stands on tiptoe, takes the double-barreled pistol down from the shelf and looks at it.* GINA, *with brush and duster, comes from the sitting room.* HEDVIG *hastily lays down the pistol unobserved.*]

GINA. Don't stand raking amongst Father's things, Hedvig.

HED. [*goes away from the bookcase*]. I was only going to tidy up a little.

GINA. You'd better go into the kitchen and see if the coffee's keeping hot; I'll take his breakfast on a tray when I go down to him.

[HEDVIG *goes out.* GINA *begins to sweep and clean up the studio. Presently the passage door is opened with hesitation and* HIALMAR EKDAL *looks in. He has on his overcoat but not his hat; he is unwashed, and his hair is disheveled and unkempt. His eyes are dull and heavy.*]

GINA [*standing with the brush in her hand and looking at him*]. Oh, there now, Ekdal—so you've come after all?

HIAL [*comes in and answers in a toneless voice*]. I come—only to depart immediately.

GINA. Yes, yes, I suppose so. But, Lord help us! what a sight you are!

HIAL. A sight?

GINA. And your nice winter coat too! Well, that's done for.

HED.[*at the kitchen door*]. Mother,

hadn't I better—— [*Sees* HIALMAR, *gives a loud scream of joy and runs to him.*] Oh, Father, Father!

HIAL. [*turns away and makes a gesture of repulsion*]. Away, away, away! [*To* GINA.] Keep her away from me, I say!

GINA [*in a low tone*]. Go into the sitting room, Hedvig.

[HEDVIG *does so without a word.*]

HIAL. [*fussily pulls out the table drawer*]. I must have my books with me. Where are my books?

GINA. Which books?

HIAL. My scientific books, of course; the technical magazines I require for my invention.

GINA [*searches in the bookcase*]. Is it these here paper-covered ones?

HIAL. Yes, of course.

GINA [*lays a heap of magazines on the table*]. Shan't I get Hedvig to cut them for you?

HIAL. I don't require to have them cut for me. [*Short silence.*]

GINA. Then you're still set on leaving us, Ekdal?

HIAL. [*rummaging amongst the books*]. Yes, that is a matter of course, I should think.

GINA. Well, well.

HIAL [*vehemently*]. How can I live here, to be stabbed to the heart every hour of the day?

GINA. God forgive you for thinking such vile things of me.

HIAL. Prove——

GINA. I think it's you as has got to prove.

HIAL. After a past like yours? There are certain claims—I may almost call them claims of the ideal——

GINA. But what about Grandfather? What's to become of him, poor dear?

HIAL. I know my duty; my helpless father will come with me. I am going out into the town to make arrangements—— H'm [*hesitatingly*]—has anyone found my hat on the stairs?

GINA. No. Have you lost your hat?

HIAL. Of course I had it on when I came in last night—there's no doubt about that—but I couldn't find it this morning.

GINA. Lord help us! Where have you been to with those two ne'er-do-wells?

HIAL. Oh, don't bother me about trifles. Do you suppose I am in the mood to remember details?

GINA. If only you haven't caught cold, Ekdal—— [*Goes out into the kitchen.*]

HIAL. [*talks to himself in a low tone of irritation while he empties the table drawer*]. You're a scoundrel, Relling! You're a low fellow! Ah, you shameless tempter! I wish I could get someone to stick a knife into you! [*He lays some old letters on one side, finds the torn document of yesterday, takes it up and looks at the pieces, puts it down hurriedly as* GINA *enters.*]

GINA [*sets a tray with coffee, etc., on the table*]. Here's a drop of something hot, if you'd fancy it. And there's some bread and butter and a snack of salt meat.

HIAL. [*glancing at the tray*]. Salt meat? Never under this roof! It's true I have not had a mouthful of solid food for nearly twenty-four hours, but no matter. My memoranda! The commencement of my autobiography! What has become of my diary and all my important papers? [*Opens the sitting-room door but draws back.*] She is there too!

GINA. Good lord! the child must be somewhere!

HIAL. Come out. [*He makes room;*

HEDVIG *comes, scared, into the studio.*]

HIAL. [*with his hand on the door handle, says to* GINA]. In these, the last moments I spend in my former home, I wish to be spared from interlopers. [*Goes into the room.*]

HED. [*with a bound toward her mother, asks softly, trembling*]. Does that mean me?

GINA. Stay out in the kitchen, Hedvig; or, no—you'd best go into your own room. [*Speaks to* HIALMAR *as she goes in to him.*] Wait a bit, Ekdal; don't rummage so in the drawers. I know where everything is.

HED. [*stands a moment immovable, in terror and perplexity, biting her lips to keep back the tears; then she clenches her hands convulsively and says softly*]. The wild duck! [*She steals over and takes the pistol from the shelf, opens the garret door a little way, creeps in and draws the door to after her.* HIALMAR *and* GINA *can be heard disputing in the sitting room.*]

HIAL. [*comes in with some manuscript books and old loose papers which he lays upon the table*]. That portmanteau is of no use! There are a thousand and one things I must drag with me.

GINA [*following with the portmanteau*]. Why not leave all the rest for the present and only take a shirt and a pair of woolen drawers with you?

HIAL. Whew! All these exhausting preparations! [*Pulls off his overcoat and throws it upon the sofa.*]

GINA. And there's the coffee getting cold.

HIAL. H'm. [*Drinks a mouthful without thinking of it and then another.*]

GINA [*dusting the backs of the chairs*]. A nice job you'll have to find such another big garret for the rabbits.

HIAL. What! Am I to drag all those rabbits with me too?

GINA. You don't suppose Grandfather can get on without his rabbits.

HIAL. He must just get used to doing without them. Have not *I* to sacrifice very much greater things than rabbits!

GINA [*dusting the bookcase*]. Shall I put the flute in the portmanteau for you?

HIAL. No. No flute for me. But give me the pistol!

GINA. Do you want to take the pigstol with you?

HIAL. Yes. My loaded pistol.

GINA [*searching for it*]. It's gone. He must have taken it in with him.

HIAL. Is he in the garret?

GINA. Yes, of course he's in the garret.

HIAL. H'm—poor lonely old man. [*He takes a piece of bread and butter, eats it and finishes his cup of coffee.*]

GINA. And if we hadn't have let that room, you could have moved in there.

HIAL. And continued to live under the same roof with—— Never—never!

GINA. But couldn't you put up with the sitting room for a day or two? You could have it all to yourself.

HIAL. Never within these walls!

GINA. Well, then, down with Relling and Molvik.

HIAL. Don't mention those wretches' names to me! The very thought of them almost takes away my appetite. Oh no, I must go out into the storm and the snowdrift—go from house to house and seek shelter for my father and myself.

GINA. But you've got no hat, Ekdal! You've been and lost your hat, you know.

HIAL. Oh, those two brutes, those slaves of all the vices! A hat must be procured. [*Takes another piece of bread and butter.*] Some arrangements must be made. For I have no mind to throw away my life either. [*Looks for something on the tray.*]

GINA. What are you looking for?

HIAL. Butter.

GINA. I'll get some at once. [*Goes out into the kitchen.*]

HIAL. [*calls after her*]. Oh, it doesn't matter; dry bread is good enough for me.

GINA [*brings a dish of butter*]. Look here; this is fresh churned. [*She pours out another cup of coffee for him; he seats himself on the sofa, spreads more butter on the already buttered bread and eats and drinks a while in silence.*]

HIAL. Could I, without being subject to intrusion–intrusion of any sort –could I live in the sitting room there for a day or two?

GINA. Yes, to be sure you could, if you only would.

HIAL. For I see no possibility of getting all Father's things out in such a hurry.

GINA. And, besides, you've surely got to tell him first as you don't mean to live with us others no more.

HIAL. [*pushes away his coffee cup*]. Yes, there is that too; I shall have to lay bare the whole tangled story to him—— I must turn matters over; I must have breathing time. I cannot take all these burdens on my shoulders in a single day.

GINA. No, especially in such horrible weather as it is outside.

HIAL. [*touching* WERLE'S *letter*]. I see that paper is still lying about here.

GINA. Yes, *I* haven't touched it.

HIAL. So far as I am concerned it is mere wastepaper——

GINA. Well, *I* have certainly no notion of making any use of it.

HIAL. –but we had better not let it get lost all the same; in all the upset when I move it might easily——

GINA. I'll take good care of it. Ekdal.

HIAL. The donation is in the first instance made to Father, and it rests with him to accept or decline it.

GINA [*sighs*]. Yes, poor old Father ——

HIAL. To make quite safe—— Where shall I find some gum?

GINA [*goes to the bookcase*]. Here's the gum pot.

HIAL. And a brush?

GINA. The brush is here too. [*Brings him the things.*]

HIAL. [*takes a pair of scissors*]. Just a strip of paper at the back—— [*Clips and gums.*] Far be it from me to lay hands upon what is not my own–and least of all upon what belongs to a destitute old man–and to–the other as well. There now! Let it lie there for a time, and when it is dry take it away. I wish never to see that document again. Never!

[GREGERS WERLE *enters from the passage.*]

GREG. [*somewhat surprised*]. What –are you sitting here, Hialmar?

HIAL. [*rises hurriedly*]. I had sunk down from fatigue.

GREG. You have been having breakfast, I see.

HIAL. The body sometimes makes its claims felt too.

GREG. What have you decided to do?

HIAL. For a man like me there is only one course possible. I am just putting my most important things together. But it takes time, you know.

GINA [*with a touch of impatience*]. Am I to get the room ready for you or am I to pack your portmanteau?

HIAL. [*after a glance of annoyance at* GREGERS]. Pack—and get the room ready!

GINA [*takes the portmanteau*]. Very well; then I'll put in the shirt and the other things. [*Goes into the sitting room and draws the door to after her.*]

GREG. [*after a short silence*]. I never dreamed that this would be the end of it. Do you really feel it a necessity to leave house and home?

HIAL. [*wanders about restlessly*]. What would you have me do? I am not fitted to bear unhappiness, Gregers. I must feel secure and at peace in my surroundings.

GREG. But can you not feel that here? Just try it. I should have thought you had firm ground to build upon now—if only you start afresh. And, remember, you have your invention to live for.

HIAL. Oh, don't talk about my invention. It's perhaps still in the dim distance.

GREG. Indeed!

HIAL. Why, great heavens, what would you have one invent? Other people have invented almost everything already. It becomes more and more difficult every day——

GREG. And you have devoted so much labor to it.

HIAL. It was that blackguard Relling that urged me to it.

GREG. Relling?

HIAL. Yes, it was he that first made me realize my aptitude for making some notable discovery in photography.

GREG. Aha—it was Relling!

HIAL. Oh, I have been so truly happy over it! Not so much for the sake of the invention itself as because Hedvig believed in it—believed in it with a child's whole eagerness of faith. At least I have been fool enough to go and imagine that she believed in it.

GREG. Can you really think Hedvig has been false toward you?

HIAL. I can think anything now. It is Hedvig that stands in my way. She will blot out the sunlight from my whole life.

GREG. Hedvig! Is it Hedvig you are talking of? How should she blot out your sunlight?

HIAL. [*without answering*]. How unutterably I have loved that child! How unutterably happy I have felt every time I came home to my humble room and she flew to meet me with her sweet little blinking eyes. Oh, confiding fool that I have been! I loved her unutterably—and I yielded myself up to the dream, the delusion, that she loved me unutterably in return.

GREG. Do you call that a delusion?

HIAL. How should I know? I can get nothing out of Gina; and besides, she is totally blind to the ideal side of these complications. But to you I feel impelled to open my mind, Gregers. I cannot shake off this frightful doubt—perhaps Hedvig has never really and honestly loved me.

GREG. What would you say if she were to give you a proof of her love? [*Listens.*] What's that? I thought I heard the wild duck——

HIAL. It's the wild duck quacking. Father's in the garret.

GREG. Is he? [*His face lights up with joy.*] I say you may yet have proof that your poor misunderstood Hedvig loves you!

HIAL. Oh, what proof can she give me? I dare not believe in any assurance from that quarter.

GREG. Hedvig does not know what deceit means.

HIAL. Oh, Gregers, that is just what I cannot be sure of. Who knows what Gina and that Mrs Sorby may many a time have sat here whispering and tattling about? And Hedvig usually has her ears open, I can tell you. Perhaps the deed of gift was not such a surprise to her after all. In fact, I'm not sure but that I noticed something of the sort.

GREG. What spirit is this that has taken possession of you?

HIAL. I have had my eyes opened. Just you notice—you'll see, the deed of gift is only a beginning. Mrs Sorby has always been a good deal taken up with Hedvig, and now she has the power to do whatever she likes for the child. They can take her from me whenever they please.

GREG. Hedvig will never, never leave you.

HIAL. Don't be so sure of that. If only they beckon to her and throw out a golden bait—— And oh! I have loved her so unspeakably! I would have counted it my highest happiness to take her tenderly by the hand and lead her, as one leads a timid child through a great dark empty room! I am cruelly certain now that the poor photographer in his humble attic has never really and truly been anything to her. She has only cunningly contrived to keep on a good footing with him until the time came.

GREG. You don't believe that yourself, Hialmar.

HIAL. That is just the terrible part of it— I don't know what to believe— I never can know it. But can you really doubt that it must be as I say? Ho-ho, you have far too much faith in the claim of the ideal, my good Gregers! If those others came, with the glamour of wealth about them, and called to the child: "Leave him; come to us; here life awaits you——"

GREG. [*quickly*]. Well, what then?

HIAL. If I then asked her: "Hedvig, are you willing to renounce that life for me?" [*Laughs scornfully.*] No, thank you! You would soon hear what answer I should get.

[*A pistol shot is heard from within the garret.*]

GREG. [*loudly and joyfully*]. Hialmar!

HIAL. There now; he must needs go shooting too.

GINA [*comes in*]. Oh, Ekdal, I can hear Grandfather blazing away in the garret by himself.

HIAL. I'll look in——

GREG. [*eagerly, with emotion*]. Wait a moment! Do you know what that was?

HIAL. Yes, of course I know.

GREG. No, you don't know. But *I* do. That was the proof!

HIAL. What proof?

GREG. It was a child's free-will offering. She has got your father to shoot the wild duck.

HIAL. To shoot the wild duck!

GINA. Oh, think of that!

HIAL. What was that for?

GREG. She wanted to sacrifice to you her most cherished possession, for then she thought you would surely come to love her again.

HIAL. [*tenderly, with emotion*]. Oh, poor child!

GINA. What things she does think of!

GREG. She only wanted your love again, Hialmar. She could not live without it.

GINA [*struggling with her tears*]. There, you can see for yourself, Ekdal.

HIAL. Gina, where is she?

GINA [*sniffs*]. Poor dear, she's sitting out in the kitchen, I daresay.

HIAL. [*goes over, tears open the kitchen door and says*]. Hedvig, come, come in to me! [*Looks around.*] No, she's not here.

GINA. Then she must be in her own little room.

HIAL. [*without*]. No, she's not here either. [*Comes in.*] She must have gone out.

GINA. Yes, you wouldn't have her anywheres in the house.

HIAL. Oh, if she would only come home quickly, so that I can tell her—— Everything will come right now, Gregers; now I believe we can begin life afresh.

GREG. [*quietly*]. I knew it; I knew the child would make amends.

[OLD EKDAL *appears at the door of his room; he is in full uniform and is busy buckling on his sword.*]

HIAL. [*astonished*]. Father! Are you there?

GINA. Have you been firing in your room?

EKD. [*resentfully, approaching*]. So you go shooting alone, do you, Hialmar?

HIAL. [*excited and confused*]. Then it wasn't you that fired that shot in the garret?

EKD. Me that fired? H'm.

GREG. [*calls out to* HIALMAR]. She has shot the wild duck herself!

HIAL. What can it mean? [*Hastens to the garret door, tears it aside, looks in and calls loudly*]. Hedvig!

GINA [*runs to the door*]. Good God! what's that?

HIAL. [*goes in*]. She's lying on the floor!

GREG. Hedvig! Lying on the floor! [*Goes in to* HIALMAR.]

GINA [*at the same time*]. Hedvig! [*Inside the garret.*] No, no, no!

EKD. Ho-ho! Does she go shooting too now?

[HIALMAR, GINA and GREGERS *carry* HEDVIG *into the studio; in her dangling right hand she holds the pistol fast clasped in her fingers.*]

HIAL. [*distracted*]. The pistol has gone off. She has wounded herself. Call for help! Help!

GINA [*runs into the passage and calls down*]. Relling! Relling! Doctor Relling, come up as quick as you can!

[HIALMAR *and* GREGERS *lay* HEDVIG *down on the sofa.*]

EKD. [*quietly*]. The woods avenge themselves.

HIAL. [*on his knees beside* HEDVIG]. She'll soon come to now. She's coming to; yes, yes, yes.

GINA [*who has come in again*]. Where has she hurt herself? I can't see anything.

[RELLING *comes hurriedly, and immediately after him* MOLVIK; *the latter without his waistcoat and necktie and with his coat open.*]

RELL. What's the matter here?

GINA. They say Hedvig shot herself.

HIAL. Come and help us!

RELL. Shot herself! [*He pushes the table aside and begins to examine her.*]

HIAL. [*kneeling and looking anxiously up at him.*] It can't be dangerous? Speak, Relling! She is scarcely bleeding at all. It can't be dangerous?

RELL. How did it happen?

HIAL. Oh, we don't know——

GINA. She wanted to shoot the wild duck.

RELL. The wild duck?

HIAL. The pistol must have gone off.

RELL. H'm. Indeed.

EKD. The woods avenge themselves. But I'm not afraid all the same. [*Goes into the garret and closes the door after him.*]

HIAL. Well, Relling, why don't you say something?

RELL. The ball has entered the breast.

HIAL. Yes, but she's coming to!

RELL. Surely you can see that Hedvig is dead.

GINA [*bursts into tears*]. Oh, my child, my child——

GREG. [*huskily*]. In the depths of the sea——

HIAL. [*jumps up*]. No, no, she must live! Oh, for God's sake, Relling—only a moment—only just till I can tell her how unspeakably I loved her all the time.

RELL. The bullet has gone through her heart. Internal hemorrhage. Death must have been instantaneous.

HIAL. And I! I hunted her from me like an animal! And she crept terrified into the garret and died for love of me! [*Sobbing.*] I can never atone to her! I can never tell her—— [*Clenches his hands and cries upward.*] Oh, Thou above—if Thou be indeed! Why hast Thou done this thing to me?

GINA. Hush, hush, you mustn't go on that awful way. We had no right to keep her, I suppose.

MOL. The child is not dead but sleepeth.

RELL. Bosh!

HIAL. [*becomes calm, goes over to the sofa, folds his arms and looks at* HEDVIG]. There she lies so stiff and still.

RELL. [*tries to loosen the pistol*]. She's holding it so tight, so tight.

GINA. No, no, Relling; don't break her fingers; let the pistol be.

HIAL. She shall take it with her.

GINA. Yes, let her. But the child mustn't lie here for a show. She shall go to her own room, so she shall. Help me, Ekdal.

[HIALMAR *and* GINA *take* HEDVIG *between them.*]

HIAL. [*as they are carrying her*]. Oh, Gina, Gina, can you survive this?

GINA. We must help each other to bear it. For now, at least, she belongs to both of us.

MOL. [*stretches out his arms and mumbles*]. Blessed be the Lord; to earth thou shalt return; to earth thou shalt return——

RELL. [whispers]. Hold your tongue, you fool; you're drunk.

[HIALMAR *and* GINA *carry the body out through the kitchen door.* RELLING *shuts it after them.* MOLVIK *slinks out into the passage.*]

RELL. [*goes over to* GREGERS *and says*]. No one shall ever convince me that the pistol went off by accident.

GREG. [*who has stood terrified, with convulsive twitchings*]. Who can say how the dreadful thing happened?

RELL. The powder has burned the body of her dress. She must have pressed the pistol right against her breast and fired.

GREG. Hedvig has not died in vain. Did you not see how sorrow set free what is noble in him?

RELL. Most people are ennobled by the actual presence of death. But how long do you suppose this nobility will last in him?

Greg. Why should it not endure and increase throughout his life?

Rell. Before a year is over, little Hedvig will be nothing to him but a pretty theme for declamation.

Greg. How dare you say that of Hialmar Ekdal?

Rell. We will talk of this again, when the grass has first withered on her grave. Then you'll hear him spouting about "the child too early torn from her father's heart"; then you'll see him steep himself in a syrup of sentiment and self-admiration and self-pity. Just you wait!

Greg. If you are right and I am wrong, then life is not worth living.

Rell. Oh, life would be quite tolerable, after all, if only we could be rid of the confounded duns that keep on pestering us, in our poverty, with the claim of the ideal.

Greg. [*looking straight before him*]. In that case I am glad that my destiny is what it is.

Rell. May I inquire–what is your destiny?

Greg. [*going*]. To be the thirteenth at table.

Rell. The devil it is.

THE MASTER BUILDER

PERSONS OF THE PLAY

HALVARD SOLNESS, *master builder.*
ALINE SOLNESS, *his wife.*
DR HERDAL, *physician.*
KNUT BROVIK, *formerly an architect now in Solness's employment.*
RAGNAR BROVIK, *his son, draughtsman.*
KAIA FOSLI, *his niece, bookkeeper.*
MISS HILDA WANGEL.
Some ladies.
A crowd in the street.
The action takes place in and about Solness's house.

ACT I

SCENE—*A plainly furnished work-room in the house of Halvard Solness. Folding doors on the left lead out to the hall. On the right is the door leading to the inner rooms of the house. At the back is an open door into the draughtsmen's office. In front, on the left, a desk with books, papers and writing materials. Further back than the folding door a stove. In the right-hand corner a sofa, a table and one or two chairs. On the table a water bottle and glass. A smaller table, with a rocking chair and armchair, in front on the right. Lighted lamps, with shades, on the table in the draughtsmen's office, on the table in the corner and on the desk.*

In the draughtsmen's office sit KNUT BROVIK *and his son* RAGNAR, *occupied with plans and calculations. At the desk in the outer office stands* KAIA FOSLI, *writing in the ledger.* KNUT BROVIK *is a spare old man with white hair and a beard. He wears a rather threadbare but well-brushed black coat, spectacles and a somewhat discolored white neckcloth.* RAGNAR BROVIK *is a well-dressed, light-haired man in his thirties, with a slight stoop.* KAIA FOSLI *is a slightly built girl, a little over twenty, carefully dressed and delicate looking. She has a green shade over her eyes. All three go on working for some time in silence.*

BRO. [*rises suddenly, as if in distress, from the table; breathes heavily and laboriously as he comes forward into the doorway*]. No, I can't bear it much longer!

KAIA [*going up to him*]. You are feeling very ill this evening, are you not, Uncle?

BRO. Oh, I seem to get worse every day.

RAG. [*has risen and advances*]. You ought to go home, Father. Try to get a little sleep.

BRO. [*impatiently*]. Go to bed, I suppose? Would you have me stifled outright?

KAIA. Then take a little walk.

RAG. Yes, do; I will come with you.

BRO. [*with warmth*]. I will not go till he comes! I am determined to have it out this evening with [*in a tone of suppressed bitterness*]—with him—with the chief.

KAIA [*anxiously*]. Oh no, Uncle—do wait a while before doing that.

RAG. Yes, better wait, Father!

BRO. [*draws his breath laboriously*]. Ha—ha! *I* haven't much time for waiting.

KAIA [*listening*]. Hush! I hear him on the stairs.

[*All three go back to their work. A short silence.* HALVARD SOLNESS *comes in through the hall door. He is a man no longer young, but healthy and vigorous, with close-cut curly hair, dark mustache and dark thick eyebrows. He wears a grayish-green buttoned jacket with an upstanding collar and broad lapels. On his head he wears a soft gray felt hat, and he has one or two light portfolios under his arm.*]

SOL. [*near the door, points toward the draughtsmen's office and asks in a whisper*]. Are they gone?

KAIA [*softly, shaking her head*]. No. [*She takes the shade off her eyes. Solness crosses the room, throws his hat on a chair, places the portfolios on the table by the sofa and approaches the desk again.* KAIA *goes on writing without intermission but seems nervous and uneasy.*]

SOL. [*aloud*]. What is that you are entering, Miss Fosli?

KAIA [*starts*]. Oh, it is only something that——

SOL. Let me look at it, Miss Fosli. [*Bends over her, pretends to be looking into the ledger and whispers.*] Kaia!

KAIA [*softly, still writing*]. Well?

SOL. Why do you always take that shade off when I come?

KAIA [*as before*]. I look so ugly with it on.

SOL. [*smiling*]. Then you don't like to look ugly, Kaia?

KAIA [*half glancing up at him*]. Not for all the world. Not in your eyes.

SOL. [*stroking her hair gently*]. Poor, poor little Kaia——

KAIA [*bending her head*]. Hush—they can hear you.

[SOLNESS *strolls across the room to the right, turns and pauses at the door of the draughtsmen's office.*]

SOL. Has anyone been here for me?

RAG. [*rising*]. Yes, the young couple who want a villa built out at Lövstrand.

SOL. [*growling*]. Oh, those two! They must wait. I am not quite clear about the plans yet.

RAG. [*advancing, with some hesitation*]. They were very anxious to have the drawings at once.

SOL. [*as before*]. Yes, of course—so they all are.

BRO. [*looks up*]. They say they are longing so to get into a house of their own.

SOL. Yes, yes—we know all that! And so they are content to take whatever is offered them. They get a—a roof over their heads—an address—but nothing to call a home. No, thank you! In that case let them apply to somebody else. Tell them that the next time they call.

BRO. [*pushes his glasses up onto his forehead and looks in astonishment at him*]. To somebody else? Are you prepared to give up the commission?

SOL. [*impatiently*]. Yes, yes, yes, devil take it! If that is to be the way of it. Rather that than build away at random. [*Vehemently.*] Besides, I know very little about these people as yet.

BRO. The people are safe enough.

Ragnar knows them. He is a friend of the family. Perfectly safe people.

SOL. Oh, safe—safe enough! That is not at all what I mean. Good lord—don't you understand me either? [*Angrily.*] I won't have anything to do with these strangers. They may apply to whom they please, so far as I am concerned.

BRO. [*rising*]. Do you really mean that?

SOL. [*sulkily*]. Yes, I do—for once in a way. [*He comes forward.* BROVIK *exchanges a glance with* RAGNAR, *who makes a warning gesture. Then* BROVIK *comes into the front room.*]

BRO. May I have a few words with you?

SOL. Certainly.

BRO. [*to* KAIA]. Just go in there for a moment, Kaia.

KAIA [*uneasily*]. Oh, but, Uncle——

BRO. Do as I say, child. And shut the door after you.

[KAIA *goes reluctantly into the draughtsmen's office, glances anxiously and imploringly at* SOLNESS *and shuts the door.*]

BRO. [*lowering his voice a little*]. I don't want the poor children to know how ill I am.

SOL. Yes, you have been looking very poorly of late.

BRO. It will soon be all over with me. My strength is ebbing—from day to day.

SOL. Won't you sit down?

BRO. Thanks—may I?

SOL. [*placing the armchair more conveniently*]. Here—take this chair. And now?

BRO. [*has seated himself with difficulty*]. Well, you see, it's about Ragnar. That is what weighs most upon me. What is to become of him?

SOL. Of course your son will stay with me as long as ever he likes.

BRO. But that is just what he does not like. He feels that he cannot stay here any longer.

SOL. Why, I should say he was very well off here. But if he wants more money, I should not mind——

BRO. No, no! It is not that. [*Impatiently.*] But sooner or later he, too, must have a chance of doing something on his own account.

SOL. [*without looking at him*]. Do you think that Ragnar has quite talent enough to stand alone?

BRO. No, that is just the heartbreaking part of it—I have begun to have my doubts about the boy. For you have never said so much as—as one encouraging word about him. And yet I cannot but think there must be something in him—he can't be without talent.

SOL. Well, but he has learned nothing—nothing thoroughly, I mean. Except, of course, to draw.

BRO. [*looks at him with covert hatred and says hoarsely*]. You had learned little enough of the business when you were in my employment. But that did not prevent you from setting to work [*breathing with difficulty*] and pushing your way up and taking the wind out of my sails—mine and so many other people's.

SOL. Yes, you see—circumstances favored me.

BRO. You are right there. Everything favored you. But then how can you have the heart to let me go to my grave—without having seen what Ragnar is fit for? And of course I am anxious to see them married too—before I go.

SOL. [*sharply*]. Is it she who wishes it?

BRO. Not Kaia so much as Ragnar

—he talks about it every day. [*Appealingly.*] You must—you must help him to get some independent work now! I must see something that the lad has done. Do you hear?

SOL. [*peevishly*]. Hang it, man, you can't expect me to drag commissions down from the moon for him!

BRO. He has the chance of a capital commission at this very moment. A big bit of work.

SOL. [*uneasily, startled*]. Has he?

BRO. If you would give your consent.

SOL. What sort of work do you mean?

BRO. [*with some hesitation*]. He can have the building of that villa out at Lövstrand.

SOL. That! Why, I am going to build that myself.

BRO. Oh, you don't much care about doing it.

SOL. [*flaring up*]. Don't care! I? Who dares to say that?

BRO. You said so yourself just now.

SOL. Oh, never mind what I say. Would they give Ragnar the building of that villa?

BRO. Yes. You see, he knows the family. And then—just for the fun of the thing—he has made drawings and estimates and so forth——

SOL. Are they pleased with the drawings? The people who will have to live in the house?

BRO. Yes. If you would only look through them and approve of them.

SOL. Then they would let Ragnar build their home for them?

BRO. They were immensely pleased with his idea. They thought it exceedingly original, they said.

SOL. Oho! Original! Not the old-fashioned stuff that *I* am in the habit of turning out!

BRO. It seemed to them different.

SOL. [*with suppressed irritation*]. So it was to see Ragnar that they came here—whilst I was out!

BRO. They came to call upon you—and at the same time to ask whether you would mind retiring——

SOL. [*angrily*]. Retire? I?

BRO. In case you thought Ragnar's drawings——

SOL. I? Retire in favor of your son!

BRO. Retire from the agreement, they meant.

SOL. Oh, it comes to the same thing. [*Laughs angrily.*] So that is it, is it? Halvard Solness is to see about retiring now! To make room for younger men! For the very youngest, perhaps! He must make room! Room! Room!

BRO. Why, good heavens! there is surely room for more than one single man——

SOL. Oh, there's not so very much room to spare either. But be that as it may—I will never retire! I will never give way to anybody! Never of my own free will. Never in this world will I do that.

BRO. [*rises with difficulty*]. Then I am to pass out of life without any certainty? Without a gleam of happiness? Without any faith or trust in Ragnar? Without having seen a single piece of work of his doing? Is that to be the way of it?

SOL. [*turns half aside and mutters*]. H'm—don't ask more just now.

BRO. I must have an answer to this one question. Am I to pass out of life in such utter poverty?

SOL. [*seems to struggle with himself; finally he says, in a low but firm voice*]. You must pass out of life as best you can.

BRO. Then be it so. [*He goes up the room.*]

SOL. [*following him, half in desperation*]. Don't you understand that I cannot help it? I am what I am, and I cannot change my nature!

BRO. No, no; I suppose you can't. [*Reels and supports himself against the sofa table.*] May I have a glass of water?

SOL. By all means. [*Fills a glass and hands it to him.*]

BRO. Thanks. [*Drinks and puts the glass down again.* SOLNESS *goes up and opens the door of the draughtsmen's office.*]

SOL. Ragnar—you must come and take your father home.

[RAGNAR *rises quickly. He and* KAIA *come into the workroom.*]

RAG. What is the matter, Father?

BRO. Give me your arm. Now let us go.

RAG. Very well. You had better put your things on too, Kaia.

SOL. Miss Fosli must stay—just for a moment. There is a letter I want written.

BRO. [*looks at* SOLNESS]. Good night. Sleep well—if you can.

SOL. Good night.

[BROVIK *and* RAGNAR *go out by the hall door.* KAIA *goes to the desk.* SOLNESS *stands with bent head, to the right, by the armchair.*]

KAIA [*dubiously*]. Is there any letter?

SOL. [*curtly*]. No, of course not. [*Looks sternly at her.*] Kaia!

KAIA [*anxiously, in a low voice*]. Yes!

SOL. [*points imperatively to a spot on the floor*]. Come here! At once!

KAIA [*hesitatingly*]. Yes.

SOL. [*as before*]. Nearer!

KAIA [*obeying*]. What do you want with me?

SOL. [*looks at her for a while*]. Is it you I have to thank for all this?

KAIA. No, no, don't think that!

SOL. But confess now—you want to get married!

KAIA [*softly*]. Ragnar and I have been engaged for four or five years, and so——

SOL. And so you think it time there were an end to it. Is not that so?

KAIA. Ragnar and Uncle say I must. So I suppose I shall have to give in.

SOL. [*more gently*]. Kaia, don't you really care a little bit for Ragnar too?

KAIA. I cared very much for Ragnar once—before I came here to you.

SOL. But you don't now? Not in the least?

KAIA [*passionately, clasping her hands and holding them out toward him*]. Oh, you know very well there is only one person I care for now! One, and one only, in all the world! I shall never care for anyone else.

SOL. Yes, you say that and yet go away from me—leave me alone here with everything on my hands.

KAIA. But could I not stay with you even if Ragnar——

SOL. [*repudiating the idea*]. No, no, that is quite impossible. If Ragnar leaves me and starts work on his own account, then of course he will need you himself.

KAIA [*wringing her hands*]. Oh, I feel as if I could not be separated from you! It's quite, quite impossible!

SOL. Then be sure you get those foolish notions out of Ragnar's head. Marry him as much as you please [*alters his tone*]—I mean—don't let him throw up his good situation with me. For then I can keep you too, my dear Kaia.

KAIA. Oh yes, how lovely that would be if it could only be managed!

SOL. [*clasps her head with his two hands and whispers*]. For I cannot get on without you, you see. I must have you with me every single day.

KAIA [*in nervous exaltation*]. My God! My God!

SOL. [*kisses her hair*]. Kaia–Kaia!

KAIA [*sinks down before him*]. Oh, how good you are to me! How unspeakably good you are!

SOL. [*vehemently*]. Get up! For goodness' sake, get up! I think I hear someone! [*He helps her to rise. She staggers over to the desk.* MRS S. *enters by the door on the right. She looks thin and wasted with grief but shows traces of bygone beauty. Blonde ringlets. Dressed with good taste, wholly in black. Speaks somewhat slowly and in a plaintive voice.*]

MRS S. [*in the doorway*]. Halvard!

SOL. [*turns*]. Oh, are you there, my dear?

MRS S. [*with a glance at* KAIA]. I am afraid I am disturbing you.

SOL. Not in the least. Miss Fosli has only a short letter to write.

MRS S. Yes, so I see.

SOL. What do you want with me, Aline?

MRS S. I merely wanted to tell you that Doctor Herdal is in the drawing room. Won't you come and see him, Halvard?

SOL. [*looks suspiciously at her*]. H'm– is the doctor so very anxious to talk to me?

MRS S. Well, not exactly anxious. He really came to see me, but he would like to say how-do-you-do to you at the same time.

SOL. [*laughs to himself*]. Yes, I daresay. Well, you must ask him to wait a little.

MRS S. Then you will come in presently?

SOL. Perhaps I will. Presently, presently, dear. In a little while.

MRS S. [*glancing at* KAIA.] Well, now, don't forget, Halvard. [*Withdraws and closes the door behind her.*]

KAIA [*softly*]. Oh dear! Oh dear! I am sure Mrs Solness thinks ill of me in some way!

SOL. Oh, not in the least. Not more than usual, at any rate. But all the same you had better go now, Kaia.

KAIA. Yes, yes, now I must go.

SOL. [*severely*]. And mind you get that matter settled for me. Do you hear?

KAIA. Oh, if it only depended on me——

SOL. I will have it settled, I say! And tomorrow too–not a day later!

KAIA [*terrified*]. If there's nothing else for it, I am quite willing to break off the engagement.

SOL. [*angrily*]. Break it off! Are you mad? Would you think of breaking it off?

KAIA [*distracted*]. Yes, if necessary. For I must–I must stay here with you! I can't leave you! That is utterly–utterly impossible!

SOL. [*with a sudden outburst*]. But deuce take it–how about Ragnar then? It's Ragnar that I——

KAIA [*looks at him with terrified eyes*]. It is chiefly on Ragnar's account that–that you——

SOL. [*collecting himself*]. No, no, of course not! You don't understand me either. [*Gently and softly.*] Of course it is you I want to keep–you above everything, Kaia. But for that very reason you must prevent Ragnar, too, from throwing up his situation. There, there–now go home.

KAIA. Yes, yes–good night, then.

SOL. Good night. [*As she is going.*]

Oh, stop a moment! Are Ragnar's drawings in there?

KAIA. I did not see him take them with him.

SOL. Then just go and find them for me. I might perhaps glance over them after all.

KAIA [*happy*]. Oh yes, please do!

SOL. For your sake, Kaia dear. Now let me have them at once, please.

[KAIA *hurries into the draughtsmen's office, searches anxiously in the table drawer, finds a portfolio and brings it with her.*]

KAIA. Here are all the drawings.

SOL. Good. Put them down there on the table.

KAIA [*putting down the portfolio*]. Good night, then. [*Beseechingly.*] And please, please think kindly of me.

SOL. Oh, that I always do. Good night, my dear little Kaia. [*Glances to the right.*] Go, go now!

[MRS SOLNESS *and* DR HERDAL *enter by the door on the right. He is a stoutish elderly man with a round, good-humored face, clean shaven, with thin light hair and gold spectacles.*]

MRS S. [*still in the doorway*]. Halvard, I cannot keep the doctor any longer.

SOL. Well, then, come in here.

MRS S. [*to Kaia, who is turning down the desk lamp*]. Have you finished the letter already, Miss Fosli?

KAIA [*in confusion*]. The letter?

SOL. Yes, it was quite a short one.

MRS S. It must have been very short.

SOL. You may go now, Miss Fosli. And please come in good time tomorrow morning.

KAIA. I will be sure to. Good night, Mrs Solness. [*She goes out by the hall door.*]

MRS S. She must be quite an acquisition to you, Halvard, this Miss Fosli.

SOL. Yes indeed. She is useful in all sorts of ways.

MRS S. So it seems.

DR H. Is she good at bookkeeping too?

SOL. Well—of course she has had a good deal of practice during these two years. And then she is so nice and willing to do whatever one asks of her.

MRS S. Yes, that must be very delightful.

SOL. It is. Especially when one is not too much accustomed to that sort of thing.

MRS S. [*in a tone of gentle remonstrance*]. Can you say that, Halvard?

SOL. Oh no, no, my dear Aline; I beg your pardon.

MRS S. There's no occasion. Well, then, Doctor, you will come back later on and have a cup of tea with us?

DR H. I have only that one patient to see and then I'll come back.

MRS S. Thank you. [*She goes out by the door on the right.*]

SOL. Are you in a hurry, Doctor?

DR H. No, not at all.

SOL. May I have a little chat with you?

DR H. With the greatest of pleasure.

SOL. Then let us sit down. [*He motions the doctor to take the rocking chair and sits down himself in the armchair. Looks searchingly at him.*] Tell me—did you notice anything odd about Aline?

DR H. Do you mean just now, when she was here?

SOL. Yes, in her manner to me. Did you notice anything?

Dr H. [*smiling*]. Well, I admit—one couldn't well avoid noticing that your wife—h'm——

Sol. Well?

Dr H. —that your wife is not particularly fond of this Miss Fosli.

Sol. Is that all? I have noticed that myself.

Dr H. And I must say I am scarcely surprised at it.

Sol. At what?

Dr H. That she should not exactly approve of your seeing so much of another woman all day and every day.

Sol. No, no, I suppose you are right there—and Aline too. But it's impossible to make any change.

Dr H. Could you not engage a clerk?

Sol. The first man that came to hand? No, thank you—that would never do for me.

Dr H. But now, if your wife—— Suppose, with her delicate health, all this tries her too much?

Sol. Even then—I might almost say—it can make no difference. I must keep Kaia Fosli. No one else can fill her place.

Dr H. No one else?

Sol. [*curtly*]. No, no one.

Dr H. [*drawing his chair closer*]. Now listen to me, my dear Mr Solness. May I ask you a question, quite between ourselves?

Sol. By all means.

Dr H. Women, you see—in certain matters they have a deucedly keen intuition——

Sol. They have indeed. There is not the least doubt of that. But——

Dr H. Well, tell me now—if your wife can't endure this Kaia Fosli——

Sol. Well, what then?

Dr H. —may she not have just—just the least little bit of reason for this instinctive dislike?

Sol. [*looks at him and rises*]. Oho!

Dr H. Now don't be offended—but hasn't she?

Sol. [*with curt decision*]. No.

Dr H. No reason of any sort?

Sol. No other reason than her own suspicious nature.

Dr H. I know you have known a good many women in your time.

Sol. Yes, I have.

Dr H. And have been a good deal taken with some of them too.

Sol. Oh yes, I don't deny it.

Dr H. But as regards Miss Fosli then? There is nothing of that sort in the case?

Sol. No, nothing at all—on my side.

Dr H. But on her side?

Sol. I don't think you have any right to ask that question, Doctor.

Dr H. Well, you know, we were discussing your wife's intuition.

Sol. So we were. And for that matter [*lowers his voice*] Aline's intuition, as you call it—in a certain sense it has not been so far astray.

Dr H. Aha! There we have it!

Sol. [*sits down*]. Doctor Herdal—I am going to tell you a strange story—if you care to listen to it.

Dr H. I like listening to strange stories.

Sol. Very well, then. I daresay you recollect that I took Knut Brovik and his son into my employment—after the old man's business had gone to the dogs.

Dr H. Yes, so I have understood.

Sol. You see, they really are clever fellows, these two. Each of them has talent in his own way. But then the son took it into his head to get engaged, and the next thing, of course, was that he wanted to get married—

and begin to build on his own account. That is the way with all these young people.

Dr H. [*laughing*]. Yes, they have a bad habit of wanting to marry.

Sol. Just so. But of course that did not suit my plans, for I needed Ragnar myself—and the old man too. He is exceedingly good at calculating bearing strains and cubic contents—and all that sort of deviltry, you know.

Dr H. Oh yes, no doubt that's indispensable.

Sol. Yes, it is. But Ragnar was absolutely bent on setting to work for himself. He would hear of nothing else.

Dr H. But he has stayed with you all the same.

Sol. Yes; I'll tell you how that came about. One day this girl, Kaia Fosli, came to see them on some errand or other. She had never been here before. And when I saw how utterly infatuated they were with each other the thought occurred to me: if I could only get her into the office here, then perhaps Ragnar would stay where he is.

Dr H. That was not at all a bad idea.

Sol. Yes, but at the time I did not breathe a word of what was in my mind; I merely stood and looked at her—and kept on wishing intently that I could have her here. Then I talked to her a little, in a friendly way—about one thing and another. And then she went away.

Dr H. Well?

Sol. Well, then, next day, pretty late in the evening, when old Brovik and Ragnar had gone home, she came here again and behaved as if I had made an arrangement with her.

Dr H. An arrangement? What about?

Sol. About the very thing my mind had been fixed on. But I hadn't said one single word about it.

Dr H. That was most extraordinary.

Sol. Yes, was it not? And now she wanted to know what she was to do here—whether she could begin the very next morning and so forth.

Dr H. Don't you think she did it in order to be with her sweetheart?

Sol. That was what occurred to me at first. But no, that was not it. She seemed to drift quite away from him—when once she had come here to me.

Dr H. She drifted over to you then?

Sol. Yes, entirely. If I happen to look at her when her back is turned, I can tell that she feels it. She quivers and trembles the moment I come near her. What do you think of that?

Dr H. H'm—that's not very hard to explain.

Sol. Well, but what about the other things? That she believed I had said to her what I had only wished and willed—silently—inwardly—to myself? What do you say to that? Can you explain that, Doctor Herdal?

Dr H. No, I won't undertake to do that.

Sol. I felt sure you would not, and so I have never cared to talk about it till now. But it's a cursed nuisance to me in the long run, you understand. Here I have to go on day after day pretending—— And it's a shame to treat her so, poor girl. [*Vehemently.*] But I cannot do anything else. For if she runs away from me—then Ragnar will be off too.

Dr H. And you have not told your wife the rights of the story?

SOL. No.

DR H. Then why on earth don't you?

SOL. [*looks fixedly at him and says in a low voice*]. Because I seem to find a sort of—of salutary self-torture in allowing Aline to do me an injustice.

DR H. [*shakes his head*]. I don't in the least understand what you mean.

SOL. Well, you see—it is like paying off a little bit of a huge, immeasurable debt——

DR H. To your wife?

SOL. Yes; and that always helps to relieve one's mind a little. One can breathe more freely for a while, you understand.

DR H. No, goodness knows, I don't understand at all.

SOL. [*breaking off, rises again*]. Well, well, well—then we won't talk any more about it. [*He saunters across the room, returns and stops beside the table. Looks at the doctor with a sly smile.*] I suppose you think you have drawn me out nicely now, Doctor?

DR H. [*with some irritation*]. Drawn you out? Again I have not the faintest notion what you mean, Mr Solness.

SOL. Oh, come, out with it; I have seen it quite clearly, you know.

DR H. What have you seen?

SOL. [*in a low voice, slowly*]. That you have been quietly keeping an eye upon me.

DR H. That *I* have! And why in all the world should I do that?

SOL. Because you think that I—— [*Passionately.*] Why, devil take it—you think the same of me as Aline does.

DR H. And what does she think about you?

SOL. [*having recovered his self-control*]. She has begun to think that I am—that I am—ill.

DR H. Ill! You! She has never hinted such a thing to me. Why, what can she think is the matter with you?

SOL. [*leans over the back of the chair and whispers*]. Aline has made up her mind that I am mad. That is what she thinks.

DR H. [*rising*]. Why, my dear good fellow——

SOL. Yes, on my soul she does! I tell you it is so. And she has got you to think the same! Oh, I can assure you, Doctor, I see it in your face as clearly as possible. You don't take me in so easily, I can tell you.

DR H. [*looks at him in amazement*]. Never, Mr Solness—never has such a thought entered my mind.

SOL. [*with an incredulous smile*]. Really? Has it not?

DR H. No, never! Nor your wife's mind either, I am convinced. I could almost swear to that.

SOL. Well, I wouldn't advise you to. For, in a certain sense, you see, perhaps—perhaps she is not so far wrong in thinking something of the kind.

DR H. Come now, I really must say——

SOL. [*interrupting, with a sweep of his hand*]. Well, well, my dear doctor—don't let us discuss this any further. We had better agree to differ. [*Changes to a tone of quiet amusement.*] But look here now, Doctor—h'm——

DR H. What then?

SOL. Since you don't believe that I am ill—and crazy and mad and so forth—then I daresay you fancy that I am an extremely happy man.

Dr H. Is that mere fancy?

Sol. [*laughs*]. No, no—of course not! Heaven forbid! Only think—to be Solness the master builder! Halvard Solness! What could be more delightful?

Dr H. Yes, I must say it seems to me you have had the luck on your side to an astounding degree.

Sol. [*suppresses a gloomy smile*]. So I have; I can't complain on that score.

Dr H. First of all that grim old robbers' castle was burned down for you. And that was certainly a great piece of luck.

Sol. [*seriously*]. It was the home of Aline's family. Remember that.

Dr H. Yes, it must have been a great grief to her.

Sol. She has not got over it to this day—not in all these twelve or thirteen years.

Dr H. Ah, but what followed must have been the worst blow for her.

Sol. The one thing with the other.

Dr H. But you—yourself—you rose upon the ruins. You began as a poor boy from a country village—and now you are at the head of your profession. Ah yes, Mr Solness, you have undoubtedly had the luck on your side.

Sol. [*looking at him with embarrassment*]. Yes, but that is just what makes me so horribly afraid.

Dr H. Afraid? Because you have the luck on your side!

Sol. It terrifies me—terrifies me every hour of the day. For sooner or later the luck must turn, you see.

Dr H. Oh, nonsense! What should make the luck turn?

Sol. [*with firm assurance*]. The younger generation.

Dr H. Pooh! The younger generation! You are not laid on the shelf yet, I should hope. Oh no—your position here is probably firmer now than it has ever been.

Sol. The luck will turn. I know it —I feel the day approaching. Someone or other will take it into his head to say: "Give me a chance!" And then all the rest will come clamoring after him and shake their fists at me and shout: "Make room—make room —make room!" Yes, just you see, Doctor—presently the younger generation will come knocking at my door——

Dr H. [*laughing*]. Well, and what if they do?

Sol. What if they do? Then there's an end of Halvard Solness. [*There is a knock at the door on the left.* Solness *starts.*] What's that? Did you not hear something?

Dr H. Someone is knocking at the door.

Sol. [*loudly*]. Come in.

[Hilda Wangel *enters by the hall door. She is of middle height, supple and delicately built. Somewhat sunburned. Dressed in a tourist costume, with skirt caught up for walking, a sailor's collar open at the throat and a small sailor hat on her head. Knapsack on back, plaid in strap and alpenstock.*]

Hilda [*goes straight up to Solness, her eyes sparkling with happiness*]. Good evening!

Sol. [*looks doubtfully at her*]. Good evening.

Hilda [*laughs*]. I almost believe you don't recognize me!

Sol. No—I must admit that—just for the moment——

Dr H. [*approaching*]. But I recognize you, my dear young lady.

HILDA [*pleased*]. Oh, is it you that——

DR H. Of course it is. [*To* SOLNESS.] We met at one of the mountain stations this summer. [*To* HILDA.] What became of the other ladies?

HILDA. Oh, they went westward.

DR H. They didn't much like all the fun we used to have in the evenings.

HILDA. No, I believe they didn't.

DR H. [*holds up his finger at her*]. And I am afraid it can't be denied that you flirted a little with us.

HILDA. Well, that was better fun than to sit there knitting stockings with all those old women.

DR H. [*laughs*]. There I entirely agree with you.

SOL. Have you come to town this evening?

HILDA. Yes, I have just arrived.

DR H. Quite alone, Miss Wangel?

HILDA. Oh yes!

SOL. Wangel. Is your name Wangel?

HILDA [*looks in amused surprise at him*]. Yes, of course it is.

SOL. Then you must be a daughter of the district doctor up at Lysanger?

HILDA [*as before*]. Yes, who else's daughter should I be?

SOL. Oh, then I suppose we met up there that summer when I was building a tower on the old church.

HILDA [*more seriously*]. Yes, of course it was then we met.

SOL. Well, that is a long time ago.

HILDA [*looks hard at him*]. It is exactly the ten years.

SOL. You must have been a mere child then, I should think.

HILDA [*carelessly*]. Well, I was twelve or thirteen.

DR H. Is this the first time you have ever been up to town, Miss Wangel?

HILDA. Yes, it is indeed.

SOL. And don't you know anyone here?

HILDA. Nobody but you. And, of course, your wife.

SOL. So you know her too?

HILDA. Only a little. We spent a few days together at the sanatorium.

SOL. Ah, up there?

HILDA. She said I might come and pay her a visit if ever I came up to town. [*Smiles.*] Not that that was necessary.

SOL. Odd that she should never have mentioned it.

[HILDA *puts her stick down by the stove, takes off the knapsack and lays it and the plaid on the sofa.* DR HERDAL *offers to help her.* SOLNESS *stands and gazes at her.*]

HILDA [*going toward him*]. Well, now I must ask you to let me stay the night here.

SOL. I am sure there will be no difficulty about that.

HILDA. For I have no other clothes than those I stand in, except a change of linen in my knapsack. And that has to go to the wash, for it's very dirty.

SOL. Oh yes, that can be managed. Now I'll just let my wife know——

DR H. Meanwhile I will go and see my patient.

SOL. Yes, do; and come again later on.

DR H. [*playfully, with a glance at* HILDA]. Oh, that I will, you may be very certain! [*Laughs.*] So your prediction has come true, Mr Solness!

SOL. How so?

DR H. The younger generation did come knocking at your door.

SOL. [*cheerfully*]. Yes, but in a very different way from what I meant.

DR H. Very different, yes. That's undeniable. [*He goes out by the hall door.* SOLNESS *opens the door on the right and speaks into the side room.*]

SOL. Aline! Will you come in here, please? Here is a friend of yours—Miss Wangel.

MRS S. [*appears in the doorway*]. Who do you say it is? [*Sees* HILDA.] Oh, is it you, Miss Wangel? [*Goes up to her and offers her hand.*] So you have come to town after all.

SOL. Miss Wangel has this moment arrived, and she would like to stay the night here.

MRS S. Here with us? Oh yes, certainly.

SOL. Till she can get things a little in order, you know.

MRS S. I will do the best I can for you. It's no more than my duty. I suppose your trunk is coming on later?

HILDA. I have no trunk.

MRS S. Well, it will be all right, I daresay. In the meantime you must excuse my leaving you here with my husband until I can get a room made a little comfortable for you.

SOL. Can we not give her one of the nurseries? They are all ready as it is.

MRS S. Oh yes. There we have room and to spare. [*To* HILDA.] Sit down now and rest a little. [*She goes out to the right.*]

[HILDA, *with her hands behind her back, strolls about the room and looks at various objects.* SOLNESS *stands in front, beside the table, also with his hands behind his back, and follows her with his eyes.*]

HILDA [*stops and looks at him*]. Have you several nurseries?

SOL. There are three nurseries in the house.

HILDA. That's a lot. Then I suppose you have a great many children?

SOL. No. We have no child. But now you can be the child here for the time being.

HILDA. For tonight, yes. I shall not cry. I mean to sleep as sound as a stone.

SOL. Yes, you must be very tired, I should think.

HILDA. Oh no! But all the same—it's so delicious to lie and dream.

SOL. Do you dream much of nights?

HILDA. Oh yes! Almost always.

SOL. What do you dream about most?

HILDA. I shan't tell you tonight. Another time, perhaps. [*She again strolls about the room, stops at the desk and turns over the books and papers a little.*]

SOL. [*approaching*]. Are you searching for anything?

HILDA. No, I am merely looking at all these things. [*Turns.*] Perhaps I mustn't?

SOL. Oh, by all means.

HILDA. Is it you that write in this great ledger?

SOL. No, it's my bookkeeper.

HILDA. Is it a woman?

SOL. [*smiles*]. Yes.

HILDA. One you employ here, in your office?

SOL. Yes.

HILDA. Is she married?

SOL. No, she is single.

HILDA. Oh, indeed!

SOL. But I believe she is soon going to be married.

HILDA. That's a good thing for her.

SOL. But not such a good thing for me. For then I shall have nobody to help me.

HILDA. Can't you get hold of someone else who will do just as well?

SOL. Perhaps you would stay here and write in the ledger?

HILDA [*measures him with a glance*]. Yes, I daresay! No, thank you—nothing of that sort for me. [*She again strolls across the room and sits down in the rocking chair.* SOLNESS *too goes to the table.*]

HILDA [*continuing*]. For there must surely be plenty of other things to be done here. [*Looks smiling at him.*] Don't you think so too?

SOL. Of course. First of all, I suppose, you want to make a round of the shops and get yourself up in the height of fashion.

HILDA [*amused*]. No, I think I shall let that alone!

SOL. Indeed.

HILDA. For you must know I have run through all my money.

SOL [*laughs*]. Neither trunk nor money then.

HILDA. Neither one nor the other. But never mind—it doesn't matter now.

SOL. Come now, I like you for that.

HILDA. Only for that?

SOL. For that among other things. [*Sits in the armchair.*] Is your father alive still?

HILDA. Yes, Father's alive.

SOL. Perhaps you are thinking of studying here?

HILDA. No, that hadn't occurred to me.

SOL. But I suppose you will be staying for some time?

HILDA. That must depend upon circumstances. [*She sits awhile rocking herself and looking at him, half seriously, half with a suppressed smile. Then she takes off her hat and puts it on the table in front of her.*] Mr Solness!

SOL. Well?

HILDA. Have you a very bad memory?

SOL. A bad memory? No, not that I am aware of.

HILDA. Then you have nothing to say to me about what happened up there?

SOL. [*in momentary surprise*]. Up at Lysanger? [*Indifferently.*] Why, it was nothing much to talk about, it seems to me.

HILDA [*looks reproachfully at him*]. How can you sit there and say such things?

SOL. Well, then, you talk to me about it.

HILDA. When the tower was finished we had grand doings in the town.

SOL. Yes, I shall not easily forget that day.

HILDA [*smiles*]. Will you not? That comes well from you.

SOL. Comes well?

HILDA. There was music in the churchyard—and many, many hundreds of people. We schoolgirls were dressed in white, and we all carried flags.

SOL. Ah yes, those flags—I can tell you I remember them!

HILDA. Then you climbed right up the scaffolding, straight to the very top; and you had a great wreath with you, and you hung that wreath right away up on the weather vane.

SOL. [*curtly interrupting*]. I always did that in those days. It was an old custom.

HILDA. It was so wonderfully thrilling to stand below and look up at you. Fancy, if he should fall over! He—the master builder himself!

SOL. [*as if to divert her from the subject*]. Yes, yes, yes, that might very well have happened too. For one of those white-frocked little devils—she went on in such a way and screamed up at me so——

Hilda [*sparkling with pleasure*]. "Hurrah for Master Builder Solness!" Yes!

Sol. —and waved and flourished with her flag, so that I—so that it almost made me giddy to look at it.

Hilda [*in a lower voice, seriously*]. That little devil—that was *I*.

Sol. [*fixes his eyes steadily upon her*]. I am sure of that now. It must have been you.

Hilda [*lively again*]. Oh, it was so gloriously thrilling! I could not have believed there was a builder in the whole world that could build such a tremendously high tower. And then that you yourself should stand at the very top of it, as large as life! And that you should not be the least dizzy! It was that above everything that made one—made one dizzy to think of.

Sol. How could you be so certain that I was not——

Hilda [*scouting the idea*]. No indeed! Oh no! I knew that instinctively. For if you had been, you could never have stood up there and sung.

Sol. [*looks at her in astonishment*]. Sung? Did *I* sing?

Hilda. Yes, I should think you did.

Sol. [*shakes his head*]. I have never sung a note in my life.

Hilda. Yes indeed, you sang then. It sounded like harps in the air.

Sol. [*thoughtfully*]. This is very strange—all this.

Hilda [*is silent awhile, looks at him and says in a low voice*]. But then—it was after that—and the real thing happened.

Sol. The real thing?

Hilda [*sparkling with vivacity*]. Yes, I surely don't need to remind you of that?

Sol. Oh yes, do remind me a little of that too.

Hilda. Don't you remember that a great dinner was given in your honor at the club?

Sol. Yes, to be sure. It must have been the same afternoon, for I left the place next morning.

Hilda. And from the club you were invited to come round to our house to supper.

Sol. Quite right, Miss Wangel. It is wonderful how all these trifles have impressed themselves on your mind.

Hilda. Trifles! I like that! Perhaps it was a trifle, too, that I was alone in the room when you came in?

Sol. Were you alone?

Hilda [*without answering him*]. You didn't call me a little devil then.

Sol. No, I suppose I did not.

Hilda. You said I was lovely in my white dress and that I looked like a little princess.

Sol. I have no doubt you did, Miss Wangel. And besides—I was feeling so buoyant and free that day——

Hilda. And then you said that when I grew up I should be your princess.

Sol. [*laughing a little*]. Dear, dear—did I say that too?

Hilda. Yes, you did. And when I asked how long I should have to wait you said that you would come again in ten years—like a troll, and carry me off—to Spain or some such place. And you promised you would buy me a kingdom there.

Sol. [*as before*]. Yes, after a good dinner one doesn't haggle about the halfpence. But did I really say all that?

Hilda [*laughs to herself*]. Yes. And

you told me, too, what the kingdom was to be called.

SOL. Well, what was it?

HILDA. It was to be called the kingdom of Orangia, you said.

SOL. Well, that was an appetizing name.

HILDA. No, I didn't like it a bit, for it seemed as though you wanted to make game of me.

SOL. I am sure that cannot have been my intention.

HILDA. No, I should hope not—considering what you did next.

SOL. What in the world did I do next?

HILDA. Well, that's the finishing touch if you have forgotten that too. I should have thought no one could help remembering such a thing as that.

SOL. Yes, yes; just give me a hint, and then perhaps—— Well?

HILDA [*looks fixedly at him*]. You came and kissed me, Mr Solness.

SOL. [*open-mouthed, rising from his chair*]. *I* did!

HILDA. Yes, indeed you did. You took me in both your arms and bent my head back and kissed me—many times.

SOL. Now, really, my dear Miss Wangel!

HILDA [*rises*]. You surely cannot mean to deny it?

SOL. Yes, I do. I deny it altogether!

HILDA [*looks scornfully at him*]. Oh, indeed! [*She turns and goes slowly close up to the stove, where she remains standing motionless, her face averted from him, her hands behind her back. Short pause.*]

SOL. [*goes cautiously up behind her*]. Miss Wangel!

[HILDA *is silent and does not move.*]

SOL. Don't stand there like a statue. You must have dreamed all this. [*Lays his hand on her arm.*] Now just listen——

[HILDA *makes an impatient movement with her arm.*]

SOL. [*as a thought flashes upon him*]. Or—— Wait a moment! There is something under all this, you may depend!

[HILDA *does not move.*]

SOL. [*in a low voice but with emphasis*]. I must have thought all that. I must have wished it—have willed it—have longed to do it. And then—— May not that be the explanation?

[HILDA *is still silent.*]

SOL. [*impatiently*]. Oh, very well, deuce take it all—then I did it, I suppose.

HILDA [*turns her head a little but without looking at him*]. Then you admit it now?

SOL. Yes—whatever you like.

HILDA. You came and put your arms around me?

SOL. Oh yes!

HILDA. And bent my head back?

SOL. Very far back.

HILDA. And kissed me?

SOL. Yes, I did.

HILDA. Many times?

SOL. As many as ever you like.

HILDA [*turns quickly toward him and has once more the sparkling expression of gladness in her eyes*]. Well, you see, I got it out of you at last!

SOL. [*with a slight smile*]. Yes—just think of my forgetting such a thing as that.

HILDA [*again a little sulky, retreats from him*]. Oh, you have kissed so many people in your time, I suppose.

SOL. No, you mustn't think that of me. [HILDA *seats herself in the arm-*

chair. SOLNESS *stands and leans against the rocking chair. Looks observantly at her.*] Miss Wangel!

HILDA. Yes!

SOL. How was it now? What came of all this—between us two?

HILDA. Why, nothing more came of it. You know that quite well. For then the other guests came in and then—bah!

SOL. Quite so! The others came in. To think of my forgetting that too!

HILDA. Oh, you haven't really forgotten anything; you are only a little ashamed of it all. I am sure one doesn't forget things of that kind.

SOL. No, one would suppose not.

HILDA [*lively again, looks at him*]. Perhaps you have even forgotten what day it was?

SOL. What day——

HILDA. Yes, on what day did you hang the wreath on the tower? Well? Tell me at once!

SOL. H'm—I confess I have forgotten the particular day. I only knew it was ten years ago. Sometime in the autumn.

HILDA [*nods her head slowly several times*]. It was ten years ago—on the nineteenth of September.

SOL. Yes, it must have been about that time. Fancy your remembering that too! [*Stops.*] But wait a moment! Yes—it's the nineteenth of September today.

HILDA. Yes, it is; and the ten years are gone. And you didn't come—as you promised me.

SOL. Promised you? Threatened, I suppose you mean?

HILDA. I don't think there was any sort of threat in that.

SOL. Well, then, a little bit of fun.

HILDA. Was that all you wanted? To make fun of me?

SOL. Well, or to have a little joke with you. Upon my soul, I don't recollect. But it must have been something of that kind, for you were a mere child then.

HILDA. Oh, perhaps I wasn't quite such a child either. Not such a mere chit as you imagine.

SOL. [*looks searchingly at her*]. Did you really and seriously expect me to come again?

HILDA [*conceals a half-teasing smile*]. Yes indeed, I did expect that of you.

SOL. That I should come back to your home and take you away with me?

HILDA. Just like a troll—yes.

SOL. And make a princess of you?

HILDA. That's what you promised.

SOL. And give you a kingdom as well?

HILDA [*looks up at the ceiling*]. Why not? Of course it need not have been an actual, everyday sort of kingdom.

SOL. But something else just as good?

HILDA. Yes, at least as good. [*Looks at him a moment.*] I thought if you could build the highest church towers in the world you could surely manage to raise a kingdom of one sort or another as well.

SOL. [*shakes his head*]. I can't quite make you out, Miss Wangel.

HILDA. Can you not? To me it seems all so simple.

SOL. No, I can't make up my mind whether you mean all you say or are simply having a joke with me.

HILDA [*smiles*]. Making fun of you, perhaps? I too?

SOL. Yes, exactly. Making fun—of both of us. [*Looks at her.*] Is it long since you found out that I was married?

HILDA. I have known it all along. Why do you ask me that?

SOL. [*lightly*]. Oh well, it just occurred to me. [*Looks earnestly at her and says in a low voice.*] What have you come for?

HILDA. I want my kingdom. The time is up.

SOL. [*laughs involuntarily*]. What a girl you are!

HILDA [*gaily*]. Out with my kingdom, Mr Solness! [*Raps with her fingers.*] The kingdom on the table!

SOL. [*pushing the rocking chair nearer and sitting down*]. Now, seriously speaking—what have you come for? What do you really want to do here?

HILDA. Oh, first of all I want to go around and look at all the things that you have built.

SOL. That will give you plenty of exercise.

HILDA. Yes, I know you have built a tremendous lot.

SOL. I have, indeed—especially of late years.

HILDA. Many church towers among the rest? Immensely high ones?

SOL. No. I build no church towers now. Nor churches either.

HILDA. What do you build then?

SOL. Homes for human beings.

HILDA [*reflectively*]. Couldn't you build a little—a little bit of a church tower over these homes as well?

SOL. [*starting*]. What do you mean by that?

HILDA. I mean—something that points—points up into the free air. With the vane at a dizzy height.

SOL. [*pondering a little*]. Strange that you should say that—for that is just what I am most anxious to do.

HILDA [*impatiently*]. Why don't you do it then?

SOL. [*shakes his head*]. No, the people will not have it.

HILDA. Fancy their not wanting it!

SOL. [*more lightly*]. But now I am building a new home for myself—just opposite here.

HILDA. For yourself?

SOL. Yes. It is almost finished. And on that there is a tower.

HILDA. A high tower?

SOL. Yes.

HILDA. Very high?

SOL. No doubt people will say it is too high—too high for a dwelling house.

HILDA. I'll go out and look at that tower the first thing tomorrow morning.

SOL. [*sits resting his cheek on his hand and gazes at her*]. Tell me, Miss Wangel—what is your name? Your Christian name, I mean.

HILDA. Why, Hilda, of course.

SOL. [*as before*]. Hilda? Indeed?

HILDA. Don't you remember that? You called me Hilda yourself—that day you misbehaved.

SOL. Did I really?

HILDA. But then you said "little Hilda," and I didn't like that.

SOL. Oh, you didn't like that, Miss Hilda?

HILDA. No, not at such a time as that. But "Princess Hilda"—that will sound very well, I think.

SOL. Very well indeed. Princess Hilda of—of—what was to be the name of the kingdom?

HILDA. Pooh! I won't have anything to do with that stupid kingdom. I have set my heart upon quite a different one!

SOL. [*has leaned back in the chair, still gazing at her*]. Isn't it strange?

The more I think of it now, the more it seems to me as though I had gone about all these years torturing myself with–h'm——

HILDA. With what?

SOL. With the effort to recover something–some experience, which I seemed to have forgotten. But I never had the least inkling of what it could be.

HILDA. You should have tied a knot in your pocket handkerchief, Mr Solness.

SOL. In that case I should simply have had to go racking my brains to discover what the knot could mean.

HILDA. Oh yes, I suppose there are trolls of that kind in the world too.

SOL. [*rises slowly*]. What a good thing it is that you have come to me now.

HILDA [*looks deeply into his eyes*]. Is it a good thing?

SOL. For I have been so lonely here. I have been gazing so helplessly at it all. [*In a lower voice.*] I must tell you –I have begun to be so afraid–so terribly afraid of the younger generation.

HILDA [*with a little snort of contempt*]. Pooh–is the younger generation a thing to be afraid of?

SOL. It is indeed. And that is why I have locked and barred myself in. [*Mysteriously.*] I tell you the younger generation will one day come and thunder at my door! They will break in upon me!

HILDA. Then I should say you ought to go out and open the door to the younger generation.

SOL. Open the door?

HILDA. Yes. Let them come in to you on friendly terms as it were.

SOL. No, no, no! The younger generation–it means retribution, you see. It comes, as if under a new banner, heralding the turn of fortune.

HILDA [*rises, looks at him and says with a quivering twitch of her lips*]. Can I be of any use to you, Mr Solness?

SOL. Yes, you can indeed! For you, too, come–under a new banner, it seems to me. Youth marshaled against youth!

[DR HERDAL *comes in by the hall door.*]

DR H. What–you and Miss Wangel here still?

SOL. Yes. We have had no end of things to talk about.

HILDA. Both old and new.

DR H. Have you really?

HILDA. Oh, it has been the greatest fun. For Mr Solness–he has such a miraculous memory. All the least little details he remembers instantly.

[MRS SOLNESS *enters by the door on the right.*]

MRS S. Well, Miss Wangel, your room is quite ready for you now.

HILDA. Oh, how kind you are to me!

SOL. [*to* MRS SOLNESS]. The nursery?

MRS S. Yes, the middle one. But first let us go in to supper.

SOL. [*nods to* HILDA]. Hilda shall sleep in the nursery, she shall.

MRS S. [*looks at him*]. Hilda?

SOL. Yes, Miss Wangel's name is Hilda. I knew her when she was a child.

MRS S. Did you really, Halvard? Well, shall we go? Supper is on the table. [*She takes* DR HERDAL'S *arm and goes out with him to the right.* HILDA *has meanwhile been collecting her traveling things.*]

HILDA [*softly and rapidly to* SOL-

NESS]. Is it true, what you said? Can I be of use to you?

SOL. [*takes the things from her*]. You are the very being I have needed most.

HILDA [*looks at him with happy, wondering eyes and clasps her hands*]. But then, great heavens——

SOL. [*eagerly*]. What?

HILDA. Then I have my kingdom!

SOL. [*involuntarily*]. Hilda!

HILDA [*again with the quivering twitch of her lips*]. Almost—I was going to say. [*She goes out to the right;* SOLNESS *follows her.*]

ACT II

SCENE—*A prettily furnished small drawing room in* SOLNESS'S *house. In the back a glass door leading out to the veranda and garden. The right-hand corner is cut off transversely by a large bay window in which are flower stands. The left-hand corner is similarly cut off by a transverse wall in which is a small door papered like the wall. On each side an ordinary door. In front, on the right, a console table with a large mirror over it. Well-filled stand of plants and flowers. In front, on the left, a sofa with a table and chairs. Further back a bookcase. Well forward in the room, before the bay window, a small table and some chairs. It is early in the day.*

SOLNESS *sits by the little table with* RAGNAR BROVIK'S *portfolio open in front of him. He is turning the drawings over and closely examining some of them.* MRS SOLNESS *moves about noiselessly with a small watering pot, attending to her flowers. She is dressed in black as before. Her hat, cloak and parasol lie on a chair near the mirror. Unobserved by her,* SOLNESS *now and again follows her with his eyes. Neither of them speaks.*

KAIA FOSLI *enters quietly by the door on the left.*

SOL. [*turns his head and says in an offhand tone of indifference*]. Well, is that you?

KAIA. I merely wished to let you know that I have come.

SOL. Yes, yes, that's all right. Hasn't Ragnar come too?

KAIA. Not well. He begs you to excuse him; he is obliged to keep his bed today.

SOL. Why, of course; by all means let him rest. But now get to work.

KAIA. Yes. [*Pauses at the door.*] Do you wish to speak to Ragnar when he comes?

SOL. No—I don't know that I have anything particular to say to him.

[KAIA *goes out again to the left.* SOLNESS *remains seated, turning over the drawings.*]

MRS S. [*over beside the plants*]. I wonder if he isn't going to die now as well?

SOL. [*looks up to her*]. As well as who?

MRS S. [*without answering*]. Yes, yes—depend upon it, Halvard, old Brovik is going to die too. You'll see that he will.

SOL. My dear Aline, ought you not to go out for a little walk?

MRS S. Yes, I suppose I ought to. [*She continues to attend to the flowers.*]

SOL. [*bending over the drawings*]. Is she still asleep?

MRS S. [*looking at him*]. Is it Miss Wangel you are sitting there thinking about?

SOL. [*indifferently*]. I just happened to recollect her.

Mrs S. Miss Wangel was up long ago.

Sol. Oh! Was she?

Mrs S. When I went in to see her she was busy putting her things in order. [*She goes in front of the mirror and slowly begins to put on her hat.*]

Sol. [*after a short pause*]. So we have found a use for one of our nurseries after all, Aline.

Mrs S. Yes, we have.

Sol. That seems to me better than to have them all standing empty.

Mrs S. That emptiness is dreadful; you are right there.

Sol. [*closes the portfolio, rises and approaches her*]. You will find that we shall get on far better after this, Aline. Things will be more comfortable. Life will be easier—especially for you.

Mrs S. [*looks at him*]. After this?

Sol. Yes, believe me, Aline——

Mrs S. Do you mean—because she has come here?

Sol. [*checking himself*]. I mean, of course, when once we have moved into the new house.

Mrs S. [*takes her cloak*]. Ah, do you think so, Halvard? Will it be better then?

Sol. I can't think otherwise. And surely you think so too?

Mrs S. I think nothing at all about the new house.

Sol. [*cast down*]. It's hard for me to hear you say that, for you know it is mainly for your sake that I have built it. [*He offers to help her on with her cloak.*]

Mrs S. [*evades him*]. The fact is, you do far too much for my sake.

Sol. [*with a certain vehemence*]. No, no, you really mustn't say that, Aline! I cannot bear to hear you say such things!

Mrs S. Very well, then I won't say it, Halvard.

Sol. But I stick to what *I* said. You'll see that things will be easier for you in the new place.

Mrs S. O heavens!—easier for me!

Sol. [*eagerly*]. Yes, indeed they will! You may be quite sure of that. For you see—there will be so very, very much there that will remind you of your own home.

Mrs S. The home that used to be Father's and Mother's—and that was burned to the ground.

Sol. [*in a low voice*]. Yes, yes, my poor Aline. That was a terrible blow for you.

Mrs S. [*breaking out in lamentation*]. You may build as much as ever you like, Halvard—you can never build up again a real home for me!

Sol. [*crosses the room*]. Well, in heaven's name, let us talk no more about it then.

Mrs S. Oh yes, Halvard, I understand you very well. You are so anxious to spare me—and to find excuses for me too—as much as ever you can.

Sol. [*with astonishment in his eyes*]. You! Is it you—yourself, that you are talking about, Aline?

Mrs S. Yes, who else should it be but myself?

Sol. [*involuntarily to himself*]. That too!

Mrs S. As for the old house, I wouldn't mind so much about that. When once misfortune was in the air—why——

Sol. Ah, you are right there. Misfortune will have its way—as the saying goes.

Mrs S. But it's what came of the

fire—the dreadful thing that followed! That is the thing! That, that, that!

Sol. [*vehemently*]. Don't think about that, Aline!

Mrs S. Ah, that is exactly what I cannot help thinking about. And now, at last, I must speak about it too; for I don't seem able to bear it any longer. And then never to be able to forgive myself——

Sol. [*exclaiming*]. Yourself!

Mrs S. Yes, for I had duties on both sides—both toward you and toward the little ones. I ought to have hardened myself—not to have let the horror take such hold upon me—nor the grief for the burning of my old home. [*Wrings her hands.*] Oh, Halvard, if I had only had the strength!

Sol. [*softly, much moved, comes closer*]. Aline—you must promise me never to think these thoughts any more. Promise me that, dear!

Mrs S. Oh, promise, promise! One can promise anything.

Sol. [*clenches his hands and crosses the room*]. Oh, but this is hopeless, hopeless! Never a ray of sunlight! Not so much as a gleam of brightness to light up our home!

Mrs S. This is no home, Halvard.

Sol. Oh no, you may well say that. [*Gloomily.*]And God knows whether you are not right in saying that it will be no better for us in the new house either.

Mrs S. It will never be any better. Just as empty—just as desolate—there as here.

Sol. [*vehemently*]. Why in all the world have we built it then? Can you tell me that?

Mrs S. No, you must answer that question for yourself.

Sol. [*glances suspiciously at her*]. What do you mean by that, Aline?

Mrs S. What do I mean?

Sol. Yes, in the devil's name! You said it so strangely—as if you had hidden some meaning in it.

Mrs S. No indeed, I assure you——

Sol. [*comes closer*]. Oh, come now—I know what I know. I have both my eyes and my ears about me, Aline—you may depend upon that!

Mrs S. Why, what are you talking about? What is it?

Sol. [*places himself in front of her*]. Do you mean to say you don't find a kind of lurking, hidden meaning in the most innocent word I happen to say?

Mrs S. *I*, do you say? *I* do that?

Sol. [*laughs*]. Ho-ho-ho! It's natural enough, Aline! When you have a sick man on your hands——

Mrs S. [*anxiously*]. Sick? Are you ill, Halvard?

Sol. [*violently*]. A half-mad man then! A crazy man! Call me what you will.

Mrs S. [*feels blindly for a chair and sits down*]. Halvard—for God's sake——

Sol. But you are wrong, both you and the doctor. I am not in the state you imagine. [*He walks up and down the room.* Mrs Solness *follows him anxiously with her eyes. Finally he goes up to her.*]

Sol. [*calmly*]. In reality there is nothing whatever the matter with me.

Mrs S. No, there isn't, is there? But then what is it that troubles you so?

Sol. Why this, that I often feel ready to sink under this terrible burden of debt.

Mrs S. Debt, do you say? But you owe no one anything, Halvard!

Sol. [*softly, with emotion*]. I owe

a boundless debt to you—to you—to you, Aline.

MRS S. [*arises slowly*]. What is behind all this? You may just as well tell me at once.

SOL. But there is nothing behind it; I have never done you any wrong—not wittingly and willfully, at any rate. And yet—and yet it seems as though a crushing debt rested upon me and weighed me down.

MRS S. A debt to me?

SOL. Chiefly to you.

MRS S. Then you are—ill after all, Halvard.

SOL. [*gloomily*]. I suppose I must be—or not far from it. [*Looks toward the door to the right, which is opened at this moment.*] Ah! Now it grows lighter.

[HILDA WANGEL *comes in. She has made some alteration in her dress and let down her skirt.*]

HILDA. Good morning, Mr Solness!

SOL. [*nods*]. Slept well?

HILDA. Quite deliciously! Like a child in a cradle. Oh—I lay and stretched myself like—like a princess!

SOL. [*smiles a little*]. You were thoroughly comfortable then?

HILDA. I should think so.

SOL. And no doubt you dreamed too.

HILDA. Yes, I did. But that was horrid.

SOL. Was it?

HILDA. Yes, for I dreamed I was falling over a frightfully high, sheer precipice. Do you never have that kind of dream?

SOL. Oh yes—now and then.

HILDA. It's tremendously thrilling—when you fall and fall——

SOL. It seems to make one's blood run cold.

HILDA. Do you draw your legs up under you while you are falling?

SOL. Yes, as high as ever I can.

HILDA. So do I.

MRS S. [*takes her parasol*]. I must go into town now, Halvard. [*To* HILDA.] And I'll try to get one or two things that you may require.

HILDA [*making a motion to throw her arms round her neck*]. Oh, you dear, sweet Mrs Solness! You are really much too kind to me! Frightfully kind——

MRS S. [*deprecatingly, freeing herself*]. Oh, not at all. It's only my duty, so I am very glad to do it.

HILDA [*offended, pouts*]. But really, I think I am quite fit to be seen in the streets—now that I've put my dress to rights. Or do you think I am not?

MRS S. To tell you the truth, I think people would stare at you a little.

HILDA [*contemptuously*]. Pooh! Is that all? That only amuses me.

SOL. [*with suppressed ill-humor*]. Yes, but people might take it into their heads that you were mad too, you see.

HILDA. Mad? Are there so many mad people here in town, then?

SOL. [*points to his own forehead*]. Here you see one, at all events.

HILDA. You—Mr Solness!

MRS S. Oh, don't talk like that, my dear Halvard!

SOL. Have you not noticed that yet?

HILDA. No, I certainly have not. [*Reflects and laughs a little.*] And yet—perhaps in one single thing.

SOL. Ah! Do you hear that, Aline?

MRS S. What is that one single thing, Miss Wangel?

HILDA. No, I won't say.

SOL. Oh yes, do!

HILDA. No, thank you—I am not so mad as that.

MRS S. When you and Miss Wangel are alone I daresay she will tell you, Halvard.

SOL. Ah—you think she will?

MRS S. Oh yes, certainly. For you have known her so well in the past. Ever since she was a child—you tell me. [*She goes out by the door on the left.*]

HILDA [*after a little while*]. Does your wife dislike me very much?

SOL. Did you think you noticed anything of the kind?

HILDA. Did you not notice it yourself?

SOL. [*evasively*]. Aline has become exceedingly shy with strangers of late years.

HILDA. Has she really?

SOL. But if only you could get to know her thoroughly—— Ah! she is so good—so kind—so excellent a creature——

HILDA [*impatiently*]. But if she is all that—what made her say that about her duty?

SOL. Her duty?

HILDA. She said that she would go out and buy something for me because it was her duty. Oh! I can't bear that ugly, horrid word!

SOL. Why not?

HILDA. It sounds so cold and sharp and stinging. Duty—duty—duty. Don't you think so too? Doesn't it seem to sting you?

SOL. H'm—haven't thought much about it.

HILDA. Yes, it does. And if she is so good—as you say she is—why should she talk in that way?

SOL. But, good lord, what would you have had her say then?

HILDA. She might have said she would do it because she had taken a tremendous fancy to me. She might have said something like that—something really warm and cordial, you understand.

SOL. [*looks at her*]. Is that how you would like to have it?

HILDA. Yes, precisely. [*She wanders about the room, stops at the bookcase and looks at the books.*] What a lot of books you have!

SOL. Yes, I have got together a good many.

HILDA. Do you read them all too?

SOL. I used to try to. Do you read much?

HILDA. No, never! I have given it up. For it all seems so irrelevant.

SOL. That is just my feeling.

[HILDA *wanders about a little, stops at the small table, opens the portfolio and turns over the contents.*]

HILDA. Are all these drawings yours?

SOL. No, they are drawn by a young man whom I employ to help me.

HILDA. Someone you have taught?

SOL. Oh yes, no doubt he has learned something from me too.

HILDA [*sits down*]. Then I suppose he is very clever. [*Looks at a drawing.*] Isn't he?

SOL. Oh, he might be worse. For my purpose——

HILDA. Oh yes—I'm sure he is frightfully clever.

SOL. Do you think you can see that in the drawings?

HILDA. Pooh—these scrawlings! But if he has been learning from you——

SOL. Oh, so far as that goes—there are plenty of people that have learned from me and have come to little enough for all that.

HILDA [*looks at him and shakes her head*]. No, I can't for the life of me understand how you can be so stupid.

SOL. Stupid? Do you think I am so very stupid?

HILDA. Yes, I do indeed. If you are content to go about here teaching all these people——

SOL. [*with a slight start*]. Well, and why not?

HILDA [*rises, half serious, half laughing*]. No indeed, Mr Solness! What can be the good of that? No one but you should be allowed to build. You should stand quite alone—do it all yourself. Now you know it.

SOL. [*involuntarily*]. Hilda!

HILDA. Well?

SOL. How in the world did that come into your head?

HILDA. Do you think I am so very far wrong then?

SOL. No, that's not what I mean. But now I'll tell you something.

HILDA. Well?

SOL. I keep on—incessantly—in silence and alone—brooding on that very thought.

HILDA. Yes, that seems to me perfectly natural.

SOL. [*looks somewhat searchingly at her*]. Perhaps you have noticed it already?

HILDA. No, indeed I haven't.

SOL. But just now—when you said you thought I was—off my balance? In one thing, you said.

HILDA. Oh, I was thinking of something quite different.

SOL. What was it?

HILDA. I am not going to tell you.

SOL. [*crosses the room*]. Well, well—as you please. [*Stops at the bow window.*] Come here, and I will show you something.

HILDA [*approaching*]. What is it?

SOL. Do you see—over there in the garden?

HILDA. Yes?

SOL. [*points*]. Right about the great quarry——

HILDA. That new house, you mean?

SOL. The one that is being built, yes. Almost finished.

HILDA. It seems to have a very high tower.

SOL. The scaffolding is still up.

HILDA. Is that your new house?

SOL. Yes.

HILDA. The house you are soon going to move into?

SOL. Yes.

HILDA. [*looks at him*]. Are there nurseries in that house too?

SOL. Three, as there are here.

HILDA. And no child.

SOL. And there never will be one.

HILDA [*with a half-smile*]. Well, isn't it just as I said?

SOL. That——?

HILDA. That you are a little—a little mad after all.

SOL. Was that what you were thinking of?

HILDA. Yes, of all the empty nurseries I slept in.

SOL. [*lowers his voice*]. We have had children—Aline and I.

HILDA [*looks eagerly at him*]. Have you?

SOL. Two little boys. They were of the same age.

HILDA. Twins, then.

SOL. Yes, twins. It's eleven or twelve years ago now.

HILDA [*cautiously*]. And so both of them—— You have lost both the twins then?

SOL. [*with quiet emotion*]. We kept them only about three weeks. Or scarcely so much. [*Bursts forth.*] Oh, Hilda, I can't tell you what a good thing it is for me that you have come!

For now at last I have someone I can talk to!

HILDA. Can you not talk to—her too?

SOL. Not about this. Not as I want to talk and must talk. [*Gloomily.*] And not about so many other things either.

HILDA [*in a subdued voice*]. Was that all you meant when you said you needed me?

SOL. That was mainly what I meant —at all events yesterday. For today I am not so sure—— [*Breaking off.*] Come here and let us sit down, Hilda. Sit there on the sofa—so that you can look into the garden. [HILDA *seats herself in the corner of the sofa.* SOLNESS *brings a chair closer.*] Should you like to hear about it?

HILDA. Yes, I shall love to sit and listen to you.

SOL. [*sits down*]. Then I will tell you all about it.

HILDA. Now I can see both the garden and you, Mr Solness. So now, tell away! Begin!

SOL. [*points toward the bow window*]. Out there on the rising ground —where you see the new house——

HILDA. Yes?

SOL. Aline and I lived there in the first years of our married life. There was an old house up there that had belonged to her mother, and we inherited it and the whole of the great garden with it.

HILDA. Was there a tower on that house too?

SOL. No, nothing of the kind. From the outside it looked like a great, dark, ugly wooden box; but all the same it was snug and comfortable enough inside.

HILDA. Then did you pull down the ramshackle old place?

SOL. No, it burned down.

HILDA. The whole of it?

SOL. Yes.

HILDA. Was that a great misfortune for you?

SOL. That depends on how you look at it. As a builder, the fire was the making of me.

HILDA. Well, but——

SOL. It was just after the birth of the two little boys——

HILDA. The poor little twins, yes.

SOL. They came healthy and bonny into the world. And they were growing too—you could see the difference from day to day.

HILDA. Little children do grow quickly at first.

SOL. It was the prettiest sight in the world to see Aline lying with the two of them in her arms. But then came the night of the fire——

HILDA [*excitedly*]. What happened? Do tell me! Was anyone burned?

SOL. No, not that. Everyone got safe and sound out of the house——

HILDA. Well, and what then?

SOL. The fright had shaken Aline terribly. The alarm—the escape—the breakneck hurry—and then the ice-cold night air—for they had to be carried out just as they lay—both she and the little ones.

HILDA. Was it too much for them?

SOL. Oh no, they stood it well enough. But Aline fell into a fever, and it affected her milk. She would insist on nursing them herself; because it was her duty, she said. And both our little boys, they—[*clenching his hands*]—they—— Oh!

HILDA. They did not get over that.

SOL. No, that they did not get over. That was how we lost them.

HILDA. It must have been terribly

hard for you.

SOL. Hard enough for me, but ten times harder for Aline. [*Clenching his hands in suppressed fury.*] Oh, that such things should be allowed to happen here in the world! [*Shortly and firmly.*] From the day I lost them I had no heart for building churches.

HILDA. Did you not like the church tower in our town?

SOL. I didn't like it. I know how free and happy I felt when that tower was finished.

HILDA. I know that too.

SOL. And now I shall never–never build anything of that sort again! Neither churches nor church towers.

HILDA [*nods slowly*]. Nothing but houses for people to live in.

SOL. Homes for human beings, Hilda.

HILDA. But homes with high towers and pinnacles upon them.

SOL. If possible. [*Adopts a lighter tone.*] But, as I said before, that fire was the making of me–as a builder, I mean.

HILDA. Why don't you call yourself an architect, like the others?

SOL. I have not been systematically enough taught for that. Most of what I know I have found out for myself.

HILDA. But you succeeded all the same.

SOL. Yes, thanks to the fire. I laid out almost the whole of the garden in villa lots, and there I was able to build after my own heart. So I came to the front with a rush.

HILDA [*looks keenly at him*]. You must surely be a very happy man as matters stand with you.

SOL. [*gloomily*]. Happy? Do you say that too–like all the rest of them?

HILDA. Yes, I should say you must be. If you could only cease thinking about the two little children––

SOL. [*slowly*]. The two little children–they are not so easy to forget, Hilda.

HILDA [*somewhat uncertainly*]. Do you still feel their loss so much–after all these years?

SOL. [*looks fixedly at her without replying*]. A happy man, you said ––

HILDA. Well, now, are you not happy–in other respects?

SOL. [*continues to look at her*]. When I told you all this about the fire –h'm––

HILDA. Well?

SOL. Was there not one special thought that you–that you seized upon?

HILDA [*reflects in vain*]. No. What thought should that be?

SOL. [*with subdued emphasis*]. It was simply and solely by that fire that I was enabled to build homes for human beings. Cosy, comfortable, bright homes, where father and mother and the whole troop of children can live in safety and gladness, feeling what a happy thing it is to be alive in the world–and most of all to belong to each other–in great things and in small.

HILDA [*ardently*]. Well, and is it not a great happiness for you to be able to build such beautiful homes?

SOL. The price, Hilda! The terrible price I had to pay for the opportunity!

HILDA. But can you never get over that?

SOL. No. That I might build homes for others I had to forego–to forego for all time–the home that might have been my own. I mean a home for a troop of children–and for father and mother too.

HILDA [*cautiously*]. But need you have done that? For all time, you say?

SOL. [*nods slowly*]. That was the price of this happiness that people talk about. [*Breathes heavily.*] This happiness—h'm—this happiness was not to be bought any cheaper, Hilda.

HILDA [*as before*]. But may it not come right even yet?

SOL. Never in this world—never. That is another consequence of the fire—and of Aline's illness afterward.

HILDA [*looks at him with an indefinable expression*]. And yet you build all these nurseries?

SOL. [*seriously*]. Have you never noticed, Hilda, how the impossible—how it seems to beckon and cry aloud to one?

HILDA [*reflecting*]. The impossible? [*With animation.*] Yes indeed! Is that how you feel too?

SOL. Yes, I do.

HILDA. There must be—a little of the troll in you too.

SOL. Why of the troll?

HILDA. What would you call it then?

SOL. [*rises*]. Well, well, perhaps you are right. [*Vehemently.*] But how can I help turning into a troll when this is how it always goes with me in everything—in everything!

HILDA. How do you mean?

SOL. [*speaking low, with inward emotion*]. Mark what I say to you, Hilda. All that I have succeeded in doing, building, creating—all the beauty, security, cheerful comfort—ay, and magnificence too—— [*Clenches his hands.*] Oh, is it not terrible even to think of!

HILDA. What is so terrible?

SOL. That all this I have to make up for, to pay for—not in money but in human happiness. And not with my own happiness only, but with other people's too. Yes, yes, do you see that, Hilda? That is the price which my position as an artist has cost me—and others. And every single day I have to look on while the price is paid for me anew. Over again and over again—and over again forever!

HILDA [*rises and looks steadily at him*]. Now I can see that you are thinking of—of her.

SOL. Yes, mainly of Aline. For Aline—she, too, had her vocation in life, just as much as I had mine. [*His voice quivers.*] But her vocation has had to be stunted and crushed and shattered—in order that mine might force its way to—to a sort of great victory. For you must know that Aline—she, too, had a talent for building.

HILDA. She! For building?

SOL. [*shakes his head*]. Not houses and towers and spires—not such things as I work away at.

HILDA. Well, but what then?

SOL. [*softly, with emotion*]. For building up the souls of little children, Hilda. For building up children's souls in perfect balance and in noble and beautiful forms. For enabling them to soar up into erect and full-grown human souls. That was Aline's talent. And there it all lies now—unused and unusable forever—of no earthly service to anyone—just like the ruins left by a fire.

HILDA. Yes, but even if this was so——

SOL. It is so! It is so! I know it!

HILDA. Well, but in any case it is not your fault.

SOL. [*fixes his eyes on her and nods slowly*]. Ah, that is the great, terrible question. That is the doubt that is gnawing me—night and day.

HILDA. That?

SOL. Yes. Suppose the fault was mine—in a certain sense.

HILDA. Your fault! The fire!

SOL. All of it, the whole thing. And yet perhaps—I may not have had anything to do with it.

HILDA [*looks at him with a troubled expression*]. Oh, Mr Solness—if you can talk like that, I am afraid you must be ill after all.

SOL. H'm—I don't think I shall ever be of quite sound mind on that point.

[RAGNAR BROVIK *cautiously opens the little door in the left-hand corner.* HILDA *comes forward.*]

RAG. [*when he sees* HILDA]. Oh, I beg pardon, Mr Solness. [*He makes a movement to withdraw.*]

SOL. No, no, don't go. Let us get it over.

RAG. Oh yes—if only we could.

SOL. I hear your father is no better.

RAG. Father is fast growing weaker—and therefore I beg and implore you to write a few kind words for me on one of the plans! Something for Father to read before he——

SOL. [*vehemently*]. I won't hear anything more about those drawings of yours!

RAG. Have you looked at them?

SOL. Yes—I have.

RAG. And they are good for nothing? And *I* am good for nothing too?

SOL. [*evasively*]. Stay here with me, Ragnar. You shall have everything your own way. And then you can marry Kaia and live at your ease—and happily too, who knows? Only don't think of building on your own account.

RAG. Well, well, then I must go home and tell Father what you say—I promised I would. Is this what I am to tell Father—before he dies?

SOL. [*with a groan*]. Oh! tell him—tell him what you will, for me. Best to say nothing at all to him. [*With a sudden outburst.*] I cannot do anything else, Ragnar.

RAG. May I have the drawings to take with me?

SOL. Yes, take them—take them by all means! They are lying there on the table.

RAG. [*goes to the table*]. Thanks.

HILDA [*puts her hand on the portfolio*]. No, no; leave them here.

SOL. Why?

HILDA. Because I want to look at them too.

SOL. But you have been—— [*To* RAGNAR.] Well, leave them here then.

RAG. Very well.

SOL. And go home at once to your father.

RAG. Yes, I suppose I must.

SOL. [*as if in desperation*]. Ragnar—you must not ask me to do what is beyond my power. Do you hear, Ragnar? You must not!

RAG. No, no. I beg your pardon. [*He bows and goes out by the corner door.* HILDA *goes over and sits down on a chair near the mirror.*]

HILDA [*looks angrily at* SOLNESS]. That was a very ugly thing to do.

SOL. Do you think so too?

HILDA. Yes, it was horribly ugly—and hard and bad and cruel as well.

SOL. Oh, you don't understand my position.

HILDA. No matter. I say you ought not to be like that.

SOL. You said yourself, only just now, that no one but *I* ought to be allowed to build.

HILDA. *I* may say such things—but you must not.

SOL. I most of all, surely, who have paid so dear for my position.

HILDA. Oh yes—with what you call

domestic comfort–and that sort of thing.

SOL. And with my peace of soul into the bargain.

HILDA [*rising*]. Peace of soul. [*With feeling.*] Yes, yes, you are right in that! Poor Mr Solness–you fancy that——

SOL. [*with a quiet chuckling laugh*]. Just sit down again, Hilda, and I'll tell you something funny.

HILDA [*sits down, with intent interest*]. Well?

SOL. It sounds such a ludicrous little thing; for, you see, the whole story turns upon nothing but a crack in a chimney.

HILDA. No more than that?

SOL. No, not to begin with. [*He moves a chair nearer to* HILDA *and sits down.*]

HILDA [*impatiently taps on her knee*]. Well, now for the crack in the chimney!

SOL. I had noticed the split in the flue long, long before the fire. Everytime I went up into the attic I looked to see if it was still there.

HILDA. And it was?

SOL. Yes, for no one else knew about it.

HILDA. And you said nothing?

SOL. Nothing.

HILDA. And did not think of repairing the flue either?

SOL. Oh yes, I thought about it–but never got any further. Every time I intended to set to work it seemed just as if a hand held me back. Not today, I thought–tomorrow; and nothing ever came of it.

HILDA. But why did you keep putting it off like that?

SOL. Because I was revolving something in my mind. [*Slowly and in a low voice.*] Through that little black crack in the chimney I might, perhaps, force my way upward–as a builder.

HILDA [*looking straight in front of her*]. That must have been thrilling.

SOL. Almost irresistible–quite irresistible. For at that time it appeared to me a perfectly simple and straightforward matter. I would have had it happen in the wintertime–a little before midday. I was to be out driving Aline in the sleigh. The servants at home would have made huge fires in the stoves.

HILDA. For of course it was to be bitterly cold that day?

SOL. Rather biting, yes–and they would want Aline to find it thoroughly snug and warm when she came home.

HILDA. I suppose she is very chilly by nature?

SOL. She is. And as we drove home we were to see the smoke.

HILDA. Only the smoke?

SOL. The smoke first. But when we came up to the garden gate the whole of the old timber box was to be a rolling mass of flames. That is how I wanted it to be, you see.

HILDA. Oh, why could it not have happened so!

SOL. You may well say that, Hilda.

HILDA. Well, but now listen, Mr Solness. Are you perfectly certain that the fire was caused by that little crack in the chimney?

SOL. No, on the contrary–I am perfectly certain that the crack in the chimney had nothing whatever to do with the fire.

HILDA. What?

SOL. It has been clearly ascertained that the fire broke out in a clothes cupboard–in a totally different part of the house.

HILDA. Then what is all this nonsense you are talking about the crack in the chimney?

SOL. May I go on talking to you a little, Hilda?

HILDA. Yes, if you'll only talk sensibly.

SOL. I will try. [*He moves his chair nearer.*]

HILDA. Out with it then, Mr Solness.

SOL. [*confidentially*]. Don't you agree with me, Hilda, that there exist special chosen people who have been endowed with the power and faculty of desiring a thing, craving for a thing, willing a thing—so persistently and so —so inexorably—that at last it has to happen? Don't you believe that?

HILDA [*with an indefinable expression in her eyes*]. If that is so, we shall see, one of these days, whether *I* am one of the chosen.

SOL. It is not one's self alone that can do such great things. Oh no—the helpers and the servers—they must do their part, too, if it is to be of any good. But they never come of themselves. One has to call upon them very persistently—inwardly, you understand.

HILDA. What are these helpers and servers?

SOL. Oh, we can talk about that some other time. For the present let us keep to this business of the fire.

HILDA. Don't you think that fire would have happened all the same—even without your wishing for it?

SOL. If the house had been old Knut Brovik's, it would never have burned down so conveniently for him. I am sure of that, for he does not know how to call for the helpers—no, nor for the servers either. [*Rises in unrest.*] So you see, Hilda—it is my fault, after all, that the lives of the two little boys had to be sacrificed. And do you think it is not my fault, too, that Aline has never been the woman she should and might have been—and that she most longed to be?

HILDA. Yes, but if it is all the work of those helpers and servers——

SOL. Who called for the helpers and servers? It was I! And they came and obeyed my will. [*In increasing excitement.*] That is what people call having the luck on your side, but I must tell you what this sort of luck feels like! It feels like a great raw place here on my breast. And the helpers and servers keep on flaying pieces of skin off other people in order to close my sore! But still the sore is not healed —never, never! Oh, if you knew how it can sometimes gnaw and burn.

HILDA [*looks attentively at him*]. You are ill, Mr Solness. Very ill, I almost think.

SOL. Say mad, for that is what you mean.

HILDA. No, I don't think there is much amiss with your intellect.

SOL. With what, then? Out with it!

HILDA. I wonder whether you were not sent into the world with a sickly conscience.

SOL. A sickly conscience? What deviltry is that?

HILDA. I mean that your conscience is feeble—too delicately built, as it were—hasn't strength to take a grip of things—to lift and bear what is heavy.

SOL. [*growls*]. H'm. May I ask, then, what sort of conscience one ought to have?

HILDA. I should like your conscience to be—to be thoroughly robust.

SOL. Indeed? Robust, eh? Is your own conscience robust, may I ask?

HILDA. Yes, I think it is. I have never noticed that it wasn't.

SOL. It has not been put very severely to the test, I should think.

HILDA [*with a quivering of the lips*]. Oh, it was no such simple matter to leave Father–I am so awfully fond of him.

SOL. Dear me! For a month or two ——

HILDA. I think I shall never go home again.

SOL. Never? Then why did you leave him?

HILDA [*half seriously, half banteringly*]. Have you forgotten that the ten years are up?

SOL. Oh, nonsense! Was anything wrong at home? Eh?

HILDA [*quite seriously*]. It was the impulse within me that urged and goaded me to come–and lured and drew me on as well.

SOL. [*eagerly*]. There we have it! There we have it, Hilda! There is a troll in you too, as in me. For it's the troll in one, you see–it is that that calls to the powers outside us. And then you must give in–whether you will or not.

HILDA. I almost think you are right, Mr Solness.

SOL. [*walks about the room*]. Oh, there are devils innumerable abroad in the world, Hilda, that one never sees!

HILDA. Devils too?

SOL. [*stops*]. Good devils and bad devils, light-haired devils and black-haired devils. If only you could always tell whether it is the light or dark ones that have got hold of you. [*Paces about.*] Ho-ho! Then it would be simple enough.

HILDA [*follows him with her eyes*]. Or if one had a really vigorous, radiantly healthy conscience–so that one dared to do what one would.

SOL. [*stops beside the console table*]. I believe now that most people are just as puny creatures as I am in that respect.

HILDA. I shouldn't wonder.

SOL. [*leaning against the table*]. In the sagas—— Have you read any of the old sagas?

HILDA. Oh yes! When I used to read books I——

SOL. In the sagas you read about vikings who sailed to foreign lands and plundered and burned and killed men——

HILDA. –and carried off women ——

SOL. –and kept them in captivity ——

HILDA. –took them home in their ships——

SOL. –and behaved to them like–like the very worst of trolls.

HILDA [*looks straight before her with a half-veiled look*]. I think that must have been thrilling.

SOL. [*with a short, deep laugh*]. To carry off women?

HILDA. To be carried off.

SOL. [*looks at her a moment*]. Oh, indeed.

HILDA [*as if breaking the thread of the conversation*]. But what made you speak of these vikings, Mr Solness?

SOL. Why, those fellows must have had robust consciences, if you like! When they got home again they could eat and drink and be as happy as children. And the women too! They often would not leave them on any account. Can you understand that, Hilda?

HILDA. Those women I can understand exceedingly well.

SOL. Oho! Perhaps you could do

the same yourself?

HILDA. Why not?

SOL. Live—of your own free will—with a ruffian like that?

HILDA. If it was a ruffian I had come to love——

SOL. Could you come to love a man like that?

HILDA. Good heavens, you know very well one can't choose whom one is going to love.

SOL. [*looks meditatively at her*]. Oh no, I suppose it is the troll within one that's responsible for that.

HILDA [*half laughing*]. And all these blessed devils that you know so well—both the light-haired and the dark-haired ones.

SOL. [*quietly and warmly*]. Then I hope with all my heart that the devils will choose carefully for you, Hilda.

HILDA. For me they have chosen already—once and for all.

SOL. [*looks earnestly at her*]. Hilda—you are like a wild bird of the woods.

HILDA. Far from it. I don't hide myself away under the bushes.

SOL. No, no. There is rather something of the bird of prey in you.

HILDA. That is nearer it—perhaps. [*Very earnestly.*] And why not a bird of prey? Why should not *I* go a-hunting—I, as well as the rest? Carry off the prey I want—if only I can get my claws into it and do with it as I will.

SOL. Hilda—do you know what you are?

HILDA. Yes, I suppose I am a strange sort of bird.

SOL. No. You are like a dawning day. When I look at you—I seem to be looking toward the sunrise.

HILDA. Tell me, Mr Solness—are you certain that you have never called me to you? Inwardly, you know?

SOL. [*softly and slowly*]. I almost think I must have.

HILDA. What did you want with me?

SOL. You are the younger generation, Hilda.

HILDA [*smiles*]. That younger generation that you are so afraid of?

SOL. [*nods slowly*]. And which, in my heart, I yearn toward so deeply.

[HILDA *rises, goes to the little table and fetches* RAGNAR BROVIK's *portfolio.*]

HILDA [*holds out the portfolio to him*]. We were talking of these drawings——

SOL. [*shortly, waving them away*]. Put those things away! I have seen enough of them.

HILDA. Yes, but you have to write your approval on them.

SOL. Write my approval on them? Never!

HILDA. But the poor old man is lying at death's door! Can't you give him and his son this pleasure before they are parted? And perhaps he might get the commission to carry them out too.

SOL. Yes, that is just what he would get. He has made sure of that—has my fine gentleman!

HILDA. Then, good heavens—if that is so—can't you tell the least bit of a lie for once in a way?

SOL. A lie? [*Raging.*] Hilda—take those devil's drawings out of my sight!

HILDA [*draws the portfolio a little nearer to herself*]. Well, well, well—don't bite me. You talk of trolls—but I think you go on like a troll yourself. [*Looks around.*] Where do you keep your pen and ink?

SOL. There is nothing of the sort in here.

Hilda [*goes toward the door*]. But in the office where that young lady is——

Sol. Stay where you are, Hilda! I ought to tell a lie, you say. Oh yes, for the sake of his old father I might well do that—for in my time I have crushed him, trodden him underfoot——

Hilda. Him too?

Sol. I needed room for myself. But this Ragnar—he must on no account be allowed to come to the front.

Hilda. Poor fellow, there is surely no fear of that. If he has nothing in him——

Sol. [*comes closer, looks at her and whispers*]. If Ragnar Brovik gets his chance, he will strike me to the earth. Crush me—as I crushed his father.

Hilda. Crush you? Has he the ability for that?

Sol. Yes, you may depend upon it he has the ability! He is the younger generation that stands ready to knock at my door—to make an end of Halvard Solness.

Hilda [*looks at him with quiet reproach*]. And yet you would bar him out. Fie, Mr Solness!

Sol. The fight I have been fighting has cost heart's blood enough. And I am afraid, too, that the helpers and servers will not obey me any longer.

Hilda. Then you must go ahead without them. There is nothing else for it.

Sol. It is hopeless, Hilda. The luck is bound to turn. A little sooner or a little later. Retribution is inexorable.

Hilda [*in distress, putting her hands over her ears*]. Don't talk like that! Do you want to kill me? To take from me what is more than my life?

Sol. And what is that?

Hilda. The longing to see you great. To see you with a wreath in your hand, high, high up upon a church tower. [*Calm again.*] Come, out with your pencil now. You must have a pencil about you.

Sol. [*takes out his pocketbook*] I have one here.

Hilda [*lays the portfolio on the sofa table*]. Very well. Now let us two sit down here, Mr Solness. [Solness *seats himself at the table.* Hilda *stands behind him, leaning over the back of the chair.*] And now we will write on the drawings. We must write very, very nicely and cordially—for this horrid Ruar—or whatever his name is.

Sol. [*writes a few words, turns his head and looks at her*]. Tell me one thing, Hilda.

Hilda. Yes!

Sol. If you have been waiting for me all these ten years——

Hilda. What then?

Sol. Why have you never written to me? Then I could have answered you.

Hilda [*hastily*]. No, no, no! That was just what I did not want.

Sol. Why not?

Hilda. I was afraid the whole thing might fall to pieces. But we were going to write on the drawings, Mr Solness.

Sol. So we were.

Hilda [*bends forward and looks over his shoulder while he writes*]. Mind now, kindly and cordially! Oh, how I hate—how I hate this Ruald!

Sol. [*writing*]. Have you never really cared for anyone, Hilda?

Hilda [*harshly*]. What do you say?

Sol. Have you never really cared for anyone?

Hilda. For anyone else, I suppose you mean?

SOL. [*looks up at her*]. For anyone else, yes. Have you never? In all these ten years? Never?

HILDA. Oh yes, now and then. When I was perfectly furious with you for not coming.

SOL. Then you did take an interest in other people too?

HILDA. A little bit—for a week or so. Good heavens, Mr Solness, you surely know how such things come about.

SOL. Hilda—what is it you have come for?

HILDA. Don't waste time talking. The poor old man might go and die in the meantime.

SOL. Answer me, Hilda. What do you want of me?

HILDA. I want my kingdom.

SOL. H'm—— [*He gives a rapid glance toward the door on the left and then goes on writing on the drawings. At the same moment* MRS SOLNESS *enters; she has some packages in her hand.*]

MRS S. Here are a few things I have got for you, Miss Wangel. The large parcels will be sent later on.

HILDA. Oh, how very, very kind of you!

MRS S. Only my simple duty. Nothing more than that.

SOL. [*reading over what he has written*]. Aline!

MRS S. Yes?

SOL. Did you notice whether the—the bookkeeper was out there?

MRS S. Yes, of course she was out there.

SOL. [*puts the drawings in the portfolio*]. H'm——

MRS S. She was standing at the desk, as she always is—when *I* go through the room.

SOL. [*rises*]. Then I'll give this to her and tell her that——

HILDA [*takes the portfolio from him*]. Oh no, let me have the pleasure of doing that! [*Goes to the door but turns.*] What is her name?

SOL. Her name is Miss Fosli.

HILDA. Pooh, that sounds too cold! Her Christian name, I mean?

SOL. Kaia—I believe.

HILDA [*opens the door and calls out*]. Kaia, come in here! Make haste! Mr Solness wants to speak to you.

[KAIA FOSLI *appears at the door.*]

KAIA [*looking at him in alarm*]. Here I am.

HILDA [*handing her the portfolio*]. See here, Kaia! You can take this home; Mr Solness has written on them now.

KAIA. Oh, at last!

SOL. Give them to the old man as soon as you can.

KAIA. I will go straight home with them.

SOL. Yes, do. Now Ragnar will have a chance of building for himself.

KAIA. Oh, may he come and thank you for all——

SOL. [*harshly*]. I won't have any thanks! Tell him that from me.

KAIA. Yes, I will.

SOL. And tell him at the same time that henceforward I do not require his services—nor yours either.

KAIA [*softly and quiveringly*]. Nor mine either?

SOL. You will have other things to think of now and to attend to, and that is a very good thing for you. Well, go home with the drawings now, Miss Fosli. At once! Do you hear?

KAIA [*as before*]. Yes, Mr Solness. [*She goes out.*]

MRS S. Heavens! what deceitful eyes she has.

SOL. She? That poor little creature?

MRS S. Oh—I can see what I can see, Halvard. Are you really dismissing them?

SOL. Yes.

MRS S. Her as well?

SOL. Was not that what you wished?

MRS S. But how can you get on without her? Oh well, no doubt you have someone else in reserve, Halvard.

HILDA [*playfully*]. Well, I for one am not the person to stand at that desk.

SOL. Never mind, never mind—it will be all right, Aline. Now all you have to do is to think about moving into our new home—as quickly as you can. This evening we will hang up the wreath—[*turns to* HILDA]—right on the very pinnacle of the tower. What do you say to that, Miss Hilda?

HILDA [*looks at him with sparkling eyes*]. It will be splendid to see you so high up once more.

SOL. Me!

MRS S. For heaven's sake, Miss Wangel, don't imagine such a thing! My husband!—when he always gets so dizzy!

HILDA. He gets dizzy! No, I know quite well he does not!

MRS S. Oh yes, indeed he does.

HILDA. But I have seen him with my own eyes right up at the top of a high church tower!

MRS S. Yes, I hear people talk of that; but it is utterly impossible.

SOL. [*vehemently*]. Impossible—impossible, yes! But there I stood all the same!

MRS S. Oh, how can you say so, Halvard? Why, you can't even bear to go out on the second-story balcony here. You have always been like that.

SOL. You may perhaps see something different this evening.

MRS S. [*in alarm*]. No, no, no! Please God I shall never see that. I will write at once to the doctor—and I am sure he won't let you do it.

SOL. Why, Aline!

MRS S. Oh, you know you're ill, Halvard. This proves it! Oh God—Oh God! [*She goes hastily out to the right.*]

HILDA [*looks intently at him*]. Is it so or is it not?

SOL. That I turn dizzy?

HILDA. That my master builder dare not—cannot—climb as high as he builds?

SOL. Is that the way you look at it?

HILDA. Yes.

SOL. I believe there is scarcely a corner of me that is safe from you.

HILDA [*looks toward the bow window*]. Up there, then. Right up there ——

SOL. [*approaches her*]. You might have the topmost room in the tower, Hilda—there you might live like a princess.

HILDA [*indefinably, between earnest and jest*]. Yes, that is what you promised me.

SOL. Did I really?

HILDA. Fie, Mr Solness! You said I should be a princess and that you would give me a kingdom. And then you went and—— Well!

SOL. [*cautiously*]. Are you quite certain that this is not a dream—a fancy that has fixed itself in your mind?

HILDA [*sharply*]. Do you mean that you did not do it?

SOL. I scarcely know myself. [*More softly.*] But now I know so much for certain that I——

HILDA. That you——? Say it at once!

SOL. —that I ought to have done it.

HILDA [*exclaims with animation*]. Don't tell me you can ever be dizzy!

SOL. This evening, then, we will hang up the wreath—Princess Hilda.

HILDA [*with a bitter curve of the lips*]. Over your new home, yes.

SOL. Over the house which will never be a home for me. [*He goes out through the garden door.*]

HILDA [*looks straight in front of her with a faraway expression and whispers to herself. The only words audible are*]—frightfully thrilling——

ACT III

SCENE—*The large broad veranda of* SOLNESS's *dwelling house. Part of the house, with outer door leading to the veranda, is seen to the left. A railing along the veranda to the right. At the back, from the end of the veranda, a flight of steps leads down to the garden below. Tall old trees in the garden spread their branches over the veranda and toward the house. Far to the right, in among the trees, a glimpse is caught of the lower part of the new villa, with scaffolding round so much as is seen of the tower. In the background the garden is bounded by an old wooden fence. Outside the fence a street with low tumble-down cottages.*

Evening sky with sunlit clouds.

On the veranda a garden bench stands along the wall of the house and in front of the bench a long table. On the other side of the table an armchair and some stools. All the furniture is of wickerwork.

MRS SOLNESS, *wrapped in a large white crape shawl, sits resting in the armchair and gazes over to the right. Shortly after,* HILDA WANGEL *comes up the flight of steps from the garden. She is dressed as in the previous act and wears her hat. She has in her bodice a little nosegay of small common flowers.*

MRS S. [*turning her head a little*]. Have you been round the garden, Miss Wangel?

HILDA. Yes, I have been taking a look at it.

MRS S. And found some flowers too, I see.

HILDA. Yes indeed! There are such heaps of them in among the bushes.

MRS S. Are there really? Still! You see, I scarcely ever go there.

HILDA [*closer*]. What! Don't you take a run down into the garden every day then?

MRS S. [*with a faint smile*]. I don't "run" anywhere nowadays.

HILDA. Well, but do you not go down now and then to look at all the lovely things there?

MRS S. It has all become so strange to me. I am almost afraid to see it again!

HILDA. Your own garden!

MRS S. I don't feel that it is mine any longer.

HILDA. What do you mean?

MRS S. No, no, it is not—not as it was in my mother's and father's time. They have taken away so much—so much of the garden, Miss Wangel. Fancy—they have parceled it out—and built houses for strangers—people that I don't know. And they can sit and look in upon me from their windows.

HILDA [*with a bright expression*]. Mrs Solness.

MRS S. Yes?

HILDA. May I stay here with you a little?

MRS S. Yes, by all means, if you care to.

[HILDA *moves a stool closer to the armchair and sits down.*]

HILDA. Ah—here one can sit and sun oneself like a cat.

MRS S. [*lays her hand softly on* HILDA'*s neck*]. It is nice of you to be willing to sit with me. I thought you wanted to go in to my husband.

HILDA. What should I want with him?

MRS S. To help him, I thought.

HILDA. No, thank you. And besides, he is not in. He is over there with the workmen. But he looked so fierce that I did not care to talk to him.

MRS S. He is so kind and gentle in reality.

HILDA. He?

MRS S. You do not really know him yet, Miss Wangel.

HILDA [*looks affectionately at her*]. Are you pleased at the thought of moving over to the new house?

MRS S. I ought to be pleased, for it is what Halvard wants.

HILDA. Oh, not just on that account, surely.

MRS S. Yes, yes, Miss Wangel; for it is only my duty to submit myself to him. But very often it is dreadfully difficult to force one's mind to obedience.

HILDA. Yes, that must be difficult indeed.

MRS S. I can tell you it is—when one has so many faults as I have.

HILDA. When one has gone through so much trouble as you have.

MRS S. How do you know about that?

HILDA. Your husband told me.

MRS S. To me he very seldom mentions these things. Yes, I can tell you I have gone through more than enough trouble in my life, Miss Wangel.

HILDA [*looks sympathetically at her and nods slowly*]. Poor Mrs Solness. First of all there was the fire——

MRS S. [*with a sigh*]. Yes, everything that was mine was burned.

HILDA. And then came what was worse.

MRS S. [*looking inquiringly at her*]. Worse?

HILDA. The worst of all.

MRS S. What do you mean?

HILDA [*softly*]. You lost the two little boys.

MRS S. Oh yes, the boys. But, you see, that was a thing apart. That was a dispensation of Providence, and in such things one can only bow in submission—yes, and be thankful too.

HILDA. Then you are so?

MRS S. Not always, I am sorry to say. I know well enough that it is my duty—but all the same I cannot.

HILDA. No, no, I think that is only natural.

MRS S. And often and often I have to remind myself that it was a righteous punishment for me.

HILDA. Why?

MRS S. Because I had not fortitude enough in misfortune.

HILDA. But I don't see that——

MRS S. Oh no, no, Miss Wangel—do not talk to me any more about the two little boys. We ought to feel nothing but joy in thinking of them, for they are so happy—so happy now. No, it is the small losses of life that cut one to the heart—the loss of all that other people look upon as almost nothing.

HILDA [*lays her arms on* MRS SOL-

NESS's *knees and looks up at her affectionately*]. Dear Mrs Solness—tell me what things you mean!

MRS S. As I say, only little things. All the old portraits were burned on the walls. And all the old silk dresses were burned, that had belonged to the family for generations and generations. And all Mother's and Grandmother's lace—that was burned too. And only think—the jewels too! [*Sadly.*] And then all the dolls.

HILDA. The dolls?

MRS S. [*choking with tears*]. I had nine lovely dolls.

HILDA. And they were burned too?

MRS S. All of them. Oh, it was hard —so hard for me.

HILDA. Had you put by all these dolls, then? Ever since you were little?

MRS S. I had not put them by. The dolls and I had gone on living together.

HILDA. After you were grown up?

MRS S. Yes, long after that.

HILDA. After you were married too?

MRS S. Oh, yes indeed. So long as he did not see it—— But they were all burned up, poor things. No one thought of saving them. Oh, it is so miserable to think of. You mustn't laugh at me, Miss Wangel.

HILDA. I am not laughing in the least.

MRS S. For you see, in a certain sense, there was life in them too. I carried them under my heart—like little unborn children.

[DR HERDAL, *with his hat in his hand, comes out through the door and observes* MRS SOLNESS *and* HILDA.]

DR H. Well, Mrs Solness, so you are sitting out here catching cold?

MRS S. I find it so pleasant and warm here today.

DR H. Yes, yes. But is there anything going on here? I got a note from you.

MRS S. [*rises*]. Yes, there is something I must talk to you about.

DR H. Very well; then perhaps we had better go in. [*To* HILDA.] Still in your mountaineering dress, Miss Wangel?

HILDA [*gaily, rising*]. Yes—in full uniform! But today I am not going climbing and breaking my neck. We two will stop quietly below and look on, Doctor.

DR H. What are we to look on at?

MRS S. [*softly, in alarm, to* HILDA]. Hush, hush—for God's sake! He is coming. Try to get that idea out of his head. And let us be friends, Miss Wangel. Don't you think we can?

HILDA [*throws her arms impetuously round* MRS SOLNESS's *neck*]. *Oh*, if we only could!

MRS S. [*gently disengages herself*]. There, there, there! There he comes, Doctor. Let me have a word with you.

DR H. Is it about him?

MRS S. Yes, to be sure it's about him. Do come in. [*She and the doctor enter the house. Next moment* SOLNESS *comes up from the garden by the flight of steps. A serious look comes over* HILDA's *face.*]

SOL. [*glances at the house door, which is closed cautiously from within*]. Have you noticed, Hilda, that as soon as I come she goes?

HILDA. I have noticed that as soon as you come you make her go.

SOL. Perhaps so. But I cannot help it. [*Looks observantly at her.*] Are you cold, Hilda? I think you look cold.

HILDA. I have just come out of a tomb.

SOL. What do you mean by that?

HILDA. That I have got chilled through and through, Mr Solness.

Sol. [*slowly*]. I believe I understand.

Hilda. What brings you up here just now?

Sol. I caught sight of you from over there.

Hilda. But then you must have seen her too.

Sol. I knew she would go at once if I came.

Hilda. Is it very painful for you that she should avoid you in this way?

Sol. In one sense it's a relief as well.

Hilda. Not to have her before your eyes?

Sol. Yes.

Hilda. Not to be always seeing how heavily the loss of the little boys weighs upon her?

Sol. Yes, chiefly that.

[Hilda *drifts across the veranda with her hands behind her back, stops at the railing and looks out over the garden.*]

Sol. [*after a short pause*]. Did you have a long talk with her?

[Hilda *stands motionless and does not answer.*]

Sol. Had you a long talk, I asked?

[Hilda *is silent as before.*]

Sol. What was she talking about, Hilda?

[Hilda *continues silent.*]

Sol. Poor Aline! I suppose it was about the little boys.

[*A nervous shudder runs through her, then she nods hurriedly once or twice.*]

Sol. She will never get over it—never in this world. [*Approaches her.*] Now you are standing there again like a statue, just as you stood last night.

Hilda [*turns and looks at him with great serious eyes*]. I am going away.

Sol. [*sharply*]. Going away!

Hilda. Yes.

Sol. But I won't allow you to!

Hilda. What am I to do here now?

Sol. Simply to be here, Hilda!

Hilda [*measures him with a look*]. Oh, thank you. You know it wouldn't end there.

Sol. [*heedlessly*]. So much the better!

Hilda [*vehemently*]. I cannot do any harm to one whom I know! I can't take away anything that belongs to her.

Sol. Who wants you to do that?

Hilda [*continuing*]. A stranger, yes! For that is quite a different thing. A person I have never set eyes on. But one that I have come into close contact with—— Oh no! Oh no! Ugh!

Sol. Yes, but I never proposed you should.

Hilda. Oh, Mr Solness, you know quite well what the end of it would be. And that is why I am going away.

Sol. And what is to become of me when you are gone? What shall I have to live for then—after that?

Hilda [*with the indefinable look in her eyes*]. It is surely not so hard for you. You have your duties to her. Live for those duties.

Sol. Too late. These powers—these—these——

Hilda. Devils?

Sol. Yes, these devils—and the troll within me as well—they have drawn all the lifeblood out of her. [*Laughs in desperation.*] They did it for my happiness! Yes, yes! [*Sadly.*] And now she is dead—for my sake. And I am chained alive to a dead woman. [*In wild anguish.*] I—I who cannot live without joy in life!

[Hilda *moves round the table and seats herself on the bench with her elbows on the table and her head supported by her hands.*]

HILDA [*sits and looks at him awhile*]. What will you build next?

SOL. [*shakes his head*]. I don't believe I shall build much more.

HILDA. Not those cosy, happy homes for mother and father and for the troop of children?

SOL. I wonder whether there will be any use of such homes in the coming time.

HILDA. Poor Mr Solness! And you have gone all these ten years–and staked your whole life–on that alone.

SOL. Yes, you may well say so, Hilda.

HILDA [*with an outburst*]. Oh! it all seems to me so foolish–so foolish!

SOL. All what?

HILDA. Not to be able to grasp at your own happiness–at your own life! Merely because someone you know happens to stand in the way!

SOL. One whom you have no right to set aside.

HILDA. I wonder whether one really has not the right! And yet, and yet–– Oh, if one could only sleep the whole thing away! [*She lays her arms flat on the table, rests the left side of her head on her hands and shuts her eyes.*]

SOL. [*turns the armchair and sits down at the table*]. Had you a cosy, happy home–up there with your father, Hilda?

HILDA [*without stirring, answers as if half asleep*]. I had only a cage.

SOL. And you are determined not to go back to it?

HILDA [*as before*]. The wild bird never wants to go into the cage.

SOL. Rather range through the free air––

HILDA [*still as before*]. The bird of prey loves to range.

SOL. [*lets his eyes rest on her*]. If only one had the viking spirit in life––

HILDA [*in her usual voice, opens her eyes but does not move*]. And the other thing? Say what that was!

SOL. A robust conscience.

[HILDA *sits erect on the bench, with animation. Her eyes have once more the sparkling expression of gladness.*]

HILDA [*nods to him*]. I know what you are going to build next!

SOL. Then you know more than I do, Hilda.

HILDA. Yes, builders are such stupid people.

SOL. What is it to be, then?

HILDA [*nods again*]. The castle.

SOL. What castle?

HILDA. My castle, of course.

SOL. Do you want a castle now?

HILDA. Don't you owe me a kingdom, I should like to know?

SOL. You say I do.

HILDA. Well–you admit you owe me this kingdom. And you can't have a kingdom without a royal castle, I should think!

SOL. [*more and more animated*]. Yes, they usually go together.

HILDA. Good! Then build it for me! This moment!

SOL. [*laughing*]. Must you have that on the instant too?

HILDA. Yes, to be sure! For the ten years are up now, and I am not going to wait any longer. So–out with the castle, Mr Solness!

SOL. It's no light matter to owe you anything, Hilda.

HILDA. You should have thought of that before. It is too late now. So–[*tapping the table*]–the castle on the table! It is my castle! I will have it at once!

SOL. [*more seriously, leans over toward her, with his arms on the table*]. What sort of castle have you imagined, Hilda?

[*Her expression becomes more and more veiled. She seems gazing inward at herself.*]

HILDA [*slowly*]. My castle shall stand on a height—on a very great height—with a clear outlook on all sides, so that I can see far—far around.

SOL. And no doubt it is to have a high tower!

HILDA. A tremendously high tower. And at the very top of the tower there shall be a balcony. And I will stand out upon it——

SOL. [*involuntarily clutches at his forehead*]. How can you like to stand at such a dizzy height?

HILDA. Yes, I will; right up there will I stand and look down on the other people—on those that are building churches and homes for mother and father and the troop of children. And you may come up and look on at it too.

SOL. [*in a low tone*]. Is the builder to be allowed to come up beside the princess?

HILDA. If the builder will.

SOL. [*more softly*]. Then I think the builder will come.

HILDA. [*nods*]. The builder—he will come.

SOL. But he will never be able to build any more. Poor builder!

HILDA [*animated*]. Oh yes, he will! We two will set to work together. And then we will build the loveliest—the very loveliest—thing in all the world.

SOL. [*intently*]. Hilda—tell me what that is!

HILDA [*looks smilingly at him, shakes her head a little, pouts and speaks as if to a child*]. Builders—they are such very, very stupid people.

SOL. Yes, no doubt they are stupid. But now tell me what it is—the loveliest thing in the world—that we two are to build together?

HILDA [*is silent a little while, then says with an indefinable expression in her eyes*]. Castles in the air.

SOL. Castles in the air?

HILDA [*nods*]. Castles in the air, yes! Do you know what sort of thing a castle in the air is?

SOL. It is the loveliest thing in the world, you say.

HILDA [*rises with vehemence and makes a gesture of repulsion with her hand*]. Yes, to be sure it is! Castles in the air—they are so easy to take refuge in. And so easy to build too—[*looks scornfully at him*]—especially for the builders who have a—a dizzy conscience.

SOL. [*rises*]. After this day we two will build together, Hilda.

HILDA [*with a half-dubious smile*]. A real castle in the air?

SOL. Yes, one with a firm foundation under it.

[RAGNAR BROVIK *comes out from the house. He is carrying a large green wreath with flowers and silk ribbons.*]

HILDA [*with an outburst of pleasure*]. The wreath! Oh, that will be glorious!

SOL. [*in surprise*]. Have you brought the wreath, Ragnar?

RAG. I promised the foreman I would.

SOL. [*relieved*]. Ah, then I suppose your father is better?

RAG. No.

SOL. Was he not cheered by what I wrote?

RAG. It came too late.

SOL. Too late!

RAG. When she came with it he was unconscious. He had had a stroke.

SOL. Why, then, you must go home to him! You must attend to your father!

RAG. He does not need me any more.

SOL. But surely you ought to be with him.

RAG. She is sitting by his bed.

SOL. [*rather uncertainly*]. Kaia?

RAG. [*looking rather darkly at him*]. Yes–Kaia.

SOL. Go home, Ragnar–both to him and to her. Give me the wreath.

RAG. [*suppressing a mocking smile*]. You don't mean that you yourself——

SOL. I will take it down to them myself. [*Takes the wreath from him.*] And now you go home; we don't require you today.

RAG. I know you do not require me any more, but today I shall remain.

SOL. Well, remain then, since you are bent upon it.

HILDA [*at the railing*]. Mr Solness, I will stand here and look on at you.

SOL. At me!

HILDA. It will be fearfully thrilling.

SOL. [*in a low tone*]. We will talk about that presently, Hilda. [*He goes down the flight of steps with the wreath and away through the garden.*]

HILDA [*looks after him, then turns to* RAGNAR]. I think you might at least have thanked him.

RAG. Thanked him? Ought I to have thanked him?

HILDA. Yes, of course you ought!

RAG. I think it is rather you I ought to thank.

HILDA. How can you say such a thing?

RAG. [*without answering her*]. But I advise you to take care, Miss Wangel! For you don't know him rightly yet.

HILDA [*ardently*]. Oh, no one knows him as I do!

RAG. [*laughs in exasperation*]. Thank him, when he has held me down year after year! When he made Father disbelieve in me–made me disbelieve in myself! And all merely that he might——

HILDA [*as if divining something*]. That he might——? Tell me at once!

RAG. That he might keep her with him.

HILDA [*with a start toward him*]. The girl at the desk?

RAG. Yes.

HILDA [*clenching her hands*]. That is not true! You are telling falsehoods about him!

RAG. I would not believe it either until today–when she said so herself.

HILDA [*as if beside herself*]. What did she say? I will know! At once! At once!

RAG. She said that he had taken possession of her mind–her whole mind –centered all her thoughts upon himself alone. She says that she can never leave him–that she will remain here, where he is——

HILDA [*with flashing eyes*]. She will not be allowed to!

RAG. [*as if feeling his way*]. Who will not allow her?

HILDA [*rapidly*]. He will not either!

RAG. Oh no–I understand the whole thing now. After this she would merely be–in the way.

HILDA. You understand nothing–since you can talk like that. No, *I* will tell you why he kept hold of her.

RAG. Well, then, why?

HILDA. In order to keep hold of you.

RAG. Has he told you so?

HILDA. No, but it is so. It must be

so! [*Wildly.*] I will—I will have it so!

RAG. And at the very moment when you came—he let her go.

HILDA. It was you—you that he let go. What do you suppose he cares about strange women like her?

RAG. [*reflects*]. Is it possible that all this time he has been afraid of me?

HILDA. He afraid! I would not be so conceited if I were you.

RAG. Oh, he must have seen long ago that I had something in me too. Besides—cowardly—that is just what he is, you see.

HILDA. He! Oh yes, I am likely to believe that!

RAG. In a certain sense he is cowardly—he, the great master builder. He is not afraid of robbing others of their life's happiness—as he has done both for my father and for me. But when it comes to climbing up a paltry bit of scaffolding—he will do anything rather than that.

HILDA. Oh, you should just have seen him—high, high up—at the dizzy height where I once saw him.

RAG. Did you see that?

HILDA. Yes, indeed I did. How free and great he looked as he stood and fastened the wreath to the church vane!

RAG. I know that he ventured that once in his life—one solitary time. It is a legend among us younger men. But no power on earth would induce him to do it again.

HILDA. Today he will do it again!

RAG. [*scornfully*]. Yes, I daresay!

HILDA. We shall see it!

RAG. That neither you nor I will see.

HILDA [*with uncontrollable vehemence*]. I will see it! I will and must see it!

RAG. But he will not do it. He simply dare not do it For, you see, he cannot get over this infirmity—master builder though he be.

[MRS SOLNESS *comes from the house onto the veranda.*]

MRS S. [*looks around*]. Is he not here? Where has he gone to?

RAG. Mr Solness is down with the men.

HILDA. He took the wreath with him.

MRS S. [*terrified*]. Took the wreath with him! Oh God! Oh God! Brovik—you must go down to him! Get him to come back here!

RAG. Shall I say you want to speak to him, Mrs Solness?

MRS S. Oh yes, do! No, no—don't say that *I* want anything! You can say that somebody is here and he must come at once.

RAG. Good. I will do so, Mrs Solness. [*He goes down the flight of steps and away through the garden.*]

MRS S. Oh, Miss Wangel, you can't think how anxious I feel about him.

HILDA. Is there anything in this to be so terribly frightened about?

MRS S. Oh yes; surely you can understand. Just think, if he were really to do it! If he should take it into his head to climb up the scaffolding!

HILDA [*eagerly*]. Do you think he will?

MRS S. Oh, one can never tell what he might take into his head. I am afraid there is nothing he mightn't think of doing.

HILDA. Aha! Perhaps you too think he is—well——

MRS S. Oh, I don't know what to think about him now. The doctor has been telling me all sorts of things, and putting it all together with several things I have heard him say——

[DR HERDAL *looks out at the door.*]

Dr H. Is he not coming soon?

Mrs S. Yes, I think so. I have sent for him at any rate.

Dr H. [*advancing*]. I am afraid you will have to go in, my dear lady.

Mrs S. Oh no! Oh no! I shall stay out here and wait for Halvard.

Dr H. But some ladies have just come to call on you.

Mrs S. Good heavens, that too! And just at this moment!

Dr H. They say they positively must see the ceremony.

Mrs S. Well, well, I suppose I must go to them after all. It is my duty.

Hilda. Can't you ask the ladies to go away?

Mrs S. No, that would never do. Now they are here it is my duty to see them. But do you stay out here in the meantime—and receive him when he comes.

Dr H. And try to occupy his attention as long as possible.

Mrs S. Yes, do, dear Miss Wangel. Keep a firm hold of him as ever you can.

Hilda. Would it not be best for you to do that?

Mrs S. Yes, God knows that is my duty. But when one has duties in so many directions——

Dr H. [*looks toward the garden*]. There he is coming.

Mrs S. And I have to go in!

Dr H. [*to* Hilda]. Don't say anything about my being here.

Hilda. Oh no! I daresay I shall find something else to talk to Mr Solness about.

Mrs S. And be sure you keep firm hold of him. I believe you can do it best.

[Mrs Solness *and* Dr Herdal *go into the house.* Hilda *remains standing on the veranda.* Solness *comes from the garden up the flight of steps.*]

Sol. Somebody wants me, I hear.

Hilda. Yes; it is I, Mr Solness.

Sol. Oh, is it you, Hilda? I was afraid it might be Aline or the doctor.

Hilda. You are very easily frightened, it seems!

Sol. Do you think so?

Hilda. Yes; people say that you are afraid to climb about—on the scaffoldings, you know.

Sol. Well, that is quite a special thing.

Hilda. Then it is true that you are afraid to do it?

Sol. Yes, I am.

Hilda. Afraid of falling down and killing yourself?

Sol. No, not of that.

Hilda. Of what, then?

Sol. I am afraid of retribution, Hilda.

Hilda. Of retribution? [*Shakes her head.*] I don't understand that.

Sol. Sit down and I will tell you something.

Hilda. Yes, do! At once! [*She sits on a stool by the railing and looks expectantly at him.*]

Sol. [*throws his hat on the table*]. You know that I began by building churches?

Hilda. [*nods*]. I know that well.

Sol. For, you see, I came as a boy from a pious home in the country; and so it seemed to me that this church building was the noblest task I could set myself.

Hilda. Yes, yes.

Sol. And I venture to say that I built those poor little churches with such honest and warm and heartfelt devotion that—that——

Hilda. That——? Well?

Sol. Well, that I think that He

ought to have been pleased with me.

HILDA. He? What he?

SOL. He who was to have the churches, of course! He to whose honor and glory they were dedicated.

HILDA. Oh, indeed! But you are certain, then, that—that He was not—pleased with you?

SOL. [*scornfully*]. He pleased with me! How can you talk so, Hilda? He who gave the troll in me leave to lord it just as it pleased. He who bade them be at hand to serve me, both day and night—all these—all these——

HILDA. Devils.

SOL. Yes, of both kinds. Oh no, He made me feel clearly that He was not pleased with me. [*Mysteriously.*] You see, that was really the reason why He made the old house burn down.

HILDA. Was that why?

SOL. Yes, don't you understand? He wanted to give me the chance of becoming an accomplished master in my own sphere—so that I might build all the more glorious churches for Him. At first I did not understand what He was driving at, but all of a sudden it flashed upon me.

HILDA. When was that?

SOL. It was when I was building the church tower up at Lysanger.

HILDA. I thought so.

SOL. For you see, Hilda—up there, amidst those new surroundings, I used to go about musing and pondering within myself. Then I saw plainly why He had taken my little children from me. It was that I should have nothing else to attach myself to. No such thing as love and happiness, you understand. I was to be only a master builder—nothing else. And all my life long I was to go on building for Him. [*Laughs.*] But I can tell you nothing came of that!

HILDA. What did you do then?

SOL. First of all I searched and tried my own heart——

HILDA. And then?

SOL. Then I did the impossible—I no less than He.

HILDA. The impossible?

SOL. I had never before been able to climb up to a great, free height. But that day I did it.

HILDA [*leaping up*]. Yes, yes, you did!

SOL. And when I stood there, high over everything, and was hanging the wreath over the vane, I said to Him: Hear me now, Thou Mighty One! From this day forward I will be a free builder—I, too, in my sphere—just as Thou in Thine. I will nevermore build churches for Thee—only homes for human beings.

HILDA [*with great sparkling eyes*]. That was the song that I heard through the air!

SOL. But afterward His turn came.

HILDA. What do you mean by that?

SOL. [*looks despondently at her*]. Building homes for human beings—is not worth a rap, Hilda.

HILDA. Do you say that now?

SOL. Yes, for now I see it. Men have no use for these homes of theirs—to be happy in. And I should not have had any use for such a home if I had had one. [*With a quiet, bitter laugh.*] See, that is the upshot of the whole affair, however far back I look. Nothing really built, nor anything sacrificed for the chance of building. Nothing, nothing! The whole is nothing!

HILDA. Then you will never build anything more?

SOL. [*with animation*]. On the contrary, I am just going to begin!

HILDA. What, then? What will you

build? Tell me at once!

SOL. I believe there is only one possible dwelling place for human happiness—and that is what I am going to build now.

HILDA [*looks fixedly at him*]. Mr Solness—you mean our castle?

SOL. The castles in the air—yes.

HILDA. I am afraid you would turn dizzy before we got halfway up.

SOL. Not if I can mount hand in hand with you, Hilda.

HILDA [*with an expression of suppressed resentment*]. Only with me? Will there be no others of the party?

SOL. Who else should there be?

HILDA. Oh—that girl—that Kaia at the desk. Poor thing—don't you want to take her with you too?

SOL. Oho! Was it about her that Aline was talking to you?

HILDA. Is it so—or is it not?

SOL. [*vehemently*]. I will not answer such a question. You must believe in me wholly and entirely!

HILDA. All these ten years I have believed in you so utterly—so utterly.

SOL. You must go on believing in me!

HILDA. Then let me see you stand free and high up!

SOL. [*sadly*]. Oh! Hilda—it is not every day that I can do that.

HILDA [*passionately*]. I will have you do it! I will have it! [*Imploringly.*] Just once more, Mr Solness! Do the impossible once again!

SOL. [*stands and looks deep into her eyes*]. If I try it, Hilda, I will stand up there and talk to Him as I did that time before.

HILDA [*in rising excitement*]. What will you say to Him?

SOL. I will say to Him: Hear me, Mighty Lord—Thou may'st judge me as seems best to Thee. But hereafter I will build nothing but the loveliest thing in the world——

HILDA [*carried away*]. Yes—yes—yes!

SOL. —build it together with a princess whom I love.

HILDA. Yes, tell Him that! Tell Him that!

SOL. Yes. And then I will say to Him: Now I shall go down and throw my arms round her and kiss her——

HILDA. —many times! Say that!

SOL. —many, many times, I will say.

HILDA. And then?

SOL. Then I will wave my hat—and come down to the earth—and do as I said to Him.

HILDA [*with outstretched arms*]. Now I see you again as I did when there was song in the air.

SOL. [*looks at her with his head bowed*]. How have you become what you are, Hilda?

HILDA. How have you made me what I am?

SOL. [*shortly and firmly*]. The princess shall have her castle.

HILDA [*jubilant, clapping her hands*]. Oh, Mr Solness! My lovely, lovely castle. Our castle in the air!

SOL. On a firm foundation.

[*In the street a crowd of people has assembled, vaguely seen through the trees. Music of wind instruments is heard far away behind the new house.*]

[MRS SOLNESS, *with a fur collar round her neck,* DR HERDAL *with her white shawl on his arm, and some ladies, come out on the veranda.* RAGNAR BROVIK *comes at the same time up from the garden.*]

MR S. [*to* RAGNAR]. Are we to have music too?

RAG. Yes. It's the band of the Mason's Union. [*To* SOLNESS.] The foreman asked me to tell you that he is ready now to go up with the wreath.

SOL. [*takes his hat*]. Good. I will go down to him myself.

MRS S. [*anxiously*]. What have you to do down there, Halvard?

SOL. [*curtly*]. I must be down below with the men.

MRS S. Yes, down below—only down below.

SOL. That is where I always stand—on everyday occasions. [*He goes down the flight of steps and away through the garden.*]

MRS S. [*calls after him over the railing*]. But do beg the man to be careful when he goes up. Promise me that, Halvard.

DR H. [*to* MRS SOLNESS]. Don't you see that I was right? He has given up all thought of that folly.

MRS S. Oh, what a relief! Twice workmen have fallen, and each time they were killed on the spot. [*Turns to* HILDA.] Thank you, Miss Wangel, for having kept such a firm hold upon him. I should never have been able to manage him.

DR H. [*playfully*]. Yes, yes, Miss Wangel, you know how to keep firm hold on a man when you give your mind to it.

[MRS SOLNESS *and* DR. HERDAL *go up to the ladies, who are standing nearer to the steps and looking over the garden.* HILDA *remains standing beside the railing in the foreground.* RAGNAR *goes up to her.*]

RAG. [*with suppressed laughter, half whispering*]. Miss Wangel—do you see all those young fellows down in the street?

HILDA. Yes.

RAG. They are my fellow students, come to look at the master.

HILDA. What do they want to look at him for?

RAG. They want to see how he daren't climb to the top of his own house.

HILDA. Oh, that is what those boys want, is it?

RAG. [*spitefully and scornfully*]. He has kept us down so long—now we are going to see him keep quietly down below himself.

HILDA. You will not see that—not this time.

RAG. [*smiles*]. Indeed! Then where shall we see him?

HILDA. High—high up by the vane! That is where you will see him!

RAG. [*laughs*]. Him! Oh yes, I daresay!

HILDA. His will is to reach the top—so at the top you shall see him.

RAG. His will, yes; that I can easily believe. But he simply cannot do it. His head would swim round long, long before he got halfway. He would have to crawl down again on his hands and knees.

DR H. [*points across*]. Look! There goes the foreman up the ladders.

MRS S. And of course he has the wreath to carry too. Oh, I do hope he will be careful!

RAG. [*stares incredulously and shouts*]. Why, but it's——

HILDA [*breaking out in jubilation*]. It is the master builder himself!

MRS S. [*screams with terror*]. Yes, it is Halvard! Oh, my great God! Halvard! Halvard!

DR H. Hush! Don't shout to him!

MRS S. [*half beside herself*]. I must go to him! I must get him to come down again!

DR H. [*holds her*]. Don't move, any of you! Not a sound!

HILDA [*immovable, follows* SOLNESS *with her eyes*]. He climbs and climbs. Higher and higher! Higher and higher! Look! Just look!

RAG. [*breathless*]. He must turn now. He can't possibly help it.

HILDA. He climbs and climbs. He will soon be at the top now.

MRS S. Oh, I shall die of terror. I cannot bear to see it.

DR H. Then don't look up at him.

HILDA. There he is, standing on the topmost planks. Right at the top!

DR H. Nobody must move! Do you hear?

HILDA [*exulting with quiet intensity*]. At last! At last! Now I see him great and free again!

RAG. [*almost voiceless*]. But this is im——

HILDA. So I have seen him all through these ten years. How secure he stands! Frightfully thrilling all the same. Look at him! Now he is hanging the wreath round the vane.

RAG. I feel as if I were looking at something utterly impossible.

HILDA. Yes, it is the impossible that he is doing now! [*With the indefinable expression in her eyes.*] Can you see anyone else up there with him?

RAG. There is no one else.

HILDA. Yes, there is one he is striving with.

RAG. You are mistaken.

HILDA. Then do you hear no song in the air either?

RAG. It must be the wind in the treetops.

HILDA. I hear a song—a mighty song! [*Shouts in wild jubilation and glee.*] Look, look! Now he is waving his hat! He is waving it to us down here! Oh, wave, wave back to him. For now it is finished! [*Snatches the white shawl from the doctor, waves it and shouts up to* SOLNESS.] Hurrah for Master Builder Solness!

DR H. Stop! Stop! For God's sake!

[*The ladies on the veranda wave their pocket handkerchiefs, and the shouts of "Hurrah" are taken up in the street below. Then they are suddenly silenced, and the crowd bursts out into a shriek of horror. A human body, with planks and fragments of wood, is vaguely perceived crashing down behind the trees.*]

MRS S. AND THE LADIES [*at the same time*]. He is falling! He is falling!

[MRS SOLNESS *totters, falls backward, swooning, and is caught, amid cries and confusion, by the ladies. The crowd in the street breaks down the fence and storms into the garden. At the same time* DR HERDAL, *too, rushes down thither. A short pause.*]

HILDA [*stares fixedly upward and says, as if petrified*]. My master builder.

RAG. [*supports himself, trembling, against the railing*]. He must be dashed to pieces—killed on the spot.

ONE OF THE LADIES [*whilst* MRS SOLNESS *is carried into the house*]. Run down for the doctor!

RAG. I can't stir a foot.

ANOTHER LADY. Then call to someone!

RAG. [*tries to call out*]. How is it? Is he alive?

A VOICE [*below in the garden*]. Mr Solness is dead!

OTHER VOICES [*nearer*]. The head is all crushed. He fell right into the quarry.

HILDA [*turns to* RAGNAR *and says quietly*]. I can't see him up there now.

RAG. This is terrible. So, after all, he could not do it.

HILDA [*as if in quiet spellbound triumph*]. But he mounted right to the top. And I heard harps in the air. [*Waves her shawl in the air and shrieks with wild intensity.*] My—my master builder!

PEER GYNT

PERSONS OF THE PLAY

ASE, *a peasant's widow.*
PEER GYNT, *her son.*
TWO OLD WOMEN.
ASLAK, *a smith.*
WEDDING GUESTS.
A MAN AND WIFE, *newcomers.*
SOLVEIG AND LITTLE HELGA, *their daughters.*
THE FARMER AT HEGSTAD.
INGRID, *his daughter.*
THE BRIDEGROOM AND HIS PARENTS.
THREE SAETER GIRLS.
THE OLD MAN OF THE DOVRE.
THE TROLLS.
KARI, *a cotter's wife.*
MASTER COTTON, MONSIEUR BALLON, HERREN VON EBERKOPF AND TRUMPETERSTRALE, *gentlemen.*
ANITRA, *daughter of a Bedouin chief.*
ARABS, FEMALE SLAVES, DANCING GIRLS.
PROFESSOR BEGRIFFENFELDT, *Dr Phil., director of the madhouse at Cairo.*
HUHU, *a language reformer.*
HUSSEIN, *an eastern minister.*
SEVERAL MADMEN, *with their* KEEPERS.
A NORWEGIAN SKIPPER AND HIS CREW.

The action takes place in Gudbrandsdale, in a Cairo madhouse and other localities.

ACT I

SCENE—*A wooded hillside near* ASE'S *farm. A river rushes down the slope. On the further side of it an old mill shed. It is a hot day in summer.*

PEER GYNT, *a strongly built youth of twenty, comes down the pathway. His mother,* ASE, *a small, slightly built woman, follows him, scolding angrily.*

ASE. Peer, you're lying!

PEER [*without stopping*]. No, I am not!

ASE. Well, then, swear that it is true!

PEER. Swear? Why should I?

ASE. See, you dare not! It's a lie from first to last.

PEER [*stopping*]. It is true—each blessed word!

ASE [*confronting him*]. Don't you blush before your mother? First you skulk among the mountains monthlong in the busiest season, stalking reindeer in the snows; home you come then, torn and tattered, gun amissing, likewise game; and at last, with open eyes, think to get me to believe all the wildest hunters' lies! Well, where did you find the buck, then?

PEER. West near Gendin.

ASE [*laughing scornfully*]. Ah! Indeed!

PEER. Keen the blast toward me swept; hidden by an alder clump, he was scraping in the snow crust after lichen——

ASE [*as before*]. Doubtless, yes!

PEER. Breathlessly I stood and listened, heard the crunching of his hoof, saw the branches of one antler. Softly then among the boulders I crept forward on my belly. Crouched in the moraine, I peered up; such a buck, so sleek and fat, you, I'm sure, have ne'er set eyes on.

ASE. No, of course not!

PEER. Bang, I fired! Clean he dropped upon the hillside. But the instant that he fell I sat firm astride his back, gripped him by the left ear tightly and had almost sunk my knife blade in his neck, behind his skull—when, behold! the brute screamed wildly, sprang upon his feet like lightning, with a backcast of his head from my fist made knife and sheath fly, pinned me tightly by the thigh, jammed his horns against my legs, clenched me like a pair of tongs; then forthwith away he flew right along the Gendin Edge!

ASE [*involuntarily*]. Jesus save us!

PEER. Have you ever chanced to see the Gendin Edge? Nigh on four miles long, it stretches sharp before you like a scythe. Down o'er glaciers, landslips, scaurs, down the toppling gray moraines, you can see, both right and left, straight into the tarns that slumber, black and sluggish, more than seven hundred fathoms deep below you. Right along the Edge we two clove our passage through the air. Never rode I such a colt! Straight before us as we rushed 'twas as though there glittered suns. Brown-backed eagles that were sailing in the wide and dizzy void halfway 'twixt us and the tarns dropped behind, like motes in air. Ice floes on the shore broke crashing, but no murmur reached my ears. Only sprites of dizziness sprang, dancing, round; they sang, they swung, circlewise, past sight and hearing!

ASE [*dizzy*]. Oh, God save me!

PEER. All at once, at a desperate, breakneck spot, rose a great cock ptarmigan, flapping, cackling, terrified, from the crack where he lay hidden at the buck's feet on the Edge. Then the buck shied half around, leaped sky-high, and down we plunged both of us into the depths! [ASE *totters and catches at the trunk of a tree.* PEER GYNT *continues.*] Mountain walls behind us, black, and below a void unfathomed! First we clove through banks of mist, then we clove a flock of sea gulls, so that they, in mid-air startled, flew in all directions, screaming. Downward rushed we, ever downward. But beneath us something shimmered, whitish, like a reindeer's belly. Mother, 'twas our own reflection in the glass-smooth mountain tarn, shooting up toward the surface with the same wild rush of speed wherewith we were shooting downward.

ASE [*gasping for breath*]. Peer! God help me! Quickly, tell——

PEER. Buck from over, buck from under, in a moment clashed together, scattering foam flecks all around. There we lay then, floating, plashing. But at last we made our way somehow to the northern shore; buck, he swam, I clung behind him; I ran homeward——

ASE. But the buck, dear?

PEER. He's still there, for aught I know. [*Snaps his fingers, turns on his heel and adds.*] Catch him, and you're welcome to him!

ASE. And your neck you haven't broken? Haven't broken both your thighs? And your backbone, too, is whole? Oh, dear Lord—what thanks, what praise, should be thine who helped my boy! There's a rent, though, in your breeches; but it's scarce worth talking of when one thinks what dreadful things might have come of such a leap—— [*Stops suddenly, looks at him open-mouthed and wide-eyed, cannot find words for some time but at last bursts out.*] Oh, you devil's storyteller, cross of Christ, how you can lie! All this screed you foist upon me, I remember now, I knew it when I was a girl of twenty. Gudbrand Glesne it befell, never you, you——

PEER. Me as well. Such a thing can happen twice.

ASE [*exasperated*]. Yes, a lie, turned topsy-turvy, can be prinked and tinseled out, decked in plumage new and fine, till none knows its lean old carcass. That is just what you've been doing, vamping up things, wild and grand, garnishing with eagles' backs and with all the other horrors, lying right and lying left, filling me with speechless dread, till at last I recognized not what of old I'd heard and known!

PEER. If another talked like that, I'd half kill him for his pains.

ASE [*weeping*]. Oh, would God I lay a corpse; would the black earth held me sleeping! Prayers and tears don't bite upon him. Peer, you're lost and ever will be!

PEER. Darling, pretty little mother, you are right in every word; don't be cross, be happy——

ASE. Silence! Could I, if I would, be happy with a pig like you for son? Think how bitter I must find it, I, a poor defenseless widow, ever to be put to shame! [*Weeping again.*] How much have we now remaining from your grandsire's days of glory? Where are now the sacks of coin left behind by Rasmus Gynt? Ah, your father lent them wings—lavished them abroad like sand, buying land in every parish, driving round in gilded chariots. Where is all the wealth he wasted at the famous winter banquet, when each guest sent glass and bottle shivering 'gainst the wall behind him?

PEER. Where's the snow of yesteryear?

ASE. Silence, boy, before your mother! See the farmhouse! Every second windowpane is stopped with clouts. Hedges, fences, all are down, beasts exposed to wind and weather, fields and meadows lying fallow, every month a new distraint——

PEER. Come now, stop this old wife's talk! Many a time has luck seemed drooping and sprung up as high as ever!

ASE. Salt-strewn is the soil it grew from. Lord, but you're a rare one, you—just as pert and jaunty still, just as bold as when the pastor, newly come from Copenhagen, bade you tell your Christian name and declared that such a headpiece many a prince down there might envy; till the cob your father gave him, with a sledge to boot, in thanks for his pleasant, friendly talk—— Ah, but things went bravely then! Provost, captain, all the rest, dropped in daily, ate and drank, swilling till they well-nigh burst. But 'tis need that tests one's neighbor. Still it grew and empty here from the day that "Gold-bag Jon" started with his pack, a peddler. [*Dries her eyes with her apron.*] Ah, you're big and strong enough; you should be a staff and pillar for your mother's frail old age—you should keep the farm work going, guard the remnants of your gear—— [*Crying again.*] Oh, God help me, small's the profit you have been to me, you scamp! Lounging by the hearth at home, grubbing in the charcoal embers; or, round all the country, frightening girls away from merrymakings—shaming me in all directions, fighting with the worst rapscallions——

PEER [*turning away from her*]. Let me be.

ASE [*following him*]. Can you deny that you were the foremost brawler in the mighty battle royal fought the other day at Lunde, when you raged like mongrels mad? Who was it but you that broke Blacksmith Aslak's arm for him—or at any rate that wrenched one of his fingers out of joint?

PEER. Who has filled you with such prate?

ASE [*hotly*]. Cotter Kari heard the yells!

PEER [*rubbing his elbow*]. Maybe, but 'twas I that howled.

ASE. You?

PEER. Yes, Mother—*I* got beaten.

ASE. What d'you say?

PEER. He's limber, *he* is.

ASE. Who?

PEER. Why, Aslak, to be sure.

ASE. Shame—and shame; I spit upon you! Such a worthless sot as that, such a brawler, such a sodden dram-sponge to have beaten you! [*Weeping again.*] Many a shame and slight I've suffered, but that this should come to pass is the worst disgrace of all. What if he be ne'er so limber, need you therefore be a weakling?

PEER. Though I hammer or am hammered, still we must have lamentations. [*Laughing.*] Cheer up, Mother.

ASE. What? You're lying now again?

PEER. Yes, just this once. Come now, wipe your tears away. [*Clenching his left hand.*] See—with this same pair of tongs thus I held the smith bent double, while my sledge hammer right fist——

ASE. Oh, you brawler! You will bring me with your doings to the grave!

PEER. No, you're worth a better fate; better twenty thousand times! Little, ugly, dear old mother, you may safely trust my word—all the parish shall exalt you; only wait till I have done something—something really grand!

ASE [*contemptuously*]. You!

PEER. Who knows what may befall one!

ASE. Would you'd get so far in sense one day as to do the darning of your breeches for yourself!

PEER [*hotly*]. I will be a king, a kaiser!

ASE. Oh, God comfort me, he's losing all the wits that he had left!

PEER. Yes, I will! Just give me time!

ASE. Give you time, you'll be a prince, so the saying goes, I think!

PEER. You shall see!

ASE. Oh, hold your tongue! You're as mad as mad can be. Ah, and yet it's true enough—*something* might have come of you had you not been steeped forever in your lies and trash and moonshine. Hegstad's girl was fond of you. Easily you could have won her had you wooed her with a will.

PEER. Could I?

ASE. The old man's too feeble not to give his child her way. He is stiff-necked in a fashion; but at last 'tis Ingrid rules, and where *she* leads, step by step, stumps the gaffer, grumbling, after. [*Begins to cry again.*] Ah, my Peer!—a golden girl—land entailed on her! Just think, had you set your mind upon it, you'd be now a bridegroom brave—you that stand here grimed and tattered!

PEER [*briskly*]. Come, we'll go a-wooing then!

ASE. Where?

PEER. At Hegstad!

ASE. Ah, poor boy; Hegstad way is barred to wooers!

PEER. How is that?

ASE. Ah, I must sigh! Lost the moment, lost the luck——

PEER. Speak!

ASE [*sobbing*]. While in the Westerhills you in air were riding reindeer, here Mads Moen's won the girl!

PEER. What! That women's bugbear! He!

ASE. Ay, she's taking him for husband.

PEER. Wait you here till I have harnessed horse and wagon. [*Going.*]

ASE. Spare your pains. They are to be wed tomorrow.

PEER. Pooh, this evening I'll be there!

ASE. Fie now! Would you crown our miseries with a load of all men's scorn?

PEER. Never fear; 'twill all go well. [*Shouting and laughing at the same time.*] Mother, jump! We'll spare the wagon; 'twould take time to fetch the mare up. [*Lifts her up in his arms*].

ASE. Put me down!

PEER. No, in my arms I will bear you to the wedding! [*Wades out into the stream.*]

ASE. Help! The Lord have mercy on us! Peer! We're drowning!

PEER. I was born for a braver death.

ASE. Ay, true; sure enough you'll hang at last! [*Tugging at his hair.*] Oh, you brute!

PEER. Keep quiet now; here the bottom's slippery-slimy.

ASE. Ass!

PEER. That's right, don't spare your tongue; that does no one any harm. Now it's shelving up again.

ASE. Don't you drop me!

PEER. Heisan! Hop! Now we'll play at Peer and reindeer. [*Curvetting.*] I'm the reindeer, you are Peer!

ASE. Oh, I'm going clean distraught!

PEER. There see; now we've reached the shallows. [*Wades ashore.*] Come, a kiss now for the reindeer; just to thank him for the ride.

ASE [*boxing his ears*]. This is how I thank him!

PEER. Ow! That's a miserable fare!

ASE. Put me down!

PEER. First to the wedding. Be my spokesman. You're so clever; talk to him, the old curmudgeon; say Mads Moen's good for nothing——

ASE. Put me down!

PEER. And tell him then what a rare lad is Peer Gynt.

ASE. Truly, you may swear to that! Fine's the character I'll give you. Through and through I'll show you up; all about your devil's pranks I will tell them straight and plain——

PEER. Will you?

ASE [*kicking with rage*]. I won't stay my tongue till the old man sets his dog at you, as you were a tramp!

PEER. H'm; then I must go alone.

ASE. Ay, but I'll come after you!

PEER. Mother dear, you haven't strength.

ASE. Strength? When I'm in such a rage I could crush the rocks to powder! Hu! I'd make a meal of flints! Put me down!

PEER. You'll promise then——

ASE. Nothing! I'll to Hegstad with you! They shall know you, what you are!

PEER. Then you'll even have to stay here.

ASE. Never! To the feast I'm coming!

PEER. That you shan't.

ASE. What will you do?

PEER. Perch you on the millhouse roof. [*He puts her up on the roof.* ASE *screams.*]

ASE. Lift me down!

PEER. Yes, if you'll listen.

ASE. Rubbish!

PEER. Dearest Mother, pray——

ASE [*throwing a sod of grass at him*]. Lift me down this moment, Peer!

PEER. If I dared, be sure I would. [*Coming nearer.*] Now remember, sit quite still. Do not sprawl and kick about; do not tug and tear the shingles—else 'twill be the worse for you; you might topple down.

ASE. You beast!

PEER. Do not kick!

ASE. I'd have you blown, like a changeling, into space!

PEER. Mother, fie!

ASE. Bah!

PEER. Rather give your blessing on my undertaking. Will you? Eh?

ASE. I'll thrash you soundly, hulking fellow though you be!

PEER. Well, good-by then, Mother dear! Patience; I'll be back ere long. [*Is going but turns, holds up his finger warningly and says.*] Careful now, don't kick and sprawl! [*Goes.*]

ASE. Peer!—God help me, now he's off! Reindeer rider! Liar! Hei! Will you listen! No, he's striding o'er the meadow! [*Shrieks.*] Help! I'm dizzy!

[TWO OLD WOMEN, *with sacks on their backs, come down the path to the mill.*]

FIRST WOMAN. Christ, who's screaming?

ASE. It is I!

SECOND WOMAN. Ase! Well, you *are* exalted!

ASE. This won't be the end of it; soon, God help me, I'll be heaven-high!

FIRST WOMAN. Bless your passing!

ASE. Fetch a ladder; I must be down! That devil Peer——

SECOND WOMAN. Peer! Your son?

ASE. Now you can say you have seen how he behaves.

FIRST WOMAN. We'll bear witness.

ASE. Only help me; straight to Hegstad I will hasten——

SECOND WOMAN. Is he there?

FIRST WOMAN. You'll be revenged then; Aslak Smith will be there too.

ASE [*wringing her hands*]. Oh, God help me with my boy; they will kill him ere they're done!

FIRST WOMAN. Oh, that lot has oft been talked off; comfort you; what must be must be!

SECOND WOMAN. She is utterly demented. [*Calls up the hill.*] Eivind, Anders! Hei! Come here!

MAN'S VOICE. What's amiss?

SECOND WOMAN. Peer Gynt has perched his mother on the millhouse roof!

SCENE—*A hillock covered with bushes and heather. The highroad runs behind it, a fence between.* PEER GYNT *comes along a footpath, goes quickly up to the fence, stops and looks out over the stretch of country below.*

PEER. There it lies, Hegstad. Soon I'll have reached it. [*Puts one leg over the fence, then hesitates.*] Wonder if Ingrid's alone in the house now? [*Shades his eyes with his hand and looks out.*] No; to the farm guests are swarming like gnats. H'm, to turn back now perhaps would be wisest. [*Draws back his leg.*] Still they must titter behind your back and whisper so that it burns right through you. [*Moves a few steps away from the fence and begins absently plucking leaves.*] Ah, if I'd only a good strong dram now. Or if I could only pass to and fro unseen. Or were I unknown. Something proper and strong were the best thing of all, for the laughter don't bite then. [*Looks around suddenly as though afraid, then hides among the bushes. Some* WEDDING GUESTS *pass by, going downward toward the farm.*]

MAN [*in conversation as they pass*]. His father was drunken, his mother is weak.

WOMAN. Ay, then it's no wonder the lad's good for nought.

[*They pass on. Presently* PEER GYNT *comes forward, his face flushed with shame. He peers after them.*]

PEER [*softly*]. Was it me they were talking of? [*With a forced shrug.*] Oh, let them chatter! After all, they can't sneer the life out of my body. [*Casts himself down upon the heathery slope, lies for some time flat on his back with his hands under his head, gazing up into the sky.*] What a strange sort of cloud! It is just like a horse. There's a man on it too—and saddle—and—bridle. And after it comes an old crone on a broomstick. [*Laughs quietly to himself.*] It is Mother. She's scolding and screaming: "You beast! Hei you, Peer Gynt——" [*His eyes gradually close.*] Ay, now she is frightened. Peer Gynt he rides first, and there follow him many. His steed is gold shod and crested with silver. Himself he has gauntlets and saber and scabbard. His cloak it is long, and its lining is silken. Full brave is the company riding behind him. None of them, though, sits his charger so stoutly. None of them glitters like him in the sunshine. Down by the fence stand the people in clusters, lifting their hats and agape gazing upward. Women are curtseying. All the world knows him, Kaiser Peer Gynt and his thousands of henchmen. Sixpenny pieces and glittering shillings over the roadway he scatters like pebbles. Rich as a lord grows each man in the parish. High o'er the ocean Peer Gynt goes a-riding. Engelland's prince on the seashore awaits him; there too await him all Engelland's maidens. Engelland's nobles and Engelland's kaiser see him come riding and rise from their banquet. Raising his crown, hear the kaiser address him——

ASLAK THE SMITH [*to some other young men passing along the road*]. Just look at Peer Gynt, the drunken swine!

PEER [*starting half up*]. What, Kaiser!

SMITH [*leaning against the fence and grinning*]. Up with you, Peer, my lad!

PEER. What the devil? The smith! What do you want here?

SMITH [*to the others*]. He hasn't got over the Lunde spree yet.

PEER [*jumping up*]. You'd better be off!

SMITH. I am going, yes. But tell us, where have you dropped from, man? You've been gone six weeks. Were you troll-taken, eh?

PEER. I have been doing strange deeds, Aslak Smith!

SMITH [*winking to the others*]. Let us hear them, Peer!

PEER. They are nought to you.

SMITH [*after a pause*]. You're going to Hegstad?

PEER. No.

SMITH. Time was they said that the girl there was fond of you.

PEER. You grimy crow!

SMITH [*falling back a little*]. Keep your temper, Peer! Though Ingrid has jilted you, others are left; think—son—of Jon Gynt! Come on to the feast; you'll find there both lambkins and widows well on——

PEER. To hell——

SMITH. You will surely find one that will have you. Good evening! I'll give your respects to the bride. [*They go off, laughing and whispering.*]

PEER [*looks after them awhile, then makes a defiant motion and turns half round*]. For my part, may Ingrid of Hegstad go marry whoever she pleases. It's all one to me. [*Looks at his clothes.*] My breeches are torn. I am ragged and grim. If only I had something new to put on now. [*Stamps on the ground.*] If only I could, with a butcher grip, tear out the scorn from their very vitals! [*Looks round suddenly.*] What was *that?* Who was it that tittered behind there? H'm, I certainly thought—— No, no, it was no one. I'll go home to Mother. [*Begins to go upward but stops again and listens toward* HEGSTAD.] They're playing a dance! [*Gazes and listens, moves downward step by step; his eyes glisten; he rubs his hands down his thighs.*] How the lasses do swarm! Six or eight to a man! Oh, galloping death—I must join in the frolic! But how about Mother, perched up on the millhouse—— [*His eyes are drawn downward again; he leaps and laughs.*] Hei, how the Halling flies over the green! Ay, Guttorm, he *can* make his fiddle speak out! It gurgles and booms like a foss o'er a scaur. And then all that glittering bevy of girls! Yes, galloping death, I must join in the frolic! [*Leaps over the fence and goes down the road.*]

SCENE—*The farmplace at Hegstad. In the background the dwelling house.* A THRONG OF GUESTS. *A lively dance in progress on the green.* THE FIDDLER *sits on a table.* THE MASTER COOK *is standing in the doorway.* COOKMAIDS *are going to and fro between the different buildings. Groups of* ELDERLY PEOPLE *sit here and there, talking.*

WOMAN [*joins a group that is seated on some logs of wood*]. The bride? Oh yes, she is crying a bit; but that, you know, isn't worth heeding.

MASTER COOK [*in another group*]. Now then, good folk, you must empty the barrel.

MAN. Thanks to you, friend; but you fill up too quick.

LAD [*to the* FIDDLER, *as he flies past, holding a* GIRL *by the hand.*] To it now, Guttorm, and don't spare the fiddlestrings!

GIRL. Scrape till it echoes out over the meadows!

OTHER GIRLS [*standing in a ring round a lad who is dancing*]. That's a rare fling!

GIRL. He has legs that can lift him!

LAD [*dancing*]. The roof here is

high and the walls wide asunder!

BRIDEGROOM [*comes whimpering up to his* FATHER, *who is standing talking with some other men, and twitches his jacket*]. Father, she will not; she is so proud!

FATHER. What won't she do?

BRIDEGROOM. She has locked herself in.

FATHER. Well, you must manage to find the key.

BRIDEGROOM. I don't know how.

FATHER. You're a nincompoop! [*Turns away to the others. The* BRIDEGROOM *drifts across the yard.*]

LAD [*comes from behind the house*]. Wait a bit, girls! Things 'll soon be lively! Here comes Peer Gynt.

SMITH [*who has just come up*]. Who invited him?

MASTER COOK. No one. [*Goes toward the house.*]

SMITH [*to the girls*]. If he should speak to you, never take notice!

GIRL [*to the others*]. No, we'll pretend that we don't even see him.

PEER GYNT [*comes in heated and full of animation, stops right in front of the group and claps his hands*]. Which is the liveliest girl of the lot of you?

GIRL [*as he approaches her*]. I am not.

ANOTHER [*similarly*]. I am not.

THIRD. No; nor I either.

PEER [*to a fourth*]. You come along, then, for want of a better.

GIRL. Haven't got time.

PEER [*to a fifth*]. Well, then, you!

GIRL [*going*]. I'm for home.

PEER. Tonight? Are you utterly out of your senses?

SMITH [*after a moment, in a low voice*]. See, Peer, she's taken a graybeard for partner.

PEER [*turns sharply to an elderly man*]. Where are the unbespoke girls?

MAN. Find them out. [*Goes away from him.* PEER GYNT *has suddenly become subdued. He glances shyly and furtively at the group. All look at him, but no one speaks. He approaches other groups. Wherever he goes there is silence; when he moves away they look after him and smile.*]

PEER [*to himself*]. Mocking looks, needle-keen whispers and smiles. They grate like a saw blade under the file! [*He slinks along close to the fence.* SOLVEIG, *leading little* HELGA *by the hand, comes into the yard, along with her* PARENTS.]

MAN [*to another, close to* PEER GYNT]. Look, here are the new folk.

OTHER. The ones from the west?

MAN. Ay, the people from Hedal.

OTHER. Ah yes, so they are.

PEER [*places himself in the path of the newcomers, points to* SOLVEIG *and asks the* FATHER]. May I dance with your daughter?

FATHER [*quietly*]. You may so, but first we must go to the farmhouse and greet the good people. [*They go in.*]

MASTER COOK [*to* PEER GYNT, *offering him drink*]. Since you *are* here, you'd best take a pull at the liquor.

PEER [*looking fixedly after the newcomers*]. Thanks; I'm for dancing; I am not athirst. [*The* MASTER COOK *goes away from him.* PEER GYNT *gazes toward the house and laughs.*] How fair! Did ever you see the like? Looked down at her shoes and her snow-white apron! And then she held onto her mother's skirt folds and carried a psalmbook wrapped up in a kerchief! I must look at that girl. [*Going into the house.*]

LAD [*coming out of the house with several others*]. Are you off so soon,

Peer, from the dance?

PEER. No, no.

LAD. Then you're heading amiss! [*Takes hold of his shoulder to turn him round.*]

PEER. Let me pass!

LAD. I believe you're afraid of the smith.

PEER. I afraid!

LAD. You remember what happened at Lunde? [*They go off, laughing, to the dancing green.*]

SOL. [*in the doorway of the house*]. Are you not the lad that was wanting to dance?

PEER. Of course it was me; don't you know me again? [*Takes her hand.*] Come, then!

SOL. We mustn't go far, Mother said.

PEER. Mother said! Mother said! Were you born yesterday?

SOL. Now you're laughing!

PEER. Why, sure, you are almost a child. Are you grown up?

SOL. I read with the pastor last spring.

PEER. Tell me your name, lass, and then we'll talk easier.

SOL. My name is Solveig. And what are you called?

PEER. Peer Gynt.

SOL. [*withdrawing her hand*]. Oh, heaven!

PEER. Why, what is it now?

SOL. My garter is loose; I must tie it up tighter. [*Goes away from him.*]

BRIDEGROOM [*pulling at his* MOTHER's *gown*]. Mother, she will not—

MOTHER. She will not? What?

BRIDEGROOM. She won't, Mother—

MOTHER. What?

BRIDEGROOM. Unlock the door.

FATHER [*angrily, below his breath*]. Oh, you're fit to be tied in a stall!

MOTHER. Don't scold him. Poor dear, he'll be all right yet. [*They move away.*]

LAD [*coming with a whole crowd of others from the dancing green*]. Peer, have some brandy?

PEER. No.

LAD. Only a drain?

PEER [*looking darkly at him*]. Got any?

LAD. Well, I won't say but I have. [*Pulls out a pocket flask and drinks.*] Ah! How it stings your throat! Well?

PEER. Let me try it. [*Drinks.*]

ANOTHER LAD. Now you must try mine as well, you know.

PEER. No!

LAD. Oh, nonsense; now don't be a fool. Take a pull, Peer!

PEER. Well, then, give me a drop. [*Drinks again.*]

GIRL [*half aloud*]. Come, let's be going.

PEER. Afraid of me, wench?

THIRD LAD. Who isn't afraid of *you?*

FOURTH. At Lunde you showed us clearly what trick you could play.

PEER. I can do more than that when once I get started!

FIRST LAD [*whispering*]. Now he's getting into swing!

SEVERAL OTHERS [*forming a circle around him*]. Tell away! Tell away! What can you—

PEER. Tomorrow!

OTHERS. No; now, tonight!

GIRL. Can you conjure, Peer?

PEER. I can call up the devil!

MAN. My grandmam could do that before I was born!

PEER. Liar! What *I* can do, that no one else can do. I one day conjured him into a nut. It was worm-bored, you see!

SEVERAL [*laughing*]. Ay, that's easily guessed!

PEER. He cursed and he wept, and he wanted to bribe me with all sorts of things.

ONE OF THE CROWD. But he had to go in?

PEER. Of course. I stopped up the hole with a peg. Hei! If you'd heard him rumbling and grumbling!

GIRL. Only think!

PEER. It was just like a humblebee buzzing.

GIRL. Have you got him still in the nut?

PEER. Why, no! By this time that devil has flown on his way. The grudge the smith bears me is all *his* doing.

LAD. Indeed?

PEER. I went to the smithy and begged that he would crack that same nutshell for me. He promised he would–laid it down on his anvil; but Aslak, you know, is so heavy of hand –forever swinging that great sledge hammer––

A VOICE FROM THE CROWD. Did he kill the foul fiend?

PEER. He laid on like a man. But the devil showed fight and tore off in a flame through the roof and shattered the wall asunder.

SEVERAL VOICES. And the smith?

PEER. Stood there with his hands all scorched. And from that day onward we've never been friends. [*General laughter.*]

SOME OF THE CROWD. That yarn is a good one.

OTHERS. About his best.

PEER. Do you think I am making it up?

MAN. Oh no, that you're certainly not; for I've heard the most on't from my grandfather.

PEER. Liar! It happened to me!

MAN. Yes, like everything else.

PEER [*with a fling*]. I can ride, I can, clean through the air, on the bravest of steeds! Oh, many's the thing I can do, I tell you! [*Another roar of laughter.*]

ONE OF THE GROUP. Peer, ride through the air a bit!

MANY. Do, dear Peer Gynt.

PEER. You may spare you the trouble of begging so hard. I will ride like a hurricane over you all! Every man in the parish shall fall at my feet!

ELDERLY MAN. Now he is clean off his head.

ANOTHER. The dolt!

THIRD. Braggart!

FOURTH. Liar!

PEER [*threatening them.*] Ay, wait till you see!

MAN [*half drunk*]. Ay, wait; you'll soon get your jacket dusted!

OTHERS. Your back beaten tender! Your eyes painted blue!

[*The crowd disperses, the elder men angry, the younger laughing and jeering.*]

BRIDEGROOM [*close to* PEER GYNT]. Peer, is it true you can ride through the air?

PEER [*shortly*]. It's all true, Mads! You must know I'm a rare one!

BRIDEGROOM. Then have you got the invisible cloak too?

PEER. The invisible hat, do you mean? Yes, I have.

[*Turns away from him.* SOLVEIG *crosses the yard, leading little* HELGA.]

PEER [*goes toward them; his face lights up*]. Solveig! Oh, it is well you have come! [*Takes hold of her wrist.*] Now will I swing you round fast and fine!

SOL. Loose me!

PEER. Wherefore?

SOL. You are so wild.

PEER. The reindeer is wild too,

when summer is dawning. Come then, lass; do not be wayward now!

SOL. [*withdrawing her arm*]. Dare not.

PEER. Wherefore?

SOL. No, you've been drinking. [*Moves off with* HELGA.]

PEER. Oh, if I had but my knife blade driven clean through the heart of them—one and all!

BRIDEGROOM [*nudging him with his elbow*]. Peer, can't you help me to get at the bride?

PEER [*absently*]. The bride? Where is *she?*

BRIDEGROOM. In the storehouse.

PEER. Ah!

BRIDEGROOM. Oh, dear Peer Gynt, you must try at least!

PEER. No, you must get on without my help. [*A thought strikes him; he says softly but sharply.*] Ingrid! The storehouse! [*Goes up to* SOLVEIG.] Have you thought better on't? [SOLVEIG *tries to go; he blocks her path.*] You're ashamed to because I've the look of a tramp.

SOL. [*hastily*]. No, that you haven't; that's not true at all!

PEER. Yes! And I've taken a drop as well, but that was to spite you because you had hurt me. Come then!

SOL. Even if I would now, I daren't.

PEER. Who are you frightened of?

SOL. Father, most.

PEER. Father! Ay, ay; he is one of the quiet ones! One of the godly, eh? Answer, come!

SOL. What shall I say?

PEER. Is your father a psalm singer? And you and your mother as well, no doubt? Come, will you speak?

SOL. Let me go in peace.

PEER. No! [*In a low but sharp and threatening tone.*] I can turn myself into a troll! I'll come to your bedside at midnight tonight. If you should hear someone hissing and spitting, you mustn't imagine it's only the cat. It's me, lass! I'll drain out your blood in a cup, and your little sister, I'll eat her up; ay, you must know I'm a werewolf at night; I'll bite you all over the loins and the back— [*Suddenly changes his tone and entreats, as if in dread.*] Dance with me, Solveig!

SOL. [*looking darkly at him*]. Then you were grim. [*Goes into the house.*]

BRIDEGROOM [*comes sidling up again*]. I'll give you an ox if you'll help me!

PEER. Then come!

[*They go out behind the house. At the some moment a crowd of men come up from the dancing green; most of them are drunk. Noise and hubbub.* SOLVEIG, HELGA *and their* PARENTS *appear among a number of elderly people in the doorway.*]

MASTER COOK [*to the* SMITH, *who is the foremost of the crowd*]. Keep peace now!

SMITH [*pulling off his jacket*]. No, we must fight it out here. Peer Gynt or I must be taught a lesson.

VOICES. Ay, let them fight for it!

OTHERS. No, only wrangle!

SMITH. Fists must decide, for the case is past words.

SOLVEIG'S FATHER. Control yourself, man!

HELGA. Will they beat him, Mother?

LAD. Let us rather tease him with all his lies!

ANOTHER. Kick him out of the company!

THIRD. Spit in his eyes!

FOURTH [*to the* SMITH]. You're not backing out, Smith?

SMITH [*flinging away his jacket*]. The jade shall be slaughtered!

SOLVEIG'S MOTHER [*to* SOLVEIG].

There, you can see how that windbag is thought of.

ASE [*coming up with a stick in her hand*]. Is that son of mine here? Now he's in for a drubbing! Oh, how heartily I will dang him!

SMITH [*rolling up his shirt sleeves*]. That switch is too light for a carcass like his.

SOME OF THE CROWD. The smith will dang him!

OTHERS. Bang him!

SMITH [*spits on his hands and nods to* ASE]. Hang him!

ASE. What? Hang my Peer? Ay, just try if you dare; Ase and I, we have teeth and claws! Where is he? [*Calls across the yard.*] Peer!

BRIDEGROOM [*comes running up*]. Oh, God's death on the cross! Come, Father, come, Mother, and——

FATHER. What is the matter?

BRIDEGROOM. Just fancy, Peer Gynt ——

ASE [*screams*]. Have they taken his life?

BRIDEGROOM. No, but Peter Gynt—— Look, there on the hillside!

CROWD. With the bride!

ASE [*lets her stick sink*]. Oh, the beast!

SMITH [*as if thunderstruck*]. Where the slope rises sheerest he's clambering upward, by God, like a goat!

BRIDEGROOM [*crying*]. He's shouldered her, Mother, as I might a pig!

ASE [*shaking her fist up at him*]. Would God you might fall and—— [*Screams out in terror.*] Take care of your footing!

THE HEGSTAD FARMER [*comes in, bare headed and white with rage*]. I'll have his life for this bride rape yet!

ASE. Oh no, God punish me if I let you!

ACT II

SCENE—*A narrow path high up in the mountains. Early morning.* PEER GYNT *comes hastily and sullenly along the path.* INGRID, *still wearing some of her bridal ornaments, is trying to hold him back.*

PEER. Get you from me!

ING. [*weeping*]. After this, Peer? Whither?

PEER. Where you will for me.

ING. [*wringing her hands*]. Oh, what falsehood!

PEER. Useless railing. Each alone must go his way.

ING. Sin—and sin again unites us!

PEER. Devil take all recollections! Devil take the tribe of women—all but *one!*

ING. Who is that one, pray?

PEER. 'Tis not you.

ING. Who is it then?

PEER. Go! Go thither whence you came! Off! To your father!

ING. Dearest, sweetest——

PEER. Peace!

ING. You cannot mean it, surely, what you're saying?

PEER. Can and do.

ING. First to lure—and then forsake me!

PEER. And what terms have you to offer?

ING. Hegstad farm and more besides.

PEER. Is your psalmbook in your kerchief? Where's the gold mane on your shoulders? Do you glance adown your apron? Do you hold your mother's skirt fold? Speak!

ING. No, but——

PEER. Went you to the pastor this last spring tide?

ING. No, but, Peer——

PEER. Is there shyness in your glances? When I beg, can you deny?

ING. Heaven! I think his wits are going!

PEER. Does your presence sanctify? Speak!

ING. No, but——

PEER. What's all the rest then? [*Going.*]

ING. [*blocking his way*]. Know you it will cost your neck should you fail me?

PEER. What do I care?

ING. You may win both wealth and honor if you take me.

PEER. Can't afford.

ING. [*bursting into tears*]. Oh, you lured me!

PEER. You were willing.

ING. I was desperate!

PEER. Frantic I.

ING. [*threatening*]. Dearly shall you pay for this!

PEER. Dearest payment cheap I'll reckon.

ING. Is your purpose set?

PEER. Like flint.

ING. Good! We'll see, then, who's the winner! [*Goes downward.*]

PEER [*stands silent a moment, then cries*]. Devil take all recollections! Devil take the tribe of women!

ING. [*turning her head and calling mockingly upward*]. All but *one!*

PEER. Yes, all but *one.*

[*They go their several ways.*]

SCENE—*Near a mountain tarn; the ground is soft and marshy round about. A storm is gathering.* ASE *enters, calling and gazing around her despairingly in every direction.* SOLVEIG *has difficulty in keeping up with her.* SOLVEIG'S FATHER *and* MOTHER, *with* HELGA, *are some way behind.*

ASE [*tossing her arms and tearing her hair*]. All things are against me with wrathful might! Heaven and the waters and the grisly mountains! Fog scuds from heaven roll down to bewilder him! The treacherous waters are lurking to murder him! The mountains would crush him with landslip and rift! And the people too! They're out after his life! God knows they shan't have it! I can't bear to lose him! Oh, the oaf! To think that the fiend should tempt him! [*Turning to* SOLVEIG.] Now isn't it clean unbelievable this? He, that did nought but romance and tell lies; he, whose sole strength was the strength of his jaw; he, that did never a stroke of true work; he—— Oh, a body could both cry and laugh! Oh, we clung closely in sorrow and need. Ay, you must know that my husband, he drank, loafed round the parish to roister and prate, wasted and trampled our gear underfoot. And meanwhile at home there sat Peerkin and I—the best we could do was to try to forget; for ever I've found it so hard to bear up. It's a terrible thing to look Fate in the eyes, and of course one is glad to be quit of one's care and try all one can to keep thought far away. Some take to brandy and others to lies, and we—why we took to fairy tales of princes and trolls and of all sorts of beasts, and of bride rapes as well. Ah, but who could have dreamed that those devil's yarns would have stuck in his head? [*In a fresh access of terror.*] Hu! What a scream! It's the nixie or droug! Peer! Peer! Up there on that hillock! [*She runs to the top of a little rise and looks out over the farm.* SOLVEIG'S FATHER *and* MOTHER *come up.*]

ASE. Not a sign to be seen!

FATHER [*quietly*]. It is worst for him!

ASE [*weeping*]. Oh, my Peer! Oh, my own lost lamb!

FATHER [*nods mildly*]. You may well say lost.

ASE. Oh no, don't talk like that! He is so clever. There's no one like him.

FATHER. You foolish woman!

ASE. Oh! ay; oh! ay; foolish I am, but the boy's all right!

FATHER [*still softly and with mild eyes*]. His heart is hardened, his soul is lost.

ASE [*in terror*]. No, no, he can't be so hard, our Lord!

FATHER. Do you think he can sigh for his debt of sin?

ASE [*eagerly*]. No, but he can ride through the air on a buck though!

MOTHER. Christ, are you mad?

FATHER. Why, what do you mean?

ASE. Never a deed is too great for him. You shall see, if only he lives so long——

FATHER. Best if you saw him on the gallows hanging.

ASE [*shrieks*]. Oh, cross of Christ!

FATHER. In the hangman's hands, it may be his heart would be turned to repentance.

ASE [*bewildered*]. Oh, you'll soon talk me out of my senses! We must find him!

FATHER. To rescue his soul.

ASE. And his body! If he's stuck in the swamp, we must drag him out; if he's taken by trolls, we must ring the bells for him.

FATHER. H'm—here's a sheep path.

ASE. The Lord will repay you your guidance and help!

FATHER. It's a Christian's duty.

ASE. Then the others, fie! they are heathens all; there wasn't one that would go with us.

FATHER. They knew him too well.

ASE. He was too good for them! [*Wrings her hands.*] And to think—and to think that his life is at stake!

FATHER. Here are tracks of a man.

ASE. Then it's here we must search!

FATHER. We'll scatter around on this side of our saeter. [*He and his wife go on ahead.*]

SOLVEIG [*to* ASE]. Say on; tell me more.

ASE [*drying her eyes*]. Of my son, you mean?

SOL. Yes; tell everything!

ASE [*smiles and tosses her head*]. Everything? Soon you'd be tired!

SOL. Sooner by far will you tire of the telling than I of the hearing.

SCENE—*Low, treeless heights, close under the mountain moorlands; peaks in the distance. The shadows are long; it is late in the day.* PEER GYNT *comes running at full speed and stops short on the hillside.*

PEER. The parish is all at my heels in a pack. Every man of them armed or with gun or with club. Foremost I hear the old Hegstad churl howling. Now it's noised far and wide that Peer Gynt is abroad! It is different, this, from a bout with a smith. This is life! Every limb grows as strong as a bear's. [*Strikes out with his arms and leaps in the air.*] To crush, overturn, stem the rush of the foss! To strike! Wrench the fir tree right up by the root! This is life! This both hardens and lifts one high! To hell then with all of the savorless lies!

THREE SAETER GIRLS [*rush across the hillside, screaming and singing*]. Trond of the Valfjeld! Bard and Kare! Troll pack! Tonight would you sleep in our arms?

PEER. To whom are you calling?

GIRLS. To the trolls! To the trolls!

FIRST GIRL. Trond, come with kindness!

SECOND GIRL. Bard, come with force!

THIRD GIRL. The cots in the saeter are all standing empty!

FIRST GIRL. Force is kindness!

SECOND GIRL. And kindness is force!

THIRD GIRL. If lads are a-wanting, one plays with the trolls!

PEER. Why, where are lads, then?

ALL THREE [*with a hoarse laugh*]. They cannot come hither!

FIRST GIRL. Mine called me his sweetheart and called me his darling. Now he has married a gray-headed widow.

SECOND GIRL. Mine met a gipsy wench north on the upland. Now they are tramping the country together.

THIRD GIRL. Mine put an end to our bastard brat. Now his head's grinning aloft on a stake.

ALL THREE. Trond of the Valfjeld! Bard and Kare! Troll pack! Tonight would you sleep in our arms?

PEER [*stands, with a sudden leap, in the midst of them*]. I'm a three-headed troll and the boy for three girls!

GIRLS. Are you *such* a lad, eh?

PEER. You shall judge for yourselves!

FIRST GIRL. To the hut! To the hut!

SECOND GIRL. We have mead!

PEER. Let it flow!

THIRD GIRL. No cot shall stand empty this Saturday night!

SECOND GIRL [*kissing him*]. He sparkles and glisters like white-heated iron.

THIRD GIRL [*doing likewise*]. Like a baby's eyes from the blackest tarn.

PEER [*dancing in the midst of them*]. Heavy of heart and wanton of mind. The eyes full of laughter, the throat of tears!

GIRLS [*making mocking gestures toward the mountaintops, screaming and singing*]. Trond of the Valfjeld! Bard and Kare! Troll pack! Tonight will you sleep in our arms? [*They dance away over the heights with* PEER GYNT *in their midst.*]

SCENE—*Among the Ronde mountains. Sunset. Shining snow peaks all around.* PEER GYNT *enters, dizzy and bewildered.*

PEER. Tower over tower arises! Hei, what a glittering gate! Stand! Will you stand! It's drifting further and further away! High on the vane the cock stands, lifting his wings for flight; blue spread the rifts and bluer, locked is the fell and barred. What are those trunks and tree roots that grow from the ridge's clefts? They are warriors heron-footed! Now they, too, are fading away. A shimmering like rainbow streamers goes shooting through eyes and brain. What is it, that far-off chiming? What's weighing my eyebrows down? Hu, how my forehead's throbbing—a tightening red-hot ring! I cannot think who the devil has bound it around my head! [*Sinks down.*] Flight o'er the Edge of Gendin—stuff and accursed lies! Up o'er the steepest hill wall with the bride—and a whole day drunk; hunted by hawks and falcons, threatened by trolls and such, sporting with crazy wenches; lies and accursed stuff! [*Gazes long upward.*] Yonder sail two brown eagles. Southward the wild geese fly. And here I must splash and stumble in quagmire and filth knee-deep! [*Springs up.*] I'll fly too! I will wash myself clean in the bath of the keenest winds! I'll fly high! I will plunge myself fair in the glorious christening font! I will soar far over the saeter; I will ride myself pure of soul; I will forth o'er the salt sea waters and high over Engelland's prince! Ay, gaze as ye may, young maidens; my ride is for none of you; you're wasting your time in waiting! Yet maybe I'll swoop down too. What has come of the two brown eagles? They've vanished, the devil knows where! There's the peak of a gable rising; it's soaring on every hand; it's growing from out the ruins; see, the gateway is standing wide! Ha-ha, yonder house, I know it; it's Grandfather's new-built farm! Gone are the clouts from the windows; the crazy old fence is gone. The lights gleam from every casement; there's a feast in the hall tonight. There, that was the provost clinking the back of his knife on his glass; there's the captain flinging his bottle and shivering the mirror to bits. Let them waste; let it all be squandered! Peace, Mother; what need we care! 'Tis the rich Jon Gynt gives the banquet; hurrah for the race of Gynt! What's all this bustle and hubbub? Why do they shout and bawl? The captain is calling the son in; oh, the provost would drink my health. In then, Peer Gynt, to the judgment; it rings forth in song and shout: Peer Gynt, thou art come of great things, and great things shall come of thee! [*Leaps forward but runs his head against a rock, falls and remains stretched on the ground.*]

SCENE—*A hillside wooded with great soughing trees. Stars are gleaming through the leaves; birds are singing in the treetops.* A GREEN-CLAD WOMAN *is crossing the hillside;* PEER GYNT *follows her with all sorts of loverlike antics.*

GREEN-CLAD ONE [*stops and turns around*]. Is it true?

PEER [*drawing his finger across his throat*]. As true as my name is Peer—as true as that you are a lovely woman! Will you have me? You'll see what a fine man I'll be; you shall neither tread the loom nor turn the spindle. You shall eat all you want, till you're ready to burst. I never will drag you about by the hair——

GREEN-CLAD ONE. Nor beat me?

PEER. No, can you think I would? We kings' sons never beat women and such.

GREEN-CLAD ONE. You're a king's son?

PEER. Yes.

GREEN-CLAD ONE. I'm the Dovre King's daughter.

PEER. Are you? See there, now, how well that fits in!

GREEN-CLAD ONE. Deep in the Ronde has father his palace.

PEER. My mother's is bigger, or much I'm mistaken.

GREEN-CLAD ONE. Do you know my father? His name is King Brose.

PEER. Do you know my mother? Her name is Queen Ase.

GREEN-CLAD ONE. When my father is angry the mountains are riven.

PEER. They reel when my mother by chance falls a-scolding.

GREEN-CLAD ONE. My father can kick e'en the loftiest rooftree.

PEER. My mother can ride through the rapidest river.

GREEN-CLAD ONE. Have you other garments besides those rags?

PEER. Ho, you should just see my Sunday clothes!

GREEN-CLAD ONE. My weekday gown is of gold and silk.

PEER. It looks to me like tow and straws.

GREEN-CLAD ONE. Ay, there is *one* thing you must remember—this is the Rondefolk's use and wont: all our possessions have twofold form. When you shall come to my father's hall it well may chance that you're on the point of thinking you stand in a dismal moraine.

PEER. Well, now, with us it's precisely the same. Our gold will seem to you litter and trash! And you'll think, mayhap, every glittering pane is nought but a bunch of old stockings and clouts.

GREEN-CLAD ONE. Black it seems white, and ugly seems fair.

PEER. Big it seems little, and dirty seems clean.

GREEN-CLAD ONE [*falling on his neck*]. Ay, Peer, now I see that we fit, you and I!

PEER. Like the leg and the trouser, the hair and the comb.

GREEN-CLAD ONE [*calls away over the hillside*]. Bridal steed! Bridal steed. Come, bridal steed mine!

[*A gigantic pig comes running in with a rope's end for a bridle and an old sack for a saddle.* PEER GYNT *vaults on its back and seats the* GREEN-CLAD ONE *in front of him.*]

PEER. Hark away! Through the Ronde gate gallop we in! Gee-up, gee-up, my courser fine!

GREEN-CLAD ONE [*tenderly*]. Ah, but lately I wandered and moped and pined. One never can tell what may happen to one!

PEER [*thrashing the pig and trotting off*]. You may know the great by their riding gear!

SCENE—*The Royal Hall of the King of the Dovre Trolls. A great assembly of* TROLL COURTIERS, GNOMES *and* BROWNIES. THE OLD MAN OF THE DOVRE *sits on the throne, crowned, and with his scepter in his hand. His* CHILDREN *and* NEAREST RELATIONS *are ranged on both sides.* PEER GYNT *stands before him. Violent commotion in the hall.*

TROLL COURTIERS. Slay him! a Christian man's son has deluded the Dovre King's loveliest maid!

TROLL IMP. May I hack him on the fingers?

ANOTHER. May I tug him by the hair?

TROLL MAIDEN. Hu, hei, let me bite him in the haunches!

TROLL WITCH [*with a ladle*]. Shall he be boiled into broth and bree?

ANOTHER TROLL WITCH [*with a chopper*]. Shall he roast on a spit or be browned in a stewpan?

OLD MAN OF THE DOVRE. Ice to your blood, friends! [*Beckons his counselors nearer around him.*] Don't let us talk big. We've been drifting astern in these latter years; we can't tell what's going to stand or to fall, and there's no sense in turning recruits away. Besides, the lad's body has scarce a blemish, and he's strongly built too, if I see aright. It's true he has only a single head, but my daughter, too, has no more than one. Three-headed trolls are going clean out of fashion; one hardly sees even a two-header now, and even those heads are but so-so ones. [*To* PEER GYNT.] It's my daughter, then, you demand of me?

PEER. Your daughter and the realm to her dowry, yes.

OLD MAN. You shall have the half while I'm still alive and the other half when I come to die.

PEER. I'm content with that.

OLD MAN. Ay, but stop, my lad; *you* also have some undertakings to give. If you break even one, the whole pact's at an end and you'll never get away from here living. First of all you must swear that you'll never give heed to aught that lies outside the Ronde hills' bounds; day you must shun, and deeds, and each sunlit spot.

PEER. Only call me king, and that's easy to keep.

OLD MAN. And next—now for putting your wits to the test. [*Draws himself up in his seat.*]

OLDEST TROLL COURTIER [*to* PEER GYNT]. Let us see if you have a wisdom tooth that can crack the Dovre King's riddle nut!

OLD MAN. What difference is there 'twixt trolls and men?

PEER. No difference at all, as it seems to me. Big trolls would roast you and small trolls would claw you; with us it were likewise, if only they dared.

OLD MAN. True enough; in that and in more we're alike. Yet morning is morning and even is even, and there *is* a difference all the same. Now let me tell you wherein it lies: Out yonder, under the shining vault, among men the saying goes: "Man, be thyself!" At home here with us, 'mid the tribe of the trolls, the saying goes: "Troll, to thyself be—enough!"

TROLL COURTIER [*to* PEER GYNT]. Can you fathom the depth?

PEER. It strikes me as misty.

OLD MAN. My son, that "Enough," that most potent and sundering word, must be graven upon your escutcheon.

PEER [*scratching his head*]. Well, but——

OLD MAN. It *must,* if you here would be master!

PEER. Oh well, let it pass; after all, it's no worse——

OLD MAN. And next you must learn to appreciate our homely, everyday way of life. [*He beckons; two* TROLLS *with pigs' heads, white nightcaps and so forth bring in food and drink.*] The cow gives cakes and the bullock mead; ask not if its taste be sour or sweet; the main matter is, and you mustn't forget it, it's all of it home brewed.

PEER [*pushing the things away from him*]. The devil fly off with your home-brewed drinks! I'll never get used to the ways of this land.

OLD MAN. The bowl's given in, and it's fashioned of gold. Whoso owns the gold bowl, him my daughter holds dear.

PEER [*pondering*]. It is written: Thou shalt bridle the natural man; and I daresay the drink may in time seem less sour. So be it! [*Complies.*]

OLD MAN. Ay, that was sagaciously said. You spit?

PEER. One must trust to the force of habit.

OLD MAN. And next you must throw off your Christian man's garb; for this you must know to our Dovre's renown: here all things are mountain made—nought's from the dale, except the silk bow at the end of your tail.

PEER [*indignant*]. I haven't a tail!

OLD MAN. Then of course you must get one. See my Sunday tail, chamberlain, fastened to him.

PEER. I'll be hanged if you do! Would you make me a fool?

OLD MAN. None comes courting my child with no tail at his rear.

PEER. Make a beast of a man!

OLD MAN. Nay, my son, you mistake; I make you a mannerly wooer, no more. A bright orange bow we'll allow you to wear, and that passes here for the highest of honors.

PEER [*reflectively*]. It's true, as the saying goes: Man's but a mote. And it's wisest to follow the fashion a bit. Tie away!

Old Man. You're a tractable fellow, I see.

Courtier. Just try with what grace you can waggle and whisk it!

Peer [*peevishly*]. Ha, would you force me to go still further? Do you ask me to give up my Christian faith?

Old Man. No, that you are welcome to keep in peace. Doctrine goes free; upon that there's no duty; it's the outward cut one must tell a troll by. If we're only at one in our manners and dress, you may hold as your faith what to us is a horror.

Peer. Why, in spite of your many conditions, you are a more reasonable chap that one might have expected.

Old Man. We troll folk, my son, are less black than we're painted; that's another distinction between you and us. But the serious part of the meeting is over; now let us gladden our ears and our eyes. Music maid, forth! Set the Dovre harp sounding! Dancing maid, forth! Tread the Dovre hall's floor! [*Music and a dance.*]

Courtier. How like you it?

Peer. Like it? Hm——

Old Man. Speak without fear! What see you?

Peer. Why, something unspeakably grim: a bell cow with her hoof on a gut harp strumming, a sow in socklets atrip to the tune.

Courtiers. Eat him!

Old Man. His sense is but human, remember!

Troll Maidens. Hu, tear away both his ears and his eyes!

Green-Clad One [*weeping*]. Hu-hu! And this we must hear and put up with when I and my sister make music and dance.

Peer. Oho, was it you? Well, a joke at the feast, you must know, is never unkindly meant.

Green-Clad One. Can you swear it was so?

Peer. Both the dance and the music were utterly charming, the cat claw me else.

Old Man. This same human nature's a singular thing; it sticks to people so strangely long. If it gets a gash in the fight with us, it heals up at once, though a scar may remain. My son-in-law, now, is as pliant as any; he's willingly thrown off his Christian man's garb, he's willingly drunk from our chalice of mead, he's willingly tied on the tail to his back—so willing, in short, did we find him in all things, I thought to myself the old Adam, for certain, had for good and all been kicked out of doors; but lo! in two shakes he's atop again! Ay, ay, my son, we must treat you, I see, to cure this pestilent human nature.

Peer. What will you do?

Old Man. In your left eye, first, I'll scratch you a bit, till you see awry; but all that you see will seem fine and brave. And then I'll just cut your right windowpane out——

Peer. Are you drunk?

Old Man. [*lays a number of sharp instruments on the table*]. See, here are the glazier's tools. Blinkers you'll wear, like a raging bull. Then you'll recognize that your bride is lovely—and ne'er will your vision be troubled, as now, with bell cows harping and sows that dance.

Peer. This is madman's talk!

Oldest Courtier. It's the Dovre King speaking; it's he that is wise, and it's you that are crazy!

Old Man. Just think how much worry and mortification you'll thus escape from, year out, year in. You must remember, your eyes are the fountain of the bitter and searing lye of tears.

Peer. That's true, and it says in our sermon book: If thine eye offend thee, then pluck it out. But tell me, when will my sight heal up into human sight?

Old Man. Nevermore, my friend.

Peer. Indeed! In that case I'll take my leave.

Old Man. What would you without?

Peer. I would go my way.

Old Man. No, stop! It's easy to slip in here, but the Dovre King's gate doesn't open outward.

Peer. You wouldn't detain me by force, I hope?

Old Man. Come now, just listen to reason, Prince Peer! You have gifts for trolldom. He acts, does he not, even now in a passably trolllike fashion? And you'd fain be a troll?

Peer. Yes, I would, sure enough. For a bride and a well-managed kingdom to boot I can put up with losing a good many things. But there is a limit to all things on earth. The tail I've accepted, it's perfectly true; but no doubt I can loose what the chamberlain tied. My breeches I've dropped; they were old and patched; but no doubt I can button them on again. And lightly enough I can slip my cable from these your Dovrefield ways of life. I am willing to swear that a cow is a maid, an oath one can always eat up again; but to know that one never can free oneself, that one can't even die like a decent soul; to live as a hill troll for all one's days—to feel that one never can beat a retreat—as the book has it—*that's* what your heart is set on, but that is a thing I can never agree to.

Old Man. Now, sure as I live, I shall soon lose my temper; and then I am not to be trifled with. You pasty-faced loon! Do you know who I am? First with my daughter you make too free——

Peer. There you lie in your throat!

Old Man. You must marry her.

Peer. Do you dare to accuse me?

Old Man. What? Can you deny that you lusted for her in heart and eye?

Peer [*with a snort of contempt*]. No more? Who the deuce cares a straw for that?

Old Man. It's ever the same with this humankind. The spirit you're ready to own with your lips, but in fact nothing counts that your fists cannot handle. So you really think, then, that lust matters nought? Wait; you shall soon have ocular proof of it.

Peer. You don't catch me with a bait of lies!

Green-Clad One. My Peer, ere the year's out you'll be a father.

Peer. Open doors! Let me go!

Old Man. In a he-goat's skin you shall have the brat after you.

Peer [*mopping the sweat off his brow*]. Would I could waken!

Old Man. Shall we send him to the palace?

Peer. You can send him to the parish!

Old Man. Well, well, Prince Peer, that's your own lookout. But one thing's certain, what's done is done; and your offspring, too, will be sure to grow; such mongrels shoot up amazingly fast.

Peer. Old man, don't act like a headstrong ox! Hear reason, maiden! Let's come to terms. You must know I'm neither a prince nor rich; and whether you measure or whether you weigh me, be sure you won't gain much by making me yours.

[THE GREEN-CLAD ONE *is taken ill and is carried out by* TROLL MAIDS.]

OLD MAN [*looks at him for a while in high disdain, then says*]. Dash him to shards on the rock walls, children!

TROLL IMPS. Oh, Dad, mayn't we play owl and eagle first! The wolf game! Gray mouse and glow-eyed cat!

OLD MAN. Yes, but quick. I am worried and sleepy. Good night! [*He goes.*]

PEER [*hunted by the* TROLL IMPS]. Let me be, devil's imps! [*Tries to escape up the chimney.*]

IMPS. Come, brownies! Come, nixies! Bite him behind!

PEER. Ow! [*Tries to slip down the cellar trap door.*]

IMPS. Shut up all the crannies!

TROLL COURTIER. Now the small fry are happy.

PEER [*struggling with a little* IMP *that has bit himself fast to his ear*]. Let go, will you, beast!

COURTIER [*hitting him across the fingers*]. Gently, you scamp, with a scion of royalty!

PEER. A rathole! [*Runs to it.*]

IMPS. Be quick, Brother Nixie, and block it!

PEER. The old one was bad, but the youngsters are worse!

IMPS. Slash him!

PEER. Oh, would I were as small as a mouse! [*Rushing around.*]

IMPS [*swarming round him*]. Close the ring! Close the ring!

PEER [*weeping*]. Would that I were a louse! [*He falls.*]

IMPS. Now into his eyes!

PEER [*buried in a heap of* IMPS]. Mother, help me, I die! [*Church bells sound far away.*]

IMPS. Bells in the mountain! The Black Frock's cows!

[THE TROLLS *take to flight amid a confused uproar of yells and shrieks. The palace collapses; everything disappears.*]

SCENE—*Pitch darkness.* PEER GYNT *is heard beating and slashing about him with a large bough.*

PEER. Answer! Who are you?

A VOICE IN THE DARKNESS. Myself.

PEER. Clear the way!

VOICE. Go roundabout, Peer! The hill's roomy enough.

PEER [*tries to force a passage at another place but strikes against something*]. Who are *you?*

VOICE. Myself. Can you say the same?

PEER. I can say what I will, and my sword can smite! Mind yourself! Hu, hei, now the blow falls crushing! King Saul slew hundreds; Peer Gynt slew thousands! [*Cutting and slashing.*] Who *are* you?

VOICE. Myself.

PEER. That stupid reply you may spare; it doesn't clear up the matter. *What* are you?

VOICE. The great Boyg.

PEER. Ah, indeed! The riddle was black; now I'd call it gray. Clear the way then, Boyg!

VOICE. Go roundabout, Peer!

PEER. No, through! [*Cuts and slashes.*] There he fell! [*Tries to advance but strikes against something.*] Ho-ho, are there more here?

VOICE. The Boyg, Peer Gynt, the one only one. It's the Boyg that's unwounded, and the Boyg that was hurt; it's the Boyg that is dead, and the Boyg that's alive.

PEER [*throws away the branch*].

The weapon is troll-smeared, but I have my fists! [*Fights his way forward.*]

VOICE. Ay, trust to your fists, lad, trust to your body. Hee-hee, Peer Gynt, so you'll reach the summit.

PEER [*falling back again*]. Forward or back, and it's just as far; out or in, and it's just as strait! He is *there!* And *there!* And he's round the bend! No sooner I'm out than I'm back in the ring. Name who you are! Let me see you! What are you?

VOICE. The Boyg.

PEER [*groping around*]. Not dead, not living; all slimy, misty. Not so much as a shape! It's as bad as to battle in a cluster of snarling, half-awakened bears! [*Screams.*] Strike back at me, can't you!

VOICE. The Boyg isn't mad.

PEER. Strike!

VOICE. The Boyg strikes not.

PEER. Fight! You shall!

VOICE. The great Boyg conquers but does not fight.

PEER. Were there only a nixie here that could prick me! Were there only as much as a year-old troll! Only something to fight with. But here there is nothing. Now he's snoring! Boyg!

VOICE. What's your will?

PEER. Use force!

VOICE. The great Boyg conquers in all things without it.

PEER [*biting his own arms and hands*]. Claws and ravening teeth in my flesh! I must feel the drip of my own warm blood.

[*A sound is heard like the wing strokes of great birds.*]

BIRD CRIES. Comes he now, Boyg.

VOICE. Ay, step by step.

BIRD CRIES. All our sisters far off! Gather here to the tryst!

PEER. If you'd save me now, lass, you must do it quick! Gaze not adown so, lowly and bending. Your clasp book! Hurl it straight into his eyes!

BIRD CRIES. He totters.

VOICE. We have him.

BIRD CRIES. Sisters! Make haste!

PEER. Too dear the purchase one pays for life in such a heart-wasting hour of strife. [*Sinks down.*]

BIRD CRIES. Boyg, there he's fallen! Seize him! Seize him!

[*A sound of bells and of psalm singing is heard far away.*]

BOYG [*shrinks up to nothing and says in a gasp*]. He was too strong. There were women behind him.

SCENE—*Sunrise. The mountainside in front of Ase's saeter. The door is shut; all is silent and deserted.* PEER GYNT *is lying asleep by the wall of the saeter.*

PEER [*wakens and looks about him with dull and heavy eyes. He spits*]. What wouldn't I give for a pickled herring! [*Spits again and at the same moment catches sight of* HELGA, *who appears carrying a basket of food.*] Ha, child, are you there? What is it you want?

HEL. It is Solveig—

PEER [*jumping up*]. Where is *she?*

HEL. Behind the saeter.

SOL. If you come nearer, I'll run away!

PEER [*stopping short*]. Perhaps you're afraid I might take you in my arms?

SOL. For shame!

PEER. Do you know where I was last night? Like a horsefly the Dovre King's daughter is after me.

SOL. Then it was well that the bells were set ringing.

PEER. Peer Gynt's not the lad they can lure astray. What do you say?

HEL. [*crying*]. Oh, she's running away! [*Running after her.*] Wait!

PEER [*catches her by the arm*]. Look here, what I have in my pocket! A silver button, child! You shall have it—only speak for me!

HEL. Let me be; let me go!

PEER. There you have it.

HEL. Let go; there's the basket of food.

PEER. God pity you if you don't——

HEL. Uf, how you scare me!

PEER [*gently, letting her go*]. No, I only meant: beg her not to forget me!

[HELGA *runs off.*]

ACT III

SCENE—*Deep in the pinewoods. Gray autumn weather. Snow is falling.* PEER GYNT *stands in his shirt sleeves, felling timber.*

PEER [*hewing at a large fir tree with twisted branches*]. Oh! ay, you are tough, you ancient churl; but it's all in vain, for you'll soon be down. [*Hews at it again.*] I see well enough you've a chain-mail shirt, but I'll hew it through were it never so stout. Ay, ay, you're shaking your twisted arms; you've reason enough for your spite and rage, but nonetheless you must bend the knee! [*Breaks off suddenly.*] Lies! 'Tis an old tree and nothing more. Lies! It was never a steel-clad churl; it's only a fir tree with fissured bark. It is heavy labor this hewing timber, but the devil and all when you hew and dream too. I'll have done with it all—with this dwelling in mist—and, broad awake, dreaming your senses away. You're an outlaw, lad! You are banned to the woods. [*Hews for a while rapidly.*] Ay, an outlaw, ay. You've no mother now to spread your table and bring your food. If you'd eat, my lad, you must help yourself, fetch your rations, raw from the wood and stream, split your own fir roots and light your own fire, bustle around and arrange and prepare things. Would you clothe yourself warmly, you must stalk your deer; would you found you a house, you must quarry the stones; would you build up its walls, you must fell the logs and shoulder them all to the building place. [*His ax sinks down; he gazes straight in front of him.*] Brave shall the building be. Tower and vane shall rise from the rooftree, high and fair. And then I will carve, for the knob on the gable, a mermaid shaped like a fish from the navel. Brass shall there be on the vane and the door locks. Glass I must see and get hold of too. Strangers, passing, shall ask amazed what that is glittering far on the hillside. [*Laughs angrily.*] Devil's own lies! There they come again. You're an outlaw, lad! [*Hewing vigorously.*] A bark-thatched hovel is shelter enough both in rain and frost. [*Looks up at the tree.*] Now he stands wavering. There; only a kick, and he topples and measures his length on the ground; the thick-swarming undergrowth shudders around him! [*Begins lopping the branches from the trunk; suddenly he listens and stands motionless with his ax in the air.*] There's someone after me! Ay, are you that sort, old Hegstad churl; would you play me false? [*Crouches behind the tree and peeps over it.*] A lad! One only. He seems afraid. He peers all round him. What's that he hides 'neath his jacket? A sickle. He stops and looks round—now he lays his hand on a fence rail flat. What's this now? Why does he lean like that? Ugh, ugh! Why, he's chopped his finger off! A whole finger off! He bleeds like an ox. Now he takes to his heels with his fist in a clout. [*Rises.*] What a devil of a lad! An unmendable finger! Right off! And with no one compelling him to it! Ho, now I remember! It's only thus you can 'scape from having to serve the king. That's it. They wanted to send him soldiering, and of course the lad didn't want to go. But to chop it off? To sever for good and all? Ay, think of it–wish it done–*will* it to boot–but *do* it! No, that's past my understanding! [*Shakes his head a little, then goes on with his work.*]

SCENE–*A room in* ASE's *house. Everything in disorder; boxes standing open, wearing apparel strewn around. A cat is lying on the bed.* ASE *and the* COTTER's WIFE *are hard at work packing things together and putting them straight.*

ASE [*running to one side*]. Kari, come here!

KARI. What now?

ASE [*on the other side*]. Come here! Where is— Where shall I find—– Tell me where—– What am I seeking? I'm out of my wits! Where is the key of the chest?

KARI. In the keyhole.

ASE. What is that rumbling?

KARI. The last cartload they're driving to Hegstad.

ASE [*weeping*]. How glad I'd be in the black chest myself to be driven away! Oh, what must a mortal abide and live through! God help me in mercy! The whole house is bare! What the Hegstad churl left now the bailiff has taken. Not even the clothes on my back have they spared. Fie! Shame on them all that have judged so hardly! [*Seats herself on the edge of the bed.*] Both the land and the farmplace are lost to our line; the old man was hard, but the law was still harder; there was no one to help me, and none would show mercy; Peer was away; not a soul to give counsel.

KARI. But here, in this house, you may dwell till you die.

ASE. Ay, the cat and I live on charity.

KARI. God help you, Mother; your Peer's cost you dear.

ASE. Peer? Why, you're out of your senses, sure! Ingrid came home none the worse in the end. The right thing had been to hold Satan to reckoning; he was the sinner, ay, he and none other; the ugly beast tempted my poor boy astray!

KARI. Had I not better send word to the parson? Mayhap you're worse than you think you are.

ASE. To the parson? Truly I almost think so. [*Starts up.*] But, oh God, I can't! I'm the boy's own mother, and help him I must; it's no more than my duty; I must do what I can when the rest forsake him. They've left him this coat; I must patch it up. I wish I dared snap up the fur rug as well! What's come of the hose?

KARI. They are there, 'mid that rubbish.

ASE [*rummaging about*]. Why, what have we here? I declare, it's an old casting ladle, Kari! With this he would play button molder, would melt and then shape and then stamp them. One day–there was company–in the boy came and begged of his father a lump of tin. "Not tin," says Jon, "but King Christian's coin–silver–to show you're the son of Jon

Gynt." God pardon him, Jon; he was drunk, you see, and then he cared neither for tin nor for gold. Here are the hose. Oh, they're nothing but holes; they want darning, Kari!

KARI. Indeed, but they do.

ASE. When that is done I must get to bed; I feel so broken and frail and ill. [*Joyfully.*] Two woolen shirts, Kari; they've passed them by!

KARI. So they have, indeed.

ASE. It's a bit of luck. One of the two you may put aside, or rather I think we'll e'en take them both; the one he has on is so worn and thin.

KARI. But, oh, Mother Ase, I fear it's a sin!

ASE. Maybe; but remember, the priest holds out pardon for this and our other sinnings.

SCENE—*In front of a settler's newly built hut in the forest. A reindeer's horns over the door. The snow is lying deep around. It is dusk.*

PEER GYNT *is standing outside the door, fastening a large wooden bar to it.*

PEER [*laughing betweenwhiles*]. Bars I must fix me; bars that can fasten the door against troll folk and men and women. Bars I must fix me; bars that can shut out all the cantankerous little hobgoblins. They come with the darkness, they knock and they rattle: Open, Peer Gynt, we're as nimble as thoughts are! 'Neath the bedstead we bustle; we rake in the ashes; down the chimney we hustle like fiery-eyed dragons. Hee-hee! Peer Gynt, think you staples and planks can shut out cantankerous hobgoblin thoughts?

[SOLVEIG *comes on snowshoes over the heath; she has a shawl over her head and a bundle in her hand.*]

SOL. God prosper your labor. You must not reject me. You sent for me hither, and so you must take me.

PEER. Solveig! It cannot be! Ay, but it is! And you're not afraid to come near to me!

SOL. One message you sent me by little Helga; others came after in storm and in stillness. All that your mother told bore me a message that brought forth others when dreams sank upon me. Nights full of heaviness, blank, empty days, brought me the message that now I must come. It seemed as though life had been quenched down there; I could nor laugh nor weep from the depths of my heart. I knew not for sure how you might be minded; I knew but for sure what I should do and must do.

PEER. But your father?

SOL. In all of God's wide earth I have none I can call either father or mother. I have loosed me from all of them.

PEER. Solveig, you fair one—and to come to me?

SOL. Ay, to you alone; you must be all to me, friend and consoler. [*In tears.*] The worst was leaving my little sister, but parting from Father was worse, still worse; and worst to leave her at whose breast I was borne —oh no, God forgive me, the worst I must call the sorrow of leaving them all, ay, all!

PEER. And you know the doom that was passed in spring? It forfeits my farm and my heritage.

SOL. Think you for heritage, goods and gear I forsook the paths all my dear ones tread?

PEER. And know you the compact? Outside the forest whoever may meet me may seize me at will.

SOL. I ran upon snowshoes; I asked

my way on; they said, "Whither go you?" I answered, "I go home."

PEER. Away, away then with nails and planks! No need now for bars against hobgoblin thoughts. If you dare dwell with the hunter here, I know the hut will be blessed from ill. Solveig! Let me look at you! Not too near! Only look at you! Oh, but you are bright and pure! Let me lift you! Oh, but you are fine and light! Let me carry you, Solveig, and I'll never be tired! I will not soil you. With outstretched arms I will hold you far out from me, lovely and warm one! Oh, who would have thought I could draw you to me? Ah, but I have longed for you, daylong and night-long. Here you may see I've been hewing and building; it must down again, dear; it is ugly and mean—

SOL. Be it mean or brave—here is all to my mind. One so lightly draws breath in the teeth of the wind. Down below it was airless; one felt as though choked; that was partly what drove me in fear from the dale. But here, with the fir branches soughing o'erhead—what a stillness and song!—I am here in my home.

PEER. And know you that surely? For all your days?

SOL. The path I have trodden leads back nevermore.

PEER. You are mine then! In! In the room let me see you! Go in! I must go to fetch fir roots for fuel. Warm shall the fire be and bright shall it shine; you shall sit softly and never be a-cold. [*He opens the door;* SOLVEIG *goes in. He stands still for a while, then laughs aloud with joy and leaps into the air.*]

PEER. My king's daughter! Now I have found her and won her! Hei! Now the palace shall rise, deeply founded! [*He seizes his ax and moves away; at the same moment an* OLD-LOOKING WOMAN, *in a tattered green gown, comes out from the wood; an* UGLY BRAT, *with an ale flagon in his hand, limps after, holding onto her skirt.*]

WOMAN. Good evening, Peer Lightfoot!

PEER. What is it? Who's there?

WOMAN. Old friends of yours, Peer Gynt! My home is near by. We are neighbors.

PEER. Indeed? That is more than I know.

WOMAN. Even as your hut was builded, mine built itself too.

PEER [*going*]. I'm in haste—

WOMAN. Yes, that you are always, my lad; but I'll trudge behind you and catch you at last.

PEER. You're mistaken, good woman!

WOMAN. I was so before; I was when you promised such mighty fine things.

PEER. I promised? What devil's own nonsense is this?

WOMAN. You've forgotten the night when you drank with my sire? You've forgot?

PEER. I've forgot what I never have known. What's this that you prate of? When last did we meet?

WOMAN. When last we met was when first we met. [*To the* BRAT.] Give your father a drink; he is thirsty, I'm sure.

PEER. Father? You're drunk, woman! Do you call him—

WOMAN. I should think you might well know the pig by its skin! Why, where are your eyes? Can't you see that he's lame in his shank, just as you too are lame in your soul?

Peer. Would you have me believe——

Woman. Would you wiggle away?

Peer. This long-legged urchin!

Woman. He's shot up apace.

Peer. Dare you, you troll snout, ther on me?

Woman. Come now, Peer Gynt, 're as rude as an ox! [*Weeping.*] t my fault if no longer I'm fair as I was when you lured me on hillside and lea? Last fall, in my labor, the Fiend held my back, and so 'twas no wonder I came out a fright. But if you would see me as fair as before, you have only to turn yonder girl out of doors, drive her clean out of your sight and your mind; do but this, dear my love, and I'll soon lose my snout!

Peer. Begone from me, troll witch!

Woman. Ay, see if I do!

Peer. I'll split your skull open!

Woman. Just try if you dare! Hoho, Peer Gynt, I've no fear of blows! Be sure I'll return every day of the year. I'll set the door ajar and peep in at you both. When you're sitting with your girl on the fireside bench—when you're tender, Peer Gynt—when you'd pet and caress her—I'll seat myself by you and ask for my share. She there and I—we will take you by turns. Farewell, dear my lad, you can marry tomorrow!

Peer. You nightmare of hell!

Woman. By the bye, I forgot! You must rear your own youngster, you light-footed scamp! Little imp, will you go to your father?

Brat [*spits at him*]. Faugh! I'll chop you with my hatchet; only wait, only wait!

Woman [*kisses the* Brat]. What a head he has got on his shoulders, the dear! You'll be father's living image when once you're a man!

Peer [*stamping*]. Oh, would you were as far——

Woman. —as we now are near?

Peer [*clenching his hands*]. And all this——

Woman. —for nothing but thoughts and desires! It is hard on you, Peer!

Peer. It is worst for another! Solveig, my fairest, my purest gold!

Woman. Oh! ay, 'tis the guiltless must smart, said the devil; his mother boxed his ears when his father was drunk! [*She trudges off into the thicket with the* Brat, *who throws the flagon at* Peer Gynt.]

Peer [*after a long silence*]. The Boyg said, "Go roundabout!"—so one must here. There fell my fine palace, with crash and clatter! There's a wall around her whom I stood so near; of a sudden all's ugly—my joy has grown old. Roundabout, lad! There's no way to be found right through all this from where you stand to her. Right through? Hm, surely there should be one. There's a text on repentance, unless I mistake. But what? What is it? I haven't the book, I've forgotten it mostly, and here there is none that can guide me aright in the pathless wood. Repentance? And maybe 'twould take whole years ere I fought my way through. 'Twere a meager life, that. To shatter what's radiant and lovely and pure and clinch it together in fragments and shards? You can do it with a fiddle but not with a bell. Where you'd have the sward green you must mind not to trample. 'Twas nought but a lie though, that witch-snout business! Now all that foulness is well out of sight. Ay, out of sight, maybe, not out of mind. Thoughts will sneak stealthily in at my heel. Ingrid! And the three, they that danced on the heights! Will they too want to join us? With vixenish spite will they claim to be folded, like her, to my breast, to be tenderly lifted on outstretched arms? Roundabout, lad; though my arms were as long as the root of the fir or the pine tree's stem—I think even then I should hold her too near, to set her down pure and untarnished again. I must roundabout here, then, as best I may, and see that it brings me nor gain nor loss. One must put such things from one and try to forget. [*Goes a few steps toward the hut but stops again.*] Go in after this? So befouled and disgraced? Go in with that troll rabble after me still? Speak, yet be silent; confess, yet conceal? [*Throws away his ax.*] It's a holy-day evening. For me to keep tryst, such as now I am, would be sacrilege.

SOL. [*in the doorway*]. Are you coming?

PEER [*half aloud*]. Roundabout!

SOL. What?

PEER. You must wait. It is dark, and I've something heavy to fetch.

SOL. Wait; I will help you; the burden we'll share.

PEER. No, stay where you are! I must bear it alone.

SOL. But don't go too far, dear!

PEER. Be patient, my girl; be my way long or short—you must wait.

SOL. [*nodding to him as he goes*]. Yes, I'll wait!

[PEER GYNT *goes down the wood path.* SOLVEIG *remains standing in the open half door.*]

SCENE—ASE'S *room. Evening. The room is lighted by a wood fire on the open hearth. A cat is lying on a chair at the foot of the bed.*

ASE *lies in the bed, fumbling about restlessly with her hands on the coverlet.*

ASE. Oh, Lord my God, isn't he coming? The time drags so heavily on. I have no one to send with a message, and I've much, oh, so much, to say. I haven't a moment to lose now! So quickly! Who could have foreseen! Oh me, if I only were certain I'd not been too strict with him!

PEER [*enters*]. Good evening!

ASE. The Lord give you gladness! You've come then, my boy, my dear! But how dare you show face in the valley? You know your life's forfeit here.

PEER. Oh, life must e'en go as it may go; I felt that I must look in.

ASE. Ay, now Kari is put to silence, and I can depart in peace.

PEER. Depart? Why, what are you saying? Where is it you think to go?

ASE. Alas, Peer, the end is nearing: I have but a short time left.

PEER [*writhing and walking toward the back of the room*]. See there, now! I'm fleeing from trouble; I thought at least *here* I'd be free! Are your hands and your feet a-cold, then?

ASE. Ay, Peer, all will soon be o'er. When you see that my eyes are glazing you must close them carefully. And then you must see to my coffin, and be sure it's a fine one, dear. Ah no, by the bye——

PEER. Be quiet! There's time yet to think of that.

ASE. Ay, ay. [*Looks restlessly around the room.*] Here you see the little they've left us! It's like them, just.

PEER [*with a writhe*]. Again! [*Harshly.*] Well, I know it was my fault. What's the use of reminding me?

Ase. You! No, that accursed liquor, from that all mischief came! Dear my boy, you know you'd been drinking, and then no one knows what he does; and besides, you'd been riding the reindeer; no wonder your head was turned!

Peer. Ay, ay; of that yarn enough now. Enough of the whole affair. All that's heavy we'll let stand over till after—some other day. [*Sits on the edge of the bed.*] Now, Mother, we'll chat together, but only of this and that—forget what's awry and crooked and all that is sharp and sore. Why, see now, the same old pussy; so she is alive then still?

Ase. She makes such a noise o' nights now; you know what that bodes, my boy!

Peer [*changing the subject*]. What news is there here in the parish?

Ase [*smiling*]. There's something about, they say, a girl who would fain to the uplands——

Peer [*hastily*]. Mads Moen, is he content?

Ase. They say that she hears and heeds not the old people's prayers and tears. You ought to look in and see them; you, Peer, might perhaps bring help.

Peer. The smith, what's become of him now?

Ase. Don't talk of that filthy smith. Her name I would rather tell you, the name of the girl, you know——

Peer. No, now we will chat together, but only of this and that—forget what's awry and crooked and all that is sharp and sore. Are you thirsty? I'll fetch you water. Can you stretch you? The bed is short. Let me see—if I don't believe, now, it's the bed that I had when a boy! Do you mind, dear, how oft in the evenings you sat at my bedside here and spread the fur coverlet o'er me and sang many a lilt and lay?

Ase. Ay, mind you? And then we played sledges when your father was far abroad. The coverlet served for sledge apron and the floor for an icebound fiord.

Peer. Ah, but the best of all, though —Mother, you mind that too?—the best was the fleet-foot horses——

Ase. Ay, think you that I've forgot? It was Kari's cat that we borrowed; it sat on the log-scooped chair——

Peer. To the castle west of the moon and the castle east of the sun, to Soria-Moria Castle the road ran both high and low. A stick that we found in the closet, for a whip shaft you made it serve.

Ase. Right proudly I perked on the box seat——

Peer. Ay, ay; you threw loose the reins and kept turning round as we traveled and asked me if I was cold. God bless you, ugly old Mother—you were ever a kindly soul! What's hurting you now?

Ase. My back aches, because of the hard, bare boards.

Peer. Stretch yourself; I'll support you. There now, you're lying soft.

Ase [*uneasily*]. No, Peer, I'd be moving!

Peer. Moving?

Ase. Ay, moving; 'tis ever my wish.

Peer. Oh, nonsense! Spread o'er you the bed fur. Let me sit at your bedside here. There; now we'll shorten the evening with many a lilt and lay.

Ase. Best bring from the closet the prayerbook; I feel so uneasy of soul.

Peer. In Soria-Moria Castle the king and the prince give a feast. On the sledge cushions lie and rest you; I'll drive you there over the heath.

ASE. But, Peer dear, am I invited?

PEER. Ay, that we are, both of us. [*He throws a string round the back of the chair on which the cat is lying, takes up a stick and seats himself at the foot of the bed.*] Gee-up! Will you stir yourself, Black Boy? Mother, you're not a-cold? Ay, ay; by the pace one knows it, when Grane begins to go!

ASE. Why, Peer, what is it that's ringing?

PEER. The glittering sledge bells, dear!

ASE. Oh, mercy, how hollow it's rumbling!

PEER. We're just driving over a fiord.

ASE. I'm afraid! What is that I hear rushing and sighing so strange and wild?

PEER. It's the sough of the pine trees, Mother, on the heath. Do you but sit still.

ASE. There's a sparkling and gleaming afar now; whence comes all that blaze of light?

PEER. From the castle's windows and doorways. Don't you hear, they are dancing?

ASE. Yes.

PEER. Outside the door stands Saint Peter and prays you to enter in.

ASE. Does he greet us?

PEER. He does, with honor, and pours out the sweetest wine.

ASE. Wine! Has he cakes as well, Peer?

PEER. Cakes? Ay, a heaped-up dish. And the dean's wife is getting ready your coffee and your dessert.

ASE. Oh, Christ, shall we two come together?

PEER. As freely as ever you will.

ASE. Oh deary, Peer, what a frolic you're driving me to, poor soul!

PEER [*cracking his whip*]. Gee-up; will you stir yourself, Black Boy!

ASE. Peer dear, you're driving right?

PEER [*cracking his whip again*]. Ay, broad is the way.

ASE. This journey, it makes me so weak and tired.

PEER. There's the cattle rising before us; the drive will be over soon.

ASE. I will lie back and close my eyes then, and trust me to you, my boy!

PEER. Come up with you, Grane, my trotter! In the castle the throng is great; they bustle and swarm to the gateway. Peer Gynt and his mother are here! What say you, Master Saint Peter? Shall Mother not enter in? You may search a long time, I tell you, ere you find such an honest old soul. Myself I don't want to speak of; I can turn at the castle gate. If you'll treat me, I'll take it kindly; if not, I'll go off just as pleased. I have made up as many flimflams as the devil at the pulpit desk and called my old mother a hen, too, because she would cackle and crow. But her you shall honor and reverence and make her at home indeed; there comes not a soul to beat her from the parishes nowadays. Ho-ho; here comes God the Father! Saint Peter! you're in for it now! [*In a deep voice.*] "Have done with these jack-in-office airs, sir; Mother Ase shall enter free!" [*Laughs loudly and turns toward his mother.*] Ay, didn't I know what would happen? Now they dance to another tune! [*Uneasily.*] Why, what makes your eyes so glassy? Mother! Have you gone out of your wits? [*Goes to the head of the bed.*] You mustn't lie there and stare so! Speak, Mother; it's I, your boy! [*Feels her forehead and hands cautiously, then throws the string on the chair and says softly.*] Ay, ay! You can rest yourself, Grane; for even now the journey's done. [*Closes her eyes and bends over her.*] For all of your days I thank you, for beatings and lullabys! But see, you must thank me back now. [*Presses his cheek against her mouth.*] There, that was the driver's fare.

COTTER'S WIFE [*entering*]. What? Peer! Ah, then we are over the worst of the sorrow and need! Dear Lord, but she's sleeping soundly—or can she be?

PEER. Hush; she is dead.

[KARI *weeps beside the body;* PEER GYNT *walks up and down the room for some time; at last he stops beside the bed.*]

PEER. See Mother buried with honor. I must try to fare forth from here.

KARI. Are you faring afar?

PEER. To seaward.

KARI. So far!

PEER. Ay, and further still. [*He goes.*]

ACT IV

SCENE—*On the southwest coast of Morocco. A palm grove. Under an awning, on ground covered with matting, a table spread for dinner. Further back in the grove hammocks are slung. In the offing lies a steam yacht, flying the Norwegian and American colors. A jolly boat drawn up on the beach. It is toward sunset.*

PEER GYNT, *a handsome middle-aged gentleman in an elegant travelling dress, with a gold-rimmed double eyeglass hanging at his waistcoat, is doing the honors at the head of the table.* MR COTTON, MONSIEUR BALLON, HERR VON EBERKOPF *and* HERR TRUMPETERSTRALE *are seated at the table finishing dinner.*

PEER. Drink, gentlemen! If man is made for pleasure, let him take his fill then. You know 'tis written: Lost is lost, and gone is gone. What may I hand you?

TRUMPET. As host you're princely, Brother Gynt!

PEER. I share the honor with my cash, with cook and steward.

MR COT. Very well, let's pledge a toast to all the four!

MONSIEUR BAL. Monsieur, you have a *gout*, a *ton*, that nowadays is seldom met with among men living *en garçon* —a certain—what's the word?

VON EBER. A dash, a tinge of free-soul contemplation and cosmopolitanization, an outlook through the cloudy rifts by narrow prejudice unhemmed, a stamp of high illumination, an *Ur-Natur*, with lore of life, to crown the trilogy, united. *Nicht wahr*, monsieur, 'twas that you meant?

MONSIEUR BAL. Yes, very possibly; not quite so loftily it sounds in French.

VON EBER. Ei was! That language is so stiff. But the phenomenon's final cause if we would seek——

PEER. It's found already. The reason is that I'm unmarried. Yes, gentlemen, completely clear that matter is. What should a man be? *Himself*, is my concise reply. He should regard *himself* and *his*. But *can* he, as a sumpter mule for others' woe and others' weal?

VON EBER. But this same in-and-for-yourselfness, I'll answer for't, has cost you strife.

PEER. Ah! yes indeed; in former days; but always I came off with honor. Yet one time I ran very near to being trapped against my will. I was a brisk and handsome lad, and she to whom my heart was given, she was of royal family——

MONSIEUR BAL. Of royal——

PEER [*carelessly*]. One of those old stocks, you know the kind.

TRUMPET. [*thumping the table*]. Those noble trolls!

PEER [*shrugging his shoulders*]. Old fossil highnesses who make it their pride to keep plebeian blots excluded from their line's escutcheon.

MR COT. Then nothing came of the affair?

MONSIEUR BAL. The family opposed the marriage?

PEER. Far from it!

MONSIEUR BAL. Ah!

PEER [*with forbearance*]. You understand that certain circumstances made for their marrying us without delay. But, truth to tell, the whole affair was, first to last, distasteful to me. I'm finical in certain ways and like to stand on my own feet. And when my father-in-law came out with delicately veiled demands that I should change my name and station and undergo ennoblement, with much else that was most distasteful, not to say quite inacceptable—why, then I gracefully withdrew, point-blank declined his ultimatum—and so renounced my youthful bride. [*Drums on the table with a devout air.*] Yes, yes; there is a ruling Fate! On that we mortals may rely, and 'tis a comfortable knowledge.

MONSIEUR BAL. And so the matter ended, eh?

PEER. Oh no, far otherwise I found it; for busybodies mixed themselves, with furious outcries, in the business. The juniors of the clan were worst; with seven of them I fought a duel. That time I never shall forget, though I came through it all in safety. It cost me blood, but that same blood attests the value of my person and points encouragingly toward the wise control of Fate aforesaid.

VON EBER. Your outlook on the course of life exalts you to the rank of thinker. Whilst the mere commonplace empiric sees separately the scattered scenes and to the last goes groping on, you in one glance can focus all things. One norm to all things you apply. You point each random rule of life, till one and all diverge like rays from one full-orbed philosophy. And you have never been to college?

PEER. I am, as I've already said, exclusively a self-taught man. Methodically naught I've learned, but I have thought and speculated and done much desultory reading. I started somewhat late in life, and then, you know, it's rather hard to plow ahead through page on page and take in all of everything. I've done my history piecemeal; I never have had time for more. And, as one needs in days of trial some certainty to place one's trust in, I took religion intermittently. That way it goes more smoothly down. One should not read to swallow all but rather see what one has use for.

MR COT. Ay, that is practical!

PEER [*lights a cigar*]. Dear friends, just think of my career in general. In what case came I to the West? A poor young fellow, empty-handed. I had to battle sore for bread; trust me,

I often found it hard. But life, my friends, ah, life is dear, and, as the phrase goes, death is bitter. Well! Luck, you see, was kind to me; old Fate, too, was accommodating. I prospered, and by versatility I prospered better still and better. In ten years' time I bore the name of Croesus 'mongst the Charleston shippers. My fame flew wide from port to port, and fortune sailed on board my vessels——

MR COT. What did you trade in?

PEER. I did most in Negro slaves for Carolina and idol images for China.

MONSIEUR BAL. Fi donc!

TRUMPET. The devil, Uncle Gynt!

PEER. You think, no doubt, the business hovered on the outer edge of the allowable? Myself, I felt the same thing keenly. It struck me even as odious. But, trust me, when you've once begun it's hard to break away again. At any rate it's no light thing, in such a vast trade enterprise that keeps whole thousands in employ, to break off wholly, once for all. That "once for all" I can't abide, but own, upon the other side, that I have always felt respect for what are known as consequences and that to overstep the bounds has ever somewhat daunted me. Besides, I had begun to age, was getting on toward the fifties; my hair was slowly growing grizzled; and, though my health was excellent, yet painfully the thought beset me: Who knows how soon the hour may strike, the jury verdict be delivered that parts the sheep and goats asunder? What could I do? To stop the trade with China was impossible. A plan I hit on—opened straightway a new trade with the selfsame land. I shipped off idols every spring, each autumn sent forth missionaries, supplying them with all they needed, as stockings, Bibles, rum and rice.

MR COT. Yes, at a profit?

PEER. Why, of course. It prospered. Dauntlessly they toiled. For every idol that was sold they got a coolie well baptized, so that the effect was neutralized. The mission field lay never fallow, for still the idol propaganda the missionaries held in check.

MR COT. Well, but the African commodities?

PEER. There, too, my ethics won the day. I saw the traffic was a wrong one for people of a certain age. One may drop off before one dreams of it. And then there were the thousand pitfalls laid by the philanthropic camp; besides, of course, the hostile cruisers and all the wind-and-weather risks. All this together won the day. I thought: Now, Peter, reef your sails; see to it you amend your faults! So in the South I bought some land and kept the last meat importation, which chanced to be a superfine one. They throve so, grew so fat and sleek, that 'twas a joy to me and them too. Yes, without boasting, I may say I acted as a father to them—and found my profit in so doing. I built them schools too, so that virtue might uniformly be maintained at a certain general *niveau,* and kept strict watch that never its thermometer should sink below it. Now, furthermore, from all this business I've beat a definite retreat; I've sold the whole plantation and its tale of livestock, hide and hair. At parting, too, I served around, to big and little, gratis grog, so men and women all got drunk and widows got their snuff as well. So that is why I trust—provided the saying is not idle breath: Whoso does not do ill does good—my former errors are forgotten, and I, much more than most, can hold my misdeeds balanced by my virtues.

VON EBER [*clinking glasses with him*]. How strengthening it is to hear a principle thus acted out, freed from the night of theory, unshaken by the outward ferment!

PEER [*who has been drinking freely during the preceding passages*]. We Northland men know how to carry our battle through! The key to the art of life's affairs is simply this: to keep one's ear close shut against the ingress of one dangerous viper.

MR COT. What sort of viper, pray, dear friend?

PEER. A little one that slyly wiles you to tempt the irretrievable. [*Drinking again.*] The essence of the art of daring, the art of bravery in act, is this: To stand with choice-free foot amid the treacherous snares of life—to know for sure that other days remain beyond the day of battle—to know that ever in the rear a bridge for your retreat stands open. This theory has borne me on, has given my whole career its color; and this same theory I inherit, a race gift, from my childhood's home.

MONSIEUR BAL. You are Norwegian?

PEER. Yes, by birth; but cosmopolitan in spirit. For fortune such as I've enjoyed I have to thank America. My amply furnished library I owe to Germany's later schools. From France, again, I get my waistcoats, my manners and my spice of wit—from England an industrious hand and keen sense for my own advantage. The Jew has taught me how to wait. Some taste for *dolce far niente* I have received from Italy—and one time, in a perilous pass, to eke the measure of my days, I had recourse to Swedish steel.

TRUMPET. [*lifting up his glass*]. Ay, Swedish steel!

VON EBER. The weapon's wielder demands our homage first of all! [*They clink glasses and drink with him. The wine begins to go to his head.*]

MR COT. All this is very good indeed; but, sir, I'm curious to know what with your gold you think of doing.

PEER [*smiling*]. Hm; doing? Eh?

ALL FOUR [*coming closer*]. Yes, let us hear!

PEER. Well, first of all I want to travel. You see, that's why I shipped you four, to keep me company at Gibraltar. I needed such a dancing choir of friends around my gold calf altar——

VON EBER. Most witty!

MR COT. Well, but no one hoists his sails for nothing but the sailing. Beyond all doubt you have a goal, and that is——?

PEER. To be emperor.

ALL FOUR. What?

PEER [*nodding*]. Emperor!

FOUR. Where?

PEER. O'er all the world.

MONSIEUR BAL. But how, friend?

PEER. By the might of gold! That plan is not at all a new one; it's been the soul of my career. Even as a boy I swept in dreams far o'er the ocean on a cloud. I soared with train and golden scabbard—and flopped down on all fours again. But still my goal, my friends, stood fast. There is a text, or else a saying, somewhere, I don't remember where, that if you gained the whole wide world but lost *yourself*, your gain were but a garland on a cloven skull. That is the text—or something like it, and that remark is sober truth.

VON EBER. But what, then, is the Gyntish Self?

PEER. The world behind my forehead's arch, in force of which I'm no one else than I, no more than God's the devil.

TRUMPET. I understand now where you're aiming!

MONSIEUR BAL. Thinker sublime!

VON EBER. Exalted poet!

PEER [*more and more elevated*]. The Gyntish Self—it is the host of wishes, appetites, desires—the Gyntish Self, it is the sea of fancies, exigencies, claims, all that, in short, makes *my* breast heave and whereby I, as I, exist. But as our Lord requires the clay to constitute him God o' the world, so I, too, stand in need of gold if I as emperor would figure.

MONSIEUR BAL. You have the gold, though!

PEER. Not enough. Ay, maybe for a nine days' flourish, as emperor *à la* Lippe-Detmold. But I must be myself *en bloc*, must be the Gynt of all the planet, Sir Gynt throughout, from top to toe!

MONSIEUR BAL. [*enraptured*]. Possess the earth's most exquisite beauty!

VON EBER. All century-old Johannisberger!

TRUMPET. And all the blades of Charles the Twelfth!

MR COT. But first a profitable opening for business——

PEER. That's already found; our anchoring here supplied me with it. Tonight we set off northward ho! The papers I received on board have brought me tidings of importance! [*Rises with uplifted glass.*] It seems that Fortune ceaselessly aids him who has the pluck to seize it.

GUESTS. Well? Tell us!

PEER. Greece is in revolt.

ALL FOUR [*springing up*]. What! Greece?

PEER. The Greeks have risen in Hellas.

FOUR. Hurrah!

PEER. And Turkey's in a fix! [*Empties his glass.*]

MONSIEUR BAL. To Hellas! Glory's gate stands open! I'll help them with the sword of France!

VON EBER. And I with war whoops —from a distance.

MR COT. And I as well—by taking contracts!

TRUMPET. Lead on! I'll find again in Bender the world-renowned spur-strap buckles!

MONSIEUR BAL. [*falling on* PEER GYNT's *neck*]. Forgive me, friend, that I at first misjudged you quite!

VON EBER. [*pressing his hands*]. I, stupid hound, took you for next door to a scoundrel!

MR COT. Too strong that; only for a fool——

TRUMPET. [*trying to kiss him*]. I, Uncle, for a specimen of Yankee riff-raff's meanest spawn! Forgive me!

VON EBER. We've been in the dark——

PEER. What stuff is this?

VON EBER. We now see gathered in glory all the Gyntish host of wishes, appetites and desires!

MONSIEUR BAL. [*admiringly*]. So *this* is being Monsieur Gynt!

VON EBER. [*in the same tone*]. This I call being Gynt with honor!

PEER. But tell me——

MONSIEUR BAL. Don't understand?

PEER. May I be hanged if I begin to!

MONSIEUR BAL. What? Are you not

upon your way to join the Greeks with ship and money?

PEER [*contemptuously*]. No, many thanks! I side with strength and lend my money to the Turks.

MONSIEUR BAL. Impossible!

VON EBER. Witty, but a jest!

PEER [*after a short silence, leaning on a chair and assuming a dignified mien*]. Come, gentlemen, I think it best we part before the last remains of friendship melt away like smoke. Who nothing owns will lightly risk it. When in the world one scarce commands the strip of earth one's shadow covers, one's born to serve as food for powder. But when a man stands safely landed, as I do, then his stake is greater. Go you to Hellas. I will put you ashore and arm you gratis too. The more you eke the flames of strife, the better will it serve my purpose. Strike home for freedom and for right! Fight! Storm! Make hell hot for the Turks—and gloriously end your days upon the Janissaries lances. But I—excuse me—[*slaps his pocket*] —I have cash and am myself, Sir Peter Gynt. [*Puts up his sunshade and goes into the grove where the hammocks are partly visible.*]

TRUMPET. The swinish cur!

MONSIEUR BAL. No taste for glory!

MR COT. Oh, glory's neither here nor there, but think of the enormous profits we'd reap if Greece should free herself.

MONSIEUR BAL. I saw myself a conqueror, by lovely Grecian maids encircled.

TRUMPET. Grasped in my Swedish hands I saw the great, heroic spurstrap buckles!

VON EBER. I my gigantic Fatherland's culture saw spread o'er earth and sea!

MR COT. The worst's the loss in solid cash. Goddam! I scarce can keep from weeping! I saw me owner of Olympus. If to its fame the mountain answers, there must be veins of copper in it that could be opened up again. And furthermore, that stream Castalia, which people talk so much about, with fall on fall, at lowest reckoning, must mean a thousand horsepower good!

TRUMPET. Still I will go! My Swedish sword is worth far more than Yankee gold!

MR COT. Perhaps; but jammed into the ranks, amid the press we'd all be drowned, and then where would the profit be?

MONSIEUR BAL. Accurst! So near to fortune's summit and now stopped short beside its grave!

MR COT. [*shakes his fist toward the yacht*]. That long black chest holds coffered up the nabob's golden nigger sweat!

VON EBER. A royal notion! Quick! Away! It's all up with his empire now! Hurrah!

MONSIEUR BAL. What would you?

VON EBER. Seize the power! The crew can easily be bought. On board then! I annex the yacht!

MR COT. You—what?

VON EBER. I grab the whole concern! [*Goes down to the jolly boat.*]

MR COT. Why, then, self-interest commands me to grab my share. [*Goes after him.*]

TRUMPET. What scoundrelism!

MONSIEUR BAL. A scurvy business—but—*enfin!* [*Follows the others.*]

TRUMPET. I'll have to follow, I suppose—but I protest to all the world! [*Follows.*]

SCENE—*Another part of the coast. Moonlight with drifting clouds. The yacht is seen far out, under full steam.* PEER GYNT *comes running along the beach, now pinching his arms, now gazing out to sea.*

PEER. A nightmare! Delusion! I'll soon be awake! She's standing to sea! And at furious speed! Mere delusion! I'm sleeping! I'm dizzy and drunk! [*Clenches his hands.*] It's not possible I should be going to die! [*Tearing his hair.*] A dream! I'm determined it shall be a dream! Oh, horror! It's only too real, worse luck! My brute beasts of friends! Do but hear me, oh Lord! Since thou art so wise and so righteous! Oh! judge! [*With upstretched arms.*] It is *I*, Peter Gynt! Oh, our Lord, give but heed! Hold thy hand o'er me, Father, or else I must perish! Make them back the machine! Make them lower the gig! Stop the robbers! Make something go wrong with the rigging! Hear me! Let other folks' business lie over! The world can take care of itself for the time! I'm blessed if He hears me! He's deaf as His wont is! Here's a nice thing! A God that is bankrupt of help! [*Beckons upward.*] Hist! I've abandoned the nigger plantation! And missionaries I've exported to Asia! Surely one good turn should be worth another! Oh, help me on board!

[*A jet of fire shoots into the air from the yacht, followed by thick clouds of smoke; a hollow report is heard.* PEER GYNT *utters a shriek and sinks down on the sands. Gradually the smoke clears away; the ship has disappeared.*]

PEER [*softly, with a pale face*]. That's the sword of wrath! In a crack to the bottom, every soul, man and mouse! Oh, forever blest be the lucky chance— [*With emotion.*] A chance? No, no, it was more than chance. I was to be rescued and they to perish. Oh, thanks and praise for that Thou has kept me, hast cared for me, spite of all my sins! [*Draws a deep breath.*] What a marvelous feeling of safety and peace it gives one to know oneself especially shielded! But the desert! What about food and drink? Oh, something I'm sure to find. *He'll* see to that. There's no cause for alarm. [*Loud and insinuatingly.*] He would never allow a poor little sparrow like me to perish! Be but lowly of spirit. And give Him time. Leave it all in the Lord's hands and don't be cast down. [*With a start of terror.*] Can that be a lion that growled in the reeds? [*His teeth chattering.*] No, it wasn't a lion. [*Mustering up courage.*] A lion, forsooth! Those beasts, they'll take care to keep out of the way. They know it's no joke to fall foul of their betters. They have instinct to guide them; they feel, what's a fact, that it's dangerous playing with elephants. But all the same— I must find a tree. There's a grove of acacias and palms over there; if I once can climb up, I'll be sheltered and safe—most of all if I knew but a psalm or two. [*Clambers up.*] Morning and evening are not alike; that text has been oft enough weighed and pondered. [*Seats himself comfortably.*] How blissful to feel so uplifted in spirit. To think nobly is more than to know oneself rich. Only trust in Him. He knows well what share of the chalice of need I can bear to drain. He takes fatherly thought for my personal weal. [*Casts a glance over the sea and whispers with a sigh.*] But economical—no, that He isn't!

SCENE—*Night. An encampment of*

Moroccan troops on the edge of the desert. Watch fires, with Soldiers *resting by them.*

A Slave [*enters, tearing his hair*]. Gone is the emperor's milk-white charger!

Another Slave [*enters, rending his garments*]. The emperor's sacred robes are stolen!

An Officer [*enters*]. A hundred stripes upon the foot soles for all who fail to catch the robber!

[*The troopers mount their horses and gallop away in every direction.*]

Scene—*Daybreak. The grove of acacias and palms.* Peer Gynt *in his tree with a broken branch in his hand, trying to beat off a swarm of monkeys.*

Peer. Confound it! A most disagreeable night. [*Laying about him.*] Are you there again? This is most accursed! Now they're throwing fruit. No, it's something else. A loathsome beast is your Barbary ape! The Scripture says: Thou shalt watch and fight. But I'm blest if I can; I am heavy and tired. [*Is again attacked; impatiently.*] I must put a stopper upon this nuisance! I must see and get hold of one of these scamps, get him hung and skinned and then dress myself up, as best I may, in his shaggy hide, that the others may take me for one of themselves. What are we mortals? Motes, no more; and it's wisest to follow the fashion a bit. Again a rabble! They throng and swarm. Off with you! Shoo! They go on as though crazy. If only I had a false tail to put on now—only something to make me a bit like a beast. What now? There's a pattering over my head! [*Looks up.*] It's the grandfather ape—with his fists full of filth! [*Huddles together apprehensively and keeps still for a while. The ape makes a motion;* Peer Gynt *begins coaxing and wheedling him, as he might a dog.*] Ay—are you there, my good old Bus! He's a good beast, he is! He will listen to reason! He wouldn't throw; I should think not, indeed! It is me! Pip-pip! We are first-rate friends! Ai-ai! Don't you hear, I can talk your language? Bus and I, we are kinsfolk, you see; Bus shall have sugar tomorrow! The beast! The whole cargo on top of me! Ugh, how disgusting! Or perhaps it was food? 'Twas in taste indefinable, and taste's for the most part a matter of habit. What thinker is it who somewhere says: You must spit and trust to the force of habit? Now here come the small fry! [*Hits and slashes around him.*] It's really too bad that man, who by rights is the lord of creation, should find himself forced to—— O! murder! murder! The old one was bad, but the youngsters are worse!

Scene—*Early morning. A stony region, with a view out over the desert. On one side a cleft in the hill and a cave.* A Thief *and a* Receiver *hidden in the cleft, with the emperor's horse and robes. The horse, richly caparisoned, is tied to a stone. Horsemen are seen afar off.*

Thief. The tongues of the lances all flickering and flashing—see, see!

Receiver. Already my head seems to roll on the sand plain! Woe, woe!

Thief [*folds his arms over his breast*]. My father he thieved; so his son must be thieving.

Receiver. My father received; so his son keeps receiving.

Thief. Thy lot shalt thou bear still; thyself shalt thou be still.

Receiver [*listening*]. Steps in the brushwood! Flee, flee! But where?

Thief. The cavern is deep and the Prophet great! [*They make off, leaving the booty behind them. The horsemen gradually disappear in the distance.*]

Peer [*enters, cutting a reed whistle*]. What a delectable morningtide! The dung beetle's rolling his ball in the dust; the snail creeps out of his dwelling house. The morning; ay, it has gold in its mouth. It's a wonderful power, when you think of it, that Nature has given to the light of day. One feels so secure and so much more courageous–one would gladly, at need, take a bull by the horns. What a stillness all round! Ah, the joys of Nature–strange enough I should never have prized them before. Why go and imprison oneself in a city, for no end but just to be bored by the mob? Just look how the lizards are whisking about, snapping and thinking of nothing at all. What innocence ev'n in the life of the beasts! Each fulfills the Creator's behest unimpeachably, preserving its own special stamp undefaced; is itself, both in sport and in strife, itself, as it was at his primal. Be! [*Puts on his eyeglasses.*] A toad. In the middle of a sandstone block. Petrification all round him. His head alone peering. There he's sitting and gazing as though through a window at the world and is–to himself–enough. [*Reflectively.*] Enough? To himself? Where is it that's written? I've read it, in youth, in some so-called classic. In the family prayerbook? Or Solomon's Proverbs? Alas, I notice that, year by year, my memory for dates and for places is fading. [*Seats himself in the shade.*] Here's a cool spot to rest and to stretch out one's feet. Why, look, here are ferns growing–edible roots. [*Eats a little.*] 'Twould be fitter food for an animal, but the text says: Bridle the natural man! Furthermore it is written: The proud shall be humbled, and whoso abaseth himself, exalted. [*Uneasily.*] Exalted? Yes, that's what will happen with me; no other result can so much as be thought of. Fate will assist me away from this place and arrange matters so that I get a fresh start. This is only a trial; deliverance will follow–if only the Lord lets me keep my health. [*Dismisses his misgivings, lights a cigar, stretches himself and gazes out over the desert.*] What an enormous, limitless waste! Far in the distance an ostrich is striding. What can one fancy was really God's meaning in all of this voidness and deadness? This desert, bereft of all sources of life; this burned-up cinder, that profits no one; this patch of the world, that forever lies fallow; this corpse, that never, since earth's creation, has brought its Maker so much as thanks –why was it created? How spendthrift is Nature! Is that sea in the east there, that dazzling expanse all gleaming? It can't be; 'tis but a mirage. The sea's to the west; it lies piled up behind me, dammed out from the desert by a sloping ridge. [*A thought flashes through his mind.*] Dammed out? Then I could—— The ridge is narrow. Dammed out? It wants but a gap, a canal–like a flood of life would the waters rush in through the channel and fill the desert! Soon would the whole of yon red-hot grave spread forth, a breezy and rippling sea. The oases would rise in the midst, like islands; Atlas would tower in green cliffs on the north; sailing ships would, like stray birds on the wing, skim to the south, on the caravan's track. Life-giving breezes would scatter the choking vapors, and dew would distill from the clouds. People would build themselves town on town, and grass would grow green round the swaying palm trees. The southland, behind the Sahara's wall, would make a new seaboard for civilization. Steam would set Timbuctoo's factories spinning; Bornu would be colonized apace; the naturalist would pass safely through Habes in his railway car to the Upper Nile. In the midst of my sea, on a fat oasis, I will replant the Norwegian race; the Dalesman's blood is next door to royal; Arabic crossing will do the rest. Skirting a bay, on a shelving strand, I'll build the chief city, Peeropolis. The world is decrepit! Now comes the turn of Gyntiana, my virgin land! [*Springs up.*] Had I but capital, soon 'twould be done. A gold key to open the gate of the sea! A crusade against Death! The close-fisted old churl shall open the sack he lies brooding upon. Men rave about freedom in every land; like the ass in the ark, I will send out a cry o'er the world and will baptize to liberty the beautiful, thrall-bounden coasts that shall be. I must on! To find capital, eastward or west! My kingdom—well, half of it, say—for a horse! [*The horse in the cleft neighs.*] A horse! Ay, and robes! Jewels too—and a sword! [*Goes closer.*] It can't be! It is, though! But how? I have read, I don't quite know where, that the will can move mountains; but how about moving a horse as well? Pooh! Here stands the horse, that's a matter of fact; for the rest, why, *ab esse ad posse*, et cetera. [*Puts on the dress and looks down at it.*] Sir Peter—a Turk too, from top to toe! Well, one never knows what may happen to one. Gee-up, now, Grane, my trusty steed! [*Mounts the horse.*] Gold-slipper stirrups beneath my feet! You may know the great by their riding gear! [*Gallops off into the desert.*]

SCENE—*The tent of an Arab chief, standing alone on an oasis.* PEER GYNT, *in his Eastern dress, resting on cushions. He is drinking coffee and smoking a long pipe.* ANITRA *and a bevy of* GIRLS *dancing and singing before him.*

CHORUS. The Prophet is come! The Prophet, the Lord, the All-Knowing One, to us, to us is he come, o'er the sand ocean riding! The Prophet, the Lord, the Unerring One, to us, to us is he come, o'er the sand ocean sailing! Wake the flute and the drum! The Prophet, the Prophet is come!

ANI. His courser is white as the milk is that streams in the rivers of Paradise. Bend every knee! Bow every head! His eyes are as bright-gleaming, mild-beaming stars. Yet none earthborn endureth the rays of those stars in their blinding splendor! Through the desert he came. Gold and pearl drops sprang forth on his breast. Where he rode there was light. Behind him was darkness; behind him raged drought and the simoom. He, the glorious one, came! Through the desert he came, like a mortal appareled. Kaaba, Kaaba stands void; he himself hath proclaimed it!

CHORUS. Wake the flute and the drum! The Phophet, the Prophet is come! [*They continue the dance, to soft music.*]

PEER. I have read it in print—and the saying is true—that no one's a prophet in his native land. This position is very much more to my mind than my life over there 'mong the

Charleston merchants. There was something hollow in the whole affair, something foreign at the bottom, something dubious behind. I was never at home in their company nor felt myself really one of the guild. What tempted me into that galley at all? To grub and grub in the bins of trade —as I think it all over I can't understand it; it *happened* so; that's the whole affair. To be oneself on a basis of gold is no better than founding one's house on the sand. For your watch and your ring and the rest the good people fawn on you, groveling to earth; they lift their hats to your jeweled breastpin, but your ring and your breastpin are not your person. A prophet; ay, that is a clearer position. At least one knows on what footing one stands. If you make a success, it's *yourself* that receives the ovation and not your pounds sterling and shillings. One is what one is, and no nonsense about it; one owes nothing to chance or to accident and needs neither license nor patent to lean on. A prophet; ay, that is the thing for me. And I slipped so utterly unawares into it—just by coming galloping over the desert and meeting these children of nature en route. The Prophet had come to them; so much was clear. It was really not my intent to deceive; there's a difference 'twixt lies and oracular answers; and then I can always withdraw again. I'm in no way bound; it's a simple matter; the whole thing is private, so to speak; I can go as I came; there's my horse ready saddled; I am master, in short, of the situation.

ANI. [*approaching from the tent door*]. Prophet and Master!

PEER. What would my slave?

ANI. The sons of the desert await at thy tent door; they pray for the light of thy countenance——

PEER. Stop! Say in the distance I'd have them assemble; say from the distance I hear all their prayers. Add that I suffer no menfolk in here! Men, my child, are a worthless crew —inveterate rascals you well may call them! Anitra, you can't think how shamelessly they have swind—— I mean they have sinned, my child! Well, enough now of that; you may dance for me, damsels! The Prophet would banish the memories that gall him.

THE GIRLS [*dancing*]. The Prophet is good! The Prophet is grieving for the ill that the sons of the dust have wrought! The Prophet is mild; to his mildness be praises; he opens to sinners his Paradise!

PEER [*his eyes following* ANITRA *during the dance*]. Legs as nimble as drumsticks flitting. She's a dainty morsel indeed, that wench! It's true she has somewhat extravagant contours—not quite in accord with the norms of beauty. But what is beauty? A mere convention—a coin made current by time and place. And just the extravagant seems most attractive when one of the normal has drunk one's fill. In the law-bound one misses all intoxication. Either plump to excess or excessively lean; either parlously young or portentously old; the medium is mawkish. Her feet—they are not altogether clean; no more are her arms; in especial one of them. But that is at bottom no drawback at all. I should rather call it a qualification—Anitra, come listen!

ANI. [*approaching*]. Thy handmaiden hears!

PEER. You are tempting, my daughter! The Prophet is touched. If you don't believe me, then hear the proof; I'll make you a houri in Paradise!

ANI. Impossible, Lord!

PEER. What? You think I am jesting? I'm in sober earnest, as true as I live!

ANI. But I haven't a soul.

PEER. Then of course you must get one!

ANI. How, Lord?

PEER. Just leave *me* alone for that; I shall look after your education. No soul? Why, truly you're not overbright, as the saying goes. I've observed it with pain. But pooh! for a soul you can always find room. Come here! Let me measure your brainpan, child. There is room, there is room, I was sure there was. It's true you never will penetrate very deep; to a *large* soul you'll scarcely attain—but never you mind; it won't matter a bit; you'll have plenty to carry you through with credit.

ANI. The Prophet is gracious——

PEER. You hesitate? Speak!

ANI. But I'd rather——

PEER. Say on; don't waste time about it!

ANI. I don't care so much about having a soul; give me rather——

PEER. What, child?

ANI. [*pointing to his turban*]. That lovely opal!

PEER [*enchanted, handing her the jewel*]. Anitra! Anitra! True daughter of Eve! I feel thee magnetic, for I am a man. And, as a much-esteemed author has phrased it: "Das Ewig-Weibliche zieht uns hinan!"

SCENE—*A moonlight night. The palm grove outside* ANITRA'S *tent.* PEER GYNT *is sitting beneath a tree with an Arabian lute in his hands. His beard and hair are clipped; he looks considerably younger.*

PEER [*plays and sings*]. I double-locked my Paradise and took its key with me. The north wind bore me seaward ho! while lovely women all forlorn wept on the ocean strand. Still southward, southward clove my keel the salt sea currents through. Where palms were swaying proud and fair, a garland round the ocean bight, I set my ship afire. I climbed aboard the desert ship, a ship on four stout legs. It foamed beneath the lashing whip; oh, catch me, I'm a flitting bird; I'm twittering on a bough! Anitra, thou 'rt the palm tree's must; that know I now full well! Ay, even the Angora goat-milk cheese is scarcely half such dainty fare, Anitra, ah, as thou! [*He hangs the lute over his shoulder and comes forward.*] Stillness! Is the fair one listening? Has she heard my little song? Peeps she from behind the curtain, veil and so forth cast aside? Hush! A sound as though a cork from a bottle burst amain! Now once more! And yet again! Love sighs, can it be? Or songs? No, it is distinctly snoring. Dulcet strain! Anitra sleepeth! Nightingale, thy warbling stay! Every sort of woe betide thee, if with gurgling trill thou darest—but, as says the text: Let be! Nightingale, thou art a singer; ah, even such an one am I. He, like me, ensnares with music tender, shrinking little hearts. Balmy night is made for music; music is our common sphere; in the act of singing, we are we, Peer Gynt and nightingale. And the maiden's very sleeping is my passion's crowning bliss; for the lips protruded o'er the beaker yet untasted quite—but she's coming, I declare! After all, it's best she should.

ANI. [*from the tent*]. Master, call'st thou in the night?

PEER. Yes indeed, the Prophet calls. I was wakened by the cat with a furious hunting hubbub——

ANI. Ah, not hunting noises, Master; it was something much, much worse.

PEER. What, then, was't?

ANI. Oh, spare me!

PEER. Speak.

ANI. Oh, I blush to——

PEER [*approaching*]. Was it, mayhap, that which filled me so completely when I let you have my opal?

ANI. [*horrified*]. Liken thee, O earth's great treasure, to a horrible old cat!

PEER. Child, from passion's standpoint viewed, many a tomcat and a prophet come to very much the same.

ANI. Master, jest like honey floweth from thy lips.

PEER. My little friend, you, like other maidens, judge great men by their outsides only. I am full of jest at bottom, most of all when we're alone. I am forced by my position to assume a solemn mask. Duties of the day constrain me; all the reckonings and worry that I have with one and all make me oft a cross-grained prophet, but it's only from the tongue out. Fudge, avaunt! En tête-à-tête I'm Peer—well, the man I am. Hei, away now with the prophet; me, myself, you have me here! [*Seats himself under a tree and draws her to him.*] Come, Anitra, we will rest us underneath the palm's green fan shade! I'll lie whispering, you'll lie smiling; afterward our roles exchange we; then shall your lips, fresh and balmy, to my smiling passion whisper!

ANI. [*lies down at his feet*]. All thy words are sweet as singing, though I understand but little. Master, tell me, can thy daughter catch a soul by listening?

PEER. Soul and spirit's light and knowledge, all in good time you shall have them. When in east, on rosy streamers, golden types print: Here is day—then, my child, I'll give you lessons; you'll be well brought up, no fear. But 'mid night's delicious stillness it were stupid if I should, with a threadbare wisdom's remnants, play the part of pedagogue. And the soul, moreover, is not, looked at properly, the main thing. It's the heart that really matters.

ANI. Speak, O Master! When thou speakest I see gleams, as though of opals!

PEER. Wisdom in extremes is folly; coward blossoms into tyrant; truth, when carried to excess, ends in wisdom written backward. Ay, my daughter, I'm forsworn as a dog if there are not folk with o'erfed souls on earth who shall scarce attain to clearness. Once I met with such a fellow, of the flock the very flower; and even he mistook his goal, losing sense in blatant sound. See the waste round this oasis. Were I but to swing my turban, I could force the ocean flood to fill up the whole concern. But I were a blockhead, truly, seas and land to go creating. Know you what it is to live?

ANI. Teach me!

PEER. It is to be wafted dry-shod down the stream of time, wholly, solely as oneself. Only in full manhood can I be the man I am, dear child! Aged eagle molts his plumage, aged fogy lags declining, aged dame has ne'er a tooth left, aged churl gets withered hands—one and all get withered souls. Youth! Ah, youth! I mean to reign, as a sultan, whole and fiery

—not on Gyntiana's shores, under trellised vines and palm leaves—but enthroned in the freshness of a woman's virgin thoughts. See you now, my little maiden, why I've graciously bewitched you—why I have your heart selected and established, so to speak, *there* my being's caliphate? All your longings shall be mine. I'm an autocrat in passion! You shall live for me alone. I'll be he who shall enthrall you like gold and precious stones. Should we part, then life is over—that is, *your* life, *nota bene!* Every inch and fiber of you, will-less, without yea or nay, I must know filled full of me. Midnight beauties of your tresses, all that's lovely to be named, shall, like Babylonian gardens, tempt your sultan to his tryst. After all, I don't complain, then, of your empty forehead vault. With a soul one's oft absorbed in contemplation of oneself. Listen, while we're on the subject—if you like it, faith, you shall have a ring about your ankle: 'twill be best for both of us. *I* will be your soul by proxy; for the rest why, *status quo.* [ANITRA *snores.*] What! She sleeps! Then has it glided bootless past her, all I've said? No; it marks my influence o'er her that she floats away in dreams on my love talk as it flows. [*Rises and lays trinkets in her lap.*] Here are jewels! Here are more! Sleep, Anitra! Dream of Peer. Sleep! In sleeping, you the crown have placed upon your emperor's brow! Victory on his person's basis has Peer Gynt this night achieved.

SCENE—*A caravan route. The oasis is seen far off in the background.* PETER GYNT *comes galloping across the desert on his white horse with* ANITRA *before him on his saddlebow.*

ANI. Let be, or I'll bite you!

PEER. You little rogue!

ANI. What would you?

PEER. What would I? Play hawk and dove! Run away with you! Frolic and frisk a bit!

ANI. For shame! An old prophet like you!

PEER. Oh, stuff! The prophet's not old at all, you goose! Do you think all this is a sign of age?

ANI. Let me go! I want to go home!

PEER. Coquette! What, home! To father-in-law! That would be fine! We madcap birds that have flown from the cage must never come into his sight again. Besides, my child, in the selfsame place it's wisest never to stay too long, for familiarity lessens respect; most of all when one comes as a prophet or such. One should show oneself glimpsewise and pass like a dream. Faith, 'twas time that the visit should come to an end. They're unstable of soul, are these sons of the desert; both incense and prayers dwindled off toward the end.

ANI. Yes, but *are* you a prophet?

PEER. Your emperor I am! [*Tries to kiss her.*] Why, just see now how coy the wee woodpecker is!

ANI. Give me that ring that you have on your finger.

PEER. Take, sweet Anitra, the whole of the trash!

ANI. Thy words are as songs! Oh, how dulcet their sound!

PEER. How blessed to know oneself loved to this pitch! I'll dismount! Like your slave, I will lead your palfrey! [*Hands her his riding whip and dismounts.*] There now, my rosebud, my exquisite flower! Here I'll go trudging my way through the sand till a sunstroke o'ertakes me and finishes me. I'm young, Anitra; bear that in mind! You mustn't be shocked at my escapades. Frolics and high jinks are youth's sole criterion! And so, if your intellect weren't so dense, you would see at a glance, oh, my fair oleander—your lover is frolicsome—*ergo*, he's young!

ANI. Yes, you are young. Have you any more rings?

PEER. Am I not? There, grab! I can leap like a buck! Were there vine leaves around, I would garland my brow. To be sure, I am young! Hei, I'm going to dance! [*Dances and sings.*] I am a blissful gamecock! Peck me, my little pullet! Hop-sa-sa! Let me trip it; I am a blissful gamecock!

ANI. You are sweating, my prophet; I fear you will melt—hand me that heavy bag hung at your belt.

PEER. Tender solicitude! Bear the purse ever; hearts that can love are content without gold. [*Dances and sings again.*] Young Peer Gynt is the maddest wag; he knows not what foot he shall stand upon. Pooh, says Peer —pooh, never mind! Young Peer Gynt is the maddest wag!

ANI. What joy when the Prophet steps forth in the dance!

PEER. Oh, bother the Prophet! Suppose we change clothes! Heisa! Strip off!

ANI. Your caftan were too long, your girdle too wide and your stockings too tight——

PEER. Eh bien! [*Kneels down.*] But vouchsafe me a vehement sorrow—to a heart full of love it is sweet to suffer! Listen, as soon as we're home at my castle——

ANI. In your Paradise; have we far to ride?

PEER. Oh, a thousand miles or——

ANI. Too far!

PEER. Oh, listen; you shall have the soul that I have promised you once.

ANI. Oh, thank you; I'll get on without the soul. But you asked for a sorrow——

PEER [*rising*]. Ay, curse me, I did! A keen one but short—to last two or three days!

ANI. Anitra obeyeth the Prophet! Farewell! [*Gives him a smart cut across the fingers and dashes off, at a tearing gallop, back across the desert.*]

PEER [*stands for a long time thunderstruck*]. Well, now, may I be——

SCENE—*The same place an hour later.* PEER GYNT *is stripping off his Turkish costume soberly and thoughtfully, bit by bit. Last of all he takes his little traveling cap out of his coat pocket, puts it on and stands once more in European dress.*

PEER GYNT [*throwing the turban far away from him*]. There lies the Turk, then, and here stand I! These heathenish doings are no sort of good. It's lucky 'twas only a matter of clothes and not, as the saying goes, bred in the bone. What tempted me into that galley at all? It's best, in the long run, to live as a Christian, to put away peacocklike ostentation, to base all one's dealings on law and morality, to be ever oneself and to earn at the last a speech at one's graveside and wreaths on one's coffin. [*Walks a few steps.*] The hussy—she was on the very verge of turning my head clean topsy-turvy. May I be a troll if I understand what it was that dazed and bemused me so. Well, it's well that's done; had the joke been carried but one step on, I'd have looked absurd. I have erred, but at least it's a consolation that my error was due to the false situation. It wasn't my personal self that fell. 'Twas in fact this prophetical way of life, so utterly lacking the salt of activity, that took its revenge in these qualms of bad taste. It's a sorry business, this prophetizing! One's office compels one to walk in a mist; in playing the prophet you throw up the game the moment you act like a rational being. In *so* far I've done what the occasion demanded, in the mere fact of paying my court to that goose. But nevertheless—— [*Bursts out laughing.*] Hm, to think of it now! To try to make time stop by jigging and dancing and to cope with the current by capering and prancing! To thrum on the lute strings, to fondle and sigh, and end, like a rooster, by getting well plucked! Such conduct is truly prophetic frenzy. Yes, plucked! Phew! I'm plucked clean enough indeed. Well, well, I've a trifle still left in reserve; I've a little in America, a little in my pocket; so I won't be quite driven to beg my bread. And at bottom this middle condition is best. I'm no longer a slave to my coachman and horses; I haven't to fret about post chaise or baggage; I am master, in short, of the situation. What path should I choose? Many paths lie before me, and a wise man is known from a fool by his choice. My business life is a finished chapter; my love sports, too, are a castoff garment. I feel no desire to live back like a crab. "Forward or back, and it's just as far; out or in, and it's just as strait" —so I seem to have read in some luminous work. I'll try something new then; ennoble my course; find a goal worth the labor and money it costs. Shall I write my life without dissimulation—a book for guidance and imitation? Or stay! I have plenty of time at command; what if, as a traveling scientist, I should study past ages and time's voracity? Ay, sure enough, *that* is the thing for me! Legends I read e'en in childhood's days, and since then I've kept up that branch of learning. I will follow the path of the human race! Like a feather I'll float on the stream of history, make it all live again, as in a dream—see the heroes battling for truth and right, as an onlooker only, in safety ensconced —see thinkers perish and martyrs bleed, see empires founded and vanish away—see world epochs grow from their trifling seeds; in short, I will skim off the cream of history. I must try to get hold of a volume of Becker and travel as far as I can by chronology. It's true—my grounding's by no means thorough, and history's wheels within wheels are deceptive; but pooh! the wilder the starting point, the result will oft be the more original. How exalting it is, now, to choose a goal and drive straight for it, like flint and steel! [*With quiet emotion.*] To break off all around one, on every side, the bonds that bind one to home and friends—to blow into atoms one's hoarded wealth —to bid one's love and its joys good night—all simply to find the arcana of truth—[*wiping a tear from his eye*]—*that* is the test of the true man of science! I feel myself happy beyond all measure. *Now* I have fathomed my destiny's riddle. Now 'tis but persevering through thick and thin! It's excusable, sure, if I hold up my head and feel my worth, as the man, Peer Gynt, also called human life's emperor. I will own the sum total of bygone days; I'll nevermore tread in the paths of the living. The present is not worth so much as a shoe sole; all faithless and marrowless the doings of men; their soul has no wings and their deeds no weight—[*shrugs his shoulders*]—and women—ah, they are a worthless crew! [*Goes off.*]

SCENE—*A summer day. Far up in the North. A hut in the forest. The door, with a large wooden bar, stands open. Reindeer horns over it. A flock of goats by the wall of the hut. A* MIDDLE-AGED WOMAN, *fair-haired and comely, sits spinning outside in the sunshine.*

WOMAN [*glances down the path and sings*]. Maybe both the winter and spring will pass by, and the next summer too, and the whole of the year; but thou wilt come one day, that know I full well; and I will await thee, as I promised of old. [*Calls the goats, spins and sings again.*] God strengthen thee, whereso thou goest in the world! God gladden thee, if at his footstool thou stand! Here will I await thee till thou comest again; and if thou wait up yonder, then there we'll meet, my friend!

SCENE—*In Egypt. Daybreak.* MEMNON'S STATUE *amid the sands.* PEER GYNT *enters on foot and looks around him for a while.*

PEER GYNT. Here I might fittingly start on my wanderings. So now, for a change, I've become an Egyptian, but Egyptian on the basis of the Gyntish I. To Assyria next I will bend my steps. To begin right back at the world's creation would lead to nought but bewilderment. I will go round about all the Bible history; its secular traces I'll always be coming on; and to look, as the saying goes, into its seams lies entirely outside both my plan and my powers. [*Sits upon a stone.*] Now I will rest me and patiently wait till the statue has sung its habitual dawn song. When breakfast is over I'll climb up the pyramid; if I've time, I'll look through its interior afterward. Then I'll go round the head of the Red Sea by land; perhaps I may hit on King Potiphar's grave. Next I'll turn Asiatic. In Babylon I'll seek for the far-renowned harlots and hanging gardens—that's to say, the chief traces of civilization. Then at one bound to the ramparts of Troy. From Troy there's a fareway by sea direct across to the glorious ancient Athens; there on the spot will I, stone by stone, survey the pass that Leonidas guarded. I will get up the works of the better philosophers, find the prison where Socrates suffered, a martyr—— Oh no, by the bye —there's a war there at present! Well, then, my Hellenism must even stand over. [*Looks at his watch.*] It's really too bad, such an age as it takes for the sun to rise. I am pressed for time. Well, then, from Troy—it was there I left off—— [*Rises and listens.*] What is that strange sort of murmur that's rushing? [*Sunrise.*]

MEMNON'S STATUE [*sings*]. From the demigod's ashes there soar, youth renewing, birds ever singing. Zeus the Omniscient shaped them contending. Owls of wisdom, my birds, where do they slumber? Thou must die if thou rede not the song's enigma!

PEER. How strange now—I really fancied there came from the statue a sound. Music, this, of the past. I heard the stone accents now rising, now sinking. I will register it, for the learned to ponder. [*Notes in his pocketbook.*] "The statue did sing. I heard the sound plainly but didn't quite follow the text of the song. The whole thing, of course, was hallucination. Nothing else of importance observed today." [*Proceeds on his way.*]

SCENE—*Near the village of Gizeh. The great* SPHINX *carved out of the rock. In the distance the spires and minarets of Cairo.* PEER GYNT *enters; he examines the* SPHINX *attentively, now through his eyeglass, now through his hollowed hand.*

PEER GYNT. Now where in the world have I met before something half forgotten that's like this hobgoblin? For met it I have, in the north or the south. Was it a person? And, if so, who? That Memnon, it afterward crossed my mind, was like the Old Men of the Dovre, so called, just as he sat there, stiff and stark, planted on end on the stumps of pillars. But this most curious mongrel here, this changeling, a lion and woman in one—does he come to me, too, from a fairy tale or from a remembrance of something real? From a fairy tale? Ho, I remember the fellow! Why, of course it's the Boyg that I smote on the skull—that is, I dreamed it—I lay in fever. [*Going closer.*] The selfsame eyes and the selfsame lips; not quite so lumpish; a little more cunning; but the same, for the rest, in all essentials. Ay, so that's it, Boyg; so you're like a lion when one sees you from behind and meets you in the daytime! Are you still good at riddling? Come, let us try. Now we shall see if you answer as last time! [*Calls out toward the* SPHINX.] Hei, Boyg, who are you?

VOICE [*behind the* SPHINX]. Ach, Sphinx, wer bist du?

PEER. What! Echo answers in German! How strange!

VOICE. Wer bist du?

PEER. It speaks it quite fluently too! That observation is new and my own. [*Notes in his book.*] "Echo in German. Dialect, Berlin."

[BEGRIFFENFELDT *comes out from behind the* SPHINX.]

BEG. A man!

PEER. Oh, then it was *he* that was chattering. [*Notes again.*] "Arrived in the sequel at other results."

BEG. [*with all sorts of restless antics*]. Excuse me, mein Herr! Eine Lebensfrage! What brings you to this place precisely today?

PEER. A visit. I'm greeting a friend of my youth.

BEG. What? The Sphinx?

PEER [*nods*]. Yes, I knew him in days gone by.

BEG. Famos! And that after such a night! My temples are hammering as though they would burst! You know him, man! Answer! Say on! Can you tell what he is?

PEER. What he is? Yes, that's easy enough. He's *himself*.

BEG. [*with a bound*]. Ha, the riddle of life lightened forth in a flash to my vision! It's certain he is himself?

PEER. Yes, he says so, at any rate.

BEG. Himself! Revolution! thine hour is at hand! [*Takes off his hat.*] Your name, pray, mein Herr?

PEER. I was christened Peer Gynt.

BEG. [*in rapt admiration*]. Peer Gynt! Allegoric! I might have foreseen it. Peer Gynt! That must clearly imply: the Unknown—the Comer whose coming was foretold to me—

PEER. What, really? And now you are here to meet——

BEG. Peer Gynt! Profound! Enigmatic! Incisive! Each word, as it were, an abysmal lesson! What are you?

PEER [*modestly*]. I've always endeavored to be myself. For the rest, here's my passport, you see.

BEG. Again that mysterious word at

the bottom. [*Seizes him by the wrist.*] To Cairo! The interpreters' kaiser is found!

PEER. Kaiser?

BEG. Come on!

PEER. Am I really known?

BEG. [*dragging him away*]. The interpreters' kaiser—on the basis of Self!

SCENE—*In Cairo. A large courtyard surrounded by high walls and buildings. Barred windows, iron cages.* THREE KEEPERS *in the courtyard.* A FOURTH *comes in.*

NEWCOMER. Schafmann, say, where's the director gone?

KEEPER. He drove out this morning some time before dawn.

FIRST. I think something must have occurred to annoy him, for last night—

ANOTHER. Hush, be quiet; he's there at the door!

[BEGRIFFENFELDT *leads* PEER GYNT *in, locks the gate and puts the key in his pocket.*]

PEER [*to himself*]. Indeed an exceedingly gifted man; almost all that he says is beyond comprehension. [*Looks around.*] So this is the Club of the Savants, eh?

BEG. Here you will find them, every man jack of them; the group of interpreters threescore and ten; it's been lately increased by a hundred and sixty. [*Shouts to the* KEEPERS.] Mikkel, Schlingelberg, Schafmann, Fuchs—into the cages with you at once!

KEEPERS. We!

BEG. Who else, pray? Get in, get in! When the world twirls around we must twirl with it too. [*Forces them into a cage.*] He's arrived this morning, the mighty Peer—the rest you can guess—I need say no more. [*Locks the cage door and throws the key into a well.*]

PEER. But, my dear Herr Doctor and Director, pray——

BEG. Neither one nor the other! I was before—— Herr Peer, are you secret? I must ease my heart.

PEER [*with increasing uneasiness*]. What is it?

BEG. Promise you will not tremble.

PEER. I will do my best, but——

BEG. [*draws him into a corner and whispers*]. The Absolute Reason departed this life at eleven last night.

PEER. God help me!

BEG. Why, yes, it's extremely deplorable. And as *I'm* placed, you see, it is doubly unpleasant; for this institution has passed up to now for what is called a madhouse.

PEER. A madhouse, ha!

BEG. Not *now*, understand!

PEER [*softly, pale with fear*]. Now I see what the place is! And the man is mad, and there's none that knows it! [*Tries to steal away.*]

BEG. [*following him*]. However, I hope you don't misunderstand me? When I said he was dead I was talking stuff. He's beside himself. Started clean out of his skin—just like my compatriot Munchausen's fox.

PEER. Excuse me a moment.

BEG. [*holding him back*]. I meant like an eel; it was not like a fox. A needle through his eye—and he writhed on the wall——

PEER. Where can rescue be found!

BEG. A snick round his neck, and whip! out of his skin!

PEER. He's raving! He's utterly out of his wits!

BEG. Now it's patent and can't be dissimulated that this from-himself-going must have for result a complete revolution by sea and land. The persons one hitherto reckoned as mad, you see, became normal last night at eleven, accordant with Reason in its newest phase. And more, if the matter be rightly regarded, it's patent that at the aforementioned hour the sane folks, so called, began forthwith to rave.

PEER. You mentioned the hour, sir; my time is but scant.

BEG. Your time, did you say? There you jog my remembrance! [*Opens a door and calls out.*] Come forth all! The time that shall be is proclaimed! Reason is dead and gone; long live Peer Gynt!

PEER. Now, my dear good fellow!

[*The* LUNATICS *come one by one, and at intervals, into the courtyard.*]

BEG. Good morning! Come forth and hail the dawn of emancipation! Your kaiser has come to you!

PEER. Kaiser?

BEG. Of course!

PEER. But the honor's so great, so entirely excessive——

BEG. Oh, do not let any false modesty sway you at an hour such as this.

PEER. But at least give me time! No indeed, I'm not fit; I'm completely dumbfounded!

BEG. A man who has fathomed the Sphinx's meaning! A man who's himself!

PEER. Ay, but that's just the rub. It's true that in everything I am myself, but here the point is, if I follow your meaning, to be, so to phrase it, outside oneself.

BEG. Outside? No, there you are strangely mistaken! It's here, sir, that one is oneself with vengeance, oneself and nothing whatever besides. We go, full sail, as our very selves. Each one shuts himself up in a barrel of self, in the self-fermentation he dives to the bottom—and with the self-bung he seals it hermetically and seasons the staves in the well of self. No one has ears for the other's woes; no one has mind for the other's ideas. We're our very selves, both in thought and tone; ourselves to the springboard's uttermost verge—and so, if a kaiser's to fill the throne, it is clear that you are the very man.

PEER. O would that the devil——

BEG. Come, don't be cast down; almost all things in nature are new at the first. "Oneself"—come, here you shall see an example; I'll choose you at random the first man that comes. [*To a gloomy figure.*] Good day, Huhu! Well, my boy, wandering round forever with misery's impress upon you?

HUHU. Can I help it, when the people, race by race, dies untranslated? [*To* PEER GYNT.] You're a stranger; will you listen?

PEER [*bowing.*] Oh, by all means!

HUHU. Lend your ear then. Eastward far, like brow-borne garlands, lie the Malabarish seaboards. Hollanders and Portuguese compass all the land with culture. There, moreover, swarms are dwelling of the pure-bred Malabaris. These have muddled up the language; they now lord it in the country. But in long-departed ages there the orangoutang was ruler. He, the forest's lord and master, freely fought and snarled in freedom. As the hand of nature shaped him, just so grinned he, just so gaped he. He could shriek unreprehended; he was ruler in his kingdom. Ah, but then the foreign yoke came, marred the forest tongue primeval. Twice two hundred years of darkness brooded o'er the race of monkeys; and, you know, nights *so* protracted bring a people to a standstill. Mute are now the wood notes primal; grunts and growls are heard no longer—if we'd utter our ideas, it must be by means of language. What constraint on all and sundry! Hollanders and Portugueses, half-caste race and Malabaris, all alike must suffer by it. I have tried to fight the battle of our real, primal wood speech—tried to bring life to its carcass—proved the people's right of shrieking—shrieked myself and shown the need of shrieks in poems for the people. Scantly, though, my work is valued. Now I think you grasp my sorrow. Thanks for lending me a hearing; have you counsel, let me hear it!

PEER [*softly*]. It is written: Best be howling with the wolves that are about you. [*Aloud.*] Friend, if I remember rightly, there are bushes in Morocco where orangoutangs in plenty live with neither bard nor spokesman; their speech sounded Malabarish; it was classical and pleasing. Why don't you, like other worthies, emigrate to serve your country?

HUHU. Thanks for lending me a hearing; I will do as you advise me. [*With a large gesture.*] East! thou hast disowned thy singer. West! thou hast orangoutangs still! [*Goes.*]

BEG. Well, was he himself? I should rather think so. He's filled with his own affairs, simply and solely. He's himself in all that comes out of him—himself, just because he's beside himself. Come here! Now I'll show you another one who's no less, since last evening, accordant with Reason. [*To a* FELLAH *with a mummy on his back.*] King Apis, how goes it, my mighty lord?

FELLAH [*wildly, to* PEER GYNT]. *Am* I King Apis?

PEER [*getting behind the* DOCTOR]. I'm sorry to say I'm not quite at home in the situation, but I certainly gather, to judge by your tone——

FELLAH. Now you too are lying.

BEG. Your Highness should state how the whole matter stands.

FELLAH. Yes, I'll tell him my tale. [*Turns to* PEER GYNT.] Do you see whom I bear on my shoulders? His name was King Apis of old. Now he goes by the title of mummy, and withal he's completely dead. All the pyramids yonder he builded and hewed out the mighty Sphinx and fought, as the doctor puts it, with the Turks, both to rechts and links. And therefore the whole of Egypt exalted him as a god and set up his image in temples, in the outward shape of a bull. But *I* am this very King Apis—I see that as clear as day; and if you don't understand it, you shall understand it soon. King Apis, you see, was out hunting and got off his horse awhile and withdrew himself unattended to a part of my ancestor's land. But the field that King Apis manured has nourished *me* with its corn; and if further proofs are remanded, know I have invisible horns. Now isn't it most accursed that no one will own my might! By birth I am Apis of Egypt but a fellah in other men's sight. Can you tell me what course to follow?—then counsel me honestly. The problem is how to make me resemble King Apis the Great.

PEER. Build pyramids then, Your Highness, and carve out a greater Sphinx and fight, as the doctor puts it, with the Turks, both to rechts and links.

FELLAH. Ay, that is all mighty fine

talking! A fellah! A hungry louse! I, who scarcely can keep my hovel clear even of rats and mice. Quick, man—think of something better that 'll make me both great and safe and, further, exactly like to King Apis that's on my back!

PEER. What if Your Highness hanged you and then, in the lap of earth, 'twixt the coffin's natural frontiers, kept still and completely dead.

FELLAH. I'll do it! My life for a halter! To the gallows with hide and hair! At first there will be some difference, but that time will smooth away. [*Goes off and prepares to hang himself.*]

BEG. There's a personality for you, Herr Peer—a man of method——

PEER. Yes, yes. I see; but he'll really hang himself! God grant us grace! I'll be ill; I can scarcely command my thoughts!

BEG. A state of transition; it won't last long.

PEER. Transition? To what? With your leave—I must go.

BEG. [*holding him*]. Are you crazy?

PEER. Not yet. Crazy? Heaven forbid!

[*A commotion. The* MINISTER HUSSEIN *forces his way through the crowd.*]

HUSSEIN. They tell me a kaiser has come today. [*To* PEER GYNT.] It is you?

PEER [*in desperation*]. Yes, that is a settled thing!

HUSSEIN. Good. Then no doubt there are notes to be answered?

PEER [*tearing his hair*]. Come on! Right you are, sir; the madder the better!

HUSSEIN. Will you do me the honor of taking a dip? [*Bowing deeply.*] I am a pen.

PEER [*bowing still deeper*]. Why, then, I am quite clearly a rubbishy piece of imperial parchment.

HUSSEIN. My story, my lord, is concisely this: they take me for a sandbox, and I am a pen.

PEER. My story, Sir Pen, is, to put it briefly: I'm a blank sheet of paper that no one will write on.

HUSSEIN. No man understands in the least what I'm good for; they all want to use me for scattering sand with!

PEER. I was, in a woman's keeping, a silver-clasped book; it's one and the same misprint to be either mad or sane!

HUSSEIN. Just fancy, what an exhausting life—to be a pen and never taste the edge of a knife!

PEER [*with a high leap*]. Just fancy, for a reindeer to leap from on high—to fall and fall—and never feel the ground beneath your hoofs!

HUSSEIN. A knife! I am blunt; quick, mend me and slit me! The world will go to ruin if they don't mend my point for me!

PEER. A pity for the world which, like other self-made things, was reckoned by the Lord to be so excellently good.

BEG. Here's a knife!

HUSSEIN [*seizing it*]. Ah, how I shall lick up the ink now! Oh, what rapture to cut oneself! [*Cuts his throat.*]

BEG. [*stepping aside*]. Pray do not sputter.

PEER [*in increasing terror*]. Hold him!

HUSSEIN. Ay, hold me! That is the word! Hold! Hold the pen! On the desk with the paper! [*Falls.*] I'm outworn. The postscript—remember it, pray: He lived and he died as a fate-guided pen.

PEER [*dizzily*]. What shall I! What am I? Thou mighty—— Hold fast! I am all that thou wilt—I'm a Turk, I'm a sinner—a hill troll; but help—there was something that burst! [*Shrieks.*] I cannot just hit on thy name at the moment; oh, come to my aid, thou—all madmen's protector! [*Sinks down insensible.*]

BEG. [*with a wreath of straw in his hand, gives a bound and sits astride of him*]. Ha! See him in the mire enthroned—beside himself! To crown him now! [*Presses the wreath on* PEER GYNT's *head and shouts.*] Long life, long life to Selfhood's Kaiser!

SCHAFMANN [*in the cage*]. Es lebe hoch der grosse Peer!

ACT V

SCENE—*On board a ship on the North Sea, off the Norwegian coast. Sunset. Stormy weather.* PEER GYNT, *a vigorous old man with grizzled hair and beard, is standing aft on the poop. He is dressed half sailor-fashion, with a pea jacket and long boots. His clothing is rather the worse for wear; he himself is weather-beaten and has a somewhat harder expression. The* CAPTAIN *is standing beside the steersman at the wheel. The crew are forward.*

PEER GYNT [*leans with his arms on the bulwark and gazes toward the land*]. Look at Hallingskarv in his winter furs; he's ruffling it, old one, in the evening glow. The Jokel, his brother, stands behind him askew; he's got his green ice mantle still on his back. The Folgefann, now, she is mighty fine—lying there like a maiden in spotless white. Don't you be madcaps, old boys that you are! Stand where you stand; you're but granite knobs.

CAPTAIN [*shouts forward*]. Two hands to the wheel and the lantern aloft!

PEER. It's blowing up stiff——

CAPTAIN. —for a gale tonight.

PEER. Can one see the Ronde hills from the sea?

CAPTAIN. No, how should you? They lie at the back of the snow fields.

PEER. Or Blaho?

CAPTAIN. No; but from up in the rigging you've a glimpse, in clear weather, of Galdhopiggen.

PEER. Where does Harteig lie?

CAPTAIN [*pointing*]. About over there.

PEER. I thought so.

CAPTAIN. You know where you are, it appears.

PEER. When I left the country I sailed by here; and the dregs, says the proverbs, hang in to the last. [*Spits and gazes at the coast.*] In there, where the scaurs and the clefts lie blue—where the valleys, like trenches, gloom narrow and black—and underneath, skirting the open fiords—it's in places like *these* human beings abide. [*Looks at the* CAPTAIN.] They build far apart in this country.

CAPTAIN. Ay, few are the dwellings and far between.

PEER. Shall we get in by daybreak?

CAPTAIN. Thereabouts; if we don't have too dirty a night altogether.

PEER. It grows thick in the west.

CAPTAIN. It does so.

PEER. Stop a bit! You might put me in mind when we make up accounts—I'm inclined, as the phrase goes, to do a good turn to the crew.

CAPTAIN. I thank you.

PEER. It won't be much. I have dug for gold and lost what I found; we are quite at loggerheads, Fate and I. You know what I've got in safekeeping on board—that's all I have left; the rest's gone to the devil.

CAPTAIN. It's more than enough, though, to make you of weight among people at home here.

PEER. I've no relations. There's no one awaiting the rich old curmudgeon. Well, that saves you, at least, any scenes on the pier!

CAPTAIN. Here comes the storm.

PEER. Well, remember then—if any of your crew are in real need, I won't look too closely after the money.

CAPTAIN. That's kind. They are most of them ill enough off; they have all got their wives and their children at home. With their wages alone they can scarce make ends meet, but if they come home with some cash to the good, it will be a return not forgot in a hurry.

PEER. What do you say? Have they wives and children? Are they married?

CAPTAIN. Married? Ay, every man of them. But the one that is worst off of all is the cook; black famine is ever at home in his house.

PEER. Married? They've folks that await them at home? Folks to be glad when they come? Eh?

CAPTAIN. Of course, in poor people's fashion.

PEER. And come they one evening, what then?

CAPTAIN. Why, I daresay the goodwife will fetch something good for a treat——

PEER. And a light in the sconce?

CAPTAIN. Ay, ay, maybe two; and a dram to their supper.

PEER. And there they sit snug! There's a fire on the hearth! They've their children about them! The room's full of chatter; not one hears another right out to an end, for the joy that is on them!

CAPTAIN. It's likely enough. So it's really kind, as you promised just now, to help eke things out.

PEER [*thumping the bulwark*]. I'll be damned if I do! Do you think I am mad? Would you have me fork out for the sake of a parcel of other folks' brats? I've slaved much too sorely in earning my cash! There's nobody waiting for old Peer Gynt.

CAPTAIN. Well, well, as you please then; your money's your own.

PEER. Right! Mine it is, and no one else's. We'll reckon as soon as your anchor is down. Take my fare, in the cabin, from Panama here. Then brandy all around to the crew. Nothing more. If I give a dolt more, slap my jaw for me, Captain.

CAPTAIN. I owe you a quittance and not a thrashing; but excuse me, the wind's blowing up to a gale. [*He goes forward. It has fallen dark; lights are lit in the cabin. The sea increases. Fog and thick clouds.*]

PEER. To have a whole bevy of youngsters at home; still to dwell in their minds as a coming delight; to have others' thoughts follow you still on your path! There's never a soul gives a thought to me. Lights in the sconces! I'll put out those lights. I will hit upon something! I'll make them all drunk; not one of the devils shall go sober ashore. They shall all come home drunk to their children and wives! They shall curse, bang the table till it rings again—they shall scare those that wait for them out of their wits! The goodwife shall scream and rush forth from the house—clutch her children along! All their joy gone to ruin! [*The ship gives a heavy lurch; he staggers and keeps his balance with difficulty.*] Why, that was a buffet and no mistake. The sea's hard at labor, as though it were paid for it; it's still itself here on the coasts of the North—a cross sea, as wry and wrongheaded as ever. [*Listens.*] Why, what can those screams be?

LOOKOUT [*forward*]. A wreck alee!

CAPTAIN [*on the main deck, shouts*]. Helm hard astarboard! Bring her up to the wind!

MATE. Are there men on the wreck?

LOOKOUT. I can just see three!

PEER. Quick! Lower the stern boat——

CAPTAIN. She'd fill ere she floated. [*Goes forward.*]

PEER. Who can think of that now? [*To some of the crew.*] If you're men, to the rescue! What the devil if you should get a bit of a ducking!

BOATSWAIN. It's out of the question in such a sea.

PEER. They are screaming again! There's a lull in the wind. Cook, will you risk it? Quick! I will pay——

COOK. No, not if you offered me twenty pounds sterling.

PEER. You hounds! You chicken hearts! Can you forget these are men that have goodwives and children at home? There they're sitting and waiting——

BOATSWAIN. Well, patience is wholesome.

CAPTAIN. Bear away from that sea!

MATE. There, the wreck turned over!

PEER. All is silent of a sudden!

BOATSWAIN. Were they married, as you think, there are three new-baked widows even now in the world.

[*The storm increases.* PEER GYNT *moves away aft.*]

PEER. There is no faith left among men any more—no Christianity—well may they say it and write it; their good deeds are few and their prayers are still fewer, and they pay no respect to the Powers above them. In a storm like tonight's he's a terror, the Lord is. These beasts should be careful and think, what's the truth, that it's dangerous playing with elephants; and yet they must openly brave his displeasure! *I* am no whit to blame, for the sacrifice I can prove I stood ready, my money in hand. But how does it profit me? What says the proverb? A conscience at ease is a pillow of down. Oh! ay, that is all very well on dry land, but I'm blest if it matters a snuff on board ship, when a decent man's out on the seas with such riffraff. At sea one never can be one's self; one must go with the others from deck to keel; if for boatswain and cook the hour of vengeance should strike, I shall no doubt be swept to the deuce with the rest; one's personal welfare is clean set aside; one counts but as a sausage in slaughtering time. My mistake is this: I have been too meek; and I've had no thanks for it after all. Were I younger, I think I would shift the saddle and try how it answered to lord it awhile. There is time enough yet! They shall know in the parish that Peer has come sailing aloft o'er the seas! I'll get back the farmstead by fair means or foul; I will build it anew; it shall shine like a palace. But none shall be suffered to enter the hall! They shall stand at the gateway, all twirling their caps; they shall beg and beseech—*that* they freely may do; but none gets so much as a farthing of mine. If *I've* had to howl 'neath the lashes of fate, trust me to find folks I can lash in my turn.

STRANGE PASSENGER [*stands in the darkness at* PEER GYNT's *side and salutes him in friendly fashion*]. Good evening!

PEER. Good evening! What? Who are you?

PASSENGER. Your fellow passenger, at your service.

PEER. Indeed? I thought I was the only one.

PASSENGER. A mistaken impression, which now is set right.

PEER. But it's singular that, for the first time tonight, I should see you.

PASSENGER. I never come out in the daytime.

PEER. Perhaps you are ill? You're as white as a sheet.

PASSENGER. No, thank you—my health is uncommonly good.

PEER. What a raging storm!

PASSENGER. Ay, a blessed one, man!

PEER. A blessed one?

PASSENGER. The sea's running high as houses. Ah, one can feel one's mouth watering! Just think of the wrecks that tonight will be shattered—and think, too, what corpses will drive ashore!

PEER. Lord save us!

PASSENGER. Have you ever seen a man strangled or hanged—or drowned?

PEER. This is going too far!

PASSENGER. The corpses all laugh. But their laughter is forced, and the most part are found to have bitten their tongues.

PEER. Hold off from me!

PASSENGER. Only one question, pray! If we, for example, should strike on a rock and sink in the darkness——

PEER. You think there is danger?

PASSENGER. I really don't know what I ought to say. But suppose, now, I float and you go to the bottom——

PEER. Oh, rubbish!

PASSENGER. It's just a hypothesis. But when one is placed with one foot in the grave one grows softhearted and openhanded——

PEER [*puts his hands in his pocket*]. Ho, money!

PASSENGER. No, no; but perhaps you would kindly make me a gift of your much-esteemed carcass?

PEER. This is *too* much!

PASSENGER. No more than your body, you know! To help my researches in science.

PEER. Begone!

PASSENGER. But think, my dear sir—the advantage is yours! I'll have you laid open and brought to the light. What I specially seek is the center of dreams—and with critical care I'll look into your seams——

PEER. Away with you!

PASSENGER. Why, my dear sir—a drowned corpse!

PEER. Blasphemer! You're goading the rage of the storm! I call it too bad! Here it's raining and blowing, a terrible sea on and all sorts of signs of something that's likely to shorten our days—and you carry on so as to make it come quicker!

PASSENGER. You're in no mood, I see, to negotiate further; but time, you know, brings with it many a change. [*Nods in a friendly fashion.*] We'll meet when you're sinking, if not before; perhaps I may then find you more in the humor. [*Goes into the cabin.*]

PEER. Unpleasant companions these scientists are! With their freethinking ways. [*To the* BOATSWAIN, *who is passing.*] Hark, a word with you, friend! That passenger? What crazy creature is he?

BOATSWAIN. I know of no passenger here but yourself.

PEER. No others? This thing's getting worse and worse. [*To the* SHIP'S BOY, *who comes out of the cabin.*] Who went down the companion just now?

BOY. The ship's dog, sir! [*Passes on.*]

LOOKOUT [*shouts*]. Land close ahead!

PEER. Where's my box? Where's my trunk? All the baggage on deck!

BOATSWAIN. We have more to attend to!

PEER. It was nonsense, Captain! 'Twas only my joke; as sure as I'm here I will help the cook——

CAPTAIN. The jib's blown away!

MATE. And there went the foresail!

BOATSWAIN [*shrieks from forward*]. Breakers under the bow!

CAPTAIN. She will go to shivers!

[*The ship strikes. Noise and confusion.*]

SCENE—*Close under the land, among sunken rocks and surf. The ship sinks. The jolly boat, with two men in her, is seen for a moment through the scud. A sea strikes her; she fills and upsets. A shriek is heard, then all is silent for a while. Shortly afterward the boat appears floating bottom upward.* PEER GYNT *comes to the surface near the boat.*

PEER. Help! Help! A boat! Help! I'll be drowned! Save me, oh Lord—as saith the text! [*Clutches hold of the boat's keel.*]

COOK [*comes up on the other side*]. Oh, Lord God—for my children's sake, have mercy! Let me reach the land! [*Seizes hold of the keel.*]

PEER. Let go!

COOK. Let go!

PEER. I'll strike!

COOK. So'll I!

PEER. I'll crush you down with kicks and blows! Let go your hold! She won't float two!

COOK. I know it! Yield!

PEER. Yield you!

COOK. Oh yes!

[*They fight; one of the* COOK'S *hands is disabled; he clings on with the other.*]

PEER. Off with that hand!

COOK. Oh, kind sir—spare! Think of my little ones at home!

PEER. I need my life far more than you, for I am lone and childless still.

COOK. Let go! You've lived, and I am young!

PEER. Quick, haste you, sink; you drag us down.

COOK. Have mercy! Yield, in heaven's name! There's none to miss and mourn for you. [*His hand slips; he screams.*] I'm drowning!

PEER [*seizing him*]. By this wisp of hair I'll hold you! Say your Lord's Prayer, quick!

COOK. I can't remember; all turns black——

PEER. Come, the essentials in a word!

COOK. Give us this day——

PEER. Skip that part, Cook; you'll get all *you* need, safe enough.

COOK. Give us this day——

PEER. The same old song! One sees you were a cook in life!

[*The* COOK *slips from his grasp.*]

COOK [sinking]. Give us this day our—— [*Disappears.*]

PEER. Amen, lad! To the last gasp you were yourself. [*Draws himself up onto the bottom of the boat.*] So long as there is life there's hope.

STRANGE PASSENGER [*catches hold of the boat*]. Good morning!

PEER. Hoy!

PASSENGER. I heard you shout. It's pleasant finding you again. Well? So my prophecy came true!

PEER. Let go! Let go! 'Twill scarce float *one!*

PASSENGER. I'm striking out with my left leg. I'll float, if only with their tips my fingers rest upon this ledge. But apropos: your body——

PEER. Hush!

PASSENGER. The rest, of course, is done for, clean——

PEER. No more!

PASSENGER. Exactly as you please. [*Silence.*]

PEER. Well?

PASSENGER. I am silent.

PEER. Satan's trick! What now?

PASSENGER. I'm waiting.

PEER [*tearing his hair*]. I'll go mad! What are you?

PASSENGER [*nods*]. Friendly.

PEER. What else? Speak!

PASSENGER. What think you? Do you know none other that's like me?

PEER. Do I know the devil?

PASSENGER [*in a low voice*]. Is it his way to light a lantern for life's night pilgrimage through fear?

PEER. Ah, come! When once the thing's cleared up you'd seem a messenger of light?

PASSENGER. Friend—have you *once* in each half year felt all the earnestness of dread?

PEER. Why, one's afraid when danger threatens; but all your words have double meanings.

PASSENGER. Ay, have you gained but *once* in life the victory that is given in dread?

PEER [*looks at him*]. Came you to ope for me a door, 'twas stupid not to come before. What sort of sense is there in choosing your time when seas gape to devour one?

PASSENGER. Were, then, the victory more likely beside your hearthstone, snug and quiet?

PEER. Perhaps not, but your talk befooled me. How could you fancy it awakening?

PASSENGER. Where I come from there smiles are prized as highly as pathetic style.

PEER. All has its time; what fits the taxman, so says the text, would damn the bishop.

PASSENGER. The host whose dust inurned has slumbered treads not on weekdays the cothurnus.

PEER. Avaunt thee, bugbear! Man, begone! I will not die! I *must* ashore!

PASSENGER. Oh, as for that, be reassured—one dies not midmost of Act Five. [*Glides away.*]

PEER. Ah, there he let it out at last; he was a sorry moralist.

SCENE—*Churchyard in a high-lying mountain parish. A funeral is going on. By the grave the* PRIEST *and a gathering of people. The last verse of the psalm is being sung.* PEER GYNT *passes by on the road.*

PEER [*at the gate*]. Here's a countryman going the way of all flesh. God be thanked that it isn't me. [*Enters the churchyard.*]

PRIEST [*speaking beside the grave*]. Now, when the soul has gone to meet its doom and here the dust lies, like an empty pod—now, my dear friends, we'll speak a word or two about this dead man's pilgrimage on earth. He was not wealthy, neither was he wise, his voice was weak, his bearing was unmanly, he spoke his mind abashed and faltering, he scarce was master at his own fireside; he sidled into church, as though appealing for leave, like other men, to take his place. It was from Gudbransdale, you know, he came. When here he settled he was but a lad; and you remember how, to the very last, he kept his right hand hidden in his pocket. That right hand in the pocket was the feature that chiefly stamped his image on the mind—and therewithal his writhing, his abashed shrinking from notice wheresoe'er he went. But though he still pursued a path aloof and ever seemed a stranger in our midst, you all know what he strove so hard to hide—the hand he muffled had four fingers only. I well remember, many years ago, one morning, there were session held at Lunde. 'Twas wartime, and the talk in every mouth turned on the country's sufferings and its fate. I stood there watching. At the table sat the captain, 'twixt the bailiff and the sergeants; lad after lad was measured up and down, passed and enrolled and taken for a soldier. The room was full; thronged the young folks; loud the laughter rang. A name was called, and forth another stepped, one pale as snow upon the glacier's edge. They bade the youth advance; he reached the table; we saw his right hand swaddled in a clout—he gasped, he swallowed, battling after words—but, though the captain urged him, found no voice. Ah yes, at last! Then with his cheek aflame, his tongue now failing him, now stammering fast, he mumbled something of a scythe that slipped by chance and shore his finger to the skin. Straightway a silence fell upon the room. Men bandied meaning glances; they made mouths; they stoned the boy with looks of silent scorn. He felt the hailstorm, but he saw it not. Then up the captain stood, the gray old man: he spat and pointed forth and thundered "Go!" And the lad went. On both sides men fell back, till through their midst he had to run the gauntlet. He reached the door; from there he took to flight—up, up he went—through wood and over hillside, up through the stone slips, rough, precipitous. He had his home up there among the mountains. It was some six months later he came here, with mother and betrothed and little child. He leased some ground upon the high hillside, there where the wastelands trend away toward Lomb. He married the first moment that he could; he built a house; he broke the stubborn soil; he throve, as many a cultivated patch bore witness, bravely clad in waving gold. At church he kept his right hand in his pocket—but sure I am at home his fingers nine toiled every bit as hard as others' ten. One spring the torrent washed it all away. Their lives were spared. Ruined and stripped of all, he set to work to make another clearing; and, ere the autumn, smoke again arose from a new, better-sheltered, mountain farmhouse. Sheltered? From torrent—not from avalanche; two years, and all beneath the snow lay buried. But still the avalanche could not daunt his spirit. He dug and raked and carted—cleared the ground—and the next winter, ere the snow blasts came, a third time was his little homestead reared. Three sons he had, three bright and stirring boys; they must to school, and school was far away; and they must clamber where the hill track failed, by narrow ledges through the headlong scaur. What did he do? The eldest had to manage as best he might, and where the path was worst his father cast a rope around him to stay him; the others on his back and arms he bore. Thus he toiled, year by year, till they were men. Now might he well have looked for some return. In the New World three prosperous gentlemen their schoolgoing and their father have forgotten. He was shortsighted. Out beyond the circle of those most near to him he nothing saw. To him seemed meaningless as cymbals' tinkling those words that to the heart should ring like steel. His race, his fatherland, all things high and shining, stood ever, to his vision, veiled in mist. But he was humble, humble, was this man; and since that sessions day his doom oppressed him, as surely as his cheeks were flushed with shame and his four fingers hidden in his pocket. Offender 'gainst his country's laws? Ay, true! But there is one thing that the law outshineth sure as the snow-white tent of Glittertind has clouds, like higher rows of peaks, above it. No patriot was he. Both for church and state a fruitless tree. But there, on the upland ridge, in the small circle where he saw his calling, *there* he was great, because he was himself. His inborn note rang true unto the end. His days were as a lute with muted strings. And therefore peace be with thee, silent warrior, that fought the peasant's little fight and fell! It is not ours to search the heart and reins; that is no task for dust but for its ruler; yet dare I freely, firmly, speak my hope: he scarce stands crippled now before his God!

[*The gathering disperses.* PEER GYNT *remains behind, alone.*]

PEER. Now *that* is what I call Christianity! Nothing to seize on one's mind unpleasantly. And the topic—immovably being oneself—that the pastor's homily turned upon—is full, in its essence, of edification. [*Looks down upon the grave.*] Was it he, I wonder, that hacked through his knuckle that day I was out hewing logs in the forest? Who knows? If I weren't standing here with my staff by the side of the grave of this kinsman in spirit, I could almost believe it was I that slept and heard in a vision my panegyric. It's a seemly and Christianlike custom indeed, this casting a so-called memorial glance in charity over the life that is ended. I shouldn't at all mind accepting my verdict at the hands of this excellent parish priest. Ah well, I dare say I have some time left ere the gravedigger comes to invite me to stay with him; and as Scripture has it: What's best is best—and: Enough for the day is the evil thereof—and further: Discount not thy funeral. Ah, the church, after all, is the true consoler. I've hitherto scarcely appreciated it, but now I feel clearly how blessed it is to be well assured upon sound authority: Even as thou sowest thou shalt one day reap. One must be oneself; for oneself and one's own one must do one's best, both in great and in small things. If the luck goes against you, at least you've the honor of a life carried through in accordance with principle. Now homeward! Though narrow and steep the path, though Fate to the end may be never so biting—still old Peer Gynt will pursue his own way and remain what he is: poor but virtuous ever. [*Goes out.*]

SCENE—*A hillside seamed by the dry bed of a torrent. A ruined mill-house beside the stream. The ground is torn up and the whole place waste. Further up the hill a large farmhouse. An auction is going on in front of the farmhouse. There is a great gathering of people, who are drinking, with much noise.* PEER GYNT *is sitting on a rubbish heap beside the mill.*

PEER. Forward and back, and it's just as far; out and in, and it's just as strait. Time wears away and the river gnaws on. Go roundabout, the Boyg said; and here one must.

MAN DRESSED IN MOURNING. Now there is only rubbish left over. [*Catches sight of* PEER GYNT.] Are there strangers here too? God be with you, good friend!

PEER. Well met! You have lively times here today. Is't a christening junket or a wedding feast?

MAN. I'd rather call it a house-warming treat; the bride is laid in a wormy bed.

PEER. And the worms are squabbling for rags and clouts.

MAN. That's the end of the ditty; it's over and done.

PEER. All the ditties end just alike, and they're all old together; I knew 'em as a boy.

LAD OF TWENTY [*with a casting ladle*]. Just look what a rare thing I've been buying! In this Peer Gynt cast his silver buttons.

ANOTHER. Look at mine, though! The moneybag bought for a halfpenny.

THIRD. No more, eh? Twopence for the peddler's pack!

PEER. Peer Gynt? Who was he?

MAN. All I know is this: he was kinsman to Death and to Aslak the Smith.

MAN IN GRAY. You're forgetting me, man! Are you mad or drunk?

MAN. You forget that at Hegstad was a storehouse door.

MAN IN GRAY. Ay, true; but we know you were never dainty.

MAN. If only she doesn't give Death the slip——

MAN IN GRAY. Come, kinsman! A dram, for our kinship's sake!

MAN. To the deuce with your kinship! You're maundering in drink——

MAN IN GRAY. Oh, rubbish; blood's never so thin as all that; one cannot but feel one's akin to Peer Gynt. [*Goes off with him.*]

PEER [*to himself*]. One meets with acquaintances.

LAD [*calls after the* MAN IN MOURNING]. Mother that's dead will be after you, Aslak, if you wet your whistle.

PEER [*rises*]. The agriculturists' saying seems scarce to hold here: The deeper one harrows the better it smells.

LAD [*with a bear's skin*]. Look, the cat of the Dovre! Well, only his fell. It was he chased the trolls out on Christmas Eve.

ANOTHER [*with a reindeer skull*]. Here is the wonderful reindeer that bore, at Gendin, Peer Gynt over edge and scaur.

THIRD [*with a hammer, calls out to* MAN IN MOURNING]. Hei, Aslak, this sledge hammer, say, do you know it? Was it this that you used when the devil clove the wall?

FOURTH [*empty-handed*]. Mads Moen, here's the invisible cloak Peer Gynt and Ingrid flew off through the air with.

PEER. Brandy here, boys! I feel I'm grown old; I must put up to auction my rubbish and lumber!

LAD. What have you to sell, then?

PEER. A palace I have; it lies in the Ronde; it's solidly built.

LAD. A button is bid!

PEER. You must run to a dram. 'Twere a sin and a shame to bid anything else.

ANOTHER. He's a jolly old boy this!

[*The bystanders crowd round him.*]

PEER [*shouts*]. Grane, my steed; who bids?

ONE OF THE CROWD. Where's he running?

PEER. Why, far in the west! Near the sunset, my lads! Ah, that courser can fly as fast, ay, as fast as Peer Gynt could lie.

VOICES. What more have you got?

PEER. I've both rubbish and gold! I bought it with ruin; I'll sell it at a loss.

LAD. Put it up!

PEER. A dream of a silver-clasped book! That you can have for an old hook and eye.

LAD. To the devil with dreams!

PEER. Here's my Kaiserdom! I throw it in the midst of you; scramble for it!

LAD. Is the crown given in?

PEER. Of the loveliest straw. It will fit whoever first puts it on. Hei, there is more yet! An addled egg! A madman's gray hair! And the Prophet's beard! All these shall be his that will show on the hillside a post that has writ on it: Here lies your path!

BAILIFF [*who has come up*]. You're carrying on, my good man, so that almost I think your path will lead straight to the lockup.

PEER [*hat in hand*]. Quite likely. But, tell me, who was Peer Gynt?

BAILIFF. Oh, nonsense——

PEER. Your pardon! Most humbly I beg!

BAILIFF. Oh, he's said to have been an abominable liar!

PEER. A liar?

BAILIFF. Yes—all that was strong and great, he made believe always that *he* had done it. But, excuse me, friend —I have other duties. [*Goes.*]

PEER. And where is he now, this remarkable man?

ELDERLY MAN. He fared over seas to a foreign land; it went ill with him there, as one well might foresee; it's many a year now since he was hanged.

PEER. Hanged? Ay, ay! Why, I thought as much; our lamented Peer Gynt was himself to the last. [*Bows.*] Good-by—and best thanks for today's merry meeting. [*Goes a few steps but stops again.*] You joyous youngsters, you comely lasses—shall I pay my shot with a traveler's tale?

SEVERAL VOICES. Yes; do you know any?

PEER. Nothing more easy. [*He comes nearer; a look of strangeness comes over him.*] I was gold digging once in San Francisco. There were mountebanks swarming all over the town. One with his toes could perform on the fiddle; another could dance a Spanish halling on his knees; a third, I was told, kept on making verses while his brainpan was having a hole bored right through it. To the mountebank meeting came also the devil—thought he'd try his luck with the rest of them. His talent was this: in a manner convincing he was able to grunt like a flesh-and-blood pig. He was not recognized, yet his manners attracted. The house was well filled; expectation ran high. He stepped forth in a cloak with an ample cape to it; *man muss sich drappiren*, as the Germans say. But under the mantle—what none suspected—he'd managed to smuggle a real live pig. And now he opened the representation; the devil he pinched, and the pig gave voice. The whole thing purported to be a fantasia on the porcine existence, both free and in bonds; and all ended up with a slaughterhouse squeal—whereupon the performer bowed low and retired. The critics discussed and appraised the affair; the tone of the whole was attacked and defended. Some fancied the vocal expression too thin, while some thought the death shriek too carefully studied; but all were agreed as to one thing: *qua* grunt, the performance was grossly exaggerated. Now *that*, you see, came of the devil's stupidity in not taking the measure of his public first. [*He bows and goes off. A puzzled silence comes over the crowd.*]

SCENE—*Whitsun Eve. In the depths of the forest. To the back, in a clearing, is a hut with a pair of reindeer horns over the porch gable.*

PEER GYNT *is creeping among the undergrowth, gathering wild onions.*

PEER. Well, this is one standpoint. Where is the next? One should try all things and choose the best. Well, I have done so—beginning from Caesar and downward as far as to Nebuchadnezzar. So I had, after all, to go through Bible history; the old boy's had to take to his mother again. After all, it is written: Of the earth art thou come. The main thing in life is to fill one's belly. Fill it with onions? That's not much good; I must take to cunning and set out snares. There's water in the beck here; I shan't suffer thirst, and I count as the first 'mong the beasts after all. When my time comes to die—as most likely it will—I shall crawl in under a wind-fallen tree; like the bear, I will heap up a leaf mound above me, and I'll scratch in big print on the bark of the tree: Here rests Peer Gynt, that decent soul, Kaiser o'er all of the other beasts. Kaiser? [*Laughs inwardly.*] Why, you old soothsayer humbug! no kaiser are you; you are nought but an onion. I'm going to peel you now, my good Peer! You won't escape either by begging or howling. [*Takes an onion and pulls off layer after layer.*] There lies the outermost layer, all torn; that's the shipwrecked man on the jolly boat's keel. Here's the passenger layer, scanty and thin; and yet in its taste there's a tang of Peer Gynt. Next underneath it the gold-digger ego; the juice is all gone—if it ever had any. This coarse-grained layer with the hardened skin is the peltry hunter by Hudson's Bay. The next one looks like a crown—oh, thanks! We'll throw it away without more ado. Here's the archaeologist, short but sturdy; and here is the Prophet, juicy and fresh. He stinks, as the Scripture has it, of lies, enough to bring the water to an honest man's eyes. This layer that rolls itself softly together is the gentleman, living in ease and good cheer. The next one seems sick. There are black streaks upon it; black symbolizes both parsons and niggers. [*Pulls off several layers at once.*] What an enormous number of swathings! Isn't the kernel soon coming to light? [*Pulls the whole onion to pieces.*] I'm blest if it is! To the innermost center it's nothing but swathings—each smaller and smaller. Nature is witty! [*Throws the fragments away.*] The devil take brooding! If one goes about thinking, one's apt to stumble. Well, *I* can at any rate laugh at that danger—for here on all fours I am firmly planted. [*Scratches his head.*] A queer enough business, the whole concern! Life, as they say, plays with cards up its sleeve; but when one snatches at them they've disappeared, and one grips something else—or else nothing at all. [*He has come near to the hut; he catches sight of it and starts.*] This hut? On the heath! Ha! [*Rubs his eyes.*] It seems exactly as though I had known this same building before. The reindeer horns jutting above the gable! A mermaid shaped like a fish from the navel! Lies! there's no mermaid! But nails—and planks—bars, too, to shut out hobgoblin thoughts!

SOL. [*singing in the hut*]. Now all is ready for Whitsun Eve. Dearest boy of mine, far away, comest thou soon? Is thy burden heavy, take time, take time; I will await thee; I promised of old.

PEER [*rises, quiet and deadly pale*]. One that's remembered—and one that's forgot. One that has squandered —and one that has saved. Oh, earnest! —and never can the game be played o'er! Oh, dread!—*here* was my kaiserdom! [*Hurries off along the wood path.*]

SCENE—*Night. A heath with fir trees. A forest fire has been raging; charred tree trunks are seen stretching for miles. White mists here and there clinging to the earth.*

PEER GYNT *comes running over the heath.*

PEER. Ashes, fog scuds, dust winddriven—here's enough for building with! Stench and rottenness within it; all a whited sepulcher. Figments, dreams and stillborn knowledge lay the pyramid's foundation, o'er them shall the work mount upward, with its step on step of falsehood. Earnest shunned, repentance dreaded, flaunt at the apex like a scutcheon, fill the trump of judgment with their *Petrus Gyntus Caesar fecit!* [*Listens.*] What is this, like children's weeping? Weeping, but halfway to song. Thread balls at my feet are rolling! [*Kicking at them.*] Off with you! You block my path!

THREAD BALLS [*on the ground*]. We are thoughts; thou shouldst have thought us; feet to run on thou shouldst have given us!

PEER [*going round about*]. I have given life to *one;* 'twas a bungled, crook-legged thing!

THREAD BALLS. We should have soared up like clangorous voices—and here we must trundle as gray-yarn thread balls.

PEER [*stumbling*]. Thread clue! You accursed scamp! Would you trip your father's heels? [*Flees.*]

WITHERED LEAVES [*flying before the wind*]. We are a watchword; thou shouldst proclaimed us! See how thy dozing has woefully riddled us. The worm has gnawed us in every crevice; we have never twined us like wreaths round fruitage.

PEER. Not in vain your birth, however; lie but still and serve as manure.

SIGHING IN THE AIR. We are songs; thou shouldst have sung us! A thousand times over hast thou cowed us and smothered us. Down in thy heart's pit we have lain and waited; we were never called forth. In thy gorge be poison!

PEER. Poison *thee,* thou foolish stave! Had I time for verse and stuff? [*Attempts a short cut.*]

DEWDROPS [*dripping from the branches*]. We are tears unshed forever. Ice spears, sharp wounding, we could have melted. Now the barb rankles in the shaggy bosom; the wound is closed over; our power is ended.

PEER. Thanks; I wept in Ronde cloisters—nonetheless they tied the tail on!

BROKEN STRAWS. We are deeds; thou shouldst have achieved us! Doubt, the throttler, has crippled and riven us. On the Day of Judgment we'll come aflock and tell the story—then woe to you!

PEER. Rascal tricks! How dare you debit what is *negative* against me? [*Hastens away.*]

ASE'S VOICE [*far away*]. Fie, what a postboy! Hu, you've upset me! Snow's newly fallen here; sadly it's smirched me. You've driven me the wrong way. Peer, where's the castle? The Fiend has misled you with the switch from the cupboard!

PEER. Better haste away, poor fellow! With the devil's sins upon you, soon you'll faint upon the hillside; hard enough to bear one's own sins. [*Runs off.*]

SCENE—*Another part of the heath.*

PEER [*sings*]. A sexton! A sexton! Where are you, hounds? A song from braying precentor mouths; around your hatbrim a mourning band; my dead are many; I must follow their biers!

[BUTTON MOLDER, *with a box of tools and a large casting ladle, comes from a side path.*]

MOLDER. Well met, old gaffer!

PEER. Good evening, friend.

MOLDER. The man's in a hurry. Why, where is he going?

PEER. To a grave feast.

MOLDER. Indeed? My sight's not very good; excuse me—your name doesn't chance to be Peer?

PEER. Peer Gynt, as the saying is.

MOLDER. That I call luck! It's precisely Peer Gynt I am sent for tonight.

PEER. You're sent for? What do you want?

MOLDER. Why, see here; I'm a button molder. You're to go into my ladle.

PEER. And what to do there?

MOLDER. To be melted up.

PEER. To be melted?

MOLDER. Here it is, empty and scoured. Your grave is dug ready, your coffin bespoke. The worms in your body will live at their ease; but I have orders, without delay, on Master's behalf to fetch in your soul.

PEER. It can't be! Like this, without any warning!

MOLDER. It's an old tradition at burials and births to appoint in secret the day of the feast, with no warning at all to the guest of honor.

PEER. Ay, ay, that's true. All my brain's awhirl. You are——?

MOLDER. Why, I told you—a button molder.

PEER. I see! A pet child has many nicknames. So that's it, Peer; it is *there* you're to harbor! But these, my good man, are most unfair proceedings! I'm sure I deserve better treatment than this; I'm not nearly so bad as perhaps you think—I've done a good deal of good in the world; at worst you may call me a sort of a bungler—but certainly not an exceptional sinner.

MOLDER. Why, that is precisely the rub, my man; you're no sinner at all in the higher sense; that's why you're excused all the torture pangs and land, like others, in the casting ladle.

PEER. Give it what name you please—call it ladle or pool; spruce ale and swipes, they are both of them beer. Avaunt from me, Satan!

MOLDER. You can't be so rude as to take my foot for a horse's hoof?

PEER. On horse's hoof or on fox's claws—be off; and be careful what you're about!

MOLDER. My friend, you're making a great mistake. We're both in a hurry, and so, to save time, I'll explain the reason of the whole affair. You are, with your own lips you told me so, no sinner on the so-called heroic scale–scarce middling even––

PEER. Ah, now you're beginning to talk common sense.

MOLDER. Just have patience a bit–but to call you virtuous would be going too far.

PEER. Well, you know I have never laid claim to that.

MOLDER. You're nor one thing nor t'other then, only so-so. A sinner of really grandiose style is nowadays not to be met on the highways. It wants much more than merely to wallow in mire, for both vigor and earnestness go to a sin.

PEER. Ay, it's very true, that remark of yours; one has to lay on, like the old berserkers.

MOLDER. You, friend, on the other hand, took your sin lightly.

PEER. Only outwardly, friend, like a splash of mud.

MOLDER. Ah, we'll soon be at one now. The sulphur pool is no place for you who but plashed in the mire.

PEER. And in consequence, friend, I can go as I came?

MOLDER. No, in consequence, friend, I must melt you up.

PEER. What tricks are these that you've hit upon at home here, while I've been in foreign parts?

MOLDER. The custom's as old as the snake's creation; it's designed to prevent loss of good material. You've worked at the craft–you must know that often a casting turns out, to speak plainly, mere dross; the buttons, for instance, have sometimes no loop to them. What did *you* do then?

PEER. Flung the rubbish away.

MOLDER. Ah yes, Jon Gynt was well known for a waster, so long as he'd aught left in wallet or purse. But Master, you see, he is thrifty, he is; and that is why he's so well to do. He flings nothing away as entirely worthless that can be made use of as raw material. Now *you* were designed for a shining button on the vest of the world, but your loop gave way; so into the waste box you needs must go and then, as they phrase it, be merged in the mass.

PEER. You're surely not meaning to melt me up with Dick, Tom and Harry into something new?

MOLDER. That's just what I do mean, and nothing else. We've done it already with plenty of folks. At Kongsberg they do just the same with money that's been current so long that its stamp's worn away.

PEER. But this is the wretchedest miserliness! My dear good friend, let me get off free; a loopless button, a worn-out farthing–what is *that* to a man in your master's position?

MOLDER. Oh, so long and inasmuch as the spirit's in one, one always has value as so much metal.

PEER. No, I say! No! With both teeth and claws I'll fight against this! Sooner anything else!

MOLDER. But what else? Come now, be reasonable. You know you're not airy enough for heaven––

PEER. I'm not hard to content; I don't aim so high, but I won't be deprived of one doit of my Self. Have me judged by the law in the old-fashioned way! For a certain time place me with Him of the Hoof; say a hundred years, come the worst to the worst; that, now, is a thing that one surely can bear; for they say the torment is only moral, so it can't after all be so pyramidal. It is, as 'tis written, a mere transition; and as the fox said: One waits; there comes an hour of deliverance; one lives in seclusion and hopes in the meantime for happier days. But this other notion—to have to be merged, like a mote, in the carcass of some outsider—this casting ladle business, this Gynt cessation—it stirs up my innermost soul in revolt!

MOLDER. Bless me, my dear Peer, there is surely no need to get so wrought up about trifles like this. Yourself you never have been at all; then what does it matter, your dying right out?

PEER. Have *I* not been? I could almost laugh! Peer Gynt, then, has been something else, I suppose! No, button molder, you judge in the dark. If you could but look into my very reins, you'd find only Peer there and Peer all through—nothing else in the world, no, nor anything more.

MOLDER. It's impossible. Here I have got my orders. Look, here it is written: Peer Gynt shalt thou summon. He has set at defiance his life's design; clap him into the ladle with other spoiled goods.

PEER. What nonsense! They must mean some other person. Is it really Peer? It's not Rasmus or Jon?

MOLDER. It is many a day since I melted them. So come quietly now and don't waste my time.

PEER. I'll be damned if I do! Ay, 'twould be a fine thing if it turned out tomorrow someone else was meant. You'd better take care what you're at, my good man! Think of the onus you're taking upon you.

MOLDER. I have it in writing.

PEER. At least give me time!

MOLDER. What good would that do you?

PEER. I'll use it to prove that I've been myself all the days of my life, and that's the question that's in dispute.

MOLDER. You'll prove it? And how?

PEER. Why, by vouchers and witnesses.

MOLDER. I'm sadly afraid Master will not accept them.

PEER. Impossible! However, enough for the day! My dear man, allow me a loan of myself; I'll be back shortly. One is born only once, and one's self, as created, one fain would stick to. Come, are we agreed?

MOLDER. Very well then, so be it. But remember, we meet at the next crossroads.

[PEER GYNT *runs off.*]

SCENE—*A further point on the heath.*

PEER [*running hard*]. Time is money, as the Scripture says. If I only knew where the crossroads are—they may be near and they may be far. The earth burns beneath me like red-hot iron. A witness! A witness! Oh, where shall I find one? It's almost unthinkable here in the forest. The world is a bungle! A wretched arrangement, when a man must prove a right that's as patent as day!

[*An* OLD MAN, *bent with age, with a staff in his hand and a bag on his back, is trudging in front of him.*]

OLD MAN [*stops*]. Dear, kind sir—a trifle to a houseless soul!

PEER. Excuse me, I've got no small change in my pocket.

OLD MAN. Prince Peer! Oh, to think we should meet again!

PEER. Who are you?

OLD MAN. You forget the Old Man in the Ronde?

Peer. Why, you're never——

Old Man. The King of the Dovre, my boy!

Peer. The Dovre King? Really? The Dovre King? Speak!

Old Man. Oh, I've come terribly down in the world!

Peer. Ruined?

Old Man. Ay, plundered of every stiver. Here I am tramping it, starved as a wolf.

Peer. Hurrah! Such a witness doesn't grow on the trees!

Old Man. My Lord Prince, too, has grizzled a bit since we met.

Peer. My dear father-in-law, the years gnaw and wear one. Well, well, a truce to all private affairs—and pray, above all things, no family jars. I was then a sad madcap.

Old Man. Oh yes! Oh yes! His Highness was young, and what won't one do then? But His Highness was wise in rejecting his bride; he saved himself thereby both worry and shame, for since then she's utterly gone to the bad.

Peer. Indeed!

Old Man. She has led a deplorable life; and, just think—she and Trond are now living together.

Peer. Which Trond?

Old Man. Of the Valfjeld.

Peer. It's he? Aha, it was he I cut out with the saeter girls.

Old Man. But my grandson has flourished—grown both stout and great and has strapping children all over the country——

Peer. Now, my dear man, spare us this flow of words; I've something quite different troubling my mind. I've got into rather a ticklish position and am greatly in need of a witness or voucher; that's how you could help me best, father-in-law, and I'll find you a trifle to drink my health with.

Old Man. You don't say so; can I be of use to His Highness? You'll give a character, then, in return?

Peer. Most gladly. I'm somewhat hard pressed for cash and must cut down expenses in every direction. Now hear what's the matter. No doubt you remember that night when I came to the Ronde a-wooing——

Old Man. Why, of course, my Lord Prince!

Peer. Oh, no more of the prince! But no matter. You wanted, by sheer brute force, to bias my sight, with a slit in the lens, and to change me about from Peer Gynt to a troll. What did *I* do then? I stood out against it—swore I would stand on no feet but my own; love, power and glory at once I renounced, and all for the sake of remaining myself. Now this fact, you see, you must swear to in court——

Old Man. No, I'm blest if I can.

Peer. Why, what nonsense is this?

Old Man. You surely don't want to compel me to lie? You pulled on the troll breeches—don't you remember? —and tasted the mead——

Peer. Ay, you lured me seductively —but I flatly declined the decisive test, and *that* is the thing you must judge your man by. It's the end of the ditty that all depends on.

Old Man. But it ended, Peer, just in the opposite way.

Peer. What rubbish is this?

Old Man. When you left the Ronde you inscribed my motto upon your scutcheon.

Peer. What motto?

Old Man. The potent and sundering word.

Peer. The word?

OLD MAN. That which severs the whole race of men from the troll folk. *Troll! To thyself be enough!*

PEER [*falls back a step*]. *Enough!*

OLD MAN. And with nerve in your body you've been living up to it ever since.

PEER. What, I? Peer Gynt?

OLD MAN [*weeps*]. It's ungrateful of you! You've lived as a troll but have still kept it secret. The word I taught you has shown you the way to swing yourself up as a man of substance—and now you must needs come and turn up your nose at me and the word you've to thank for it all.

PEER. *Enough!* A hill troll! An egoist! This must be all rubbish; that's perfectly certain!

OLD MAN [*pulls out a bundle of old newspapers*]. I daresay you think that we've no newspapers? Wait; here I'll show you in red and black how the *Bloksberg Post* eulogizes you, and the *Heklefjeld Journal* has done the same ever since the winter you left the country. Do you care to read them? You're welcome, Peer. Here's an article, look you, signed "Stallion-hoof." And here too is one: "On Troll Nationalism." The writer points out and lays stress on the truth that horns and a tail are of little importance so long as one has but a strip of the hide. "Our *enough*," he concludes, "gives the hallmark of trolldom to man"—and proceeds to cite you as an instance.

PEER. A hill troll? I?

OLD MAN. Yes, that's perfectly clear.

PEER. Might as well have stayed quietly where I was? Might have stopped in the Ronde in comfort and peace? Saved my trouble and toil and no end of shoe leather? Peer Gynt—a troll? Why, it's rubbish! It's stuff! Good-by! There's a halfpenny to buy you tobacco.

OLD MAN. Nay, my good Prince Peer!

PEER. Let me go! You're mad or else doting. Off to the hospital with you!

OLD MAN. Oh, that is exactly what I'm in search of. But, as I told you, my grandson's offspring have become overwhelmingly strong in the land, and they say that I only exist in books. The saw says: One's kin are unkindest of all. I've found to my cost that that saying is true. It's cruel to count as mere figment and fable——

PEER. My dear man, there are others who share the same fate.

OLD MAN. And ourselves we've no mutual aid society, no alms box or penny savings bank; in the Ronde, of course, they'd be out of place.

PEER. No, that cursed *To thyself be enough* was the word there!

OLD MAN. Oh, come now, the prince can't complain of the word. And if he could manage by hook or by crook ——

PEER. My man, you have got on the wrong scent entirely; I'm myself, as the saying goes, fairly cleaned out.

OLD MAN. You surely can't mean it? His Highness a beggar?

PEER. Completely. His Highness's ego's in pawn. And it's all your fault, you accursed trolls! That's what comes of keeping bad company.

OLD MAN. So there came my hope toppling down from its perch again! Good-by! I had best struggle on to the town.

PEER. What would you do there?

OLD MAN. I will go to the theater. The papers are clamoring for national talents.

PEER. Good luck on your journey.

and greet them from me. If I can but get free, I will go the same way. A farce I will write them, a mad and profound one; its name shall be: *Sic transit gloria mundi.* [*He runs off along the road; the* OLD MAN *shouts after him.*]

SCENE—*At a crossroad.*

PEER. Now comes the pinch, Peer, as never before! This Dovrish *enough* has passed judgment upon you. The vessel's a wreck; one must float with the spars. All else; not only to the spoiled-goods heap!

MOLDER [*at the crossroads*]. Well, now, Peer Gynt, have you found your voucher?

PEER. Have we reached the cross-road? Well, that's short work!

MOLDER. I can see on your face, as it were a signboard, the gist of the paper before I've read it.

PEER. I got tired of the hunt; one might lose one's way—

MOLDER. Yes, and what does it lead to after all?

PEER. True enough; in the wood, and by night as well—

MOLDER. There's an old man, though, trudging. Shall we call him here?

PEER. No, let him go. He is drunk, my dear fellow!

MOLDER. But perhaps he might—

PEER. Hush; no—let him be!

MOLDER. Well, shall we turn to, then?

PEER. One question only: What is it, at bottom, this "being oneself"?

MOLDER. A singular question, most odd in the mouth of a man who just now—

PEER. Come, a straightforward answer.

MOLDER. To be oneself is: to slay oneself. But on you that answer is doubtless lost, and therefore we'll say: to stand forth everywhere with Master's intention displayed like a signboard.

PEER. But suppose a man never has come to know what Master meant with him?

MOLDER. He must divine it.

PEER. But how oft are divinings beside the mark?—then one's carried *ad undas* in middle career.

MOLDER. That is certain, Peer Gynt; in default of divining the cloven-hoofed gentleman finds his best hook.

PEER. This matter's excessively complicated. See here! I no longer plead being myself; it might not be easy to get it proven. That part of my case I must look on as lost. But just now, as I wandered alone o'er the heath, I felt my conscience shoe pinching me; I said to myself: After all, you're a sinner—

MOLDER. You seem bent on beginning all over again.

PEER. No, very far from it; a *great* one I mean; not only in deeds but in words and desires. I've lived a most damnable life abroad.

MOLDER. Perhaps; I must ask you to show me the schedule!

PEER. Well, well, give me time; I will find out a parson, confess with all speed and then bring you his voucher.

MOLDER. Ay, if you can bring me that, then it is clear you escape this business of the casting ladle. But, Peer, I'd my orders—

PEER. The paper is old; it dates no doubt from a long-past period; at one time I lived with disgusting slackness, went playing the prophet and trusted in Fate. Well, may I try?

MOLDER. But—

PEER. My dear fellow, I'm sure you

can't have so much to do. Here, in this district, the air is so bracing it adds an ell to the people's ages. Recollect what the Justedal parson wrote: It's seldom that anyone dies in this valley.

MOLDER. To the next crossroads, then, but not a step further.

PEER. A priest I must catch, if it be with the tongs. [*He starts running.*]

SCENE—*A heather-clad hillside with a path following the windings of the ridge.*

PEER. This may come in useful in many ways, said Esben as he picked up a magpie's wing. Who could have thought one's account of sins would come to one's aid on the last night of all? Well, whether or no, it's a ticklish business; a move from the frying pan into the fire—but then there's a proverb of well-tried validity which says that as long as there's life there's hope.

[A LEAN PERSON, *in a priest's cassock, kilted up high, and with a birding net over his shoulder, comes hurrying along the ridge.*]

PEER. Who goes there? A priest with a fowling net! Hei, hop! I'm the spoiled child of fortune indeed! Good evening, Herr Pastor, the path is bad.

LEAN ONE. Ah yes, but what wouldn't one do for a soul?

PEER. Aha! Then there's someone bound heavenward?

LEAN ONE. No; I hope he is taking a different road.

PEER. May I walk with Herr Pastor a bit of the way?

LEAN ONE. With pleasure; I'm partial to company.

PEER. I should like to consult you——

LEAN ONE. *Heraus!* Go ahead!

PEER. You see here before you a good sort of man. The laws of the state I have strictly observed, have made no acquaintance with fetters or bolts; but it happens at times that one misses one's footing and stumbles——

LEAN ONE. Ah yes, that occurs to the best of us.

PEER. Now these trifles, you see——

LEAN ONE. Only trifles?

PEER. Yes; from sinning *en gros* I have ever refrained.

LEAN ONE. Oh! then, my dear fellow, pray leave me in peace; I'm not the person you seem to think me. You look at my fingers? What see you in them?

PEER. A nail system somewhat extremely developed.

LEAN ONE. And now? You are casting a glance at my feet?

PEER [*pointing*]. That's a natural hoof?

LEAN ONE. So I flatter myself.

PEER [*raises his hat*]. I'd have taken my oath you were simply a parson, and I find I've the honor—— Well, best is best; when the hall door stands wide, shun the kitchen way; when the king's to be met with, avoid the lackey.

LEAN ONE. Your hand! You appear to be free from prejudice. Say on then, my friend; in what way can I serve you? Now you mustn't ask me for wealth or power; I couldn't supply them although I should hang for it. You can't think how slack the whole business is; transactions have dwindled most pitiably. Nothing doing in souls; only now and again a stray one——

PEER. The race has improved so remarkably?

LEAN ONE. No, just the reverse; it's sunk shamefully low—the majority end in a casting ladle.

PEER. Ah yes—I have heard that

ladle mentioned; in fact, 'twas the cause of my coming to you.

LEAN ONE. Speak out!

PEER. If it were not too much to ask, I should like——

LEAN ONE. A harbor of refuge, eh?

PEER. You've guessed my petition before I have asked. You tell me the business is going awry, so I daresay you will not be overparticular.

LEAN ONE. But, my dear——

PEER. My demands are in no way excessive. I shouldn't insist on a salary, but treatment as friendly as things will permit.

LEAN ONE. A fire in your room?

PEER. Not too much fire—and chiefly the power of departing in safety and peace—the right, as the phrase goes, of freely withdrawing should an opening offer for happier days.

LEAN ONE. My dear friend, I vow I'm sincerely distressed; but you cannot imagine how many petitions of similar purport good people send in when they're quitting the scene of their earthly activity.

PEER. But now that I think of my past career I feel I've an absolute claim to admission——

LEAN ONE. 'Twas but trifles, you said.

PEER. In a certain sense; but, now I remember, I've trafficked in slaves.

LEAN ONE. There are men who have trafficked in wills and souls but who bungled it so that they failed to get in.

PEER. I've shipped Brahma figures in plenty to China.

LEAN ONE. Mere fustian again! Why, we laugh at such things. There are people that ship off far gruesomer figures in sermons, in art and in literature—yet have to stay out in the cold.

PEER. Ah, but then, do you know—I once went and set up as Prophet!

LEAN ONE. In foreign parts? Humbug! Why, most people's *sehen ins Blaue* ends in the casting ladle. If you've no more than that to rely upon, with the best of good will, I can't possibly house you.

PEER. But hear this: in a shipwreck I clung to a boat's keel—and it's written: A drowning man grasps at a straw—furthermore it is written: You're nearest yourself—so I halfway divested a cook of his life.

LEAN ONE. It were all one to me if a kitchenmaid you had halfway divested of something else. What sort of stuff is this halfway jargon, saving your presence? Who, think you, would care to throw away dearly bought fuel in times like these on such spiritless rubbish as this? There now, don't be enraged; 'twas your sins that I scoffed at, and excuse my speaking my mind so bluntly. Come, my dearest friend, banish this stuff from your head and get used to the thought of the casting ladle. What would you gain if I lodged you and boarded you? Consider: I know you're a sensible man. Well, you'd keep your memory, that's so far true; but the retrospect o'er recollection's domain would be, both for heart and for intellect, what the Swedes call "mighty poor sport" indeed. You have nothing either to howl or to smite about, no cause for rejoicing nor yet for despair, nothing to make you feel hot or cold; only a sort of a something to fret over.

PEER. It is written: It's never so easy to know where the shoe is tight that one isn't wearing.

LEAN ONE. Very true; I have—praise be to so-and-so!—no occasion for more than a single odd shoe. But it's lucky we happened to speak of shoes; it reminds me that I must be hurrying on. I'm after a roast that I hope will prove fat, so I really mustn't stand gossiping here.

PEER. And may one inquire, then, what sort of sin diet the man has been fattened on?

LEAN ONE. I understand he has been himself both by night and by day, and that, after all, is the principal point.

PEER. Himself? Then do such folks belong to your parish?

LEAN ONE. That depends; the door, at least, stands ajar for them. Remember, in two ways a man can be himself—there's a right and wrong side to the jacket. You know they have lately discovered in Paris a way to take portraits by help of the sun. One can either produce a straightforward picture or else what is known as a negative one. In the latter the lights and the shades are reversed, and they're apt to seem ugly to commonplace eyes; but, for all that, the likeness is latent in them, and all you require is to bring it out. If, then, a soul shall have pictured itself in the course of its life by the negative method, the plate is not therefore entirely cashiered —but without more ado they consign it to me. I take it in hand, then, for further treatment and by suitable methods effect its development. I steam it, I dip it, I burn it, I scour it, with sulphur and other ingredients like that, till the image appears which the plate was designed for—that, namely, which people call positive. But if one, like *you*, has smudged himself out, neither sulphur nor potash avails in the least.

PEER. I see; one must come to you black as a raven to turn out a white ptarmigan? Pray, what's the name inscribed 'neath the negative counterfeit that you're now to transfer to the positive side?

LEAN ONE. The name's Peter Gynt.

PEER. Peter Gynt? Indeed? Is Herr Gynt himself?

LEAN ONE. Yes, he vows he is.

PEER. Well, he's one to be trusted, that same Herr Peter.

LEAN ONE. You know him, perhaps?

PEER. Oh yes, after a fashion; one knows all sorts of people.

LEAN ONE. I'm pressed for time; where saw you him last?

PEER. It was down at the Cape.

LEAN ONE. Di Buona Speranza?

PEER. Just so; but he sails very shortly again, if I'm not mistaken.

LEAN ONE. I must hurry off then without delay. I only hope I may catch him in time! That Cape of Good Hope—I could never abide it; it's ruined by missionaries from Stavanger. [*He rushes off southward.*]

PEER. The stupid hound! There he takes to his heels with his tongue lolling out. He'll be finely sold. It delights me to humbug an ass like that. He to give himself airs and to lord it forsooth! He's a mighty lot, truly, to swagger about! He'll scarcely grow fat at his present trade; he'll soon drop from his perch with his whole apparatus. Hm, *I'm* not oversafe in the saddle either; I'm expelled, one may say, from self-owning nobility. [*A shooting star is seen; he nods after it.*] Bear all hail from Peer Gynt, Brother Starry-Flash! To flash forth, to go out and be nought at a gulp——[*Pulls himself together as though in terror and goes deeper in among the mists; stillness for a while; then he cries.*] Is there no one, no one in all the turmoil —in the void no one, no one in heaven

— [*He comes forward again further down, throws his hat upon the ground and tears at his hair. By degrees a stillness comes over him.*] So unspeakably poor, then, a soul can go back to nothingness, into the gray of the mist. Thou beautiful earth, be not angry with me that I trampled thy grasses to no avail. Thou beautiful sun, thou hast squandered away thy glory of light in an empty hut. There was no one within it to hearten and warm; the owner, they tell me, was never at home. Beautiful sun and beautiful earth, you were foolish to bear and give light to my mother. The spirit is niggard and nature lavish, and dearly one pays for one's birth with one's life. I will clamber up high, to the dizziest peak; I will look once more on the rising sun, gaze till I'm tired o'er the promised land; then try to get snowdrifts piled over me. They can write above then: "Here *No One* lies buried"; and afterward–then!–let things go as they can.

CHURCHGOERS [*singing on the forest path*]. Oh, morning thrice blessed, when the tongues of God's kingdom struck the earth like to flaming steel! from the earth to His dwelling now the heirs' song ascendeth in the tongue of the kingdom of God.

PEER [*crouches as in terror*]. Never look there! *There* all's desert and waste. I fear I was dead long before I died. [*Tries to slink in among the bushes but comes upon the cross-roads.*]

MOLDER. Good morning, Peer Gynt! Where's the list of your sins?

PEER. Do you think that I haven't been whistling and shouting as hard as I could?

MOLDER. And met no one at all?

PEER. Not a soul but a tramping photographer.

MOLDER. Well, the respite is over.

PEER. Ay, everything's over. The owl smells the daylight. Just list to the hooting!

MOLDER. It's the matin bell ringing—

PEER [*pointing*]. What's that shining yonder?

MOLDER. Only light from a hut.

PEER. And that wailing sound?

MOLDER. But a woman singing.

PEER. Ay, there–there I'll find the list of my sins.

MOLDER [*seizing him*]. Set your house in order!

[*They have come out of the underwood and are standing near the hut. Day is dawning.*]

PEER. Set my house in order? It's there! Away! Get you gone! Though your ladle were huge as a coffin, it were too small, I tell you, for me and my sins!

MOLDER. Well, to the third cross-road, Peer; but then— [*Turns aside and goes.*]

PEER [*approaches the hut*]. Forward and back, and it's just as far. Out and in, and it's just as strait. [*Stops.*] No!–like a wild, an unending lament is the thought: to come back, to go in, to go home. [*Takes a few steps on but stops again.*] Round about, said the Boyg! [*Hears singing in the hut.*] Ah no! This time at least right through, though the path may be never so strait! [*He runs toward the hut; at the same moment* SOLVEIG *appears in the doorway, dressed for church, with a psalmbook wrapped in a kerchief and a staff in her hand. She stands there erect and mild.*]

PEER [*flings himself down on the threshold*]. Hast thou doom for a sinner, then speak it forth!

SOL. He is here! He is here! Oh, to God be the praise! [*Stretches out her arms as though groping for him.*]

PEER. Cry out all my sins and my trespasses!

SOL. In nought hast thou sinned, oh! my own only boy. [*Gropes for him again and finds him.*]

MOLDER [*behind the house*]. The sin list, Peer Gynt?

PEER. Cry aloud my crime!

SOL. [*sits down beside him*]. Thou hast made all my life as a beautiful song. Blessed be thou that at last thou hast come! Blessed, thrice blessed our Whitsun-morn meeting!

PEER. Then I am lost!

SOL. There is one that rules all things.

PEER [*laughs*]. Lost! Unless thou canst answer riddles.

SOL. Tell me them.

PEER. Tell them! Come on! To be sure! Canst thou tell where Peer Gynt has been since we parted?

SOL. Been?

PEER. With his destiny's seal on his brow; been, as in God's thought he first sprang forth! Canst thou tell me? If not, I must get me home–go down to the mist-shrouded regions.

SOL. [*smiling*]. Oh, that riddle is easy.

PEER. Then tell what thou knowest! Where was I, as myself, as the whole man, the true man? Where was I, with God's sigil upon my brow?

SOL. In my faith, in my hope and in my love.

PEER [*starts back*]. What sayest thou? Peace! These are juggling words. Thou art mother thyself to the man that's there.

SOL. Ay, that I am, but who is his father? Surely he that forgives at the mother's prayer.

PEER [*a light shines in his face; he cries*]. My mother; my wife; oh, thou innocent woman!–in thy love–oh, there hide me, hide me! [*Clings to her and hides his face in her lap. A long silence. The sun rises.*]

SOL. [*sings softly*]. Sleep thou, dearest boy of mine! I will cradle thee, I will watch thee–– The boy has been sitting on his mother's lap. They two have been playing all the lifeday long. The boy has been resting at his mother's breast all the lifeday long. God's blessing on my joy! The boy has been lying close in to my heart all the lifeday long. He is weary now. Sleep thou, dearest boy of mine! I will cradle thee, I will watch thee.

MOLDER'S VOICE [*behind the house*]. We'll meet at the last crossroad again, Peer; and *then* we'll see whether–– I say no more.

SOL. [*sings louder in the full daylight*]. I will cradle thee, I will watch thee. Sleep and dream thou, dear my boy!

PILLARS OF SOCIETY

PERSONS OF THE PLAY

KARSTEN BERNICK, *a shipbuilder.*
MRS BERNICK, *his wife.*
OLAF, *their son, thirteen years old.*
MARTHA BERNICK, *Karsten Bernick's sister.*
JOHAN TONNESEN, *Mrs Bernick's younger brother.*
LONA HESSEL, *Mrs Bernick's elder half sister.*
HILMAR TONNESEN, *Mrs Bernick's cousin.*
DINA DORF, *a young girl living with the Bernicks.*
RORLUND, *a schoolmaster.*
RUMMEL, *a merchant.*
VIGELAND, SANDSTAD } *tradesmen.*
KRAP, *Bernick's confidential clerk.*
AUNE, *foreman of Bernick's shipbuilding yard.*
MRS RUMMEL.
HILDA RUMMEL, *her daughter.*
MRS HOLT.
NETTA HOLT, *her daughter.*
MRS LYNGE.
Townsfolk and visitors, foreign sailors, steamboat passengers, etc., etc.

The action takes place at the house of BERNICK *in one of the smaller coast towns in Norway.*

ACT I

SCENE—*A spacious garden room in the* BERNICK's *house. In the foreground on the left is a door leading to* BERNICK's *business room; farther back in the same wall a similar door. In the middle of the opposite wall is a large entrance door which leads to the street. The wall in the background is almost wholly composed of plate glass; a door in it opens upon a broad flight of steps which lead down to the garden; a sun awning is stretched over the steps. Below the steps a part of the garden is visible, bordered by a fence with a small gate in it. On the other side of the fence runs a street, the opposite side of which is occupied by small wooden houses painted in bright colors. It is summer, and the sun is shining warmly. People are seen every now and then, passing along the street and stopping to talk to one another; others going in and out of a shop at the corner; etc., etc.*

In the room a gathering of ladies is seated round a table. MRS BERNICK *is presiding; on her left side are* MRS HOLT *and her daughter* NETTA, *and next to them* MRS RUMMEL *and* HILDA RUMMEL. *On* MRS BERNICK'S *right are* MRS LYNGE, MARTHA BERNICK *and* DINA DORF. *All the ladies are busy working. On the table lie great piles of linen garments and other articles of clothing, some half finished and some merely cut out. Farther back, at a small table on which two pots of flowers and a glass of sugared water are standing,* RORLUND *is sitting, reading aloud from a book with gilt edges, but only loud enough for the spectators to catch a word now and then. Out in the garden* OLAF BERNICK *is running about and shooting at a target with a toy crossbow.*

After a moment AUNE *comes in quietly through the door on the right. There is a slight interruption in the reading.* MRS BERNICK *nods to him and points to the door on the left.* AUNE *goes quietly across, knocks softly at the door of* BERNICK'S *room and after a moment's pause knocks again.* KRAP *comes out of the room with his hat in his hand and some papers under his arm.*

KRAP. Oh, it was you knocking?

AUNE. Mr Bernick sent for me.

KRAP. He did, but he cannot see you. He has deputed me to tell you——

AUNE. Deputed you? All the same, I would much rather——

KRAP. —deputed me to tell you what he wanted to say to you. You must give up these Saturday lectures of yours to the men.

AUNE. Indeed? I supposed I might use my own time——

KRAP. You must not use your own time in making the men useless in working hours. Last Saturday you were talking to them of the harm that would be done to the workmen by our new machines and the new working methods at the yard. What makes you do that?

AUNE. I do it for the good of the community.

KRAP. That's curious, because Mr Bernick says it is disorganizing the community.

AUNE. My community is not Mr Bernick's, Mr Krap! As president of the Industrial Association, I must——

KRAP. You are, first and foremost, president of Mr Bernick's shipbuilding yard; and, before everything else, you have to do your duty to the community known as the firm of Bernick & Co.; that is what every one of us lives for. Well, now you know what Mr Bernick had to say to you.

AUNE. Mr Bernick would not have put it that way, Mr Krap! But I know well enough whom I have to thank for this. It is that damned American boat. Those fellows expect to get work done here the way they are accustomed to it over there, and that——

KRAP. Yes, yes, but I can't go into all these details. You know now what Mr Bernick means, and that is sufficient. Be so good as to go back to the yard; probably you are needed there. I shall be down myself in a little while. Excuse me, ladies! [*Bows to the ladies and goes out through the garden and down the street.* AUNE *goes quietly out to the right.* RORLUND, *who has continued his reading during the foregoing conversation, which has been carried on in low tones, has now come to the end of the book and shuts it with a bang.*]

ROR. There, my dear ladies, that is the end of it.

Mrs R. What an instructive tale!

Mrs H. And such a good moral!

Mrs B. A book like that really gives one something to think about.

Ror. Quite so; it presents a salutary contrast to what, unfortunately, meets our eyes every day in the newspapers and magazines. Look at the gilded and painted exterior displayed by any large community and think what it really conceals!—emptiness and rottenness, if I may say so; no foundation of morality beneath it. In a word, these large communities of ours nowadays are whited sepulchers.

Mrs H. How true! How true!

Mrs R. And for an example of it we need look no farther than at the crew of the American ship that is lying here just now.

Ror. Oh, I would rather not speak of such offscourings of humanity as that. But even in higher circles—what is the case there? A spirit of doubt and unrest on all sides, minds never at peace and instability characterizing all their behavior. Look how completely family life is undermined over there! Look at their shameless love of casting doubt on even the most serious truths!

Dina [*without looking up from her work*]. But are there not many big things done there too?

Ror. Big things done? I do not understand.

Mrs H. [*in amazement*]. Good gracious, Dina!

Mrs R. [*in the same breath*]. Dina, how can you?

Ror. I think it would scarcely be a good thing for us if such "big things" became the rule here. No indeed, we ought to be only too thankful that things are as they are in this country. It is true enough that tares grow up amongst our wheat here too, alas; but we do our best conscientiously to weed them out as well as we are able. The important thing is to keep society pure, ladies—to ward off all the hazardous experiments that a restless age seeks to force upon us.

Mrs H. And there are more than enough of them in the wind, unhappily.

Mrs R. Yes, you know last year we only by a hairsbreadth escaped the project of having a railway here.

Mrs B. Ah, my husband prevented that.

Ror. Providence, Mrs Bernick. You may be certain that your husband was the instrument of a higher Power when he refused to have anything to do with the scheme.

Mrs B. And yet they said such horrible things about him in the newspapers! But we have quite forgotten to thank you, Mr Rorlund. It is really more than friendly of you to sacrifice so much of your time to us.

Ror. Not at all. This is holiday time, and——

Mrs B. Yes, but it is a sacrifice all the same, Mr Rorlund.

Ror. [*drawing his chair nearer*]. Don't speak of it, my dear lady. Are you not all of you making some sacrifice in a good cause?—and that willingly and gladly? These poor fallen creatures for whose rescue we are working may be compared to soldiers wounded on the field of battle; you, ladies, are the kindhearted sisters of mercy who prepare the lint for these stricken ones, lay the bandages softly on their wounds, heal them and cure them——

Mrs B. It must be a wonderful gift

to be able to see everything in such a beautiful light.

ROR. A good deal of it is inborn in one—but it can be, to a great extent, acquired too. All that is needful is to see things in the light of a serious mission in life. [*To* MARTHA.] What do you say, Miss Bernick? Have you not felt as if you were standing on firmer ground since you gave yourself up to your schoolwork?

MARTHA. I really do not know what to say. There are times, when I am in the schoolroom down there, that I wish I were far away out on the stormy seas.

ROR. That is merely temptation, dear Miss Bernick. You ought to shut the doors of your mind upon such disturbing guests as that. By the "stormy seas"—for of course you do not intend me to take your words literally—you mean the restless tide of the great outer world, where so many are shipwrecked. Do you really set such store on the life you hear rushing by outside? Only look out into the street. There they go, walking about in the heat of the sun, perspiring and tumbling about over their little affairs. No, we undoubtedly have the best of it, who are able to sit here in the cool and turn our backs on the quarter from which disturbance comes.

MARTHA. Yes, I have no doubt you are perfectly right.

ROR. And in a house like this—in a good and pure home, where family life shows in its fairest colors—where peace and harmony rule—— [*To* MRS BERNICK.] What are you listening to, Mrs Bernick?

MRS B. [*who has turned toward the door of* BERNICK's *room*]. They are talking very loud in there.

ROR. Is there anything particular going on?

MRS B. I don't know. I can hear that there is somebody with my husband.

[HILMAR TONNESEN, *smoking a cigar, appears in the doorway on the right but stops short at the sight of the company of ladies.*]

HILMAR. Oh, excuse me. [*Turns to go back.*]

MRS B. No, Hilmar, come along in; you are not disturbing us. Do you want something?

HILMAR. No, I only wanted to look in here. Good morning, ladies. [*To* MRS BERNICK.] Well, what is the result?

MRS B. Of what?

HILMAR. Karsten has summoned a meeting, you know.

MRS B. Has he? What about?

HILMAR. Oh, it is this railway nonsense over again.

MRS R. Is it possible?

MRS B. Poor Karsten, is he to have more annoyance over that?

ROR. But how do you explain that, Mr Tonnesen? You know that last year Mr Bernick made it perfectly clear that he would not have a railway here.

HILMAR. Yes, that is what I thought too; but I met Krap, his confidential clerk, and he told me that the railway project had been taken up again and that Mr Bernick was in consultation with three of our local capitalists.

MRS R. Ah, I was right in thinking I heard my husband's voice.

HILMAR. Of course Mr Rummel is in it, and so are Sandstad and Michael Vigeland—"Saint Michael," as they call him.

ROR. Ahem!

HILMAR. I beg your pardon, Mr Rorlund?

MRS B. Just when everything was so nice and peaceful.

HILMAR. Well, as far as I am concerned, I have not the slightest objection to their beginning their squabbling again. It will be a little diversion anyway.

ROR. I think we can dispense with that sort of diversion.

HILMAR. It depends how you are constituted. Certain natures feel the lust of battle now and then. But unfortunately life in a country town does not offer much in that way, and it isn't given to everyone to—— [*Turns the leaves of the book* RORLUND *has been reading.*] *Woman as the Handmaid of Society*. What sort of drivel is this?

MRS B. My dear Hilmar, you must not say that. You certainly have not read the book.

HILMAR. No, and I have no intention of reading it, either.

MRS B. Surely you are not feeling quite well today.

HILMAR. No, I am not.

MRS B. Perhaps you did not sleep well last night?

HILMAR. No, I slept very badly. I went for a walk yesterday evening for my health's sake, and I finished up at the club and read a book about a polar expedition. There is something bracing in following the adventures of men who are battling with the elements.

MRS R. But it does not appear to have done you much good, Mr Tonnesen.

HILMAR. No, it certainly did not. I lay all night tossing about, only half asleep, and dreamed that I was being chased by a hideous walrus.

OLAF [*who meanwhile has come up the steps from the garden*]. Have you been chased by a walrus, Uncle?

HILMAR. I dreamed it, you duffer! Do you mean to say you are still playing about with that ridiculous bow? Why don't you get hold of a real gun?

OLAF. I should like to, but——

HILMAR. There is some sense in a thing like that; it is always an excitement every time you fire it off.

OLAF. And then I could shoot bears, Uncle. But Daddy won't let me.

MRS B. You really mustn't put such ideas into his head, Hilmar.

HILMAR. Hm!—it's a nice breed we are educating nowadays, isn't it? We *talk* a great deal about manly sports, goodness knows—but we only play with the question all the same; there is never any serious inclination for the bracing discipline that lies in facing danger manfully. Don't stand pointing your crossbow at me, blockhead—it might go off.

OLAF. No, Uncle, there is no arrow in it.

HILMAR. You don't know that there isn't—there may be all the same. Take it away, I tell you! Why on earth have you never gone over to America on one of your father's ships? You might have seen a buffalo hunt, then, or a fight with red Indians.

MRS B. Oh, Hilmar!

OLAF. I should like that awfully, Uncle; and then perhaps I might meet Uncle Johan and Aunt Lona.

HILMAR. Hm! Rubbish.

MRS B. You can go down into the garden again now, Olaf.

OLAF. Mother, may I go out into the street too?

MRS B. Yes, but not too far, mind.

[OLAF *runs down into the garden and out through the gate in the fence.*]

ROR. You ought not to put such fancies into the child's head, Mr Tonnesen.

HILMAR. No, of course he is destined to be a miserable stay-at-home, like so many others.

ROR. But why do you not take a trip over there yourself?

HILMAR. I? With my wretched health? Of course I get no consideration on that account. But, putting that out of the question, you forget that one has certain obligations to perform toward the community of which one forms a part. There must be *someone* here to hold aloft the banner of the Ideal. Ugh, there he is shouting again!

THE LADIES. Who is shouting?

HILMAR. I am sure I don't know. They are raising their voices so loud in there that it gets on my nerves.

MRS B. I expect it is my husband, Mr Tonnesen. But you must remember he is so accustomed to addressing large audiences——

ROR. I should not call the others low-voiced either.

HILMAR. Good lord, no!—not on any question that touches their pockets. Everything here ends in these petty material considerations. Ugh!

MRS B. Anyway, that is a better state of things than it used to be, when everything ended in mere frivolity.

MRS L. Used things really to be as bad as that here?

MRS R. Indeed they were, Mrs Lynge. You may think yourself lucky that you did not live here then.

MRS H. Yes, times have changed, and no mistake. When I look back to the days when I was a girl——

MRS R. Oh, you need not look back more than fourteen or fifteen years. God forgive us, what a life we led! There used to be a dancing society and a musical society——

MRS B. And the dramatic club. I remember it very well.

MRS R. Yes, that was where your play was performed, Mr Tonnesen.

HILMAR [*from the back of the room*]. What, what?

ROR. A play by Mr Tonnesen?

MRS R. Yes, it was long before you came here, Mr Rorlund. And it was only performed once.

MRS L. Was that not the play in which you told me you took the part of a young man's sweetheart, Mrs Rummel?

MRS R. [*glancing toward* RORLUND]. I? I really cannot remember, Mrs Lynge. But I remember well all the riotous gaiety that used to go on.

MRS H. Yes, there were houses I could name in which two large dinner parties were given in one week.

MRS L. And surely I have heard that a touring theatrical company came here too?

MRS R. Yes, that was the worst thing of the lot.

MRS H. [*uneasily*]. Ahem!

MRS R. Did you say a theatrical company? No, I don't remember that at all.

MRS L. Oh yes, and I have been told they played all sorts of mad pranks. What is really the truth of those stories?

MRS R. There is practically no truth in them, Mrs Lynge.

MRS H. Dina, my love, will you

give me that linen?

MRS B. [*at the same time*]. Dina dear, will you go and ask Katrine to bring us our coffee?

MARTHA. I will go with you, Dina.

[DINA *and* MARTHA *go out by the farther door on the left.*]

MRS B. [*getting up*]. Will you excuse me for a few minutes? I think we will have our coffee outside. [*She goes out to the veranda and sets to work to lay a table.* RORLUND *stands in the doorway talking to her.* HILMAR *sits outside smoking.*]

MRS R. [*in a low voice*]. My goodness, Mrs Lynge, how you frightened me!

MRS L. I?

MRS H. Yes, but you know it was you that began it, Mrs Rummel.

MRS R. I? How can you say such a thing, Mrs Holt? Not a syllable passed my lips!

MRS L. But what does it all mean?

MRS R. What made you begin to talk about—— Think—did you not see that Dina was in the room?

MRS L. Dina? Good gracious, is there anything wrong with——

MRS H. And in this house too! Did you not know it was Mrs Bernick's brother——

MRS L. What about him? I know nothing about it at all; I am quite new to the place, you know.

MRS R. Have you not heard that—— Ahem! [*To her daughter.*] Hilda dear, you can go for a little stroll in the garden.

MRS H. You go too, Netta. And be very kind to poor Dina when she comes back.

[HILDA *and* NETTA *go out into the garden.*]

MRS L. Well, what about Mrs Bernick's brother?

MRS R. Don't you know the dreadful scandal about him?

MRS L. A dreadful scandal about Mr Tonnesen?

MRS R. Good heavens, no; Mr Tonnesen is her cousin, of course, Mrs Lynge. I am speaking of her brother.

MRS H. The wicked Mr Tonnesen.

MRS R. His name was Johan. He ran away to America.

MRS H. Had to run away, you must understand.

MRS L. Then it is he the scandal is about?

MRS R. Yes; there was something—how shall I put it?—there was something of some kind between him and Dina's mother. I remember it all as if it were yesterday. Johan Tonnesen was in old Mrs Bernick's office then; Karsten Bernick had just come back from Paris—he had not yet become engaged——

MRS L. Yes, but what was the scandal?

MRS R. Well, you must know that Moller's company were acting in the town that winter——

MRS H. And Dorf, the actor, and his wife were in the company. All the young men in the town were infatuated with her.

MRS R. Yes, goodness knows how they could think *her* pretty. Well, Dorf came home late one evening——

MRS H. Quite unexpectedly.

MRS R. And found his—— No, really it isn't a thing one can talk about.

MRS H. After all, Mrs Rummel, he didn't find anything, because the door was locked on the inside.

MRS R. Yes, that is just what I was going to say—he found the door locked. And—just think of it—the man that was in the house had to jump out of the window.

Mrs H. Right down from an attic window.

Mrs L. And that was Mrs Bernick's brother?

Mrs R. Yes, it was he.

Mrs L. And that was why he ran away to America?

Mrs H. Yes, he had to run away, you may be sure.

Mrs R. Because something was discovered afterward that was nearly as bad; just think—he had been making free with the cashbox——

Mrs H. But you know no one was certain of that, Mrs Rummel; perhaps there was no truth in the rumor.

Mrs R. Well, I must say! Wasn't it known all over the town? Did not old Mrs Bernick nearly go bankrupt as the result of it? However, God forbid *I* should be the one to spread such reports.

Mrs H. Well, anyway, Mrs Dorf didn't get the money, because she——

Mrs L. Yes, what happened to Dina's parents afterward?

Mrs R. Well, Dorf deserted both his wife and his child. But Madam was impudent enough to stay here a whole year. Of course she had not the face to appear at the theater any more, but she kept herself by taking in washing and sewing——

Mrs H. And then she tried to set up a dancing school.

Mrs R. Naturally that was no good. What parents would trust their children to such a woman? But it did not last very long. The fine madam was not accustomed to work; she got something wrong with her lungs and died of it.

Mrs L. What a horrible scandal!

Mrs R. Yes, you can imagine how hard it was upon the Bernicks. It is the dark spot among the sunshine of their good fortune, as Rummel once put it. So never speak about it in this house, Mrs Lynge.

Mrs H. And, for heaven's sake, never mention the stepsister either!

Mrs L. Oh, so Mrs Bernick has a stepsister too?

Mrs R. *Had,* luckily; for the relationship between them is all over now. She was an extraordinary person too! Would you believe it, she cut her hair short and used to go about in men's boots in bad weather!

Mrs H. And when her stepbrother —the black sheep—had gone away, and the whole town naturally was talking about him—what do you think she did? She went out to America to him!

Mrs R. Yes, but remember the scandal *she* caused before she went, Mrs Holt!

Mrs H. Hush, don't speak of it.

Mrs L. My goodness, did she create a scandal too?

Mrs R. I think you ought to hear it, Mrs Lynge. Mr Bernick had just got engaged to Betty Tonnesen, and the two of them went arm in arm into her aunt's room to tell her the news——

Mrs H. The Tonnesens' parents were dead, you know.

Mrs R. —when, suddenly, up got Lona Hessel from her chair and gave our refined and well-bred Karsten Bernick such a box on the ear that his head swam.

Mrs L. Well, I am sure I never——

Mrs H. It is absolutely true.

Mrs R. And then she packed her box and went away to America.

Mrs L. I suppose she had had her eye on him for herself.

MRS R. Of course she had. She imagined that he and she would make a match of it when he came back from Paris.

MRS H. The idea of her thinking such a thing! Karsten Bernick—a man of the world and the pink of courtesy—a perfect gentleman—the darling of all the ladies——

MRS R. And, with it all, such an excellent young man, Mrs Holt—so moral.

MRS L. But what has this Miss Hessel made of herself in America?

MRS R. Well, you see, over that—as my husband once put it—has been drawn a veil which one should hesitate to lift.

MRS L. What do you mean?

MRS R. She no longer has any connection with the family, as you may suppose; but this much the whole town knows, that she has sung for money in drinking saloons over there——

MRS H. And has given lectures in public——

MRS R. And has published some mad kind of book.

MRS L. You don't say so!

MRS R. Yes, it is true enough that Lona Hessel is one of the spots on the sun of the Bernick family's good fortune. Well, now you know the whole story, Mrs Lynge. I am sure I would never have spoken about it except to put you on your guard.

MRS L. Oh, you may be sure I shall be most careful. But that poor child Dina Dorf! I am truly sorry for her.

MRS R. Well, really it was a stroke of good luck for her. Think what it would have meant if she had been brought up by such parents! Of course we did our best for her, every one of us, and gave her all the good advice we could. Eventually Miss Bernick got her taken into this house.

MRS H. But she has always been a difficult child to deal with. It is only natural—with all the bad example she has had before her. A girl of that sort is not like one of our own; one must be lenient with her.

MRS R. Hush—here she comes. [*In a louder voice.*] Yes, Dina is really a clever girl. Oh, is that you, Dina? We are just putting away the things.

MRS H. How delicious your coffee smells, my dear Dina. A nice cup of coffee like that——

MRS B. [*calling in from the veranda*]. Will you come out here?

[*Meanwhile* MARTHA *and* DINA *have helped the maid to bring out the coffee. All the ladies seat themselves on the veranda and talk with a great show of kindness to* DINA. *In a few moments* DINA *comes back into the room and looks for her sewing.*]

MRS B. [*from the coffee table*]. Dina, won't you——

DINA. No, thank you. [*Sits down to her sewing.* MRS BERNICK *and* RORLUND *exchange a few words; a moment afterward he comes back into the room, makes a pretext for going up to the table and begins speaking to* DINA *in low tones.*]

ROR. Dina.

DINA. Yes?

ROR. Why don't you want to sit with the others?

DINA. When I came in with the coffee I could see from the strange lady's face that they had been talking about me.

ROR. But did you not see as well how agreeable she was to you out there?

DINA. That is just what I will not stand!

ROR. You are very self-willed, Dina.

DINA. Yes.

ROR. But why?

DINA. Because it is my nature.

ROR. Could you not try to alter your nature?

DINA. No.

ROR. Why not?

DINA [*looking at him*]. Because I am one of the "poor fallen creatures," you know.

ROR. For shame, Dina.

DINA. So was my mother.

ROR. Who has spoken to you about such things?

DINA. No one; they never do. Why don't they? They all handle me in such a gingerly fashion, as if they thought I should go to pieces if they—— Oh, how I hate all this kind-heartedness.

ROR. My dear Dina, I can quite understand that you feel repressed here, but——

DINA. Yes, if only I could get right away from here. I could make my own way quite well if only I did not live amongst people who are so—so——

ROR. So what?

DINA. So proper and so moral.

ROR. Oh! But, Dina, you don't mean that.

DINA. You know quite well in what sense I mean it. Hilda and Netta come here every day, to be exhibited to me as good examples. I can never be so beautifully behaved as they; I don't *want* to be. If only I were right away from it all, I should grow to be worth something.

ROR. But you are worth a great deal, Dina dear.

DINA. What good does that do me here?

ROR. Get right away, you say? Do you mean it seriously?

DINA. I would not stay here a day longer if it were not for you.

ROR. Tell me, Dina—why is it that you are fond of being with me?

DINA. Because you teach me so much that is beautiful.

ROR. Beautiful? Do you call the little I can teach you beautiful?

DINA. Yes. Or perhaps, to be accurate, it is not that you teach me anything; but when I listen to you talking I see beautiful visions.

ROR. What do you mean, exactly, when you call a thing beautiful?

DINA. I have never thought it out.

ROR. Think it out now then. What do you understand by a beautiful thing?

DINA. A beautiful thing is something that is great—and far off.

ROR. Hm! Dina, I am so deeply concerned about you, my dear.

DINA. Only that?

ROR. You know perfectly well that you are dearer to me than I can say.

DINA. If I were Hilda or Netta, you would not be afraid to let people see it.

ROR. Ah, Dina, you can have no idea of the number of things I am forced to take into consideration. When it is a man's lot to be a moral pillar of the community he lives in he cannot be too circumspect. If only I could be certain that people would interpret my motives properly—— But no matter for that; you must, and shall be, helped to raise yourself. Dina, is it a bargain between us that when I come—when circumstances allow me to come—to you and say: "Here is my hand," you will take it and be my wife? Will you promise me that, Dina?

DINA. Yes.

ROR. Thank you, thank you! Because for my part too—— Oh, Dina, I love you so dearly. Hush! Someone is coming. Dina—for my sake—go out to the others. [*She goes out to the coffee table. At the same moment* RUMMEL, SANDSTAD *and* VIGELAND *come out of* BERNICK'S *room, followed by* BERNICK, *who has a bundle of papers in his hand.*]

BER. Well, then, the matter is settled.

VIG. Yes, I hope to goodness it is.

RUM. It is settled, Bernick. A Norseman's word stands as firm as the rocks on Dovrefjeld, you know!

BER. And no one must falter, no one give way, no matter what opposition we meet with.

RUM. We will stand or fall together, Bernick.

HILMAR [*coming in from the veranda*]. Fall? If I may ask, isn't it the railway scheme that is going to fall?

BER. No, on the contrary it is going to proceed.

RUM. Full steam, Mr Tonnesen.

HILMAR [*coming nearer*]. Really?

ROR. How is that?

MRS B. [*at the veranda door*]. Karsten dear, what is it that——

BER. My dear Betty, how can it interest you? [*To the three men.*] We must get out lists of subscribers, and the sooner the better. Obviously our four names must head the list. The positions we occupy in the community make it our duty to make ourselves as prominent as possible in the affair.

SAN. Obviously, Mr Bernick.

RUM. The thing *shall* go through, Bernick; I swear it shall!

BER. Oh, I have not the least anticipation of failure. We must see that we work, each one among the circle of his own acquaintances; and if we can point to the fact that the scheme is exciting a lively interest in all ranks of society, then it stands to reason that our Municipal Corporation will have to contribute its share.

MRS B. Karsten, you really must come out here and tell us——

BER. My dear Betty, it is an affair that does not concern ladies at all.

HILMAR. Then you are really going to support this railway scheme after all?

BER. Yes, naturally.

ROR. But last year, Mr Bernick——

BER. Last year it was quite another thing. At that time it was a question of a line along the coast——

VIG. Which would have been quite superfluous, Mr Rorlund; because, of course, we have our steamboat service——

SAN. And would have been quite unreasonably costly——

RUM. Yes, and would have absolutely ruined certain important interests in the town.

BER. The main point was that it would not have been to the advantage of the community as a whole. That is why I opposed it, with the result that the inland line was resolved upon.

HILMAR. Yes, but surely that will not touch the towns about here.

BER. It will eventually touch *our* town, my dear Hilmar, because we are going to build a branch line here.

HILMAR. Aha—a new scheme then?

RUM. Yes, isn't it a capital scheme? What?

ROR. Hm!

VIG. There is no denying that it

looks as though Providence had just planned the configuration of the country to suit a branch line.

ROR. Do you really mean it, Mr Vigeland?

BER. Yes, I must confess it seems to me as if it had been the hand of Providence that caused me to take a journey on business this spring, in the course of which I happened to traverse a valley through which I had never been before. It came across my mind like a flash of lightning that this was where we could carry a branch line down to our town. I got an engineer to survey the neighborhood and have here the provisional calculations and estimate; so there is nothing to hinder us.

MRS B. [*who is still with the other ladies at the veranda door*]. But, my dear Karsten, to think that you should have kept it all a secret from us!

BER. Ah, my dear Betty, I knew you would not have been able to grasp the exact situation. Besides, I have not mentioned it to a living soul till today. But now the decisive moment has come, and we must work openly and with all our might. Yes, even if I have to risk all I have for its sake, I mean to push the matter through.

RUM. And we will back you up, Bernick; you may rely upon that.

ROR. Do you really promise us so much, then, from this undertaking, gentlemen?

BER. Yes, undoubtedly. Think what a lever it will be to raise the status of our whole community. Just think of the immense tracts of forest land that it will make accessible; think of all the rich deposits of minerals we shall be able to work; think of the river with one waterfall above another! Think of the possibilities that open out in the way of manufactories!

ROR. And are you not afraid that an easier intercourse with the depravity of the outer world——

BER. No, you may make your mind quite easy on that score, Mr Rorlund. Our little hive of industry rests nowadays, God be thanked, on such a sound moral basis; we have all of us helped to drain it, if I may use the expression; and that we will continue to do, each in his degree. You, Mr Rorlund, will continue your richly blessed activity in our schools and our homes. We, the practical men of business, will be the support of the community by extending its welfare within as wide a radius as possible; and our women—yes, come nearer, ladies, you will like to hear it—our women, I say, our wives and daughters—you ladies will work on undisturbed in the service of charity and moreover will be a help and a comfort to your nearest and dearest, as my dear Betty and Martha are to me and Olaf—— [*Looks round him.*] Where is Olaf today?

MRS B. Oh, in the holidays it is impossible to keep him at home.

BER. I have no doubt he is down at the shore again. You will see he will end by coming to some harm there.

HILMAR. Bah! A little sport with the forces of nature——

MRS R. Your family affection is beautiful, Mr Bernick!

BER. Well, the family is the kernel of society. A good home, honored and trusty friends, a little snug family circle where no disturbing elements can cast their shadow——

[Krap *comes in from the right, bringing letters and papers.*]

Krap. The foreign mail, Mr Bernick—and a telegram from New York.

Ber. [*taking the telegram*]. Ah—from the owners of the Indian Girl.

Rum. Is the mail in? Oh, then you must excuse me.

Vig. And me too.

San. Good day, Mr Bernick.

Ber. Good day, good day, gentlemen. And remember, we have a meeting this afternoon at five o'clock.

The Three Men. Yes—quite so—of course. [*They go out to the right.*]

Ber. [*who has read the telegram*]. This is thoroughly American! Absolutely shocking!

Mrs B. Good gracious, Karsten, what is it?

Ber. Look at this, Krap! Read it!

Krap [*reading*]. "Do the least repairs possible. Send over Indian Girl as soon as she is ready to sail; good time of year; at a pinch her cargo will keep her afloat." Well, I must say——

Ror. You see the state of things in these vaunted great communities!

Ber. You are quite right; not a moment's consideration for human life when it is a question of making a profit. [*To* Krap.] Can the Indian Girl go to sea in four—or five—days?

Krap. Yes, if Mr Vigeland will agree to our stopping work on the Palm Tree meanwhile.

Ber. Hm—he won't. Well, be so good as to look through the letters. And look here, did you see Olaf down at the quay?

Krap. No, Mr Bernick. [*Goes into* Bernick's *room.*]

Ber. [*looking at the telegram again*]. These gentlemen think nothing of risking eight men's lives——

Hilmar. Well, it is a sailor's calling to brave the elements; it must be a fine tonic to the nerves to be like that, with only a thin plank between one and the abyss——

Ber. I should like to see the shipowner amongst us who would condescend to such a thing! There is not one that would do it—not a single one! [*Sees* Olaf *coming up to the house.*] Ah, thank heaven, here he is, safe and sound.

[Olaf, *with a fishing line in his hand, comes running up the garden and in through the veranda.*]

Olaf. Uncle Hilmar, I have been down and seen the steamer.

Ber. Have you been down to the quay again?

Olaf. No, I have only been out in a boat. But just think, Uncle Hilmar, a whole circus company has come on shore, with horses and animals; and there were such lots of passengers.

Mrs R. No, are we really to have a circus?

Ror. We? I certainly have no desire to see it.

Mrs R. No, of course I don't mean we, but——

Dina. I should like to see a circus very much.

Olaf. So should I.

Hilmar. You are a duffer. Is that anything to see? Mere tricks. No, it would be something quite different to see the gaucho careering over the pampas on his snorting mustang. But, heaven help us, in these wretched little towns of ours——

Olaf [*pulling at* Martha's *dress*]. Look, Aunt Martha! Look, there they come!

Mrs H. Good lord, yes—here they come.

Mrs L. Ugh, what horrid people!

[*A number of passengers and a whole crowd of townsfolk are seen coming up the street.*]

MRS R. They *are* a set of mountebanks, certainly. Just look at that woman in the gray dress, Mrs Holt—the one with a knapsack over her shoulder.

MRS H. Yes—look—she has slung it on the handle of her parasol. The manager's wife, I expect.

MRS R. And there is the manager himself, no doubt. He looks a regular pirate. Don't look at him, Hilda!

MRS H. Nor you, Netta!

OLAF. Mother, the manager is bowing to us.

BER. What?

MRS B. What are you saying, child?

MRS R. Yes, and—good heavens—the woman is bowing to us too.

BER. That is a little *too* cool!

MARTHA [*exclaims involuntarily*]. Ah!

MRS B. What is it, Martha?

MARTHA. Nothing, nothing. I thought for a moment——

OLAF [*shrieking with delight*]. Look, look, there are the rest of them, with the horses and animals! And there are the Americans too! All the sailors from the Indian Girl!

[*The strains of "Yankee Doodle," played on a clarinet and a drum, are heard.*]

HILMAR [*stopping his ears*]. Ugh, ugh, ugh!

ROR. I think we ought to withdraw ourselves from sight a little, ladies; we have nothing to do with such goings on. Let us go to our work again.

MRS B. Do you think we had better draw the curtains?

ROR. Yes, that was exactly what I meant.

[*The ladies resume their places at the worktable;* RORLUND *shuts the veranda door and draws the curtains over it and over the windows, so that the room becomes half dark.*]

OLAF [*peeping out through the curtains*]. Mother, the manager's wife is standing by the fountain now, washing her face.

MRS B. What? In the middle of the market place?

MRS R. And in broad daylight too!

HILMAR. Well, I must say if I were traveling across a desert waste and found myself beside a well, I am sure I should not stop to think whether—— Ugh, that frightful clarinet!

ROR. It is really high time the police interfered.

BER. Oh no; we must not be too hard on foreigners. Of course these folk have none of the deep-seated instincts of decency which restrain us within proper bounds. Suppose they do behave outrageously, what does it concern us? Fortunately this spirit of disorder, that flies in the face of all that is customary and right, is absolutely a stranger to our community, if I may say so. What is this!

[LONA HESSEL *walks briskly in from the door on the right.*]

THE LADIES [*in low, frightened tones*]. The circus woman! The manager's wife!

MRS B. Heavens, what does this mean?

MARTHA [*jumping up*]. Ah!

LONA. How do you do, Betty dear! How do you do, Martha! How do you do, brother-in-law!

MRS B. [*with a cry*]. Lona!

BER. [*stumbling backward*]. As sure as I am alive——

MRS H. Mercy on us!

MRS R. It cannot possibly be!

HILMAR. Well! Ugh!

MRS B. Lona! Is it really——

LONA. Really me? Yes, indeed it is; you may fall on my neck if you like.

HILMAR. Ugh, ugh!

MRS B. And coming back here as——

MRS B. And actually mean to appear in——

LONA. Appear? Appear in what?

BER. Well, I mean—in the circus.

LONA. Ha, ha, ha! Are you mad, brother-in-law? Do you think I belong to the circus troupe? No; certainly I have turned my hand to a good many things and made a fool of myself in a good many ways——

MRS R. Hm!

LONA —but I have never tried circus riding.

BER. Then you are not——

MRS B. Thank heaven!

LONA. No, we traveled like other respectable folk—second class, certainly, but we are accustomed to that.

MRS B. We, did you say?

BER. [*taking a step forward*]. Whom do you mean by "we"?

LONA. I and the child, of course.

THE LADIES [*with a cry*]. The child!

HILMAR. What!

ROR. I really must say——

MRS B. But what do you mean, Lona?

LONA. I mean John, of course; I have no other child, as far as I know, but John—or Johan, as you used to call him.

MRS B. Johan!

MRS R. [*in an undertone to* MRS LYNGE]. The scapegrace brother!

BER. [*hesitatingly*]. Is Johan with you?

LONA. Of course he is; I certainly would not come without him. Why do you look so tragical? And why are you sitting here in the gloom, sewing white things? There has not been a death in the family, has there?

ROR. Madam, you find yourself in the Society for Fallen Women.

LONA [*half to herself*]. What? Can these nice quiet-looking ladies possibly be——

MRS R. Well, really!

LONA. Oh, I understand! But, bless my soul, that is surely Mrs Rummel? And Mrs Holt sitting there too! Well, we three have not grown younger since the last time we met. But listen now, good people; let the fallen women wait for a day—they will be none the worse for that. A joyful occasion like this——

ROR. A home-coming is not always a joyful occasion.

LONA. Indeed? How do you read your Bible, Mr Parson?

ROR. I am not a parson.

LONA. Oh, you will grow into one then. But—faugh!—this moral linen of yours smells tainted—just like a winding sheet. I am accustomed to the air of the prairies, let me tell you.

BER. [*wiping his forehead*]. Yes, it certainly is rather close in here.

LONA. Wait a moment; we will resurrect ourselves from this vault. [*Pulls the curtains to one side.*] We must have broad daylight in here when the boy comes. Ah, you will see a boy then that has washed himself——

HILMAR. Ugh!

LONA [*opening the veranda door and window*]. I should say *when* he has washed himself, up at the hotel—for on the boat he got piggishly dirty.

HILMAR. Ugh, ugh!

LONA. Ugh? Why, surely isn't that—— [*Points at* HILMAR *and asks the others.*] Is *he* still loafing about here saying "Ugh"?

HILMAR. I do not loaf; it is the state of my health that keeps me here.

ROR. Ahem! Ladies, I do not think——

LONA [*who has noticed* OLAF]. Is he yours, Betty? Give me a paw, my boy! Or are you afraid of your ugly old aunt?

ROR. [*putting his book under his arm*]. Ladies, I do not think any of us is in the mood for any more work today. I suppose we are to meet again tomorrow?

LONA [*while the others are getting up and taking their leave*]. Yes, let us. I shall be on the spot.

ROR. You? Pardon me, Miss Hessel, but what do you propose to do in *our* society?

LONA. I will let some fresh air into it, Mr Parson.

ACT II

SCENE—*The same room.* MRS BERNICK *is sitting alone at the worktable sewing.* BERNICK *comes in from the right, wearing his hat and gloves and carrying a stick.*

MRS B. Home already, Karsten?

BER. Yes, I have made an appointment with a man.

MRS B. [*with a sigh*]. Oh yes, I suppose Johan is coming up here again.

BER. With a *man*, I said. [*Lays down his hat.*] What has become of all the ladies today?

MRS B. Mrs Rummel and Hilda hadn't time to come.

BER. Oh—did they send any excuse?

MRS B. Yes, they had so much to do at home.

BER. Naturally. And of course the others are not coming either?

MRS B. No, something has prevented them today too.

BER. I could have told you that beforehand. Where is Olaf?

MRS B. I let him go out a little with Dina.

BER. Hm—she is a giddy little baggage. Did you see how she at once started making a fuss of Johan yesterday?

MRS B. But, my dear Karsten, you know Dina knows nothing whatever of——

BER. No, but in any case Johan ought to have had sufficient tact not to pay her any attention. I saw quite well, from his face, what Vigeland thought of it.

MRS B. [*laying her sewing down on her lap*]. Karsten, can you imagine what his object is in coming here?

BER. Well—I know he has a farm over there, and I fancy he is not doing particularly well with it; *she* called attention yesterday to the fact that they were obliged to travel second class.

MRS B. Yes, I am afraid it must be something of that sort. But to think of her coming with him! She! After the deadly insult she offered you!

BER. Oh, don't think about that ancient history.

MRS B. How can I help thinking of it just now? After all, he is my brother—still, it is not on his account that I am distressed but because of all the unpleasantness it would mean for you. Karsten, I am so dreadfully afraid—

BER. Afraid of what?

MRS B. Isn't it possible that they may send him to prison for stealing that money from your mother?

BER. What rubbish! Who can prove that the money *was* stolen?

MRS B. The whole town knows it, unfortunately; and you know you said yourself——

BER. I said nothing. The town knows nothing whatever about the affair; the whole thing was no more than idle rumor.

MRS B. How magnanimous you are, Karsten!

BER. Do not let us have any more of these reminiscences, please! You don't know how you torture me by raking up all that. [*Walks up and down, then flings his stick away from him.*] And to think of their coming home now—just now, when it is particularly necessary for me that I should stand well in every respect with the town and with the press. Our newspapermen will be sending paragraphs to the papers in the other towns about here. Whether I receive them well or whether I receive them ill, it will all be discussed and talked over. They will rake up all those old stories—as you do. In a community like ours—— [*Throws his gloves down on the table.*] And I have not a soul here to whom I can talk about it and to whom I can go for support.

MRS B. No one at all, Karsten?

BER. No—who is there? And to have them on my shoulders just at this moment! Without a doubt they will create a scandal in some way or another—she in particular. It is simply a calamity to be connected with such folk in any way!

MRS B. Well, *I* can't help their——

BER. What can't you help? Their being your relations? No, that is quite true.

MRS B. And I did not ask them to come home.

BER. That's it—go on! "I did not ask them to come home; I did not write to them; I did not drag them home by the hair of their heads!" Oh, I know the whole rigmarole by heart.

MRS B. [*bursting into tears*]. You need not be so unkind.

BER. Yes, that's right—begin to cry, so that our neighbors may have that to gossip about too. Do stop being so foolish, Betty. Go and sit outside; someone may come in here. I don't suppose you want people to see the lady of the house with red eyes? It would be a nice thing, wouldn't it, if the story got about that—— There, I hear someone in the passage. [*A knock is heard at the door.*] Come in!

[MRS BERNICK *takes her sewing and goes out down the garden steps.* AUNE *comes in from the right.*]

AUNE. Good morning, Mr Bernick.

BER. Good morning. Well, I suppose you can guess what I want you for.

AUNE. Mr Krap told me yesterday that you were not pleased with——

BER. I am displeased with the whole management of the yard, Aune. The work does not get on as quickly as it ought. The Palm Tree ought to have been under sail long ago. Mr Vigeland comes here every day to complain about it; he is a difficult man to have with one as part owner.

AUNE. The Palm Tree can go to sea the day after tomorrow.

BER. At last. But what about the American ship, the Indian Girl, which has been laid up here for five weeks and——

AUNE. The American ship? I understood that, before everything else, we were to work our hardest to get your own ship ready.

BER. I gave you no reason to think so. You ought to have pushed on as fast as possible with the work on the American ship also, but you have not.

AUNE. Her bottom is completely rotten, Mr Bernick; the more we patch it, the worse it gets.

BER. That is not the reason. Krap has told me the whole truth. You do not understand how to work the new machines I have provided—or rather you will not try to work them.

AUNE. Mr Bernick, I am well on in the fifties, and ever since I was a boy I have been accustomed to the old way of working.

BER. We cannot work that way nowadays. You must not imagine, Aune, that it is for the sake of making profit; I do not need that, fortunately, but I owe consideration to the community I live in and to the business I am at the head of. I must take the lead in progress, or there would never be any.

AUNE. I welcome progress too, Mr Bernick.

BER. Yes, for your own limited circle—for the working class. Oh, I know what a busy agitator you are; you make speeches, you stir people up; but when some concrete instance of progress presents itself—as now, in the case of our machines—you do not want to have anything to do with it; you are afraid.

AUNE. Yes, I really am afraid, Mr Bernick. I am afraid for the number of men who will have the bread taken out of their mouths by these machines. You are very fond, sir, of talking about the consideration we owe to the community; it seems to me, however, that the community has its duties too. Why should science and capital venture to introduce these new discoveries into labor before the community has had time to educate a generation up to using them?

BER. You read and think too much, Aune; it does you no good, and that is what makes you dissatisfied with your lot.

AUNE. It is not, Mr Bernick; but I cannot bear to see one good workman dismissed after another, to starve because of these machines.

BER. Hm! When the art of printing was discovered many a quill driver was reduced to starvation.

AUNE. Would you have admired the art so greatly if you had been a quill driver in those days, sir?

BER. I did not send for you to argue with you. I sent for you to tell you that the Indian Girl must be ready to put to sea the day after tomorrow.

AUNE. But, Mr Bernick——

BER. The day after tomorrow, do you hear?—at the same time as our own ship, not an hour later. I have good reasons for hurrying on the work. Have you seen today's paper? Well, then you know the pranks these American sailors have been up to again. The rascally pack are turning the whole town upside down. Not a night passes without some brawling in the taverns or the streets—not to speak of other abominations.

AUNE. Yes, they certainly are a bad lot.

BER. And who is it that has to bear the blame for all this disorder? It is I! Yes, it is I who have to suffer for it. These newspaper fellows are making all sorts of covert insinuations because we are devoting all our energies to the Palm Tree. I, whose task in life it is to influence my fellow citizens by the force of example, have to endure this sort of thing cast in my face. I am not going to stand that. I have no fancy for having my good name smirched in that way.

AUNE. Your name stands high enough to endure that and a great deal more, sir.

BER. Not just now. At this particular moment I have need of all the respect and good will my fellow citizens can give me. I have a big undertaking on the stocks, as you probably have heard; but, if it should happen that evil-disposed persons succeed in shaking the absolute confidence I enjoy, it might land me in the greatest difficulties. That is why I want, at any price, to avoid these shameful innuendoes in the papers, and that is why I name the day after tomorrow as the limit of the time I can give you.

AUNE. Mr Bernick, you might just as well name this afternoon as the limit.

BER. You mean that I am asking an impossibility?

AUNE. Yes, with the hands we have now at the yard.

BER. Very good; then we must look about elsewhere.

AUNE. Do you really mean, sir, to discharge still more of your old workmen?

BER. No, I am not thinking of that.

AUNE. Because I think it would cause bad blood against you, both among the townsfolk and in the papers, if you did that.

BER. Very probably; therefore we will not do it. But if the Indian Girl is not ready to sail the day after tomorrow, I shall discharge *you.*

AUNE [*with a start*]. Me! [*He laughs.*] You are joking, Mr Bernick.

BER. I should not be so sure of that if I were you.

AUNE. Do you mean that you can contemplate discharging *me?* Me, whose father and grandfather worked in your yard all their lives, as I have done myself?

BER. Who is it that is forcing me to do it?

AUNE. You are asking what is impossible, Mr Bernick.

BER. Oh, where there's a will there's a way. Yes or no; give me a decisive answer, or consider yourself discharged on the spot.

AUNE [*coming a step nearer to him*]. Mr Bernick, have you ever realized what discharging an old workman means? You think he can look about for another job? Oh yes, he can do that; but does that dispose of the matter? You should just be there once, in the house of a workman who has been discharged, the evening he comes home bringing all his tools with him.

BER. Do you think I am discharging you with a light heart? Have I not always been a good master to you?

AUNE. So much the worse, Mr Bernick. Just for that very reason those at home will not blame *you;* they will say nothing to me, because they dare not, but they will look at me when I am not noticing and think that I must have deserved it. You see, sir, that is —that is what I cannot bear. I am a mere nobody, I know; but I have always been accustomed to stand first in my own home. My humble home is a little community too, Mr Bernick—a little community which I have been able to support and maintain because my wife has believed in me and because my children have believed in me. And now it is all to fall to pieces.

BER. Still, if there is nothing else

for it, the lesser must go down before the greater; the individual must be sacrificed to the general welfare. I can give you no other answer; and that, and no other, is the way of the world. You are an obstinate man, Aune! You are opposing me, not because you cannot do otherwise but because you will not exhibit the superiority of machinery over manual labor.

AUNE. And you will not be moved, Mr Bernick, because you know that if you drive me away you will at all events have given the newspapers proof of your good will.

BER. And suppose that were so? I have told you what it means for me—either bringing the press down on my back or making them well disposed to me at a moment when I am working for an object which will mean the advancement of the general welfare. Well, then, can I do otherwise than as I am doing? The question, let me tell you, turns upon this—whether your home is to be supported, as you put it, or whether hundreds of new homes are to be prevented from existing—hundreds of homes that will never be built, never have a fire lighted on their hearth, unless I succeed in carrying through the scheme I am working for now. That is the reason why I have given you your choice.

AUNE. Well, if that is the way things stand, I have nothing more to say.

BER. Hm—my dear Aune, I am extremely grieved to think that we are to part.

AUNE. We are not going to part, Mr Bernick.

BER. How is that?

AUNE. Even a common man like myself has something he is bound to maintain.

BER. Quite so, quite so—then I presume you think you may promise——

AUNE. The Indian Girl shall be ready to sail the day after tomorrow. [*Bows and goes out to the right.*]

BER. Ah, I have got the better of that obstinate fellow! I take it as a good omen.

[HILMAR *comes in through the garden door, smoking a cigar.*]

HILMAR [*as he comes up the steps to the veranda*]. Good morning, Betty! Good morning, Karsten!

MRS B. Good morning.

HILMAR. Ah, I see you have been crying, so I suppose you know all about it too?

MRS B. Know all about what?

HILMAR. That the scandal is in full swing. Ugh!

BER. What do you mean?

HILMAR [*coming into the room*]. Why, that our two friends from America are displaying themselves about the streets in the company of Dina Dorf.

MRS B. [*coming in after him*]. Hilmar, is it possible?

HILMAR. Yes, unfortunately it is quite true. Lona was even so wanting in tact as to call after me, but of course I appeared not to have heard her.

BER. And no doubt all this has not been unnoticed.

HILMAR. You may well say that. People stood still and looked at them. It spread like wildfire through the town—just like a prairie fire out West. In every house people were at the windows waiting for the procession to pass, cheek by jowl behind the curtains—ugh! Oh, you must excuse me, Betty, for saying "ugh"—this has got on my nerves. If it is going on, I shall be forced to think about getting right away from here.

Mrs B. But you should have spoken to him and represented to him that ——

Hilmar. In the open street? No, excuse me, I could not do that. To think that the fellow should dare to show himself in the town at all! Well, we shall see if the press doesn't put a stopper on him; yes—forgive me, Betty, but——

Ber. The press, do you say? Have you heard a hint of anything of the sort?

Hilmar. There *are* such things flying about. When I left here yesterday evening I looked in at the club, because I did not feel well. I saw at once, from the sudden silence that fell when I went in, that our American couple had been the subject of conversation. Then that impudent newspaper fellow, Hammer, came in and congratulated me at the top of his voice on the return of my rich cousin.

Ber. Rich?

Hilmar. Those were his words. Naturally I looked him up and down in the manner he deserved and gave him to understand that I knew nothing about Johan Tonnesen's being rich. "Really," he said, "that is very remarkable. People usually get on in America when they have something to start with, and I believe your cousin did not go over there quite empty-handed."

Ber. Hm—now will you oblige me by——

Mrs B. [*distressed*]. There, you see, Karsten——

Hilmar. Anyhow, I have spent a sleepless night because of them. And here he is, walking about the streets as if nothing were the matter. Why couldn't he disappear for good and all? It really is insufferable how hard some people are to kill.

Mrs B. My dear Hilmar, what are you saying?

Hilmar. Oh, nothing. But here this fellow escapes with a whole skin from railway accidents and fights with California grizzlies and Blackfoot Indians—has not even been scalped —— Ugh, here they come!

Ber. [*looking down the street*]. Olaf is with them too!

Hilmar. Of course! They want to remind everybody that they belong to the best family in the town. Look there!—look at the crowd of loafers that have come out of the chemist's to stare at them and make remarks. My nerves really won't stand it; how a man is to be expected to keep the banner of the Ideal flying under such circumstances, I——

Ber. They are coming here. Listen, Betty, it is my particular wish that you should receive them in the friendliest possible way.

Mrs B. Oh, may I, Karsten?

Ber. Certainly, certainly—and you too, Hilmar. It is to be hoped they will not stay here very long, and when we are quite by ourselves—no allusions to the past; we must not hurt their feelings in any way.

Mrs B. How magnanimous you are, Karsten!

Ber. Oh, don't speak of that.

Mrs B. But you must let me thank you, and you must forgive me for being so hasty. I am sure you had every reason to——

Ber. Don't talk about it, please!

Hilmar. Ugh!

[Johan Tonnesen *and* Dina *come*

up through the garden, followed by Lona *and* Olaf.]

Lona. Good morning, dear people!

Johan. We have been out having a look round the old place, Karsten.

Ber. So I hear. Greatly altered, is it not?

Lona. Mr Bernick's great and good works everywhere. We have been up into the recreation ground you have presented to the town——

Ber. Have you been *there?*

Lona. "The gift of Karsten Bernick," as it says over the gateway. You seem to be responsible for the whole place here.

Johan. Splendid ships you have got too. I met my old schoolfellow, the captain of the Palm Tree.

Lona. And you have built a new schoolhouse too, and I hear that the town has to thank you for both the gas supply and the water supply.

Ber. Well, one ought to work for the good of the community one lives in.

Lona. That is an excellent sentiment, brother-in-law; but it is a pleasure, all the same, to see how people appreciate you. I am not vain, I hope, but I could not resist reminding one or two of the people we talked to that we were relations of yours.

Hilmar. Ugh!

Lona. Do you say "Ugh" to that?

Hilmar. No, I said "Ahem."

Lona. Oh, poor chap, you may say that if you like. But are you all by yourselves today?

Ber. Yes, we are by ourselves today.

Lona. Ah yes, we met a couple of members of your morality society up at the market; they made out they were very busy. You and I have never had an opportunity for a good talk yet. Yesterday you had your three pioneers here, as well as the parson——

Hilmar. The schoolmaster.

Lona. I call him the parson. But now tell me what you think of *my* work during these fifteen years? Hasn't he grown a fine fellow? Who would recognize the madcap that ran away from home?

Hilmar. Hm!

Johan. Now, Lona, don't brag too much about me.

Lona. Well, I can tell you I am precious proud of him. Goodness knows, it is about the only thing I have done in my life; but it does give me a sort of right to exist. When I think, Johan, how we two began over there with nothing but our four bare fists——

Hilmar. Hands.

Lona. I say fists, and they were dirty fists——

Hilmar. Ugh!

Lona. And empty too.

Hilmar. Empty? Well, I must say ——

Lona. What must you say?

Ber. Ahem!

Hilmar. I must say—ugh! [*Goes out through the garden.*]

Lona. What is the matter with the man?

Ber. Oh, do not take any notice of him; his nerves are rather upset just now. Would you not like to take a look at the garden? You have not been down there yet, and I have got an hour to spare.

Lona. With pleasure. I can tell you my thoughts have been with you in this garden many and many a time.

Mrs B. We have made a great many alterations there too, as you will see.

[BERNICK, MRS BERNICK *and* LONA *go down to the garden, where they are visible every now and then during the following scene.*]

OLAF [*coming to the veranda door*]. Uncle Hilmar, do you know what Uncle Johan asked me? He asked me if I would go to America with him.

HILMAR. You, you duffer, who are tied to your mother's apron strings!

OLAF. Ah, but I won't be that any longer. You will see, when I grow big——

HILMAR. Oh, fiddlesticks! You have no really serious bent toward the strength of character necessary to——

[*They go down to the garden.* DINA *meanwhile has taken off her hat and is standing at the door on the right, shaking the dust off her dress.*]

JOHAN [*to* DINA]. The walk has made you pretty warm.

DINA. Yes, it was a splendid walk. I have never had such a splendid walk before.

JOHAN. Do you not often go for a walk in the morning?

DINA. Oh yes—but only with Olaf.

JOHAN. I see. Would you rather go down into the garden than stay here?

DINA. No, I would rather stay here.

JOHAN. So would I. Then shall we consider it a bargain that we are to go for a walk like this together every morning?

DINA. No, Mr Tonnesen, you mustn't do that.

JOHAN. What mustn't I do? You promised, you know.

DINA. Yes, but—on second thoughts—you mustn't go out with me.

JOHAN. But why not?

DINA. Of course you are a stranger—you cannot understand, but I must tell you——

JOHAN. Well?

DINA. No, I would rather not talk about it.

JOHAN. Oh, but you must; you can talk to me about whatever you like.

DINA. Well, I must tell you that I am not like the other young girls here. There is something—something or other about me. That is why you mustn't.

JOHAN. But I do not understand anything about it. You have not done anything wrong?

DINA. No, not I, but—— No, I am not going to talk any more about it now. You will hear about it from the others sure enough.

JOHAN. Hm!

DINA. But there is something else I want very much to ask you.

JOHAN. What is that?

DINA. I suppose it is easy to make a position for oneself over in America?

JOHAN. No, it is not always easy; at first you often have to rough it and work very hard.

DINA. I should be quite ready to do that.

JOHAN. You?

DINA. I can work now; I am strong and healthy, and Aunt Martha has taught me a lot.

JOHAN. Well, hang it, come back with us!

DINA. Ah, now you are only making fun of me; you said that to Olaf too. But what I wanted to know is if people are so very—so very moral over there?

JOHAN. Moral?

DINA. Yes; I mean are they as—as proper and as well behaved as they are here?

JOHAN. Well, at all events they are not so bad as people here make out. You need not be afraid on that score.

DINA. You don't understand me. What I want to hear is just that they are *not* so proper and so moral.

JOHAN. Not? What would you wish them to be, then?

DINA. I would wish them to be natural.

JOHAN. Well, I believe that is just what they are.

DINA. Because in that case I should get on if I went there.

JOHAN. You would, for certain!—and that is why you must come back with us.

DINA. No, I don't want to go with you; I must go alone. Oh, I would make something of my life; I would get on——

BER. [*speaking to* LONA *and his wife at the foot of the garden steps*]. Wait a moment—I will fetch it, Betty dear; you might so easily catch cold. [*Comes into the room and looks for his wife's shawl.*]

MRS B. [*from outside*]. You must come out too, Johan; we are going down to the grotto.

BER. No, I want Johan to stay here. Look here, Dina; you take my wife's shawl and go with them. Johan is going to stay here with me, Betty dear. I want to hear how he is getting on over there.

MRS B. Very well—then you will follow us; you know where you will find us.

[MRS BERNICK, LONA *and* DINA *go out through the garden to the left.* BERNICK *looks after them for a moment, then goes to the farther door on the left and locks it, after which he goes up to* JOHAN, *grasps both his hands and shakes them warmly.*]

BER. Johan, now that we are alone you must let me thank you.

JOHAN. Oh, nonsense!

BER. My home and all the happiness that it means to me—my position here as a citizen—all these I owe to you.

JOHAN. Well, I am glad of it, Karsten; some good came of that mad story after all, then.

BER. [*grasping his hands again*]. But still you must let me thank you! Not one in ten thousand would have done what you did for me.

JOHAN. Rubbish! Weren't we, both of us, young and thoughtless? One of us had to take the blame, you know.

BER. But surely the guilty one was the proper one to do that?

JOHAN. Stop! At the moment the innocent one happened to be the proper one to do it. Remember, I had no ties—I was an orphan; it was a lucky chance to get free from the drudgery of the office. You, on the other hand, had your old mother still alive; and, besides that, you had just become secretly engaged to Betty, who was devoted to you. What would have happened between you and her if it had come to her ears?

BER. That is true enough, but still——

JOHAN. And wasn't it just for Betty's sake that you broke off your acquaintance with Mrs Dorf? Why, it was merely in order to put an end to the whole thing that you were up there with her that evening.

BER. Yes, that unfortunate evening when that drunken creature came home! Yes, Johan, it was for Betty's sake; but all the same it was splendid of you to let all the appearances go against you and to go away.

JOHAN. Put your scruples to rest, my dear Karsten. We agreed that it should be so; you had to be saved, and you were my friend. I can tell you I was uncommonly proud of that friendship. Here was I, drudging away like a miserable stick-in-the-mud, when you came back from your grand tour abroad, a great swell who had been to London and to Paris; and you chose me for your chum, although I was four years younger than you—it is true it was because you were courting Betty, I understand that now—but I *was* proud of it! Who would not have been? Who would not willingly have sacrificed himself for you?—especially as it only meant a month's talk in the town and enabled me to get away into the wide world.

BER. Ah, my dear Johan, I must be candid and tell you that the story is not so completely forgotten yet.

JOHAN. Isn't it? Well, what does that matter to me once I am back over there on my farm again?

BER. Then you mean to go back?

JOHAN. Of course.

BER. But not immediately, I hope?

JOHAN. As soon as possible. It was only to humor Lona that I came over with her, you know.

BER. Really? How so?

JOHAN. Well, you see, Lona is no longer young, and lately she began to be obsessed with homesickness; but she never would admit it. [*Smiles.*] How could she venture to risk leaving such a flighty fellow as me alone, who before I was nineteen had been mixed up in——

BER. Well, what then?

JOHAN. Well, Karsten, now I am coming to a confession that I am ashamed to make.

BER. You surely haven't confided the truth to her?

JOHAN. Yes. It was wrong of me, but I could not do otherwise. You can have no conception what Lona has been to me. You never could put up with her, but she has been like a mother to me. The first year we were out there, when things went so badly with us, you have no idea how she worked! And when I was ill for a long time, and could earn nothing and could not prevent her, she took to singing ballads in taverns and gave lectures that people laughed at; and then she wrote a book that she has both laughed and cried over since then—all to keep the life in me. Could I look on when in the winter she, who had toiled and drudged for me, began to pine away? No, Karsten, I couldn't. And so I said, "You go home for a trip, Lona; don't be afraid for me, I am not so flighty as you think." And so—the end of it was that she had to know.

BER. And how did she take it?

JOHAN. Well, she thought, as was true, that as I knew I was innocent nothing need prevent me from taking a trip over here with her. But make your mind easy; Lona will let nothing out, and I shall keep my mouth shut as I did before.

BER. Yes, yes—I rely on that.

JOHAN. Here is my hand on it. And now we will say no more about that old story; luckily it is the only mad prank either of us has been guilty of, I am sure. I want thoroughly to enjoy the few days I shall stay here. You cannot think what a delightful walk we had this morning. Who would have believed that that little imp who used to run about here and play angels' parts on the stage—— But tell me, my dear fellow, what became of her parents afterward?

BER. Oh, my boy, I can tell you no more than I wrote to you immediately after you went away. I suppose you got my two letters?

JOHAN. Yes, yes, I have them both. So that drunken fellow deserted her?

BER. And drank himself to death afterward.

JOHAN. And *she* died soon afterward too?

BER. She was proud; she betrayed nothing and would accept nothing.

JOHAN. Well, at all events you did the right thing by taking Dina into your house.

BER. I suppose so. As a matter of fact it was Martha that brought that about.

JOHAN. So it was Martha? By the way, where is she today?

BER. She? Oh, when she hasn't her school to look after she has her sick people to see to.

JOHAN. So it was Martha who interested herself in her.

BER. Yes, you know Martha has always had a certain liking for teaching, so she took a post in the board school. It was very ridiculous of her.

JOHAN. I thought she looked very worn yesterday; I should be afraid her health was not good enough for it.

BER. Oh, as far as her health goes, it is all right enough. But it is unpleasant for me; it looks as though I, her brother, were not willing to support her.

JOHAN. Support her? I thought she had means enough of her own.

BER. Not a penny. Surely you remember how badly off our mother was when you went away? She carried things on for a time with my assistance, but naturally I could not put up with that state of affairs permanently. I made her take me into the firm, but even then things did not go well. So I had to take the whole business myself, and when we made up our balance sheet it became evident that there was practically nothing left as my mother's share. And when mother died soon afterward, of course Martha was left penniless.

JOHAN. Poor Martha!

BER. Poor! You surely do not suppose I let her want for anything? No, I venture to say I am a good brother. Of course she has a home here with us; her salary as a teacher is more than enough for her to dress on; what more could she want?

JOHAN. Hm—that is not our idea of things in America.

BER. No, I dare say not—in such a revolutionary state of society as you find there. But in our small circle—in which, thank God, depravity has not gained a footing, up to now at all events—women are content to occupy a seemly, as well as modest, position. Moreover, it is Martha's own fault; I mean, she might have been provided for long ago if she had wished.

JOHAN. You mean she might have married?

BER. Yes, and married very well too. She has had several good offers—curiously enough, when you think that she is a poor girl, no longer young and, besides, quite an insignificant person.

JOHAN. Insignificant?

BER. Oh, I am not blaming her for that. I most certainly would not wish her otherwise. I can tell you it is always a good thing to have a steady-going person like that in a big house like this—someone you can rely on in any contingency.

JOHAN. Yes, but what does *she*——

BER. She? How? Oh well, of course *she* has plenty to interest herself in; she has Betty and Olaf and me. People should not think first of themselves—women least of all. We have all got some community, great or small, to work for. That is my principle, at all events. [*Points to* KRAP, *who has come in from the right.*] Ah, here is an example of it ready to hand. Do you suppose that it is my own affairs that are absorbing me just now? By no means. [*Eagerly to* KRAP.] Well?

KRAP [*in an undertone, showing him a bundle of papers*]. Here are all the sale contracts, completed.

BER. Capital! Splendid! Well, Johan, you must really excuse me for the present. [*In a low voice, grasping his hand.*] Thanks, Johan, thanks! And rest assured that anything I can do for you—— Well, of course you understand. Come along, Krap. [*They go into* BERNICK's *room.*]

JOHAN [*looking after them for a moment*]. Hm! [*Turns to go down to the garden. At the same moment* MARTHA *comes in from the right with a little basket over her arm.*] Martha!

MARTHA. Ah, Johan—is it you?

JOHAN. Out so early?

MARTHA. Yes. Wait a moment; the others are just coming. [*Moves toward the door on the left.*]

JOHAN. Martha, are you always in such a hurry?

MARTHA. I?

JOHAN. Yesterday you seemed to avoid me so that I never managed to have a word with you—we two old playfellows.

MARTHA. Ah, Johan, that is many, many years ago.

JOHAN. Good lord—why, it is only fifteen years ago, no more and no less. Do you think I have changed so much?

MARTHA. You? Oh yes, you have changed too, although——

JOHAN. What do you mean?

MARTHA. Oh, nothing.

JOHAN. You do not seem to be very glad to see me again.

MARTHA. I have waited so long, Johan—too long.

JOHAN. Waited? For me to come?

MARTHA. Yes.

JOHAN. And why did you think I would come?

MARTHA. To atone for the wrong you had done.

JOHAN. I?

MARTHA. Have you forgotten that it was through you that a woman died in need and in shame? Have you forgotten that it was through you that the best years of a young girl's life were embittered?

JOHAN. And you can say such things to me? Martha, has your brother never——

MARTHA. Never what?

JOHAN. Has he never—— Oh, of course, I mean has he never so much as said a word in my defense?

MARTHA. Ah, Johan, you know Karsten's high principles.

JOHAN. Hm! Oh, of course I know my old friend Karsten's high principles! But really this is—— Well, well. I was having a talk with him just now. He seems to me to have altered considerably.

MARTHA. How can you say that? I am sure Karsten has always been an excellent man.

JOHAN. Yes, that was not exactly what I meant—but never mind. Hm! Now I understand the light you have seen me in; it was the return of the prodigal that you were waiting for.

MARTHA. Johan, I will tell you what light I have seen you in. [*Points down to the garden.*] Do you see that girl playing on the grass down there with Olaf? That is Dina. Do you remember that incoherent letter you wrote me when you went away? You asked me to believe in you. I have believed in you, Johan. All the horrible things that were rumored about you after you had gone must have been done through being led astray—from thoughtlessness, without premeditation.

JOHAN. What do you mean?

MARTHA. Oh, you understand me well enough—not a word more of that. But of course you had to go away and begin afresh—a new life. Your duties here which you never remembered to undertake—or never were able to undertake—I have undertaken for you. I tell you this so that you shall not have that also to reproach yourself with. I have been a mother to that much-wronged child; I have brought her up as well as I was able.

JOHAN. And have wasted your whole life for that reason.

MARTHA. It has not been wasted. But you have come late, Johan.

JOHAN. Martha—if only I could tell you—— Well, at all events let me thank you for your loyal friendship.

MARTHA [*with a sad smile*]. Hm. Well, we have had it out now, Johan. Hush, someone is coming. Good-by, I can't stay now. [*Goes out through the farther door on the left.* LONA *comes in from the garden, followed by* MRS BERNICK.]

MRS B. But, good gracious, Lona—what are you thinking of?

LONA. Let me be, I tell you! I must and will speak to him.

MRS B. But it would be a scandal of the worst sort! Ah, Johan—still here?

LONA. Out with you, my boy; don't stay here indoors; go down into the garden and have a chat with Dina.

JOHAN. I was just thinking of doing so.

MRS B. But——

LONA. Look here, Johan—have you had a good look at Dina?

JOHAN. I should think so!

LONA. Well, look at her to some purpose, my boy. That would be somebody for *you!*

MRS B. But, Lona!

JOHAN. Somebody for me?

LONA. Yes, to look at, I mean. Be off with you!

JOHAN. Oh, I don't need any pressing. [*Goes down into the garden.*]

MRS B. Lona, you astound me! You cannot possibly be serious about it?

LONA. Indeed I am. Isn't she sweet and healthy and honest? She is exactly the wife for Johan. She is just what he needs over there; it will be a change from an old stepsister.

MRS B. Dina? Dina Dorf? But think——

LONA. I think first and foremost of the boy's happiness. Because help him I must; he has not much idea of that sort of thing; he has never had much of an eye for girls or women.

MRS B. He? Johan? Indeed, I think we have had only too sad proofs that——

LONA. Oh, devil take all those stupid stories! Where is Karsten? I mean to speak to him.

MRS B. Lona, you must not do it, I tell you!

LONA. I am going to. If the boy takes a fancy to her—and she to him—then they shall make a match of it. Karsten is such a clever man, he must find some way to bring it about.

MRS B. And do you think these

American indecencies will be permitted here?

LONA. Bosh, Betty!

MRS B. Do you think a man like Karsten, with his strictly moral way of thinking——

LONA. Pooh! He is not so terribly moral.

MRS B. What have you the audacity to say?

LONA. I have the audacity to say that Karsten is not any more particularly moral than anybody else.

MRS B. So you still hate him as deeply as that! But what are you doing here if you have never been able to forget that? I cannot understand how you dare look him in the face after the shameful insult you put upon him in the old days.

LONA. Yes, Betty, that time I did forget myself badly.

MRS B. And to think how magnanimously he has forgiven you—he, who has never done any wrong! It was not *his* fault that you encouraged yourself with hopes. But since then you have always hated me too. [*Bursts into tears.*] You have always grudged me my good fortune. And now you come here to heap all this on my head—to let the whole town know what sort of a family I have brought Karsten into. Yes, it is me that it all falls upon, and that is what you want. Oh, it is abominable of you! [*Goes out by the door on the left, in tears.*]

LONA [*looking after her*]. Poor Betty!

[BERNICK *comes in from his room. He stops at the door to speak to* KRAP.]

BER. Yes, that is excellent, Krap—capital! Send twenty pounds to the fund for dinners to the poor. [*Turns round.*] Lona! [*Comes forward.*] Are you alone? Is Betty not coming in?

LONA. No. Would you like me to call her?

BER. No, no—not at all. Oh, Lona, you don't know how anxious I have been to speak openly to you—after having begged for your forgiveness.

LONA. Look here, Karsten—do not let us be sentimental; it doesn't suit us.

BER. You *must* listen to me, Lona. I know only too well how much appearances are against me, as you have learned all about that affair with Dina's mother. But I swear to you that it was only a temporary infatuation; I was really, truly and honestly, in love with you once.

LONA. Why do you think I have come home?

BER. Whatever you have in your mind, I entreat you to do nothing until I have exculpated myself. I can do that, Lona! At all events I can excuse myself.

LONA. Now you are frightened. You once were in love with me, you say. Yes, you told me that often enough in your letters; and perhaps it was true too—in a way—as long as you were living out in the great free world which gave you the courage to think freely and greatly. Perhaps you found in me a little more character and strength of will and independence than in most of the folk at home here. And then we kept it secret between us; nobody could make fun of your bad taste.

BER. Lona, how can you think——

LONA. But when you came back—when you heard the gibes that were made at me on all sides—when you noticed how people laughed at what they called my absurdities——

BER. You *were* regardless of people's

opinion at that time.

Lona. Chiefly to annoy the petticoated and trousered prudes that one met at every turn in the town. And then when you met that seductive young actress——

Ber. It was a boyish escapade—nothing more; I swear to you that there was no truth in a tenth part of the rumors and gossip that went about.

Lona. Maybe. But then when Betty came home—a pretty young girl, idolized by everyone—and it became known that she would inherit all her aunt's money and that I would have nothing——

Ber. That is just the point, Lona; and now you shall have the truth without any beating about the bush. I did not love Betty then; I did not break off my engagement with you because of any new attachment. It was entirely for the sake of the money. I needed it; I *had* to make sure of it.

Lona. And you have the face to tell me that?

Ber. Yes, I have. Listen, Lona——

Lona. And yet you wrote to me that an unconquerable passion for Betty had overcome you—invoked my magnanimity—begged me, for Betty's sake, to hold my tongue about all that had been between us.

Ber. I *had* to, I tell you.

Lona. Now, by heaven, I don't regret that I forgot myself as I did that time!

Ber. Let me tell you the plain truth of how things stood with me then. My mother, as you remember, was at the head of the business, but she was absolutely without any business ability whatever. I was hurriedly summoned home from Paris; times were critical, and they relied on me to set things straight. What did I find? I found—and you must keep this a profound secret—a house on the brink of ruin. Yes—as good as on the brink of ruin, this old respected house which had seen three generations of us. What else could I—the son, the only son—do than look about for some means of saving it?

Lona. And so you saved the house of Bernick at the cost of a woman.

Ber. You know quite well that Betty was in love with me.

Lona. But what about me?

Ber. Believe me, Lona, you would never have been happy with me.

Lona. Was it out of consideration for my happiness that you sacrificed me?

Ber. Do you suppose I acted as I did from selfish motives? If I had stood alone, then I would have begun all over again with cheerful courage. But you do not understand how the life of a man of business, with his tremendous responsibilities, is bound up with that of the business which falls to his inheritance. Do you realize that the prosperity or the ruin of hundreds—or thousands—depends on him? Can you not take into consideration the fact that the whole community in which both you and I were born would have been affected to the most dangerous extent if the house of Bernick had gone to smash?

Lona. Then is it for the sake of the community that you have maintained your position these fifteen years upon a lie?

Ber. Upon a lie?

Lona. What does Betty know of all this that underlies her union with you?

Ber. Do you suppose that I would

hurt her feelings to no purpose by disclosing the truth?

Lona. To no purpose, you say? Well, well—you are a man of business; you ought to understand what is to the purpose. But listen to me, Karsten. *I* am going to speak the plain truth now. Tell me, are you really happy?

Ber. In my family life, do you mean?

Lona. Yes.

Ber. I am, Lona. You have not been a self-sacrificing friend to me in vain. I can honestly say that I have grown happier every year. Betty is good and willing; and if I were to tell you how, in the course of years, she has learned to model her character on the lines of my own——

Lona. Hm!

Ber. At first, of course, she had a whole lot of romantic notions about love; she could not reconcile herself to the idea that little by little it must change into a quiet comradeship.

Lona. But now she is quite reconciled to that?

Ber. Absolutely. As you can imagine, daily intercourse with me has had no small share in developing her character. Everyone, in their degree, has to learn to lower their own pretensions if they are to live worthily of the community to which they belong. And Betty, in her turn, has gradually learned to understand this; and that is why our home is now a model to our fellow citizens.

Lona. But your fellow citizens know nothing about the lie!

Ber. The lie?

Lona. Yes—the lie you have persisted in for these fifteen years.

Ber. Do you mean to say that you call that——

Lona. I call it a lie—a threefold lie: first of all there is the lie toward me, then the lie toward Betty and then the lie toward Johan.

Ber. Betty has never asked me to speak.

Lona. Because she has known nothing.

Ber. And *you* will not demand it—out of consideration for her.

Lona. Oh no—I shall manage to put up with their gibes well enough; I have broad shoulders.

Ber. And Johan will not demand it either; he has promised me that.

Lona. But you yourself, Karsten? Do you feel within yourself no impulse urging you to shake yourself free of this lie?

Ber. Do you suppose that of my own free will I would sacrifice my family happiness and my position in the world?

Lona. What right have you to the position you hold?

Ber. Every day during these fifteen years I have earned some little right to it—by my conduct and by what I have achieved by my work.

Lona. True, you have achieved a great deal by your work, for yourself as well as for others. You are the richest and most influential man in the town; nobody in it dares do otherwise than defer to your will, because you are looked upon as a man without a spot or blemish; your home is regarded as a model home and your conduct as a model of conduct. But all this grandeur, and you with it, is founded on a treacherous morass. A moment may come and a word may be spoken—and you and all your grandeur will be engulfed in the morass if you do not save yourself in time.

BER. Lona—what is your object in coming here?

LONA. I want to help you to get firm ground under your feet, Karsten.

BER. Revenge!—you want to revenge yourself! I suspected it. But you won't succeed! There is only one person here that can speak with authority, and he will be silent.

LONA. You mean Johan?

BER. Yes, Johan. If anyone else accuses me, I shall deny everything. If anyone tries to crush me, I shall fight for my life. But you will never succeed in that, let me tell you! The one who could strike me down will say nothing—and is going away.

[RUMMEL *and* VIGELAND *come in from the right.*]

RUM. Good morning, my dear Bernick, good morning. You must come up with us to the Commercial Association. There is a meeting about the railway scheme, you know.

BER. I cannot. It is impossible just now.

VIG. You really must, Mr Bernick.

RUM. Bernick, you must. There is an opposition to us on foot. Hammer and the rest of those who believe in a line along the coast are declaring that private interests are at the back of the new proposals.

BER. Well, then, explain to them——

VIG. Our explanations have no effect, Mr Bernick.

RUM. No, no, you must come yourself. Naturally no one would dare suspect you of such duplicity.

LONA. I should think not.

BER. I cannot, I tell you; I am not well. Or, at all events, wait—let me pull myself together.

[RORLUND *comes in from the right.*]

ROR. Excuse me, Mr Bernick, but I am terribly upset.

BER. Why, what is the matter with you?

ROR. I must put a question to you, Mr Bernick. Is it with your consent that the young girl who has found a shelter under your roof shows herself in the open street in the company of a person who——

LONA. What person, Mr Parson?

ROR. With the person from whom, of all others in the world, she ought to be kept farthest apart!

LONA. Ha! ha!

ROR. Is it with your consent, Mr Bernick?

BER. [*looking for his hat and gloves*]. I know nothing about it. You must excuse me; I am in a great hurry. I am due at the Commercial Association.

[HILMAR *comes up from the garden and goes over to the farthest door on the left.*]

HILMAR. Betty, Betty, I want to speak to you.

MRS B. [*coming to the door*]. What is it?

HILMAR. You ought to go down into the garden and put a stop to the flirtation that is going on between a certain person and Dina Dorf! It has quite got on my nerves to listen to them.

LONA. And what has the certain person been saying?

HILMAR. Oh, only that he wishes she would go off to America with him. Ugh!

ROR. Is it possible?

MRS B. What do you say?

LONA. But that would be perfectly splendid!

BER. Impossible! You cannot have heard aright.

HILMAR. Ask him yourself then.

Here comes the pair of them. Only leave me out of it, please.

BER. [*to* RUMMEL *and* VIGELAND]. I will follow you—in a moment.

[RUMMEL *and* VIGELAND *go out to the right.* JOHAN *and* DINA *come up from the garden.*]

JOHAN. Hurrah, Lona, she is going with us!

MRS B. But, Johan—are you out of your senses?

ROR. Can I believe my ears! Such an atrocious scandal! By what arts of seduction have you——

JOHAN. Come, come, sir—what are you saying?

ROR. Answer me, Dina; do you mean to do this—entirely of your own free will?

DINA. I must get away from here.

ROR. But with *him!*—with *him!*

DINA. Can you tell me of anyone else here who would have the courage to take me with him?

ROR. Very well, then—you shall learn who he is.

JOHAN. Do not speak!

BER. Not a word more!

ROR. If I did not, I should be unworthy to serve a community of whose morals I have been appointed a guardian and should be acting most unjustifiably toward this young girl, in whose upbringing I have taken a material part and who is to me——

JOHAN. Take care what you are doing!

ROR. She *shall* know! Dina, this is the man who was the cause of all your mother's misery and shame.

BER. Mr Rorlund——

DINA. He! [*To* JOHAN.] Is this true?

JOHAN. Karsten, you answer.

BER. Not a word more! Do not let us say another word about it today.

DINA. Then it is true.

ROR. Yes, it is true. And more than that—this fellow, whom you were going to trust, did not run away from home empty-handed; ask him about old Mrs Bernick's cashbox—Mr Bernick can bear witness to that!

LONA. Liar!

BER. Ah!

MRS B. My God! My God!

JOHAN [*rushing at* RORLUND *with uplifted arm*]. And you dare to——

LONA [*restraining him*]. Do not strike him, Johan!

ROR. That is right, assault me! But the truth will out, and it *is* the truth—Mr Bernick has admitted it, and the whole town knows it. Now, Dina, you know him. [*A short silence.*]

JOHAN [*softly, grasping* BERNICK *by the arm*]. Karsten, Karsten, what have you done?

MRS B. [*in tears*]. Oh, Karsten, to think that I should have mixed you up in all this disgrace!

SANDSTAD [*coming in hurriedly from the right and calling out, with his hand still on the door handle*]. You positively *must* come now, Mr Bernick. The fate of the whole railway is hanging by a thread.

BER. [*abstractedly*]. What is it? What have I to——

LONA [*earnestly and with emphasis*]. You have to go and be a pillar of society, brother-in-law.

SAN. Yes, come along; we need the full weight of your moral excellence on our side.

JOHAN [*aside to* BERNICK]. Karsten, we will have a talk about this tomorrow. [*Goes out through the garden.* BERNICK, *looking half dazed, goes out to the right with* SANDSTAD.]

ACT III

SCENE—*The same room.* BERNICK, *with a cane in his hand and evidently in a great rage, comes out of the farthest room on the left, leaving the door half open behind him.*

BER. [*speaking to his wife, who is in the other room*]. There! I have given it him in earnest now; I don't think he will forget that thrashing! What do you say? . . . And *I* say that you are an injudicious mother! You make excuses for him and countenance any sort of rascality on his part. . . . Not rascality? What do you call it then? Slipping out of the house at night, going out in a fishing boat, staying away till well on in the day and giving me such a horrible fright when I have so much to worry me! And then the young scamp has the audacity to threaten that he will run away! Just let him try it! . . . You? No, very likely; you don't trouble yourself much about what happens to him. I really believe that if he were killed—— Oh, really? Well, *I* have work to leave behind me in the world; I have no fancy for being left childless. . . . Now do not raise objections, Betty; it shall be as I say—he is confined to the house. [*Listens.*] Hush; do not let anyone notice anything.

[KRAP *comes in from the right.*]

KRAP. Can you spare me a moment, Mr Bernick?

BER. [*throwing away the cane*]. Certainly, certainly. Have you come from the yard?

KRAP. Yes. Ahem!

BER. Well? Nothing wrong with the Palm Tree, I hope?

KRAP. The Palm Tree can sail tomorrow, but——

BER. Is it the Indian Girl then? I had a suspicion that that obstinate fellow——

KRAP. The Indian Girl can sail tomorrow too, but I am sure that she will not get very far.

BER. What do you mean?

KRAP. Excuse me, sir; that door is standing ajar, and I think there is someone in the other room——

BER. [*shutting the door*]. There, then! But what is this that no one else must hear?

KRAP. Just this—that I believe Aune intends to let the Indian Girl go to the bottom with every mother's son on board.

BER. Good God!—what makes you think that?

KRAP. I cannot account for it any other way, sir.

BER. Well, tell me as briefly as you can.

KRAP. I will. You know yourself how slowly the work has gone on in the yard since we got the new machines and the new inexperienced hands?

BER. Yes, yes.

KRAP. But this morning, when I went down there, I noticed that the repairs to the American boat had made extraordinary progress; the great hole in the bottom—the rotten patch, you know——

BER. Yes, yes—what about it?

KRAP. Was completely repaired—to all appearance, at any rate—covered up—looked as good as new. I heard that Aune himself had been working at it by lantern light the whole night.

BER. Yes, yes—well?

KRAP. I turned it over in my head for a bit; the hands were away at their breakfast, so I found an opportunity to have a look round the boat, both outside and in, without anyone seeing me. I had a job to get down to the bottom through the cargo, but I learned the truth. There is something very suspicious going on, Mr Bernick.

BER. I cannot believe it, Krap. I cannot and will not believe such a thing of Aune.

KRAP. I am very sorry—but it is the simple truth. Something very suspicious is going on. No new timbers put in, as far as I could see; only stopped up and tinkered at and covered over with sailcloth and tarpaulins and that sort of thing—an absolute fraud. The Indian Girl will never get to New York; she will go to the bottom like a cracked pot.

BER. This is most horrible! But what can be his object, do you suppose?

KRAP. Probably he wants to bring the machines into discredit—wants to take his revenge—wants to force you to take the old hands on again.

BER. And to do this he is willing to sacrifice the lives of all on board.

KRAP. He said the other day that there were no men on board the Indian Girl—only wild beasts.

BER. Yes, but—apart from that—has he no regard for the great loss of capital it would mean?

KRAP. Aune does not look upon capital with a very friendly eye, Mr Bernick.

BER. That is perfectly true; he is an agitator and a fomenter of discontent, but such an unscrupulous thing as this—— Look here, Krap; you must look into the matter once more. Not a word of it to anyone. The blame will fall on our yard if anyone hears anything of it.

KRAP. Of course, but——

BER. When the hands are away at their dinner you must manage to get down there again; I must have absolute certainty about it.

KRAP. You shall, sir; but, excuse me, what do you propose to do?

BER. Report the affair, naturally. We cannot, of course, let ourselves become accomplices in such a crime. I could not have such a thing on my conscience. Moreover, it will make a good impression, both on the press and on the public in general, if it is seen that I set all personal interests aside and let justice take its course.

KRAP. Quite true, Mr Bernick.

BER. But first of all I must be absolutely certain. And meanwhile do not breathe a word of it.

KRAP. Not a word, sir. And you shall have your certainty. [*Goes out through the garden and down the street.*]

BER. [*half aloud*]. Shocking! But no, it is impossible!—inconceivable! [*As he turns to go into his room* HILMAR *comes in from the right.*]

HILMAR. Good morning, Karsten. Let me congratulate you on your triumph at the Commercial Association yesterday.

BER. Thank you.

HILMAR. It was a brilliant triumph, I hear; the triumph of intelligent public spirit over selfishness and prejudice —something like a raid of French troops on the Kabyles. It is astonishing that after that unpleasant scene here you could——

BER. Yes, yes—quite so.

HILMAR. But the decisive battle has not been fought yet.

BER. In the matter of the railway, do you mean?

HILMAR. Yes; I suppose you know the trouble that Hammer is brewing?

BER. [*anxiously*]. No, what is that?

HILMAR. Oh, he is greatly taken up with the rumor that is going round and is preparing to dish up an article about it.

BER. What rumor?

HILMAR. About the extensive purchase of property along the branch line, of course.

BER. What? Is there such a rumor as that going about?

HILMAR. It is all over the town. I heard it at the club when I looked in there. They say that one of our lawyers has quietly bought up, on commission, all the forest land, all the mining land, all the waterfalls——

BER. Don't they say whom it was for?

HILMAR. At the club they thought it must be for some company, not connected with this town, that has got a hint of the scheme you have in hand and has made haste to buy before the price of these properties went up. Isn't it villainous—ugh!

BER. Villainous?

HILMAR. Yes, to have strangers putting their fingers into our pie—and one of our own local lawyers lending himself to such a thing! And now it will be outsiders that will get all the profits.

BER. But, after all, it is only an idle rumor.

HILMAR. Meanwhile people are believing it, and tomorrow or next day I have no doubt Hammer will nail it to the counter as a fact. There is a general sense of exasperation in the town already. I heard several people say that if the rumor were confirmed they would take their names off the subscription lists.

BER. Impossible!

HILMAR. Is it? Why do you suppose these mercenary-minded creatures were so willing to go into the undertaking with you? Don't you suppose they have scented profit for themselves——

BER. It is impossible, I am sure; there is so much public spirit in our little community——

HILMAR. In our community? Of course you are a confirmed optimist, and so you judge others by yourself. But I, who am a tolerably experienced observer! There isn't a single soul in the place—excepting ourselves, of course—not a single soul in the place who holds up the banner of the Ideal. [*Goes toward the veranda.*] Ugh, I can see them there!

BER. See whom?

HILMAR. Our two friends from America. [*Looks out to the right.*] And who is that they are walking with? As I am alive, if it is not the captain of the Indian Girl. Ugh!

BER. What can they want with *him?*

HILMAR. Oh, he is just the right company for them. He looks as if he had been a slave dealer or a pirate, and who knows what the other two may have been doing all these years.

BER. Let me tell you that it is grossly unjust to think such things about them.

HILMAR. Yes—you are an optimist. But here they are, bearing down upon us again; so I will get away while there is time. [*Goes toward the door on the left.* LONA *comes in from the right.*]

LONA. Oh, Hilmar, am I driving you away?

HILMAR. Not at all; I am in rather a hurry; I want to have a word with Betty. [*Goes into the farthest room on the left.*]

BER. [*after a moment's silence*]. Well, Lona?

LONA. Yes?

BER. What do you think of me to-day?

LONA. The same as I did yesterday. A lie more or less——

BER. I must enlighten you about it. Where has Johan gone?

LONA. He is coming; he had to see a man first.

BER. After what you heard yesterday you will understand that my whole life will be ruined if the truth comes to light.

LONA. I can understand that.

BER. Of course it stands to reason that *I* was not guilty of the crime there was so much talk about here.

LONA. That stands to reason. But who was the thief?

BER. There was no thief. There was no money stolen—not a penny.

LONA. How is that?

BER. Not a penny, I tell you.

LONA. But those rumors? How did that shameful rumor get about that Johan——

BER. Lona, I think I can speak to you as I could to no one else. I will conceal nothing from you. *I* was partly to blame for spreading the rumor.

LONA. You? You could act in that way toward a man who for your sake——

BER. Do not condemn me without bearing in mind how things stood at that time. I told you about it yesterday. I came home and found my mother involved in a mesh of injudicious undertakings; we had all manner of bad luck—it seemed as if misfortunes were raining upon us, and our house was on the verge of ruin. I was half reckless and half in despair. Lona, I believe it was mainly to deaden my thoughts that I let myself drift into that entanglement that ended in Johan's going away.

LONA. Hm!

BER. You can well imagine how every kind of rumor was set on foot after he and you had gone. People began to say that it was not his first piece of folly—that Dorf had received a large sum of money to hold his tongue and go away; other people said that she had received it. At the same time it was obvious that our house was finding it difficult to meet its obligations. What was more natural than that scandalmongers should find some connection between these two rumors? And as the woman remained here, living in poverty, people declared that he had taken the money with him to America; and every time rumor mentioned the sum it grew larger.

LONA. And you, Karsten?

BER. I grasped at the rumor like a drowning man at a straw.

LONA. You helped to spread it?

BER. I did not contradict it. Our creditors had begun to be pressing, and I had the task of keeping them quiet. The result was the dissipating of any suspicion as to the stability of the firm; people said that we had been hit by a temporary piece of ill luck—that all that was necessary was that they should not press us—only give us time and every creditor would be paid in full.

LONA. And every creditor was paid in full?

BER. Yes, Lona, that rumor saved our house and made me the man I now am.

LONA. That is to say, a lie has made you the man you now are.

BER. Whom did it injure at the time? It was Johan's intention never to come back.

LONA. You ask whom it injured. Look into your own heart and tell me if it has not injured you.

BER. Look into any man's heart you please and you will always find, in every one, at least one black spot which he has to keep concealed.

LONA. And you call yourselves pillars of society!

BER. Society has none better.

LONA. And of what consequence is it whether such a society be propped up or not? What does it all consist of? Show and lies—and nothing else. Here are you, the first man in the town, living in grandeur and luxury, powerful and respected—you, who have branded an innocent man as a criminal.

BER. Do you suppose I am not deeply conscious of the wrong I have done him? And do you suppose I am not ready to make amends to him for it?

LONA. How? By speaking out?

BER. Would you have the heart to insist on that?

LONA. What else can make amends for such a wrong?

BER. I am rich, Lona; Johan can demand any sum he pleases——

LONA. Yes, offer him money, and you will hear what he will say.

BER. Do you know what he intends to do?

LONA. No; since yesterday he has been dumb. He looks as if this had made a grown man of him all at once.

BER. I must talk to him.

LONA. Here he comes.

[JOHAN *comes in from the right.*]

BER. [*going toward him*]. Johan!

JOHAN [*motioning him away*]. Listen to me first. Yesterday morning I gave you my word that I would hold my tongue.

BER. You did.

JOHAN. But then I did not know——

BER. Johan, only let me say a word or two to explain the circumstances.

JOHAN. It is unnecessary; I understand the circumstances perfectly. The firm was in a dangerous position at the time; I had gone off, and you had my defenseless name and reputation at your mercy. Well, I do not blame you so very much for what you did; we were young and thoughtless in those days. But now I have need of the truth, and now you must speak.

BER. And just now I have need of all my reputation for morality, and therefore I *cannot* speak.

JOHAN. I don't take much account of the false reports you spread about me; it is the other thing that you must take the blame of. I shall make Dina my wife, and here—here in your town —I mean to settle down and live with her.

LONA. Is that what you mean to do?

BER. With Dina? Dina as your wife? —in this town?

JOHAN. Yes, here and nowhere else. I mean to stay here to defy all these liars and slanderers. But before I can win her you must exonerate me.

BER. Have you considered that, if I confess to the one thing, it will inevitably mean making myself responsible for the other as well? You will say that I can show by our books that nothing dishonest happened. But I cannot; our books were not so accurately kept in those days. And even if I could, what good would it do? Should I not in any case be pointed at as the man who had once saved himself by an untruth and for fifteen years had allowed that untruth and all its consequences to stand without having raised a finger to demolish it? You do not know our community very much, or you would realize that it would ruin me utterly.

Johan. I can only tell you that I mean to make Mrs Dorf's daughter my wife and live with her in this town.

Ber. [*wiping the perspiration from his forehead*]. Listen to me, Johan—and you too, Lona. The circumstances I am in just now are quite exceptional. I am situated in such a way that if you aim this blow at me you will not only destroy me but will also destroy a great future, rich in blessings, that lies before the community which, after all, was the home of your childhood.

Johan. And if I do not aim this blow at you, I shall be destroying all my future happiness with my own hand.

Lona. Go on, Karsten.

Ber. I will tell you, then. It is mixed up with the railway project, and the whole thing is not quite so simple as you think. I suppose you have heard that last year there was some talk of a railway line along the coast? Many influential people backed up the idea—people in the town and the suburbs, and especially the press; but I managed to get the proposal quashed, on the ground that it would have injured our steamboat trade along the coast.

Lona. Have you any interest in the steamboat trade?

Ber. Yes. But no one ventured to suspect me on that account; my honored name fully protected me from that. For the matter of that, I could have stood the loss, but the place could not have stood it. So the inland line was decided upon. As soon as that was done I assured myself—without saying anything about it—that a branch line could be laid to the town.

Lona. Why did you say nothing about it, Karsten?

Ber. Have you heard the rumors of extensive buying up of forest lands, mines and waterfalls?

Johan. Yes, apparently it is some company from another part of the country.

Ber. As these properties are situated at present, they are as good as valueless to their owners, who are scattered about the neighborhood; they have therefore been sold comparatively cheap. If the purchaser had waited till the branch line began to be talked of, the proprietors would have asked exorbitant prices.

Lona. Well—what then?

Ber. Now I am going to tell you something that can be construed in different ways—a thing to which, in our community, a man could only confess provided he had an untarnished and honored name to take his stand upon.

Lona. Well?

Ber. It is I that have bought up the whole of them.

Lona. You?

Johan. On your own account?

Ber. On my own account. If the branch line becomes an accomplished fact, I am a millionaire; if it does not, I am ruined.

Lona. It is a big risk, Karsten.

Ber. I have risked my whole fortune on it.

Lona. I am not thinking of your fortune, but if it comes to light that——

Ber. Yes, that is the critical part of it. With the unblemished and honored name I have hitherto borne, I can take the whole thing upon my shoulders, carry it through and say to my fellow citizens: "See, I have taken this risk for the good of the community."

LONA. Of the community?

BER. Yes; and not a soul will doubt my motives.

LONA. Then some of those concerned in it have acted more openly —without any secret motives or considerations.

BER. Who?

LONA. Why, of course, Rummel and Sandstad and Vigeland.

BER. To get them on my side I was obliged to let them into the secret.

LONA. And then?

BER. They have stipulated for a fifth part of the profits as their share.

LONA. Oh, these pillars of society!

BER. And isn't it society itself that forces us to use these underhand means? What would have happened if I had not acted secretly? Everybody would have wanted to have a hand in the undertaking; the whole thing would have been divided up, mismanaged and bungled. There is not a single man in the town except myself who is capable of directing so big an affair as this will be. In this country, almost without exception, it is only foreigners who have settled here who have the aptitude for big business schemes. That is the reason why my conscience acquits me in the matter. It is only in my hands that these properties can become a real blessing to the many who have to make their daily bread.

LONA. I believe you are right there, Karsten.

JOHAN. But I have no concern with the many, and my life's happiness is at stake.

BER. The welfare of your native place is also at stake. If things come out which cast reflections on my earlier conduct. then all my opponents will fall upon me with united vigor. A youthful folly is never allowed to be forgotten in our community. They would go through the whole of my previous life, bring up a thousand little incidents in it, interpret and explain them in the light of what has been revealed; they would crush me under the weight of rumors and slanders. I should be obliged to abandon the railway scheme; and, if I take my hand off that, it will come to nothing, and I shall be ruined and my life as a citizen will be over.

LONA. Johan, after what we have just heard you must go away from here and held your tongue.

BER. Yes, yes, Johan—you must!

JOHAN. Yes, I will go away and I will hold my tongue; but I shall come back, and then I shall speak.

BER. Stay over there, Johan; hold your tongue, and I am willing to share with you——

JOHAN. Keep your money but give me back my name and reputation.

BER. And sacrifice my own!

JOHAN. You and your community must get out of that the best way you can. I must and shall win Dina for my wife. And therefore I am going to sail tomorrow in the Indian Girl——

BER. In the Indian Girl?

JOHAN. Yes. The captain has promised to take me. I shall go over to America, as I say; I shall sell my farm and set my affairs in order. In two months I shall be back.

BER. And then you will speak?

JOHAN. Then the guilty man must take his guilt on himself.

BER. Have you forgotten that if I

do that I must also take on myself guilt that is not mine?

JOHAN. Who is it that for the last fifteen years has benefited by that shameful rumor?

BER. You will drive me to desperation! Well, if you speak, I shall deny everything! I shall say it is a plot against me—that you have come here to blackmail me!

LONA. For shame, Karsten!

BER. I am a desperate man, I tell you, and I shall fight for my life. I shall deny everything—everything!

JOHAN. I have your two letters. I found them in my box among my other papers. This morning I read them again; they are plain enough.

BER. And will you make them public?

JOHAN. If it becomes necessary.

BER. And you will be back here in two months?

JOHAN. I hope so. The wind is fair. In three weeks I shall be in New York—if the Indian Girl does not go to the bottom.

BER. [*with a start*]. Go to the bottom? Why should the Indian Girl go to the bottom?

JOHAN. Quite so—why should she?

BER. [*scarcely audibly*]. Go to the bottom?

JOHAN. Well, Karsten, now you know what is before you. You must find your own way out. Good-by! You can say good-by to Betty for me, although she has not treated me like a sister. But I must see Martha. She shall tell Dina; she shall promise me — [*Goes out through the farther door on the left.*]

BER. [*to himself*]. The Indian Girl — [*Quickly.*] Lona, you *must* prevent that!

LONA. You see for yourself, Karsten—I have no influence over him any longer. [*Follows* JOHAN *into the other room.*]

BER. [*a prey to uneasy thoughts*]. Go to the bottom——

[AUNE *comes in from the right.*]

AUNE. Excuse me, sir, but if it is convenient——

BER. [*turning round angrily*]. What do you want?

AUNE. To know if I may ask you a question, sir.

BER. Be quick about it then. What is it?

AUNE. I wanted to ask if I am to consider it as certain—absolutely certain—that I should be dismissed from the yard if the Indian Girl were not ready to sail tomorrow?

BER. What do you mean? The ship *is* ready to sail.

AUNE. Yes—it is. But suppose it were not, should I be discharged?

BER. What is the use of asking such idle questions?

AUNE. Only that I should like to know, sir. Will you answer me that? Should I be discharged?

BER. Am I in the habit of keeping my word or not?

AUNE. Then tomorrow I should have lost the position I hold in my house and among those near and dear to me—lost my influence over men of my own class—lost all opportunity of doing anything for the cause of the poorer and needier members of the community?

BER. Aune, we have discussed all that before.

AUNE. Quite so—then the Indian Girl will sail. [*A short silence.*]

BER. Look here—it is impossible for me to have my eyes everywhere—I cannot be answerable for everything. You can give me your assurance, I suppose, that the repairs have been satisfactorily carried out?

AUNE. You gave me very short grace, Mr Bernick.

BER. But I understand you to warrant the repairs?

AUNE. The weather is fine, and it is summer. [*Another pause.*]

BER. Have you anything else to say to me?

AUNE. I think not, sir.

BER. Then—the Indian Girl will sail——

AUNE. Tomorrow?

BER. Yes.

AUNE. Very good. [*Bows and goes out.* BERNICK *stands for a moment irresolute, then walks quickly toward the door, as if to call* AUNE *back, but stops, hesitatingly, with his hand on the door handle. At that moment the door is opened from without, and* KRAP *comes in.*]

KRAP [*in a low voice*]. Aha, he has been here. Has he confessed?

BER. Hm; have you discovered anything?

KRAP. What need of that, sir? Could you not see the evil conscience looking out of the man's eyes?

BER. Nonsense—such things don't show. Have you discovered anything, I want to know?

KRAP. I could not manage it; I was too late. They had already begun hauling the ship out of the dock. But their very haste in doing that plainly shows that——

BER. It shows nothing. Has the inspection taken place then?

KRAP. Of course, but——

BER. There, you see! And of course they found nothing to complain of?

KRAP. Mr Bernick, you know very well how much this inspection means, especially in a yard that has such a good name as ours has.

BER. No matter—it takes all responsibility off us.

KRAP. But, sir, could you really not tell from Aune's manner that——

BER. Aune has completely reassured me, let me tell you.

KRAP. And let me tell you, sir, that I am morally certain that——

BER. What does this mean, Krap? I see plainly enough that you want to get your knife into this man, but if you want to attack him you must find some other occasion. You know how important it is to me—or I should say to the owners—that the Indian Girl should sail tomorrow.

KRAP. Very well—so be it; but if ever we hear of *that* ship again—hm!

[VIGELAND *comes in from the right.*]

VIG. I wish you a very good morning, Mr Bernick. Have you a moment to spare?

BER. At your service, Mr Vigeland.

VIG. I only want to know if you are also of opinion that the Palm Tree should sail tomorrow?

BER. Certainly; I thought that was quite settled.

VIG. Well, the captain came to me just now and told me that storm signals have been hoisted.

BER. Oh! Are we to expect a storm?

VIG. A stiff breeze, at all events; but not a contrary wind—just the opposite.

BER. Hm—well, what do you say?

VIG. I say, as I said to the captain, that the Palm Tree is in the hands of Providence. Besides, they are only going across the North Sea at first; and in England freights are running tolerably high just now, so that——

BER. Yes, it would probably mean a loss for us if we waited.

VIG. Besides, she is a stout ship and

fully insured as well. It is more risky now for the Indian Girl——

BER. What do you mean?

VIG. She sails tomorrow too.

BER. Yes, the owners have been in such a hurry, and besides——

VIG. Well, if that old hulk can venture out—and with such a crew into the bargain—it would be a disgrace to us if we——

BER. Quite so. I presume you have the ship's papers with you?

VIG. Yes, here they are.

BER. Good; then will you go in with Mr Krap?

KRAP. Will you come in here, sir, and we will dispose of them at once.

VIG. Thank you. And the issue we leave in the hands of the Almighty, Mr Bernick. [*Goes with* KRAP *into* BERNICK'S *room.* RORLUND *comes up from the garden.*]

ROR. At home at this time of day, Mr Bernick?

BER. [*lost in thought*]. As you see.

ROR. It was really on your wife's account I came. I thought she might be in need of a word of comfort.

BER. Very likely she is. But I want to have a little talk with you too.

ROR. With the greatest of pleasure, Mr Bernick. But what is the matter with you? You look quite pale and upset.

BER. Really? Do I? Well, what else could you expect—a man so loaded with responsibilities as I am? There is all my own big business—and now the planning of this railway. But tell me something, Mr Rorlund; let me put a question to you.

ROR. With pleasure, Mr Bernick.

BER. It is about a thought that has occurred to me. Suppose a man is face to face with an undertaking which will concern the welfare of thousands, and suppose it should be necessary to make a sacrifice of one——

ROR. What do you mean?

BER. For example, suppose a man were thinking of starting a large factory. He knows for certain—because all his experience has taught him so—that sooner or later a toll of human life will be exacted in the working of that factory.

ROR. Yes, that is only too probable.

BER. Or say a man embarks on a mining enterprise. He takes into his service fathers of families and young men in the first flush of their youth. Is it not quite safe to predict that all of them will not come out of it alive?

ROR. Yes, unhappily that is quite true.

BER. Well—a man in that position will know beforehand that the undertaking he proposes to start must undoubtedly, at some time or other, mean a loss of human life. But the undertaking itself is for the public good; for every man's life that it costs it will undoubtedly promote the welfare of many hundreds.

ROR. Ah, you are thinking of the railway- of all the dangerous excavating and blasting and that sort of thing.

BER. Yes—quite so—I am thinking of the railway. And, besides, the coming of the railway will mean the starting of factories and mines. But do not think, nevertheless——

ROR. My dear Mr Bernick, you are almost overconscientious. What I think is that if you place the affair in the hands of Providence——

BER. Yes—exactly; Providence——

ROR. —you are blameless in the matter. Go on and build your railway hopefully.

BER. Yes, but now I will put a

special instance to you. Suppose a charge of blasting powder had to be exploded in a dangerous place and that unless it were exploded the line could not be constructed? Suppose the engineer knew that it would cost the life of the workman who lit the fuse, but that it had to be lit and that it was the engineer's duty to send a workman to do it?

ROR. Hm——

BER. I know what you will say. It would be a splendid thing if the engineer took the match himself and went and lit the fuse. But that is out of the question, so he must sacrifice a workman.

ROR. That is a thing no engineer here would ever do.

BER. No engineer in the bigger countries would think twice about doing it.

ROR. In the bigger countries? No, I can quite believe it. In those depraved and unprincipled communities——

BER. Oh, there is a good deal to be said for those communities.

ROR. Can you say that? You, who yourself——

BER. In the bigger communities a man finds space to carry out a valuable project—finds the courage to make some sacrifice in a great cause; but here a man is cramped by all kinds of petty considerations and scruples.

ROR. Is human life a petty consideration?

BER. When that human life threatens the welfare of thousands.

ROR. But you are suggesting cases that are quite inconceivable, Mr Bernick! I do not understand you at all today. And you quote the bigger countries—well, what do they think of human life there? They look upon it simply as part of the capital they have to use. But *we* look at things from a somewhat different moral standpoint, I should hope. Look at our respected shipping industry! Can you name a single one of our shipowners who would sacrifice a human life for the sake of paltry gain? And then think of those scoundrels in the bigger countries, who for the sake of profit send out freights in one unseaworthy ship after another——

BER. I am not talking of unseaworthy ships!

ROR. But I am, Mr Bernick.

BER. Yes, but to what purpose? They have nothing to do with the question. Oh, these small, timid considerations! If a general from this country were to take his men under fire and some of them were shot, I suppose he would have sleepless nights after it! It is not so in other countries. You should hear what that fellow in there says.

ROR. He? Who? The American?

BER. Yes. You should hear how in America——

ROR. He, in there? And you did not tell me? I shall at once——

BER. It is no use; you won't be able to do anything with him.

ROR. We shall see. Ah, here he comes.

[JOHAN *comes in from the other room.*]

JOHAN [*talking back through the open door*]. Yes, yes, Dina—as you please; but I do not mean to give you up, all the same. I shall come back, and then everything will come right between us.

ROR. Excuse me, but what did you mean by that? What is it you propose to do?

JOHAN. I propose that that young

girl, before whom you blackened my character yesterday, shall become my wife.

ROR. Your wife? And can you really suppose that——

JOHAN. I mean to marry her.

ROR. Well, then, you shall know the truth. [*Goes to the half-open door.*] Mrs Bernick, will you be so kind as to come and be a witness—and you too, Miss Martha. And let Dina come. [*Sees* LONA *at the door.*] Ah, you here too?

LONA. Shall I come too?

ROR. As many as you please—the more the better.

BER. What are you going to do?

[LONA, MRS BERNICK, MARTHA, DINA *and* HILMAR *come in from the other room.*]

MRS B. Mr Rorlund, I have tried my hardest, but I cannot prevent him——

ROR. I shall prevent him, Mrs Bernick. Dina, you are a thoughtless girl, but I do not blame you so greatly. You have too long lacked the necessary moral support that should have sustained you. I blame myself for not having afforded you that support.

DINA. You mustn't speak now!

MRS B. What is it?

ROR. It is now that I *must* speak, Dina, although your conduct yesterday and today has made it ten times more difficult for me. But all other considerations must give way to the necessity for saving you. You remember that I gave you my word; you remember what you promised you would answer when I judged that the right time had come. Now I dare not hesitate any longer, and therefore—— [*Turns to* JOHAN.] This young girl, whom you are persecuting, is my betrothed.

MRS B. What?

BER. Dina!

JOHAN. She? Your——

MARTHA. No, no, Dina!

LONA. It is a lie!

JOHAN. Dina—is this man speaking the truth?

DINA [*after a short pause*]. Yes.

ROR. I hope this has rendered all your arts of seduction powerless. The step I have determined to take for Dina's good I now wish openly proclaimed to everyone. I cherish the certain hope that it will not be misinterpreted. And now, Mrs Bernick, I think it will be best for us to take her away from here and try to bring back peace and tranquility to her mind.

MRS B. Yes, come with me. Oh, Dina—what a lucky girl you are! [*Takes* DINA *out to the left;* RORLUND *follows them.*]

MARTHA. Good-by, Johan! [*Goes out.*]

HILMAR [*at the veranda door*]. Hm—I really must say——

LONA [*who has followed* DINA *with her eyes, to* JOHAN]. Don't be downhearted, my boy! I shall stay here and keep my eye on the parson. [*Goes out to the right.*]

BER. Johan, you won't sail in the Indian Girl now?

JOHAN. Indeed I shall.

BER. But you won't come back?

JOHAN. I am coming back.

BER. After this? What have you to do here after this?

JOHAN. Revenge myself on you all; crush as many of you as I can. [*Goes out to the right.* VIGELAND *and* KRAP *come in from* BERNICK'S *room.*]

VIG. There, now the papers are in order, Mr Bernick.

BER. Good, good.

KRAP [*in a low voice*]. And I suppose it is settled that the Indian Girl is to sail tomorrow?

BER. Yes. [*Goes into his room.* VIGELAND *and* KRAP *go out to the right.* HILMAR *is just going after them when* OLAF *puts his head carefully out of the door on the left.*]

OLAF. Uncle! Uncle Hilmar!

HILMAR. Ugh, is it you? Why don't you stay upstairs? You know you are confined to the house.

OLAF [*coming a step or two nearer*]. Hush! Uncle Hilmar, have you heard the news?

HILMAR. Yes, I have heard that you got a thrashing today.

OLAF [*looking threateningly toward his father's room*]. He shan't thrash me any more. But have you heard that Uncle Johan is going to sail tomorrow with the Americans?

HILMAR. What has that got to do with you? You had better run upstairs again.

OLAF. Perhaps I shall be going for a buffalo hunt, too, one of these days, Uncle.

HILMAR. Rubbish! A coward like you——

OLAF. Yes—just you wait! You will learn something tomorrow!

HILMAR. Duffer! [*Goes out through the garden.* OLAF *runs into the room again and shuts the door as he sees* KRAP *coming in from the right.*]

KRAP [*going to the door of* BERNICK's *room and opening it slightly*]. Excuse my bothering you again, Mr Bernick, but there is a tremendous storm blowing up. [*Waits a moment, but there is no answer.*] Is the Indian Girl to sail for all that? [*After a short pause the following answer is heard.*]

BER. [*from his room*]. The Indian Girl is to sail for all that.

[KRAP *shuts the door and goes out again to the right.*]

ACT IV

SCENE—*The same room. The work-table has been taken away. It is a stormy evening and already dusk. Darkness sets in as the following scene is in progress. A manservant is lighting the chandelier; two maids bring in pots of flowers, lamps and candles, which they place on tables and stands along the walls.* RUMMEL, *in dress clothes, with gloves and a white tie, is standing in the room giving instructions to the servants.*

RUM. Only every other candle, Jacob. It must not look as if it were arranged for the occasion—it has to come as a surprise, you know. And all these flowers? Oh well, let them be; it will probably look as if they stood there every day.

[BERNICK *comes out of his room.*]

BER. [*stopping at the door*]. What does this mean?

RUM. Oh dear, is it you? [*To the servants.*] Yes, you might leave us for the present.

[*The servants go out.*]

BER. But, Rummel, what is the meaning of this?

RUM. It means that the proudest moment of your life has come. A procession of his fellow citizens is coming to do honor to the first man of the town.

BER. What!

RUM. In procession—with banners and a band! We ought to have had torches too, but we did not like to risk that in this stormy weather. There will be illuminations—and that always sounds well in the newspapers.

BER. Listen, Rummel—I won't have anything to do with this.

RUM. But it is too late now; they will be here in half an hour.

BER. But why did you not tell me about this before?

RUM. Just because I was afraid you would raise objections to it. But I consulted your wife; she allowed me to take charge of the arrangements, while she looks after the refreshments.

BER. [*listening*]. What is that noise? Are they coming already? I fancy I hear singing.

RUM. [*going to the veranda door*]. Singing? Oh, that is only the Americans. The Indian Girl is being towed out.

BER. Towed out? Oh yes. No, Rummel, I cannot this evening; I am not well.

RUM. You certainly do look bad. But you must pull yourself together; devil take it—you *must!* Sandstad and Vigeland and I all attach the greatest importance to carrying this thing through. We have got to crush our opponents under the weight of as complete an expression of public opinion as possible. Rumors are getting about the town; our announcement about the purchase of the property cannot be withheld any longer. It is imperative that this very evening—after songs and speeches amidst the clink of glasses—in a word, in an ebullient atmosphere of festivity—you should inform them of the risk you have incurred for the good of the community. In such an ebullient atmosphere of festivity—as I just now described it—you can do an astonishing lot with the people here. But you must have that atmosphere, or the thing won't go.

BER. Yes, yes.

RUM. And especially when so delicate and ticklish a point has to be negotiated. Well, thank goodness you have a name that will be a tower of strength, Bernick. But listen now; we must make our arrangements, to some extent. Mr Hilmar Tonnesen has written an ode to you. It begins very charmingly with the words: "Raise the Ideal's banner high!" And Mr Rorlund has undertaken the task of making the speech of the evening. Of course you must reply to that.

BER. I cannot tonight, Rummel. Couldn't you——

RUM. It is impossible, however willing I might be; because, as you can imagine, his speech will be especially addressed to you. Of course it is possible he may say a word or two about the rest of us; I have spoken to Vigeland and Sandstad about it. Our idea is that, in replying, you should propose the toast of "Prosperity to our community"; Sandstad will say a few words on the subject of harmonious relations between the different strata of society; then Vigeland will express the hope that this new undertaking may not disturb the sound moral basis upon which our community stands; and I propose, in a few suitable words, to refer to the ladies, whose work for the community, though more inconspicuous, is far from being without its importance. But you are not listening to me.

BER. Yes—indeed I am. But, tell me, do you think there is a very heavy sea running outside?

RUM. Why, are you nervous about the Palm Tree? She is fully insured, you know.

BER. Yes, she is insured, but——

RUM. And in good repair—and that is the main thing.

BER. Hm. Supposing anything does happen to a ship, it doesn't follow that human life will be in danger, does it? The ship and the cargo may be lost—and one might lose one's boxes and papers——

RUM. Good lord—boxes and papers are not of much consequence.

BER. Not of much consequence! No, no; I only meant—— Hush—I hear voices again.

RUM. It is on board the Palm Tree.

[VIGELAND *comes in from the right.*]

VIG. Yes, they are just towing the Palm Tree out. Good evening, Mr Bernick.

BER. And you, as a seafaring man, are still of opinion that——

VIG. I put my trust in Providence, Mr Bernick. Moreover, I have been on board myself and distributed a few small tracts which I hope may carry a blessing with them.

[SANDSTAD *and* KRAP *come in from the right.*]

SAN. [*to someone at the door*]. Well, if that gets through all right, anything will. [*Comes in.*] Ah, good evening, good evening!

BER. Is anything the matter, Krap?

KRAP. I say nothing, Mr Bernick.

SAN. The entire crew of the Indian Girl are drunk; I will stake my reputation on it that they won't come out of it alive.

[LONA *comes in from the right.*]

LONA. Ah, now I can say his good-bys for him.

BER. Is he on board already?

LONA. He will be directly, at any rate. We parted outside the hotel.

BER. And he persists in his intention?

LONA. As firm as a rock.

RUM. [*who is fumbling at the window*]. Confound these newfangled contrivances; I cannot get the curtains drawn.

LONA. Do you want them drawn? I thought, on the contrary——

RUM. Yes, drawn at first, Miss Hessel. You know what is in the wind, I suppose?

LONA. Yes. Let me help you. [*Takes hold of the cords.*] I will draw down the curtains on my brother-in-law—though I would much rather draw them up.

RUM. You can do that too, later on. When the garden is filled with a surging crowd, then the curtains shall be drawn back, and they will be able to look in upon a surprised and happy family. Citizens' lives should be such that they can live in glass houses!

[BERNICK *opens his mouth as though he were going to say something, but he turns hurriedly away and goes into his room.*]

RUM. Come along; let us have a final consultation. Come in too, Mr Krap; you must assist us with information on one or two points of detail.

[*All the men go into* BERNICK'S *room.* LONA *has drawn the curtains over the windows and is just going to do the same over the open glass door when* OLAF *jumps down from the room above onto the garden steps; he has a wrap over his shoulders and a bundle in his hand.*]

LONA. Bless me, child, how you frightened me!

OLAF [*hiding his bundle*]. Hush, Aunt!

LONA. Did you jump out of the window? Where are you going?

OLAF. Hush!—don't say anything. I want to go to Uncle Johan—only onto the quay, you know—only to say good-by to him. Good night, Aunt! [*Runs out through the garden.*]

LONA. No—stop! Olaf—Olaf!

[JOHAN, *dressed for his journey, with a bag over his shoulder, comes warily in by the door on the right.*]

JOHAN. Lona!

LONA [*turning round*]. What! Back again?

JOHAN. I have still a few minutes. I must see her once more; we cannot part like this.

[*The farther door on the left opens, and* MARTHA *and* DINA, *both with cloaks on and the latter carrying a small traveling bag in her hand, come in.*]

DINA. Let me go to him! Let me go to him!

MARTHA. Yes, you shall go to him, Dina!

DINA. There he is!

JOHAN. Dina!

DINA. Take me with you!

JOHAN. What!

LONA. You mean it?

DINA. Yes, take me with you. The other has written to me that he means to announce to everyone this evening——

JOHAN. Dina—you do not love him?

DINA. I have never loved the man! I would rather drown myself in the fiord than be engaged to him! Oh, how he humiliated me yesterday with his condescending manner! How clear he made it that he was lifting up a poor despised creature to his own level! I do not mean to be despised any longer. I mean to go away. May I go with you?

JOHAN. Yes, yes—a thousand times yes!

DINA. I will not be a burden to you long. Only help me to get over there; help me to go the right way about things at first——

JOHAN. Hurrah, it is all right after all, Dina!

LONA [*pointing to* BERNICK'S *door*]. Hush!—gently, gently!

JOHAN. Dina, I shall look after you.

DINA. I am not going to let you do that. I mean to look after myself; over there I am sure I can do that. Only let me get away from here. Oh, these women!—you don't know—they have written to me today too—exhorting me to realize my good fortune—impressing on me how magnanimous he has been. Tomorrow, and every day afterward, they would be watching me to see if I were making myself worthy of it all. I am sick and tired of all this goodiness!

JOHAN. Tell me, Dina—is that the only reason you are coming away? Am I nothing to you?

DINA. Yes, Johan, you are more to me than anyone else in the world.

JOHAN. Oh, Dina!

DINA. Everyone here tells me I ought to hate and detest you—that it is my duty; but I cannot see that it is my duty and shall never be able to.

LONA. No more you shall, my dear!

MARTHA. No, indeed you shall not; and that is why you shall go with him as his wife.

JOHAN. Yes, yes!

LONA. What! Give me a kiss, Martha. I never expected that from *you!*

MARTHA. No, I dare say not; I would not have expected it myself. But I was bound to break out sometime! Ah, what we suffer under the tyranny of habit and custom! Make a stand against that, Dina. Be his wife. Let me see you defy all this convention.

JOHAN. What is your answer, Dina?

DINA. Yes, I will be your wife.

JOHAN. Dina!

DINA. But first of all I want to work —to make something of myself—as you have done. I am not going to be merely a thing that is taken.

LONA. Quite right—that is the way.

JOHAN. Very well, I shall wait and hope——

LONA. And win, my boy! But now you must get on board!

JOHAN. Yes, on board! Ah, Lona, my dear sister, just one word with you. Look here—— [*He takes her into the background and talks hurriedly to her.*]

MARTHA. Dina, you lucky girl, let me look at you and kiss you once more—for the last time.

DINA. Not for the last time; no, my darling aunt, we shall meet again.

MARTHA. Never! Promise me, Dina, never to come back! [*Grasps her hands and looks at her.*] Now go to your happiness, my dear child—across the sea. How often, in my schoolroom, I have yearned to be over there! It must be beautiful; the skies are loftier than here—a freer air plays about your head——

DINA. Oh, Aunt Martha, someday you will follow us.

MARTHA. I? Never—never. I have my little vocation here, and now I really believe I can live to the full the life that I ought.

DINA. I cannot imagine being parted from you.

MARTHA. Ah, one can part from much, Dina. [*Kisses her.*] But I hope you may never experience that, my sweet child. Promise to make him happy.

DINA. I will promise nothing; I hate promises; things must happen as they will.

MARTHA. Yes, yes, that is true; only remain what you are—true and faithful to yourself.

DINA. I will, Aunt.

LONA [*putting into her pocket some papers that* JOHAN *has given her*]. Splendid, splendid, my dear boy. But now you must be off.

JOHAN. Yes, we have no time to waste now. Good-by, Lona, and thank you for all your love. Good-by, Martha, and thank you, too, for your loyal friendship.

MARTHA. Good-by, Johan! Good-by, Dina! And may you be happy all your lives! [*She and* LONA *hurry them to the door at the back.* JOHAN *and* DINA *go quickly down the steps and through the garden.* LONA *shuts the door and draws the curtains over it.*]

LONA. Now we are alone, Martha. You have lost her and I him.

MARTHA. You—lost him?

LONA. Oh, I had already half lost him over there. The boy was longing to stand on his own feet; that was why I pretended to be suffering from homesickness.

MARTHA. So that was it? Ah, then I understand why you came. But he will want you back, Lona.

LONA. An old stepsister—what use will he have for her now? Men break many very dear ties to win their happiness.

MARTHA. That sometimes is so.

LONA. But we two will stick together, Martha.

MARTHA. Can I be anything to you?

LONA. Who more so? We two foster sisters—haven't we both lost our children? Now we are alone.

MARTHA. Yes, alone. And therefore you ought to know this too—I loved him more than anything in the world.

LONA. Martha! [*Grasps her by the arm.*] Is that true?

MARTHA. All my existence lies in

those words. I have loved and waited for him. Every summer I waited for him to come. And then he came—but he had no eyes for me.

LONA. You loved him! And it was you yourself that put his happiness into his hands.

MARTHA. Ought I not to be the one to put his happiness into his hands, since I loved him? Yes, I have loved him. All my life has been for him, ever since he went away. What reason had I to hope, you mean? Oh, I think I had some reason, all the same. But when he came back—then it seemed as if everything had been wiped out of his memory. He had no eyes for me.

LONA. It was Dina that overshadowed you, Martha.

MARTHA. And it is a good thing she did. At the time he went away we were of the same age, but when I saw him again—oh, that dreadful moment!—I realized that now I was ten years older than he. He had gone out into the bright sparking sunshine and breathed in youth and health with every breath, and here I sat meanwhile, spinning and spinning——

LONA. Spinning the thread of his happiness, Martha.

MARTHA. Yes, it was a golden thread I spun. No bitterness! We have been two good sisters to him, haven't we, Lona?

LONA [*throwing her arms round her*]. Martha!

[BERNICK *comes in from his room.*]

BER. [*to the other men who are in his room*]. Yes, yes, arrange it any way you please. When the time comes I shall be able to—— [*Shuts the door.*] Ah, you are here. Look here, Martha—I think you had better change your dress, and tell Betty to do the same. I don't want anything elaborate, of course—something homely but neat. But you must make haste.

LONA. And a bright, cheerful face, Martha; your eyes must look happy.

BER. Olaf is coming downstairs too; I will have him beside me.

LONA. Hm! Olaf——

MARTHA. I will give Betty your message. [*Goes out by the farther door on the left.*]

LONA. Well, the great and solemn moment is at hand.

BER. [*walking uneasily up and down*]. Yes, it is.

LONA. At such a moment I should think a man would feel proud and happy.

BER. [*looking at her*]. Hm!

LONA. I hear the whole town is to be illuminated.

BER. Yes, they have some idea of that sort.

LONA. All the different clubs will assemble with their banners—your name will blaze out in letters of fire—tonight the telegraph will flash the news to every part of the country: "In the bosom of his happy family, Mr Bernick received the homage of his fellow citizens as one of the pillars of society."

BER. That is so; and they will begin to cheer outside, and the crowd will shout in front of my house until I shall be obliged to go out and bow to them and thank them.

LONA. Obliged to?

BER. Do you suppose I shall feel happy at that moment?

LONA. No, I don't suppose you will feel so very happy.

BER. Lona, you despise me.

LONA. Not yet.

BER. And you have no right to,

no right to *despise* me! Lona, you can have no idea how utterly alone I stand in this cramped and stunted community—where I have had, year after year, to stifle my ambition for a fuller life. My work may seem many sided, but what have I really accomplished? Odds and ends—scraps. They would not stand anything else here. If I were to go a step in advance of the opinions and views that are current at the moment, I should lose all my influence. Do you know what we are—we who are looked upon as pillars of society? We are nothing more nor less than the tools of society.

LONA. Why have you only begun to realize that now?

BER. Because I have been thinking a great deal lately—since you came back—and this evening I have thought more seriously than ever before. Oh, Lona, why did I not really know you then—in the old days, I mean?

LONA. And if you had?

BER. I should never have let you go; and if I had had you, I should not be in the position I am in tonight.

LONA. And do you never consider what *she* might have been to you—she whom you chose in my place?

BER. I know, at all events, that she has been nothing to me of what I needed.

LONA. Because you have never shared your interests with her; because you have never allowed her full and frank exchange of thoughts with you; because you have allowed her to be borne under by self-reproach for the shame you cast upon one who was dear to her.

BER. Yes, yes; it all comes from lying and deceit.

LONA. Then why not break with all this lying and deceit?

BER. Now? It is too late now, Lona.

LONA. Karsten, tell me—what gratification does all this show and deception bring you?

BER. It brings *me* none. I must disappear someday, and all this community of bunglers with me. But a generation is growing up that will follow us; it is my son that I work for—I am providing a career for *him.* There will come a time when truth will enter into the life of the community, and on that foundation he shall build up a happier existence than his father.

LONA. With a lie at the bottom of it all? Consider what sort of an inheritance it is that you are leaving to your son.

BER. [*in tones of suppressed despair*]. It is a thousand times worse than you think. But surely someday the curse must be lifted, and yet—nevertheless—— [*Vehemently.*] How could I bring all this upon my own head! Still, it is done now; I must go on with it now. You *shall* not succeed in crushing me!

[HILMAR *comes in hurriedly and agitatedly from the right with an open letter in his hand.*]

HILMAR. But this is—— Betty, Betty!

BER. What is the matter? Are they coming already?

HILMAR. No, no—but I must speak to someone immediately. [*Goes out through the farther door on the left.*]

LONA. Karsten, you talk about our having come here to crush you. So let me tell you what sort of stuff this prodigal son, whom your moral community shuns as if he had the plague, is made of. He can do without any of you—for he is away now.

BER. But he said he meant to come back.

LONA. Johan will never come back. He is gone for good, and Dina with him.

BER. Never come back?—and Dina with him?

LONA. Yes, to be his wife. That is how these two strike your virtuous community in the face, just as I did once—but never mind that.

BER. Gone—and she too—in the Indian Girl——

LONA. No; he would not trust so precious a freight to that rascally crew. Johan and Dina are on the Palm Tree.

BER. Ah! Then it is all in vain. [*Goes hurriedly to the door of his room, opens it and calls in.*] Krap, stop the Indian Girl—she must not sail tonight!

KRAP [*from within*]. The Indian Girl is already standing out to sea, Mr Bernick.

BER. [*shutting the door and speaking faintly*]. Too late—and all to no purpose.

LONA. What do you mean?

BER. Nothing, nothing. Leave me alone!

LONA. Hm! Look here, Karsten. Johan was good enough to say that he entrusted to me the good name and reputation that he once lent to you and also the good name that you stole from him while he was away. Johan will hold his tongue, and I can act just as I please in the matter. See, I have two letters in my hand.

BER. You have got them! And you mean now—this very evening—perhaps when the procession comes——

LONA. I did not come back here to betray you but to stir your conscience so that you should speak of your own free will. I did not succeed in doing that—so you must remain as you are, with your life founded upon a lie. Look, I am tearing your two letters in pieces. Take the wretched things—there you are. Now there is no evidence against you, Karsten. You are safe now; be happy too—if you can.

BER. [*much moved*]. Lona—why did you not do that sooner! Now it is too late; life no longer seems good to me; I cannot live on after today.

LONA. What has happened?

BER. Do not ask me. But I *must* live on nevertheless! I *will* live—for Olaf's sake. He shall make amends for everything—expiate everything——

LONA. Karsten!

[HILMAR *comes hurriedly back.*]

HILMAR. I cannot find anyone; they are all out—even Betty!

BER. What is the matter with you?

HILMAR. I daren't tell you.

BER. What is it? You *must* tell me!

HILMAR. Very well—Olaf has run away on board the Indian Girl!

BER. [*stumbling back*]. Olaf—on board the Indian Girl! No, no!

LONA. Yes, he is! Now I understand—I saw him jump out of the window.

BER. [*calls in through the door of his room in a despairing voice*]. Krap, stop the Indian Girl at any cost!

KRAP. It is impossible, sir. How can you suppose——

BER. We *must* stop her; Olaf is on board!

KRAP. What!

RUM. [*coming out of* BERNICK'S *room*]. Olaf run away? Impossible!

SAN. [*following him*]. He will be sent back with the pilot, Mr Bernick.

HILMAR. No, no; he has written to me. [*Shows the letter.*] He says he means to hide among the cargo till they are in the open sea.

BER. I shall never see him again!

RUM. What nonsense! A good strong ship, newly repaired——

VIG. [*who has followed the others out of* BERNICK's *room*]. And in your own yard, Mr Bernick!

BER. I shall never see him again, I tell you. I have lost him, Lona, and—I see it now—he never was really mine. [*Listens.*] What is that?

RUM. Music. The procession must be coming.

BER. I cannot take any part in it—I will not.

RUM. What are you thinking of! That is impossible.

SAN. Impossible, Mr Bernick; think what you have at stake.

BER. What does it all matter to me now? What have I to work for now?

RUM. Can you ask? You have us and the community.

VIG. Quite true.

SAN. And surely, Mr Bernick, you have not forgotten that we——

[MARTHA *comes in through the farther door to the left. Music is heard in the distance, down the street.*]

MARTHA. The procession is just coming, but Betty is not in the house. I don't understand where she——

BER. Not in the house! There, you see, Lona—no support to me, either in gladness or in sorrow.

RUM. Draw back the curtains! Come and help me, Mr Krap—and you, Mr Sandstad. It is a thousand pities that the family should not be united just now; it is quite contrary to the program.

[*They draw back all the curtains. The whole street is seen to be illuminated. Opposite the house is a large transparency bearing the words: Long live Karsten Bernick, Pillar of our Society!*]

BER. [*shrinking back*]. Take all that away! I don't want to see it! Put it out, put it out!

RUM. Excuse me, Mr Bernick, but are you not well?

MARTHA. What is the matter with him, Lona?

LONA. Hush! [*Whispers to her.*]

BER. Take away those mocking words, I tell you! Can't you see that all these lights are grinning at us?

RUM. Well, really, I must confess——

BER. Oh, how could you understand! But I, I! It is all like candles in a dead room!

RUM. Well, let me tell you that you are taking the thing a great deal too seriously.

SAN. The boy will enjoy a trip across the Atlantic, and then you will have him back.

VIG. Only put your trust in the Almighty, Mr Bernick.

RUM. And in the vessel, Bernick; it is not likely to sink, I know.

KRAP. Hm——

RUM. Now if it were one of those floating coffins that one hears are sent out by men in the bigger countries——

BER. I am sure my hair must be turning gray!

[MRS BERNICK *comes in from the garden with a shawl over her head.*]

MRS B. Karsten, Karsten, do you know?

BER. Yes, I know; but you—you, who see nothing that is going on—you, who have no mother's eyes for your son——

MRS B. Listen to me, do!

BER. Why did you not look after

him? Now I have lost him. Give him back to me if you can.

MRS B. I can! I have got him!

BER. You have got him!

THE MEN. Ah!

HILMAR. Yes, I thought so.

MARTHA. You have got him back, Karsten!

LONA. Yes—make him your own now.

BER. You have got him? Is that true? Where is he?

MRS B. I shall not tell you till you have forgiven him.

BER. Forgiven! But how did you know?

MRS B. Do you not think a mother sees? I was in mortal fear of your getting to know anything about it. Some words he let fall yesterday—and then his room was empty and his knapsack and clothes missing——

BER. Yes, yes?

MRS B. I ran and got hold of Aune; we went out in his boat; the American ship was on the point of sailing. Thank God we were in time—got on board—searched the hold—found him! Oh, Karsten, you must not punish him!

BER. Betty!

MRS B. Nor Aune either!

BER. Aune? What do you know about him? Is the Indian Girl under sail again?

MRS B. No, that is just it.

BER. Speak, speak!

MRS B. Aune was just as agitated as I was; the search took us some time; it had grown dark, and the pilot made objections; and so Aune took upon himself—in your name——

BER. Well?

MRS B. To stop the ship's sailing till tomorrow.

KRAP. Hm——

BER. Oh, how glad I am!

MRS B. You are not angry?

BER. I cannot tell you how glad I am, Betty!

RUM. You really take things far too seriously.

HILMAR. Oh yes, as soon as it is a question of a little struggle with the elements—ugh!

KRAP [*going to the window*]. The procession is just coming through your garden gate, Mr Bernick.

BER. Yes, they can come now.

RUM. The whole garden is full of people.

SAN. The whole street is crammed.

RUM. The whole town is afoot, Bernick. It really is a moment that makes one proud.

VIG. Let us take it in a humble spirit, Mr Rummel.

RUM. All the banners are out! What a procession! Here comes the committee, with Mr Rorlund at their head.

BER. Yes, let them come in!

RUM. But, Bernick—in your present agitated frame of mind——

BER. Well, what?

RUM. I am quite willing to speak instead of you, if you like.

BER. No, thank you; I will speak for myself tonight.

RUM. But are you sure you know what to say?

BER. Yes, make your mind easy, Rummel—I know now what to say.

[*The music grows louder. The veranda door is opened.* RORLUND *comes in at the head of the committee, escorted by a couple of hired waiters who carry a covered basket. They are followed by townspeople of all classes, as many as can get into the room. An apparently endless crowd of people, waving banners and flags, is visible in the garden and the street.*]

ROR. Mr Bernick! I see, from the surprise depicted upon your face, that it is as unexpected guests that we are intruding upon your happy family circle and your peaceful fireside, where we find you surrounded by honored and energetic fellow citizens and friends. But it is our hearts that have bidden us come to offer you our homage—not for the first time, it is true, but for the first time on such a comprehensive scale. We have on many occasions given you our thanks for the broad moral foundation upon which you have, so to speak, reared the edifice of our community. On this occasion we offer our homage especially to the clear-sighted, indefatigable, unselfish—nay, self-sacrificing—citizen who has taken the initiative in an undertaking which, we are assured on all sides, will give a powerful impetus to the temporal prosperity and welfare of our community.

VOICES. Bravo, bravo!

ROR. You, sir, have for many years been a shining example in our midst. This is not the place for me to speak of your family life, which has been a model to us all; still less to enlarge upon your unblemished personal character. Such topics belong to the stillness of a man's own chamber, not to a festal occasion such as this! I am here to speak of your public life as a citizen, as it lies open to all men's eyes. Well-equipped vessels sail away from your shipyard and carry our flag far and wide over the seas. A numerous and happy band of workmen look up to you as to a father. By calling new branches of industry into existence you have laid the foundations of the welfare of hundreds of families. In a word—you are, in the fullest sense of the term, the mainstay of our community.

VOICES. Hear, hear! Bravo!

ROR. And, sir, it is just that disinterestedness, which colors all your conduct, that is so beneficial to our community—more so than words can express—and especially at the present moment. You are now on the point of procuring for us what I have no hesitation in calling bluntly by its prosaic name—a railway!

VOICES. Bravo, bravo!

ROR. But it would seem as though the undertaking were beset by certain difficulties, the outcome of narrow and selfish considerations.

VOICES. Hear, hear!

ROR. For the fact has come to light that certain individuals, who do not belong to our community, have stolen a march upon the hard-working citizens of this place and have laid hands on certain sources of profit which by rights should have fallen to the share of our town.

VOICES. That's right! Hear, hear!

ROR. This regrettable fact has naturally come to your knowledge also, Mr Bernick. But it has not had the slightest effect in deterring you from proceeding steadily with your project, well knowing that a patriotic man should not solely take local interests into consideration.

VOICES. Oh! No, no! Yes, yes!

ROR. It is to such a man—to the patriot citizen whose character we all should emulate—that we bring our homage this evening. May your undertaking grow to be a real and lasting source of good fortune to this community. It is true enough that a railway may be the means of our exposing ourselves to the incursion of pernicious influences from without, but it gives us also the means of quickly expelling them from within. For even we, at the present time, cannot boast of being entirely free from the danger of such outside influences; but as we have, on this very evening—if rumor is to be believed—fortunately got rid of certain elements of that nature, sooner than was to be expected——

VOICES. Order, order!

ROR. I regard the occurrence as a happy omen for our undertaking. My alluding to such a thing at such a moment only emphasizes the fact that the house in which we are now standing is one where the claims of morality are esteemed even above ties of family.

VOICES. Hear, hear! Bravo!

BER. [*at the same moment*]. Allow me——

ROR. I have only a few more words to say, Mr Bernick. What you have done for your native place we all know has not been done with any underlying idea of its bringing tangible profit to yourself. But, nevertheless, you must not refuse to accept a slight token of grateful appreciation at the hands of your fellow citizens—least of all at this important moment when, according to the assurances of practical men, we are standing on the threshold of a new era.

VOICES. Bravo! Hear, hear!

[RORLUND *signs to the servants, who bring forward the basket. During the following speech members of the committee take out and present the various objects mentioned.*]

ROR. And so, Mr Bernick, we have the pleasure of presenting you with this silver coffee service. Let it grace your board when in the future, as so often in the past, we have the happiness of being assembled under your hospitable roof. You, too, gentlemen, who have so generously seconded the leader of our community, we ask to accept a small souvenir. This silver goblet is for you, Mr Rummel. Many a time have you, amidst the clink of glasses, defended the interests of your fellow citizens in well-chosen words; may you often find similar worthy opportunities to raise and empty this goblet in some patriotic toast! To you, Mr Sandstad, I present this album containing photographs of your fellow citizens. Your well-known and conspicuous liberality has put you in the pleasant position of being able to number your friends amongst all classes of society. And to you, Mr Vigeland, I have to offer this book of family devotions, printed on vellum and handsomely bound, to grace your study table. The mellowing influence of time has led you to take an earnest view of life; your zeal in carrying out your daily duties has, for a long period of years, been purified and ennobled by thoughts of higher and holier things. [*Turns to the crowd.*] And now, friends, three cheers for Mr Bernick and his fellow workers! Three cheers for the Pillars of our Society!

THE WHOLE CROWD. Bernick! Pillars of Society! Hurrah—hurrah—hurrah!

LONA. I congratulate you, brother-in-law!

[*An expectant hush follows.*]

BER. [*speaking seriously and slowly*]. Fellow citizens—your spokesman said just now that tonight we are standing on the threshold of a new era. I hope that will prove to be the case. But before that can come to pass we must lay fast hold of *truth*—truth which, till tonight, has been altogether and in all circumstances a stranger to this community of ours. [*Astonishment among the audience.*] To that end I must begin by deprecating the praises with which you, Mr Rorlund, according to custom on such occasions, have overwhelmed me. I do not deserve them; because, until today, my actions have by no means been disinterested. Even though I may not always have aimed at pecuniary profit, I at all events recognize now that a craving for power, influence and position has been the moving spirit of most of my actions.

RUM. [*half aloud*]. What next!

BER. Standing before my fellow citizens, I do not reproach myself for that; because I still think I am entitled to a place in the front rank of our capable men of affairs.

VOICES. Yes, yes, yes!

BER. But what I charge myself with is that I have so often been weak enough to resort to deceitfulness, because I knew and feared the tendency of the community to espy unclean motives behind everything a prominent man here undertakes. And now I am coming to a point which will illustrate that.

RUM. [*uneasily*]. Hm-hm!

BER. There have been rumors of extensive purchases of property outside of town. These purchases have been made by me—by me alone and by no one else. [*Murmurs are heard:* "What does he say? He? Bernick?"] The properties are, for the time being, in my hands. Naturally I have confided in my fellow workers, Mr Rummel, Mr Vigeland and Mr Sandstad, and we are all agreed that——

RUM. It is not true! Prove it—prove it!

VIG. We are not all agreed about anything!

SAN. Well, really, I must say!

BER. That is quite true—we are not yet agreed upon the matter I was going to mention. But I confidently hope that these three gentlemen will agree with me when I announce to you that I have tonight come to the decision that these properties shall be exploited as a company of which the shares shall be offered for public subscription; anyone that wishes can take shares.

VOICES. Hurrah! Three cheers for Bernick!

RUM. [*in a low voice to* BERNICK]. This is the basest treachery!

SAN. [*also in an undertone*]. So you have been fooling us!

VIG. Well, then, devil take—— Good lord, what am I saying?

[*Cheers are heard without.*]

BER. Silence, gentlemen. I have no right to this homage you offer me, because the decision I have just come to does not represent what was my first intention. My intention was to keep the whole thing for myself, and even now I am of opinion that these properties would be worked to best advantage if they remained in one man's hands. But you are at liberty to choose. If you wish it, I am willing to administer them to the best of my abilities.

VOICES. Yes, yes, yes!

BER. But first of all my fellow townsmen must know me thoroughly. And let each man seek to know himself thoroughly too, and so let it really come to pass that tonight we begin a new era. The old era—with its affectations, its hypocrisy and its emptiness, its pretense of virtue and its miserable fear of public opinion—shall be for us like a museum, open for purposes of instruction; and to that museum we will present—shall we not, gentlemen?—the coffee service and the goblet and the album and the family devotions printed on vellum and handsomely bound.

RUM. Oh, of course.

VIG. [*muttering*]. If you have taken everything else, then——

SAN. By all means.

BER. And now for the principal reckoning I have to make with the community. Mr Rorlund said that certain pernicious elements had left us this evening. I can add what you do not yet know. The man referred to did not go away alone; with him, to become his wife, went——

LONA [*loudly*]. Dina Dorf.

ROR. What?

MRS B. What?

[*Great commotion.*]

ROR. Fled? Run away—with him! Impossible!

BER. To become his wife, Mr Rorlund. And I will add more. [*In a low voice to his wife.*] Betty, be strong to bear what is coming. [*Aloud.*] This is what I have to say: hats off to that man, for he has nobly taken another's guilt upon his shoulders. My friends, I want to have done with falsehood; it has very nearly poisoned every fiber of my being. You shall know all. Fifteen years ago *I* was the guilty man.

MRS B. [*softly and tremblingly*]. Karsten!

MARTHA [*similarly*]. Ah, Johan!

LONA. Now at last you have found yourself!

[*Speechless consternation among the audience.*]

BER. Yes, friends, I was the guilty one, and he went away. The vile and lying rumors that were spread abroad afterward it is beyond human power to refute now, but I have no right to complain of that. For fifteen years I have climbed up the ladder of success by the help of those rumors; whether now they are to cast me down again or not, each of you must decide in his own mind.

ROR. What a thunderbolt! Our leading citizen! [*In a low voice to Betty.*] How sorry I am for you, Mrs Bernick!

HILMAR. What a confession! Well, I must say!

BER. But come to no decision tonight. I entreat everyone to go home—to collect his thoughts—to look into his own heart. When once more you can think calmly, then it will be seen whether I have lost or won by speaking out. Good-by! I have still much—very much—to repent of; but that concerns my own conscience only. Good night! Take away all these signs of rejoicing. We must all feel that they are out of place here.

ROR. That they certainly are. [*In an undertone to* MRS BERNICK.] Run away! So then she was completely unworthy of me. [*Louder, to the committee.*] Yes, gentlemen, after this I think we had better disperse as quietly as possible.

HILMAR. How, after this, anyone is to manage to hold the Ideal's banner high—— Ugh!

[*Meantime the news has been whispered from mouth to mouth. The crowd gradually disperses from the garden.* RUMMEL, SANDSTAD *and* VIGELAND *go out, arguing eagerly but in a low voice.* HILMAR *slinks away to the right. When silence is restored there only remain in the room* BER-

NICK, MRS BERNICK, MARTHA, LONA *and* KRAP.]

BER. Betty, can you forgive me?

MRS B. [*looking at him with a smile*]. Do you know, Karsten, that you have opened out for me the happiest prospect I have had for many a year?

BER. How?

MRS B. For many years I have felt that once you were mine and that I had lost you. Now I know that you never have been mine yet, but I shall win you.

BER. [*folding her in his arms*]. Oh, Betty, you *have* won me. It was through Lona that I first learned really to know you. But now let Olaf come to me.

MRS B. Yes, you shall have him now. Mr Krap! [*Talks softly to* KRAP *in the background. He goes out by the garden door. During what follows the illuminations and lights in the houses are gradually extinguished.*]

BER. [*in a low voice*]. Thank you, Lona—you have saved what was best in me—and for me.

LONA. Do you suppose I wanted to do anything else?

BER. Yes, was that so—or not? I cannot quite make you out.

LONA. Hm——

BER. Then it was not hatred? Not revenge? Why did you come back then?

LONA. Old friendship does not rust.

BER. Lona!

LONA. When Johan told me about the lie I swore to myself that the hero of my youth should stand free and true.

BER. What a wretch I am! And how little I have deserved it of you!

LONA. Oh, if we women always looked for what we deserve, Karsten——

[AUNE *comes in with* OLAF *from the garden.*]

BER. [*going to meet them*]. Olaf!

OLAF. Father, I promise I will never do it again.

BER. Never run away?

OLAF. Yes, yes, I promise you, Father.

BER. And I promise you you shall never have reason to. For the future you shall be allowed to grow up, not as the heir to *my* life's work but as one who has his own life's work before him.

OLAF. And shall I be allowed to be what I like when I grow up?

BER. Yes.

OLAF. Oh, thank you! Then I won't be a pillar of society.

BER. No? Why not?

OLAF. No—I think it must be so dull.

BER. You shall be yourself, Olaf; the rest may take care of itself. And you, Aune——

AUNE. I know, Mr Bernick; I am dismissed.

BER. We remain together, Aune; and forgive me——

AUNE. What? The ship has not sailed tonight.

BER. Nor will it sail tomorrow either. I gave you too short grace. It must be looked to more thoroughly.

AUNE. It shall, Mr Bernick—and with the new machines!

BER. By all means—but thoroughly and conscientiously. There are many among us who need thorough and conscientious repairs, Aune. Well, good night.

AUNE. Good night, sir—and thank you, thank you. [*Goes out.*]

MRS B. Now they are all gone.

BER. And we are alone. My name is not shining in letters of fire any longer; all the lights in the windows are out.

LONA. Would you wish them lit again?

BER. Not for anything in the world. Where have I been! You would be horrified if you knew. I feel now as if I had come back to my right senses after being poisoned. But I feel this—that I *can* be young and healthy again. Oh, come nearer—come closer round me. Come, Betty! Come, Olaf, my boy! And you, Martha—it seems to me as if I had never seen you all these years.

LONA. No, I can believe that. Your community is a community of bachelor souls; you do not see women.

BER. That is quite true, and for that very reason—this is a bargain, Lona—you must not leave Betty and me.

MRS B. No, Lona, you must not.

LONA. No, how could I have the heart to go away and leave you young people who are just setting up housekeeping? Am I not your foster mother? You and I, Martha, the two old aunts—— What are you looking at?

MARTHA. Look how the sky is clearing and how light it is over the sea. The Palm Tree is going to be lucky.

LONA. It carries its good luck on board.

BER. And we—we have a long earnest day of work ahead of us; I most of all. But let it come; only keep close round me, you true, loyal women. I have learned *this* too, in these last few days: it is you women that are the pillars of society.

LONA. You have learned a poor sort of wisdom, then, brother-in-law. [*Lays her hand firmly upon his shoulder.*] No, my friend; the spirit of truth and the spirit of freedom—they are the pillars of society.